T0188958

Lecture Notes in Artificial Intelligence 12817

Subseries of Lecture Notes in Computer Science

More information about this subseries at http://www.springer.com/series/1244

Han Qiu · Cheng Zhang ·
Zongming Fei · Meikang Qiu ·
Sun-Yuan Kung (Eds.)

Knowledge Science, Engineering and Management

14th International Conference, KSEM 2021
Tokyo, Japan, August 14–16, 2021
Proceedings, Part III

 Springer

Editors
Han Qiu
Tsinghua University
Beijing, China

Zongming Fei
University of Kentucky
Lexington, KY, USA

Sun-Yuan Kung
Princeton University
Princeton, NJ, USA

Cheng Zhang
Ibaraki University
Hitachi, Japan

Meikang Qiu 🆔
Texas A&M University – Commerce
Commerce, TX, USA

ISSN 0302-9743   ISSN 1611-3349   (electronic)
Lecture Notes in Artificial Intelligence
ISBN 978-3-030-82152-4   ISBN 978-3-030-82153-1   (eBook)
https://doi.org/10.1007/978-3-030-82153-1

LNCS Sublibrary: SL7 – Artificial Intelligence

This Springer imprint is published by the registered company Springer Nature Switzerland AG
The registered company address is: Gewerbestrasse 11, 6330 Cham, Switzerland

Preface

The three-volume set contains the papers presented at the 14th International Conference on Knowledge Science, Engineering, and Management (KSEM 2021), held during August 14–16, 2021, in Tokyo, Japan.

There were 492 submissions. Each submission was reviewed by at least 3 reviewers, and on average 3.5 Program Committee members. The committee decided to accept 164 full papers, resulting in an acceptance rate of 33%. We have separated the proceedings into three volumes: LNCS 12815, 12816, and 12817.

KSEM 2021 was the 14th edition in this conference series which started in 2006. The aim of this interdisciplinary conference is to provide a forum for researchers in the broad areas of knowledge science, knowledge engineering, and knowledge management to exchange ideas and to report state-of-the-art research results. KSEM is in the list of CCF (China Computer Federation) recommended conferences (C series, Artificial Intelligence).

KSEM 2021 was held in Tokyo, Japan, following the traditions of the 13 previous successful KSEM events in Guilin, China (KSEM 2006); Melbourne, Australia (KSEM 2007); Vienna, Austria (KSEM 2009); Belfast, UK (KSEM 2010); Irvine, USA (KSEM 2011); Dalian, China (KSEM 2013); Sibiu, Romania (KSEM 2014); Chongqing, China (KSEM 2015), Passau, Germany (KSEM 2016), Melbourne, Australia (KSEM 2017), Changchun, China (KSEM 2018); Athens, Greece (KSEM 2019), and Hangzhou, China (KSEM 2020).

We would like to express our gratitude to the honorary general and Steering Committee chairs, Ruqian Lu (Chinese Academy of Sciences, China), and Dimitris Karagiannis (University of Vienna, Austria), and the members of the Steering Committee, who provided insight and guidance at all stages. The KSEM 2021 general co-chairs, Meikang Qiu (Texas A&M University-Commerce, USA), and Sun-Yuan Kung (Princeton University, USA) were extremely supportive in the conference organizing, call for papers, and paper review process, and played an important role in the general success of the conference.

The objective of KSEM 2021 was to bring together researchers and practitioners from academia, industry, and government to advance the theories and technologies in knowledge science, engineering, and management. KSEM 2021 focused on three broad areas: Knowledge Science with Learning and AI (KSLA), Knowledge Engineering Research and Applications (KERA), and Knowledge Management with Optimization and Security (KMOS).

We would like to thank the conference sponsors: Springer LNCS, Waseda University, the North America Chinese Talents Association, and the Longxiang High Tech Group Inc.

August 2021   Han Qiu
                                                                    Cheng Zhang
                                                                    Zongming Fei
                                                                    Meikang Qiu
                                                                  Sun-Yuan Kung

Organization

Honorary General Chairs

Ruqian Lu — Chinese Academy of Sciences, China
Dimitris Karagiannis (Chair) — University of Vienna, Austria

General Chairs

Meikang Qiu — Texas A&M University-Commerce, USA
Sun-Yuan Kung — Princeton University, USA

Program Chairs

Han Qiu — Tsinghua University, China
Cheng Zhang — Waseda University, Japan
Zongming Fei — University of Kentucky, USA

Steering Committee

Ruqian Lu (Honorary Chair) — Chinese Academy of Sciences, China
Dimitris Karagiannis (Chair) — University of Vienna, Austria
Hui Xiong — The State University of New Jersey, USA
Yaxin Bi — Ulster University, UK
Zhi Jin — Peking University, China
Claudiu Kifor — Sibiu University, Romania
Gang Li — Deakin University, Australia
Yoshiteru Nakamori — Japan Advanced Institute of Science and Technology, Japan
Jorg Siekmann — German Research Centre of Artificial Intelligence, Germany
Martin Wirsing — Ludwig-Maximilians-Universität München, Germany
Bo Yang — Jilin University, China
Chengqi Zhang — University of Technology Sydney, Australia
Zili Zhang — Southwest University, China
Christos Douligeris — University of Piraeus, Greece
Xiaoyang Wang — Zhejiang Gongshang University, China

Publicity Chair

Peng Zhang   Stony Brook University, USA

Finance Chair

Hui Zhao   Henan University, China

Technical Committee

Chao Feng   National University of Defense Technology, China
Zhong Ming   Shenzhen University, China
Hiroyuki Sato   The University of Tokyo, Japan
Shuangyin Ren   Chinese Academy of Military Science, China
Thomas Austin   San Jose State University, USA
Zehua Guo   Beijing Institute of Technology, China
Wei Yu   Towson University, USA
Keke Gai   Beijing Institute of Technology, China
Chunxia Zhang   Beijing Institute of Technology, China
Hansi Jiang   SAS Institute Inc., USA
Weiying Zhao   University College London, UK
Shangwei Guo   Chongqing University, China
Jianlong Tan   Chinese Academy of Sciences, China
Songmao Zhang   Chinese Academy of Sciences, China
Bo Ning   Dalian Maritime University, China
Leilei Sun   Beihang University, China
Tong Xu   University of Science and Technology of China, China
Ye Zhu   Monash University, Australia
Jianye Yang   Hunan University, China
Lifei Chen   Fujian Normal University, China
Fan Zhang   Guangzhou University, China
Xiang Zhao   National University of Defense Technology, China
Massimo Benerecetti   University di Napoli "Federico II", Italy
Knut Hinkelmann   FHNW University of Applied Sciences
                                 and Arts Northwestern Switzerland, Switzerland
Shuang Li   Beijing Institute of Technology, China
Yuliang Ma   Northeastern University, China
Xin Bi   Northeastern University, China
Cheng Li   National University of Singapore, Singapore
Hechang Chen   Jilin University, China
Chen Chen   Zhejiang Gongshang University, China
Mouna Kamel   IRIT, Paul Sabatier University, France
Yuan Li   North China University of Technology, China
Shu Li   Chinese Academy of Sciences, China
Serge Autexier   DFKI, Germany
Huawen Liu   Zhejiang Normal University, China

Bo Ma	Chinese Academy of Sciences, China
Zili Zhang	Deakin University, Australia
Long Yuan	Nanjing University of Science and Technology, China
Shuiqiao Yang	UTS, Australia
Robert Andrei Buchmann	Babeş-Bolyai University of Cluj Napoca, Romania
Yong Deng	Southwest University, China
Dawei Cheng	Tongji University, China
Jun-Jie Peng	Shanghai University, China
Oleg Okun	Cognizant Technology Solutions GmbH, USA
Jianxin	Deakin University, Australia
Jiaojiao Jiang	RMIT University, Australia
Guangyan Huang	Deakin University, Australia
Li Li	Southwest University, China
Ge Li	Peking University, China
Ximing Li	Jilin University, China
Daniel Volovici	Lucian Blaga University of Sibiu, Romania
Zhenguang Liu	Zhejiang Gongshang University, China
Yi Zhuang	Zhejiang Gongshang University, China
Bo Yang	Jilin University, China
Maheswari N.	VIT University, India
Min Yu	Chinese Academy of Sciences, China
Krzysztof Kluza	AGH University of Science and Technology, Poland
Jia Xu	Guangxi University, China
Jihe Wang	Northwestern Polytechnical University, China
Shaowu Liu	University of Technology, Sydney, Australia
Wei Luo	Deakin University, Australia
Yong Lai	Jilin University, China
Ulrich Reimer	University of Applied Sciences St. Gallen, Switzerland
Klaus-Dieter Althoff	DFKI/University of Hildesheim, Germany
Jiali Zuo	Jiangxi Normal University, China
Hongtao Wang	North China Electric Power University, China
Salem Benferhat	University d'Artois, France
Xiaofei Zhou	Hangzhou Dianzi University, China
Shiyu Yang	East China Normal University, China
Zhisheng Huang	Vrije Universiteit Amsterdam, the Netherlands
Guilin Qi	Southeast University, China
Qingtian Zeng	Shandong University of Science and Technology, China
Jing Wang	The University of Tokyo, Japan
Jun Zheng	New Mexico Institute of Mining and Technology, USA
Paolo Trunfio	University of Calabria, Italy
Kewei Sha	University of Houston-Clear Lake, USA
David Dampier	University of Texas at San Antonio, USA
Richard Hill	University of Huddersfield, UK
William Glisson	University of South Alabama, USA
Petr Matousek	Brno University of Technology, Czech Republic

Javier Lopez	University of Malaga, Spain
Dong Dai	Texas Tech University, USA
Ben Martini	University of South Australia, Australia
Ding Wang	Peking University, China
Xu Zheng	Shanghai University, China
Nhien An Le Khac	University College Dublin, Ireland
Tan Guo	Chongqing University of Posts and Telecommunications, China
Shadi Ibrahim	Rennes Bretagne Atlantique Research Center, France
Neetesh Saxena	Bournemouth University, UK

Contents – Part III

Knowledge Management
with Optimization and Security (KMOS)

An Adversarial Training Method for Improving Model Robustness in Unsupervised Domain Adaptation

Zhishen Nie[1] , Ying Lin[1,2(✉)], Meng Yan[1], Yifan Cao[1], and Shengfu Ning[1]

[1] School of Software, Yunnan University, Kunming, Yunnan, China
linying@ynu.edu.cn
[2] Key Laboratory in Software Engineering of Yunnan Province, Kunming, China

Abstract. The easily-perturbed nature of deep neural network makes it vulnerable to adversarial attacks, and such vulnerability has become a major threat to the security of machine learning. The transferability of adversarial samples further increases the threat. Adversarial training has made considerable progress in defending against adversarial samples. In transfer learning, unsupervised domain adaptation is an important research branch, however, due to the label of the target domain samples can't be obtained, it is difficult to implement adversarial training. In this paper, we found that using source domain data for adversarial training and adding the generated adversarial perturbation to the target domain data could effectively enhance the robustness of the transferred model. Experimental results showed that our proposed method can not only ensure the model's classification accuracy, but also greatly improve the model's defense performance against adversarial attacks. In simple, our proposed method not only guarantees the transfer of knowledge, but also realizes the transfer of model robustness. It is the main contribution of this paper.

Keywords: Unsupervised domain adaption · Adversarial training · Robustness · Adversarial attack · Transfer learning

1 Introduction

Deep learning is an important research direction in machine learning and has been successfully applied in many fields. However, recent studies have shown that deep neural networks (DNNs) are vulnerable to adversarial attacks [1]. Figure 1 shows the process of generating an adversarial sample by FGSM (Fast Gradient Sign Method) attack using GoogLeNet [2]. Although image Fig. 1(a) and Fig. 1(c) look the same, GoogLeNet has confidence of 57.7% for distinguishing image Fig. 1(a) as panda, and confidence of 99.3% for distinguishing image Fig.

This work has been supported by the Open Foundation of Key Laboratory in Software Engineering of Yunnan Province under Grant No. 2020SE305.

1(c) as gibbon. Furthermore, adversarial attack has transferable characteristics, which poses a great threat to the DNNs, therefore, designing effective defense mechanisms against adversarial attacks is very necessary.

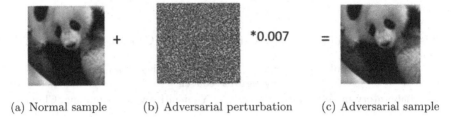

(a) Normal sample   (b) Adversarial perturbation   (c) Adversarial sample

Fig. 1. Adversarial sample illustration.

With the increasing cost of manually labeling data, transfer learning has made rapid progress. However, previous studies mainly focused on solving the problem of knowledge transfer, but did not consider that the transfer process also faces the threat of adversarial samples. Therefore, how to enhance the robustness of the model in the migration process has become an issue that need to be solved. In literature [3], the authors explored whether the robustness of the model could be transferred from the source domain to the target domain, and they used the method of fine-tuning to make the transferred model gain a certain degree of robustness. However, as far as we know, relevant literatures about model robustness in transfer learning are still scarce. In this paper, we put our attention on this topic and the main contributions of this article are as follows:

(1) Combing the adversarial training and transfer learning to complete the domain transfer learning and greatly improve the robustness of the transferred model.
(2) By randomly adding the adversarial perturbation generated from the source domain data to the target domain data, it can improve the transferred model's capability to defend against adversarial samples.
(3) Experiments were conducted on multiple benchmark datasets to verify the effectiveness of the proposed method.

The remaining parts of this paper are organized as follows. Section 2 surveys related work. Section 3 describes our method, Sect. 4 illustrates experimental results, and Sect. 5 analyzes the experimental results, and some directions are given for future improvements.

2   Related Work

2.1   Adversarial Attacks and Defense

There are multiple category standards for adversarial attacks. The category of white-box attack [1,4] and black-box attack [5–7] depends on whether the adversary knows the internal information of the attack model. It can be divided into gradient-based attack, optimization-based attack and decision-surface-based attack according to attack methods. Furthermore, according to attack results, it can be divided into targeted attack and untargeted attack. The targeted attack can induce the model to output some specific wrong results, while untargeted attack only let the model to output wrong results and dosen't care what the wrong results are. Table 1 summarizes some commonly used adversarial attacks.

Adversarial training is an important means to defend against adversarial attacks. The FGSM adversarial training method learns both normal samples and adversarial samples simultaneously [4]. With the emergence of various attack methods, FGSM adversarial training method is unable to effectively defend against most new adversarial attacks. Paper [8] proposed a PGD-based adversarial training method, which uses adversarial samples generated by PGD method. It is generally believed now that the PGD is the most versatile and vigorous first-order attack. If a model can defend against the adversarial samples generated by PGD, then the model may also be able to defend against other first-order attacks.

Table 1. Common adversarial attacks.

Name	Type of attack	Define of attacks
Fast gradient sign method, FGSM [4]	White-box, Gradient-based	$x^{adv} = x + \varepsilon \cdot sign(\nabla_x J(x, y))$
Basic iteractive method, BIM [9]	White-box, Gradient-based	$x_{t+1}^{adv} = clip_{x,\varepsilon}(x_t^{adv} + \alpha \cdot sign(\nabla_x J(x_t^{adv}, y)))$, $x_0^{adv} = x$
Project Gradient Descent, PGD [8]	White-box, Gradient-based	$x_{t+1}^{adv} = clip_{x,\varepsilon}(x_t^{adv} + \alpha \cdot sign(\nabla_x J(x_t^{adv}, y)))$, $x_0^{adv} = x + \alpha \cdot sign(N(\mu, \sigma))$
Carlini & Wagner, C& W [10]	Black-box, Optimization-based	$\|\delta\| + c \cdot f(x + \delta)$, $x + \delta \in [0, 1]$

However, the PGD based adversarial training has high computational complexity and it needs a large number of hardware resources and time consumptions. Therefore, some work has been proposed to improve its performance [11–13]. Fast adversarial training [13] uses random initialization samples and a single-step iterative method to construct adversarial samples for training and has achieved a better performance, but when the perturbation increases, it will cause severe overfitting. To solve the problem, the authors [14] introduced gradient regularization as shown in formula (1). It can reduce the calculation cost by reducing the number of back-propagation.

$$\Omega(x, y, \theta) = \mathbb{E}_{(x,y)\sim D, \eta\sim\mu([-\varepsilon,\varepsilon])}[1 - cos(\nabla_x L(x, y, \theta), \nabla_x L(x + \eta, y, \theta)] \quad (1)$$

Literature [15] effectively defends against white-box attacks through lightweight defense methods based on data augmentation.

2.2   Maximum Classifier Discrepancy

In 2018, Saito et al. [16] proposed the Maximum Classifier Discrepancy (MCD) for the unsupervised domain adaptation. The MCD mainly uses the differentiated prediction information of two classifiers and a feature extractor to achieve mutual adversarial learning. The main advantage is that it considers the task-specific decision boundary and uses it to effectively promote the knowledge positive transfer. MCD is insensitive to hyper-parameters and has good performance on multiple benchmark data sets. Literature [17] improved this method and applied it to the Internet of Things.

3   Methodology

3.1   Motivation

In transfer learning, considering that the data in the target domain has no label, so it is difficult to directly use the data of the target domain for adversarial training. Since many studies have shown that well-designed adversarial perturbations [6,18] are transferable, would the robustness also be transferable? In this work, we found and experimentally proved that the robustness is also transferable in unsupervised deep transfer learning. Robust transferability is very useful, as it can solve the threat of adversarial attacks in unsupervised transfer learning.

3.2   Method Overview

The main training architecture of our model is MCD. It consists of a feature extractor G and two classifiers F_1, F_2. The output is represented as $p_1(y|x_t)$ and $p_2(y|x_t)$ respectively. $D_s = \{X_s, Y_s\}$ represents the source domain data and its corresponding label, whereas $D_t = \{X_t\}$ represents the target domain data, which has no label. The pseudo code of our algorithm is shown in Algorithm 1 and it mainly consists of three steps:

Step 1. Randomly select F_1 or F_2 to generate adversarial samples, which are used to train the model. The parameters for calculating the gradient alignment loss $\theta = \theta_g \cup \theta_{f_1}$ or $\theta = \theta_g \cup \theta_{f_2}$ depends on which classifier is selected when generating adversarial examples. The optimization goals in this step are as follows:

$$\min_{G, F_1, F_2} L(X_s^{adv}, Y_s) + \gamma \cdot \Omega(X_s, Y_s) \tag{2}$$

$$L(X_s^{adv}, Y_s) = -\mathbb{E}_{(x_s^{adv}, y_s) \sim (X_s, Y_s)} \sum_{k=1}^{k} \mathbb{I}_{k=y_s} \log p(y|x_s^{adv}) \tag{3}$$

Where γ is the weight of the gradient alignment loss.

Algorithm 1: MCD with FAT

Input: θ_g: the feature extractor; θ_{f_1} and θ_{f_2}: two classifiers; X_s and Y_s: the source domain data and its corresponding label; X_t: the target domain data; *Epoch*: The maximum number of iterations; *lr*: Learning rates;

1 for $i = 1; i < Epoch; i++$ **do**

      /* step 1   */

2 $X_s^{adv} \leftarrow X_s + \alpha \cdot \nabla_x L(X_s, Y_s)$;

3 $grad \leftarrow \nabla_{\theta_g, \theta_{f_1}, \theta_{f_2}} [L(X_s^{adv}, Y_s) + \gamma \cdot \Omega(X_s, Y_s)]$;

4 $\theta_g, \theta_{f_1}, \theta_{f_2} \leftarrow \theta_g, \theta_{f_1}, \theta_{f_2} - lr \cdot grad$;

      /* step 2   */

5 $delta \leftarrow \alpha \cdot \nabla_x L(X_s, Y_s)$;

6 $X_s^{adv}, X_t^{adv} \leftarrow X_s + delta, X_t + delta$;

7 $grad \leftarrow \nabla_{\theta_{f_1}, \theta_{f_2}} [L(X_s^{adv}, Y_s) + \gamma \cdot \Omega(X_s, Y_s) - L_{adv}(X_t)]$;

8 $\theta_{f_1}, \theta_{f_2} \leftarrow \theta_{f_1}, \theta_{f_2} - lr \cdot grad$;

      /* step 3   */

9   **for** $j = 1; j < N; j++$ **do**

10 $delta \leftarrow \alpha \cdot \nabla_x L(X_s, Y_s)$;

11 $X_t^{adv} \leftarrow X_t + delta$;

12 $grad \leftarrow \nabla_g L_{adv}(X_s^{adv})$;

13 $\theta_g \leftarrow lr \cdot grad$;

14   **end**

15 end

Step 2. The generated adversarial perturbations are first added to all the source domain data. Especially, in this step, it is necessary to randomly select a part of the target domain data to add the perturbation. We call the target data added the perturbation as Fake Adversarial Samples (FAS). Then the feature extractor G is fixed, and the classifier F_1 and F_2 are trained to increase the difference between the two classifiers as much as possible. We use L_1 distance to measure the difference between $p_1(y|x_t)$ and $p_2(y|x_t)$. The optimization goal is shown in formula (4):

$$\min_{F_1, F_2} L(X_s^{adv}, Y_s) + \gamma \cdot \Omega(X_s, Y_s) - L_{adv}(X_t) \tag{4}$$

$$L_{adv}(X_t) = \mathbb{E}_{x_t \sim X(t)}[d(p_1(y|x_t), p_2(y|x_t))] \tag{5}$$

$$d(p_1, p_2) = \frac{1}{K} \sum_{k=1}^{K} |p_{1k} - p_{2k}| \tag{6}$$

Step 3. Randomly select a part of the target domain data to add the adversarial perturbation. The classifier F_1 and F_2 are fixed, and only the feature extractor G is trained to reduce the difference between the two classifiers, i.e.

$$\min_G L_{adv}(X_t) \tag{7}$$

4 Experiment

4.1 Datasets

Four datasets, SVHN (The Street View House Numbers) [19], MNIST (National Institute of Standards and Technology) [20], SYN SIGN (Synthesized Signal) [21] and GTSRB (The German Traffic Sign Recognition Benchmark) [22] are used to evaluate our method.

4.2 Training

In the training process, the optimizer was Adam, the learning rate was unified to 2e−4, the batch size was 256, the number of iterations N in step 3 was set to 4, and the maximum number of iterations of the entire training was set to 100. We used the FGSM attack with random initialization to generate adversarial samples, where the step-size was set to 2/255 and the perturbation upper limit was 8/255. We used 0.05 for the gradient alignment parameter γ.

    We set up four unsupervised domain adaptation tasks:

(1) SVHN → MNIST: We uniformly converted the image size of these two datasets to 32 * 32. MNIST was converted to RGB format, and the values of the three channels were consistent with the original single-channel data. During the training process, we first conducted 30 normal training, and then conducted adversarial training;

(2) SYN SIGN → GTSRB: These two datasets are traffic signal sign datasets with 43 categories. They are more complex than the other three datasets as the sample distributions among those categories are not balanced. We uniformly converted the image size of these two data sets to 40 * 40;

(3) MNIST ↔ USPS: These two datasets have the similar distributions. They are both handwritten digits 0–9, and both are single-channel grayscale images. However, the size of the MNIST data set is 28 * 28, with 70,000 pictures, and the size of USPS is 16 * 16, with 20,000 pictures. We uniformly converted them to 32 * 32.

4.3 Test

During the test phase, we selected three attack methods, FGSM attack, PGD attack and C&W attack. The perturbation upper limit ε means the maximum value by which each feature of the sample can be changed. t represents the number of iterations of PGD and C&W. And α represents the step size of PGD in each iteration. c is used to balance the perturbation and attack success rate. The relevant parameters of these attacks were set as Table 2.

Table 2. Parameter settings.

Attack	Name of parameter	SVHN to MNIST	SYN SIGN to GTSRB	MNIST to USPS	USPS to MNIST
FGSM	Perturbation upper bound ε	25/255	10/255	20/255	25/255
PGD	Perturbation upper bound ε	25/255	10/255	20/255	25/255
	Number of iterations t	30			
	Perturbation step-size α	2/255			
C& W	Number of iterations t	1000			
	Constant c	2	1	2	2

5 Results

Table 3 shows the classification accuracy of the mode on target domain data under no attacks.

Table 3. The classification accuracy under no attacks.

Method	SVHN to MNIST	SYN SIGN to GTSRB	MNIST to USPS	SUPS to MNIST
Source Only	67.1	85.1	76.7	63.4
MMD	71.1	91.1	–	–
DANN	71.1	88.7	77.1 ± 1.8	73.0 ± 0.2
DSN	82.7	93.1	91.3	–
ADDA	76.0 ± 1.8	–	89.4 ± 0.2	90.1 ± 0.8
CoGAN	–	–	91.2 ± 0.8	89.1 ± 0.8
MCD (N=4)	96.2 ± 0.4	94.4 ± 0.3	94.2 ± 0.7	94.1 ± 0.3
MCD with FAT (ours)	91.1	90.3	92.2	92.8

It can be seen that compared with the original method MCD, our proposed method has a slight decrease in the recognition performance on normal samples. For example, in the task of SVHN to MNIST, MCD achieved 96.2% recognition accuracy, whereas ours achieved 91.1%. The reason is that the added adversarial perturbation on the training data makes it inconsistent with the data distribution of the test data. However, except for MCD, our method is better than other methods.

Table 4 shows the classification accuracy of the transferred model on target domain data under different adversarial attacks.

Table 4. The classification accuracy under different adversarial attacks.

ATTACK	METHOD	SVHN to MNIST	SYN SIGN to GTSRB	MNIST to USPS	SUPS to MNIST
FGSM	MCD	35.8	16.1	31.0	33.2
	MCD with FAT (ours)	51.8	39.2	61.6	57.8
PGD	MCD	0.4	1.3	0.0	5.4
	MCD with FAT (ours)	28.4	21.0	40.6	43.7
C& W	MCD	24.3	4.1	5.9	12.5
	MCD with FAT (ours)	74.2	13.2	44.1	62.0

It can be seen from Table 4 that our method significantly improves the model's defense performance against adversarial samples. Especially, in the task of USPS to MNIST, under the attack of FGSM, PGD and C&W, the defense performance are increased by 24.6%, 42.6% and 49.5% respectively.

In general, the method we proposed greatly improves the robustness of the trained model while maintaining its original performance.

6 Discussion and Analysis

6.1 Transferability

Through thoroughly experiments, we found that the higher the similarity between the source domain data and the target domain data, the more similar the generated adversarial perturbation will be. To verify our findings, we adopted the method of calculating adversarial distribution proposed in literature [23], which is given in formula (8) where μ_i and σ_i are the mean and standard deviation of the diagonal Gaussian distribution, γ is random noise, j represents the j-th element of the vector.

$$\sum_{j=1}^{d}(\frac{1}{2}(\gamma^{(j)})^2 + \frac{log\,2\pi}{2} + log\,\sigma_i^{(j)} + log(1 - tanh(\mu_i^{(j)}) + \sigma_i^{(j)}\gamma^{(j)})^2 + log\,\varepsilon) \quad (8)$$

Figure 2 and Fig. 3 shows the adversarial distribution, where it obeys the Gaussian distribution. Figure 2 and Fig. 3 separately illustrate the mean and standard deviation of the adversarial distribution trained on the source domain data and target domain data. As it can be seen from the experimental results, the closer the two adversarial distributions are, the more robust the model after adaptation by our method. We can see that the distribution of MNIST and USPS is the closest, and the experimental results also proved that the model migrated under this task has strong robustness.

6.2 The Effect of Adversarial Perturbation

We randomly select classifier F_1 or F_2 to generate adversarial perturbation in the training process. The reason is to produce a similar effect of ensemble adversarial training [24], which can increase the perturbation generalization capabilities, and defend against black-box attacks effectively.

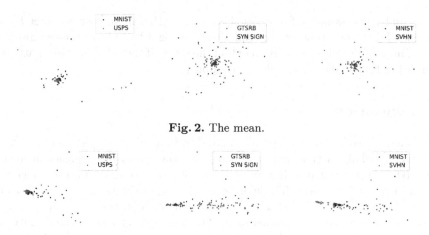

Fig. 2. The mean.

Fig. 3. The standard deviation.

In our adversarial training process, we used fake adversarial samples (FAS) to add perturbation. However, in regular adversarial training, the adversarial perturbation is generated based on the data of the source domain, not the data of the target domain. Considering that the data distribution of the two domains has certain similarity, so fake adversarial perturbation is somewhat between adversarial perturbation and random noise.

Figure 4 shows the impact on the performance of the transferred model considering whether add adversarial perturbation to the target domain data during the training process.

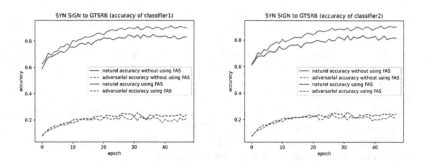

Fig. 4. Accuracy of two classifiers with or without adversarial perturbation.

The green line (including the solid line and the dashed line) indicates that no fake adversarial samples were used in the training process. The red line (including the solid line and the dashed line) indicates that fake adversarial samples were used in the training process. The dashed line represents the accuracy of the model under the PGD attack, and the solid line represents the accuracy of the model on normal samples. From Fig. 4, we can see that no matter classifier F_1 or classifier F_2, if there is no adversarial attack, using FAS reduces the recognition rate of normal samples to a certain extent, however, if there is adversarial attack, then using FAS makes the model more robust.

7   Conclusion

In this paper, we proposed a fast adversarial training method based on the MCD architecture. This method not only completes the knowledge transfer in unsupervised learning, but also improve the transferred model's robustness against various adversarial attacks. Through exhaustive experiments, we have confirmed that although adversarial attacks are transferable, robustness is also transferable in unsupervised transfer learning. The principle of the transferability of robustness lies in the similarity of the distribution of adversarial samples in the source domain and target domain, the closer the two adversarial distributions are, the more robust the model after adaptation by our method. What needs to be explained here is that the method of combing adversarial training with transfer learning is not limited to one specific transfer learning and adversarial defense method. In this paper, due to various methods of transfer learning and adversarial defense mechanisms, we only choose some classic and effective methods to demonstrate experimental results. In the future, there are still many things to do, such as how to make the adversarial perturbation closer to that generated from the data of the target domain and how to apply this method to the field of partial transfer learning.

References

1. Szegedy, C., et al.: Intriguing properties of neural networks. arXiv preprint arXiv:1312.6199 (2013)
2. Szegedy, C., et al.: Going deeper with convolutions. In: Proceedings of the IEEE Conference on Computer Vision and Pattern Recognition, pp. 1–9 (2015)
3. Shafahi, A., et al.: Adversarially robust transfer learning. arXiv preprint arXiv:1905.08232 (2019)
4. Goodfellow, I.J., Shlens, J., Szegedy, C.: Explaining and harnessing adversarial examples. arXiv preprint arXiv:1412.6572 (2014)
5. Su, J., Vargas, D.V., Sakurai, K.: One pixel attack for fooling deep neural networks. IEEE Trans. Evol. Comput. **23**(5), 828–841 (2019)
6. Moosavi-Dezfooli, S.-M., Fawzi, A., Fawzi, O., Frossard, P.: Universal adversarial perturbations. In: Proceedings of the IEEE Conference on Computer Vision and Pattern Recognition, pp. 1765–1773 (2017)
7. Qiu, H., Dong, T., Zhang, T., Lu, J., Memmi, G., Qiu, M.: Adversarial attacks against network intrusion detection in IoT systems. IEEE Internet Things J. (2020)
8. Madry, A., Makelov, A., Schmidt, L., Tsipras, D., Vladu, A.: Towards deep learning models resistant to adversarial attacks. arXiv preprint arXiv:1706.06083 (2017)
9. Kurakin, A., Goodfellow, I., Bengio, S., et al.: Adversarial examples in the physical world (2016)

10. Carlini, N., Wagner, D.: Towards evaluating the robustness of neural networks. In: 2017 IEEE symposium on security and privacy (SP), pp. 39–57. IEEE (2017)
11. Shafahi, A., et al.: Adversarial training for free! arXiv preprint arXiv:1904.12843 (2019)
12. Zhang, D., Zhang, T., Lu, Y., Zhu, Z., Dong, B.: You only propagate once: accelerating adversarial training via maximal principle. arXiv preprint arXiv:1905.00877 (2019)
13. Wong, E., Rice, L., Kolter, J.Z.: Fast is better than free: revisiting adversarial training. arXiv preprint arXiv:2001.03994 (2020)
14. Andriushchenko, M., Flammarion, N.: Understanding and improving fast adversarial training. arXiv preprint arXiv:2007.02617 (2020)
15. Zeng, Y., Qiu, H., Memmi, G., Qiu, M.: A data augmentation-based defense method against adversarial attacks in neural networks. In: Qiu, M. (ed.) ICA3PP 2020. LNCS, vol. 12453, pp. 274–289. Springer, Cham (2020). https://doi.org/10.1007/978-3-030-60239-0_19
16. Saito, K., Watanabe, K., Ushiku, Y., Harada, T.: Maximum classifier discrepancy for unsupervised domain adaptation. In: Proceedings of the IEEE Conference on Computer Vision and Pattern Recognition, pp. 3723–3732 (2018)
17. Li, Y., Song, Y., Jia, L., Gao, S., Li, Q., Qiu, M.: Intelligent fault diagnosis by fusing domain adversarial training and maximum mean discrepancy via ensemble learning. IEEE Trans. Ind. Inf. **17**, 2833–2841 (2020)
18. Zhou, W., et al.: Transferable adversarial perturbations. In: Proceedings of the European Conference on Computer Vision (ECCV), pp. 452–467 (2018)
19. Netzer, Y., Wang, T., Coates, A., Bissacco, A., Wu, B., Ng, A.Y.: Reading digits in natural images with unsupervised feature learning (2011)
20. LeCun, Y.: The MNIST database of handwritten digits (1998). http://yann.lecun.com/exdb/mnist/
21. Moiseev, B., Konev, A., Chigorin, A., Konushin, A.: Evaluation of traffic sign recognition methods trained on synthetically generated data. In: Blanc-Talon, J., Kasinski, A., Philips, W., Popescu, D., Scheunders, P. (eds.) ACIVS 2013. LNCS, vol. 8192, pp. 576–583. Springer, Cham (2013). https://doi.org/10.1007/978-3-319-02895-8_52
22. Stallkamp, J., Schlipsing, M., Salmen, J., Igel, C.: The German traffic sign recognition benchmark: a multi-class classification competition. In: The 2011 International Joint Conference on Neural Networks, pp. 1453–1460. IEEE (2011)
23. Dong, Y. Deng, Z., Pang, T., Su, H., Zhu, J.: Adversarial distributional training for robust deep learning. arXiv preprint arXiv:2002.05999 (2020)
24. Tramèr, F., Kurakin, A., Papernot, N., Goodfellow, I., Boneh, D., McDaniel, P.: Ensemble adversarial training: attacks and defenses. arXiv preprint arXiv:1705.07204 (2017)

Context-Aware Anomaly Detection in Attributed Networks

Ming Liu[✉], Jianxin Liao, Jingyu Wang, Qi Qi, and Haifeng Sun

State Key Laboratory of Networking and Switching Technology,
Beijing University of Posts and Telecommunications, Beijing, China
liuming@ebupt.com

Abstract. Anomaly detection in attributed networks has received increasing attention due to its broad applications in various high-impact domains. Compared to traditional anomaly detection, the main challenge of this task lies in how to integrate the network structure and node attributes to spot anomalies. However, existing methods attempt to integrate two kinds of information into a fixed representation and neglect the contextual information. Specifically, a fixed feature vector is directly adopted to evaluate its abnormality without considering the node's diverse roles when interacting with different neighbors. In this paper, we propose a novel Context-Aware Anomaly Detection (CAAD) framework in attributed networks. CAAD derives context-aware embeddings for each node pair with a mutual attention mechanism. The embeddings extracted by feature interactions can concentrate on the most relevant attributes of network structures. Numerous context information provides us with multiple perspectives to understand the structure connection and detect local anomaly structure. Moreover, we develop an anomaly gated mechanism to assign global anomalous scores to node pairs. The anomalous scores are learnable and applied to reduce the adverse effect of anomalies during the training process. By jointly optimizing network embeddings and anomaly gated mechanism, our model can spot anomalies in local and global collaborations. Experiments on various real-world network datasets indicate that the proposed model achieves state-of-the-art results.

Keywords: Attributed networks · Anomaly detection · Context-aware

1 Introduction

Networks, such as social networks and citation networks, provide a potent tool to represent various information systems. Nodes in the networks can represent entities, e.g., articles, users, and web pages, while edges express interactions or relationships between entities, e.g., citations, friendships, and hyperlinks. Meanwhile, nodes are often associated with a rich set of attributes [15]. For example, in citation networks, papers have substantial text contents; in social networks, users

ⓒ Springer Nature Switzerland AG 2021
H. Qiu et al. (Eds.): KSEM 2021, LNAI 12817, pp. 14–26, 2021.
https://doi.org/10.1007/978-3-030-82153-1_2

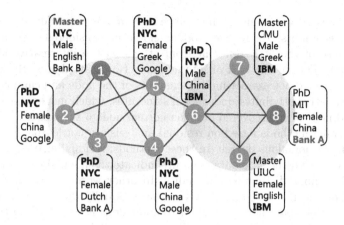

Fig. 1. A toy example on an attributed networks for anomaly detection via selecting informative attributes.

are affiliated with rich profile information. Such networks with extra attributes are called attributed networks.

Anomaly detection is a branch of data mining to discover rare, unexpected, and suspicious instances that are obviously deviating from the patterns of majority. Nowadays, detecting anomalies from attributed networks becomes an important research problem. It has significant implications in many security-related applications, ranging from social spam detection, financial fraud detection to network intrusion detection [6]. Traditional methods study the problem based on the ego-network [9] or community analysis [4]. The anomalies are identified in feature subspace by comparing with other nodes within the same community. Recently, the residual analysis [10] provides a general way to measure anomaly and has made progress compared with the traditional two-step approaches. Nodes with larger residual errors between true data and estimated data are more likely to be anomalies because their patterns do not conform to the majority. On this basis, several methods based on matrix decomposition [8] or network embeddings [2,16] are successfully combined with residual analysis and applied to anomaly detection. All methods can effectively integrate network structure and attribute information, providing a unified framework for the estimated process.

Despite their impressive success, existing methods have the following limitations: (1) They neglect the use of contextual information in the detection process. Anomaly is a relative concept which needs to specify a detection range. When the detection range changes, the relative anomalous degree of the instance changes. Similarly, some features play crucial roles in detecting when dealing with specific neighbors, but might have little relevance when dealing with other neighbors. We take a toy example in Fig. 1 to illustrate this phenomenon. The structure represents the friendship relations, where node attributes denote the degree, graduated school, gender, location and work. On the left, node 1 is taken as an anomaly due to its different education degree and graduate school. On the right, node 8 is viewed as an anomaly since its company value deviates obviously from other neighbors. Meanwhile, node 6 should be considered normal on both sides, because of the little different from others on the informative attributes of both sides. Due to the lack of interaction between attributes, the detection methods above cannot extract multiple aspects of the node and cannot focus on the discriminative attributes under local structures, which makes the anomalies node 1 and node 8 undiscovered and the normal node 6 suspicious.

(2) Existing methods based on residual analysis are not learnable about the calculation of anomalous degree. In these methods, residual errors between the estimated data and the true data can only indicate the anomalous degree, while the models cannot distinguish anomalies. In other words, these models learn patterns from normal and anomalous instances equally during the training. It forces the models' parameters to adapt to anomalous noise, which in turn leads to deviations in the estimated data. To avoid overfitting anomalous data, it is very important to weaken their influence during the training process.

To address these issues, we propose a Context-Aware Anomaly Detection (CAAD) framework for anomaly detection in attributed networks. More specifically, CAAD assigns various embeddings to a vertex according to different neighbors it interacts with. The context-aware embeddings are extracted by modeling feature interactions between vertices. Compared with original features, the interactive embeddings are more discriminative in understanding the local anomalous structure. According to the homogeneity assumption [7], links exist between instances with similar attributes in the networks. Therefore, two nodes in the same edge are considered as anomalous candidates if there remains a large gap between their context-aware embeddings. Different from residual analysis, which uses reconstruction errors as nodes' anomalous scores, we design an anomalous gated mechanism to calculate the learnable anomalous score for each node pair. The gated mechanism provides a global comparison and constrain for these local anomaly scores. The learned anomalous scores can not only replace the residuals to indicate the abnormal degree, but also weaken the adverse effect of anomalous node pairs during learning. By jointly optimizing network embeddings and the gated mechanism, anomalous edges will be assigned higher anomalous scores, and nodes with higher average scores are considered as anomalous ones. In summary, we have the following contributions:

- We propose a novel framework, CAAD, for anomaly detection in attributed networks. CAAD focuses on the informative attributes when facing with different neighborhoods. The context-aware embeddings can flexibly capture various relations and detect the local anomaly structure.
- We demonstrate the limitations of the existing residual analysis methods and propose an anomalous gated mechanism to assign a learnable anomalous score to each instance pair. The gated mechanism provides a global framework for comparing and constraining local anomalous scores. By jointly optimizing the context-aware embeddings and the gated mechanism, scores can simultaneously indicate the anomaly degree and weaken their adverse effects during the network embedding learning process.

– We carry out experiments on various real-world datasets. The results show that CAAD significantly outperforms the state-of-the-art methods.

2 Problem Formulation

We first give basic notations and definitions in this section. An attributed network is represented by a graph $G = (V, E, T)$, where V is the set of vertices, $E \subseteq V \times V$ are edges between vertices. The network structure is represented by an adjacency matrix A, where $A_{ij} = 1$ if $e_{i,j} \in E$ and $A_{ij} = 0$ otherwise. T denotes the text information of vertices. The text information of a specific vertex $v \in V$ is represented as a word sequence $S_v = (w_1, w_2, \ldots, w_{n_v})$, where $n_v = |S_v|$. The task of anomaly detection in an attributed network G is to identify anomalous nodes which contain very different attributes from the majority of their structurally connected nodes, by considering both network structure A and attribute information T.

3 Method

In this section, we present CAAD, a context-aware embedding framework for anomaly detection. As shown in Fig. 2, CAAD first adopt a mutual attention mechanism to learn the context-aware embeddings for given node pairs. Then, the anomaly gated mechanism provides a global perspective to distinguish anomalies and reduce their adverse effects. Finally, a novel loss function is used to jointly optimizing these two parts.

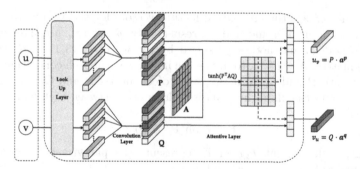

Fig. 2. Architecture of context-aware embedding module. It calculates the interactive embedding for each node pair. The attentive layer flexibly focuses on the most informative attributes of a node according to the different neighborhoods.

3.1 Context-Aware Embedding

The context-aware module derives embeddings through three layers, i.e., looking-up, convolution, and attentive pooling.

Looking-up Layer: Given a word sequence $S_v = (w_1, w_2, \ldots, w_{n_v})$, the looking-up layer transforms each word $w_i \in S_v$ into its corresponding word embedding $w_i \in \mathbb{R}^{d'}$ and obtains embedding sequence as $\mathbf{S}_v = (\mathbf{w_1}, \mathbf{w_2}, \ldots, \mathbf{w_{n_v}})$. Here, d' indicates the dimension of word embeddings.

Convolution Layer: Convolution operation is used to extract local features covered by the input embedding sequence $\mathbf{S}_v$. Specifically, a convolution filter over a sliding window of size i is used to extract the contextual feature c_h from the local context. It can be written as:

$$c_h = \sigma(\mathbf{W}_c \mathbf{S}_{h:h+i-1}), \tag{1}$$

where σ is the nonlinear activation function, $\mathbf{W}_c \in \mathbb{R}^{d \times (l \times d')}$ is the convolution weight vector and $\mathbf{S}_{h:h+i-1}$ is the slice of matrix S_v within the sliding window starting at the h-th position. Here, we pad zero vectors at the end of word sequence $\mathbf{S}_v$ to produce n_v contextual features.

Attentive Layer: As stated before, we assume that a specific vertex plays different roles when interacting with others. In other words, not all information contained in the node attributes will be useful for understanding the relationship between a specific node pair. To effectively capture useful information, we employ a mutual attention layer on attributes of the corresponding node pair.

Given an edge $e_{u,v}$ with two corresponding text sequences S_u and S_v, we can get the matrices $P \in \mathbb{R}^{d \times n_u}$ and $Q \in \mathbb{R}^{d \times n_v}$ after convolution layer.

$$P = [c_1^u; \ldots; c_{n_u}^u],$$
$$Q = [c_1^v; \ldots; c_{n_v}^v], \tag{2}$$

where c_k^u and c_l^v are the contextual feature vectors for the k-th word and the l-th word in the node u and node v, respectively. n_u and n_v are the respective lengths of node u and node v. Inspired by the work in [13,17], we utilize an attentive matrix, $\mathbf{A} \in R^{d \times d}$, to derive the importance of each contextual feature vector for both $\mathbf{P}$ and $\mathbf{Q}$. In detail, we project matrix $\mathbf{P}$ and $\mathbf{Q}$ into the same latent space and calculate the pairwise relatedness between each pair of vector as follows:

$$\mathbf{F} = \tanh(\mathbf{P}^T \mathbf{A} \mathbf{Q}). \tag{3}$$

Note that, each element $F_{l,k}$ in $\mathbf{F}$ represents the pairwise correlation score between two hidden vectors, c_k^u and c_l^v.

Based on Eq. 3, a row $F_{l,*}$ contains the correlation scores between the contextual feature vector c_l^u in $\mathbf{P}$ and all the contextual feature vectors in $\mathbf{Q}$. Similarly, a column $F_{*,k}$ contains the correlation scores between the contextual feature vector c_k^v in $\mathbf{Q}$ and all the contextual feature vectors in $\mathbf{P}$. A mean-pooling operation is then applied to each row/column of F as follows:

$$g_l^u = \mathbf{mean}(F_{l,1}, \ldots, F_{l,n_u}),$$
$$g_k^v = \mathbf{mean}(F_{1,k}, \ldots, F_{n_v,k}). \tag{4}$$

To make coefficients easily comparable, we employ softmax function to transform importance vectors to attention vectors as follows:

$$
\begin{aligned}
a_l^u &= \frac{\exp(g_l^u)}{\Sigma_h^{n_u} \exp(g_h^u)}, \\
a_k^v &= \frac{\exp(g_k^v)}{\Sigma_h^{n_v} \exp(g_h^v)},
\end{aligned}
\tag{5}
$$

where a_l^u and a_k^v are the attentive weights of $P_{l,*}$ and $Q_{*,k}$, respectively. We obtain the attentive weight vectors $a^p = [a_1^u, \ldots, a_{n_u}^u]^T$ and $a^q = [a_1^v, \ldots, a_{n_v}^v]^T$ through the attentive layer. Finally, the context-aware embeddings of u and v are computed as:

$$
\begin{aligned}
u_{(v)} &= \mathbf{P}a^p, \\
v_{(u)} &= \mathbf{Q}a^q,
\end{aligned}
\tag{6}
$$

Finally, given an edge $e_{u,v}$, we can derives the context-aware embeddings of vertices as $u_{(v)}$ and $v_{(u)}$.

In the embedding learning process, we use the same objective as [13], which measures the log-likelihood of an edge using the structure-based embeddings as:

$$
L(e_{u,v}) = \log p(u_{(v)}|v_{(u)}).
\tag{7}
$$

Without loss of generality, we assume the network is directed. Because an undirected edge can be considered as two directed edges with opposite directions.

Following LINE [12], the conditional probability of v generated by u in Eq. 7 is formalized as:

$$
p(v_{(u)}|u_{(v)}) = \frac{\exp(v_{(u)} \cdot u_{(v)})}{\sum_{z \in V} \exp(v_{(z)} \cdot z_{(v)})}.
\tag{8}
$$

Intuitively, optimizing the conditional probability using softmax function is computationally expensive. Thus, we employ negative sampling and transform the objective into the following form:

$$
L(e_{u,v}) = \log\sigma(u_{(v)} \cdot v_{(u)}) + \sum_{i=1}^{k} E_{z \sim P(v)}[\log\sigma(-u_{(z)} \cdot z_{(u)})],
\tag{9}
$$

where k is the number of negative samples and σ represents the sigmoid function. $P(v) \propto d_v^{3/4}$ denotes the distribution of vertices, where d_v is the out-degree of v.

3.2 Anomalous Score Gated Mechanism

In order to use context-aware embeddings for anomaly detection, a straightforward approach is to use the idea of residual analysis. First term of Eq. 9 can be regarded as the reconstruction of the network structure A. A lager reconstruction error $L(e_{u,v})$ indicates that the interaction pattern of two nodes u and v on one edge deviates obviously from the pattern of most other pairs. The edge between u and v can be considered as an anomalous one. Since we do not need to consider the anomalies in negative sampling pairs, the anomaly score based on the residual analysis can be calculated in the following formula:

$$R_u = \frac{1}{|\mathcal{N}_u|} \sum_{t \in \mathcal{N}_u} \log \sigma(u_{(t)} \cdot t_{(u)}) \tag{10}$$

where $\mathcal{N}_u$ is the neighborhood set of node u, $|\mathcal{N}_u|$ is the number of set.

The direct adoption of residual analysis can find anomalies to some extent. However, it cannot distinguish the anomalous instance during the learning process. Thus, the powerful fitting ability of neural networks makes it difficult to prevent itself from learning biased patterns in anomalies. We designed an anomaly gated mechanism to avoid bias. This mechanism assigns a learnable parameter to each edge to replace the reconstruction error, and reduce the adverse effects brought by anomalies. The calculation formula for this parameter is as follows:

$$s_{u,v} = \mathbf{W}_u^T \sigma(\mathbf{W}_s^T [u_v || v_u] + \mathbf{b}_s) \tag{11}$$

where $\mathbf{W}_s \in \mathbb{R}^{2d \times d}$ is the weight matrix, $||$ is the concatenation operation, $\mathbf{b}_s$ is the bias vector, $\mathbf{W}_u \in \mathbb{R}^{d \times 1}$ is the weight vector for generating the scalar value, and σ is the non-linear activation function.

The parameter $s_{u,v}$ is unbounded and unscaled. To make the local anomalous parameter globally comparable, we normalize them with softmax function:

$$\alpha_{u,v} = \frac{\exp(s_{u,v})}{\Sigma_{e_{i,j} \in E_B} \exp(s_{i,j})}, \tag{12}$$

where $E_B \in E$ is the edge set of a mini-batch. The anomalous score α is affected and constrained by all the edges in a mini-batch. Softmax is responsible for comparing and distinguishing the anomalies whose parameter s are much larger than other normal edges.

After that we obtain the anomalous score $\alpha_{u,v}$ for each edge $e_{u,v} \in E$, where $0 < \alpha_{u,v} \leq 1$. The larger the value of $\alpha_{u,v}$, the more likely $e_{u,v}$ is an anomalous edge, with a lesser contribution to the embedding process. To jointly optimize the embedding learning and anomaly score assignment, and minimize the impacts of the abnormal network structure, we update the Eq. 9 to the following cost function:

$$
\begin{aligned}
L &= L_p + L_n \\
&= \sum_{u \in V} \sum_{v \in \mathcal{N}_u} ((\frac{1}{\gamma + \alpha_{u,v}}) \log \sigma(u_{(v)} \cdot v_{(u)}) \\
&\quad + \sum_{i=1}^{k} E_{z \sim P(v)} [\log \sigma(-u_{(z)} \cdot z_{(u)})]),
\end{aligned}
\tag{13}
$$

where L_p is the reconstruct loss, L_n is the negative sampling loss, γ is a hyperparameter used to balance the influence of normal and anomalous data. It can be easily seen that, when the embedding of u and v has a large gap than other edges, in order to optimize the loss function in Eq. 13, we need a larger α to make the first term negligible. Conversely, the normal edges are assigned small α under the comparison of softmax. So naturally, α can replace the reconstruction error to indicate the anomaly degree. In addition, a large α forces the optimization process concentrating more on minimizing the contributions of anomalous edges. And parameters update also tend to adapt normal data rather than all data.

In addition, under the joint optimization of softmax and γ, the weight $\frac{1}{\gamma+\alpha}$ is constrained between $(\frac{1}{1+\gamma}, \frac{1}{\gamma})$. It ensures that in any case, the gated module will not assign 0 to the weight of all node pair, which will cause the loss to become 0. On the other hand, due to the Matthew effect of softmax, the weight of most normal edges are distributed at $\frac{1}{\gamma}$, while some others are close to $\frac{1}{1+\gamma}$. Therefore, γ controls the difference between the influence of normal and anomalous data in the overall objective.

After we obtain the anomaly score for each edge, the anomaly score for each node is calculated as follows:

$$R_u = \sum_{t \in \mathcal{N}_u} \frac{1}{|\mathcal{N}_u||\mathcal{N}_t|} \alpha_{u,t}. \tag{14}$$

4 Experiments

4.1 Datasets Used and Seeding Anomaly

In order to have a comprehensive evaluation, we select multiple real-world network datasets that have been widely used in previous research as follows:

Books[1] is a co-purchase network of books, the attributes include prices, ratings. The ground truth (anomalies) are obtained by amazonfail tag information.
Enron[2] is an email network dataset, and regards email addresses as nodes. Each node has several attributes including average content length, average number of recipients and so on. In particular, spam messages are viewed as anomalies.
Cora[3] is a paper citation network where nodes are papers, and edges indicate citations. Each paper contains variable-length text as node attributes.
BlogCatalog[4] is a blog sharing website. Bloggers in BlogCatalog can follow each other forming a social network. Users are allowed to generate keywords as short descriptions of their blogs which are severed as node attributes.

In order to make our experiments more convincing, the datasets we adopted contain as many cases as possible. Among them, Books and Enron are two public dataset with ground truth (anomalies), while Cora and BlogCatalog are two datasets with artificially inject anomalies. In particular, we refer to two anomaly injection methods that have been used in previous research [3,11] to generate

---

[1] http://www.ipd.kit.edu/~muellere/consub/.
[2] https://www.cs.cmu.edu/~./enron/.
[3] https://people.cs.umass.edu/~mccallum/data.html.
[4] http://people.tamu.edu/~xhuang/Code.html.

Table 1. Detailed information of the datasets

Dataset	Nodes	Edges	Attributes	Ratio
Books	1,418	3,695	28	2.0%
Enron	13,533	176,987	20	0.4%
Cora	2,277	6,262	1,433	6.6%
BlogCatalog	5,196	171,743	8189	5.8%

anomalies for each dataset. First, we adopt the method introduced by [3] to generate some small cliques to perturb the topological structure. The intuition behind this method is that in many real-world scenarios, a small clique is a typical anomalous sub-structure in which a small set of nodes are much more closely linked to each other than average. Therefore, we randomly select m nodes from the network and make those nodes fully connected. Then all the m nodes in the clique are regarded as anomalies. This process is iteratively repeated until n cliques are generated. The total number of structural anomalies is $m \times n$. In our experiments, we fix the clique size m to 15 and set n to 5, 10, 15 for Cora and BlogCatalog, respectively. Besides, we adopt another attribute perturbation schema introduced by [11] to generate anomalies. We randomly select another $m \times n$ nodes as the attribute perturbation candidates. For each selected node i, we randomly sample another k nodes from the data and select the node j whose attributes have the maximum deviation with node i among the sampled k nodes by maximizing the Euclidean distance $||S_i - S_j||_2$. After that, we change the attributes S_i of node i to S_j. In our experiments, we set the value of k to 50. The statistical information of these datasets is summarized in Table 1.

4.2 Experimental Settings

In this section, we introduce the detailed experimental settings, including the compared baseline methods and evaluation metrics. We compare the proposed CAAD with the following popular anomaly detection methods:

- **LOF** [1] performs the k-Nearest Neighbors to find contextual anomalies and only uses attribute information.
- **SCAN** [14] detects anomalies in a structural level and only considers network information.
- **AMEN** [9] utilizes both attribute and network structure information to spot anomalous neighborhoods from the ego-network point of view.
- **Radar** [5] detects anomalies that deviate from the majority by characterizing residuals of the attribute and its coherence with network information.
- **REMAD** [16] combines network embeddings and residual analysis together to spot anomalous and obtains the representative attributes that are closely coherent with the network structure.
- **Dominant** [2] is the state-of-the-art unsupervised method for anomaly detection in attributed networks. It performs graph convolution auto-encoder with residual analysis to detect the anomaly.

Table 2. Performance of different anomaly detection on different datasets.

Precision@K

Methods	Books			Enron			Cora			BlogCatalog		
K	20	50	100	20	50	100	20	50	100	20	50	100
LOF	0.100	0.080	0.060	0.250	0.180	0.150	0.300	0.220	0.190	0.200	0.120	0.090
Radar	0.250	0.160	0.120	0.400	0.340	0.320	0.450	0.420	0.370	0.500	0.320	0.250
REMAD	0.600	0.360	0.230	0.650	0.580	0.510	0.500	0.540	0.430	0.600	0.560	0.470
Dominant	0.400	0.260	0.200	0.700	0.680	0.580	0.650	0.620	0.490	0.600	0.520	0.420
CAAD	**0.700**	**0.400**	**0.260**	**0.800**	**0.700**	**0.620**	**0.750**	**0.680**	**0.570**	**0.700**	**0.640**	**0.510**

Recall@K

Methods	Books			Enron			Cora			BlogCatalog		
K	20	50	100	20	50	100	20	50	100	20	50	100
LOF	0.067	0.133	0.200	0.017	0.030	0.050	0.080	0.146	0.253	0.027	0.040	0.060
Radar	0.167	0.267	0.400	0.026	0.056	0.107	0.120	0.280	0.493	0.067	0.107	0.167
REMAD	0.400	0.600	0.767	0.043	0.097	0.170	0.133	0.360	0.573	0.080	0.187	0.313
Dominant	0.267	0.433	0.667	0.043	0.113	0.193	0.173	0.413	0.653	0.080	0.173	0.280
CAAD	**0.467**	**0.667**	**0.867**	**0.053**	**0.117**	**0.207**	**0.200**	**0.450**	**0.767**	**0.093**	**0.213**	**0.340**

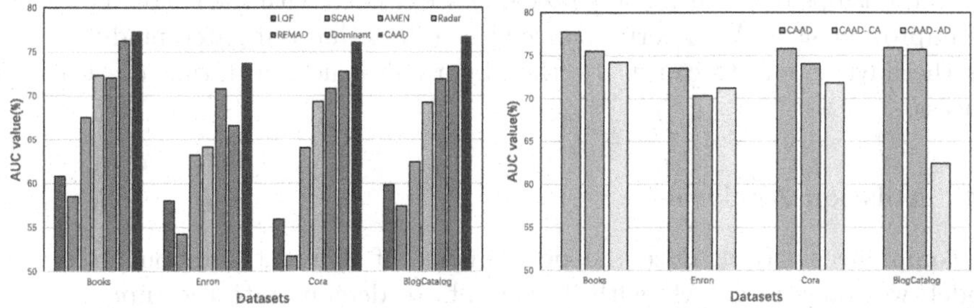

Fig. 3. AUC scores of all methods on different datasets.

Evaluation Metrics. In the experiments, we adopt AUC value to measure the performance of different anomaly detection algorithms. The higher the AUC value, the better the performance of the algorithm. We also user Precision@K and Recall@K to evaluate the ranking performance.

Parameter Settings. In the experiments on different datasets, we propose to optimize the loss function with Adam algorithm and set the learning rate to 0.001. The hyper-parameter γ is set to 1. For a fair comparison, we set the embedding dimension to 128 for REMAD, Dominant, and our method. For the other baselines, we retain the settings described in the corresponding papers.

4.3 Performance Comparison

We first present the overall experimental results in terms of AUC value on these datasets in Fig. 3(a). Then we present the Precision@K and Recall@K of each detection method in Table 2. Note that we do not include the results of SCAN and AMEN in Table 2 as they are clustering-based methods that cannot provide a precise ranking list. From the results, we have the following observations:

Most methods that take both structure and attributes into account achieve better AUC scores than methods (LOF, SCAN) that use only single information. Another interesting observation is that SCAN gains better results compared with LOF in most of the datasets. This can be interpreted as that the information provided by the network topology alone is very limited (compared to node attributes), especially in large-scale and sparse networks.

Among the methods that consider both attributes and structure, the residual analysis methods get superior AUC scores to AMEN. These methods optimize the task as a whole rather than treats subspace selection as a pre-processing step before anomaly detection. Within the method based on residual analysis, it is obvious that the methods using network embedding show better AUC performance. This is due to their deep architecture and strong integration abilities to network structure and node attributes.

CAAD achieves significant improvement on both real-world datasets and manually injected datasets. Compared to network embedding baselines, it demonstrates that context-aware embedding has a stronger capability of modeling relationships between vertices precisely. Compared with the residual method, the improvement in AUC performance also verifies that our gated module weakens the adverse effects caused by the abnormal structure during the learning process.

4.4   Ablation Analysis

To comprehensively analyze the performance of different components of our model, we compare CAAD with its variants to demonstrate the superiority of CAAD's unique design.

In order to prove that our method can jointly train context-aware network embeddings and anomaly detection, we compare our model and its two variants. First, we remove the mutual attention mechanism in the learning process of context-aware embeddings. All vectors after going through the look-up and convolution layer will be directly averaged to get the final embedding vector, the formula is as follows:

$$u_{(v)}' = \mathbf{P}a^{p'},$$
$$v_{(u)}' = \mathbf{Q}a^{q'}, \tag{15}$$

where $a^{p'} = [\frac{1}{|n_u|}, \ldots, \frac{1}{|n_u|}]^T$ and $a^{q'} = [\frac{1}{|n_v|}, \ldots, \frac{1}{|n_v|}]^T$. Other parts remain the same, and we mark this baseline as "CAAD-CA". For the other variant, we replace the anomaly gated mechanism with the residual analysis. In this variant, we keep the learning process of context-aware embeddings to reconstruct the network structure, and rank the anomalous nodes according to the reconstruction errors in Eq. 10 instead of Eq. 14. This baseline is named "CAAD-AD".

We show the performance of each anomaly detection method in Fig. 3(b). As can be observed, the AUC values of "CAAD-CA" and "CAAD-AD" are both lower than CAAD on all datasets. This phenomenon indicates that: (1) By introducing the attention mechanisms, the learned context-aware embeddings obtain considerable improvements than ones without attention. It verifies our assumption that a specific vertex might play different roles when interacting with other vertices. (2) The anomaly gated mechanism we designed is well combined with network embeddings. It provides a global perspective to compare local anomalies with others and alleviates the adverse effects brought from these anomalies.

5   Conclusion

In this paper, we presented a Context-Aware Anomaly Detection (CAAD) framework in attributed networks. The proposed model can learn various context-aware embeddings for a vertex according to different neighbors it interacts with. By jointly learning network embeddings and the anomaly gated mechanism, CAAD can detect anomalies and mitigate the adverse effects of model deviation caused by fitting anomalies. Experiments on multiple real-world datasets demonstrated our superior performance in anomaly detection. As a part of future work, we focus on how to combine anomaly detection with adversarial learning.

Acknowledgement. This work was supported in part by the National Key R&D Program of China 2020YFB1807805, in part by the National Natural Science Foundation of China under Grants 62071067, 62001054, 61771068, in part by the National Postdoctoral Program for Innovative Talents under Grant BX20200067.

References

1. Breunig, M.M., Kriegel, H., Ng, R.T., Sander, J.: LOF: identifying density-based local outliers. In: SIGMOD (2000)
2. Ding, K., Li, J., Bhanushali, R., Liu, H.: Deep anomaly detection on attributed networks. In: SDM (2019)
3. Ding, K., Li, J., Liu, H.: Interactive anomaly detection on attributed networks. In: WSDM (2019)
4. Gao, J., Liang, F., Fan, W., Wang, C., Sun, Y., Han, J.: On community outliers and their efficient detection in information networks. In: SIGKDD (2010)
5. Li, J., Dani, H., Hu, X., Liu, H.: Radar: residual analysis for anomaly detection in attributed networks. In: IJCAI (2017)
6. Liu, M., Liao, J., Wang, J., Qi, Q.: AGRM: attention-based graph representation model for telecom fraud detection. In: ICC (2019)
7. McPherson, M., Smith-Lovin, L., Cook, J.M.: Birds of a feather: homophily in social networks. Ann. Rev. Sociol. **27**, 415–444 (2001)
8. Peng, Z., Luo, M., Li, J., Liu, H., Zheng, Q.: ANOMALOUS: a joint modeling approach for anomaly detection on attributed networks. In: IJCAI (2018)
9. Perozzi, B., Akoglu, L.: Scalable anomaly ranking of attributed neighborhoods. In: SIAM (2016)
10. She, Y., Owen, A.B.: Outlier detection using nonconvex penalized regression. J. Ame. Stat. Assoc. **106**, 626–639 (2011)
11. Song, X., Wu, M., Jermaine, C.M., Ranka, S.: Conditional anomaly detection. IEEE Trans. Knowl. Data Eng. **19**, 631–645 (2007)

12. Tang, J., Qu, M., Wang, M., Zhang, M., Yan, J., Mei, Q.: LINE: large-scale information network embedding. In: WWW (2015)
13. Tu, C., Liu, H., Liu, Z., Sun, M.: CANE: context-aware network embedding for relation modeling. In: ACL (2017)
14. Xu, X., Yuruk, N., Feng, Z., Schweiger, T.A.J.: SCAN: a structural clustering algorithm for networks. In: SIGKDD (2007)
15. Yang, C., Liu, Z., Zhao, D., Sun, M., Chang, E.Y.: Network representation learning with rich text information. In: IJCAI (2015)
16. Zhang, L., Yuan, J., Liu, Z., Pei, Y., Wang, L.: A robust embedding method for anomaly detection on attributed networks. In: IJCNN (2019)
17. Zhang, Q., Lei, Z., Li, S.Z.: Neighborhood-aware attention network for semi-supervised face recognition. In: IJCNN (2020)

An Efficient Hybrid Approach to Detecting and Correcting Auxiliary Word Errors in Chinese Text

Yang Cao[1,2]([✉]) and Shi Wang[1]([✉])

[1] Key Laboratory of Intelligent Information Processing, Institute of Computer Technology, Chinese Academy of Sciences, Beijing, China
wangshi@ict.ac.cn
[2] University of Chinese Academy of Sciences, Beijing, China

Abstract. Chinese spell checking is an important research topic, and it is needed in several applications, such as optical character recognition, speech recognition, and search engines. Due to the specialties of Chinese characters, such as shape and pronunciation similarity, it is still a problem for the computer to detect and correct Chinese spell errors automatically. In this paper, we propose a hybrid approach to detecting and correcting a common class of Chinese word errors, called auxiliary word errors. First, to address the lack of dataset containing Chinese auxiliary errors, we generate artificial dataset of auxiliary errors by an auxiliary confusion set and a large Web corpus. Second, we propose a neural network detection model which adopts BERT as the embedding layer, and combines BiLSTM with CRF. Third, we utilize an auxiliary confusion set and a recurrent neural network language model (RNNLM) to correct auxiliary errors in text. Experimental results on different test datasets show our hybrid approach achieves better performance than traditional baseline methods.

Keywords: Chinese spell checking · Hybrid approach · Auxiliary confusion set · Auxiliary word errors · Artificial dataset

1 Introduction

When we type Chinese characters, Chinese keyboard input methods convert "pinyin" or "five-strokes" to a list of Hanzi characters (i.e. Chinese characters) from which we choose the "right" characters or words. Due to the specialties of Chinese characters, such as their shape and pronunciation similarity or mistaken usage of Chinese syntax, we tend to make errors in typing Chinese text.

© Springer Nature Switzerland AG 2021
H. Qiu et al. (Eds.): KSEM 2021, LNAI 12817, pp. 27–40, 2021.
https://doi.org/10.1007/978-3-030-82153-1_3

In this paper, we propose a hybrid approach to detecting and correcting a common yet difficult type of errors in Chinese text, i.e. auxiliary word errors (or auxiliary errors for short). Through a comprehensive analysis of Chinese auxiliary errors, we found the major difficulty of detecting Chinese auxiliary errors as below:

1. **Contextual opaqueness of auxiliaries.** Chinese auxiliaries appear frequently in Chinese text, such as "的" and "得". However, the left and right neighboring words of the Chinese auxiliaries have no obvious features in the Chinese text, so that the Chinese auxiliary errors are sometimes hard to detect.
2. **Pronunciation similarity of Chinese auxiliaries.** There are some Chinese auxiliaries with similar pronunciation, such as "的" and "得", and they are often confused even by native Chinese people. For example, people often incorrectly type the sentence "大家最后闹的不欢而散 (Everyone broke up in the end)" instead of "大家最后闹得不欢而散 (Everyone broke up in the end)".
3. **Word boundary problem.** There is no word boundary between words in Chi-nese sentences, we should use word segmentation tools to determine word boundaries, it makes difficult to identify Chinese auxiliary word error.

In this paper, we adopt a hybrid method to detecting and correcting auxiliary errors, mainly because the BERT can generate different word vector representations for the same word in different contexts which help us yield dynamic auxiliary word vector, and the BERT-BiLSTM-CRF model can capture long-term contextual information of an auxiliary error. In some cases, long-distance contextual information is important for the auxiliary word error detection. For example, given a Chinese sentence "他买了苹果、香蕉、橘子登水果 (He bought fruits like apples, bananas, and oranges)", detecting auxiliary word error "登 (etc.)" needs "苹果、香蕉、橘子 (apples, bananas, and oranges)" as the contextual basis.

Our main contributions are summarized as follows. First, for the lack of training sentence dataset of auxiliary errors, we propose a method to automatically generate such a training set. Second, instead of annotating an auxiliary error in a training sentence with a single tag, we annotate an auxiliary error and the k characters before and after the auxiliary error in a training sentence, which obtain much better detection performance, since auxiliary errors are highly context-dependent. Finally, we propose BERT-BiLSTM-CRF model for detecting auxiliary errors and a RNNLM combine with auxiliary confusion set for correcting them.

The rest of the paper is organized as follows. Section 2 presents the related work. Section 3 describes our hybrid method for detecting and correcting auxiliary word errors. Section 4 gives experimental results, and Sect. 5 concludes the work.

2 Related Work

Different methods have been proposed to detect and correct Chinese spelling errors in text in the past three decades. Chang [1] used a confusion set to replace words in original sentences and then used a bigram language model to calculate the probability of sentences after replacement; Finally, the likelihoods of the sentences before and after the replacement were compared to determine the errors in the sentence. Ren et al. [2] proposed a proofreading method which combined a rule-based method and a statistics-based method. Huang et al. [3] proposed a learning model based on the Chinese phonemic alphabets to improve error detection and correction rates. Chiu et al. [4] proposed a Chinese spelling checker based on statistical machine translation. Jia et al. [5] proposed a graph model for Chinese spell checking. Han et al. [6] proposed a checking method based on the maximum entropy. Yu et al. [7] proposed a method that utilized a language model, pronunciation and shape of Chinese characters to detect and correct spelling errors. Yeh et al. [8] proposed Chinese word spelling correction based on rule induction. Lin et al. [9] proposed a method that used a confusion set and a N-gram model to address Chinese spelling check. Yeh et al. [10] utilized the N-gram language model and the string matching algorithm to detect and correct Chinese errors in the text. Yu et al. [11] proposed a classifier to detect word-ordering errors in Chinese sentences. Wang et al. [12] proposed a CRF parser and a language model for a traditional Chinese spelling checker. Chiu et al. [13] proposed Chinese spell checking based on a noisy channel model.

3 The Methods of Detecting and Correcting Auxiliary Errors

Our hybrid approach to detecting and correcting auxiliary errors in Chinese text is mainly divided into two phrases: detecting and correcting phrases. In the detecting phrase, we split input sentences into sequences of Chinese characters, then use a BERT-BiLSTM-CRF model to predict the position of the auxiliary errors in sentences. If a sentence is predicted to contain "E" tags and it contains auxiliary errors, then we enter the correcting phrase. In this correcting phrase, we use a RNNLM and an auxiliary word confusion set to correct the auxiliary errors in the sentence. The whole process is shown in Fig. 1.

3.1 The BERT-BiLSTM-CRF Model for Detecting Auxiliary Errors

The BERT-BiLSTM-CRF model consists of three major parts: the BERT embedding layer, the BiLSTM layer and the CRF layer. Note that, in the training dataset, each auxiliary error, together with one character before and after it, which is annotated with an "E" tag. the whole architecture is depicted in Fig. 2.

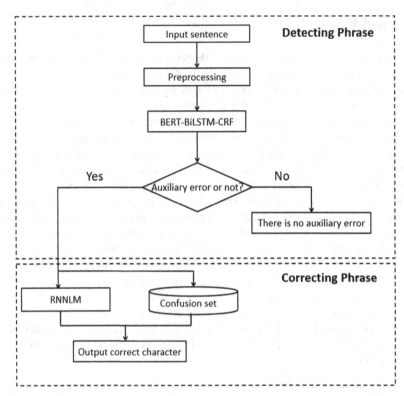

Fig. 1. The process of detecting and correcting Chinese auxiliary errors in sentences

BERT Embedding Layer. The main function of the BERT [14] embedding layer is to encode Chinese characters to vector representations of fixed dimension, while the BERT model is mainly composed of self-attention and feedforward networks. The self-attention can get the relationship between the characters of sentences, and is calculated with formula (1).

$$Attention(Q, \ K, \ V) = softmax\left(\frac{QK^T}{\sqrt{d_k}}\right)V \tag{1}$$

Where Q, K, V are the word vector matrix and d_k is the dimension of the input vector. For the sentence $S = c_1 \cdots c_i \cdots c_n$, where c_i is the i-th character of S, and the n is the number of characters in the sentence S. Through the BERT embedding layer, the sentence S is mapped to S' ($S' = c'_1 \cdots c'_i \cdots c'_n$, where $c'_i \in \mathbb{R}^d$, d represents the dimension of the embedded character).

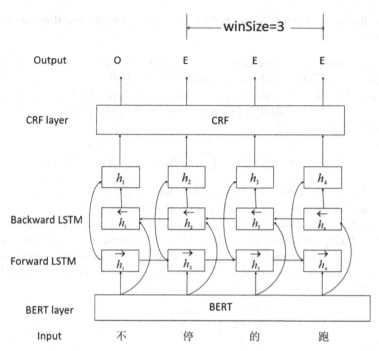

Fig. 2. The BERT-BiLSTM-CRF model for detecting auxiliary errors

BiLSTM Layer and CRF Layer. The LSTM [15] network is a variant of RNN, and it is mainly controlled by several gates. It utilizes the input gate, forget gate and update gate to address the vanishing gradient problem of RNN, and we adopt the BiLSTM to memorize the contextual information of characters in sentences, as we argued in the introduction that the contextual information of auxiliaries is significant when we judge whether they are errors or not. In using BiLSTM, $\overrightarrow{h_i}$ indicates the hidden state corresponding to the i-th character of the forward LSTM output, $\overleftarrow{h_i}$ indicates the hidden state corresponding to the i-th character of the backward LSTM output. We combine the forward LSTM $\overrightarrow{h_i}$ with the backward LSTM $\overleftarrow{h_i}$ as BiLSTM output h_i.

$$h_i = \left[\overrightarrow{h_i}, \overleftarrow{h_i}\right] \tag{2}$$

The final output of the BiLSTM layer is $H = h_1 \cdots h_i \cdots h_n$, and we pass H through the CRF [21] layer to predict the correlated tag sequence under consideration of outputs from the BiLSTM layer.

3.2 The Recurrent Neural Network Language Model for Correcting Auxiliary Errors

The language model of Chinese auxiliaries is trained from a training dataset containing sentences with auxiliary words, and it assigns a probability to each sentence. If we want to calculate the joint probability of characters in segmented Chinese sentence S $= c_1 \cdots c_i \cdots c_n$, the probability of Chinese sentence S can be calculated by using the following Eq. (3).

$$P(c_1, \cdots, c_i, \cdots, c_n) = \prod_{k=1}^{k=n} P(c_k|c_1, \cdots, c_i, \cdots, c_{k-1}) \tag{3}$$

According to the Markovian assumption, when we utilize bigram model to predict the probability of the next word, it can be approximated to $P(c_k|c_1, \cdots, c_i, \cdots, c_{k-1}) \approx P(c_k|c_{k-1})$ [16], and we use the (MLE) maximum likelihood estimation to calculate the probability of a bigram language model. Let $D(c_{k-1}, c_k)$ represent the number of occurrences of "$c_{k-1}c_k$" in the training dataset, and $D(c_{k-1})$ is the number of occurrences of c_{k-1} in the training dataset, we use the MLE to calculate the conditional probability of c_k in Eq. (4).

$$P(c_k|c_{k-1}) = \frac{D(c_{k-1}, c_k)}{D(c_{k-1})} \tag{4}$$

Unlike the traditional language model, the RNN language model is capable of memorizing all the previous characters [17]. For a sentence $S = c_1^1 \cdots c_i^t \cdots c_n^T$, the c_i^t represents the i-th character of the sentence S, and we initialize the hidden state h_0 with zero.

$$E_i^t = onehot(c_i^t) \tag{5}$$

$$ec_i^t = embedding(E_i^t) \tag{6}$$

$$h_t = \sigma \left(W_{hh}h_{t-1} + W_{ch}(ec_i^t) + b_1\right) \tag{7}$$

$$\tilde{y}_t = Softmax(Uh_t + b_2) \tag{8}$$

In the above equations, the E_i^t denotes a one-hot encoding of c_i^t, the ec_i^t represents the character vector, denotes sigmoid function, the W_{hh} denotes a recurrent weight matrix between hidden states, the W_{ch} denotes the weight matrix between the input layer and the hidden layer, the h_t denotes hidden state at time t, the U represents the weight matrix between the hidden state layer and the output layer.

For example, given a sentence S_2 = "你 如 果 仔 细 的 看" (If you watch carefully), and we want to calculate the probability of $P(的|你如果仔细)$. Figure 3 depicts the idea of identifying auxiliary errors by RNNLM. Using an auxiliary confusion set to replace the "的" in S_2, we have $P(你如果仔细地看) > P(你如果仔细的看) > P(你如果仔细得看)$ through the RNN language model, the inequalities indicate that the auxiliary "的" in S_2 is an error, and it should be corrected to the auxiliary "地".

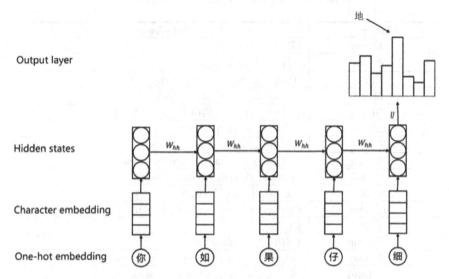

Fig. 3. Correcting auxiliary errors by recurrent neural network language model

4 Experimentation

4.1 Building Confusion Sets for Chinese Auxiliaries

For a given Chinese auxiliary, a confusing Chinese character is a character that is similar in shape or pronunciation to the auxiliary. For example, the auxiliary word "的" and "地" are phonetically similar, and thus they are often misused in Chinese text. The confusion set of a Chinese auxiliary c is defined as a set containing whose characters which are confused with c. For example, the confusion set of "地" is {的(de), 得(de)}, meaning that when "地" appears in a sentence and there is evidence to suspect that "地" is an error, the corresponding correct auxiliary for "地" may be "的" or "得".

In this paper, our main research focuses on detecting the Chinese auxiliary errors, so the confusion sets of Chinese auxiliaries are projected from Liu et al.'s confusion set of all Chinese characters [18]. Table 1 shows 21 main Chinese auxiliaries and their projected confusion set. It should be noticed that there are some other Chinese auxiliaries, e.g. 其 (zhe), 者 (zhe), 也 (ye) and 在 (zai), which were used in ancient Chinese, and are seldomly used in modern Chinese, and therefore Table 1 does not include them.

Table 1. Confusion sets of main Chinese auxiliaries.

Auxiliary	Confusion set
般(ban)	{班(ban), 搬(ban), ⋯ }
的(de)	{地(de), 得(de), 莳(di), ⋯}
地(de)	{的(de), 得(de), 炮(xie), 池(chi), ⋯}
得(de)	{的(de), 地(de), 德(de), 喝(de), ⋯}
为(wei)	{未(wei), 维(wei), 伪(wei), 卫(wei), ⋯}
过(guo)	{国(guo), 果(guo), 挝(wo), ⋯}
之(zhi)	{芝(zhi), 止(zhi), 支(zhi), 只(zhi), ⋯}
将(jiang)	{讲(jiang), 江(jiang), 奖(jiang), 降(jiang), ⋯}
看(kan)	{刊(kan), 坎(kan), 瞰(kan), 堪(kan), ⋯}
来(lai)	{莱(lai), 睐(lai), 铼(lai), 徕(lai), ⋯}
连(lian)	{链(lian), 联(lian), 梿(lian), 涟(lian), 莲(lian), ⋯}
了(le)	{乐(le), 辽(liao), ⋯ }
等(deng)	{登(deng), 邓(deng), ⋯ }
吗(ma)	{码(ma), 马(ma), 犸(ma), 冯(feng), ⋯ }
所(suo)	{锁(suo), 索(suo), 琐(suo), 嗦(suo), ⋯ }
呀(ya)	{牙(ya), 讶(ya), 芽(ya), 伢(ya), ⋯ }
嘛(ma)	{麻(ma), 吗(ma), 码(ma), 玛(ma), ⋯ }
着(zhe)	{著(zhu), 这(zhe), 哲(zhe), 浙(zhe), ⋯}
给(gei)	{饸(he), 绤(xi), 恰(qia), 洽(qia)⋯}
到(dao)	{倒(dao), 道(dao), ⋯}
以(yi)	{已(yi), 依(yi), 仪(yi), 衣(yi)⋯}

4.2 Generating Auxiliary Training Dataset.

Before constructing the auxiliary training set, we should collect the original raw corpus at first. Since both the quality and the coverage of the training dataset determine the precision and recall rates of the final auxiliary word error detection and correction, after a preliminary study, we chose four common topics, i.e. latest affairs, technological news, financial news, and entertainment news, and we individually chose two websites for each topic as shown in Table 2.

Table 2. Topics and websites of the training dataset

Topic	Website
Latest affairs	http://www.chinanews.com/
	http://www.people.com.cn/
Technological news	http://news.sciencenet.cn/
	http://www.people.com.cn/
Financial news	http://www.financialnews.com.cn
	http://www.shfinancialnews.com/
Entertainment news	http://ent.sina.com.cn/
	http://ent.qq.com/

We crawled webpages from the websites above, and downloaded about 3498 webpages. After removing the HTML tags and segmenting the webpages at Chinese punctuations, such as "。", "?" and "!", we obtained 482,086 Chinese sentences, which are used as our auxiliary training dataset in this work.

Auxiliary Error Training Dataset for BERT-BiLSTM-CRF Model. After sentence segmentation and POS tagging of the training sentences, we extracted the context of the window size surrounding the auxiliary word, and we denoted auxiliary word w_0 with a context of sequence $S = w_{-i} \cdots w_0 \cdots w_i$, the tag sequence T is represented as $T = t_{-i} \cdots t_0 \cdots t_i$, where each tag in T is initialized to "O". We use suspicious Chinese auxiliary word error $\tilde{w}_{err}$ to replace w_0 in S, and replace t_0 to "E", the context of the words surrounding the auxiliary word are also tagged "E". For example, we have an example of "闹的不欢而散", the "的" is auxiliary word error, the window size is set to 3, and the format of BERT-BiLSTM-CRF dataset sample is shown in Table 3:

Table 3. The format of BERT-BiLSTM-CRF dataset sample

Input character	TAG
闹	E
的	E
不	E
欢	O
而	O
散	O

Datasets. We used 982,375 sentence pairs for training dataset which are introduced in Sect. 4.2, to prove the effectiveness of our method, we use four test datasets: the artificial test dataset (ATD), the real test dataset (RTD), the SIGHAN-2014 [19] and the SIGHAN-2015 [20]. The RTD contains the auxiliary words errors appearing frequently in the real text, and those auxiliary errors are collected from web and newspapers. Since there are few auxiliary errors in the public dataset SIGHAN-2014 and SIGHAN-2015, we replace the part of correct auxiliary word in the public dataset to generate a test set of auxiliary errors. Table 4 shows the statistic of each test dataset.

Table 4. The statistic of test datasets

Dataset	Testing sentences
Artificial test dataset	7321
Real test dataset	1228
SIGHAN-2014	1823
SIGHAN-2015	1532

Baseline Models. We compare the performance of our proposed method with the following models: CRF, BiLSTM, CNN-BiLSTM, BiLSTM-CRF, these models are listed as follows.

1. CRF [21]. The model utilize the context of auxiliary words and part-of-speech of words as input feature.
2. BiLSTM [22]. The model uses BiLSTM to learn a context representation vector for each character.
3. CNN-BiLSTM [23]. The model utilizes CNN to capture continous representation of char-level feature.
4. BiLSTM-CRF [22]. The model utilizes BiLSTM to learn representation of character representation, the role of BiLSTM mainly plays feature extractor, the another role of CRF is mainly to predict sequence labeling.

Parameter Setting. We set the dimension of the character vector to 300 dimensions, and adopt the cross-entropy as the loss function. The initial learning rate is set to 0.0001 and dropout is set to 0.001, the optimizer is set to Adam. The size of BiLSTM hidden cell is set to 200, and the layer of BiLSTM is set to 3. The training batch size is set to 256. We trained our model on GTX-1080ti for 20 epoch, and all experiments were conducted on the Tensorflow platform.

To evaluate the performance of our proposed hybrid method, we adopted the criteria of the precision rate, recall rate and F1-score for all models, in Table 5, we compare different window sizes of auxiliary errors detection performance on ATD, compared with marking only a single auxiliary word error, marking the auxiliary word error with context improves the precision rate, recall rate and F1-score, when the auxiliary context window is set to 7, the precision rate, recall rate and F1-score reach the maximum. Table 6 shows the auxiliary word error detection performance comparison on four test datasets, and Table 7 shows the auxiliary error correction performance comparison on four test datasets, we observe that our proposed hybrid approach achieve higher precision rate, recall rate and the F1-score than all comparative methods from Table 6 and Table 7.

Table 5. Different window sizes of auxiliary errors detection performance on ATD

Model	Precision	Recall	F1-score
BERT-BiLSTM-CRF	85.23%	78.32%	81.63%
BERT-BiLSTM-CRF(win = 3)	91.23%	82.66%	86.73%
BERT-BiLSTM-CRF(win = 5)	91.53%	83.32%	87.23%
BERT-BiLSTM-CRF(win = 7)	**93.18%**	**85.76%**	**89.32%**
BERT-BiLSTM-CRF(win = 9)	92.48%	85.13%	88.65%

Table 6. Comparison of auxiliary errors detection performance on four test datasets

Dataset	Model	Precision	Recall	F1-score
ATD	CRF	81.38%	72.65%	76.77%
	BiLSTM	85.42%	79.31%	82.25%
	CNN-BiLSTM	87.52%	79.08%	83.09%
	BiLSTM-CRF	89.12%	80.34%	84.50%
	BERT-BiLSTM-CRF	**91.23%**	**82.66%**	**86.73%**
RTD	CRF	74.02%	76.65%	75.31%
	BiLSTM	79.42%	78.31%	78.86%
	CNN-BiLSTM	80.13%	79.08%	79.60%
	BiLSTM-CRF	82.97%	78.34%	80.59%
	BERT-BiLSTM-CRF	**84.23%**	**80.66%**	**82.41%**
SIGHAN-2014	CRF	78.02%	73.65%	75.77%
	BiLSTM	79.42%	79.22%	79.32%
	CNN-BiLSTM	81.27%	79.88%	80.57%
	BiLSTM-CRF	82.35%	81.79%	82.07%
	BERT-BiLSTM-CRF	**86.23%**	**83.42%**	**84.80%**
SIGHAN-2015	CRF	77.37%	72.31%	74.75%
	BiLSTM	78.52%	78.37%	78.44%
	CNN-BiLSTM	80.16%	79.35%	79.75%
	BiLSTM-CRF	81.65%	81.26%	81.45%
	BERT-BiLSTM-CRF	**85.43%**	**83.42%**	**84.41%**

5   Conclusion

In this paper, we proposed a hybrid approach to dealing with auxiliary errors in Chinese text based on a BERT-BiLSTM-CRF model and a recurrent neural network language model (RNNLM). The BERT-BiLSTM-CRF model was proposed to detect auxiliary errors, while the RNNLM was proposed to correct the detected errors. Compared with other models, the precision rate, recall rate and F1-score of BERT-BiLSTM-CRF model are much higher. When marking a single auxiliary error with context, the precision rate, recall rate and F1-score were further improved. It should be mentioned that our

Table 7. Comparsion of auxiliary errors correction performance on four test datasets

Dataset	Model	Precision	Recall	F1-score
ATD	BIGRAM	91.02%	84.65%	87.72%
	TRIGRAM	93.52%	86.77%	90.02%
	RNNLM	**95.81%**	**87.28%**	**91.35%**
RTD	BIGRAM	90.72%	82.43%	86.38%
	TRIGRAM	91.26%	83.51%	87.21%
	RNNLM	**95.37%**	**85.18%**	**89.99%**
SIGHAN-2014	BIGRAM	90.53%	80.81%	85.39%
	TRIGRAM	92.76%	81.75%	86.91%
	RNNLM	**96.43%**	**83.18%**	**89.32%**
SIGHAN-2015	BIGRAM	88.23%	79.45%	83.61%
	TRIGRAM	90.76%	80.35%	85.24%
	RNNLM	**95.46%**	**82.42%**	**88.46%**

hybrid approach had its limitation, the performance of the BERT-BiLSTM-CRF model and RNNLM depended on the scale and the domain of training dataset. In the future research, we will integrate the rules into the method to identify the auxiliary errors.

Acknowledgements. The work are supported by the National Key Research and Development Program of China (Grants no. 2017YFC1700302 and 2017YFB1002300) and Beijing NOVA Program (Cross-discipline, grant no. 191100001119014).

References

1. Chang, C.H.: A new approach for automatic Chinese spelling correction. In: Proceedings of Natural Language Processing Pacific Rim Symposium, pp. 278–283 (1995)
2. Ren, F., Shi, H., Zhou, Q.: A hybrid approach to automatic Chinese text checking and error correction. In: 2001 IEEE International Conference on Systems, Man and Cybernetics. e-Systems and e-Man for Cybernetics in Cyberspace (Cat. No. 01CH37236), pp. 1693–1698 (2001)
3. Huang, C.M., Mei-Chen, W., Chang, C.C.: Error detection and correction based on Chinese phonemic alphabet in Chinese text. In: Torra, V., Narukawa, Y., Yoshida, Y. (eds.) Modeling Decisions for Artificial Intelligence, pp. 463–476. Springer, Berlin, Heidelberg (2007). https://doi.org/10.1007/978-3-540-73729-2_44
4. Chiu, H.W., Wu, J.C., Chang, J.S.: Chinese spelling checker based on statistical machine translation. In: Proceedings of the Seventh SIGHAN Workshop on Chinese Language Processing, pp. 49–53 (2013)
5. Jia, Z., Wang, P., Zhao, H.: Graph model for Chinese spell checking. In: Proceedings of the Seventh SIGHAN Workshop on Chinese Language Processing, pp. 88–92 (2013)
6. Han, D., Chang, B.: A maximum entropy approach to Chinese spelling check. In: Proceedings of the Seventh SIGHAN Workshop on Chinese Language Processing, pp. 74–78 (2013)

7. Yu, J., Li, Z.: Chinese spelling error detection and correction based on language model, pronunciation, and shape. In: Proceedings of the Third CIPS-SIGHAN Joint Conference on Chinese Language Processing, pp. 220–223 (2014)
8. Yeh, J.F., Lu, Y.Y., Lee, C.H., Yu, Y.H., Chen, Y.T.: Chinese word spelling correction based on rule induction. In: Proceedings of The Third CIPS-SIGHAN Joint Conference on Chinese Language Processing, pp. 139–145 (2014)
9. Lin, C.J., Chu, W.C.: A study on Chinese spelling check using confusion sets and N-gram statistics. Int. J. Comput. Linguist. Chin. Langu. Process. **20**(1), 23–48 (2015)
10. Yeh, J.F., Chang, L.T., Liu, C.Y., Hsu, T.W.: Chinese spelling check based on n-gram and string matching algorithm. In: Proceedings of the 4th Workshop on Natural Language Processing Techniques for Educational Applications, pp. 35–38 (2017)
11. Yu, C.H., Chen, H.H.: Detecting word ordering errors in Chinese sentences for learning Chinese as a foreign language. In: Proceedings of COLING, pp. 3003–3018 (2012)
12. Wang, Y.R., Liao, Y.F., Wu, Y.K., Chang, L.C.: Conditional random field-based parser and language model for traditional Chinese spelling checker. In: Proceedings of the Seventh SIGHAN Workshop on Chinese Language Processing, pp. 69–73 (2013)
13. Chiu, H.W., Wu, J.C., Chang, J.S.: Chinese spell checking based on noisy channel model. In: Proceedings of the Third CIPS-SIGHAN Joint Conference on Chinese Language Processing, pp. 202–209 (2014)
14. Devlin, J., et al.: BERT: pre-training of deep bidirectional transformers for language understanding. CoRR abs/1810.04805 (2018)
15. Zaremba, W., Sutskever, I., Vinyals, O.: Recurrent neural network regularization. In: Proceedings of International Conference on Learning Representations 2015, pp. 1310–1318, San Diego, California (2015)
16. Jelinek, F.: Statistical Methods for Speech Recognition. MIT press, USA (1998)
17. Mikolov, Tomáš, et al.:Recurrent neural network based language model. In: Eleventh Annual Conference of the International Speech Communication Association, pp. 1045–1048 (2010)
18. Liu, L., Cao, C.: A seed-based method for generating Chinese confusion sets. ACM Trans. Asian Low-Resour. Lang. Inf. Process. (TALLIP) **16**(1), 1–16 (2016). https://doi.org/10.1145/2933396
19. Yu, L.C., Lee, L.H., Tseng, Y.H., Chen, H.H.: Overview of SIGHAN 2014 bake-off for Chinese spelling check. In: Proceedings of the Third CIPS-SIGHAN Joint Conference on Chinese Language Processing, pp. 126–132 (2014)
20. Tseng, Y.H., Lee, L.H., Chang, L.P., Chen, H.H.: Introduction to SIGHAN 2015 bake-off for Chinese spelling check. In: Proceedings of the Eighth SIGHAN Workshop on Chinese Language Processing, pp. 32–37(2015)
21. Lafferty, J., McCallum, A., Pereira, F.C.: Conditional random fields: probabilistic models for segmenting and labeling sequence data. In: Proceedings of the 18th International Conference on Machine Learning, vol. 951, pp. 282–289 (2001)
22. Huang, Z., Xu, W., Yu, K.: Bidirectional LSTM-CRF models for sequence tagging. arXiv preprint arXiv:1508.01991 (2015)
23. Chiu, J.P., Nichols, E.: Named entity recognition with bidirectional LSTM-CNNs. Trans. Assoc. Comput. Linguist. **4**, 357–370 (2016)

Traffic Accident Prediction Methods Based on Multi-factor Models

HaoZhe Zhao[1] and Guozheng Rao[1,2(✉)]

[1] College of Intelligence and Computing, Tianjin University, Tianjin 300350, China
{3018216249,rgz}@tju.edu.cn
[2] Tianjin Key Laboratory of Cognitive Computing and Applications,
Tianjin 300350, China

Abstract. Road traffic accident prediction has always been a complex problem for intelligent transportation since it is affected by many factors. However, to simplify the calculation complexity, most of the current research considers the impact of a few key factors and ignores multiple factors' impact in reality. To address this problem, we propose traffic accident prediction methods based on multi-factor models. The model introduces information including the severity of the traffic accident, the weather in which the accident occurred, and the external geographic environment to construct a multiple factors model to improve the prediction accuracy. Also, we can use more factors to construct the multi-factor model with the enrichment of data information. The multi-factor model can overcome the shortcomings of existing models in filtering data fluctuations and achieve more accurate predictions by extracting time-periodic features in time series. Furthermore, we combine the multi-factor models with different deep learning models to propose multiple traffic accident prediction methods to explore multi-factor models' effects in traffic accident prediction. The experimental results on the 2004–2018 Connecticut Crash Date Repository data of the University of Connecticut show that the $C(T) + R + W + RC$ multi-factor model has better prediction performance than other multi-factor models. Moreover, Multi Factors $(C(T) + R + W + RC)$ Based Bi-LSTM-Attention Method for Traffic Accident Prediction achieved the best performance on this data set.

Keywords: Road traffic safety · Traffic accident prediction · Time series · Multi-factor model · Bi-LSTM-attention

1 Introduction

Nowadays, Traffic safety is one of the focal problems in the realization of intelligent transportation [1]. The World Health Organization report shows that about 20–50 million people are injured in traffic accidents, and 1.35 million people die of road traffic accidents every year [2,3]. For instance, an estimated 6.74 million police-reported motor vehicle traffic crashes in the United States resulted in 36,096 fatalities and 2.74 million people injured in 2019 [5]. So, it is necessary

© Springer Nature Switzerland AG 2021
H. Qiu et al. (Eds.): KSEM 2021, LNAI 12817, pp. 41–52, 2021.
https://doi.org/10.1007/978-3-030-82153-1_4

to build an accurate early warning system with the accurate prediction of traffic accidents under the specific situation to ensure road traffic safety and prevent road traffic accidents. The authority can reasonably allocate public resources such as traffic police and medical personnel based on the prediction results, and maximize the usage of rescue resources. Also, rescuers can respond accurately to the accident, minimizing the property damage and casualties [4].

Complex and diverse climate and weather conditions often lead to traffic accidents [6–8], which significantly affects the periodicity of the time series of traffic accidents. Many studies have shown a strong connection between weather and road condition factors and the formation of road traffic accidents [6,8]. Also, traffic accidents' crash results are closely related to weather and road environment [9,10]. Besides the common factors, traffic accidents are also susceptible to emergencies and low-probability events, such as sudden breakdowns of vehicles or sudden diseases of drivers [7,11].

In a word, traffic accidents are affected by multiple factors, including amounts of abnormal data, and have a certain periodicity in the macroscopic view. Moreover, based on this, many researchers have done much valuable work. For example, Wang et al. estimated the crashes by type and severity using the Integrated Nested Laplace Approximation (INLA) Multivariate Poisson Lognormal (MVPLN) model [12]. Naik et al. used Random parameters ordinal and multinomial regression to find the relationship between traffic accident injuries and detailed weather conditions [10]. Li et al. also used mixed logit and latent class models to investigate the relationship between traffic accidents and rainfall in rural areas [13]. Yuan proposes a Hetero-Conv-LSTM framework to address the spatial heterogeneity challenge in the data, which involves several factors [14].

Although there is research on the screening and analyzing traffic accident data based on the severity of traffic accidents, weather conditions, rainfall conditions, and road conditions, the researchers often focus on a single factor. However, the data's periodicity is determined by the collective impact of multiple factors. The analysis of a single factor often has problems in capturing the actual periodic characteristics of the data. Therefore, we conduct a comprehensive analysis of multiple factors to explore their effects on the data sequence.

This paper proposes multi-factor models, which have excellent effects in filtering outliers in the data and capturing local characteristics and periodic changes of accident time series. The prediction method with the multi-factor model can effectively learn the local characteristics and the periodic changes of time series. Factors can participate in the construction of the prediction model in the form of parameters. With the multi-factor model, we can build a specific prediction model based on specific information, making the prediction model more realistic. For example, "rain', "highway", and "injury" can be used as parameters to construct a predictive model to predict the number of traffic accidents in which people are injured on the highway on a rainy day. After comparing with the other models, we eventually proposed the multi-factor-based Bi-LSTM-Attention method for traffic accident prediction.

The main contributions of this paper can be summarized as follows:

1) A method of extracting accident features based on different factors to build multi-factor models is proposed to improve the accuracy of the prediction.
2) Combined with the multi-factor model, we proposed the multi-factor-based Bi-LSTM-Attention method for traffic accident prediction. It has the best performance on the data set and significantly reduces the MAE of the predicted accidents to 0.91.

The structure of this paper is as follows: We summarize related research in Sect. 2, introduces the construction of the multi-factor model and the Bi-LSTM-Attention prediction method based on multi-factor models in Sect. 3. Furthermore, in Sect. 4, we summarize the experimental results and make a discussion. Finally, we give a conclusion in Sect. 5.

2   Related Works

Researchers have proposed many studies about the relationship between traffic accidents and different factors. For instance, Mussone et al. focused on analyzing road and weather factors in urban traffic accidents [15]. Lin et al. use FP trees to select features that are more helpful for the prediction [16]. Wang et al. employ a copula-based multivariate temporal ordered probit model to simultaneously estimate the four common intersection crash consequence metrics: driver error, crash type, vehicle damage, and injury severity [17].

Given the accident result factor, weather factor, and other factors, researchers launched many studies aim at the influence of the result factors on traffic accidents. Sharaf et al. divided the road risk into four levels, i.e., minor, moderate, severe, death, and used the K-means algorithm to improve the performance of the ANN model [18]. Biswajeet and Maher model traffic accident severity using neural networks and support vector machines to find out determining factors that significantly affect the severity of driver injuries caused by traffic accidents [19]. Mondal et al. comprehensively considered the weather factors that are most closely related to traffic accidents [20]. Wenqi et al. combined traffic flow, weather, and light factors to build a TAP-CNN model for highway traffic accident prediction [21].

In order to handle complex and periodic traffic accident time series and make accurate predictions, Zhou et al. used the Attention mechanism to predict traffic accidents [22].

3   Methodology

3.1   Single-Factor Model $(C(T))$

The traditional traffic accident prediction mehtod can be further formulated as the Eq. 1.

$$\begin{cases} f(x_1) = m \\ f(x_i) = F(f(x_1), f(x_2), \cdots, f(x_{i-1})) \, (i = 2, 3, \cdots, n) \end{cases} \tag{1}$$

In the Eq. 1, $f(x_1)$ is the num of accidents on the first day. $f(x_i)$ is the function that calculates the number of accidents on the i day based on a series of daily accidents on previous $i - 1$ days.

We called Eq. 1 as $C(T)$ model, which is based on the time series of traffic accidents. Traffic accidents will be affected by many factors, such as the environment and road conditions. Due to insufficient information, prediction only based on the time factor of the series will result in low-performance prediction results. So we introduce more factors to the $C(T)$ model to construct a multi-factor model for improving the prediction.

3.2 Multi-factor Model

We propose traffic accident prediction methods based on multi-factor models, using various information for accurate predictions.

We take the $C(T)$ model as the baseline to propose a novel multi-factor model combining different factors. The multi-factor model can act as a filter by checking all traffic accident data during a day and then selecting a series of data that can meet the requirements of the factors.

The multi-factor model can be further formulated as the Eq. 2.

$$\begin{cases} h(f_i) = \begin{cases} 1 \\ 0 \end{cases} (i = 1, 2, 3, \cdots, m) \\ V = [h(r_i), h(w_i), h(rc_i), \cdots] \\ f(x_j) = t_j * \sum_{i=1}^{m} V/dim(V) \\ T_n = [f(x_1), f(x_2), \cdots, f(x_{n-1})] \\ f(x_n) = F(T_{n-1}) \end{cases} \quad (2)$$

In the Eq. 2, $h(f_i)$ is the factor selected to build the multi-factor model. V is a feature vector formed by selected factors. Vector V determines whether a traffic accident can be used in the prediction method based on the information it carries. $f(x_j)$ is the function that calculates the number of accidents on the j day and m is the number of total accidents. We use the $f(x_j)$ function to multiply the time vector by the feature vector and then sum them up. After the normalization, we calculate the number of accidents that occurred on the day j based on the time factor. Furthermore, we serialize $f(x)$ and build the time series of traffic accidents T, and use the time series of past $n - 1$ days as the input to calculate $f(x_n)$, which is the number of accidents that occurred on the day n under the selected situation.

As described in Eq. 2, this paper improves the traditional traffic accident prediction methods by combining multiple factors, such as the accident results factor(R), weather factor (W), and road condition factor (RC) of traffic accidents. Based on the $C(T)$ model and those factors, the data features are extracted to construct the three multi-factor models, i.e., $C(T)+R$, $C(T)+R+W$ and $C(T)+R+W+RC$, these three multi-factor models, to explore the contribution of multi-factor models to traffic accident prediction. By combining traffic accident data variables to extract features of accident time series in advance, we can build a multi-factor model. The prediction method based on the multi-factor model can obtain more accident information and carry out machine learning targets on data features to make more accurate predictions (Fig. 1).

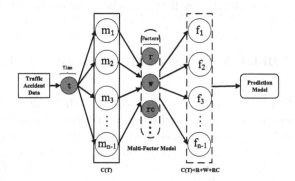

Fig. 1. Multi-factor model, where the m_i stands for accident data on the i day and the f_i stands for the output result of the multi-factor model, which is used to form the time series to build the prediction model.

Accident Results Factor. Generally, the accident result (R) is divided into three categories which are "Property Damage Only", "Injury of any type (Serious, Minor, Possible)" and "Fatal (Kill)", by the injury situation of the passengers and drivers. We found significant differences in the periodicity of traffic accidents of different results by analyzing traffic accidents [17]. However, most of the traditional methods ignore the impact of the accident result factor.

To address this problem, we extract the R from traffic accidents to establish a $C(T) + R$ multi-factor model based on the $C(T)$ model.

Weather Factor. On the other hand, the statistical results between weather conditions and traffic accidents show a strong correlation. Bad weather conditions (such as snow or fog) will reduce road visibility and traffic capacity, increasing traffic accidents. Although the research on the impact of the weather factor on traffic accidents has achieved outstanding results [7], most researchers ignore the joint impact of the weather factors and other factors on traffic accidents. Therefore, it is necessary to extract the weather factor (W) from the data feature and integrate it into the multi-factor model.

Road Condition Factor. The incidence of traffic accidents varies significantly in different road conditions(such as Interstate and Route). Besides the R and W, with the road condition factor added to the multi-factor model, the prediction of traffic accidents will be more accurate. In order to determine the collective impact of various factors on traffic accidents, we extract the road condition factor (*RC*) from the data feature and integrate it into the multi-factor model.

We can also get other multi-factor models by extracting features from the data. Furthermore, We propose deep learning methods based on the multi-factor model to make traffic accident predictions. The multi-factor model delivers the data as an input vector to the prediction method and eventually improves the prediction accuracy.

3.3 Proposed Bi-LSTM-Attention Method Based on Multi-factor Model

We propose a Bi-LSTM-Attention model based on the multi-factor model to predict traffic accidents. This method consists of 5 components: convolutional layer, bidirectional LSTM layer(Bi-LSTM layer), attention layer, and dense layer.

The multi-factor model extracts the features of the traffic accidents based on the factors to form the input vector. Furthermore, it then passes the data with apparent features to the prediction method:

1. The convolutional layer receives the input vector.
2. The convolutional layer passes the data to the Bi-LSTM layer.
3. The attention layer accepts the data delivered from the Bi-LSTM layer and learn key features scattered in the series.
4. Dense layers receive the data and flatten it to output the prediction result.

The Convolutional Neural Network (CNN) can filter the abnormal data caused by random factors and capture the local features of the data that came from the multi-factor model [23]. At the same time, traffic accident data is affected by long-term factors such as climate and weather during a short period. Hence, we can assume that all accident data in this period are related to each other. Consequently, we use the self-attention mechanism [24] to enable the model to assign the importance of traffic accidents so that the model can focus on learning the critical features scattered in the time series. Combining the advantages of the attention mechanism, Bi-LSTM can specifically learn the multiple periodicities of traffic accident time series due to the bidirectional learning mechanism [25]. It further overcomes the week learning effect in capturing the multiple periodicities of varying strengths under multiple factors.

Because of the joint action of CNN, Bi-LSTM, and the attention mechanism, the model can capture the periodicity of traffic accident time series despite multiple factors and abnormal data. In conclusion, the model's ability to capture the periodicity of time series is greatly enhanced, which solves the critical problem of traffic accident prediction (Fig. 2).

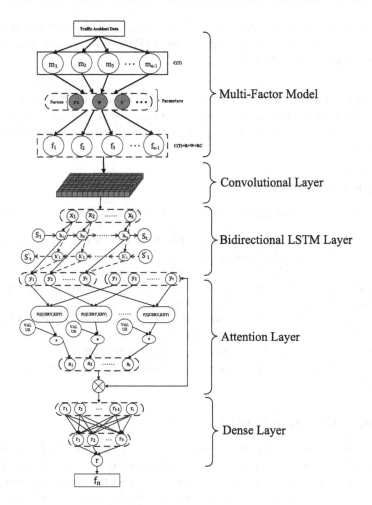

Fig. 2. The framework of Bi-LSTM-attention method based on multi-factor model

4   Experiments

4.1   Experiments Settings

Data Preparation. To verify the effectiveness of our proposed model, we use Connecticut traffic data from 2004 to 2018 from Connecticut Crash Data Repositor (CTCDR) as the data set. In this paper, the variables are set as R = "Injury of any type (Serious, Minor, Possible)", W = "Rain", RC = "State" (State Highways), to construct a multi-factor model, and combine the comparison models to make predictions. We divide the entire data set (5479 days) into two groups. The first 13 years (5114 days) are used as the training set, and data of 2017 (365 days) is used as the verification set. The last year (365 days) is used as the test set.

Evaluation Metrics. This article uses the following methods to evaluate the accuracy of the model: mean absolute error(MAE), mean squared error (MSE), root mean square error (RMSE).

Parameter Configurations. We set the window size to 90 and batch size to 365. We compile the model with the mean squared error loss function and the stochastic gradient descent optimizer with the settings: $lr=1e-5$, $momentum=0.9$.

4.2 Comparison Models

We compare our proposed framework with the following baseline models:

(1) Prophet model [26]. This model is built using the Prophet framework.
(2) DNN [27]. This model consists of a convolutional layer with 64 filters, and four DNN layers, which have 64, 32, 10 and 1 units respectively.
(3) LSTM [28,29]. This model consists of a convolutional layer with 64 filters, a 16-unit LSTM layer, and three DNN layers.
(4) Bi-LSTM [30]. This model consists of a convolutional layer with 64 filters, a 64-unit Bi-LSTM layer, and three DNN layers.
(5) Bi-LSTM-Attention. This model consists of a convolutional layer with 16 filters, a 64-unit Bi-LSTM layer, a Self-Attention layer, and three DNN layers.

4.3 Experiment Result and Discussion

This experiment aims to verify the effectiveness of the multi-factor model for improving the traffic accident prediction method and test the prediction effect of the proposed Bi-LSTM-Att model. We choose to reflect the prediction results and model effects by predicting the number of daily traffic accidents in Connecticut during 2018. Through the comparison between comparison models, we test the effectiveness of the multi-factor model.

To determine the impact of factors on the prediction, we use three multi-factor models: $C(T) + R$, $C(T) + R + W$, $C(T) + R + W + RC$. We combined the multi-factor model with different prediction methods to predict the traffic accidents in Connecticut during 2018 and measured the MAE, MSE, RMSE of the prediction results. The results are summarized in Table 1. The performance of the multi-factor models is shown in Fig. 3.

Based on the experimental results, we can first find that, in general, with the addition of a multi-factor model, the prediction model's performance is greatly improved. After combining the multi-factor model, the Mean-MAE of the $C(T)$ model has been dramatically reduced from 44.32 to 8.276 for the $C(T) + R$ model. At the same time, we found that as the factor increases, the accuracy of the prediction increases. Compared with the $C(T) + R$ model, with the addition of weather factor, the Mean-MAE of $C(T) + R + W$ model reduces to 7.04.

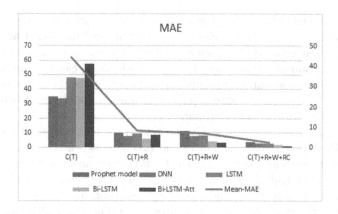

Fig. 3. The performance of different multi-factor models

Table 1. RESULTS of Multi-factor MODEL

Multi-factor modle	Method	MAE	MSE	RMSE
$C(T)$	Prophet	35.13	2929.09	54.12
	DNN	33.59	2394.23	48.93
	LSTM	47.92	4716.45	68.68
	Bi-LSTM	47.48	4775.38	69.10
	Bi-LSTM-Att	57.47	6310.34	79.44
$C(T) + R$	Prophet	9.88	166.28	12.89
	DNN	7.64	95.05	9.75
	LSTM	9.40	147.82	12.16
	Bi-LSTM	5.87	65.33	8.08
	Bi-LSTM-Attention	8.59	222.79	14.93
$C(T) + R + W$	Prophet	11.42	287.43	16.95
	DNN	7.90	265.60	16.30
	LSTM	8.38	301.20	17.36
	Bi-LSTM	4.36	109.49	10.46
	Bi-LSTM-Attention	3.13	44.28	6.65
$C(T) + R + W + RC$	Prophet	3.90	37.96	6.16
	DNN	2.60	34.71	5.89
	LSTM	2.62	34.82	5.90
	Bi-LSTM	1.70	14.79	3.84
	Bi-LSTM-Attention	**0.91**	**4.00**	**2.00**

Moreover, the $C(T)+R+W+RC$ model has the best effect on improving the prediction model's predictive ability. It reduces the Mean-MAE to 2.35. As factors increase, the ability of prediction models to capture the periodicity of time series has been enhanced. The addition of a multi-factor model allows the prediction model to obtain more traffic accident information and targeted learning data features while ensuring training speed and efficiency and eventually achieving accurate prediction of the number of traffic accidents. It can be concluded that the multi-factor model can more significantly highlight the data feature affected by the factors and can pass more explicit information about data feature to the prediction model for machine learning.

Among comparison models, DNN and LSTM models have similar poor performance. Because the information in the LSTM network is a one-way transmission, which can only use past information, there is no obvious manifestation when dealing with traffic accident prediction. However, many factors still exist after the accident, which are not immediate but continuous. These effects will be reflected in the time series as data changes over a period, which means future traffic accident data can also reflect past traffic accidents. Thus, the effect of Bi-LSTM has reflected in the experimental results that the Bi-LSTM model obtains far better performance than DNN and LSTM. The Bi-LSTM-Attention model based on the $C(T) + R + W + RC$ model reaches the best performance and reduces the MAE to 0.91, shown in Fig. 4.

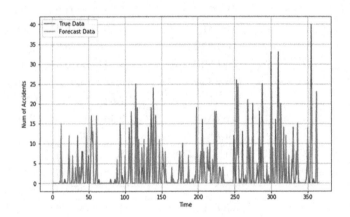

Fig. 4.   The   prediction   result   of   the   Bi-LSTM-Attention   combined   with C(T)+R+W+RC model, and the x-axis represents time, 0 represents January 1, 2018, and y represents the number of traffic accidents that occurred that day.

Interestingly, combined with the $C(T) + R + W$ and $C(T) + R + W + RC$ multi-factor model, the Bi-LSTM-Attention model reduces the MAE to 3.13 and 0.91, respectively, and achieves the best performance. Nevertheless, the performance of the Bi-LSTM-Attention model on the $C(T)$ and $C(T) + R$ model is poor. The attention mechanism can ignore irrelevant information and amplify the functional characteristics of the required information. However, because the key data features scattered in the time series are affected by many factors, the information conveyed by the $C(T) + R$ and $C(T)$ model is unclear, making the critical information mixed, even covered by each other.

5   Conclusion

This paper studies the method of traffic accident prediction based on the multi-factor model. Traffic accidents are affected by multiple factors, under the influence of which the accident time series presents complex periodicity. Hence, we propose the multi-factor model. Combined with the multi-factor model, the prediction model will have the ability to filter abnormal data in the time series, capture local features of the series, and recognize the pattern which shows strong periodicity in traffic accident time series. The experimental results show that the participation of the multi-factor model dramatically improves the accuracy of the prediction, and as the factor increase, the accuracy of the prediction also increases. The Bi-LSTM-Attention method based on the $C(T) + R + W + RC$ model has the best performance and reduces the MAE value of prediction to 0.91. The multi-factor model has specific research value in predicting events involving multiple factors, and it is a promising solution.

References

1. Zhu, M., et al.: Public vehicles for future urban transportation. IEEE Trans. Intell. Transp. Syst. **17**, 3344–3353 (2016)
2. Chen, M., Zhang, Y., Qiu, M., Guizani, N., Hao, Y.: SPHA: smart personal health advisor based on deep analytics. IEEE Commun. Mag. **56**, 164–169 (2018)
3. (WHO), W.H.O., others: Global status report on road safety 2018 (2018). Geneva WHO (2019)
4. Qiu, M., Ming, Z., Wang, J., Yang, L.T., Xiang, Y.: Enabling cloud computing in emergency management systems. IEEE Cloud Comput. **1**, 60–67 (2014)
5. National Highway Traffic Safety Administration: Overview of motor vehicle crashes in 2019. No. DOT HS 813 060 (2020)
6. Dastoorpoor, M., Idani, E., Khanjani, N., Goudarzi, G., Bahrampour, A.: Relationship between air pollution, weather, traffic, and traffic-related mortality. Trauma Mon. **21**, e37585 (2016)
7. Park, S.J., Kho, S.-Y., Park, H.-C.: The effects of road geometry on the injury severity of expressway traffic accident depending on weather conditions. J. Korea Inst. Intell. Transp. Syst. **18**, 12–28 (2019)
8. Malin, F., Norros, I., Innamaa, S.: Accident risk of road and weather conditions on different road types. Accid. Anal. Prev. **122**, 181–188 (2019)
9. Abdel-Aty, M.: Analysis of driver injury severity levels at multiple locations using ordered probit models. J. Saf. Res. **34**, 597–603 (2003)
10. Naik, B., Tung, L.W., Zhao, S., Khattak, A.J.: Weather impacts on single-vehicle truck crash injury severity. J. Saf. Res. **58**, 57–65 (2016)
11. Harirforoush, H.: Spatial and temporal analysis of seasonal traffic accidents. Am. J. Traffic Transp. Eng. **4**, 7 (2019)
12. Wang, K., Ivan, J.N., Ravishanker, N., Jackson, E.: Multivariate poisson lognormal modeling of crashes by type and severity on rural two lane highways. Accid. Anal. Prev. **99**, 6–19 (2017)
13. Li, Z., et al.: Investigation of driver injury severities in rural single-vehicle crashes under rain conditions using mixed logit and latent class models. Accid. Anal. Prev. **124**, 219–229 (2019)

14. Yuan, Z., Zhou, X., Yang, T.: Hetero-ConvLSTM: A deep learning approach to traffic accident prediction on heterogeneous spatio-temporal data. In: Proc. ACM SIGKDD International Conference on Knowledge Discovery and Data Mining, pp. 984–992 (2018)

15. Mussone, L., Bassani, M., Masci, P.: Analysis of factors affecting the severity of crashes in urban road intersections. Accid. Anal. Prev. **103**, 112–122 (2017)

16. Lin, L., Wang, Q., Sadek, A.W.: A novel variable selection method based on frequent pattern tree for real-time traffic accident risk prediction. Transp. Res. Part C Emerg. Technol. **55**, 444–459 (2015)

17. Wang, K., Bhowmik, T., Yasmin, S., Zhao, S., Eluru, N., Jackson, E.: Multivariate copula temporal modeling of intersection crash consequence metrics: a joint estimation of injury severity, crash type, vehicle damage and driver error. Accid. Anal. Prev. **125**, 188–197 (2019)

18. Alkheder, S., Taamneh, M., Taamneh, S.: Severity prediction of traffic accident using an artificial neural network. J. Forecast. **36**, 100–108 (2017)

19. Pradhan, B., Ibrahim Sameen, M.: Modeling traffic accident severity using neural networks and support vector machines. In: Pradhan, B., Ibrahim Sameen, M. (eds.) Laser Scanning Systems in Highway and Safety Assessment. ASTI, pp. 111–117. Springer, Cham (2020). https://doi.org/10.1007/978-3-030-10374-3_9

20. Mondal, A.R., Bhuiyan, M.A.E., Yang, F.: Advancement of weather-related crash prediction model using nonparametric machine learning algorithms. SN Appl. Sci. **2**, 1–11 (2020)

21. Wenqi, L., Dongyu, L., Menghua, Y.: A model of traffic accident prediction based on convolutional neural network. In: 2017 2nd IEEE International Conference on Intelligent Transportation Engineering, ICITE 2017, pp. 198–202 (2017)

22. Zhou, Z., Chen, L., Zhu, C., Wang, P.: Stack ResNet for short-term accident risk prediction leveraging cross-domain data. In: Proceedings - 2019 Chinese Automation Congress, CAC 2019, pp. 782–787 (2019)

23. Rao, G., Zhang, Y., Zhang, L., Cong, Q., Feng, Z.: MGL-CNN: a hierarchical posts representations model for identifying depressed individuals in online forums. IEEE Access **8**, 32395–32403 (2020)

24. Vaswani, A., et al.: Attention is all you need. In: Advances in Neural Information Processing Systems, pp. 5999–6009 (2017)

25. Pang, N., Xiao, W., Zhao, X.: Chinese text classification via bidirectional lattice LSTM BT - knowledge science, engineering and management. Presented at the (2020)

26. Taylor, S.J., Letham, B.: Business time series forecasting at scale. PeerJ Prepr. 5e3190v2. **35**, 48–90 (2017)

27. Yuan, Z., Zhou, X., Yang, T., Tamerius, J., Mantilla, R.: Predicting traffic accidents through heterogeneous urban data: a case study. In: Proceedings of the 6th International Workshop on Urban Computing (UrbComp 2017), Halifax, NS, Canada, p. 10 (2017)

28. Wang, J., Cao, Y., Du, Y., Li, L.: DST: a deep urban traffic flow prediction framework based on spatial-temporal features BT - knowledge science, engineering and management. Presented at the (2019)

29. Rao, G., Huang, W., Feng, Z., Cong, Q.: LSTM with sentence representations for document-level sentiment classification. Neurocomputing **308**, 49–57 (2018)

30. Wang, J., Hu, F., Li, L.: Deep bi-directional long short-term memory model for short-term traffic flow prediction. Presented at the (2017). B.T.-I.C. on N.I.P

Combining BERT and Multiple Embedding Methods with the Deep Neural Network for Humor Detection

Rida Miraj$^{(\boxtimes)}$ (iD) and Masaki Aono$^{(\boxtimes)}$ (iD)

Toyohashi University of Technology, Toyohashi, Japan
aono@tut.jp

Abstract. Humor detection from written sentences has been an interesting and challenging task in the last few years. Most of the prior studies have been explored the traditional approaches of embedding, e.g., Word2Vec or Glove. Recently Bidirectional Encoder Representations from Transformers (BERT) sentence embedding has also been used for this task. In this paper, we propose a framework for humor detection in short texts taken from news headlines. Our proposed framework attempts to extract information from written text via the use of different layers of BERT. After several trials, weights were assigned to different layers of the BERT model. The extracted information was then sent to a Bi-GRU neural network as an embedding matrix. We utilized the properties of some external embedding models. A multi-kernel convolution in our neural network was also employed to extract higher-level sentence representations. This framework performed very well on the task of humor detection.

Keywords: Humor detection · Embedding · BERT · Text · CNN · Bi-GRU

1 Introduction

Humor is a ubiquitous, elusive event that exists all around the world. In previous research and studies, mostly the problems related to humor were based on binary classification or based on the selection of linguistic features. Purandare and Litman analyzed humorous spoken conversations as data from a classic comedy television and used standard supervised learning classifiers to identify humorous speech in the conversation [21]. Taylor and Mazlack used the methodology that was based on the extraction of structural patterns and peculiar structure of jokes newcite [23]. Luke de Oliveira and Alfredo applied recurrent neural network (RNN) and convolutional neural networks (CNNs) to humor detection from reviews in Yelp dataset [10]. The detection of humor from a small and formal sentence is a unique challenge to the research community. To address the challenge of humor detection, Hossain et al. [12] presented a task that focuses on

© Springer Nature Switzerland AG 2021
H. Qiu et al. (Eds.): KSEM 2021, LNAI 12817, pp. 53–61, 2021.
https://doi.org/10.1007/978-3-030-82153-1_5

detecting humor in English news headlines with micro-edits. The edited head-lines have one selected word or entity that is replaced by editors, which are then graded by the degree of funniness. Accurate scoring of the funniness from micro-edits can serve as a footstone of humorous text generation [12]. Figure 1 depicts how a single word is replaced with another word to make the sentence funny or humicroedit(dataset formed for this task is named as humicroedit in the article [12]).

 News Headline:
California and President Trump are going to war with each other.

Word that is replaced: President trump
Used word: monkeys

 Edited Headline:
California and Monkeys are going to war with each other.

Fig. 1. Example of edited news headline.

However, most of the related work of humor detection explored the traditional way of embeddings in their methods. In this paper, we propose a framework that combines the inner layers information of BERT with Bi-GRU and uses the multiple word embeddings with the multi-kernel convolution and Bi-GRU in a unified architecture. Experimental results on edited news headlines demonstrate the efficacy of our framework.

The rest of the paper is structured as follows: Sect. 2 presents a summary of previous studies. In Sect. 3, we introduce our proposed humor detection frame-work. Section 4 includes experiments and evaluations. Some concluded remarks of our work are described in Sect. 5.

2   Related Research

In the related work of humor identification, there are a lot of work that is done over the year which includes statistical and N-gram analysis [23], Regression Trees [21], Word2Vec combined with K-NN Human Centric Features, and Con-volutional Neural Networks [8]. When working with a limited number of charac-teristics, neural networks function exceptionally effectively. When dealing with changing length sequences, sequence variants to prior states, as in recurrent neu-ral networks, can be introduced to the network. To identify jokes from non-jokes, several humor detection algorithms include hand-crafted (typically word-based) characteristics [5, 14, 17, 24]. Such word-based features work well when the non-joke dataset contains terms that are entirely distinct from the humor dataset. According to humor theory, the sequence of words matters, because announcing the punchline before the setup would merely lead to the discovery of the second interpretation of the joke, causing the joke to lose its humorous component [22]. Thus, using a big pre-trained model, such as the latest BERT-like models, is an intriguing fit for the humor detection problem. One potential disadvantage is that these models are not well adapted for comprehending complicated word-play since their tokens are ignorant of relative morphological similarities since the models are oblivious of the tokens' letters [6]. BERT-like models, on the other hand, have done well on English humor recognition datasets [4, 26]. In this paper, we used BERT layers for extracting more information regarding words in a sentence and used it as an embedding matrix for our neural network.

3 Framework

In this section, we describe the details of our proposed framework for humor detection. Figure 2 depicts an overview of our proposed framework.

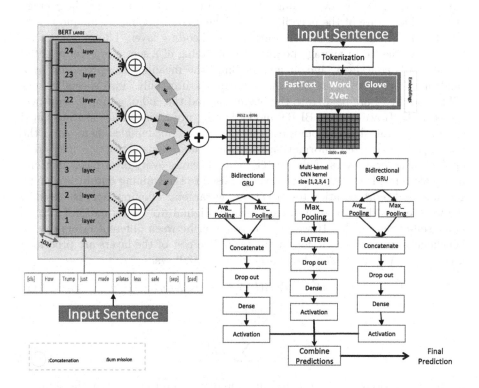

Fig. 2. Proposed framework.

On one side, we utilize the BERT layers for word embedding purposes. The embedding matrix is fed into the embedding layer of our neural network. On the other part, we utilize the multi-kernel convolution filters to extract higher-level feature sequences from the appended embeddings. After getting the predictions from these modules, results are blended and used to determine the degree of funniness. Next, we describe each component elaborately.

3.1   BERT Feature Extraction

BERT [11] is a recent language representation model that has remarkably accomplished well in diverse language understanding benchmarks which indicates the possibility that BERT networks capture structural information about the language. BERT builds on Transformer networks [25] to pre-train bidirectional representations by conditioning on both left and right contexts jointly in all layers. The transformer network inside BERT uses the encoder which has a self-attention layer. The self-attention helps the current node not only focus on the current word but also obtain the semantics of the context. Different BERT layers capture different information. Our target is to extract those hidden information denoted as $\{h_L = h_1, h_2, ..., h_{24}\}$ where L is the no. of layers in BERT model. For extraction, we use two pooling strategies together. One is taking the average of the hidden state of the encoding layer. The second pooling technique is taking the maximum of the hidden state of the encoding layer. The reason to use these strategies is: In average pooling, the meaning of a sentence is represented by all words contained, and in max-pooling, the meaning is represented by a small number of keywords and their salient features only. Two special tokens [CLS] and [SEP] are padded to the beginning and the end of an input sequence, respectively. However, our BERT model is only pre-trained and not fine-tuned on our task, embeddings from those two symbols are meaningless here. After the pooling, the extracted information is concatenated. This extraction method is applied on several layers of the BERT model because every layer has something informative inside it. i.e., the last layer is closed to the training output, so it may give a biased representation towards training targets. The first layer is closed to the word embedding, may preserve the very original word information (with no fancy self-attention) [3]. However, this trade-off between different layers can be beneficial in feature extraction in our task. The rest of the layers are processed accordingly. We can define the above process as follows:

$$h_L^o = AVG(h_L) \odot MAX(h_L), \tag{1}$$

$$h_o^l = (h_L^o) \odot (h_{L-1}^o), \tag{2}$$

$$E_h^o = \sum_{l=1}^{l} \alpha[h_o^l] \tag{3}$$

In above equations, $\odot$ sign is concatenation operation. In next step, the summation E_h^o of concatenated layers are done after adding some weights to them as shown in Fig. 2.

3.2   Embedding

In prior work, target information for humor detection is gained from traditional methods of embedding. As shown in Fig. 2, we also use these embedding techniques in our proposed framework. To integrate the target information, we generate a unified word vector matrix by concatenating the vector representations of the news. The dimensionality of the matrix $E_{glove,fasttext,word2vec}$ will be $L \times D$, where length L is the target length, and D denotes the word-vector dimension. We utilize a pre-trained word embedding model for obtaining the vector representation of words.

3.3   Bi-GRU

Recurrent Neural Network is widely used in the NLP field, which can learn context information of one word. Long Short Term Memory is designed to solve the RNN gradient vanishing problem, especially learning long sentence [7]. Grate Recurrent Unit is a simplified LSTM cell structure [9]. It is a bidirectional recurrent neural network with only the input and forget gates as shown in Fig. 3.

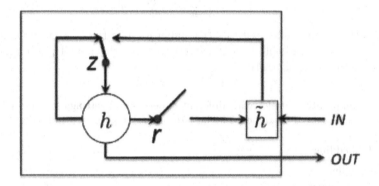

Fig. 3. Simple GRU unit

Taking advantage of its simple cell, GRU can get a close performance to LSTM with less time. With the emerging trend of deep learning, recurrent networks are the most popular for sequential tasks. A Bidirectional GRU, or BiGRU, is a sequence processing model that consists of two GRUs. One taking the input in a forward direction, and the other in a backward direction. It is a bidirectional recurrent neural network with only the input and forget gates. GRUs use less training parameters and therefore use less memory, execute faster and train faster than LSTM's. In our proposed framework, we utilize the Bi-GRU model. The embeddings E_h^o and $E_{glove,fasttext,word2vec}$ passes through the Bi-GRU layer separately. A max & avg pooling functions are then applied which are concatenated to form a feature vector.

3.4   Multi-kernel Convolution

In our multi-kernel convolution, we adopt the idea proposed by [15] to extract the higher-level features. The input of this module is the embedding matrix generated in the embedding layer. We then perform the convolution on it by using a filter. We apply multiple convolutions based on four different kernel sizes, i.e., the size of the convolution filters: 1, 2, 3, and 4. After performing convolutions, each filter generates the corresponding feature maps, and a max-pooling function is then applied to generate a univariate feature vector. Finally, the feature vectors generated from each kernel are concatenated to form a single high-level feature vector.

3.5   Humor Prediction and Model Training

We concatenate the final results from the BERT based Bi-GRU model and Embedding based CNN & Bi-GRU after passing them to a fully connected linear layer for humor detection. We consider mean square error (mse) as the loss function and train the models by minimizing the error, which is defined as:

$$mse = \sum_{i=1}^{n} |y_i - \hat{y}_i| \tag{4}$$

where i is the sample index with its true label y_i. $\hat{y}_i$ is the estimated value. We use the stochastic gradient descent (SGD) to learn the model parameter and adopt the Adam optimizer [16].

Table 1. Comparative results with different experimental settings for original news headlines and for edited headlines. The best results are highlighted in boldface.

Embedding	Model	RMSE
Baseline		.5750
Our Framework		**.5516**
Edited headlines		
Glove	Bi-GRU	.6291
Glove+FastText	Bi-GRU	.6212
Glove+FastText+GoogleNews	CNN	.6057
BERT (using layers (1, 2, 23, 24))	Bi-GRU	.5879
BERT (using layers (1, 2, 3, 4, 24, 23, 22, 21))	Bi-GRU	.5701
Original headline		
Glove	Bi-GRU	.6311
Glove+FastText	Bi-GRU	.6232
Glove+FastText+GoogleNews	CNN	.6370
BERT (using layers (1, 2, 23, 24))	Bi-GRU	.6194
BERT (using layers (1, 2, 3, 4, 21, 22, 23, 24))	Bi-GRU	.6045

4   Evaluation

4.1   Dataset

To validate the effectiveness of our proposed framework for the humor detection, we made use of a dataset used in the SemEval-2020 Task 7 [13]. The training set consists of 9652 news headlines, the validation set and the test set consist of 2419 and 3024 news headlines respectively. The dataset collected from the Reddit website used for predicting the funniness score. The score ranges from **0** to **3**, where 0 means not funny and 3 means funny among all. Before training, the original headlines are changed with the given edit words. Next, we need to pad the input. The reason behind padding the input is that text sentences have varying length, however models used in our framework expects input instances with the same length. Therefore, we need to convert our sentences into fixed-length vectors. For padding, the maximum sentence length that is set in our framework is 40. For the evaluation measure, root mean square error (rmse) is employed.

$$rmse = \sqrt{\frac{1}{n} \sum_{i=1}^{n} (y_i - \hat{y_i})^2} \tag{5}$$

4.2   Model Configuration

In the following, we describe the set of parameters that we have used in our framework during experiments. We used three embedding models to initialize the word embeddings in the embedding layer. The embedding models are 300-dimensional **FastText** embedding model pre-trained on Wikipedia with 16B tokens [18], 300-dimensional **Glove** embedding model with 2.2M vocab and 840B tokens [20] and 300-dimensional **Word2Vec** embedding model pre-trained on part of Google News dataset [1].

For the multi-kernel convolution, we employed 4 kernel sizes (1, 2, 3, 4), and the number of filters was set to 36. We use Bert-as-Service [27] for extracting information from the BERT model. In our system, the layers of BERT-Large(uncased) are used in the following manner. $h_1^l \odot h_2^l, h_3^l \odot h_4^l, ..., h_{21}^l \odot h_{22}^l, h_{23}^l \odot h_{24}^l$. The framework which we used to design our model was based on TensorFlow [2] and training of our model is done on a GPU [19] to capture the benefit from the efficiency of parallel computation of tensors. We trained all models for a max of 25 epochs with a batch size of 16 and an initial learning rate of 0.001 by Adam optimizer. In this paper, we reported the results based on these settings. Unless otherwise stated, default settings were used for the other parameters.

4.3   Results and Analysis

Our target is to detect the level of funniness from the news headlines that are not supposed to be funny. Here, we used the dataset in two different manners to show the efficacy of our framework. We showed some summarized experimental results of original and edited headlines both in Table 1. At first, we reported the results based on a naive baseline system. Next, we reported the results of our proposed framework. In order to estimate the effect of each component of our framework, we showed the performances of each component individually. From the results, it can be observed that the simple embedding technique on original and edited headlines gave almost the same RMSE error, which shows it cannot significantly distinguish between being funny or not. For the validation dataset, these techniques produced biased results for most of the cases. However, having in-depth knowledge of a sentence via BERT layers make it better regarding original and edited headlines. We did not perform multi-kernel convolution on BERT based Embedding due to large computational time.

Humor is a difficult achievement for computational models. True humor comprehension would need extensive language expertise as well as common sense about the world to recognize that a first interpretation is being revealed to be incompatible with the second, concealed meaning that fits the entire joke rather than just the premise. Due to the cultural effect and short length of a sentence, this work becomes more challenging. We tries to contribute in this area by proposing the BERT and traditional embedding based neural network. Each component performs efficiently when combine with each other.

5   Conclusion

In this paper, we proposed a framework to detect the level of funniness. The integration of the BERT and external embeddings with Bi-GRU and CNN models provides the great understanding of sentence. The results show the performance of our framework.

In a nutshell, the main contribution of our unified framework is to learn the contextual information effectively which in turn improved the humor detection performance. In the future, we want to use external information to generalize our model for humor identification in the same area.

Acknowledgments. This research was supported by the Japan International Cooperation Agency – JICA under Innovative Asia program.

References

1. Google code archive - long-term storage for google code project hosting, July 2013. https://code.google.com/archive/p/word2vec/
2. Abadi, M., et al.: Tensorflow: a system for large-scale machine learning. In: 12th {USENIX} Symposium on Operating Systems Design and Implementation ({OSDI} 16), pp. 265–283 (2016)
3. Alammar, J.: The illustrated BERT, ELMo, and co. (How NLP cracked transfer learning), December 2018. http://jalammar.github.io/illustrated-bert/
4. Annamoradnejad, I., Zoghi, G.: ColBERT: using BERT sentence embedding for humor detection. arXiv preprint arXiv:2004.12765 (2020)

5. van den Beukel, S., Aroyo, L.: Homonym detection for humor recognition in short text. In: Proceedings of the 9th Workshop on Computational Approaches to Subjectivity, Sentiment and Social Media Analysis, pp. 286–291 (2018)
6. Branwen, G.: GPT-3 creative fiction (2020)
7. Cascade-correlation, R., Chunking, N.S.: 2 Previous work **9**(8), 1–32 (1997)
8. Chen, P.Y., Soo, V.W.: Humor recognition using deep learning, pp. 113–117 (2018). https://doi.org/10.18653/v1/n18-2018
9. Chung, J.: Gated recurrent neural networks on sequence modeling. arXiv:1412.3555v1 [cs. NE], pp. 1–9, 11 December 2014
10. De Oliveira, L., Rodrigo, A.L.: Humor detection in yelp reviews (2015). Accessed 15 Dec 2019
11. Devlin, J., Chang, M.W., Lee, K., Toutanova, K.: BERT: pre-training of deep bidirectional transformers for language understanding. In: NAACL HLT 2019 – 2019 Conference of the North American Chapter of the Association for Computational Linguistics: Human Language Technologies - Proceedings of the Conference 1(Mlm), pp. 4171–4186 (2019)
12. Hossain, N., Krumm, J., Gamon, M.: "President vows to cut <Taxes> hair": dataset and analysis of creative text editing for humorous headlines (iv), pp. 133–142 (2019). https://doi.org/10.18653/v1/n19-1012
13. Hossain, N., Krumm, J., Gamon, M., Kautz, H., Corporation, M.: SemEval-2020 Task 7: assessing humor in edited news headlines (2019) (2020)
14. Kiddon, C., Brun, Y.: That's what she said: double entendre identification. In: Proceedings of the 49th Annual Meeting of the Association for Computational Linguistics: Human Language Technologies, pp. 89–94 (2011)
15. Kim, Y.: Convolutional neural networks for sentence classification, pp. 1746–1751 (2014)
16. Kingma, D.P., Ba, J.L.: A: a m s o, pp. 1–15 (2015)
17. Mihalcea, R., Strapparava, C.: Making computers laugh: investigations in automatic humor recognition. In: Proceedings of Human Language Technology Conference and Conference on Empirical Methods in Natural Language Processing, pp. 531–538 (2005)
18. Mikolov, T., Grave, E., Bojanowski, P., Puhrsch, C., Joulin, A.: Advances in pre-training distributed word representations. In: Proceedings of the International Conference on Language Resources and Evaluation (LREC 2018) (2018)
19. Owens, J.D., Houston, M., Luebke, D., Green, S., Stone, J.E., Phillips, J.C.: GPU computing. Proc. IEEE **96**(5), 879–899 (2008)
20. Pennington, J.: Blue. https://nlp.stanford.edu/projects/glove/
21. Purandare, A., Litman, D.: Humor: prosody analysis and automatic recognition for f* r* i* e* n* d* s. In: Proceedings of the 2006 Conference on Empirical Methods in Natural Language Processing, pp. 208–215 (2006)
22. Ritchie, G.: Developing the incongruity-resolution theory. Technical report (1999)
23. Taylor, J.M., Mazlack, L.J.: Computationally recognizing wordplay in jokes theories of humor (1991) (2000)
24. Taylor, J.M., Mazlack, L.J.: Computationally recognizing wordplay in jokes. In: Proceedings of the Annual Meeting of the Cognitive Science Society, vol. 26 (2004)
25. Vaswani, A., et al.: Attention is all you need. In: Advances in Neural Information Processing Systems (NIPS), pp. 5999–6009, December 2017
26. Weller, O., Seppi, K.: Humor detection: a transformer gets the last laugh. arXiv preprint arXiv:1909.00252 (2019)
27. Xiao, H.: BERT-as-service (2018). https://github.com/hanxiao/bert-as-service

An Efficient Link Prediction Model in Dynamic Heterogeneous Information Networks Based on Multiple Self-attention

Beibei Ruan[✉] and Cui Zhu

College of Computer Science, Faculty of Information Technology,
Beijing University of Technology, Beijing, China
ruanbeibei@emails.bjut.edu.cn

Abstract. The existing link prediction researches of information networks mainly focus on the dynamic homogeneous network or the static heterogeneous network. It has always been a challenge to predict future relationships between nodes while learning both continuous-time and heterogeneous information simultaneously. In this paper, we propose a Heterogeneous and Continuous-Time Model Based on Self-Attention (HTAT) to complete the link prediction task by learning temporal evolution and heterogeneity jointly. The HTAT model consists of the base layer and the heterogeneous layer. The base layer incorporates a functional time encoding with self-attention mechanism to capture continuous-time evolution. And the heterogeneous layer consists of multi-view attention to learn heterogeneous information. Experimental results show that HTAT is significantly competitive compared with four state-of-the-art baselines on three real-world datasets.

Keywords: Dynamic heterogeneous network · Link prediction · Heterogeneous layer · Base layer · Self-attention

1 Instruction

In social networks, Q&A forums, and user-item interaction systems, people and items are all regarded as nodes. There are dynamic information interactions between people and items, which are viewed as links between nodes. These nodes and links form a vast information network graph.

By analyzing existing information in the network, we can perform an essential task of link prediction. Link prediction tasks predict interactive information between nodes based on historical data [9]. It is widely used in practical applications, such as analyzing the diffusion law of information on Q&A forums and recommending suitable commodities to users on shopping platforms [18]. Therefore, link prediction tasks on information network graph have become a focus issue in recent years.

© Springer Nature Switzerland AG 2021
H. Qiu et al. (Eds.): KSEM 2021, LNAI 12817, pp. 62–74, 2021.
https://doi.org/10.1007/978-3-030-82153-1_6

Network embedding (NE) encodes the network structure into a nonlinear space [1]. Network embedding methods have achieved remarkable performance for link prediction in various domains. However, most real information networks are dynamic and heterogeneous [5]. In fact, information networks typically contain multiple types of nodes and links, and the structure of the network changes over time. To achieve effectively link prediction, we need to learn both heterogeneity and temporal evolution. Unfortunately, most approaches satisfy only one requirement (dynamic [3,8,11,15] or heterogeneity [4,14]). The network embedding method for learning dynamic heterogeneous networks has not been proposed until recent years. The DHNE model [17] builds the history-current network graph and learns dynamic heterogeneous information by proximity based on meta-path. The DyHATR model [16] uses hierarchical attention to learn heterogeneous information and incorporates recurrent neural networks with temporal attention to capture evolutionary patterns. Although they can learn both evolutionary and heterogeneous information simultaneously, learning from snapshots may truncate the expression of information and fail to grasp the critical network changes. Moreover, some nodes' interaction is usually regular and periodical. This heterogeneous potential information cannot be captured well by learning snapshots. Therefore, the link prediction task of dynamic heterogeneous networks faces the following enormous challenges:

- **Temporal evolution.** As the structure of dynamic heterogeneous networks changes over time, learning continuous time is a considerable challenge.
- **Multiplex edges.** There are many types of nodes and links in the network, and each node pair may have multiple different types of relationships [2]. Therefore, it is crucial for link prediction tasks to learn and integrate different interaction information between nodes.
- **Applicability.** The model proposed should be able to deal with complex and different networks. It's an important metric that approach can be well extended to large networks' learning.

To solve the problem of continuous time, we use the time encoding proposed by TGAT [15], which encodes the time information of links as time features and embeds them in node embeddings. In our base layer, the model is more light. Specifically, we improve the generalization of the model. When using self-attention mechanism [12], initial embeddings of central node and its neighbors that have interacted are different. Our base layer's output is nodes' base embeddings. To solve multiplex edges, we adopt the multiple view theory [2] to temporal evolution. The node self-attention is carried out in each subgraph, and then, we can get the edge embedding on all views by integrating node features of other views. We finally obtain overall embedding by integrating base embedding and edge embedding, which learns both temporal evolution and complex structure.

Our contributions are briefly summarized as follows: (i) We provide a framework for link prediction task on dynamic heterogeneous networks, which can learn continuous time to capture networks' evolutionary features. (ii) We adapt the multiple view theory to temporal evolution to analyze network's structure.

(iii) We distinguish center node and its neighbors when using self-attention mechanism. And we improve the training efficiency and lighten the model. Taken together, our model outperforms some of the most advanced methods on three real-world datasets.

The rest of this paper is organized as follows. Section 2 discusses the related work. Section 3 discusses the problem definition. Section 4 presents our method. Section 5 presents the experimental setup and results. Finally, Sect. 6 concludes the paper.

2 Related Work

2.1 The Functional Time Encoding

The TGAT [15] proposes a continuous functional mapping $\Phi : T \rightarrow R^{d_T}$, which maps the time domain to the d_T-dimensional vector space. The interval in the time domain is $T = [0, t_{max}]$, which t_{max} is the maximum time of all the edges. Assume that we have two time points t_1, t_2, and the inner product $\langle \Phi(t_1), \Phi(t_2) \rangle$, which directly reveals the effect of timespan. To obtain the expression of the inner product, let the time kernel function be $K(t_1, t_2) = \langle \Phi(t_1), \Phi(t_2) \rangle, K : T \times T \rightarrow R$. If the sample size is reasonable, it is assumed that $K(t_1, t_2) \approx \langle \Phi(t_1), \Phi(t_2) \rangle$. The kernel K depends only on the timespan at any time point, that is $K(t_1 + c, t_2 + c) = K(t_1, t_2)$. Also, the kernel K defined above satisfy the assumptions of the Bochners theorem [15]. Consequently, when scaled properly, the kernel K has the alternate expression [15]:

$$K(t_1, t_2) = \int_R e^{iw(t_1 - t_2)} p(w) dw = E_w[\xi(t_1)\xi(t_2)^*] \tag{1}$$

where $\xi_w(t) = e^{jwt}$. The formula is converted to:

$$K(t_1, t_2) = E_w[cos(w(t_1 - t_2))] = E_w[cos(wt_1)cos(wt_2) + sin(wt_1)sin(wt_2)] \tag{2}$$

After approximating the expectation by Monte Carlo integration [7], the finite dimensional functional mapping to R^d as:

$$t \rightarrow \Phi_d(t) := \sqrt{\frac{1}{d}}[cos(w_1 t), sin(w_1 t), ..., cos(w_d t), sin(w_d t)] \tag{3}$$

2.2 Self-attention Mechanism

The GAT [13] weights neighboring nodes features, which represents dependencies between nodes. The input is $h = \{h_1, h_2, ..., h_n\}, h_i \in R^m$, where n is the number of nodes, and m is the node features' dimension. The output of the GAT is $h' = \{h'_1, h'_2, ..., h'_n\}, h'_i \in R^{m'}$, where m' is the dimension of output features. It needs to train a weight matrix $W \in R^{m' \times m}$ representing the relationship between input features and output features, and all nodes share it. Implement attention mechanism for each node pair to get value $e_{i,j}$, which represents the importance of neighbor node v_j to node v_i. The softmax function is used to normalize, making the weight easier to calculate and compare. The weight coefficient of node pair (v_i, v_j) can be calculated as:

$$\alpha_{ij} = softmax_j(e_{ij}) = \frac{exp(e_{ij})}{\sum\limits_{k \in N_i} exp(e_{ik})} = \frac{exp(LeakyReLU(a^T[Wh_i \parallel Wh_j]))}{\sum\limits_{k \in N_i} exp(LeakyReLU(a^T[Wh_i \parallel Wh_k]))}$$

(4)

where N_i is the set of neighbors of node v_i, $W \in R^{m' \times m}$ is the weight matrix that you need to learn, and $LeakyReLU(.)$ is the activation function. As shown in the following formula, the embedding of node v_i is obtained by weighting neighbor features as:

$$h'_i = \sigma(\sum_{j \in N_i} \alpha_{ij} W h'_j)$$

(5)

Multi-head attention [13] is used to make the learning model process more stable by joining features together:

$$h'_i = \mathop{\Big\Vert}_{k=1}^{K} \sigma(\sum_{j \in N_i} \alpha^k{}_{ij} W^k h'_j)$$

(6)

where $\parallel$ denotes concatenation operation.

3   Problem Definition

Definition 1 (Heterogeneous Network). A heterogeneous network is a network $G = (V, E, A, R)$, where the set of nodes $V = \{v_1, v_2, ..., v_n\}$ represents all nodes in the network and n is the number of nodes. $E = \{e(v_i, v_j, r_k)\}, v_i, v_j \in V, r_k \in R$. $E = V \times V, e(v_i, v_j, r_k)$ represents the connection where node v_i and node v_j have relation r_k. $\Phi(v) : V \rightarrow A$ is a node type mapping function and $\Psi(e) : E \rightarrow R$ is an edge type mapping function, where A and R represent the set of all node types and the set of all edge types, respectively. If $\mid A \mid + \mid R \mid > 2$, the network is called heterogeneous; otherwise homogeneous.

Definition 2 (Dynamic Heterogeneous Network). A dynamic heterogeneous network is a network $G_T = (V, E, A, R, T)$. $t_h \in T$ is the time of link between node v_i and v_j, where $T = \{t_1, t_2, ..., t_{max}\}$ represents the set of all time points. $e(v_i, v_j, r_k, t_h) \in E$ is the link of type r_k between node v_i and v_j at time t_h. A pair of nodes may have multiple different relationships at different times. For example, on the Q&A forum, user v_1 answers user v_2's question at time t_1, and user v_1 responds to user v_2's confusion at time t_2, which meets conditions $e(v_1, v_2, r_1, t_1), e(v_1, v_2, r_2, t_2) \in E$.

Definition 3 (Link Prediction). Link prediction task is to predict possible links by analyzing historical nodes and edges, which is essentially a prediction task.

As shown in Fig. 1, it contains two parts network embedding and link prediction. In network embedding, the input is the network $G_T = (V, E, A, R, T)$ associated with the time limit $t_{max} < t$. The output is a low-dimensional vector representation of each node $v_i \in V$ on each edge type $r_k \in R$. In link prediction, for example, a link of edge type r_2 between node v_1 and v_3 will generate in the future network $G'_{T'}$. We firstly take node v_1 and v_3's embedding vectors in the edge type r_2. Then, calculate the inner product of the vector as the probability of the link.

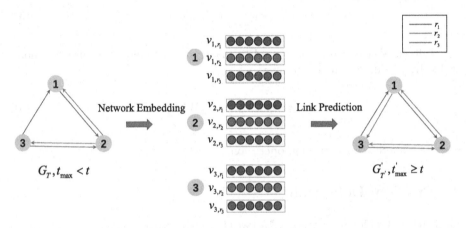

Fig. 1. Network embedding and link prediction in dynamic heterogeneous network.

4   Methodology

The overall architecture is shown in Fig. 2. We divide our model into two parts called base layer and heterogeneous layer, respectively. Specifically, the base layer gets base embedding, and the heterogeneous layer gets edge embedding on multiple views. We think of one edge type as one view. Ultimately, base embedding and edge embedding of all views are aggregated to nodes' overall embedding for link prediction.

4.1   The Base Layer

Given the limitations of TGAT model, we make the following improvements. First, we remove multiply layers to lighten the model. Second, the central node and the neighbor nodes are initialized from two different embeddings when using

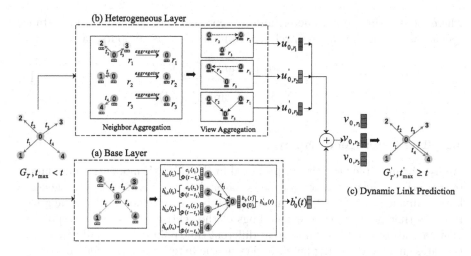

Fig. 2. The overall framework of Heterogeneous and Continuous-Time Model Based on Self-Attention (HTAT). The model proposed contains three parts, (a) Base Layer, (b) Heterogeneous Layer and (c) Dynamic Link Prediction.

self-attention mechanism. Third, we make the model adapted to heterogeneous networks.

As shown in the base layer in Fig. 2, at current time t, $b_i(t)$ is initial embedding of node v_i, and $c = \{c_1(t_1), ..., c_N(t_N)\}$ is its neighbor nodes initial embedding. To integrate more information, we take the existing heterogeneous network as homogeneous graph.

The core of the self-attention mechanism is aggregrate information between nodes and neighbor nodes. We use $\{t - t_1, ..., t - t_N\}$ as the interaction time and obtain the temporal features $\{\Phi(t - t_1), ..., \Phi(t - t_N)\}$ by the functional time encoding. Therefore, we get the entity-temporal feature of node v_i to itself and node v_i to its neighbor node v_j, respectively as:

$$b'_{i,i}(t) = b_i(t) \parallel \Phi(0) \tag{7}$$

$$b'_{i,j}(t_j) = c_j(t_j) \parallel \Phi(t - t_j) \tag{8}$$

Then, collect the entity-temporal feature of all neighbor nodes as:

$$B_i(t) = [b'_{i,1}(t_1), ..., b'_{i,N}(t_N)]^T \tag{9}$$

we can normalize the importance matrix of neighbor nodes to node v_i and computed as:

$$\beta_i = softmax(w^T \tanh(W B_i(t)))^T \tag{10}$$

where w and W are trainable parameters. Subsequently, the base embedding of node v_i is obtained by weighting the embedding of neighbor nodes:

$$b''_i(t) = M^T B_i(t) \beta_i = M^T \sum_{j=1}^{N} \lambda_j b'_{i,j}(t_j) \tag{11}$$

where M is trainable parameter. and λ_j represents the normalized importance coefficient of neighbor node v_j relative to node v_i. λ_j is computed as:

$$\lambda_j = \frac{\exp(w^T \tanh(Wb'_{i,j}))}{\sum\limits_{k}^{N} \exp(w^T \tanh(Wb'_{i,k}))} \tag{12}$$

4.2 The Heterogeneous Layer

We use the multiple view theory proposed in the GATNE model [2] and adapt it to temporal evolution. In heterogeneous layer shown in Fig. 2, the heterogeneous layer is divided into two steps, that are neighbor aggregation and view aggregation. As time goes by, edge embeddings of the central nodes on corresponding view can be obtained and updated at different time points. Eventually, we collect the latest node embedding on each view as the heterogeneous layer's output.

As shown in Fig. 2, for example, the current time is t. At the neighbor aggregation step, the network graph is divided into different subgraphs according to edge types. Each subgraph contains only one type of edge. In each subgraph, the central node v_i and its neighbor nodes are differently initialized like center word and context of skip-gram [10]. Then, the node v_i gets embedding by aggregating itself and its neighbor nodes' feature:

$$u_{i,r_t} = aggregator(\{u_{j,r_t}, \forall v_j \in N_{i,r_t}\}) \tag{13}$$

where, u_{j,r_t} is neighbor node v_j's embedding on view r_t, N_{i,r_t} is the neighbors of node v_i on edge type $r_t \in R$. The aggregator function takes the mean aggregator as:

$$u_{i,r_t} = \sigma(mean(\{u_{j,r_t}, \forall v_j \in N_{i,r_t}\})) \tag{14}$$

where $\sigma(.)$ is an activation function.

At the step of view aggregation, we firstly concatenate all the edge embeddings for node v_i as U_i, where m is the number of edge types [2]:

$$U_i = (u_{i,r_1}, u_{i,r_2}, ..., u_{i,r_m}) \tag{15}$$

Then, we aggregate node embedding on different views based on self-attention mechanism to get edge embedding on view r_t at current time. Node v_i's importance matrix of other views to view r_t is calculated as:

$$\alpha_{i,r_t} = softmax(w_{r_t}^T \tanh(W_{r_t} U_i))^T \tag{16}$$

where w_{r_t} and W_{r_t} are trainable parameters for view r_t. Finally, after weighting the embedding of nodes on other views, the edge embedding of node v_i on view r_t is:

$$u'_{i,r_t} = M_{r_t}^T U_i \alpha_{i,r_t} = M_{r_t}^T \sum_{k=1}^{m} \lambda_k u_{i,r_k} \tag{17}$$

where M_{r_t} is trainable parameters, and λ_k represents the normalized importance coefficient that is view r_k relative to view r_t. λ_k is computed as:

$$\lambda_k = \frac{\exp(w_{r_t}^T \tanh(W_{r_t} u_{i,r_k})}{\sum\limits_{j}^{m} \exp(w_{r_t}^T \tanh(W_{r_t} u_{i,r_j}))} \tag{18}$$

4.3 Aggregation

We aggregate the base embedding and the edge embedding to the overall embedding of node v_i:

$$v_{i,r_t} = b_i''(t) + a u_{i,r_t}' \tag{19}$$

where a is a hyper-parameter denoting the importance of edge embeddings towards the overall embedding. We get the overall embedding of node v_i with different views as:

$$V_i = \{v_{i,r_1}, v_{i,r_2}, ..., v_{i,r_m}\} \tag{20}$$

4.4 Objective Function

We use the temporal loss function to train our model and compute the value according to the view of links between nodes as:

$$L = \sum_{e(v_i,v_j,r_t,t_h)\in\varepsilon} -\log(\sigma(-v_{i,r_t}^T v_{j,r_t}))$$
$$-Q.E_{v_q\sim P_n(v)} \log(\sigma(v_{i,r_t}^T v_{q,r_t})) \tag{21}$$

where $\sigma(.)$ is the sigmoid function, Q is the number of negative samples and $P_n(v)$ is the negative sampling distribution over the node space, ε is the set of edges, and $e(v_i, v_j, r_t, t_h)$ represents the link of type r_t between node v_i and node v_j at time t_h.

We get all nodes' overall embedding on all views. Links are generated over time. According to each generated edge, we take two nodes' overall embedding of this view to calculate the loss.

5 Experiments

This part introduces three datasets, four baselines, the experimental setup and experimental results. Experimental results show that our model significantly outperforms other baselines on three real-world datasets. We further conduct an ablation study to demonstrate the effectiveness of our revised framework (Base Layer) and the added heterogeneous layer.

Table 1. Statistics of three real-world datasets

Dataset	Nodes	Edges	Node types	Edge types
Math-overflow	24818	506550	1	3
Super-user	194085	1443339	1	3
EComm	50000	974766	2	4

5.1 Datasets

We use three real datasets of dynamic heterogeneous network in our experiment. Table 1 shows the statistics for these datasets.

- **Math-Overflow**[1]. This temporal network dataset is collected from the stack exchange website Math Overflow. It includes three different interactions between users over 2,350 days [16].
- **Super-User**[2]. This temporal network dataset is collected from the stack exchange website Super User. It includes three different interactions between users over 2,773 days.
- **EComm**[3]. This temporal network dataset is a heterogeneous bipartite network of e-commerce, extracted from the AnalytiCup challenge of CIKM-2019 [16]. It mainly records people's shopping behavior during time, consisting of two types of nodes and four types of edge.

5.2 Baselines

We compare four baselines to evaluate the performance of HTAT. Node2vec [6] is a typical static homogeneous network embedding method that maps network nodes from a high dimensional space to a low dimensional vector. The GATNE [2] proposes a unified framework to address the problem of heterogeneity. The TGAT [15] suiting for dynamic homogeneous network is based on self-attention mechanism. The DyHATR [16] is proposed for dynamic heterogeneous network, which uses hierarchical attention to learn heterogeneous information, and uses a recurrent neural network with temporal attention to capture the evolution.

To make the baselines suit the datasets of dynamic heterogeneous network, we make following adjustments in our experiment. For the node2vec method, we treat datasets as a static homogeneous network. For the GATNE method, we take away the dynamics of networks and retain the heterogeneity. For the TGAT method, we regard the datasets as dynamic homogeneous network by ignoring the heterogeneity of nodes and edges. For the DyHATR method, according to its paper's parameter index, we divide the training sets into ten snapshots, and the

---

[1] http://snap.stanford.edu/data/sx-mathoverflow.html.

[2] http://snap.stanford.edu/data/sx-superuser.html.

[3] https://tianchi.aliyun.com/competition/entrance/231721/information.

test set is taken as the eleventh snapshot. Eventually, we set the same dimension (100) of node embedding as HTAT and baselines to make a fair comparison. The hyper-parameters for different baselines are explicitly adjusted to be optimal.

Table 2. The experimental results of dynamic link prediction

Methods	Math-Overflow		Super-User		EComm	
	AUROC	AUPRC	AUROC	AUPRC	AUROC	AUPRC
node2vec	62.10	58.86	–	–	–	–
GATNE	74.25	74.19	67.88	63.04	67.71	68.74
TGAT	76.08	74.19	71.15	73.12	73.29	76.35
DyHATR	75.10	79.00	73.37	77.10	69.60	73.40
HTAT(ours)	**85.99**	**86.86**	**80.04**	**83.27**	**73.56**	**77.19**

5.3 Experimental Setup

Parameters. As for parameters of HTAT, we select twenty as the number of neighbors, two attention heads in the base layer, and one attention head in the heterogeneous layer with dropout rate of 0.1. And the results are relatively stable when the learning rate is 1e−5.

Evaluation Metrics. To evaluate HTAT, we divide each dataset into training set, validation set, and test set according to the time epochs of edges. The first 70% is used as training set, 15% as the validation set, and the last 15% as test set. As for the link prediction task, similar to previous works [19], we train a Logistic Regression model to a classifier. Therefore, we use the area under the ROC curve (AUROC) and area under the precision-recall curve (AUPRC) as metrics to evaluate the model's performance on the link prediction task.

5.4 Experimental Results

Link Prediction Task. We train and test four baselines and HTAT. The final performance of link prediction task is shown in Table 2. The HTAT significantly improve the scores of AUROC and AUPRC comparing to other baselines. For Math-Overflow, the highest metrics obtained by HTAT are 85.99% and 86.86%, respectively, which are significantly higher than the baselines. For Super-User, HTAT's AUROC and AUPRC scores are 80.04% and 83.27%, respectively, significantly higher than the second highest scores. Besides, Our model for EComm achieve the best performance (73.56% for AUROC and 77.19% for AUPRC).

Table 3. The average time of an epoch taken by TGAT (before improvement) and TAT (after improvement) during training

Methods	Math-Overflow	Super-User
	Time (ms)	
TGAT	503400	5517000
TAT	409000	5171000

Table 4. The ablation experimental results

Methods	Math-Overflow		Super-User	
	AUROC	AUPRC	AUROC	AUPRC
TGAT	76.08	74.19	71.15	73.12
TAT	79.36	83.87	76.13	80.63
HTAT	85.99	86.86	80.04	83.27

Effectiveness of Base Layer. First, due to the redundancy problem of the TGAT model, we use a single base layer to lighten the model. We calculate and compare the average time of an epoch taken by the TGAT (with original base layer) and the TAT (with base layer but without heterogeneous layer) during training. As shown in Table 3, TAT is 94,400 ms less than TGAT on the Math-Overflow dataset and 346,000 ms less than TGAT on the Super-User dataset. Second, we differentiate central node and neighbor nodes' embedding during self-attention, and their initial embedding sources are different. In order to verify the effectiveness of the improved base layer, we compare the results before and after the improvement. As the ablation experimental results are shown in Table 4, the TAT outperforms TGAT model on both Math-Overflow and Super-User datasets.

Effectiveness of Heterogeneous Layer. We add a heterogeneous layer to capture complex structure and heterogeneity. In order to verify the effectiveness of the added heterogeneous layer, we compare the results before and after. As shown in Table 4, the HTAT model is significantly improved in the ablation experimental results compared with the TAT model. For example, AUROC and AUPRC are increased by 6.63% and 2.99% on the Math-Overflow dataset.

6   Conclusions

Our approach completes the link prediction in dynamic heterogeneous information networks. It is a challenging task due to continuous time, implicit relationship and multi-source heterogeneous. We propose a dynamic heterogeneous network embedding model named HTAT to meet the above challenges. Our model's advantages are as follows: (i) we use the base layer by learning continuous time to avoid redundant accumulation and information loss. (ii) The HTAT can learn heterogeneous information network by heterogeneous layer. (iii) Experimental results show that HTAT performs well at dynamic link prediction tasks compared to other state-of-the-art baselines.

References

1. Cai, H., Zheng, V.W., Chang, K.C.C.: A comprehensive survey of graph embedding: problems, techniques, and applications. IEEE Trans. Knowl. Data Eng. **30**(9), 1616–1637 (2018)
2. Cen, Y., Zou, X., Zhang, J., Yang, H., Zhou, J., Tang, J.: Representation learning for attributed multiplex heterogeneous network. In: Proceedings of the 25th ACM SIGKDD International Conference on Knowledge Discovery & Data Mining, pp. 1358–1368 (2019)
3. Chen, J., Zhang, J., Xu, X., Fu, C., Zhang, D., Zhang, Q., Xuan, Q.: E-LSTM-D: a deep learning framework for dynamic network link prediction. IEEE Trans. Syst. Man Cybern.: Syst. (2019)
4. Dong, Y., Chawla, N.V., Swami, A.: metapath2vec: scalable representation learning for heterogeneous networks. In: Proceedings of the 23rd ACM SIGKDD International Conference on Knowledge Discovery and Data Mining, pp. 135–144 (2017)
5. Gai, K., Qiu, M., Zhao, H., Sun, X.: Resource management in sustainable cyber-physical systems using heterogeneous cloud computing. IEEE Trans. Sustain. Comput. **3**(2), 60–72 (2017)
6. Grover, A., Leskovec, J.: node2vec: scalable feature learning for networks. In: Proceedings of the 22nd ACM SIGKDD International Conference on Knowledge Discovery and Data Mining, pp. 855–864 (2016)
7. Lee, D.D., Pham, P., Largman, Y., Ng, A.: Advances in neural information processing systems 22. Technical report (2009)
8. Li, T., Zhang, J., Philip, S.Y., Zhang, Y., Yan, Y.: Deep dynamic network embedding for link prediction. IEEE Access **6**, 29219–29230 (2018)
9. Lü, L., Zhou, T.: Link prediction in complex networks: a survey. Phys. A **390**(6), 1150–1170 (2011)
10. Mikolov, T., Sutskever, I., Chen, K., Corrado, G., Dean, J.: Distributed representations of words and phrases and their compositionality. arXiv preprint arXiv:1310.4546 (2013)
11. Pareja, A., et al.: EvolveGCN: evolving graph convolutional networks for dynamic graphs. In: Proceedings of the AAAI Conference on Artificial Intelligence, vol. 34, pp. 5363–5370 (2020)
12. Vaswani, A., et al.: Attention is all you need. arXiv preprint arXiv:1706.03762 (2017)
13. Veličković, P., Cucurull, G., Casanova, A., Romero, A., Lio, P., Bengio, Y.: Graph attention networks. arXiv preprint arXiv:1710.10903 (2017)
14. Wang, X., et al.: Heterogeneous graph attention network. In: The World Wide Web Conference, pp. 2022–2032 (2019)
15. Xu, D., Ruan, C., Korpeoglu, E., Kumar, S., Achan, K.: Inductive representation learning on temporal graphs. arXiv preprint arXiv:2002.07962 (2020)
16. Xue, H., Yang, L., Jiang, W., Wei, Y., Hu, Y., Lin, Y.: Modeling dynamic heterogeneous network for link prediction using hierarchical attention with temporal RNN. arXiv preprint arXiv:2004.01024 (2020)

17. Yin, Y., Ji, L.X., Zhang, J.P., Pei, Y.L.: DHNE: network representation learning method for dynamic heterogeneous networks. IEEE Access **7**, 134782–134792 (2019)
18. Zhang, L., Li, J., Zhang, Q., Meng, F., Teng, W.: Domain knowledge-based link prediction in customer-product bipartite graph for product recommendation. Int. J. Inf. Technol. Decis. Making **18**(01), 311–338 (2019)
19. Zhou, L., Yang, Y., Ren, X., Wu, F., Zhuang, Y.: Dynamic network embedding by modeling triadic closure process. In: Proceedings of the AAAI Conference on Artificial Intelligence, vol. 32 (2018)

A Clustering-Prediction Pipeline for Customer Churn Analysis

Hanming Zheng, Ling Luo$^{(\boxtimes)}$, and Goce Ristanoski

School of Computing and Information Systems,
The University of Melbourne, Melbourne, Australia
Hanmingz@student.unimelb.edu.au, {ling.luo,gri}@unimelb.edu.au

Abstract. Customer churn is the event when customers using the products or services of an organization decide to no longer do so by either switching to another organization or by stopping using those products/services. It takes much more effort to attract new customers than to retain the existing clientele, which makes predicting customer churn and imposing retention strategies an essential task for many organizations. Though methodologies that deliver accurate predictions are available, there exists no general and transparent pipeline designed for churn prediction on different domains with high interpretability. In our work, we propose two domain-agnostic, inference-friendly, and easy-interpreting novelties: 1) a general and interpretable clustering-based churn prediction pipeline, ClusPred, which incorporates both demographics and transaction records; 2) an Inhomogeneous Poisson Process (IHPP) specifically designed to model customer behaviors to predict churners. We evaluated the prediction performance of ClusPred with IHPP using datasets from banking, retails, and mobile application fields. The experiments illustrated the ClusPred pipeline with IHPP have increased the performance while ensuring domain independence, making it a more standardized churner prediction process. With competitive accuracy and running time, our proposed models are also suitable for big data applications, which is rarely addressed by customer churn methods.

Keywords: Customer churn prediction · Prediction pipeline · Poisson Process · Interpretable model · Time-series data

1 Introduction

Customer churn occurs when a regular customer terminates the use of a product or service after a certain period. The availability of products and services in a globalized environment puts even more stress on companies in their effort to keep loyal customers. With different types of products and services available to the public, designing an efficient customer churn prediction strategy is more complex than ever. Innovation in this area is therefore guided more by the need for an accurate model in a specific domain rather than a general methodology with wide application scope. This limits the design of a strategy for predicting customer churn efficiently over the entire market.

© Springer Nature Switzerland AG 2021
H. Qiu et al. (Eds.): KSEM 2021, LNAI 12817, pp. 75–84, 2021.
https://doi.org/10.1007/978-3-030-82153-1_7

The complexity of the customer cohorts and types of products and services is additionally matched with another challenge: diversity in customer data records. With organizations choosing their own IT structure and database designs, it becomes increasingly difficult to investigate customer churn prediction with a standardized process. Some of the most common challenges in customer churn predictions originating in the structure and content of the datasets are: 1) **Demographics may be anonymized or contain little information.** Customers often refuse to provide demographic information, or services simply do not collect them. 2) **Transactional data has not been widely utilized.** Analysts often ignore valuable time-series user behavior records, which are not easy to evaluate due to flexible length, complexity, and sparsity. 3) **The pipeline and prediction methods are case-specific rather than problem-specific.** With case-specific problems focusing on results, methods such as deep learning are often applied, which allows for little interpretation and transferability. 4) **The pipeline and prediction methods are not efficient enough for large-scale data.** When the churn prediction pipeline is too complex, it may not be feasible for small or mid-sized businesses from both technical and AI expertise aspects.

Our research focuses on providing a customer churn paradigm that can tackle these challenges and provide transferable and adaptable models that can be used in several projects within an organization. We provide two main contributions:

- We propose a clustering-prediction pipeline for customer churn, called ClusPred, to tackle the aforementioned challenges. ClusPred is interpretable and compatible with datasets from different domains and handles the limited information from demographics data. **The experimental results show that ClusPred could significantly boost the True Positive Rate (TPR) of machine learning methods.**
- We propose an Inhomogeneous Poisson Process (IHPP) prediction method and integrate it into ClusPred. The simplicity and efficiency of IHPP make it possible to apply on a large-scale dataset. **The experimental results delineate that IHPP obtained the highest TPR compared to other popular methods.**

By combining these two approaches, we can address the main challenges in the churn prediction task and help fill the gap in designing more reliable and practical churn prediction models, while still accounting for efficiency and accuracy.

2 Related Work

The usefulness of customer churn can be observed in industries where many companies are competing for the same customers. In these cases, we can see how the challenges listed in the introduction are significant, and how they are often addressed.

The telecommunications industry is quite invested in predicting customer churn. Diversity in data quality and structure means we have cases where graph-based features are used [1], and other models include standard Decision Trees (DT) and Linear Regression (LR) with profit function [2], logit leaf model [3], rough set theory with some focus on interpretability [4] and Axiomatic Fuzzy Set using manually defined features [5]. Other industries such as banking also use LR as well as Support Vector Machine

(SVM) [6]. SVM-based model is useful for data that has a mixed structure of communication networks and numeric values [7], which addressed the challenge of incorporating demographics data. Social networks churn forecasting has the same challenge [8, 9], with solutions that cannot be easily adjusted for transactional data. Financial industries have been successful in incorporating unstructured demographics data by translating customer behaviors into different features [10], showing again the importance of feature engineering.

Despite simpler models such as clustering algorithms and decision tree style models being quite popular, others have resorted to more complex methods, having also met the challenges of transactions' utilization and attempted to overcome them. Several versions of Artificial Neural Networks have been used for the gaming industry [11], social media [12], and text analysis [13]. All these models propose domain-specific feature engineering or case-specific application, making it difficult to transfer the models to other domains. To address this challenge, we propose a generic prediction pipeline, ClusPred, for different domains and an Inhomogeneous Poisson prediction method for interpretability.

3   General Pipeline for Churn Prediction

It can be highly inefficient to attempt to adjust a customer churn prediction model designed for one domain to another. The datasets can have different structures, and the amount of feature engineering and data preprocessing depends more on the quality of the data than the prediction task. The main setback in current methods is that they are too focused on the individual use case of customer churn, rather than the general process and common tasks. To tackle the variety of domains and complications of feature engineering, we propose a more general pipeline for churn prediction, ClusPred.

ClusPred contains three phases: 1) user clustering; 2) behavior clustering; 3) churner prediction. The flow chart of ClusPred is shown in Fig. 1.

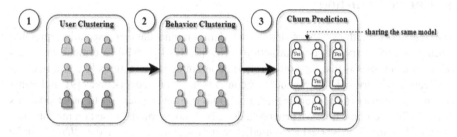

Fig. 1. The flow chart of ClusPred

1. **Phase One: User Clustering.** Users are separated into different groups based on demographics using unsupervised methods. Since user groups have varied intrinsic demographic properties, the initial leaving probability for each group varies. This phase extracts prior knowledge of customer churn, which stands for the initial leaving motivation related to user backgrounds. K-Means is used to do clustering with the demographic features, of which categorical features are encoded by one-hot encoding, and the numbers of groups are determined by the Silhouette Method. If there is no demographic information, all customers will be in one group.
2. **Phase Two: Behavior Clustering.** Users are grouped based on their behaviors, i.e., transactional records. For users with different behavior, if applying identical learners to them, it probably makes false predictions since the trends of transactional series are different. This phase reflects how user behaviors represent their willingness of leaving. Due to the nature of unfixed lengths of transactions, Dynamic Time Warping (DTW) based K-Means is used to cluster them, in which DTW is used to calculate the distance of transactional series. The numbers of groups are also determined by Silhouette Method.
3. **Phase Three: Churner Prediction.** Combining the demographics and behavior clustering results, various models can be applied to predict churners. The same model is applied to users having the same behavior and demographic group, so the prediction considers both the initial motivation and fluctuation of actual behaviors.

The overall procedure is: clustering customers based on demographics and behaviors to obtain groups, then applying prediction models on groups to predict final leaving probabilities. The prediction method we proposed will be described in Sect. 4.

ClusPred considers demographic data as prior knowledge of behaviors, so the churn prediction is more specific for different users. However, if demographics are missing, the prediction performance will not be affected, given that the prediction will mainly rely on the third phase. This makes demographic information no longer compulsory.

4   Churn Prediction

The prevailing methods either depend on demographic data or use uninterpretable machine learning models on transaction series [3, 12–14]. Also, a critical weakness of previous models is that they often rely on domain-specific features like internet logs in telecom industries [1], user-generated contents in social network areas [9], and transaction information in the Banking area [6], making the application to other domains difficult. To overcome this, we propose a domain-agnostic model based on the Inhomogeneous Poisson Process (IHPP) to predict churn using transactional data. *IHPP can be integrated into the ClusPred pipeline to complete Phase Three.*

Customers and users are regarded as churners if they leave some service for a certain time. To quantify the definition, intervals between two adjacent transactions are used to measure customers' intention to leave. We assume that if the average transaction interval becomes longer, then the users have more likely quitted. Once the time interval between the last record of a customer and the end of observation is greater than 99.9% of their previous intervals, then we label that the customer is a churner.

Homogeneous and Inhomogeneous Poisson Process

Poisson Process (PP) is used to describe the occurrences of events during a period. The number of events of PP in a period follows the Poisson distribution. The probability of n events occurred in the time range of $(a, b]$ is given by:

$$P\{\Lambda(a, b] = n\} = \frac{[\Lambda(a, b)]^n}{n!}e^{-\Lambda(a, b)} \tag{1}$$

The expectation of a random variable $\Lambda(a, b]$, i.e. the number of events that occurred during the period $t = (a, b]$, is:

$$E(\Lambda(a, b)) = \int_a^b \lambda(t)dt \tag{2}$$

where $\lambda(t)$ is an intensity function. The integral of one customer's buying records from the time a to the time b is the expectation of $\Lambda(a, b]$, and the integral is approximated by the accumulation of discrete records during a period. Considering the approximation is more accurate when the granularity approaches 0, we assume that the time unit is one day, and each day can only have one or no events, as two events cannot occur at the same time. All transactions that happened during the same day are considered as a single event. Regarding the intensity function, user behaviors can be adequately described by trends plus seasonal patterns [15], so polynomial and trigonometric intensity functions are introduced to fit user behaviors, which are transactions.

Polynomial Fitting

The polynomial fitting indicates customer behaviors can be decomposed as multiple trends, so the density function is:

$$\lambda(t) = \sum_{i=0} \alpha_i t^i \tag{3}$$

where i is the order. To avoid overfitting, the initial orders of curves are selected via the Akaike Information Criterion of records of each customer.

Trigonometric Fitting

While polynomial functions roughly fit the trends, sine functions can be important to describe periodic patterns. E.g., for a sine-like pattern, polynomial fitting cannot describe the periodic changes when time is long, while trigonometric fitting could depict the fluctuations more precisely. The Discrete Fourier Transform (DFT) is introduced to solve the decomposition problem, and the intensity function is defined as:

$$\lambda(t) = \sum_{i=0} \alpha_i t^i + \sum_{j=1} \left(b_j \sin\left(c_j t + d_j\right)\right) \tag{4}$$

The final fitting curves are the polynomial fitting adding the trigonometric components, which are harmonics decomposed by DFT. The harmonics are sorted by tension, and $log_N(M)$ harmonics will be selected to reconstruct the fitted curves, where M is the length of a user's records, and N is a parameter. Then, our model summates polynomial trends and those harmonics with corresponding phases to predict churn. The churner

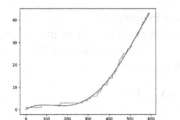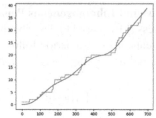

Fig. 2. Examples of poly-fitted (left) and trig-fitted (right) results. The orange curves are accumulated records, and the blue curves are fitted results. (Color figure online)

probability of a certain user can be obtained by computing the probability of not buying anything and comparing it with the threshold of churn definition.

There are two fitting examples in Fig. 2, which can be interpreted based on their intense functions. The left graph shows a customer with few transactions initially, but the customer increased the usage to one record per 10 days after the 300th day. This change is captured by the polynomial intensity function. While the right one illustrates that a customer stockpiled every 100 days and increased usage after the 500th day. The trigonometric fitting is more advanced since it captures the periodic stockpiling and increase of usage due to the trigonometric and polynomial components, respectively.

5 Experiments

5.1 Datasets and Experimental Setup

To testify to the generalizability and usability of our model, four open-source transactional datasets from different domains were used. The information is in Table 1.

Table 1. Information about datasets.

Name	Area	Length	Demographic	Number of Customers	Non-churner (label) Rate
Music[a]	App	2-year	Yes	869,900	**0.894**
Carbo[b]	Retail	2-year	No	510,000	**0.440**
CJ[c]	Retail	2-year	Yes	801	**0.969**
Bank[d]	Banking	6-year	No	4,500	**0.994**

[a]https://www.kaggle.com/c/kkbox-churn-prediction-challenge/data
[b]https://www.dunnhumby.com/careers/engineering/sourcefiles
[c]https://www.dunnhumby.com/careers/engineering/sourcefiles
[d]https://www.kaggle.com/bhadreshsavani/bank-transaction-data#transections.csv

In ClusPred, after demographical clustering and behavioral clustering, prediction models such as IHPP and baselines will be trained on clusters. The baselines are Logistic

Regression (LR), Decision Tree (DT), and LightGBM [16]. LR and DT are state-of-the-art interpretable methods for Customer Churn Prediction [3, 10], and LightGBM is a state-of-the-art tree-based prediction model. As these baselines require structured input, i.e. data frames, they will be trained with the statistics of ACF, which is often used to analyze transactions, instead of the original transactional series. Specifically, the ACF statistics used are maximum, minimum, median, mean, kurtosis, skewness, variance, and entropy of ACF. Additionally, Homogeneous Poisson Process (HPP), i.e. $\lambda(t) = \lambda_0 \times t$, will also be tested as a baseline.

We used 5-fold cross-validation to prepare training and test datasets. The performance evaluation metrics include the True Positive Rate (TPR) and accuracy. TPR measures the proportion of churners that are correctly identified.

5.2 Results and Discussion

In this section, we present the comparison between non-pipeline and pipeline, and the performance and running time of ClusPred and baselines which are state-of-the-art interpretable customer churn prediction methods in other papers, i.e. DT, LR [1], and LightGBM [16].

ClusPred Pipeline

This experiment is to examine if using the pipeline ClusPred can improve the prediction performance. The performance is shown in Table 2. Overall, using the ClusPred can achieve higher TPR, but accuracies remain stable. The TPR of DT, LR, and LightGBM have been increased by at least 10% after using ClusPred.

Since customers have been subsumed into different groups before training, the origin space has been split into smaller pieces. Therefore, the borders between positive labels and negative labels will become smoother and simpler. We found some groups have no churners, so other groups became less imbalanced after clustering, which partly solved the problem that learners tend to label all customers as non-churners because that may attain the least error. Clustering before training can there help companies find high-value groups and make specific marketing strategies for them.

Prediction Performance

This experiment is to examine the performance of ClusPred with different prediction models, including an LSTM model [12] and the proposed IHPP. The results of TPR and accuracy are presented in Table 3. The models with the prefix 'Trig' are for trigonometric intensity function and 'Poly' is for polynomial intensity function.

Generally, IHPP outperforms all baselines. Especially, the trigonometric fitting obtains the highest accuracy on every dataset. The TPR of IHPP is higher than baselines by 20% on average.

Most of the models achieved high accuracies except on the Carbo dataset. Since all the datasets except Carbo are highly imbalanced, learners will obtain high accuracy easily by predicting the majority label (the ratios of two classes are given in Table 1).

For example, LR achieved high accuracy, but it got very low TPR on three datasets. When training LSTM on Carbo, it attempted to identify more samples as churners (the majority label of the Carbo dataset) to attain a higher TPR. But, since it also misclassified

Table 2. Prediction performance of the ClusPred pipeline and non-pipeline models.

Dataset	Model	True Positive Rate		Accuracy	
		No Pipeline	ClusPred	No Pipeline	ClusPred
CJ	DT	0.080	**0.240**	0.938	**0.946**
	LightGBM	0.120	**0.200**	0.968	**0.970**
	LR	0.000	**0.120**	0.969	**0.969**
Music	DT	0.023	**0.553**	**0.867**	0.783
	LightGBM	0.442	**0.502**	**0.919**	**0.919**
	LR	0.001	**0.002**	0.894	**0.897**
Bank	DT	0.289	**0.313**	**0.992**	0.991
	LightGBM	0.189	**0.200**	**0.994**	0.992
	LR	0.000	0.000	**0.994**	0.993
Carbo	DT	0.843	**0.862**	**0.838**	0.828
	LightGBM	0.888	**0.893**	**0.854**	0.853
	LR	0.754	**0.873**	**0.856**	0.850

Table 3. Prediction performance of different models.

	Dataset	DT	LightGBM	LR	LSTM	HPP	Poly-IHPP	Trig-IHPP
Accuracy	CJ	0.946	**0.973**	0.969	0.966	0.929	0.960	0.959
	Music	0.828	0.934	0.894	0.933	0.923	0.925	**0.943**
	Bank	0.992	0.994	0.995	0.995	**0.996**	**0.996**	**0.996**
	Carbo	0.828	0.853	0.850	0.560	0.771	0.840	**0.859**
True Positive Rate	CJ	0.240	0.200	0.120	0.089	0.507	0.741	**0.881**
	Music	0.553	0.502	0.002	0.465	**0.714**	0.707	0.691
	Bank	0.313	0.200	0.000	0.229	0.759	0.794	**0.944**
	Carbo	0.862	0.893	0.873	**0.989**	0.981	0.929	0.937

many non-churners as churners, the accuracy was low. If we increased the ratio of non-churners: churners to 90:10 by randomly deleting some churners in Carbo, which made it an imbalanced dataset like the other three, the accuracy increased to 0.885, and TPR became 0.013. It means this LSTM model made a random guess and learned few patterns since it still assigned samples to the majority class.

Apart from accuracy, IHPP-based methods attained much higher TPR, so the results attested that feature engineering is not compulsory to acquire high TPR if using IHPP. The only exception was baselines achieved a few competitive outcomes as IHPP did in the Carbo. To explore the reason why the TPRs of baselines were poor, we conducted

F-tests on those features and found they are highly correlated to labels only in the Carbo. Therefore, better features are needed. Considering sophisticated feature engineering may need rich domain knowledge and end-to-end methods may lose interpretability, it could be helpful to characterize customers purchasing behaviors as trends plus oscillations individually because that could extract serial correlation adequately and are also friendly to making retention strategies.

There are some disadvantages for trigonometric fitting IHPP since the overfitting problems might be a concern. The numbers of harmonics should be carefully selected, due to the overfitting nature of DFT. Linear fitting, i.e., HPP, can be more viable on datasets that have intervals with small variance because customers' usage patterns in them are simple and consistent. Besides, with the increase of the scale of the dataset, the time increases linearly. IHPP has the least prediction time and preprocessing time. Therefore, prediction models based on IHPP can be applied to large datasets.

6 Conclusion

In this paper, we proposed a general scalable prediction pipeline ClusPred for customer churn prediction. We applied our pipeline to four datasets from different domains and with different data structures. The experiments demonstrate that by using the pipeline, the quality of the demographics will not interfere with the performance of the model. Moreover, ClusPred could boost the TPR of state-of-the-art customer churn prediction models. The results also showed Inhomogeneous Poisson Process (IHPP) with trigonometric and polynomial intensity functions can tackle the deficiency of traditional methods that did not utilize time-series data. The experimental results indicate that IHPP methods obtained the highest TPR, compared to other popular methods.

We also notice that when fitting the intensity functions, Fourier Transform (FT) may not be perfect, since FT could not precisely fit irregular cyclical patterns. This is a potentially fruitful area of future work. Apart from that, our approach opens the door for the use of a complete single pipeline as a framework for customer churn prediction on large-scale data in multiple real-life scenarios.

References

1. Huang, Y., et al.: Telco churn prediction with big data. In: Proceedings of the ACM SIGMOD International Conference on Management of Data. Association for Computing Machinery, pp. 607–618 (2015)
2. Zhang, Z., Wang, R., Zheng, W., Lan, S., Liang, D., Jin, H.: Profit maximization analysis based on data mining and the exponential retention model assumption with respect to customer churn problems. In: Proceedings - 15th IEEE International Conference on Data Mining Workshop, ICDMW 2015. Institute of Electrical and Electronics Engineers Inc., pp 1093–1097 (2016)
3. De Caigny, A., Coussement, K., De Bock, K.W.: A new hybrid classification algorithm for customer churn prediction based on logistic regression and decision trees. Eur. J. Oper. Res. **269**, 760–772 (2018). https://doi.org/10.1016/j.ejor.2018.02.009
4. Amin, A., et al.: Customer churn prediction in the telecommunication sector using a rough set approach. Neurocomputing **237**, 242–254 (2017). https://doi.org/10.1016/j.neucom.2016.12.009

5. Bi, W., Cai, M., Liu, M., Li, G.: A big data clustering algorithm for mitigating the risk of customer churn. IEEE Trans. Ind. Inform. **12**, 1270–1281 (2016). https://doi.org/10.1109/TII. 2016.2547584
6. Li, Y., Wang, B.: A study on customer churn of commercial banks based on learning from label proportions. In: IEEE International Conference on Data Mining Workshops, ICDMW. IEEE Computer Society, pp. 1241–1247 (2019)
7. Yang, Y., Liu, Z., Tan, C., Wu, F., Zhuang, Y., Li, Y.: To stay or to leave: Churn prediction for urban migrants in the initial period. In: The Web Conference 2018 - Proceedings of the World Wide Web Conference, WWW 2018. Association for Computing Machinery, Inc., pp. 967–976 (2018)
8. Das, M., Elsner, M., Nandi, A., Ramnath, R.: TopChurn: maximum entropy churn prediction using topic models over heterogeneous signals. In: WWW 2015 Companion - Proceedings of the 24th International Conference on World Wide Web. Association for Computing Machinery, Inc., pp 291–297 (2015)
9. Lu, Y., et al.: Uncovering the co-driven mechanism of social and content links in user churn phenomena. In: Proceedings of the ACM SIGKDD International Conference on Knowledge Discovery and Data Mining. Association for Computing Machinery, pp. 3093–3101 (2019)
10. Shirazi, F., Mohammadi, M.: A big data analytics model for customer churn prediction in the retiree segment. Int. J. Inf. Manage. **48**, 238–253 (2019). https://doi.org/10.1016/j.ijinfomgt. 2018.10.005
11. Liu, X., et al.: A Semi-Supervised and Inductive Embedding Model for Churn Prediction of Large-Scale Mobile Games (2018)
12. Yang, C., Shi, X., Luo, J., Han, J.: I know you'll be back: interpretable new user clustering and churn prediction on a mobile social application. In: Proceedings of the ACM SIGKDD International Conference on Knowledge Discovery and Data Mining. Association for Computing Machinery, pp. 914–922 (2018)
13. De Caigny, A., Coussement, K., De Bock, K.W., Lessmann, S.: Incorporating textual information in customer churn prediction models based on a convolutional neural network. Int. J. Forecast. **36**, 1563–1578 (2020). https://doi.org/10.1016/j.ijforecast.2019.03.029
14. Mitrović, S., Baesens, B., Lemahieu, W., Weerdt, J.: Churn prediction using dynamic RFM-augmented Node2vec. In: Guidotti, R., Monreale, A., Pedreschi, D., Abiteboul, S. (eds.) PAP 2017. LNCS, vol. 10708, pp. 122–138. Springer, Cham (2017). https://doi.org/10.1007/978-3-319-71970-2_11
15. Luo, L., Li, B., Koprinska, I., Berkovsky, S., Chen, F.: Discovering temporal purchase patterns with different responses to promotions. In: International Conference on Information and Knowledge Management, Proceedings (2016)
16. Ke, G., et al.: LightGBM: A highly efficient gradient boosting decision tree. In: Advances in Neural Information Processing Systems (2017)

Fine-Grained Unbalanced Interaction Network for Visual Question Answering

Xinxin Liao[1] , Mingyan Wu[1], Heyan Chai[1], Shuhan Qi[1], Xuan Wang[1],
and Qing Liao[1,2(✉)]

[1] School of Computer Science and Technology, Harbin Institute of Technology
Shenzhen, Shenzhen, China
liaoqing@hit.edu.cn
[2] Peng Cheng Laboratory, Shenzhen, China

Abstract. Learning an effective interaction mechanism is important for
Visual Question Answering (VQA). It requires an understanding of both
the visual content of images and the textual content of questions. Existing approaches consider both the inter-modal and intra-modal interactions, while neglecting the irrelevant information in the interactions. In
this paper, we propose a novel Fine-grained Unbalanced Interaction Network (FUIN) to adaptively capture the most useful information from
interactions. It contains a parallel interaction module to model the two-
way interactions and a fine-grained adaptive activation module to adaptively activate the interactions for each component according to their specific context. Experimental evaluation results on the benchmark VQA-v2
dataset demonstrate that FUIN achieves state-of-the-art VQA performance, we achieve an overall accuracy of 71.14% on the test-std set.

Keywords: Visual question answering · Multi-modal learning ·
Self-attention · Co-attention

1 Introduction

Visual question answering aims at automatically predicting the correct answer
to a natural language question related to the contents of a given picture. The
visual attention mechanism has been applied in many VQA methods introduced
in recent years [1–3]. Learning visual attention and textual attention are both
important. Some recent works [4,5] have proposed co-attention methods that
simultaneously learning these attentions for visual and textual modalities. However, these co-attention methods learn the coarse interaction between different
modalities and unable to infer the interactions between each image region and
each question word. To overcome the above limitation, [6,7] have been proposed
to model dense interactions between regions and words, which greatly improved
VQA performance by enhancing the understanding of the image-question relationship.

Although the current multi-modal dense co-attention models have achieved
good performance, we still find that their interactions between the modalities

H. Qiu et al. (Eds.): KSEM 2021, LNAI 12817, pp. 85–97, 2021.
https://doi.org/10.1007/978-3-030-82153-1_8

have a shortcoming. These models use the information from intra-modal and inter-modal interactions to reconstruct the original features, while ignores the irrelevant information of them. Such reconstructing will hinder VQA model's understanding process. For example, some image regions in the image may obtain more information from its associate words/phrases in the question and some regions may more rely on the understanding of related image regions to infer the answer to the question. For addressing the above issues, we propose a novel Fine-grained Unbalanced Interaction Network (FUIN), which consists of a new Fine-grained Adaptive Activation (FAA) module to model the unbalanced interactions between modalities for each component adaptively. Concretely, our main contributions are as follows:

- A novel Multimodal Fine-grained Unbalanced Interaction Network (FUIN) is proposed, which can simultaneously capture the fine-grained intra- and inter-modal interactions.
- We proposed a new Fine-grained Adaptive Activation (FAA) module to capture the most salient information from interactions adaptively.
- Evaluation results on the benchmark VQA-v2 dataset demonstrate that FUIN performs favorably against the state-of-the-art methods.

The remaining organizational structure of this paper is as follows. Section 2 introduces the research work related to VQA. Section 3 illustrates the overall framework research and design of FUIN. Section 4 verifies the effectiveness of FUIN through some experiments. Section 5 concludes the full paper and the future work.

2   Related Work

In this section, we review fusion-based approaches and attention-based models for visual question answering that are relevant to our work.

2.1   Fusion Methods

VQA task requires an understanding of image and question contents as well as the relation between them. For this reason, in the early stage of VQA methods, simple element-wise summation and element-wise multiplication are used in [8, 9]. To capture the high-level interactions between image and question, MCB [10] based on bilinear pooling was applied to VQA. With better performance but less weighted parameters than MCB, MLB [11] and MFB [12] were proposed. Then, [5] proposed the MFH method that outperforms the aforementioned methods. Additionally, the method MUTAN [13] was proposed, indicating that both MCB and MLB are the special case of this method. Multimodal feature fusion is key to improve VQA performance.

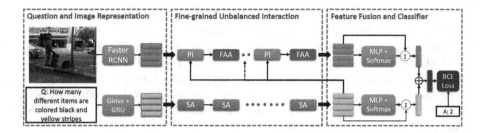

Fig. 1. The framework overview of FUIN

2.2 Attention Mechanisms

It is important to learn about visual attention and question attention simultaneously in VQA. Hierarchical relational attention network [14] jointly reasoned visual attention and question attention with a hierarchical co-attention model. However, these co-attention methods cannot catch the dense relationship between each question word and each image region. To address this issue, the deep co-attention model DFAF [15] establishes the complete interaction between each question word and each image region delivering significantly better VQA performance. MEDAN [16] designs a multi-modal encoder-decoder attention module and stacks them in depth to achieve a new state-of-the-art performance in VQA. Despite the great success of existing methods, they ignore the impact of irrelevant information in the multimodal interactions. In this paper, we propose a fine-grained adaptive activation mechanism to adaptively capture key information from the interactions.

3 Methodology

The overall architecture of FUIN is given in Fig. 1. The proposed framework first extracts visual region features and word features from the input image and question by utilizing the Faster RCNN and GRU models respectively. Then, the Fine-grained unbalanced interaction layer is applied to model the interactions of two modalities. Finally, we employ a fusion mechanism to obtain the joint embedding of the attended image features and attended question features, and then feed it into a classifier to predict the most likely answer.

3.1 Question and Image Representation

The base visual features are represented as a set of regional visual features from the bottom-up & top-down attention model. These features are extracted from a Faster R-CNN model pre-trained on Visual Genome dataset. Give an image I, we encode it as a series of m visual-region features, denoted as $R \in \mathbb{R}^{m \times 2048}$, where the ith region feature is denoted as $r_i \in \mathbb{R}^{2048}$. Then these features transform to 512-dimensional through a fully connected layer.

Given a question Q which is tokenized into words, we firstly transform each word of the question into a vector. Then we use the 300-dimensional GLoVe [17] word embeddings to pre-trained these vectors on a large-score corpus. Take these vectors as the inputs of the GRU, we obtain the final textual features $E \in \mathbb{R}^{l \times 512}$, where the jth word feature is denoted as $e_j \in \mathbb{R}^{512}$ and l is the number of words in the question.

3.2   Fine-Grained Unbalanced Interaction

The Fine-grained Unbalanced Interaction (FUI) layer showed in Fig. 1 consists of Self-Attention (SA) module, Parallel Interaction (PI) module, and Fine-grained Adaptive Activation (FAA) module. We stack the SA module to reconstruct the question features. The PI module and FAA module are cascaded in-depth to capture the high-level interactions between question and image features.

Self-Attention. Self-Attention (SA) module is inspired by scaled dot-product attention proposed in [18]. Each word features are first transformed into query, key and value features. Transformed word features are denoted as $E_Q, E_K, E_V \in \mathbb{R}^{l \times d}$, where d is the common dimension of transformed features. Updated question features $E_{update} \in \mathbb{R}^{l \times d}$ is the weighted summation over all values E_V with respect to the attention learned from the scaled dot-product of E_Q and E_K

$$E_{update} = softmax(\frac{E_Q E_K^T}{\sqrt{d}})E_V \qquad (1)$$

Then the output of SA module E_{output} is obtained by the updated word features E_{update} and original word features $E_{original}$ via residual

$$E_{output} = \mathrm{F}(E_{update} + E_{original}) \qquad (2)$$

where F is a learnable transformation composed of a linear layer. A stacked SA module can help the model to better understand the content of the question [19].

Parallel Interaction. Take image region features R as input, Parallel interaction (PI) module considers the intra-modal interaction and inter-modal interaction simultaneously. Intra-modal interaction model the relationship between all region pairs and the inter-modal interaction model the relationship between all region-word pairs. The information from intra-modal interaction $R_{intra} \in \mathbb{R}^{m \times d}$ is computed as

$$R_{intra} = softmax(\frac{R_Q R_K^T}{\sqrt{d}})R_V \qquad (3)$$

where $R_Q, R_K, R_V \in \mathbb{R}^{m \times d}$ are the transformed region features. And the information from inter-modal interaction $R_{inter} \in \mathbb{R}^{m \times d}$ is computed as

$$R_{inter} = softmax(\frac{R_Q E_K^T}{\sqrt{d}})E_V \qquad (4)$$

Fine-Grained Adaptive Activation. Take R_{intra} and R_{inter} as input, Fine-grained Adaptive Activation (FAA) module adaptively reconstructs the original image region features $R_{original}$. The information from inter-modal interaction or intra-modal interaction may contain some uninformative or even misleading information. Directly fusing them to reconstruct the original features may degrades the performance. Therefore, our proposed FAA module automatically activates R_{intra} and R_{inter} according the specific context of each region feature. The context of each region consists of two parts, self-context and cross-context. Self-context denotes the extent to which the region is mentioned in the image and cross-context denotes the extent to which the region is mentioned in the question. We assume that if a region is well represented in a context, and then it is more inclined to use the information extracted from this context to reconstruct itself. Take the ith region of image for example. For the self-context, we first compute the cosine similarity matrix for all possible region-region pairs, $i.e.$

$$s_{ij} = \frac{r_i^T r_j}{||r_i||||r_j||}, i \in [1, m], j \in [1, m] \tag{5}$$

Here, s_{ij} represents the similarity between the ith region and the jth region. To attend on all regions with respect to each target image region, we define a weighted combination of region representations ($i.e.$ the attended image vector a_i, with respect to the ith image region)

$$a_i = \sum_{j=1}^{m} \alpha_{ij} r_j, \tag{6}$$

where

$$\alpha_{ij} = \frac{exp(s_{ij})}{\sum_{j=1}^{m} exp(s_{ij})} \tag{7}$$

Then intra-modal gate g_i^{intra} is obtained as

$$g_i^{intra} = \sigma(r_i \odot a_i) \tag{8}$$

where $\odot$ denotes the element-wise product and σ denotes the sigmoid function.

For the cross-context, similar to the self-context, given a question Q with l words, we first compute the cosine similarity matrix for all possible region-word pairs, $i.e.$ $c_{ij} = \frac{r_i^T e_j}{||r_i||||e_j||}, i \in [1, m], j \in [1, l]$. Here, c_{ij} represents the similarity between the ith region and the jth word. To attend on entire question with respect to each target image region, we define a weighted combination of word representations $b_i = \sum_{j=1}^{l} \beta_{ij} e_j,$, where $\beta_{ij} = \frac{exp(c_{ij})}{\sum_{j=1}^{l} exp(c_{ij})}$. Then inter-modal gate g_i^{inter} is obtained as $g_i^{inter} = \sigma(r_i \odot b_i)$. Jointly consider the self-context and cross-context to activate the refactoring information from modalities can help us to limit the uninformative information more effective. Therefore, we get the final gates by calculate as

$$g_i^{intra} = \frac{exp(g_i^{intra})}{exp(g_i^{intra}) + exp(g_i^{inter})} \tag{9}$$

$$g_i^{inter} = \frac{exp(g_i^{inter})}{exp(g_i^{intra}) + exp(g_i^{inter})} \tag{10}$$

We represents the region-level gates for all regions of intra-modal interaction as $G_{intra} = [g_1^{intra}, \ldots, g_m^{intra}] \in \mathbb{R}^{m \times d}$, gates of inter-model interaction as $G_{inter} = [g_1^{inter}, \ldots, g_m^{inter}] \in \mathbb{R}^{m \times d}$. These gates control how much information should be passed for reconstruction. Then, the output of FAA module R_{output} can be calculated as

$$R_{output} = R_{original} + F(G_{intra} \odot R_{intra} + G_{inter} \odot R_{inter}) \tag{11}$$

where $R_{original}$ are original image region features.

3.3 Feature Fusion and Classifier

After the FUI layer, we obtain the question features $E = [e_1, e_2, \ldots, e_l] \in R^{l \times 512}$ and image features $R = [r_1, r_2, \ldots, r_m] \in R^{m \times 512}$. Then the final attended feature r is computed as

$$\alpha^R = softmax(\text{MLP}(R)) \tag{12}$$

$$r = \sum_i^m \alpha_i^R r_i \tag{13}$$

where MLP(.) represents a two-layer multi-layer perception and α^R are the learned attention weights of regions in image. Similarity, we can get the final attended question feature e by E. Using the computed e and r, final classification result $Z \in \mathbb{R}^A$ is as

$$Z = sigmoid(W_z(W_e e + W_r r)) \tag{14}$$

where W_e, W_r and W_z are three linear projection matrixes, A represents the number of most frequency answers and *sigmoid* is used for classification.

4 Experiments

In this section, we conduct extensive experiments to evaluate the performance of our FUIN models on the largest VQA benchmark dataset, VQA-v2 [20]. A series of ablation studies and attention visualization demonstrate the effectiveness of FUIN model.

4.1 Datasets

VQA-v2 is the most commonly used large-scale VQA benchmark dataset. It contains human-annotated question-answer pairs relating to the images from the MS-COCO dataset, with 3 questions per image and 10 answers per question from different annotators. Answers with the highest frequency are treated as the

Table 1. Performance evaluated on the test-dev and test-std splits of the VQA-v2 dataset

Method	Test-std				Test-std
	Yes/No	Number	Other	All	All
BUTD [21]	81.82	44.21	56.05	65.32	65.37
DFAF [15]	86.09	53.32	60.49	70.22	70.34
MLIN [22]	85.96	52.93	60.49	70.18	70.28
MCAN [19]	87.06	53.26	60.66	70.63	70.90
SelRes [23]	86.74	53.05	60.47	70.45	70.74
RA [24]	87.00	53.06	60.19	70.43	70.72
MESAN [25]	87.05	53.21	60.72	71.71	71.08
MEDAN [16]	86.90	52.83	60.67	70.59	70.91
FAIN (ours)	**87.07**	53.19	**60.77**	**70.76**	**70.76**

ground truth. The dataset is split into three: *train* (80k images and 444 QA pairs); *val* (40k images and 214k QA pairs); and *test* (80k images and 449k QA pairs). Particularly, the test set is divided into two test subsets, called *test-dev* and *test-standard* to evaluate model performance online. The results consist of three per-type accuracies (*Yes/No*, *Number*, and *Other*) and overall accuracy.

4.2 Implementation Details

The hyper-parameters of our model used in the experiments are as follows. The dimensionality of image, question, multi-modal fusion features are 2048, 512, and 1024, respectively. The number of answer candidates A is 3129 and the stacked depth of modules in FUI layer is 6. The dropout rate used in model is 0.1 and the training batch size is set to 64 and 32 for evaluation.

To train the FUIN model, we use the Adam solver with parameters ($\beta_1 = 0.9, \beta_2 = 0.8$) following [19]. The base learning rate is set to $min(2.5te^{-5}, 1e^{-4})$, where t is the current epoch number starting from 1. After 10 epochs, the learning rate decays by 1/5 every 2 epochs. Only the *train* split of dataset is used for train when evaluating the model on the *val* split, and both the *train* and *val* split are used for training when testing on the *test*.

4.3 Comparison with State-of-the-Art Methods

Table 1 shows the performance of our FUIN model and baseline models trained with the widely used VQA-v2 dataset. For a fair comparison, all the models are based on single-model performance and use the image features extracted by bottom-up attention. BUTD [21] proposed the Bottom-up attention method based on Faster RCNN for the extraction of visual features which becomes one

Table 2. Ablation studies of FUIN on *val* split

Method	Yes/No	Number	Other	All
FAIN	**84.95**	**49.09**	**58.52**	**67.21**
PI w/o inter-modal	69.53	37.08	49.96	55.52
PI w/o intra-modal	84.51	45.23	58.19	66.38
FAA w/o self-context	84.84	49.05	58.4	67.13
FAA w/o cross-context	84.82	48.48	58.52	67.08
w/o FAA	84.76	48.65	58.49	67.07

of the most common and advanced methods used in VQA models. DFAF [15] is a multi-layer stacked network dynamically fusing intra- and inter-modality information. MLIN [22] learns the cross-modality relationships between latent visual and language summarizations. RA [24] utilizes the information in answer. Based on the deep co-attention mechanism, MCAN [19] proposes an encoder-decoder strategy for VQA and models the SA and GA units in a sequential stage. MEDAN [16] and MESAN [25] are the most advanced deep co-attention models following MCAN. Our proposed model FUIN is also based on deep co-attention using encoder-decoder strategy. As shown in Table 1, our model increases the overall (*All*) accuracy of DFAF and MCAN by 0.54 point and 0.13 point on the test-dev set respectively and also outperforms the MEDAN and MESAN. Although our model cannot achieve comparable performance in the category of *Num* to DFAF, our model outperforms DFAF in other categories. DFAF uses the dynamic intra-modal interaction, which is the advanced intra-modal interaction and intra-modal interaction plays a key role in object counting performance [19] (*i.e.*, the number type). We guess that if using dynamic intra-model interaction, the accuracy of our model may be further improved. In summary, these comparisons illustrate the adequate effectiveness of our proposed FUIN.

4.4   Ablation Study

We run several ablations to investigate the reasons why FUIN is effective. The results shown in Table 2 are discussed in detail below.

The Effectiveness of Parallel Interaction Module. The Parallel Interaction (PI) module simultaneously captures the information from intra-modal and inter-modal interaction. We implement a FUIN model with PI module without intra-modal or inter-modal interaction, denoted as "PI w/o inter-modal" and "PI w/o intra-modal" in Table 2. By comparing the performance with our FUIN model, we demonstrate that both intra-modal and inter-modal interactions are effective.

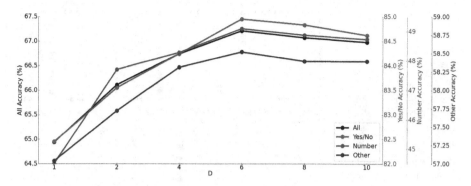

Fig. 2. Ablation studies of the depth D of FUI layer on *val* split, where $D \in \{1, 2, 4, 6, 8, 10\}$

The Effectiveness of Fine-Grained Adaptive Activation Module. In the Fine-grained Adaptive Activation (FAA) module, we adaptively activate the interaction according to the context of each component. We first experiment removing the FAA module and simply add the information features from interactions up. Results are shown as "w/o FAA" in Table 2, indicating that removing the FAA module would decrease the performance. Furthermore, our proposed FAA module considers both the self-context and cross-context. We also experiment with the FUIN model with FAA module which only uses self-context or cross-context, denoted by "FAA w/o self-context" and "FAA w/o cross-context". We can see that "FAA w/o self-context" and "FAA w/o cross-context" both outperform the "w/o FAA". This verifies the usefulness of self-context and cross-context for FAA module.

The Depth of FUI Layer. We then investigate the influence of the depth D of FUI layer. As one can see from Fig. 2, as the depth of FUI layer increases, the accuracy of the model also continues to improve. The model can gradually focus on the most critical regions and words when depth increases. But from the depth is 8, the performance of the model is no longer improved due to the overfitting.

4.5 Visualization

In Fig. 3, we visualize the learned attention and the activation weights of the inter-modal interaction and intra-model interaction from the visual modality. Due to the space limitation, we only show one example and visualize attention and activation weights from three layers. From the results, we have the following observations. The attention maps of intra-6 focus on the 4th, 9th, and 11th columns, which correspond to the three types of foods in the image. Values in

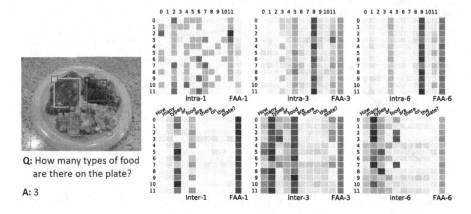

Fig. 3. Visualizations of the learned attention maps and the FAA module from some typical layers $D \in \{1, 3, 6\}$. The intra-D and inter-D denote the intra-model and inter-modal attention maps. FAA-D stands for the activation weight of interactions learned from the D-th FAA module, respectively. The darker the color, the bigger the parameter. For the better visualization effect, we highlight in the image three objects which correspond to 4th, 9th and 11th objects, respectively.

the attention maps of inter-6 occur on the "many", "types" and "foods" columns which are the keywords of the question. That is to say when reconstructing the attended region features, intra-model interaction tends to focus on the correct target regions and the inter-model interaction grasps the nature of the problem. This explains why our model can answer questions correctly. And we can find that values in the question maps of intra-1 are uniformly distributed, suggesting that the module is unclear to focus on which object region. In such a situation, directly feeding it to co-attention may damage the feature of attended region. Therefore, our model does not activate the fuse of intra-model interaction to block it (FAA-1 set low weight to intra-1), preventing the model from fusing noisy information. On the contrary, the words like "types" and "foods" obtain large attention weights. And the value of activation is large, revealing that the attended features tend to use the feature of these keywords for reconstruction.

4.6 Analysis of Imbalance Between Interactions

In this section, we explore the impact of the imbalance between the inter-modal interaction and intra-modal interaction on the VQA model performance. We manually set the activation weight of the interactions to control how much information is used for constructing ("unbalanced" model in Fig. 4). For example, if we set a high weight for intra-modal interaction, VQA model would use more information from intra-modal interaction. From the Fig. 4, we can find that the performance of the model is sensitive to the weight of interactions, and the model can perform better at some optimal weight. Our proposed FUIN model can outperform these optimal weight models, which indicated that our model can balance the two interactions adaptively.

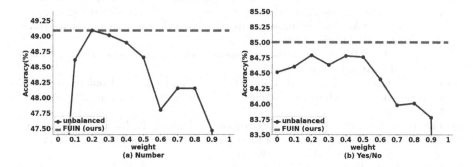

Fig. 4. *Number* and *Yes/No* accuracies of unbalanced model. The red line is the result of our FUIN model. All the reported results are evaluated on the *val* split. (Color figure online)

5   Conclusion

In this paper, we proposed a novel Fine-grained Unbalanced Interaction Network (FUIN) for VQA. The core idea is to design an FUI layer, which consists of the Parallel Interaction module (PI) and Fine-grained Adaptive Activation (FAA) module. The PI module models the fine-grained inter- and intra-interaction simultaneously. The FAA module aims to adaptively encourage the fusing of positive interaction. Extensive experiments on the VQA-v2 datasets demonstrate that our model achieves comparable performance with the state-of-the-art approaches.

Acknowledgement. This work is supported in part by the National Natural Science Foundation of China under grant No. U1711261 and the Guangdong Major Project of Basic and Applied Basic Research under grant No. 2019B030302002.

References

1. Gai, K., Qiu, M.: Reinforcement learning-based content-centric services in mobile sensing. IEEE Netw. **32**(4), 34–39 (2018)
2. Tao, L., Golikov, S., Gai, K., Qiu, M.: A reusable software component for integrated syntax and semantic validation for services computing. In: 2015 IEEE Symposium on Service-Oriented System Engineering, pp. 127–132. IEEE (2015)
3. Chen, M., Zhang, Y., Qiu, M., Guizani, N., Hao, Y.: SPHA: smart personal health advisor based on deep analytics. IEEE Commun. Mag. **56**(3), 164–169 (2018)
4. Lu, J., Yang, J., Batra, D., Parikh, D.: Hierarchical question-image co-attention for visual question answering. arXiv preprint arXiv:1606.00061 (2016)

5. Yu, Z., Yu, J., Xiang, C., Fan, J., Tao, D.: Beyond bilinear: Generalized multimodal factorized high-order pooling for visual question answering. IEEE Trans. Neural Netw. Learn. Syst. **29**(12), 5947–5959 (2018)

6. Yu, Z., Cui, Y., Yu, J., Tao, D., Tian, Q.: Multimodal unified attention networks for vision-and-language interactions. arXiv preprint arXiv:1908.04107 (2019)

7. He, S., Han, D.: An effective dense co-attention networks for visual question answering. Sensors **20**(17), 4897 (2020)

8. Wang, X., Cao, W.: Non-iterative approaches in training feed-forward neural networks and their applications (2018)

9. Cao, W., Gao, J., Ming, Z., Cai, S., Shan, Z.: Fuzziness-based online sequential extreme learning machine for classification problems. Soft. Comput. **22**(11), 3487–3494 (2018)

10. Fukui, A., Park, D.H., Yang, D., Rohrbach, A., Darrell, T., Rohrbach, M.: Multi-modal compact bilinear pooling for visual question answering and visual grounding. arXiv preprint arXiv:1606.01847 (2016)

11. Kim, J.H., On, K.W., Lim, W., Kim, J., Ha, J.W., Zhang, B.T.: Hadamard product for low-rank bilinear pooling. arXiv preprint arXiv:1610.04325 (2016)

12. Yu, Z., Yu, J., Fan, J., Tao, D.: Multi-modal factorized bilinear pooling with co-attention learning for visual question answering. In: Proceedings of the IEEE International Conference on Computer Vision, pp. 1821–1830 (2017)

13. Ben-Younes, H., Cadene, R., Cord, M., Thome, N.: MUTAN: multimodal tucker fusion for visual question answering. In: Proceedings of the IEEE International Conference on Computer Vision, pp. 2612–2620 (2017)

14. Cao, W., Hu, L., Gao, J., Wang, X., Ming, Z.: A study on the relationship between the rank of input data and the performance of random weight neural network. Neural Comput. Appl. **32**(16), 12685–12696 (2020)

15. Gao, P., et al.: Dynamic fusion with intra-and inter-modality attention flow for visual question answering. In: Proceedings of the IEEE/CVF Conference on Computer Vision and Pattern Recognition, pp. 6639–6648 (2019)

16. Chen, C., Han, D., Wang, J.: Multimodal encoder-decoder attention networks for visual question answering. IEEE Access **8**, 35662–35671 (2020)

17. Pennington, J., Socher, R., Manning, C.D.: GloVe: global vectors for word representation. In: Proceedings of the 2014 Conference on Empirical Methods in Natural Language Processing (EMNLP), pp. 1532–1543 (2014)

18. Vaswani, A., et al.: Attention is all you need. arXiv preprint arXiv:1706.03762 (2017)

19. Yu, Z., Yu, J., Cui, Y., Tao, D., Tian, Q.: Deep modular co-attention networks for visual question answering. In: Proceedings of the IEEE/CVF Conference on Computer Vision and Pattern Recognition, pp. 6281–6290 (2019)

20. Goyal, Y., Khot, T., Summers-Stay, D., Batra, D., Parikh, D.: Making the V in VQA matter: elevating the role of image understanding in visual question answering. In: Proceedings of the IEEE Conference on Computer Vision and Pattern Recognition, pp. 6904–6913 (2017)

21. Anderson, P., et al.: Bottom-up and top-down attention for image captioning and visual question answering. In: Proceedings of the IEEE Conference on Computer Vision and Pattern Recognition, pp. 6077–6086 (2018)

22. Gao, P., You, H., Zhang, Z., Wang, X., Li, H.: Multi-modality latent interaction network for visual question answering. In: Proceedings of the IEEE/CVF International Conference on Computer Vision, pp. 5825–5835 (2019)

23. Hong, J., Park, S., Byun, H.: Selective residual learning for visual question answering. Neurocomputing **402**, 366–374 (2020)

24. Guo, W., Zhang, Y., Wu, X., Yang, J., Cai, X., Yuan, X.: Re-attention for visual question answering. In: Proceedings of the AAAI Conference on Artificial Intelligence, pp. 91–98 (2020)
25. Guo, Z., Han, D.: Multi-modal explicit sparse attention networks for visual question answering. Sensors **20**(23), 6758 (2020)

Swarm Intelligence-Based Feature Selection: An Improved Binary Grey Wolf Optimization Method

Wenqi Li, Hui Kang, Tie Feng$^{(\boxtimes)}$, Jiahui Li, Zhiru Yue, and Geng Sun

College of Computer Science and Technology, Jilin University,
Changchun 130012, China
{liwq19,yuezr2118}@mails.jlu.edu.cn,
{kanghui,fengtie,sungeng}@jlu.edu.cn

Abstract. Feature selection can effectively reduce the number of features and improve the accuracy of classification, so that reducing the computational burden and improving the performance of machine learning. In this paper, we propose an improved binary grey wolf optimization (IBGWO) algorithm for a wrapper-based feature selection method. Aiming at the shortcomings of grey wolf optimization (GWO) for feature selection, we first propose a enhanced opposition-based learning (E-OBL) initialization method to enhance the performance of initial solutions. Second, a local search strategy is introduced to balance the exploitation and exploration abilities of the IBGWO. Finally, a novel update mechanism is proposed for improving the population diversity and exploration capability of the algorithm. Simulations are conducted by using 16 well-known datasets, and the results show that the proposed method outperforms other benchmark algorithms on 12 datasets, and the introduced improved factors are suitable and effective.

Keywords: Feature selection · Classification · Swarm intelligence algorithm · Grey wolf optimization

1 Introduction

With the progress of information technology, a large number of datasets have been generated in medical imaging [20], bioinformatics [3], finance [8] and other fields [7]. However, part of the datasets, especially high-dimensional datasets, cannot be processed effectively by machine learning since they contain some redundant, irrelevant, or noisy features [4]. The existence of these features increases the consumption of computing resources and reduces classification accuracy. Thus, it is necessary to use feature selection method to preprocess the dataset.

As an important preprocessing step, feature selection aims to select the informative feature subset from a large number of features by eliminating worthless features [22], so that saving computing resources and improving the classification

© Springer Nature Switzerland AG 2021
H. Qiu et al. (Eds.): KSEM 2021, LNAI 12817, pp. 98–110, 2021.
https://doi.org/10.1007/978-3-030-82153-1_9

accuracy for machine learning. In general, feature selection methods can be divided into two categories, i.e., filter-based methods and wrapped-based methods. Specifically, wrapper-based methods can be more effective than filter-based methods in terms of classification accuracy. However, the wrapper-based method may take more computing resources than the filter-based method.

The feature selection problem is proven as an NP-hard combination optimization problem that is difficult to be solved by exhaustive strategies [9]. Thus, it is impractical to generate all possible subsets to search the optimal feature subset when dealing with a high-dimensional dataset. In recent years, metaheuristic algorithms are regarded as powerful tools for solving feature selection problem. There are some works that conduct feature selection by using some metaheuristic algorithms such as particle swarm optimization (PSO) [18], genetic algorithm (GA) [11], ant colony optimization (ACO) [12], dragonfly algorithm (DA) [14], whale optimization algorithm (WOA) [15], and salp swarm algorithm (SSA) [19].

Among the abovementioned algorithms, grey wolf optimization (GWO) is a population-based metaheuristic algorithm proposed by Mirjalili et al. [16], which shows the outperformance and superiority in comparison with other algorithms. Thus, GWO has some potential and value to be applied in the field of feature selection. For instance, Al-Tashi et al. [2] propose a binary version of the hybrid GWO and PSO algorithm to search for optimal feature subset. Moreover, Abdel-Basset et al. [1] introduce a two-phase mutation strategy into GWO to solve the feature selection problems. However, according to the no free lunch (NFL) theory, no algorithm can solve all feature selection problems suitably. Thus, this motivates us to propose a more effective algorithm for solving more feature selection problems.

In this paper, we propose an improved binary GWO (IBGWO) to solve the feature selection problem. Firstly, we utilize a enhanced opposition-based learning (E-OBL) initialization strategy to improve the initial solution. Then, based on Lévy flight mechanism, a local search strategy is introduced. Finally, mutation and crossover operators are introduced into the update mechanism, so that enhancing the exploration ability. Moreover, simulations are conducted which demonstrates that the proposed approach performs better than other comparison algorithms.

The rest of this paper is organized as follows. Section 2 describes some preliminaries and theoretical background. Section 3 presents the details of the proposed approach. The results are presented in Sect. 4. Finally, a summary of conclusions is given in Sect. 5.

2   Preliminaries

In this section, the preliminaries and models used in this paper are presented.

2.1   Conventional GWO

GWO is mainly inspired by the social hierarchy and hunting behaviors of grey wolf. In nature, the grey wolf pack has a strict social hierarchy, which is organized into four main levels: alpha (α), beta (β), delta (δ), and omega (ω). The α, β, δ wolves are leaders that guide the hunting process, while ω wolves are dominated by all three. In the GWO algorithm, the potential optimal position is considered as prey, the best three solutions of the population are considered as α, β and δ wolves, respectively, and the remaining solutions are considered as ω. To find the optimal position, the ω wolves will encircle the prey based on the positions of α, β and δ. Specifically, the mathematical models of ith ω wolf of the population can be described as follows:

$$\begin{aligned} \overrightarrow{D_\alpha} &= |\overrightarrow{C_1} \cdot \overrightarrow{X_\alpha} - \overrightarrow{X}_i(t)| \\ \overrightarrow{D_\beta} &= |\overrightarrow{C_2} \cdot \overrightarrow{X_\beta} - \overrightarrow{X}_i(t)| \\ \overrightarrow{D_\delta} &= |\overrightarrow{C_3} \cdot \overrightarrow{X_\delta} - \overrightarrow{X}_i(t)| \end{aligned} \tag{1}$$

$$\begin{aligned} \overrightarrow{X_1} &= \overrightarrow{X_\alpha} - \overrightarrow{A_1} \cdot \overrightarrow{D_\alpha} \\ \overrightarrow{X_2} &= \overrightarrow{X_\beta} - \overrightarrow{A_2} \cdot \overrightarrow{D_\beta} \\ \overrightarrow{X_3} &= \overrightarrow{X_\delta} - \overrightarrow{A_3} \cdot \overrightarrow{D_\delta} \end{aligned} \tag{2}$$

where D_α, D_β, and D_δ denote the approximate distances between the ith wolf and α, β and δ, respectively. X_1, X_2, and X_3 indicate the estimated positions of the prey based on the position of α, β and δ, respectively. $\overrightarrow{X_\alpha}$, $\overrightarrow{X_\beta}$ and $\overrightarrow{X_\delta}$ represent the positions of the α, β, δ, respectively. Moreover, $\overrightarrow{X}_i(t)$ denotes the current position of the ith ω wolf. In addition, A and C are two coefficient vectors which can be calculated as follows:

$$\overrightarrow{A} = 2\overrightarrow{a} \cdot \overrightarrow{r_1} - \overrightarrow{a} \tag{3}$$

$$\overrightarrow{C} = 2\overrightarrow{r_2} \tag{4}$$

where $\overrightarrow{r_1}$ and $\overrightarrow{r_2}$ are random vectors between $[0,1]$. $\overrightarrow{a}$ is vector linearly decreases from 2 to 0 [16].

Accordingly, the position of ith ω wolf can be updated as follows:

$$\overrightarrow{X}_i(t+1) = \frac{\overrightarrow{X_1} + \overrightarrow{X_2} + \overrightarrow{X_3}}{3} \tag{5}$$

2.2 Binary Grey Wolf Optimization (BGWO)

In conventional GWO, the position of each wolf is in a continuous space, which can be updated easily by using Eq. (5). However, BGWO is proposed for binary optimization problems, and each wolf's position is represented by a vector whose value is only 0 or 1. Consequently, the update mechanism needs to be changed to make the algorithm suitable for binary space.

Accordingly, the update mechanism of BGWO is modified as follows:

$$x_{t+1}^d = \begin{cases} 1 & if \quad sigmoid(\frac{x_1^d + x_2^d + x_3^d}{3}) \geq rand \\ 0 & else \end{cases} \tag{6}$$

where x_{t+1}^d is the value of the dth dimension of the position vector $X(t+1)$, $rand$ is a random number between $[0,1]$, and $sigmoid(x)$ is defined as follows:

$$sigmoid(x) = \frac{1}{1 + e^{-10(x-0.5)}} \tag{7}$$

Moreover, the values of x_1^d, x_2^d, x_3^d are the dth dimension of X_1, X_2 and X_3, and more details about BGWO can be found in reference [6].

3   The Proposed Approach

In this section, we first propose the IBGWO with several improved factors. Then, we use it for solving feature selection problem. Finally, a fitness evaluation method is presented.

3.1   IBGWO

GWO has certain shortcomings for solving optimization problems, e.g., its search strategy is relatively simple, resulting in the lack of exploration capability. Thus, we propose an IBGWO that introduces the E-OBL initialization, local search strategy and novel update mechanisms to improve the performance of GWO. The pseudo code of the proposed IBGWO is presented in Algorithm 1, and the details of the introduced improved factors are as follows.

E-OBL Initialization Mechanism. Conventional GWO algorithm builds the initial solution in a random way, which is easy to implement. However, this randomly generating initial solutions method may lead to the blindness of the algorithm. Thus, we introduce E-OBL approach to improve the initial solution.

Specifically, the main idea of opposition-based learning (OBL) is to search both directions of the search space, it may generate some solutions according to some strategies and then generate the opposite solutions of them, so that making the distribution of the initial solutions more reasonable. As can be seen, OBL can be combined with some other solution initialization techniques for accessing higher performance. Thus, we propose a E-OBL initialization strategy by combining OBL with the small initialization strategy proposed in [21] since it can achieve the better performance than random ways in the tests, and the details are summarized as follows:

First, we use the small initialization strategy to generate N_{pop} initial solutions. Specifically, solutions are initialized by randomly setting $\varphi \cdot N_{dim}$ dimensions of them to 1, which means that $\varphi \cdot N_{dim}$ features of a dataset are selected randomly. Note that φ is a parameter that less than 0.5.

Second, the N_{pop} opposition solutions of the initial solutions are generated by using OBL, and each dimension of opposition solutions is calculated as follows:

$$\tilde{x}_d = a_d + b_d - x_d \tag{8}$$

Algorithm 1: Pseudo-code of the IBGWO

---

1 Define and initialize the related parameters: population size N_{pop}, solution dimension N_{dim}, maximum iteration t_{max} and fitness function, etc.;

2 Generate the population P by using small initialization;

3 Calculate the opposite population OP by using Eq. (8);

4 Select N_{pop} fittest ones from $\{P \cup OP\}$ as the initial population; //**E-OBL initialization mechanism**

5 **for** $t = 1$ *to* t_{max} **do**

6   Calculate the fitness function values of solutions;

7   Sort these solutions in descending order according to their fitness function values;

8   Update X_α, X_β, X_δ;

9   Apply the **local search strategy** to improve X_α, X_β, X_δ by using Eq. (9);

10   Update the parameters of GWO;

11   **for** $i = 1$ *to* N_{pop} **do**

12   Update the position of X_i by using Algorithm 2; //**Novel update mechanism**

13   **end**

14 **end**

15 Return X_α;

16 //X_α **is the best solution obtained by the algorithm**

---

where x_d and $\tilde{x}_d$ are the dth dimension of a solution and its opposition solution, respectively. a_d and b_d are the upper and lower bounds of dth dimension, respectively.

Finally, the fitness function values of the generated $2 \cdot N_{pop}$ initial solutions are computed and ranked. Then, the best N_{pop} solutions are selected as the final initial solutions.

Local Search Strategy. In conventional BGWO, the solutions are updated under the guidance of X_α, X_β and X_δ. If the positions of X_α, X_β and X_δ are far from the optimal solution or fall into local optimum, the performance of the algorithm may be greatly reduced. Therefore, we introduce the Lévy flight mechanism to enhance the local search ability, so that optimizing the positions of X_α, X_β and X_δ and it is described as follows:

$$X^{new} = X + \zeta \oplus L\acute{e}vy(\lambda) \tag{9}$$

where ζ is the step factor that depends on the scales of the applications, and ζ is set as 0.01 in this work. Moreover, $L\acute{e}vy(\lambda)$ indicates random step length that can be calculated briefly by Mantegna's algorithm as in literature [10].

By using Eq. (9), X_α^{new}, X_β^{new} and X_δ^{new} can be generated, and then their fitness functions can be evaluated, if the fitness functions of new solution are better than the original ones, X_α, X_β and X_δ are replaced by X_α^{new}, X_β^{new} and X_δ^{new}, respectively. As such, the exploitation ability of the BGWO can be improved by short-distance and long-distance searches of Lévy flight mechanism.

Novel Update Mechanism with Mutation/Crossover Operators. The update method of conventional GWO may reduce the population diversity and make the GWO insufficient in global search capability. To tackle this issue, a new two-stage mutation and crossover operators are introduced to enrich the update mechanism, so that improving the population diversity while enhancing the global search efficiency.

Specifically, we use the two-stage mutation operator to obtain the solution around the randomly selected solution or the best solution. In the early iteration stage, the mutation operator tends to randomly select solutions with better fitness values for mutation operation so that enhancing the exploration ability. In the later iteration stage, mutation operation is carried out on the best solution so that the updated solution can converge to the best solution. Accordingly, the two-stage mutation operator is designed as follows:

$$
X_M = \begin{cases} X_{r_0} + F \cdot (X_{r_1} - X_{r_2}) & if \ \theta < 0.5 \\ X_\alpha + F \cdot (X_{r_0} - X_{r_1}) & otherwise \end{cases} \tag{10}
$$

where X_M is the result solution of mutation operation, X_{r_0}, X_{r_1} and X_{r_2} are randomly selected solutions from half population that with better fitness function values, and $r_0 \neq r_1 \neq r_2$. F is a mutation scaling factor that set as 0.5, and θ is a parameter used to judge the iteration phase that calculated as $\theta = \frac{t}{t_{max}}$.

On the other hand, the crossover operator is introduced to update the solutions of half of the population with the worst fitness function values by crossing with X_M. As for each dimension of X_M, the crossover operation can be described as follows:

$$
x^d(t+1) = \begin{cases} x_M^d & if \ \ rand < 0.5 \\ x^d(t) & otherwise \end{cases} \tag{11}
$$

where x_M^d is dth dimension of X_M obtained by Eq. (10). Accordingly, the update mechanism with mutation and crossover operators is shown in Algorithm 2. By using this mechanism, the algorithm has a good balance between exploitation and exploration.

3.2 The Complexity of the Proposed IBGWO

We suppose that the maximum number of iteration and population size are t_{max} and N_{pop}, respectively, then the complexity of IBGWO can computed as follows. The most time-consuming step is the calculation of fitness function value. In IBGWO, E-OBL initialization, local search strategy and main loop of algorithm need to calculate fitness function $\mathcal{O}(2 \cdot N_{pop})$, $\mathcal{O}(3 \cdot t_{max})$ and $\mathcal{O}(t_{max} \cdot N_{pop})$, respectively. Thus, the overall complexity of IBGWO is $\mathcal{O}(t_{max} \cdot N_{pop})$.

Algorithm 2: Novel update mechanisms with mutation/crossover operators

---
1 Define and initialize the related parameters: population size N_{pop}, and the array of solutions sorted by fitness function values in descending order *Array*, etc.;
2 **for** $i = 1$ *to* $\frac{N_{pop}}{2}$ **do**
3 $\quad$ Randomly select three solutions X_{r_0}, X_{r_1} and X_{r_2} from the best half of *Array*;
4 $\quad$ Calculate the mutated solution X_M by using Eq. (10);
5 $\quad$ Cross X_M with the ith solution of *Array* by using Eq. (11);
6 **end**
7 **for** $i = \frac{N_{pop}}{2}$ *to* N_{pop} **do**
8 $\quad$ Calculate A, C by using Eqs. (3), (4);
9 $\quad$ Update the position of the ith solution of *Array* by using Eq. (6);
10 **end**
11 Return *Array*;
12 //*Array* **is the array of updated solutions**

3.3 Feature Selection with IBGWO

To solve the feature selection problems, we consider each wolf as a solution to the problem. Therefore, each wolf consists of a one-dimensional binary vector and each dimension expresses a feature candidate. If the dimension has a value of 1, the feature is selected, and vice versa. Thus, the population of IBGWO is expressed as follows:

$$P = \begin{bmatrix} X_1 \\ X_2 \\ \vdots \\ X_{N_{pop}} \end{bmatrix} = \begin{bmatrix} x_1^1 & x_2^1 & \cdots & x_{N_{dim}}^1 \\ x_1^2 & x_2^2 & \cdots & x_{N_{dim}}^2 \\ \vdots & \vdots & & \vdots \\ x_1^{N_{pop}} & x_2^{N_{pop}} & \cdots & x_{N_{dim}}^{N_{pop}} \end{bmatrix} \qquad (12)$$

3.4 Fitness Evaluation

In this work, the fitness function has two objectives, one is to reduce the number of selected features, and the other is to improve the accuracy of classification. Thus, by using the linear weighting method, the fitness function can be defined as follows:

$$fitness = a \cdot Err + b \cdot \frac{N_S}{N_F} \qquad (13)$$

where Err is the classification error rate, N_S and N_F respectively indicate the number of selected features and the total number of features, respectively. Moreover, $a \in [0, 1]$ and $b = 1 - a$ are the weights of these two objectives.

Note that the K nearest neighbor (KNN, $k = 5$) is employed in this paper to compute the classification error rate due to it is effective, easy to be implemented and low computational cost [13].

4   Experimental Results and Analysis

In this section, the performance of the proposed IBGWO for the feature selection problem is evaluated.

4.1   Datasets and Setups

In this work, we use 16 datasets that are selected from the UCI repository [5] to conduct the simulations. Table 1 presents the details of the employed datasets.

Moreover, we set the population size and maximum iterations at 10 and 100 [17], respectively. Due to the stochastic of metaheuristics algorithm, each algorithm is independently run 30 times. To assess the selected features, we use 10-fold cross-validation to randomly partition datasets. Nine folds are used for training the classification algorithm while the remaining fold is used for testing. In addition, a and b in the fitness function are set to 0.99 and 0.01, respectively. The CPU of the used computer is Intel(R) Core(TM) i7-4790 CPU with 3.60 GHz and the RAM is 4 GB.

Table 1. Benchmark datasets.

No.	Dataset	No. of Features	No. of instance
1	Arrhythmia	278	452
2	Breastcancer	10	699
3	BreastEW	30	569
4	Congress	16	435
5	Dermatology	34	366
6	Hillvalley	100	606
7	Ionosphere	34	351
8	Krvskp	36	3196
9	Lung	325	73
10	Lymphography	18	148
11	Sonar	60	208
12	Spect	22	267
13	Tic-tac-toe	9	958
14	Vehicule	18	846
15	Wine	13	178
16	Zoo	16	101

4.2   Parameter Tuning

In this section, we tune the key parameter φ of IBGWO by evaluating the fitness function value. Specifically, the proposed IBGWO algorithm with different settings of the parameter φ, i.e., $\varphi = 0.1$, $\varphi = 0.2$, $\varphi = 0.3$, and $\varphi = 0.4$.

Table 2 shows the results of the proposed IBGWO algorithm with different settings of the parameter φ in terms of the fitness function value. Note that the best fitness function values are highlighted in bold font. The results show that when $\varphi = 0.3$, the IBGWO algorithm obtains the best performance on 10 datasets, which means that IBGWO with $\varphi = 0.3$ achieves the best optimization results. Thus, we use this parameter value in subsequent simulations.

Table 2. The fitness function values obtained by IBGWO that based on different settings of φ.

	$\varphi = 0.1$	$\varphi = 0.2$	$\varphi = 0.3$	$\varphi = 0.4$
Arrhythmia	0.3336	0.3321	**0.3208**	0.3343
Breastcancer	**0.0272**	**0.0272**	**0.0272**	**0.0272**
BreastEW	0.0430	0.0422	**0.0400**	0.0414
Congress	**0.0254**	0.0262	0.0258	0.0260
Dermatology	0.0120	0.0134	**0.0107**	**0.0107**
Hillvalley	**0.3572**	0.3710	0.3730	0.3827
Ionosphere	**0.0841**	0.0869	0.0859	0.1105
Krvskp	0.0251	0.0275	**0.0236**	0.0240
Lung	**0.0955**	0.1023	0.0960	0.1062
Lymphography	**0.5630**	0.5662	0.5651	0.5664
Sonar	0.1124	0.0937	**0.0932**	0.0937
Spect	0.2712	0.2736	**0.2629**	0.2695
Tic-tac-toe	**0.1564**	**0.1564**	**0.1564**	**0.1564**
Vehicule	0.2752	0.2766	**0.2744**	0.2769
Wine	0.0517	**0.0489**	0.0500	0.0497
Zoo	0.0746	0.0715	**0.0693**	0.0737

4.3 Comparison with Other Feature Selection Methods

In this section, the performance of the proposed IBGWO is compared with the following metaheuristic-based feature selection algorithms: BGWO [6], BPSO [10], binary salp swarm algorithm (BSSA) [19] and WOA [15]. Moreover, the settings of the key parameters used to run these comparison algorithms are listed in Table 3.

Table 4 shows the average fitness function values obtained by different algorithms for each dataset. It can be observed that the performance of IBGWO outperforms other algorithms as it obtains the best results on 12 out of 16 datasets, and BPSO, WOA and SCA achieves the best results on 6, 2 and 1 datasets, respectively. The reason may be that the introduced novel update mechanism can enhance the population diversity and improve the exploration ability of the algorithm.

Table 3. Key parameters of different algorithms.

No.	Algorithm	Parameters
1	BGWO	$\alpha = [2, 0]$
2	BPSO	Acceleration constants ($c_1 = 2$, $c_2 = 2$)
		Inertia weights ($w_1 = 0.9$, $w_2 = 0.4$)
3	BSSA	c_2 and c_3 random numbers over [0,1]
4	WOA	$a = 2$, $b = 1$
5	IBGWO	$\alpha = [2, 0]$, $\varphi = 0.3$

Table 4. Fitness function values obtained by different algorithms.

	BGWO	BPSO	BSSA	WOA	IBGWO
Arrhythmia	0.3321	0.3392	0.3504	0.3518	**0.3208**
Breastcancer	0.0288	**0.0272**	0.0277	**0.0272**	**0.0272**
BreastEW	0.0436	0.0404	0.0438	0.0437	**0.0400**
Congress	0.0287	0.0262	0.0305	0.0295	**0.0258**
Dermatology	0.0154	0.0123	0.0174	0.0171	**0.0107**
Hillvalley	0.3881	0.3992	0.4097	0.4111	**0.3730**
Ionosphere	0.1126	0.1026	0.1336	0.1343	**0.0859**
Krvskp	0.0242	0.0295	0.0409	0.0387	**0.0236**
Lung	0.1159	0.1038	0.1277	0.1295	**0.0960**
Lymphography	0.5745	**0.5616**	0.5738	0.5777	0.5651
Sonar	0.1072	0.0991	0.1146	0.1165	**0.0932**
Spect	0.2723	0.2687	0.2820	0.2858	**0.2629**
Tic-tac-toe	0.1919	**0.1564**	**0.1564**	**0.1564**	**0.1564**
Vehicule	0.2811	**0.2721**	0.2775	0.2772	0.2744
Wine	0.0573	**0.0485**	0.0524	0.0513	0.0500
Zoo	0.0881	**0.0611**	0.0755	0.0684	0.0693

For more intuitive, Fig. 1 shows the convergence rates of different algorithms during the optimization processes. Note that each curve is selected from the 15th test. As can be seen, the proposed IBGWO obtains the best curves on 12 datasets, which performs the best convergence ability among all the comparison methods. The reason may be that the introduced E-OBL initialization strategy improves the quality of the initial solutions. Note that it can be observed in Fig. 1 that IBGWO has the lowest fitness function values at initial iterations in most datasets.

Table 5 presents the results in terms of the classification accuracy (acc.) and the number of the selected features (N_{fea}). As can be seen, the proposed IBGWO outperforms other algorithms as it obtains the best average accuracy on 11 out of

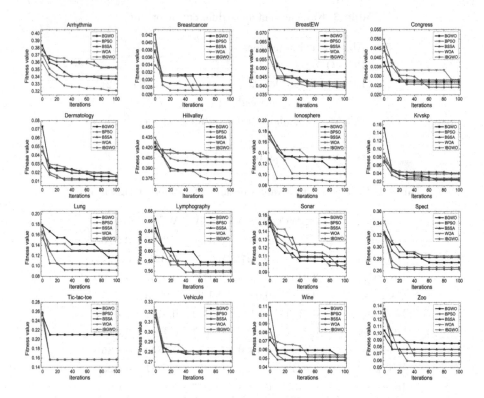

Fig. 1. Convergence rates obtained by different algorithms.

Table 5. Classification accuracies and number of selected features obtained by different algorithms.

	BGWO		BPSO		BSSA		WOA		IBGWO	
	acc.	N_{fea}	acc.	N_{fea}	acc.	N_{fea}	acc.	N_{fea}	acc.	N_{fea}
Arrhythmia	66.98	142.9	66.22	132.0	65.13	144.2	65.04	159.2	**68.07**	**130.2**
Breastcancer	97.69	**5.9**	**97.86**	6.0	97.80	**5.9**	**97.86**	6.0	**97.86**	6.0
BreastEW	95.68	**2.7**	**96.12**	6.1	95.98	12.0	95.98	11.9	96.09	3.9
Congress	97.59	7.8	**97.80**	7.0	97.34	6.6	97.52	8.0	**97.80**	**6.4**
Dermatology	98.95	**17.0**	99.32	19.0	98.81	19.3	98.92	21.7	**99.43**	17.4
Hillvalley	61.39	59.4	60.16	**48.3**	59.15	52.5	59.02	54.1	**62.84**	50.7
Ionosphere	89.00	12.6	89.89	8.4	86.86	12.0	86.86	14.3	**91.51**	**6.2**
Krvskp	98.12	**20.0**	97.64	22.3	96.48	21.7	96.75	23.5	**98.22**	21.4
Lung	88.75	148.0	90.00	154.9	87.63	167.3	87.50	186.4	**90.75**	**142.3**
Lymphography	42.47	8.8	**43.73**	**8.2**	42.60	9.9	42.13	8.7	43.47	9.7
Sonar	89.62	**26.5**	90.48	28.9	88.95	31.4	88.81	34.0	**91.05**	27.2
Spect	73.07	12.7	73.33	**10.5**	72.07	12.2	71.70	12.4	**74.00**	12.2
Tic-tac-toe	81.48	**7.7**	85.21	9.0	**85.21**	9.0	**85.21**	9.0	**85.21**	9.0
Vehicule	72.19	10.4	**73.07**	9.9	72.51	**9.6**	72.59	10.4	72.86	10.3
Wine	94.67	5.9	**95.50**	**5.1**	95.17	5.9	95.22	5.2	95.39	5.6
Zoo	91.64	8.5	**94.27**	7.0	92.91	8.5	93.64	8.7	93.55	8.7

16 datasets. Moreover, the proposed IBGWO selects more features than BGWO, which means that IBGWO tends to select more features to achieve higher accuracy. Note that the classification accuracy and the number of the selected features are trade-offs, which means that it is very hard to obtain the best results in all terms. Thus, the proposed IBGWO can be regarded as achieving the best performance for feature selection.

In summary, IBGWO has the best performance in all comparison algorithms, and the introduced operators can improve the performance of conventional GWO in a reasonable way.

5   Conclusion

In this paper, the feature selection problem is investigated. We propose an IBGWO algorithm as the learning algorithm of the wrapper-based method for feature selection. In IBGWO, we first propose an E-OBL initialization method to enhance the performance of initial solutions. Then, we introduce a local search strategy to improve the exploitation ability of IBGWO. Finally, a novel update mechanism is proposed for improving population diversity and exploration capability. Moreover, simulations are conducted by using 16 well-known datasets from UCI repository, and the results show that the proposed method outperforms other benchmark algorithms. In the future, we will investigate more enhanced OBL methods and combine them with the GWO algorithm for feature selection.

Acknowledgment. This work is supported in part by the National Key Research and Development Program of China (2018YFC0831706), in part by the National Natural Science Foundation of China (62002133, 61872158, 61806083), in part by the Science and Technology Development Plan Project of Jilin Province (20200201166JC, 20190701019GH, 20190701002GH), in part by Youth Science and Technology Talent Lift Project of Jilin Province (QT202013), and in part by the Excellent Young Talents Program for Department of Science and Technology of Jilin Province (Grant 20190103051JH).

References

1. Abdel-Basset, M., El-Shahat, D., El-henawy, I., de Albuquerque, V.H.C., Mirjalili, S.: A new fusion of grey wolf optimizer algorithm with a two-phase mutation for feature selection. Exp. Syst. Appl. **139**, 112824 (2020)
2. Al-Tashi, Q., Kadir, S.J.A., Rais, H.M., Mirjalili, S., Alhussian, H.: Binary optimization using hybrid grey wolf optimization for feature selection. IEEE Access **7**, 39496–39508 (2019)
3. Alber, M., et al.: Integrating machine learning and multiscale modeling-perspectives, challenges, and opportunities in the biological, biomedical, and behavioral sciences. NPJ Digital Med. **2**(1), 1–11 (2019)
4. Aljarah, I., et al.: A dynamic locality multi-objective salp swarm algorithm for feature selection. Comput. Ind. Eng. **147**, 106628 (2020)
5. Dua, D., Graff, C.: UCI machine learning repository (2017). http://archive.ics.uci.edu/ml

6. Emary, E., Zawbaa, H.M., Hassanien, A.E.: Binary grey wolf optimization approaches for feature selection. Neurocomputing **172**, 371–381 (2016)
7. Gai, K., Qiu, M.: Optimal resource allocation using reinforcement learning for iot content-centric services. Appl. Soft Comput. **70**, 12–21 (2018)
8. Ghoddusi, H., Creamer, G.G., Rafizadeh, N.: Machine learning in energy economics and finance: a review. Energy Econ. **81**, 709–727 (2019)
9. Guyon, I., Elisseeff, A.: An introduction to variable and feature selection. J. Mach. Learn. Res. **3**(Mar), 1157–1182 (2003)
10. Jensi, R., Jiji, G.W.: An enhanced particle swarm optimization with levy flight for global optimization. Appl. Soft Comput. **43**, 248–261 (2016)
11. Kabir, M.M., Shahjahan, M., Murase, K.: A new local search based hybrid genetic algorithm for feature selection. Neurocomputing **74**(17), 2914–2928 (2011)
12. Kashef, S., Nezamabadi-pour, H.: An advanced ACO algorithm for feature subset selection. Neurocomputing **147**, 271–279 (2015)
13. Mafarja, M., Aljarah, I., Faris, H., Hammouri, A.I., Ala'M, A.Z., Mirjalili, S.: Binary grasshopper optimisation algorithm approaches for feature selection problems. Exp. Syst. Appl. **117**, 267–286 (2019)
14. Mafarja, M., Aljarah, I., Heidari, A.A., Faris, H., Fournier-Viger, P., Li, X., Mirjalili, S.: Binary dragonfly optimization for feature selection using time-varying transfer functions. Knowl.-Based Syst. **161**, 185–204 (2018)
15. Mafarja, M., Mirjalili, S.: Whale optimization approaches for wrapper feature selection. Appl. Soft Comput. **62**, 441–453 (2018)
16. Mirjalili, S., Mirjalili, S.M., Lewis, A.: Grey wolf optimizer. Adv. Eng. Softw. **69**, 46–61 (2014)
17. Neggaz, N., Ewees, A.A., Abd Elaziz, M., Mafarja, M.: Boosting salp swarm algorithm by sine cosine algorithm and disrupt operator for feature selection. Exp. Syst. Appl. **145**, 113103 (2020)
18. Qi, C., Zhou, Z., Sun, Y., Song, H., Hu, L., Wang, Q.: Feature selection and multiple kernel boosting framework based on PSO with mutation mechanism for hyperspectral classification. Neurocomputing **220**, 181–190 (2017)
19. Tubishat, M., et al.: Dynamic salp swarm algorithm for feature selection. Exp. Syst. Appl. **164**, 113873 (2021)
20. Wernick, M.N., Yang, Y., Brankov, J.G., Yourganov, G., Strother, S.C.: Machine learning in medical imaging. IEEE Signal Process. Mag. **27**(4), 25–38 (2010)
21. Xue, B., Zhang, M., Browne, W.N.: Particle swarm optimisation for feature selection in classification: novel initialisation and updating mechanisms. Appl. Soft Comput. **18**, 261–276 (2014)
22. Yin, H., Gai, K.: An empirical study on preprocessing high-dimensional class-imbalanced data for classification. In: 2015 IEEE 17th International Conference on High Performance Computing and Communications, 2015 IEEE 7th International Symposium on Cyberspace Safety and Security, and 2015 IEEE 12th International Conference on Embedded Software and Systems, pp. 1314–1319. IEEE (2015)

Integrating Real-Time Entity Resolution with Top-*N* Join Query Processing

Liang Zhu[1](✉), Xinfeng Li[1], Yonggang Wei[1], Qin Ma[1], and Weiyi Meng[2]

[1] Hebei University, Baoding 071002, Hebei, China
{zhu,wyg}@hbu.edu.cn
[2] State University of New York at Binghamton, Binghamton, NY 13902, USA

Abstract. Real-time entity resolution (ER) is a challenging problem for large datasets. Traditional techniques of top-*N* join query processing are based on clean data without ER. For dirty datasets with duplicate tuples referring to the same real-world entity, these techniques may yield duplicates of top-*N* tuples for a query, and as a result some useful tuples may fail to be retrieved from the datasets, which leads to poor effectiveness. Based on "sorted and/or random accesses" and "no wild guesses", in this paper, we discuss the models that integrate real-time entity resolution with top-*N* join queries over dirty datasets of real vectors. For finite dimensional ℓ_p spaces and p-norm distances as nonmonotone ranking functions, using the norm equivalence theorem in Functional Analysis as a foundation, and designing buffers to join tuples with an outer-join mechanism and to cluster candidates for ER, we propose two database-friendly algorithms to answer the top-*N* join queries with the following two cases of data access methods: restricting sorted access and no random access. Extensive experiments are conducted to measure the effectiveness and efficiency of our approaches over various dirty datasets.

Keywords: Top-*N* join query · Entity resolution · Dirty data · Cluster · Algorithm · d-dimensional ℓ_p space

1 Introduction

Join queries are necessary in (distributed) database systems with Primary-Foreign key relationships or vertical fragmentations [18]. Processing and optimization of join queries are critical issues for developing high performance database management systems, which have received significant attention in the database community [9].

H. Qiu et al. (Eds.): KSEM 2021, LNAI 12817, pp. 111–123, 2021.
https://doi.org/10.1007/978-3-030-82153-1_10

A top-N query against a relation/dataset is to find a sorted set of N (e.g., $N = 10$, 50, or 100) tuples that best, but not necessarily completely, satisfy the query condition. In general, top-N query techniques contain two categories: top-N selection queries and top-N join queries. A survey on this topic can be found in [13].

Most proposed techniques for top-N queries take into account a fixed query point Q and monotone ranking functions including linear functions. For this query model, the algorithms TA, TA_Z and NRA introduced by Fagin et al. [7] are based on the situations of "sorted and/or random accesses" and "no wild guesses". However, few proposed approaches handle general functions as using nonmonotone ranking functions in top-N queries is a challenge [13]. Moreover, integrating real-time entity resolution (ER) with top-N queries is one of the open directions for future investigation [1].

ER is the process of identifying tuples/records in one or multiple data sources that refer to the same real-world entity and then merging the matching duplicate tuples into a cluster or a single tuple. ER has become an important issue in artificial intelligence, cloud computing, big data research and the database community due to its applications in a wide variety of commercial, scientific and security domains [6, 8, 10, 14]. In spite of several decades of research, ER remains a challenging problem [4].

In general, ER techniques are classified into two categories: generic ER and real-time ER. The traditional techniques for generic ER are offline and enormously expensive, and in general cannot be directly applied to query processing, which needs the techniques for real-time ER [1].

Real-time ER (also known as on-the-fly ER, query-time ER, or query-driven ER) is the process of matching a query record in sub-second time with records in a database that represent the same real-world entity, or in (near) real time, ideally within a few seconds at most [3]. Real-time ER is a challenging problem for large datasets, and how to make approximate blocking approaches scalable to large datasets and effective for ER in real-time remains an open challenge [16].

To address the problems above, in this paper, we discuss the top-N join query models based on "sorted and/or random accesses" and "no wild guesses". Our contributions are summarized below: (1) For an arbitrary query point in a finite dimensional ℓ_p space with nonmonotone ℓ_p-norm (or p-norm) distance as ranking function ($1 \leq p \leq \infty$), we define a model of integrating real-time ER with top-N join queries over dirty datasets. TA-like methods are based on monotone ranking functions, and thus are not suitable for this query model. (2) We propose database-friendly algorithms ErTAz and ErNRA to answer the top-N join queries of this model. (3) Using three p-norm distances ($p = 1, 2$ and ∞), extensive experiments are conducted to measure the performance of our proposed methods over various dirty datasets.

The rest of this paper is organized as follows. In Sect. 2, we briefly review some related work. In Sect. 3, the problem definition is introduced. Section 4 presents our methods of integrating real-time ER with top-N join queries. In Sect. 5, we present the experimental results. Finally, we conclude the paper in Sect. 6.

2 Related Work

Numerous researches on the processing of top-N queries have been proposed, and most of the current techniques are for processing top-N selection queries. Here, we only review some of the related researches involving top-N join queries.

For the data access mode of "no random access", Ilyas et al. [12] proposed their NRA-RJ algorithm by using tuple keys. Considering the order of binary rank joins at query-planning time, Li et al. [15] introduced the RankSQL framework, which extended operators of relational algebra for query processing and optimization. Adapting and improving TA-like algorithms in [7, 23] presented the processing methods for top-N join queries over Web-accessible databases. Han et al. [11] presented the TJJE algorithm which is suitable for handling massive data by using pre-computed information. Lin et al. [17] formally defined a model of top-N query, i.e., top-N, m query, to find the top-N combination of attributes according to the total score of top-m objects in each combination. For the processing of top-N spatial join query, an efficient algorithm STKSJ was proposed based on the Spark platform in [19]. Tziavelis et al. [22] analyzed and compared the assumptions, concepts and algorithms of top-N query, including TA algorithm and optimized join algorithm using the standard RAM model of computation to determine algorithm complexity, and then demonstrated the challenge of top-N join queries, which deserve renewed attention. Notice that the above techniques of top-N join query processing have not integrated with ER.

Based on cleaning only the necessary parts of data needed to answer the SQL-SPJ queries over dirty data, [1] presented a framework QuERy integrating with real-time ER. For join with two datasets $\{C, M\}$ ($|C| = 89{,}070$ and $|M| = 2{,}144$), QuERy takes from 4 to 61 s to evaluate a query, being much faster than SS (the Standard Solution), while SS needs more than 140 s to do so [1].

3 Problem Definition

Let $\Re$ be the set of all real numbers, and $(\Re^d, \rho(\cdot,\cdot))$ be a d-dimensional real vector space with distance function $\rho(\cdot,\cdot)$. Suppose that $R \subset \Re^d$ is a finite dataset/relation, its schema is $R(tid, A_1, \cdots, A_d)$ with d attributes $(A_1, \cdots, A_d)$ corresponding to $\Re^d = \Re_1 \times \cdots \times \Re_d$ where the ith axis $\Re_i = \Re$ for every i, and each tuple $t = (tid, t_1, \cdots, t_d) \in R$ is associated with a tid (tuple identifier). R is stored generally as a base table in a relational database system, and $|R|$ indicates the size of R, i.e., the number of tuples in R.

In this paper, the distance function $\rho(\cdot,\cdot)$ is induced by the ℓ_p-norm or p-norm $\|\cdot\|_p$ ($1 \leq p \leq \infty$). For $x = (x_1, x_2, \cdots, x_d)$ and $y = (y_1, y_2, \cdots, y_d)$ in $\Re^d$, $\rho(x, y)$ will be

$$\rho_p(x, y) = \|x - y\|_p = \left(\sum_{i=1}^{d} |x_i - y_i|^p\right)^{1/p} \text{ for } 1 \leq p < \infty \tag{1}$$

$$\rho_\infty(x, y) = \|x - y\|_\infty = \max_{1 \leq i \leq d}(|x_i - y_i|) \text{ for } p = \infty \tag{2}$$

Moreover, $\|x\|_p \to \|x\|_\infty$ as $p \to \infty$. When $p = 1, 2$, and ∞, $\rho_p(x, y)$ will be the *Manhattan distance* $\rho_1(x, y)$, *Euclidean distance* $\rho_2(x, y)$, and *Maximum distance* $\rho_\infty(x, y)$ respectively, which are useful in many applications.

The relation/dataset $R = \{t_1, t_2, \cdots, t_{|R|}\}$ with its schema above is considered dirty if there exist at least two tuples $t_i, t_j \in R$ that refer to the same real-world entity e, that is, $t_i[A_1, \cdots, A_d] = t_j[A_1, \cdots, A_d]$ but $t_i[tid] \neq t_j[tid]$ in this paper. Hence t_i and t_j are duplicates $(1 \leq i, j \leq |R|, i \neq j)$, and they will be grouped into a cluster C to act as "one tuple". An arbitrary tuple t in a nonempty cluster C will be chosen as the **representative** tuple of C (usually, it is the first one inserted into C), which refers to the entity e.

Formally, let $E = \{e_1, e_2, \cdots, e_{|E|}\}$ be the set of real-world entities described by the dataset R, and $\mathcal{E}$ be a mapping from R to E. $\forall t_i, t_j \in R, t_i \sim t_j$ if and only if $\exists e \in E$ $(e = \mathcal{E}(t_i) = \mathcal{E}(t_j))$. We denote $\mathbb{R} = R/\sim = \{[t'_1], [t'_2], \cdots, [t'_M]\}$, where $[t'_1], [t'_2], \cdots, [t'_M]$ are the equivalence classes with respect to "$\sim$". Thus, $\mathbb{R}$ is the quotient set of R by the equivalence relation "$\sim$". $[t'_i]$ is indicated by C_i $(1 \leq i \leq M)$. It is clear that (1) $R = C_1 \cup C_2 \cup \cdots \cup C_M$ and (2) $C_i \cap C_j = \varnothing$ $(1 \leq i, j \leq M, i \neq j)$. The goal of ER is to design $\mathcal{E}$s comprising data structures, indices, and algorithms, which are effective and efficient.

For a query point $Q = (q_1, \cdots, q_d) \in \Re^d$, a set $T \subset R$, and a tuples $t \in R$, we define $\rho(t, Q) = \rho(t[A_1, \cdots, A_n], Q)$, and $\rho(T, Q) = \min\{\rho(t, Q): t \in T\}$. If a cluster C is an equivalence class of tuples with respect to the equivalence relation "$\sim$" given by "$t_i[A_1, \cdots, A_d] = t_j[A_1, \cdots, A_d]$", we can define $\rho(C, Q) = \min\{\rho(t, Q): t \in C\} = \rho(t, Q)$ for any $t \in C$, and t is usually the **representative** tuple of C.

For a (clean) dataset R, consider a query point $Q = (q_1, \cdots, q_d) \in \Re^d$ and an integer $N > 0$. A top-N selection query (Q, N) is to find a sorted set of N tuples in R that are closest to Q according to the given distance function $\rho(\cdot, \cdot)$. The results of a top-N query are called top-N tuples. We assume $N < |R|$; otherwise, we just retrieve all tuples in R. For simplicity, sometimes, a top-N query (Q, N) is just denoted by Q. Equivalently, a sorted subset $Y = \langle t_1, t_2, \cdots, t_N \rangle$ of R is one of the answers to (Q, N) if and only if $\rho(t_1, Q) \leq \rho(t_2, Q) \leq \cdots \leq \rho(t_N, Q)$ and $\rho(t_N, Q) \leq \rho(t, Q)$ for arbitrary $t \in R - Y$ (ties are broken arbitrarily).

For a dirty dataset R, let $\mathbb{C} = \langle C_1, C_2, \cdots, C_N \rangle \subset \mathbb{R}$ be a sorted set of N clusters, that is, $C_i \subset R, C_i \cap C_j = \varnothing, \forall t_{i1}, t_{i2} \in C_i(t_{i1}[A_1, \cdots, A_n] = t_{i2}[A_1, \cdots, A_n])$, and $\forall t_i \in C_i \forall t_j \in C_j(t_i[A_1, \cdots, A_n] \neq t_j[A_1, \cdots, A_n])$ $(1 \leq i, j \leq N, i \neq j)$. The set $\mathbb{C} = \langle C_1, C_2, \cdots, C_N \rangle \subset \mathbb{R}$ is an answer to a top-N selection query (Q, N) according to $\rho(\cdot, \cdot)$ if and only if $\rho(C_1, Q) \leq \rho(C_2, Q) \leq \cdots \leq \rho(C_N, Q)$ and $\rho(C_N, Q) \leq \rho(t, Q)$ for $\forall t \in R - (C_1 \cup C_2 \cup \cdots \cup C_N)$ (ties are broken arbitrarily). Sometimes, we do not distinguish between C_i and its representative t_i (or $C_i.t$) in C_i $(1 \leq i \leq N)$.

Consider a relation R and s relations $R_1, R_2, \cdots,$ and R_s, their schemas are $R(tid, U)$, $R_1(tid, U_1), R_2(tid, U_2), \cdots,$ and $R_s(tid, U_s)$ respectively, where $U = (A_1, \cdots, A_d), U_1 = (A_{11}, \cdots, A_{1m}), U_2 = (A_{21}, \cdots, A_{2n}), \cdots, U_s = (A_{s1}, \cdots, A_{sr})$, and $U = U_1 \cup U_2 \cup \cdots \cup U_s$, i.e., R is the natural join of $\{R_1, R_2, \cdots, R_s\}$ with the primary key tid denoted by $R = R_1 \bowtie R_2 \bowtie \cdots \bowtie R_s$, or $\{R_1, R_2, \cdots, R_s\}$ is the lossless join schema decomposition of R and each $R_h(1 \leq h \leq s)$ contains the tid of R in a (distributed) database system [18]. Without loss of generality, let $U_1 \cap U_2 \cap \cdots \cap U_s = \varnothing$, then $d = m + n + \cdots + r$. If the s relations $\{R_1, R_2, \cdots, R_s\}$ are dirty, $R = R_1 \bowtie R_2 \bowtie \cdots \bowtie R_s$, then R may also be dirty.

Suppose that R is cleaned, and its clean version is denoted by R_c ($= \{C_i.t: C_i \in \mathbb{R}\}$). For a top-$N$ query $Q = (q_1, \cdots, q_d) \in \Re^d$, we decompose $Q = (Q_1, Q_2, \cdots, Q_s)$, and Q_h is a top-N_h query over R_h ($1 \le h \le s$), where $Q_1 = (q_{11}, \cdots, q_{1m}) \in \Re^m$, $Q_2 = (q_{21}, \cdots, q_{2n}) \in \Re^n$, and $Q_s = (q_{s1}, \cdots, q_{sr}) \in \Re^r$. We will define effective and efficient algorithm $\mathcal{A}$ with $(Q_1, Q_2, \cdots, Q_s)$ over $\{R_1, R_2, \cdots, R_s\}$ to obtain a set $T_\mathcal{A}$ of deduplicated top-N results of Q, which is equivalent to an answer T of the top-N selection query (Q, N) over the clean dataset R_c, i.e., $T_\mathcal{A} \equiv T$, the two answers to (Q, N) obtained over $\{R_1, R_2, \cdots, R_s\}$ and R_c respectively contain the same tuples except for the different identifiers because of duplicates, or the different tuples with the identical distance from Q since ties are broken arbitrarily.

For attribute A_i of a relation $R(tid, A_1, \cdots, A_h) \subset \Re^h$ ($h = d, m, n, \ldots$, or r), its values are sorted in ascending order from $\min(A_i)$ to $\max(A_i)$, $1 \le i \le h$. For attribute A_i, assume that there is a B$^+$-tree in which all leaf nodes form a *doubly linked list L_i* in sorted A_i-values [20]. The B$^+$-tree is used to locate q_i in L_i quickly for a given query $Q = (q_1, \cdots, q_h) \in \Re^h$, $1 \le i \le h$. Alternately, we may use a dynamic array L_i in sorted A_i-values, and determine the position of q_i in L_i by binary search. Therefore, the cost of locating q_i is $O(\log|R|)$ in the worst case.

Each entry of L_i is of the form (tid, a), where $a = t[A_i]$ is the value of t with tid under attribute A_i. We sometimes use $a_{ij} = L_i.a_j$ to indicate L_i's jth attribute-value. Let $\{L_1, \cdots, L_v\}$ be the set of v sorted lists of the relation $R \subset \Re^h$ ($1 \le v \le h$). We say that an algorithm $\mathcal{A}_L$ locates $Q = (q_1, \cdots, q_h)$ on R if $\mathcal{A}_L$ can locate Q over $\{L_1, \cdots, L_v\}$, that is, can find a_{ij} and a_{ij+1} in L_i such that $a_{ij} \le q_i \le a_{ij+1}$ for $i = 1, \cdots, v$.

The meaning of "random access" in our paper is the same as in [7], i.e., the value of a tuple's attribute is obtained by providing the tid. "Sorted access" in [7] is "to obtain the attribute value of a tuple in one of the sorted lists by proceeding through the list sequentially from the top". "No wild guesses" means that a tuple must be "discovered" under sorted access before it can be probed using random access [7].

We define the direction(s) of "sorted access" used in this paper as follows. Suppose that the query $Q = (q_1, \cdots, q_h)$ has been located on R, say, we have determined the position of q_i in L_i with $a_{ij} \le q_i \le a_{ij+1}$ for every i by binary search. If $q_i \le \min(A_i)$, then $a_{ij+1} = \min(A_i)$, the direction is "$q_i \to \max(A_i)$". If $\max(A_i) \le q_i$, then $a_{ij} = \max(A_i)$, "$\min(A_i) \leftarrow q_i$". For the two cases, sorted access has the same meaning as in [7]. If $\min(A_i) < q_i < \max(A_i)$, we use two directions "$\min(A_i) \leftarrow q_i \to \max(A_i)$" for sorted access, i.e., from a_{ij} to $\min(A_i)$ for the interval $[\min(A_i), a_{ij}]$, and from a_{ij+1} to $\max(A_i)$ for $[a_{ij+1}, \max(A_i)]$.

4 Algorithms

This paper is a continuation and extension of the previous work in [24, 25]. [25] studied top-N selection queries over single relations in n-dimensional normed spaces without ER. [24] discussed the same query model as in this paper, using a complex region-tree structure and a divide-and-conquer mechanism to design an ER-Index and algorithms without considering the situations of "sorted and/or random accesses" and "no wild guesses". Motivated by the spirit of the elegant algorithms in the TA-family with instance optimality [7], in this section, we introduce two algorithms ErTAz and ErNRA that are also simple and powerful for the two cases of data access methods: (1) *restricting sorted access* and (2) *no random access* [7, 13], where prefix "Er" in the algorithm names means "Entity resolution".

We denote the dimensionality of R_h by $d[h]$ in our algorithms, i.e., $d[h]$ is the number of attributes in U_h. Then, for a query Q with the decomposition $Q = (Q_1, Q_2, \cdots, Q_s)$, we have $Q_h = (q_{h1}, \cdots, q_{hd[h]})$ $(1 \le h \le s)$, then $Q = (q_{11}, \cdots, q_{1d[1]}, q_{21}, \cdots, q_{2d[2]}, \cdots, q_{s1}, \cdots, q_{sd[s]})$. Sometimes, we use $Q_h.q_k$ to indicate q_{hk} $(1 \le k \le d[h])$.

4.1 ErTAz for Restricting Sorted Access

We first discuss the situation of "*restricting sorted access*", in which top-N processing techniques assume the availability of at least one sorted access *List* for each $R_h \in \{R_1, R_2, \cdots, R_s\}$. Let $Z_h = \{i_1, i_2, \cdots, i_{mh}\}$ with $1 \le m_h = |Z_h| < d[h]$ be the set of indices i of those lists L_i that can be accessed under sorted access for R_h. Without loss of generality, we assume that $Z = \{1, 2, \cdots, m_h\}$, $1 \le m_h < d[h]$, and $m_h = 1$ in our experiments. Obviously, "*restricting sorted access*" will be "*both sorted and random accesses*" in [7] when $m_h = d[h]$ for R_h $(1 \le h \le s)$.

For a query $Q = (q_1, \cdots, q_d) \in \Re^d$ with the decomposition $Q = (Q_1, Q_2, \cdots, Q_s)$ over $\{R_1, R_2, \cdots, R_s\}$, in the following algorithm ErTAz, we map a top-N_h query Q_h over R_h to a *range selection query* $S(Q_h, r)$ that is a $d[h]$-dimensional square centered at Q_h with side length $2r$. The candidate tuples of Q_h are obtained from $S(Q_h, r)$ by doing sorted access for L_i $(i = 1, 2, \cdots, m_h)$ to find m_h attribute values and then doing random accesses to find the other attribute values of each seen tuple $t^{(h)}$ in R_h. Then candidate tuples of Q_h will be insert into a buffer **CandidatesL**[h], the tuples $\{t^{(h)}\}$ $(h = 1, 2, \cdots, s)$ will be joined in a buffer **S**, and every complete joined tuple $t = t^{(1)} \bowtie t^{(2)} \bowtie \cdots \bowtie t^{(s)}$ will be grouped into a cluster for ER in the buffer **CandidatesList**, and the *representative* tuple $C.t$ in each cluster C is a candidate tuple of top-N query Q over $R = R_1 \bowtie R_2 \bowtie \cdots \bowtie R_s$. If $\rho_p(t, Q) \le r$, then t will be a top-N tuple of Q according to the norm equivalence theorem "$\|\cdot\|_\infty \le \|\cdot\|_p \le d^{1/p} \|\cdot\|_\infty$" in Functional Analysis [5, 25]. Each $S(Q_h, r)$ is enlarged again and again, and more and more candidate tuples of Q_h will be seen until all of top-N tuples of Q are obtained.

Algorithm ErTAz

Input: (Q, N), $\{R_1, R_2, \cdots, R_s\}$ $//Q = (Q_1, Q_2, \cdots, Q_s)$ with dimensionality $d = d[1] + \cdots + d[s]$
Output: Y   //a sorted set of N tuples in $R_1 \bowtie R_2 \bowtie \cdots \bowtie R_s$ with distances $\{\rho(t_i, Q)\}$.

1 Let $\mathbf{Y}$ = null;   //$\mathbf{Y}$ is a heap, cache and sorting top-N tuples of query (Q, N)
2 Let $r = 0$;   //r is the search radius of all $\{S(Q_h, r)\}$
3 Let **CandidatesList** = null;   //cache the set of top-N candidates
   // locate Q_h by B+-tree or binary search with $Q_h = (q_1, \cdots, q_{mh})$, and update the radius r
4 **For** $h = 1$ to s
5   Let $r[h] = 0$ //$r[h]$ is the h-th relation's radius
6   **For** $i = 1$ to m_h // $1 \leq m_h = |Z_h| < d[h]$ for each R_h
7   Find $L_i.a_j$ and $L_i.a_k$ in L_i of R_h such that $L_i.a_j \leq Q_h.q_i \leq L_i.a_k$;   //where $k = j + 1$;
8          $r[i] = \min(Q_h.q_i - L_i.a_j, L_i.a_k - Q_h.q_i)$;
9          $r[h] = \max(r[h], r[i])$;
10   **End for**
11     $r = \max(r, r[h])$;   // the search radius r is the max of the radius of s relations
12 **End for**
   // obtain top-N tuples, which will be inserted in $\mathbf{Y}$
13 **While** ($\mathbf{Y}$.size $< N$ and some L_i is not exhausted)   //$\mathbf{Y}$.size is the number of tuples in $\mathbf{Y}$
14     $r_{max} = 0$;   // r_{max} is the increment of the search radius r
15   **For** $h = 1$ to s //get candidate tuples from R_h
16   Let $r[h] = 0$;
17         $S(Q_h, r) = \prod_{k=1}^{d[h]}[Q_h.q_k - r, Q_h.q_k + r]$;   // map (Q_h, N_h) to $S(Q_h, r)$
18   Let **CandidatesL**$[h]$ = null; //cache the candidates set for each R_h
19   **For** each L_i of R_h, $i = 1$ to m_h
20   Do sorted access in $S(Q_h, r)$ to get $t.tid$ and $t.a_j$ and/or $t.a_k$;
               /*from $Q_h.q_i$, by direction(s) in §2, and j-- for $L_i.a_j$ and/or k++ for $L_i.a_k$ until
               $L_i.a_j < Q_h.q_i - r$ or j is exhausted, and/or $Q_h.q_i + r < L_i.a_k$ or k is exhausted*/
21   As a tuple t is seen under sorted access in L_i, do random access in other lists to
               find the other attribute values of tuple t by $t.tid$;
22             $r[i] = \min(\ (Q_h.q_i - r) - L_i.a_j, L_i.a_k - (Q_h.q_i + r)\ )$;
23             $r[h] = \max(r[h], r[i]\ )$;   // update the $r[h]$
24   **End for**
25   Insert t into **CandidatesL**$[h]$ when all attribute values of t are in $S(Q_h, r)$;
26         $r_{max} = \max(r_{max}, r[h])$;   //obtain the incremental r_{max} of the search radius r
27   **End for**
       /*Call the Function JOINandER() to join the tuples in **CandidatesL**$[h]$
         and cluster complete tuples for ER */
28   Call JOINandER(Q, s, &**CandidatesL**, &**CandidatesList**);
29   **Scan sequentially** each $C.t \in$**CandidatesList** in ascending order of $\rho(C.t\ Q)$
30   **If** ($\rho(C.t\ Q) \leq r$ and C.inY = False and $\mathbf{Y}$.size $< N$) //obtain a top-N result
31   Insert ($C.t$, $\rho(t, Q)$) into $\mathbf{Y}$;   // Insert result cluster into result set $\mathbf{Y}$
32   C.inY = True;   //flagging cluster C in result set $\mathbf{Y}$
33             $\mathbf{Y}$.size ++;
34   **End if**
35   **End scan**
36     $r = r + r_{max}$;   // enlarge r and then $S(Q_h, r)$ is enlarged
37 **End while**
38 **Return Y**   //or **Return $\mathfrak{C}$** = $\langle C_1, \cdots, C_N \rangle$, i.e., $C.t$ with other tids, for some applications.

For the tuples in the buffers $\{$**CandidatesL**$[h]\}$, the function JOINandER() below will be used to join them in the buffer $\mathbf{S}$ for generating candidates of top-N query Q, and to cluster the candidates in the buffer **CandidatesList** for ER.

Function JOINandER (Q, s, *CandidatesL, *CandidatesList)
1   S = CandidatesL[1] $\bowtie$ ⋯ $\bowtie$ CandidatesL[s] //sorted and outer joined with *tid*
2   **For each** $t \in S$
3   **If** t.size = Q.size // i.e., t is a complete joined tuple with $t = t^{(1)} \bowtie t^{(2)} \bowtie \dots \bowtie t^{(s)}$
4   Remove t from S, and delete $t^{(h)}$ from **CandidatesL**[h] for all h = 1 to s;
5   Compute $\rho(t, Q)$; // t is a candidate of top-N query Q
//Insert t into **CandidatesList** in ascending order of $\rho(t, Q)$;
6   **If** $\rho(t, Q) \neq \rho(C, Q)$ for $\forall C \in$ **CandidatesList**
7   Create a new cluster C and insert t into C;
8                $C.t = t$; // $C.t$ means the representative tuple of C.
9   **Else if** $C.t \neq t$ for all $C \in$ **CandidatesList** with $\rho(t, Q) = \rho(C, Q)$
10   Create a new cluster C and insert t into C;
11               $C.t = t$;
12   **Else**
13   Insert $t.tid$ into C; //i.e., $C.t = t$ for only one $C \in$ **CandidatesList**
14   **End if**
15   **End if**
16   **End for**

4.2 ErNRA for no Random Access

In this section, we discuss the situations where random accesses are impossible, and modify ErTAz to obtain our algorithm ErNRA for the data access mode of "no random access". Let the number m_h of the For-loop in Line 6 be replaced by $d[h]$, and let the For-loop "**For each** L_i of R_h, i = 1 to m_h,…, **End for**" from Line 19 to Line 25 of algorithm ErTAz be replaced by the following the For-loop, then we obtain ErNRA.

1   **For each** L_i of R_h, i = 1 to $d[h]$
2   Do sorted access in $S(Q_h, r)$ to get $t.tid$ and $t.a_j$ and/or $t.a_k$;
/* from $Q_h.q_i$ and by direction(s) in §2, and j-- for $L_i.a_j$ and/or k++ for $L_i.a_k$
until $L_i.a < Q_h.q_i - r$ or j is exhausted, and/or $Q_h.q_i + r < L_i.a_k$ or k is exhausted*/
3        $r[i] = \min((Q_h.q_i - r) - L_i.a_j, L_i.a_k - (Q_h.q_i + r))$;
4        $r[h] = \max(r[h], r[i])$;
5   **End for** //sorted access each attribute of s relations to obtain candidate tuples

5 Experimental Results

Using GoLand and Windows 10, all the experiments are conducted on a PC with Intel(R) Core(TM) i7-6700 CPU@3.40 GHz 3.41 GHz, and the memory is 16 GB.

Two original datasets Cover54D [2] and Sift128D [21] are used to generate eleven relations, including eight relations {C4D, C6D, S6D, S9D, S10D, S15D, S20D, S30D} used in [24] for comparing algorithms, where the suffix "hD" means that the dataset has h dimensions. Each of the eight datasets contains 100,000 tuples. The other three relations S_d30D, S_d9D and S_d10D come from S30D, S9D and S10D, respectively. For each tuple t in S30D, t is duplicated 1, 2 or 3 times randomly, and then S_d30D contains the first 100,000 tuples of them. For each tuple t in S9D or S10D, t is duplicated 1 to

5 times randomly, and then S_d9D or S_d10D contain the first 600,000 tuples of them respectively.

Each R of the eleven relations is decomposed vertically into two or three relations, and each one has 100,000 or 600,000 tuples. For example, S6D$(tid, A_1, \cdots, A_6)$ is decomposed vertically into $\{R_1(tid, A_1, A_2, A_3), R_2(tid, A_4, A_5, A_6)\}$; while C6D$(tid, A_1, \cdots, A_6)$ is decomposed into $\{R_1(tid, A_1, A_2), R_2(tid, A_3, A_4), R_3(tid, A_5, A_6)\}$.

We use the following default settings: (1) For each dataset, the workload includes 1000 queries that are the tuples randomly selected from the respective d-dimensional dataset ($4 \leq d \leq 30$). Each $Q = (q_1, \cdots, q_d)$ is decomposed into (Q_1, Q_2) or (Q_1, Q_2, Q_3). (2) The three distance functions are the Manhattan distance $\rho_1(x, y)$, Euclidean distance $\rho_2(x, y)$, and Maximum distance $\rho_\infty(x, y)$. (3) $N = 100$ for top-N queries against all datasets. (4) The average values will be reported for each workload.

The following measures are used to assess the efficiency of our join algorithms. (1) *The elapsed time (millisecond, ms)*: the time needed to find the top-N tuples from the respective dataset for a query $Q = (q_1, \cdots, q_d)$ over $\{R_1, R_2\}$ or $\{R_1, R_2, R_3\}$. (2) *The number of sorted accesses*: the average number of sorted accesses for all queries in the workload. Note that $Z = \{1\}$ for ErTAz, which will do $d[h]$-1 random accesses for each sorted access over $R_h(tid, A_1, \cdots, A_{d[h]})$.

For a given query $Q = (q_1, \cdots, q_d) \in \Re^d$, one top-$N$ selection algorithm TSA over the *single* relation R ($= R_1 \bowtie R_2$ or $R_1 \bowtie R_2 \bowtie R_3$) will be utilized as a baseline to compare the performance of ErTAz and ErNRA. The TSA is a Naïve algorithm over R as follows: it retrieves all tuple $t \in R$, computes the distance $\rho(t, Q)$ between each tuple t and Q, ranks tuples based on the distances, deduplicates/clusters the top-N tuples, and then returns the top-N tuples with the smallest distances. The complexity of TSA is at least $O(|R|\log|R|)$ for the dataset of size $|R|$, and it is not efficient for a large relation. Notice that TSA does not contain the cost of $R_1 \bowtie R_2$ or $R_1 \bowtie R_2 \bowtie R_3$.

5.1 The Effectiveness of Algorithms

For each R of the eleven datasets, (1) we use the Naïve top-N selection algorithm TSA to get the sorted set T of the top-100 tuples for each query in a workload over R. (2) Our join algorithm ErTAz or ErNRA is used to obtain two sorted sets T' and T'' of top-100 tuples for the same workload over $\{R_1, R_2\}$ and $\{R_1, R_2, R_3\}$, respectively. (3) By comparing the top-100 tuples of each query, we obtain $T \equiv T'$ and $T \equiv T''$, which show that ErTAz and ErNRA are effective.

5.2 The Elapsed Time

Using Euclidean distance, Fig. 1 shows that the elapsed time of the Naïve top-N selection algorithm TSA over a single relation R is between 76 ms and 145 ms in Fig. 1(a), and from 84 ms to 183 ms in Fig. 1(b). For join with two relations $\{R_1, R_2\}$ in Fig. 1(a), the elapsed times are between 61 ms and 236 ms with our ErTAz, between 105ms and 1,622 ms with our ErNRA, and from 2546 ms to 3741 ms with TupleJoin in [24]. For join with three relations $\{R_1, R_2, R_3\}$ in Fig. 1(b), the elapsed times are from 156 ms to 406 ms with ErTAz, from 375 ms to 3,519 ms with ErNRA, and from 7332 ms to 8624 ms with TupleJoin. Therefore, ErTAz and ErNRA are significantly better than TupleJoin.

Moreover, for two join datasets C and M with $|C| = 89{,}070$ and $|M| = 2{,}144$ respectively, QuERy in [1] takes from 4 to 61 s to process a SQL-SPJ query with real-time ER. To the best of our knowledge, the query model in [1] is most related to our model in this paper. Consequently, ErTAz and ErNRA are highly competitive compared with existing techniques.

Notice that the naïve join operation "nested loop" will be too expensive to handle top-N join queries over two dirty datasets $\{R_1, R_2\}$. It takes from several minutes to several hours to process a top-N join query by the naïve join operation in our experiments. Hence, we omit it in the algorithm comparison.

The elapsed times of ErTAz are illustrated in Fig. 2 using three types of distances: Manhattan distance, Euclidean distance and Maximum distance. Figure 2(a) is of two join relations, and Fig. 2(b) is of three join relations. For ErTAz over S_d9D in Fig. 2(b), the elapsed times are 1,144 ms and 1,048 ms with the Manhattan distance and Euclidian distance respectively, the other elapsed times of ErTAz are smaller than 1,000 ms.

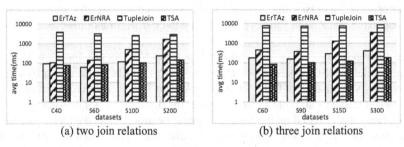

(a) two join relations   (b) three join relations

Fig. 1. The elapsed time of four algorithms ErTAz, ErNRA, TupleJoin and TSA

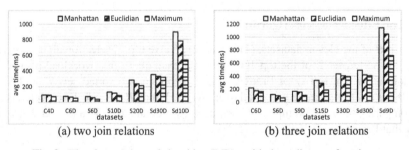

(a) two join relations   (b) three join relations

Fig. 2. The elapsed time of algorithm ErTAz with three distance functions

Figure 3 depicts the elapsed times of ErNRA with the three types of distance functions over two join relations in Fig. 3(a) and three join relations in Fig. 3(b). For ErNRA, Fig. 3(a) shows that the elapsed times are smaller than 580 ms over C4D, C6D, S6D and S10D, between 1,335 ms and 1,675 ms over S20D, and from 2,537 ms to 3,828 ms over S_d30D and S_d10D. Moreover, for ErNRA, Fig. 3(b) illustrates the elapsed times are smaller than 1,294 ms over C6D, S6D, S9D and S15D, and from 2,531 ms to 3,590 ms over S30D, S_d30D and S_d9D.

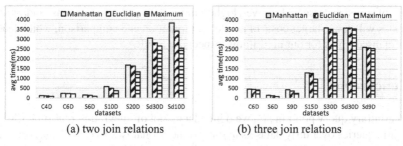

(a) two join relations   (b) three join relations

Fig. 3. The elapsed time of algorithm ErNRA with three distance functions

From Fig. 2, and Fig. 3, we can see that higher dimensions (≥ 10 dimensions) and/or more duplicates incur longer elapsed times for the two algorithms.

5.3 The Number of Sorted Accesses

Figure 4 and Fig. 5 show the average numbers of sorted accesses for a query by using ErTAz and ErNRA with the three types of distance functions.

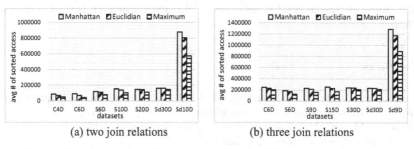

(a) two join relations   (b) three join relations

Fig. 4. The number of sorted accesses of algorithm ErTAz with three distances

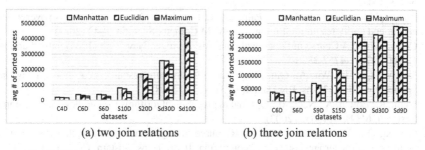

(a) two join relations   (b) three join relations

Fig. 5. The number of sorted accesses of algorithm ErNRA with three distances

Larger execution costs (including costs of the sorted and/or random accesses) will lead to larger elapsed times. Comparing Fig. 4 with Fig. 2, and Fig. 5 with Fig. 3, respectively, the trends of elapsed times of our algorithms are similar to those of the number of sorted accesses. Moreover, higher dimensions ($\geq$ 10 dimensions) and/or more duplicates will cause larger costs of access, computation and comparison, which lead to longer elapsed times for our algorithms, especially ErNRA.

6 Conclusions

For an arbitrary query point in $\mathfrak{R}^d$, we defined a model of integrating real-time ER with top-N join queries over dirty datasets in finite dimensional ℓ_p spaces ($\mathfrak{R}^d$, $\|\cdot\|_p$) ($1 \leq p \leq \infty$). Based on "sorted and/or random accesses" and "no wild guesses", we proposed two algorithms ErTAz and ErNRA to answer top-N join queries with the following two cases of data access methods: (1) restricting sorted access, and (2) no random access. Moreover, the norm equivalence theorem in Functional Analysis can guarantee the retrieval of top-N tuples for each query with both ErTAz and ErNRA.

Using eleven datasets with various dimensions, we carried out extensive experiments to measure the effectiveness and efficiency of the two methods. The sorted sets of top-N tuples of a query by ErTAz and ErNRA over relations $\{R_1, R_2\}$ or $\{R_1, R_2, R_3\}$ are equivalent to the results by a Naïve top-N selection algorithm TSA over $R = R_1 \bowtie R_2$ or $R = R_1 \bowtie R_2 \bowtie R_3$, which showed the effectiveness of our proposed methods; meanwhile, the average elapse times of processing a top-100 join query over two or three relations are less than 1,144 ms using ErTAz, and are smaller than 3,828 ms using ErNRA.

References

1. Altwaijry, H., Mehrotra, S., Kalashnikov, D.V.: QuERy: a framework for integrating entity resolution with query processing. Proc. VLDB Endow. **9**(3), 120–131 (2015)
2. Blake, C., Merz, C.: UCI repository of machine learning databases (1998). http://archive.ics. uci.edu/ml/datasets/Covertype. Accessed 5 Sept 2019
3. Christen, P.: Data Matching: Concepts and Techniques for Record Linkage, Entity Resolution, and Duplicate Detection. Springer, Berlin, Heidelberg (2012). https://doi.org/10.1007/978-3-642-31164-2
4. Christophides, V., Efthymiou, V., Palpanas, T., Papadakis, G., Stefanidis, K.: An overview of end-to-end entity resolution for big data. ACM Comput. Surv. **53**, 1–42 (2021)
5. Conway, J.B.: A Course in Functional Analysis. Springer, New York (1985). https://doi.org/10.1007/978-1-4757-3828-5
6. Dai, W., Qiu, L., Wu, A., Qiu, M.: Cloud infrastructure resource allocation for big data applications. IEEE Trans. Big Data **4**(3), 313–324 (2018)
7. Fagin, R., Lotem, A., Naor, M.: Optimal aggregation algorithms for middleware. J. Comput. Syst. Sci. **66**(4), 614–656 (2003)
8. Gai, K., Qiu, M., Zhao, H., Sun, X.: Resource management in sustainable cyber-physical systems using heterogeneous cloud computing. IEEE Trans. Sustain. Comput. **3**(2), 60–72 (2017)
9. Gao, J., Liu, W., Li, Z., Zhang, J., Shen, L.: A general fragments allocation method for join query in distributed database. Inf. Sci. **512**, 1249–1263 (2020)
10. Getoor, L., Machanavajjhala, A.: Entity resolution for big data. Tutorial at ACM SIGKDD. In: KDD (2013). http://www.umiacs.umd.edu/~getoor/Tutorials/ER_KDD2013.pdf

11. Han, X., Li, J., Wang, J., Yang, D.: TJJE: An efficient algorithm for top-k join on massive data. Inf. Sci. **222**, 362–383 (2013)
12. Ilyas, I.F., Aref, W.G., Elmagarmid, A.K.: Joining ranked inputs in practice. In: Proceedings of the 28th International Conference on Very Large Data Bases (VLDB) (2002)
13. Ilyas, I.F., Beskales, G., Soliman, M.A.: A survey of top-k query processing techniques in relational database systems. ACM Comput. Surv. **40**(4), Article 11 (2008)
14. Kejriwal, M.: Entity resolution in a big data framework. In: Proceedings of Twenty-Ninth AAAI Conference on Artificial Intelligence, pp. 4243–4244 (2015)
15. Li, C., Chang, K., Ilyas, I.F., Song, S.: RankSQL: query algebra and optimization for relational top-k queries. In: SIGMOD, pp. 131–142 (2005)
16. Liang, H., Wang, Y., Christen, P., Gayler, R.: Noise-tolerant approximate blocking for dynamic real-time entity resolution. In: Tseng, V.S., Ho, T.B., Zhou, Z.-H., Chen, A.L.P., Kao, H.-Y. (eds.) PAKDD 2014. LNCS (LNAI), vol. 8444, pp. 449–460. Springer, Cham (2014). https://doi.org/10.1007/978-3-319-06605-9_37
17. Lin, C., Lu, J., Wei, Z., Wang, J., Xiao, X.: Optimal algorithms for selecting top-k combinations of attributes: theory and applications. VLDB J. **27**, 27–52 (2018)
18. Özsu, M.T., Valduriez, P.: Principles of Distributed Database Systems, 3rd edn. Springer, New York (2011)
19. Qiao, B., Hu, B., Zhu, J., Wu, G., Giraud-Carrier, C., Wang, G.: A top-k spatial join querying processing algorithm based on spark. Inf. Syst. **87**, 101419 (2020)
20. Ramakrishnan, R.: Database Management Systems. WCB/McGraw-Hill, Boston (1998)
21. Singh, V., Singh, A. K.: SIMP: accurate and efficient near neighbor search in high dimensional spaces. In: EDBT, pp. 492–503 (2012)
22. Tziavelis, N., Gatterbauer, W., Riedewald, M.: Optimal join algorithms meet top-k. In: SIGMOD, pp. 2659–2665 (2020)
23. Wu, M., Berti-Equille, L., Marian, A., Procopiuc, C., Srivastava, D.: Processing top-k join queries. Proc. VLDB Endow. **3**(1), 860–870 (2010)
24. Zhu, L., Cheng, Y., Wang, Y., Ma, Q., Meng, W.: Evaluating top-N join queries with real-time entity resolution. J. Phys.: Conf. Ser. **1575**(1), 012084 (2020)
25. Zhu, L., Liu, F., Meng, W., Ma, Q., Wang, Y., Yuan, F.: Evaluating top-N queries in n-dimensional normed spaces. Inf. Sci. **374**, 255–275 (2016)

Incorporating Question Information to Enhance the Performance of Automatic Short Answer Grading

Shuang Chen and Li Li[✉]

School of Computer and Information Science, Southwest University,
Chongqing, China
chen60423351@email.swu.edu.cn, lily@swu.edu.cn

Abstract. Automatic short answer grading (ASAG) is focusing on tackling the problem of automatically assessing students' constructed responses to open-ended questions. ASAG is still far from being a reality in NLP. Previous work mainly concentrates on exploiting feature extraction from the textual information between the student answer and the model answer. A grade will be assigned to the student based on the similarity of his/her answers and the model answer. However, ASAG models trained by the same type of features lack the capacity to deal with a diversity of conceptual representations in students' responses. To capture multiple types of features, prior knowledge is utilized in our work to enrich the obtained features. The whole model is based on the Transformer. More specifically, a novel training approach is proposed. Forward propagation is added in the training step randomly to exploit the textual information between the provided questions and student answers in a training step. A feature fusion layer followed by an output layer is introduced accordingly for fine-tuning purposes. We evaluate the proposed model on two datasets (the University of North Texas dataset and student response analysis (SRA) dataset). A comparison is conducted on the ASAG task between the proposed model and the baselines. The performance results show that our model is superior to the recent state-of-the-art models.

Keywords: Automatic short answer grading · Natural language processing · Classification

1 Introduction

With the rapid development of online education, there are many challenges for educators. One challenge is for instructors scoring work to assess the gained knowledge from students and to be able to provide instructive feedback to teachers. However, manual grading is tedious and has a low degree of reproducibility. The computer-aided assessment has been facilitated in schools and colleges for several years currently, but primarily for the objective test with strained answers such as Multiple Choice Questions. A previous study did specify which nature

© Springer Nature Switzerland AG 2021
H. Qiu et al. (Eds.): KSEM 2021, LNAI 12817, pp. 124–136, 2021.
https://doi.org/10.1007/978-3-030-82153-1_11

of objective tests was deficient capture multiple aspects of acquired knowledge from the student. Such as reasoning and comprehension [1].

Thus, assessment of some form of a free response by students on open-ended questions could be a major focus of current research. Specifically, We are interested in fill-in-the-gap and essay-style short answers that are between a few words and a few sentences long [2,3]. Previously Automatic Short-Answer Grading (ASAG) is the procedure of assigning grades to student provided free-text answers either by comparing it with the corresponding model answers or pattern-based answers extracted from student answer [4,5]. Grading student-constructed answers could be a complicated natural language task attributed to linguistic diversity (the same answer can be phrased in numerous ways). Therefore ASAG is an important research area.

The methods of calculating the semantic similarity of two texts have been well researched in Natural Language Processing(NLP) literature [6]. These works mainly based on supervised learning technology are all around the text-similarity (synonymously, overlap, correspondence, entailment etc.) in NLP [7,8]. The ASAG system's general procedure is that features are extracted from model answers and student answers that have been graded by the instructor or grader and fed these features into various classification or regression models for training. The trained model will automatically mark raw student answers fraction. ASAG systems can be regarded in two ways:

Classification/labeling task (Table 1, the 2rd column): The student answer will be assigned to one of a set of categories i.e., 'correct', 'partially correct incomplete', 'contradictory', 'irrelevant', 'non domain'.

Regression task (Table 1, the 3rd column): Assign a mark/grade to the student answer based on the similarity with the corresponding model answer.

Table 1. Sample in the middle are from the ScientsBank [9] subset of student response analysis(SRA dataset) corpus, and the 3rd column are from the undergraduate Data Structure course(CS dataset) [8], the scores or label of each student's answer are manually assigned.

Question	Throwing a ball uses a hinge joint and a ball-and-socket joint. Describe how each of these 2 joints moves when you throw a ball. The hinge joint —	What is the role of a prototype program in problem solving?
Reference answer	Moves back-and-forth	To simulate the behaviour of portions of the desired software product
Student answer-1	Up and down if it did not go up and down you could not throw a ball. (correct)	You can break the whole program into prototype programs to simulate parts of the final program. (5.0/5.0)
Student answer-2	The socket joint makes sure that you do not break your wrist. (irrelevant)	A prototype program is a part of the Specification phase of Software Problem Solving. It is employed to illustrate how the key problem or problems will be solved in a program, and sometimes serves as a base program to expand upon. (4.5/5.0)

However, the previous ASAG model had remarkable shortcomings. With the diversity of the conceptual representation in the context, student-constructed responses are diverse and sophisticated. A correct answer has relevance to the question and the reference answer. Meanwhile, students' responses may be different from the reference answer but still correct, they may be similar to the reference answer but incorrect. For example, in Table 1, both questions have a brief reference answer. Each answer is different from the reference answer but is correct, and interestingly is highly similar to the question. We analyze that the feature extracted from the answer and the reference answer pair does not effectively address the variety of conceptual representations. We can use the method of adding prior knowledge to capture multiple types of features to enhance performance. Here, we want to exploit the textual information of the questions and student answers to enable the ASAG system to mine meaningful semantic features that the previous model could not hit.

In this paper, we propose a novel ASAG system based on the Transformer [10] network. We proposed a novel Feature Fusion layer based on the pooling layer that was deployed as fine-tuning. Then, we design a novel train approach by adding a forward propagation on a random training step, which takes the string of the reference answer and answers into the model to do forward propagation to get the first output. Consequently, we input the string of the question and student answer into the same model to do another forward propagation to get the second output. Finally, feed the two outputs obtained above into the Feature Fusion layer filtering out multiple facets of semantic features, followed by a flexible output layer for generating a score/label. Our contribution is as follows

- We propose a novel training approach to incorporate textual information of questions and answers. The method has the capacity to enable the ASAG system to capture multiple aspects of semantic features.
- We customize an ASAG system for the proposed training method comprising a novel Feature Fusion layer based on the pooling layer over the Transformer-Encoder network, followed by a flexible output layer for generating a score/label.
- Experiments were evaluated on two publicly available datasets. We compare the performance of several popular Transformer models on the ASAG task. Extensive experimental results illustrate the effectiveness of our model and outperform the previous ASAG model in most metrics.

2   Related Work

Numerous approaches have been proposed for the grading of short answers. The Oxford-UCLES system [4] requires manually crafted patterns by using a set of keywords and synonyms to search for a new pattern through a text window. C-Rater [11] generates a word set that is extracted from the model answer set, and then the corresponding student's answer is matched with this word set for scoring. Many text similarity methods have been considered, and the assigned scores are measured relying on the correlation between the student and model answers, using text similarity measures such as knowledge-based, corpus-based [7,8,12]and word embedding [13].

To improve the performance of the model, many researchers have tried to combine ensemble learning. Divide the feature set into several feature subsets to train the classifier, and ensemble the different classifiers trained [14]. Similarly, there is the ensemble of different regression models with the same feature set [13]. The ASAG system, which combines domain adaptive techniques and ensemble two classifiers, is designed to grade students [15]. The above work requires feature engineering. There is also a deep learning model in the ASAG system. Which contains three neural network blocks: Siamese bidirectional LSTMs(bi-LSTMs), EMD(Earth mover's distance) pooling layer, and regression layer. It can assign a score to student answers by optimizing above mentioned neural network blocks in order [16]. However, ASAG similar to other nontrivial NLP tasks that have limited training data.

The NLP community has recently proposed many general pre-trained language models, which can be transferred and fine-tuned seamlessly for any downstream tasks. Bidirectional Encoder Representations from Transformers(BERT [17]) has been proven to achieve state-of-the-art results through fine-tuning in a large number of tasks. It is a trained deep language model that can simultaneously combine left and right context information on all layers. By training the BERT model from corpus resources in a specific domain, fine-tuning it in the ASAG task will achieve superior performance [18].

However, all of these ASAG systems leverage the same type of features extracted from textual information between the reference answer and the student answer. The results in the ASAG system lack of capability to tackle the diversity of conceptual representations in response. More specifically, these ASAG systems are incapable to discriminate against the ground truth for student answers with low or no similarity to the reference answer. In this article, we focus on methods to add prior knowledge through textual information of the question that was discarded by most previous researchers to capture multiple aspects of semantic features.

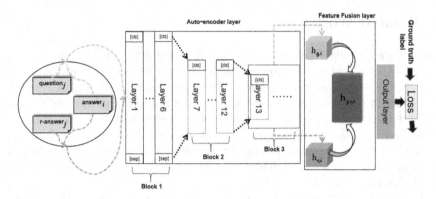

Fig. 1. Schematic of ASAG system.

3   Our System

The black circle on the left of Fig. 1 shows input data for the system. $question_j$, $r - answer_j$ and $answer_i$ represents the case of the input data. $question_j$ represents the jth question in the dataset, $r - answer_j$ represents the $question_j$ corresponding reference answer, $answer_i$ denotes the ith responses to jth question. Auto-encoder Layer is based on the Funnel-Transformer-Encoder model, with three blocks and six layers in each block. We propose a novel approach to training a model by dividing each training step into two stages. The blue dotted line represents the first stage fed the sequence of $question_j$ and $answer_i$ into the Auto-encoder Layer do forward propagation. Immediately, the green dotted line represents the second stage fed the sequence of $r-answer_j$ and $answer_i$ into the same Encoder Layer do another forward propagation. The output of two forward propagations are fed into our proposed Feature Fusion layer based pooling layer to filter out meaningful semantic features blue cube $h_{q,i}$, green cube $h_{r,i}$. Further fusing semantic features $h_{q,i}$ and $h_{r,i}$ in Feature Fusion Layer to obtain the dark blue square $h_{q,r,i}$, which is the capture multiple aspects of the semantic feature. Then drop $h_{q,r,i}$ into the output layer and the assessment score of the ith response by the ASAG system.

3.1   Auto-Encoder Layer

Funnel-Transformer [19] is proposed to compress the hidden layer computation reduction of the whole sequence, and the structure is similar to the Transformer. But the difference is made up of multiple layers of blocks stacked and the sequence length of each block is gradually reduced through a pooling as follow:

$$\mathbf{h}' \leftarrow Pooling(\mathbf{h}) \tag{1}$$

After a pooling, the sequence length of $\mathbf{h}'$ will be less than the sequence length of $\mathbf{h}$, which is $L' < L$. The new multi-head self-attention can be expressed as

$$\mathbf{h} \leftarrow LayerNorm(\mathbf{h}' + S - Attn(Q = \mathbf{h}', KV = \mathbf{h})) \tag{2}$$

Where h is still used as a role of key and value vector, which is to reduce the loss of information after passing through the pooling. In this article, the Funnel-Transformer-encoder will be used as the Auto-encoder of the proposed system.

3.2   Feature Fusion Layer

In this article, We propose a novel approach to divide each training step into a two-stage. More specifically, the first stage is to input the answer and question pairs in the form of "[CLS] answer [SEP] question [SEP]" into the Auto-encoder layer to do forward propagation to obtain the output of sequence representation as Eq. (3). Similarly, in the second stage, to input the answer and model answer pairs in the form of "[CLS] answer [SEP] model answer [SEP]" into the same Auto-encoder layer does a second forward propagation to obtain the sequence representation as Eq. (4). Due to Funnel-Transformer-encoder, the length of the sequence decreases as the number of blocks increases. Then the sequence length of all layers in the last block is greatly reduced. Avoid waste the sequence representation, distinct from takes the hidden state of the first position token ([cls] token) of the sequence as aggregate representation, we can filter the sequence representation as aggregate representation. Therefore, we propose a novel Feature Fusion layer based on the pooling layer and put the output of two forward propagations into the Feature Fusion layer, which can be described as.

$$h_{q,i}'' \leftarrow LayerNorm(h_{q,i}' + S - Attn(Q = h_{q,i}', KV = h_{q,i})) \tag{3}$$

$$h_{r,i}'' \leftarrow LayerNorm(h_{r,i}' + S - Attn(Q = h_{r,i}', KV = h_{r,i})) \tag{4}$$

$$h_{q,i}''' \leftarrow Pooling(h_{q,i}'') \tag{5}$$

$$h_{r,i}''' \leftarrow Pooling(h_{r,i}'') \tag{6}$$

where $h_{q,i}''$ is sequence representation of questions and corresponding student responses. $h_{q,i}'''$ is meaningful semantic features filtered out from textual information of questions and answers. $h_{r,i}''$ and $h_{r,i}'''$ is also obtained in the above manner. The difference is $h_{r,i}''$ captured another type of semantic feature. Further we can fuse both $h_{q,i}'''$ and $h_{r,i}'''$ semantic features aim to capture multiple aspects of semantic feature, which can be described as.

$$\mathbf{h}'' \leftarrow Pooling([h_{q,r,i}^1 : \cdots : h_{q,r,i}^j]) \tag{7}$$

where $h_{q,r,i}^j = [h_{q,i}''' : h_{r,i}''']$ is expressed as a matrix of $h_{q,i}'''$ and $h_{r,i}'''$ of the j-th ($j \in num\_layer$) layer concatenated according to feature dimensions. To better filter out meaningful semantic features, $h_{q,r,i}^1, \cdots, h_{q,r,i}^j$ means that output of each layer of the last block in the Auto-encoder layer, concatenated according to the sequence dimension. Finally it is filtered the sequence dimension to obtain $\mathbf{h}''$.

3.3 Output Layer

Here, we have captured multiple aspects of semantic feature $\mathbf{h}''$. Further, the following.

$$S = softmax(tanh(\mathbf{h}''W_0)W_1) \tag{8}$$

where W_0 and $\mathbf{h}''$ have the same dimensions. After nonlinear mapping is performed through tanh function, linear matrix transformation is performed through W_1. For classification tasks and fed to the softmax classifier. Although the output after the Compress layer is a set of values and the number of dimensions and label categories are the same, it did not directly correspond to answer labels. It needs to be fed into a softmax classifier. The loss function on all labeled data is defined as cross-entropy error:

$$\mathcal{L}_{cls} = -\sum_{i \in T_I} \sum_{f=0}^{F} T_{if} ln S_{if} \tag{9}$$

where T_I is the set of graded student answers, F is the dimension of the output features, and T_{if} is the ground truth of the ith answer in T_I.

For regression tasks, remove the softmax classifier and the output is a single value, but it will not directly match the answer score. The final loss function can be the L2 (mean square) error between the above output prediction and ground truth. The overall ASAG system is schematically illustrated in Fig. 1.

4 Experiments

4.1 Dataset

We use two publicly available datasets for evaluation, shwon as follows:

CS dataset[1] [8]: This dataset is provided by the two examinations of the Data Structure course of a class of undergraduates at the University of North Texas. It contains 2442 student answers and 87 questions and the corresponding model answers are spread across ten assignments. The answer has been scored from 0 to 5 independently by two human graders. Their average score will be used as the gold standard, The Inter Annotator Agreement(IAA) between the two annotators Pearson Correlation Coefficient = 0.586.

SRA dataset[2]: This dataset is part of the "Student Response Analysis" (SRA) in the Semantic Evaluation (SemEval) workshop in 2013 [20], it contains two types of datasets:

- **ScientsBank:** This dataset has about 10,000 student answers to around 197 questions, which belonging to 15 different scientific domains. The answers have been graded as explained in [9].

- **Beetle:** This dataset has about 3000 answers and 56 questions in Basic Electricity and Electronics domains extracted from the interactions with the

---

[1] http://web.eecs.umich.edu/~mihalcea/downloads/ShortAnswerGrading_v2.0.zip.

[2] https://www.cs.york.ac.uk/semeval-2013/task7/index.php%3Fid=data.html

Beetle-II Tutorial Dialogue system [21]. The student answers can refer to single or multiple reference answers. Each reference answer has a category from 'BEST', 'GOOD', 'MINIMAL' or 'KEYWORD'.

All student answers contained in the SRA dataset [20] are labeled by manual graders, and categories are in any of the five categories named, Correct, Partially Correct Incomplete, Contradictory, Irrelevant, Non-domain. In case of ScientsBank corpus, it contains three types of test sets [9]: Unseen-answers (UA), Unseen-questions (UQ) and Unseen-domains (UD). However, for Beetle corpus, only two types of test sets are included: Unseen-answers (UA) and Unseen-questions (UQ). All the above five-way datasets are considered for optimization.

4.2   Experiment Design

Settings. Our system will evaluate on classification tasks and regression tasks, so we have two sets of experimental settings. For classification tasks on the SRA dataset, experiment and debug other parameters, set the learning rate to 3e-5, the drop out to 0.1, and the epoch to 6. The cross-entropy loss function sets the parameter weight, which is set to (5., 2., 1., 2., 1.) for scientbank's UQ test set, and (1., 1., 1., 1., 15.) for the rest of the test sets. For the regression task on the CS dataset, we randomly divide 10% of the dataset used for testing, and the remaining dataset (about 2197 student answers) for training (in 12-fold cross-validation), the learning rate is set to 4e−5, the rest of the settings are a similar as the classified tasks. Besides, we use the AdamW [22] optimizer, with a linear learning rate schedule with 20% of train steps to warm-up. The padding size of the two experiments is 90.

Evaluation Metrics. The results reported using evaluation metrics Weighted-average F1 score and Macro-average F1 score consider all categories for the classification task. In the regression task, there are two types of evaluation metrics for the ordinal labels predicted by ASAG. RMSE is used here as a metric of value deviation, and Pearson's is the most popular correlation coefficient.

Table 2. We make tests on ScientBank, Beetle and CS dataset. Where UA is denoted as Unseen-answers test set, UQ is denoted as Unseen-questions test set and UD is denoted as Unseen-domains test set.

Model	Scientbank						Beetle				CS dataset	
	Wighted F1			Macro F1			Wighted F1		Macro F1		Pearson	RMSE
	UA	UQ	UD	UA	UQ	UD	UA	UQ	UA	UQ		
BERT-question	0.541	0.365	0.394	0.455	0.251	0.375	0.687	0.579	0.626	0.557	0.621	0.880
BERT-reference	0.644	**0.556**	0.526	0.480	**0.398**	0.510	0.784	**0.702**	0.704	0.615	0.722	0.778
Our approach	**0.659**	0.541	**0.534**	**0.498**	0.388	**0.512**	**0.790**	0.693	**0.713**	**0.660**	**0.754**	**0.736**

4.3 Proposed Training Approach

In this experimental part, we only use BERT [10] as the encoder layer in our ASAG system, because we want to verify that the idea of incorporating question information is feasible. As shown in Table 2, BERT-reference indicates that the input is the reference answer and answer pair, BERT-question is also the same meaning. The result is our proposed approach has better results. We analyze that the proposed method can capture multiple aspects of semantic features compared to other systems, and the model can learn a better feature distribution. The following experiments will all adopt this training approach.

Table 3. Influence of encoder and ablation experiment table

Model	Scientbank						Beetle				CS dataset	
	Wighted F1			Macro F1			Wighted F1		Macro F1		Pearson	RMSE
	UA	UQ	UD	UA	UQ	UD	UA	UQ	UA	UQ		
A BERT-base	0.659	0.541	0.534	0.498	0.388	0.512	0.790	0.693	0.713	0.660	0.754	0.736
ROBERTA-base	0.678	0.572	0.560	0.625	0.407	0.538	**0.794**	0.722	0.720	**0.685**	0.767	0.735
ELECTRA-base	0.706	**0.603**	0.583	0.549	0.438	0.597	0.764	0.720	0.637	0.616	0.754	0.741
Funnel-B6-6-6	**0.717**	0.600	**0.602**	**0.667**	**0.582**	**0.630**	0.789	**0.735**	**0.768**	0.622	**0.796**	**0.678**
Funnel-B4-4-4	0.689	0.597	0.562	0.587	0.434	0.575	0.779	0.697	0.728	0.616	0.795	0.683
Funnel-B6-3*2-3*2	0.655	0.585	0.565	0.488	0.398	0.560	0.775	0.714	0.688	0.606	0.782	0.698
B Funnel-layers(−6)	0.717	**0.600**	0.602	**0.662**	**0.582**	**0.630**	0.789	0.735	0.768	0.622	0.796	0.678
Funnel-layers (−5)	**0.724**	0.575	0.593	0.562	0.513	0.589	0.779	0.707	0.692	0.602	0.747	0.760
Funnel-layers (−4)	0.708	0.589	0.571	0.609	0.529	0.590	0.780	0.729	0.689	0.618	0.789	0.690
Funnel-layers (−3)	0.684	0.572	0.574	0.513	0.516	0.558	0.768	0.687	0.710	0.576	0.751	0.745
Funnel-layers (−2)	0.703	0.510	**0.604**	0.543	0.449	0.629	0.767	0.725	0.698	0.614	0.761	0.733
Funnel-layers (−1)	0.707	0.552	0.596	0.609	0.501	0.612	0.787	0.684	0.728	0.606	0.760	0.731
C Funnel-Avg_pooling	**0.717**	**0.600**	**0.602**	**0.662**	**0.582**	**0.630**	0.789	0.735	0.768	0.622	0.796	0.678
Funnel-Max_pooling	0.676	0.479	0.561	0.502	0.414	0.544	0.769	0.712	0.715	0.609	0.768	0.743
Funnel-Dropping	0.707	0.310	0.596	0.609	0.260	0.612	0.787	0.684	0.728	0.606	0.775	0.710
D Funnel-Normal_set	−	−	−	−	−	−	**0.789**	**0.735**	**0.768**	0.622	−	−
Funnel-Optimal_set	−	−	−	−	−	−	0.772	0.717	0.685	0.664	−	−
Funnel-GOOD_set	−	−	−	−	−	−	0.773	0.659	0.675	0.563	−	−
Funnel-BEST_set	−	−	−	−	−	−	0.755	0.676	0.657	**0.668**	−	−

4.4 Influence of Encoder

In this section, we selected the few most popular transformers to replace Funnel-Transformer for comparison experiments. It is BERT-uncased-base, ROBERTA [23]-base, ELECTRA [24]-base-discriminator, Funnel-B6-6-6, Funnel-B4-4-4 and Funnel-B6-3*2-3*2. The above six pre-trained models are all from huggingface[3]. Except for Funnel-B6-6-6 (6 represent each six layers as a block) and Funnel-B6-3*2-3*2 has 18 layers, each other pre-trained model has 12 layers, every layer has 12 heads, and the hidden layer size is 768 dimensions.

The results of Block A in Table 3 show that Funnel-B6-6-6 has the best performance compared to other models. We believe that the number of layers of

---

[3] https://huggingface.co/.

Funnel-B6-6-6 is the key point. The reason is sequence length becomes shorter after a pooling operation, which leads to savings memory, further can increase the number of layers of stacked transformers from 12 to 18 and boost the model capacity. However, Funnel-B6-3*2-3*2 also has the same number of stacked layers and the difference is that every two layers share parameters in the 2nd and 3rd blocks. The reason for the loss performance is the number of parameters will be less than Funnel-B6-6-6. Compared with the model mentioned above, Funnel-B6-6-6 can achieve better results at the expense of more computing power.

4.5   Ablation Experiment

We compare some important points about our system in this section.

Encoder Layer Comparative: In this section, we want to know which aggregate representation of layers is worth utilizing(can be regarded as the multi_layer of Sect. 3 and formula 7). According to [25], Attention heads in the last few layers of BERT in medium metastable states [25], and still have learning ability after pre-trained. Therefore, we only compare the last six layers of the encoder for experimental validation. The result is shown in block B in Table 3. We believe that splicing the aggregate representation of the last six layers (expressed as layers(-6)) and the best result can be achieved. In the following ablation experiments, we adopt this fixed setting.

Feature Fusion Layer Comparative: Our Feature Fusion layer uses the Average pooling operations (as shown in block C in Table 3). For simplicity, we only experiment with stride 6 and window size 6 in this work. We compared the results after replacing it with another Max pooling operation and the ASAG system after dropping Feature Fusion layer (denoted as Funnel-Dropping). Through the results, we believe that compared to Average pooling, Max pooling operation will lose more valuable feature information during the compression sequence.

Beetle Dataset Analysis: We use all the reference answers corresponding to the question as a Normal set, the previous experiments also used the Normal set. Then we manually filter out the model answers, we put the categories of each conference answers are 'BEST' and 'GOOD' as BEST set and GOOD set, respectively, and further combine the above two sets as an Optimal set. We have done four comparative experiments and aim to analyze whether the category of the reference answer will have a significant impact on the result. As shown block D in Table 3, from top to bottom, indicates that used reference answer set in the experiment. Our analysis that the category of the reference answer will not lead to improve the result, but the number of reference answers will increase the result. This is because the more prior knowledge the model can mine meaningful semantic features.

4.6   Comparison with State-of-the-Art Systems

Our proposed ASAG system will be compared with other state-of-art ASAG systems. The ASAG systems that have been considered are Mohler [8], Earth

Mover's Distance-based ASAG System [16], Iterative Ensemble [15], ETS [14] and Feature Engineering and Ensemble-Based [13]. Table 4 shows that the comparison between our proposed system and the above systems includes regression tasks and classification tasks.

Table 4. Our proposed system is compared with the recently out-of-the-art ASAG system

ASAG systems	Scientbank						Beetle				CS dataset	
	Wighted F1			Macro F1			Wighted F1		Macro F1		Pearson	RMSE
	UA	UQ	UD	UA	UQ	UD	UA	UQ	UA	UQ		
Mohler [8]	–	–	–	–	–	–	–	–	–	–	0.518	0.978
Earth Mover's Distancebased [16]	–	–	–	–	–	–	–	–	–	–	0.649	0.830
ETS [14]	0.625	0.356	0.434	0.581	0.274	0.339	0.705	0.614	0.619	0.552	–	–
Iterative Ensemble [15]	0.672	0.518	0.507	0.612	0.415	0.402	–	–	–	–	–	–
Feature Engineering and Ensemble-Based [13]	**0.925**	**0.658**	**0.656**	**0.899**	0.527	0.505	0.7091	0.6248	0.5969	0.5923	0.703	0.793
Our System	0.717	0.6004	0.6019	0.6671	**0.5823**	**0.6298**	**0.7889**	**0.7348**	**0.7683**	**0.6219**	**0.7961**	**0.6776**

The results show that the performance of the proposed system exceeds the most recent ASAG systems. Compared with [13], our system has highly improved performance both in the case of regression tasks and for classification tasks in Beetle. But for the classification task on ScientsBank, we only have a huge improvement on the Macro F1 metric of UQ and UD compared to [13], and the Weighted F1 and Macro F1 of UA have a significant improvement over [16] but lower than [13]. We analyze that our proposed system perform poorly on long-tailed dataset such as ScientsBank. More specifically, the number of students answers in category Non_doamin is minimal just 23 compared to 4969 students answers, which makes it difficult for our proposed neural network based system to learn the feature distribution of samples. Therefore, the performance of the proposed system on classification tasks for the ScientBank dataset will under-performance compared to the beetle. We analyze that feature engineering in [13] tackle long-tailed dataset is helpful, which it can extract a variety of text similarity features. In summary, our model achieved the best grading performance on the regression task with Pearson = 0.796 and RMSE = 0.678. The best labeling performance on the classification task in case of Beetle Dataset with Weighted F1-score = 0.789, Macro F1-score = 0.768 (UA test set) and Weighted F1-score = 0.735, Macro F1-score = 0.622 (UQ test set).

5   Conclusion

In this work, we tested with several popular Transformers on the ASAG task, and the Funnel-Transformer has significant results compared to other models. We propose a novel ASAG system comprising a novel Feature Fusion layer based on the pooling layer over the Transformer-Encoder network. Further, our proposed novel training approach incorporates question information to obtain more prior knowledge. Our proposed ASAG system can effectively tackle the diversity of conceptual representations in a student response. Extensive experiments demonstrate the superior performance on the two publicly available datasets and surpass the most recent out-of-the-art ASAG systems.

Acknowledgement. This research was supported by NSFC (Grants No. 61877051). Li Li is the corresponding author for the paper.

References

1. Conole, G., Warburton, B.: A review of computer-assisted assessment. Res. Learn. Technol. **13**(1), 17–31 (2005)
2. Burrows, S., Gurevych, I., Stein, B.: The eras and trends of automatic short answer grading. Int. J. Artif. Intell. Educ. **25**(1), 60–117(2015)
3. Roy, S., Narahari, Y., Deshmukh, O.D.: A perspective on computer assisted assessment techniques for short free-text answers. In: Ras, E., Joosten-ten Brinke, D. (eds.) CAA 2015. CCIS, vol. 571, pp. 96–109. Springer, Cham (2015). https://doi.org/10.1007/978-3-319-27704-2_10
4. Pulman, S.: Automarking 2: an update on the uclesoxford university research into using computational linguistics to score short free text responses (2004)
5. Thomas, P.: The evaluation of electronic marking of examinations. In: Proceedings of the 8th Annual Conference on Innovation and Technology in Computer Science Education, pp. 50–54 (2003). https://doi.org/10.1145/961511.961528
6. Pedersen, T., Patwardhan, S., WordNet, J.M.: Similarity - measuring the relatedness of concepts. In: AAAI, pp. 1024–1025. AAAI Press/The MIT Press (2004)
7. Mohler, M., Mihalcea, R.: Text-to-text semantic similarity for automatic short answer grading. In: EACL, pp. 567–575. The Association for Computer Linguistics (2009)
8. Mohler, M., Bunescu, R., Mihalcea, R.: Learning to grade short answer questions using semantic similarity measures and dependency graph alignments. In: ACL, pp. 752–762. The Association for Computer Linguistics (2011)
9. Dzikovska, M.O., Nielsen, R.D., Brew, C.: Semeval-2013 task 7: the joint student response analysis and 8th recognizing textual entailment challenge. In: SemEval@NAACL-HLT, pp. 263–274. The Association for Computer Linguistics (2013)
10. Vaswani, A., Shazeer, N., Parmar, N.: Attention is all you need. In: NIPS, pp. 5998–6008 (2017)
11. Claudia, L., Martin, et al.: Automated scoring of short-answer questions. Comput. Hum. **37**, 92–96 (2003)
12. Mihalcea, R., Corley, C., Strapparava, C.: Corpus-based and knowledge-based measures of text semantic similarity. Unt Scholarly Works **1**, 775–780 (2006)
13. Sahu, A., Bhowmick, P.K.: Feature engineering and ensemble-based approach for improving automatic short-answer grading performance. IEEE Trans. Learn. Technol. **13**(1), 77–90 (2020)
14. Heilman, M., Madnani, N.: ETS: domain adaptation and stacking for short answer scoring. In: SemEval@NAACL-HLT, pp. 275–279. The Association for Computer Linguistics (2013)

15. Roy, S., Bhatt, H.S., Narahari, Y.: An iterative transfer learning based ensemble technique for automatic short answer grading. CoRR, abs/1609.04909 (2016)
16. Kumar, S., Chakrabarti, S., Roy, S.: Earth mover's distance pooling over siamese LSTMs for automatic short answer grading. In: IJCAI, pp. 2046–2052. ijcai.org (2017)
17. Devlin, J., Chang, M.W., Lee, K.: BERT: pre-training of deep bidirectional transformers for language understanding. In: NAACL-HLT (1), pp. 4171–4186. Association for Computational Linguistics (2019)
18. Sung, C., Dhamecha, T., Saha, S.: Pre-training BERT on domain resources for short answer grading. In: EMNLP/IJCNLP (1), pp. 6070–6074. Association for Computational Linguistics (2019)
19. Dai, Z., Lai, G., Yang, Y.: Funnel-transformer: filtering out sequential redundancy for efficient language processing. CoRR, abs/2006.03236 (2020)
20. Dzikovska, M.O., Nielsen, R., Brew, C.: Towards effective tutorial feedback for explanation questions: a dataset and baselines. In: HLT-NAACL, pp. 200–210. The Association for Computational Linguistics (2012)
21. Dzikovska, M.O., Isard, A., Bell, P.: BEETLE II: an adaptable tutorial dialogue system. In: SIGDIAL Conference, pp. 338–340. The Association for Computer Linguistics (2011)
22. Loshchilov, I., Hutter, F.: Fixing weight decay regularization in adam. CoRR, abs/1711.05101 (2017)
23. Liu, Y., Ott, M., Roberta, N.G.: A robustly optimized BERT pretraining approach. CoRR, abs/1907.11692 (2019)
24. Clark, K., Luong, M.T., Le, Q.V., Manning, C.D.: ELECTRA: pre-training text encoders as discriminators rather than generators. In: ICLR. OpenReview.net (2020)
25. Ramsauer, H., Schäfl, B., Lehner, J.: Hopfield networks is all you need. CoRR, abs/2008.02217 (2020)

Integrating Task Information into Few-Shot Classifier by Channel Attention

Zhaochen Li$^{(\boxtimes)}$ and Kedian Mu

School of Mathematical Sciences, Peking University, Beijing 100871, China
zhaochenli@pku.edu.cn, mukedian@math.pku.edu.cn

Abstract. It has been increasingly recognized that meta-learning-based approaches provide a promising way to handle challenges to few-shot learning. In this paper, we incorporate the channel attention in the main framework of simple-CNAPS proposed by Bateni et al. to develop a model more appropriate for few-shot image classification. In detail, we replace FiLM layers in simple-CNAPS with channel attention blocks which scale the image channels according to the relationship between task information and feature maps rather than only the task information. This replacement makes the feature extractor more expressive. Moreover, it allows us to take the interaction of different image channels into account. In addition, to alleviate the computational bias caused by small sample size, we provide a method to estimate class centers with perturbations. Finally, the effectiveness of the model is verified by experiments on the few-shot image classification benchmark datasets.

Keywords: Few-shot learning · Meta-learning · Channel attention · Image classification · Machine learning

1 Introduction

Nowadays, deep learning has made great achievements in a wide range of fields including natural language [1], computer vision [2], medicine [5], etc. The success of deep learning, however, relies on a large number of data and powerful computing resources [3,7]. Unfortunately, there are many areas, such as biomedical science, that cannot provide sufficient data resources because of personal privacy, high data acquisition costs and other factors. Therefore, how to make machines acquire useful information efficiently from a small number of samples has attracted much attention, which inspires the emergence of few-shot learning [22]. In this paper, we focus on few-shot image classification to develop a classification model which can perform well at test time in the case where only a small number of training samples are provided.

Meta-learning, which learns meta-parameters such that it can get the optimal model parameters for any new task by further adjustment, has become one of the most common methods to deal with few-shot learning problems [7]. Generally, it can be divided into 3 categories: *1) Optimization-based methods*, represented

© Springer Nature Switzerland AG 2021
H. Qiu et al. (Eds.): KSEM 2021, LNAI 12817, pp. 137–148, 2021.
https://doi.org/10.1007/978-3-030-82153-1_12

by MAML [6] and its variants FOMAML [9], iMAML [8], Reptile [9], etc. *2) Model-based (or black box) methods* which train a neural network, including recurrent networks [10], convolutional networks [11] ect., to embed the training tasks into activation state and make predictions for test tasks based on this state. *3) Non-parametric (metric-based) methods*, such as matching network [12] and prototypical network [13]. Numerous experiments indicate that the studies on non-parametric methods perform better in the field of few-shot classification [12,13,15,17]. The regular non-parametric models consist of two structures: a feature extractor and a classifier, which provides two directions of designing models that are constructing a well-trained feature extractor and applying an appropriate similarity measure in the classifier.

Tian [14] et al. argued that a good embedding model (feature extractor) plays a key role in meta-learning algorithms. Consequently, designing a powerful feature extractor becomes a major current focus in this field. In most non-parametric models, the parameters of feature extractors are fixed at meta-test time, which limits the flexibility and, especially, the expression ability of the model. In order to solve this problem, Requeima et al. [15] proposed an adaptive system for the multi-task classification called Conditional Neural Adaptive Processes (CNAPS for shot). CNAPS trains adaptation networks to produce task related parameters for the feature extractor and the classifier. To integrate task information into the feature extractor, CNAPS applies the Feature-wise Linear Modulation (FiLM for shot) layers [16] to adjust the feature embeddings according to the current task information. However, it seems inappropriate that scaling feature maps according to the parameters only related to the task information. We figure that the scaling parameters should be determined by the relationship between the feature maps and the task information. In order to improve the expression ability of the feature extractor and, at the same time, introduce the task information, we put forward an embedding model with conditional channel attentions based on SE-ResNet [18].

As for the classifier, in order to model the sample distribution more accurately, Bateni et al. [17] proposed simple-CNAPS with a non-parametric classifier based on squared Mahalanobis distance, which not only greatly reduces the number of parameters, but also improves the accuracy of few-shot image classification. Nonetheless, the class center represented by the average of samples might lead to a computational bias in the case of small sample size. To alleviate this problem, we provide a novel approach to introduce a slight disturbance to the class center.

The remaining sections of this paper are organized as follows. The related works will be given in Sect. 2. In order to model the problem conveniently, the formulation of few-shot classification problem will be illustrated in Sect. 3. Our models will be proposed in Sect. 4. To verify the effect of our models, we will present the classification experiments in Sect. 5. Finally, we conclude this paper in Sect. 6.

The contributions of this paper are as follows:

- The conditional channel attention improves the expression ability of the embedding model and, at the meanwhile, integrates the task information into the feature extractor.
- The conditional channel attention takes the relationship among feature maps into consideration while scaling the feature maps.
- This paper proposes a novel approach to estimate the center of each category for non-parametric classifiers.

2 Related Work

Most popular few-shot learning models can be considered as a combination of a feature extractor and a classifier. Many methods, hence, can be viewed as designing a good feature extractor or constructing an efficient classifier.

As for the feature extractor, some models adapt their feature extractors by updating the task related parameters in the embedding model. MAML fine-tunes the whole feature extractor while training, which confronts the model with the risk of over-fitting and the heavy burden of calculation [21]. In order to adjust proper parameters of the feature extractor, a modular meta-learning method with shrinkage [21] can automatically discover both task-specific modules and meta modules. It models the modules of the feature extractor as normal distribution with variance of σ^2 and mean of the meta-parameter. The σ^2 for each module is treated as the standard whether the corresponding module needs to be updated at test-time. However, the number of parameters to be modified at test-time is largely determined by the way to partition modules, and often quite a few. CNAPS [15] mitigates this issue by utilizing sparse FiLM layers within the task-specific information so that only a few parameters need to be adjusted at test-time. CNAPS trains a ResNet18 network as the feature extractor with 2 FiLM layers inserted in each block. Each FiLM layer augments the features with the help of task-specific parameters provided by adaptation networks which take the task embedding as input and scales and shifts the feature map in the feature extractor with the guide of task information. However, the scaling parameters ignore the relationship among feature maps.

As for the classifier, some models mainly focus on choosing an appropriate metric to measure the relationship among samples. Matching Networks construct two distinct feature extractors by using the variants of LSTM [19] models for training samples and query samples, and then compute the cosine similarity between training samples and the query sample for one-shot classification. Prototypical Networks extend the Matching Networks to few-shot classification. It produces a linear classifier by using squared Euclidean distance rather than a weighted nearest neighbor classifier like Matching Networks. Moreover, the theorem of regular Bregman divergences ensures that squared Euclidian distance, Mahalanobis distance and any other examples of Bregman divergences are effectively performing mixture density estimation [13]. For this reason, simple-CNAPS uses a nearest neighbor classifier based on squared Mahalanobis distance in place of a linear classifier in CNAPS, which achieves encouraging results on the standard few-shot image classification benchmark datasets. In these models, the prototype of each category is expressed by average of support samples, which might induce some deviation in the case of small data size.

Therefore, our model is constructed from two aspects. On the one hand, we put forward an adaptive feature extractor based on the structure of CNAPS. The main difference is that the adaptation parameters computed according to task-specific information are provided to calculate the channel attention in each block. The FiLM layers are substituted by channel attention layers, which contributes to improving the expression ability of embedding networks. Moreover, the weights added to the feature maps consider the relationship between feature maps and task information, rather than being determined only by task information like those in CNAPS and simple-CNAPS. On the other hand, we add a slight perturbation when computing the class centers in the classifier to alleviate the computational deviation.

3 Problem Formulation

In this section, we provide a formulation of few-shot image classification problem. Assume that we have a large dataset denoted by $\mathcal{D} = \{(x_i, y_i)\}_{i=1}^{N}$, where x_i is an image and y_i is a label. Then, we can construct different tasks from the large dataset. We denote the τ-th classification task as $\mathcal{D}^\tau$, where each pair of data is sampled from dataset $\mathcal{D}$. To apply meta-learning algorithm, we seperate each task $\mathcal{D}^\tau$ into a support set $\mathcal{S}^\tau = \{(x_i, y_i)\}_{i=1}^{N_\tau}$ and a query set $\mathcal{Q}^\tau = \{(x_i^\star, y_i^\star)\}_{i=1}^{M_\tau}$ to implement episodic training strategy [20], where $\mathcal{D}^\tau = \mathcal{S}^\tau \cup \mathcal{Q}^\tau$ and $\mathcal{S}^\tau \cap \mathcal{Q}^\tau = \varnothing$, N_τ and M_τ denote the data scale of support set and query set, respectively. The objective is to find a set of model parameters θ to make the image classification accuracy as high as possible.

According to the episodic training strategy, parameters of the classifier can be divided into meta-parameters ϕ and task-specific parameters ψ^τ. Meta-parameters are updated according to the query data, so that the model has strong generalization ability. Task-specific parameters are related to the specific task, and they are updated according to the support data of each task. After the training phase, the classifier is tested by new tasks. In testing phase, task-specific parameters are updated according to the support data while meta-parameters are fixed to generate the predictive labels for query data. The predictive distributions can be written as $p(y^\star|x^\star, \theta) = p(y^\star|x^\star, \phi, \psi^\tau = \psi_\phi(\mathcal{S}^\tau))$, where ψ_ϕ denotes the algorithm to produce parameter ψ^τ. Thus the objective of the few-shot classification problem is to maximize $\mathbb{E}_\tau[\prod_{\mathcal{Q}^\tau} p(y^\star|x^\star, \theta)]$.

4 Classification Models

As mentioned before, our model can be seperated into a feature extractor and a metric learning based classifier. Our model shares the same framework with simple-CNAPS, except for two changes, that is, we modify the feature extractor by replacing the FiLM layers with channel attentions, and adjust the class centers by introducing a perturbation.

4.1 Feature Extractor

Our model adopt the framework of the feature extractor in CNAPS and simple-CNAPS but deviates from them by replacing the way to scale feature maps with a more expressive method.

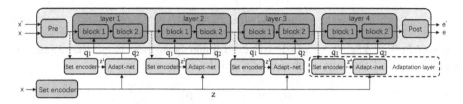

Fig. 1. The architecture of feature extractor. The upper block represents ResNet18, and the lower part is adaptation networks with 4 adaptation layers

The structure of our feature extractor is shown in the Fig. 1. It consists of a ResNet18 [19] network with channel attention blocks and an adaptation network.

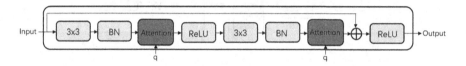

Fig. 2. The architechture of blocks in each ResNet18 layer. (Color figure online)

There are 4 layers in the ResNet18, and each layer is made up of 2 basic blocks. The structure of basic block is constructed based on the traditional block of ResNet18. As Fig. 2 shows, the difference between them is the channel attention blocks (shown in yellow) which absorb the parameters q computed by adaptation networks from support images. The concrete structure of channel attention block used in this paper is illustrated in Fig. 3. Suppose that there are r channels, and each channel of the network is a real feature map matrix with the size of $H \times W$, namely $\boldsymbol{U}_1, \boldsymbol{U}_2, ..., \boldsymbol{U}_r \in \mathcal{R}^{H \times W}$. After the pooling layer in the attention block, the results can be computed as follows:

$$s_i = \text{pooling}(\boldsymbol{U}_i) \tag{1}$$

where s_i is the i-th component of the output vector $\boldsymbol{s}$ of the global pooling, pooling($\cdot$) presents the global pooling function, which can be average pooling or max pooling calculated as follows:

$$\text{avgpool}(\boldsymbol{U}_i) = \frac{1}{HW} \sum_{h=1}^{H} \sum_{w=1}^{W} \boldsymbol{U}_i(h, w) \tag{2}$$

$$\text{maxpool}(\boldsymbol{U}_i) = \max_{h,w} \boldsymbol{U}_i(h,w) \tag{3}$$

where $\boldsymbol{U}_i(h,w)$ presents the element of the h-th row and the w-th column of the matrix $\boldsymbol{U}_i$, and $i = 1, ..., r$. After pooling the input feature maps, the results are used to calculate weights of channels with the parameter $\boldsymbol{q}$ after passing through a two-layer linear network:

$$\boldsymbol{p} = \boldsymbol{M}_2 \text{ReLU}(\boldsymbol{M}_1 \boldsymbol{s}) \tag{4}$$

where $\boldsymbol{M}_1$ and $\boldsymbol{M}_2$ are weight matrices of linear networks. Then, the weights of channels $\boldsymbol{\alpha}$ and the output channel $\boldsymbol{U}'_i$ can be computed by:

$$\boldsymbol{\alpha} = \text{sigmoid}(\boldsymbol{q} \odot \boldsymbol{p}) \tag{5}$$

$$\boldsymbol{U}'_i = \alpha_i \boldsymbol{U}_i \quad i = 1, ..., r \tag{6}$$

where $\odot$ in (5) represents Hadamard product.

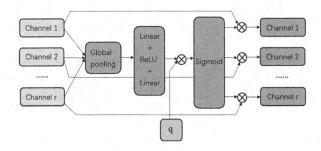

Fig. 3. Channel attention.

Adaptation networks(Adapt-net in Fig. 1) are used to compute the parameter $\boldsymbol{q}$ that contains information of the specific task. The networks operate as follows:

1. The images in support dataset are absorbed in a 5-layer convolutional network and get the set embedding vector $\boldsymbol{z}$.
2. The parameters $\boldsymbol{z}^i$ are computed by a network with 2 linear layers and 3 residual linear layers whose inputs are the intermediate results positioned before the i-th layer in the ResNet18 network.
3. The concatenation of $\boldsymbol{z}$ and $\boldsymbol{z}^i$ is fed into 4 adaptation networks abbreviated as Adapt-nets. Each Adapt-net has 2 parallel networks which consists of 1 linear layer and 3 residual linear layers to seperatively calculate parameters $\boldsymbol{q}_1$ and $\boldsymbol{q}_2$ for each block in 4 layers in ResNet18.

We refer to the concrete architecture of set encoder networks and adaptation layers. More details about them can be found in [15] if readers are interested.

4.2   Classifier

After getting the embedding vectors of image data from the feature extractor, the classifier is performed directly in this embedding vector space. We adopt the metric-learning-based classifier with Mahalanobis distance and introduce a slight disturbance into class centers.

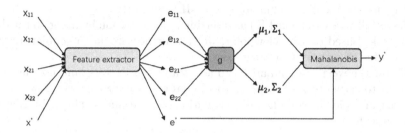

Fig. 4. Classifier architecture.

The overview of the classifier is illustrated in Fig. 4. For example, there are 4 samples in support set, $\{x_{11}, x_{12}\}$ belongs to the first category, and $\{x_{21}, x_{22}\}$ belongs to the second category. The query sample $x^\star$ and support samples are passed into feature extractor and obtain their embedding vectors $e^\star, e_{11}, e_{12}, e_{21}, e_{22}$. Function g is used to compute the mean and covariance for each category. It should be noted that the method of computing covariance we use is consist with that in simple-CNAPS. The prediction of $x^{\star}$'s label $y^\star$ is the class with the minimum Mahalanobis distance between the query's embedding and the center of each category.

When comes across few-shot image classification problem, the means of image categories are calculated by a small number of samples, which might results in a small bias. To alleviate the problem as much as possible, we apply an estimation of each center from the bayesian perspective.

For each category, the sample variable is denoted as x_i, where i is the index of the sample and $i = 1, ..., N$. It is assumed that the sample variables are independent of each other and obey normal distribution with the mean of μ and the covariance of Σ, namely $x_1, ..., x_N \overset{i.i.d}{\sim} \mathcal{N}(\mu, \Sigma)$. Suppose the prior distribution of μ is $\mathcal{N}(\mu_0, \Sigma_0)$. According to bayesian formula $p(\mu|x) = \frac{p(\mu)p(x|\mu)}{p(x)}$ where x denotes the set of sample variables, the bayesian estimation can be computed as follow:

$$\hat{\mu}_{bayes} = (N\Sigma^{-1} + \Sigma_0^{-1})^{-1}(N\Sigma^{-1}\bar{x} + \Sigma_0^{-1}\mu_0) \tag{7}$$

where $\bar{x} = \frac{\sum_{i=1}^{N} x_i}{N}$.

According to (7), $\hat{\mu}_{bayes}$ can be considered as a weighted average of $\bar{x}$ and μ_0 and the weights are $\frac{N\Sigma^{-1}}{N\Sigma^{-1}+\Sigma_0^{-1}}$ and $I - \frac{N\Sigma^{-1}}{N\Sigma^{-1}+\Sigma_0^{-1}}$. In practice, N is the number of samples in each category, Σ is the covariance of samples in the specific category, μ_0 and Σ_0 are computed based on the total samples in a specific task. We apply an MLP network with 4 linear layers and a mean pooling layer to calculate μ_0 and Σ_0 seperately with the embedding vectors of data in support set as input. Suppose that $\hat{\mu}_0 = \mathrm{MLP}(S^\tau)$ and $\hat{\Sigma}_0 = \mathrm{MLP}(S^\tau)$ and the MLP can be trained according to the classification loss function for each calss. In addition, we can also add a parameter to balance the results and to train a better model, such as $\hat{\mu}_0 = \epsilon\bar{x} + (1-\epsilon)\hat{\mu}_0$ and $\hat{\Sigma}_0 = \epsilon\Sigma + (1-\epsilon)\hat{\Sigma}_0$, but for simplicity, we directly use the results calculated by the MLP networks.

Essentially, we can regard (7) as inserting a perturbation by using all the data of the task. Based on this viewpoint, we can further provide a simpler method to compute the center of each category.

We set the weights of $\bar{x}$ and μ_0 to adjustable parameters, and use the same networks to estimate μ_0 according to the data in the specific category. In this way, we can avoid the complicated calculation of covariances. This naive method is shown as follow:

$$\hat{\mu}_{naive} = (1-\delta)\bar{x} + \delta\mu_0 \tag{8}$$

where δ is an adjustable parameter. When δ is set to 0, the center becomes the average of samples.

5   Experiments

As the capacity of feature extractor is more than other structures', we adapt the same two-stage training strategy as simple-CNAPS, and we use the pre-trained parameters of the feature extractor directly from simple-CNAPS. The experiments tackle the in-domain few-shot image classification challenge.

5.1   Datasets

Our experiments are conducted on 5 benchmark datasets for few-shot image classification.

Mini/TieredImageNet are both subsets of ILSVRC_2012 [23]. The mini-ImageNet [12] was proposed by Vinyals et al. for few-shot learning evaluation. It consists of 100 classes with 600 color images per class. These classes are divided into 64, 16 and 20 classes respectively to train, evaluate and test. TieredIma-geNet [4] is a larger subset of ILSVRC_2012 with 608 classes. These classes are grouped into 34 nodes in the ImageNet hierarchy, which is partitioned into 20, 6 and 8 nodes for training, evaluating and testing.

ILSVRC_2012 is one of the most famous hierarchical image dataset in the field of computer vision. It is made up for 1000 classes with at most 1300 samples of hand-labeled color images for each class. These 1000 classes are divided into 712, 158 and 130 for training, validation and testing.

Omniglot [24] is a handwritten character dataset. There are 1623 classes consists of 50 kinds of alphabets. The dataset is divided into 883, 81 and 659 classes corresponding to 25, 5 and 20 alphabets for training, evaluating and testing seperatively.

Fungi [25] is a dataset with 1394 fungi species. There are 85578 training images, 4182 validation images and 9758 testing images in this dataset. It is proposed for a 2018 competition which is part of a workshop at IEEE conference on computer vision.

5.2   Results

Because of the different experimental settings for different data, the experiments are two-fold. On the one hand we test the validity of our model on miniImageNet and tieredImageNet, on the other hand we apply the remaining datasets to verify the effectiveness of our model architectures relative to the original model structures.

Table 1. Classification accuracy (%) on mini/tieredImageNet baselines.

Models	miniImageNet		tieredImageNet	
	1-shot	5-shot	1-shot	5-shot
ProtoNet [13]	46.14	65.77	48.58	69.57
TADAM [26]	58.50	76.70	N/A	N/A
TPN [27]	55.51	69.86	59.91	73.70
LEO [28]	61.76	77.59	66.33	81.44
CNAPS [15]	77.99	87.31	75.12	86.57
Simple-CNAPS [17]	**82.16**	89.80	78.29	89.01
Ours	77.76	**91.49**	**82.53**	**93.82**

Table 1 shows the results of the standard 5-way 1 and 5-shot classification tasks. We compared six models in [17] with ours. In this experiment, we set δ in (8) to 0.3, set the dimension of feature embedding to 512, and use the max pooling in attention blocks for 5-shot miniImageNet and average pooling for others. We test the two center estimation methods shown in formula 7 and formula 8. The result of 5-shot miniImageNet uses $\hat{\mu}_{bayes}$, and the rest results are based on $\hat{\mu}_{naive}$. As results of this experiment show, our model generally outperforms recent baselines on the basic few-shot classification task, which priliminarily verifies the validity of our model, espetially for 5-shot learning. The performance of 1-shot learning in miniImageNet approximates that of CNAPS, which might due to the perturbation added to the center will reduce the accuracy of the estimation when there is only one sample for each category. Therefore, we can conclude that the perturbation added to class centers can work with a certain amount of data.

In order to further illustrate that the architectures of our model make sense, we use the training strategy in [25] and set the upper bound of support size in training phase to 350 to test our model on the remaining three datasets mentioned in Sect. 5.1 one by one. In order to prevent over-fitting, we use the augmentation techniques including blurring, adjusting brightness, rotation, random noise and translation in some datasets. As Table 2 shows, we compare simple-CNAPS model and our model with different settings, where 'att' indicates the attention model without using the novel class center estimations, and 'att+naive' and 'att+bayes' represent the attention model integrated with the naive and bayesian class center estimation method, which corresponds to max pooling and average pooling seperatively.

Table 2. Classification accuracy (%) on three datasets for meta-learning.

Datasets	ILSVRC_2012	Omniglot	Fungi
Simple-CNAPS	55.4 ± 1.1	88.2 ± 0.7	47.2 ± 1.1
Ours (att)	$\mathbf{56.6 \pm 1.1}$	$\mathbf{88.4 \pm 0.7}$	45.0 ± 1.1
Ours (att+naive)	55.1 ± 1.1	88.0 ± 0.7	48.4 ± 1.0
Ours (att+bayes)	56.2 ± 1.1	85.9 ± 0.8	$\mathbf{50.0 \pm 1.0}$

From the results of Table 2, we can generally conclude that our models outperform simple-CNAPS when the models are adjusted appropriately for different datasets. For fungi dataset, the architecture of the novel method to calculate class centers makes the poor performance model surpass the benchmark model, which shows, at least in some scenarios, the effectiveness of the class center estimation method. And for the ILSVRC_2012 dataset, we can get higher classification accuracy than the original model with attention blocks, which confirms the validity of the channel attention model. However, as for the omniglot dataset, the classification accuracy is slightly reduced by introducing disturbance into class centers, but it is still close to the result of the original model. Comparing the two class estimation methods, we can see that the bayesian method performs better than the naive method on ILSVRC_2012 and Fungi. It can be conjectured that the naive method is more suitable for some simple datasets, whilst the bayesian method performs better on slightly complex datasets.

The experiments demonstrate that our model has acquired improvements to a certain extend on some datasets. We can tentatively conclude that our model is more effective when the number of training samples of each category increases slightly. And both the novel architectures of embedding model and center estimation are verified to be effective on different datasets.

6   Conclusions

Few-shot learning has attracted the attention of many researchers on account of insufficient data in various fields. Taking the few-shot image classification problem as an example, we propose an improved non-parametric meta-learning-based approach from two aspects: feature extractor and classifier. We use channel attention to integrate the task information to improve the expression ability of the embedding model and provide a method to add learnable perturbation into class centers to promote the classifier's quality. Compared with other models, our model has achieved different degree of improvements on different datasets. Exploration of other ways of incorporating task information in embedding models can be a potential research. In addition, how to relieve the bias of the center of dataset in the case of small sample size more efficiently also needs to be taken into account.

Acknowledgements. This work was partly supported by the National Natural Science Foundation of China under Grant No. 61572002, No. 61690201, and No. 61732001.

References

1. Sutskever, I., Vinyals, O., Le, Q.V.: Sequence to sequence learning with neural networks. In: 27th International Conference on Neural Information Processing Systems (NeurIPS), pp. 3104–3112. MIT, Montreal (2014)
2. He, K., Zhang, X., Ren, S., Sun, J.: Deep residual learning for image recognition. In: 2016 IEEE Conference on Computer Vision and Pattern Recognition (CVPR), pp. 770–778. IEEE, Las Vegas (2016)
3. Chen, M., Zhang, Y., Qiu, M., Guizani, N., Hao, Y.: SPHA: smart personal health advisor based on deep analytics. IEEE Commun. Mag. **56**(3), 164–169 (2018)
4. Ren, M., Triantafillou, E., Ravi, S., Snell, J., et al.: Meta learning for semi-supervised few-shot classification. CoRR, abs/1803.00676(2018)
5. Esteva, A., et al.: Dermatologist-level classification of skin cancer with deep neural networks. Nature **542**(7639), 115–118 (2017)
6. Finn, C., Abbeel, P., Levine, S.: Model-agnostic meta-learning for fast adaptation of deep networks. In: 34th International Conference on Machine Learning, pp. 1126–1135. JMLR, Sydney (2017)
7. Hospedales, T., Antoniou, A., Micaelli, P., Storkey, A.: Meta-learning in neural networks: a survey. arXiv preprint arXiv:2004.05439 (2020)
8. Rajeswaran, A., Finn, C., Kakade, S.M., Levine, S.: Meta-learning with implicit gradients. In: 33rd Conference on Neural Information Processing Systems (NeurIPS), pp. 113–124. MIT, Vancouver (2019)
9. Nichol, A., Achiam, J., Schulman, J.: On first-order meta-learning algorithms. arXiv preprint arXiv:1803.02999 (2018)
10. Ravi, S., Larochelle, H.: Optimization as a model for few shot learning. In: 5th International Conference on Learning Representations (ICLR), OpenReview.net, Toulon (2016)
11. Mishra, N., Rohaninejad, M., Chen, X., Abbeel, P.: A simple neural attentive meta-learner. In: 6th International Conference on Learning Representations (ICLR), OpenReview.net, Vancouver (2018)
12. Vinyals, O., Blundell, C., Lillicrap, T., Wierstra, D., et al.: Matching networks for one shot learning. In: 29th Annual Conference on Neural Information Processing Systems (NeurIPS), pp. 3630–3638. MIT, Barcelona (2016)
13. Snell, J., Swersky, K., Zemel, R.: Prototypical networks for few-shot learning. In: 30rd Annual Conference on Neural Information Processing Systems (NeurIPS), Long Beach, USA, pp. 4077–4087 (2017)

14. Tian, Y., Wang, Y., Krishnan, D., Tenenbaum, J.B., Isola, P.: Rethinking few-shot image classification: a good embedding is all you need? In: Vedaldi, A., Bischof, H., Brox, T., Frahm, J.-M. (eds.) ECCV 2020. LNCS, vol. 12359, pp. 266–282. Springer, Cham (2020). https://doi.org/10.1007/978-3-030-58568-6_16

15. Requeima, J., Gordon, J., Bronskill, J., Nowozin, S., Turner, R.E.: Fast and flexible multi-task classification using conditional neural adaptive processes. In: 32rd Conference on Neural Information Processing Systems(NeurIPS), Vancouver, Canada, pp. 7957–7968 (2019)

16. Perez, E., Strub, F., Vries, H.D., Dumoulin, V., Courville, A.: FiLM: visual reasoning with a general conditioning layer. In: 32nd AAAI Conference on Artificial Intelligence (AAAI), pp. 3942–3951. AAAI press, New Orleans (2018)

17. Bateni, P., Goyal, R., Masrani, V., Wood, F., Sigal, L.: Improved few-shot visual classification. In: 2020 IEEE Conference on Computer Vision and Pattern Recognition (CVPR), pp. 14481–14490. IEEE, Seattle (2020)

18. Hu, J., Shen, L., Sun, G.: Squeeze-and-excitation networks. In: 2018 IEEE Conference on Computer Vision and Pattern Recognition (CVPR), pp. 7132–7141. IEEE, Salt Lake City (2018)

19. Hochreiter, S., Schmidhuber, J.: Long short-term memory. Neural Comput. 9(8), 1735–1780 (1997)

20. Chen, J., Wu, X., Li, Y., Li, Q., Zhan, L., Chung, F.: A closer look at the training strategy for modern meta-learning. In: 33th International Conference on Neural Information Processing Systems (NeurIPS). Virtual (2020)

21. Chen, Y., et al.: Modular meta-learning with shrinkage. In: 33th International Conference on Neural Information Processing Systems (NeurIPS). Virtual (2020)

22. Lu, J., Gong, P., Ye, J.: Learning from very few samples: a survey. CoRR: abs/2009.02653 (2020)

23. Russakovsky, O., et al.: ImageNet large scale visual recognition challenge. Int. J. Comput. Vis. 115(3), 211–252 (2015)

24. Lake, B.M., Salakhutdinov, R., Tenenbaum, J.B.: Human-level concept learning through probabilistic program induction. Science 350(6266), 1332–1338 (2015)

25. Triantafillou, E., et al.: Meta-dataset: a dataset of datasets for learning to learn from examples. In: 8th International Conference on Learning Representations (ICLR). OpenReview.net, Addis Ababa (2020)

26. Oreshkin, B., Rodrıguez Lopez, P., Lacoste, A.: TADAM: task dependent adaptive metric for improved few-shot learning. In: 31st Annual Conference on Neural Information Processing Systems (NeurIPS), Montreal, Canada, pp. 721–731 (2018)

27. Liu, Y., Lee, J., Park, M., Kim, S., Yang, Y.: Transductive propagation network for few-shot learning. CoRR, abs/1805.10002 (2018)

28. Rusu, A.A., et al.: Meta-learning with latent embedding optimization. CoRR, abs/1807.05960 (2018)

Rumor Verification on Social Media with Stance-Aware Recursive Tree

Xiaoyun Han[1], Zhen Huang[1(✉)], Menglong Lu[1], Dongsheng Li[1], and Jinyan Qiu[2]

[1] National Key Laboratory of Parallel and Distributed Processing, National University of Defense Technology, Changsha, China
{hxy_1021,huangzhen,lumenglong,dsli}@nudt.edu.cn
[2] H. R. Support Center, Beijing, China

Abstract. Since rumors have affected real society harmfully, automatic rumor verification attracts much attention from researchers. Incorporating the stance-aware knowledge into rumor verification is a hot direction, because its great potential to boost verification performance has been revealed in many studies. However, existing methods are still limited by two problems, the existence of short retweets and fraud nodes. For short retweets, since it is hard to extract the semantic information from short retweets, modeling the stance between a tweet and its short retweets could carry out training noises. For fraud nodes, they might perturb the normal propagation structure of rumors, so the model could be misled to capture those wrong stance information. To mitigate them, we propose a Credibility and Stance Aware recursive Tree (CSATree) for rumor verification. Firstly, we utilize a self-attention mechanism and a multi-task learning module to explore the context of short retweets, which could help to enrich the semantics and stance information in short retweets. In detail, the context of short retweets refers to those retweets that respond to a same tweet, i.e., sibling nodes in a conversation tree. Secondly, we take the node credibility into account and adopt another novel attention mechanism to reduce the impact of fraud nodes. Experiments on two public datasets demonstrate that CSATree significantly outperforms the current best stance-aware model by around 9%.

Keywords: Rumor verification · Stance-aware knowledge · Recursive tree · Attention mechanism · Node credibility

1 Introduction

Rumor refers to information whose truthfulness has not yet to be verified at the time of posting. Along with the extensive application of social media, rumors have spread virally on social platforms, which seriously affects the acquisition of knowledge from web content. Therefore, automatic rumor verification is an important task in the upstream of open-domain knowledge acquisition.

© Springer Nature Switzerland AG 2021
H. Qiu et al. (Eds.): KSEM 2021, LNAI 12817, pp. 149–161, 2021.
https://doi.org/10.1007/978-3-030-82153-1_13

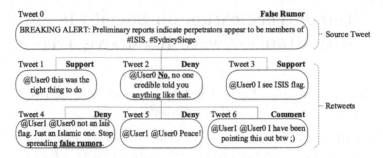

Fig. 1. A conversation tree of a false rumor on social media. The stance of the retweets is annotated above the text.

On social platforms (e.g., Twitter), a source tweet and its retweets can be formalized as a conversation tree according to their response relationship, as shown in Fig. 1. To improve the performance and the interpretability of rumor verification, [20] proposed to utilize the correlation between the stance of retweets and the veracity of the source tweet (i.e., the rumor). Their assumption is that different kinds of rumors would lead to different kinds of discussions, which is also proved by many other sociology researches [12]. For example, false rumors tend to lead to tremendous controversies while true rumors do not. To exploit such correlation, some studies [6–8,10,17] tried multi-task learning (MTL), i.e., joint training of rumor verification and stance classification, to boost the performance of rumor verification. In specific, the stance classification is conducted on every tweet pair which refers to a sentence pair containing a tweet and a retweet. However, such kind of methods is still limited by two problems, the existence of short retweets and the existence of fraud nodes.

A short retweet refers to a response tweet that contains very few words, so its stance would be ambiguous unless its complementary context is provided. For example, the stance of retweet *"@User1 @User0 Peace!"* in Fig. 1 is "deny", which is hard to be determined by observing the single sentence pair <Tweet 5, Tweet 2>. However, if the context {Tweet 4, Tweet 6} is provided, it could be easily inferred that the stance of Tweet 5 is "deny". In addition, since the fraud nodes are commonly registered by rumor publishers to mislead people, the existence of fraud nodes will affect the process of integrating stances. In Fig. 1, Tweet 1 and Tweet 3 support the source Tweet 0 while Tweet 2 holds the "deny" stance, which makes Tweet 0 more like a true rumor. If we know that Tweet 1 and Tweet 3 are posted by fraudulent users, we would not trust these fraud nodes, which may draw the opposite conclusion that Tweet 0 is a false rumor.

In this paper, we propose a novel model to address the above problems, named Credibility and Stance Aware recursive Tree (CSATree). Firstly, CSATree employs a self-attention mechanism to extract the contextual information from sibling nodes. As mentioned earlier, ambiguous semantics and stances in short retweets can be complemented by the context from sibling nodes. Besides, we introduce a MTL module to enhance the stance representation of nodes.

Secondly, based on social aspect characteristics and user profiles, we propose another attention mechanism to determine the credibility of nodes, which could alleviate the disturbance from fraud nodes in the process of semantics and stance information aggregation. The contributions of this paper are summarized as follows.

- We propose CSATree, a novel recursive tree that not only extracts the structural information from the conversation tree but also utilizes the stance and semantic information from sibling nodes.
- We design a novel attention mechanism to learn node credibility, which eliminates the impact of fraud nodes and enhances the representation of rumors.
- Extensive experiments on two public datasets demonstrate that the proposed CSATree achieves superior improvements over existing approaches.

The rest of the paper is organized as follows. In Sect. 2, we review related works. Section 3 presents the details of our CSATree and Sect. 4 shows the experimental results. Finally, we conclude our work in Sect. 5.

2   Related Work

Conventional rumor verification methods develop hand-crafted features to classify rumors, but these methods are time-consuming and labor-intensive. Recent studies exploit deep learning methods to automatically extract features from rumors [19]. T-FNN [1] is a fusion neural network based on Bi-GRU and CNN to extract the textural feature. BranchLSTM [6] is a LSTM model to learn the representation of each chronological branch in a conversation. TD-RvNN [11] is a top-down recursive tree model to capture the structural information from conversation trees. HiTPLAN [5] exploits token-level and post-level attention networks to model interactions between tweets. Tree Transformer [9] leverages Transformer as units to further enhance the representation of rumors.

More recently, some efforts are put on MTL of stance classification and rumor verification [10]. According to the organization of the conversation, MTL methods can be mainly categorized into two genres: (i) Sequential classification methods, which organize the conversation into a tweet sequence, and utilize RNN or Transformer to learn the representation of the tweet sequence. Among them, BranchLSTM + NileTMRG [6] classifies stances with BranchLSTM and verifies rumors with a SVM. MTL2 [6] is a multi-task learning framework, which includes a shared LSTM layer and task-specific layers for jointly predicting stance and rumor. Coupled Hierarchical TFM [18] extends BERT and uses coupled Transformers for MTL, which further improves the MTL2 framework. However, the learned sequence representation could be less effective because the tweet sequence discards structural information; (ii) Structure-based methods, which organize the conversation as a tree, and utilize tree LSTM or GCN to extract propagation patterns. Hierarchical GCN-RNN [17] is an architecture that utilizes a GCN at the bottom to capture propagation patterns and a RNN at the top to capture temporal dynamics, and Hierarchical PSV [17] is a MTL framework that employs GCN for stance classification and Hierarchical GCN-RNN for rumor verification. TreeLSTM [7] is a recursive tree model that exploits LSTM with convolution units to recursively aggregate node features, predicts rumors at the root node, and predicts stances at each node. However, these methods are flawed in the inadequate exploration of short retweets and the neglecting of fraud nodes, which makes the potential of MTL methods is not fully exploited.

3   Approach

In this section, we introduce the proposed approach, a credibility and stance aware recursive tree via MTL for jointly predicting stance and rumor veracity. In Sect. 3.1, we formulate our rumor verification and stance classification tasks. In Sect. 3.2, we give an overview of the framework and describe the details of our CSATree. Section 3.3 presents the training procedure of our MTL approach.

3.1   Task Definition

Assume we have a set of rumors $\mathbf{T} = \{T\}$, every rumor can be organized as a conversation tree $T = <V, E>$. In the denotation of $T = <V, E>$, $V = \{p_0, p_1, ..., p_n\}$ refers to the node set of the conversation tree, where p_0 is the root node (i.e., source tweet), $p_1, ..., p_n$ are the retweets directly or indirectly responded to p_0, and n denotes the number of retweets. Moreover, E denotes the directed edge set that describes the response relationship in V. For example, if $p_i, p_j \in V$ and the edge $<p_i, p_j>$ exists in E, it means that there is a directed edge from p_i to p_j, i.e., p_i responds to p_j.

The goal of the **rumor verification task** is to predict the rumor class for each conversation tree T. More specifically, the goal is to learn a multiple classifier $f : T \rightarrow Y_R$, $Y_R \in \{false\ rumor, true\ rumor, unverified\ rumor\}$.

For the **stance classification task**, it is a special case of natural language inference task, whose goal is to determine the relationship between two sentences. In this paper, the stance label between two sentences is from $\{support, deny, query, comment\}$, the goal of the stance classification task is to learn a multiple classifier on a sentence pair, i.e., $g: <s_0, s_1> \rightarrow y_s$, where s_0 is the head sentence, s_1 is the tail sentence, and y_s is the ground truth stance of s_0 for s_1.

3.2   Stance-Aware Recursive Tree for Rumor Verification

Framework Overview. Figure 2 illustrates the overall architecture of our model. Our model is mainly composed of three components, i.e., *multi-task learning module*, *credibility and stance aware module* and *recursive tree*. In specific, we model a rumor conversation tree as a bottom-up recursive tree. Before recursive aggregation, we introduce an extra multi-task learning module to generate the initial stance feature of nodes on the recursive tree. The module achieves stance classification via MTL, which can enhance the stance representation. During the bottom-up recursion on the recursive tree, if a non-leaf node is found, all the features of its child nodes are aggregated by the credibility and stance aware module. Finally, we verify the rumor at the root node.

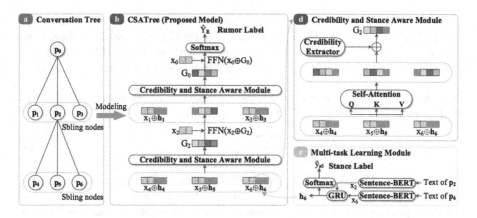

Fig. 2. The overview of CSATree. The textural content of p_* is transformed to the sentence embedding x_* by Sentence-BERT. h_* is the stance representation generated by the multi-task learning module. The aggregation process of G_i is detailed in Sect. 3.2.

Multi-task Learning Module. Now, we detail the multi-task learning module. The module can receive a sentence pair to obtain the initial stance feature of each node towards its parent node on the recursive tree. Moreover, we perform the stance classification task on the module to enhance the stance representation.

We first use Sentence-BERT [14] to obtain the sentence embedding of each tweet in the conversation tree. As such, this transforms the textural content of $\{p_0, p_1, ..., p_n\}$ to $\{x_0, x_1, ..., x_n\}$. Let $<x_j, x_i>$ denote a sentence pair, where their relationship is that x_j responds to x_i. We feed $<x_j, x_i>$ into a GRU [2] to obtain the feature h_j:

$$h_j = \mathrm{GRU}(x_j, x_i) \tag{1}$$

where x_j is the input vector of the GRU and x_i is the hidden vector of the GRU.

In particular, for the stance classification task, a softmax layer after the GRU is used to produce the stance prediction for the j-th tweet:

$$\hat{y}_{sj} = \mathrm{softmax}(W_S^T h_j + b_S) \tag{2}$$

where $W_S \in \mathbb{R}^{d_{model} \times 4}$ and $b_S \in \mathbb{R}^{d_{model}}$ are the weight and bias of the softmax layer, and $\hat{y}_{sj} \in \mathbb{R}^4$ is the predicted stance distribution.

Credibility and Stance Aware Module. Let $X(i) = \{x_i, x_j, ..., x_k\}$ denote a set of sentence vectors of a substree, where $x_j, ..., x_k$ are all sibling nodes that directly respond to x_i. For any leaf node x_t in $X(i)$, we concatenate x_t and h_t as the initial feature of the t-th tweet, denoted as H_t. After initializing the features, we aggregate the features from sibling nodes to capture their global semantics and stance information. We can generalize the aggregation process of the sbutree $X(i)$ with the following formula:

$$G_i = O_{* \in X(i) \wedge * \neq i} H_* \tag{3}$$

where $G_i \in \mathbb{R}^{2d_{model}}$ is the aggregated feature, and O is a series of operators acting on the child feature H_*. In this work, we investigate three operations: *Sum*, *Self Attention*, and *Credibility-weighted Self Attention*. These three operations correspond to three models called STree, SATree, and CSATree, respectively.

Sum. Inspired by [7], we use the child-sum operation, which directly sums all the features of $\{x_j, ..., x_k\}$, i.e., $O = \sum$. Therefore

$$G_i = \sum\nolimits_{* \in X(i) \wedge * \neq i} H_* \tag{4}$$

Self Attention. We use a multi-head self-attention (MHA) mechanism for the features of sibling nodes and aggregate them into a feature representation. The feature representation attended to some other long retweets would reduce the perplexity of short retweets. The aggregation process is as below:

$$[\tilde{H}_j; ...; \tilde{H}_k] = \text{MHA}([H_j; ...; H_k]), \quad G_i = \sum\nolimits_{* \in X(i) \wedge * \neq i} \tilde{H}_* \tag{5}$$

where $\text{MHA}(\cdot)$ refers to the multi-head attention [15] and the query, key, and value vectors of MHA all come from $[H_j; ...; H_k]$.

Credibility-weighted Self Attention. We utilize another self-attention mechanism to determine node credibility. We select salient social aspect characteristics to represent the credibility of a tweet: (1) posting user is verified or not; (2) the number of followers of the posting user; (3) the number of friends of the posting user; (4) the number of likes of the tweet. We generate a four-dimensional credibility vector for every node. We add a self-attention layer on the basis of *Self Attention*, feed the credibility vectors of sibling nodes into the layer, and the calculated attention weights matrix is denoted as $\alpha \in \mathbb{R}^{(|X(i)|-1) \times (|X(i)|-1)}$. Then we aggregate the credibility-weighted features of the sibling nodes:

$$[\hat{H}_j; ...; \hat{H}_k] = \alpha[\tilde{H}_j; ...; \tilde{H}_k], \quad G_i = \sum\nolimits_{* \in X(i) \wedge * \neq i} \hat{H}_* \tag{6}$$

FFN Unit on Recursive Tree. Next, we concatenate the feature x_i and G_i, and feed it into a FFN layer to capture the global semantics and stance information of the subtree $X(i)$. FFN refers to the feed forward network [15]. M_i is the representation of $X(i)$:

$$M_i = \text{FFN}(x_i \oplus G_i) \tag{7}$$

Output Layer on Recursive Tree. Lastly, we add a softmax layer at the root node to predict the veracity distribution over rumor classes:

$$\hat{Y}_R = \text{softmax}(W_R^T M_0 + b_R) \tag{8}$$

where $W_R \in \mathbb{R}^{2d_{model} \times 3}$ and $b_R \in \mathbb{R}^{2d_{model}}$ are the weight and bias of the softmax layer, and $\hat{Y}_R \in \mathbb{R}^3$ is the predicted rumor distribution.

3.3 Jointly Training Two Tasks

Due to the interrelation between the tweet stances and the rumor veracity in a conversation, we adopt a multi-task learning loss function inspired by a work in the field of computer vision [4]. This loss function L can automatically learn a relative weighting between two tasks:

$$L_{stance} = -\frac{1}{n} \sum_{i=1}^{n} y_{si} \log \hat{y}_{si} \qquad (9)$$

$$L_{rumor} = -Y_R \log \hat{Y}_R \qquad (10)$$

$$L = \frac{1}{2\sigma_1^2} L_{stance} + \frac{1}{2\sigma_2^2} L_{rumor} + \log \sigma_1 \sigma_2 \qquad (11)$$

where L_{stance} is the cross-entropy loss of the stance classification task, y_{si} is the ground-truth label of the i-th tweet, and $\hat{y}_{si}$ is the predicted stance distribution of the i-th tweet. L_{rumor} is the cross-entropy loss of the rumor verification task, Y_R is the ground-truth label of the rumor, and $\hat{Y}_R$ is the predicted distribution over rumor classes. σ_1 and σ_2 are two learnable parameters.

4 Experiments

In this section, we report the experimental results of the proposed approach. Firstly, we evaluate its superiority on rumor verification task in Sect. 4.2, followed by its superiority on stance classification task in Sect. 4.3. Then, in Sect. 4.4 and Sect. 4.5, we conduct an ablation study and a case study to show the effect of our model.

4.1 Experiment Setting

Datasets. We conduct experiments on two datasets: SemEval-2017 and PHEME.

- **SemEval-2017** [3] comes from SemEval-2017 Task 8 competition. It contains 325 rumors, of which a total of 5,568 tweets. It has veracity annotation for each rumor and stance annotation for each tweet. This dataset has been split into training, development, and testing sets.
- **PHEME** [20] contains 2,402 rumors, of which a total of 105,354 tweets related to nine events. It has veracity annotation for each rumor. We follow the previous works [6,17,18] to perform leave-one-event-out (LOEO) cross-validation: for each event, all its rumors are used for testing, and the rumors of the remaining events are used for training.

Table 1 provides the statistics of the two datasets. SemEval-2017 has rumor labels and stance labels, while PHEME only has rumor labels. Hence, we use SemEval-2017 for evaluation of stance classification and rumor verification tasks, and PHEME for evaluation of rumor verification task, same as [17,18].

Table 1. Statistics of two datasets.

Dataset	#Rumors	#Tweets	Rumor Veracity Labels			Stance Labels			
			#True	#False	#Unverified	#Support	#Deny	#Query	#Comment
SemEval-2017	325	5,568	145	74	106	1,004	415	464	3,685
PHEME	2,402	105,354	1,067	638	697	–	–	–	–

Implementation Details. We use the pre-trained Sentence-BERT$_{base}$ model to obtain the sentence representations of tweets, so our model dimension d_{model} is 768. The number of heads of the MHA layer is 8. In the training procedure of our proposed models, we use the Adam optimizer. We set the learning rate as 1e−4 and the weight decay coefficient as 1e−2. We train our models for 50 epochs.

Baselines. We compare our approaches with several state-of-the-art baselines: *TD-RvNN* [11], *BranchLSTM* [6], *BranchLSTM+NileTMRG* [6], *MTL2 (Veracity+Stance)* [6], *Hierarchical GCN-RNN* [17], *Hierarchical PSV* [17], *TreeLSTM* [7], *HiTPLAN* [5], *Hierarchical TFM* [18], and *Coupled Hierarchical TFM* [18]. All baselines are briefly introduced in Sect. 2, and more details about the mentioned methods could be found in the referenced paper.

For the approaches we proposed, we compare several variants of the proposed approaches according the way to aggregate features, i.e., **STree**, **SATree**, and **CSATree**, in which STree acts *Sum* operation to aggregate features, SATree acts *Self Attention* operation to aggregate features, and CSATree acts *Credibility-weighted Self Attention* operation to aggregate features.

4.2   Results of Rumor Verification

Table 2 shows the experimental results of the rumor verification task. We can see that: (1) In the single-task case, our models outperform all the compared single-task baselines on macro-averaged F1 and accuracy metrics. Moreover, our models perform better than TD-RvNN and TreeLSTM, which shows the effectiveness of our proposed recursive tree; (2) In the multi-task case, our models outperform the current best stance-aware model on two metrics and CSATree is the best performer, improving the performance by around 9%. Besides, our multi-task approaches perform better than our single-task approaches, which demonstrates the effective auxiliary of our stance classification task for our rumor verification task; (3) For the three approaches we proposed, SATree achieves better performance than STree, which indicates the effectiveness of the self-attention mechanism in the credibility and stance aware module. Meanwhile, CSATree outperforms SATree, which shows that CSATree can model the conversation tree more effectively than our other models by attending to node credibility; (4) The performance on PHEME is worse than that on SemEval-2017. Concerning the ways of splitting training and testing sets, PHEME is split by events, while SemEval-2017 is split randomly. Domains of different events may be different, which hurts the performance on PHEME.

Table 2. Results of rumor verification. Single-Task means that there is no supervised learning for stance labels.

Setting	Method	SemEval-2017		PHEME	
		Macro-F1	Accuracy	Macro-F1	Accuracy
Single-task	BranchLSTM	0.491	0.500	0.259	0.314
	TD-RvNN	0.509	0.536	0.264	0.341
	Hierarchical GCN-RNN	0.540	0.536	0.317	0.356
	TreeLSTM	0.567	0.571	0.349	0.365
	HiTPLAN	0.581	0.571	0.361	0.438
	Hierarchical TFM	0.592	0.607	0.372	0.441
	STree	0.617	0.607	0.427	0.455
	SATree	0.651	0.643	0.438	0.478
	CSATree	**0.666**	**0.679**	**0.483**	**0.515**
Multi-task	BranchLSTM+NileTMRG	0.539	0.570	0.297	0.360
	MTL2 (Veracity+Stance)	0.558	0.571	0.318	0.357
	Hierarchical PSV	0.588	0.643	0.333	0.361
	TreeLSTM-Multitask	0.638	0.643	-	-
	Coupled Hierarchical TFM	0.680	0.678	0.396	0.466
	STree	0.681	0.679	0.492	0.514
	SATree	0.711	0.714	0.520	0.537
	CSATree	**0.747**	**0.750**	**0.549**	**0.570**

4.3 Results of Stance Classification

Table 3. Results of stance classification on SemEval-2017 dataset.

Method	Macro-F1	Accuracy
SVM	0.470	0.795
BranchLSTM	0.434	0.784
TemporalAttention	0.482	**0.820**
Conversational-GCN	0.499	0.751
Hierarchical TFM	0.509	0.763
BERT-GRU	**0.524**	0.770

Stance information provides important clues for rumor verification in CSATree. To enhance the stance representation of our model, we perform stance classification task on the BERT-GRU of the multi-task learning module. We compare our *BERT-GRU* with several state-of-the-art baselines: *SVM* [13] is a machine learning method. *TemporalAttention* [16] is a CNN-LSTM model to learn the sequence features to classify stances. *Conversational-GCN* [17] and *Hierarchical TFM* [17], are part of Hierarchical GCN-RNN and Coupled Hierarchical TFM respectively. The experimental results are shown in Table 3. We can observe that our BERT-GRU performs better than all baselines on macro-averaged F1 metric, outperforming Hierarchical TFM by 1.5%. Therefore, our BERT-GRU in the multi-task learning module has a strong capability for stance representation.

4.4 Ablation Study

Table 4. Ablation study.

Setting	Method	SemEval-2017		PHEME	
		Macro-F1	Accuracy	Macro-F1	Accuracy
Single-Task	CSATree	**0.666**	**0.679**	**0.483**	**0.515**
	-Stance	0.604	0.607	0.449	0.487
	-Attention	0.638	0.643	0.461	0.488
Multi-Task	CSATree	**0.747**	**0.750**	**0.549**	**0.570**
	-Attention	0.678	0.679	0.503	0.521

Effect of Stance Feature. To evaluate the importance of stance feature and show the effect of our multi-task learning module, we remove the multi-task learning module (i.e., -Stance), so CSATree is modified to a text-based recursive tree model. The experimental results on two datasets are shown in Table 4. We can see that "-Stance" performs worse than CSATree, which indicates that our multi-task learning module is essential to capture the stance information.

Effect of Attention Mechanism. To examine the effect of the self-attention mechanism, we remove the self-attention mechanism that captures text and stance features between sibling nodes in CSATree (i.e., -Attention), so Eq. 6 is modified to $[\hat{H}_j; ...; \hat{H}_k] = \alpha[H_j; ...; H_k]$. As shown in Table 4, "-Attention" hurts the performance. Also, Table 2 shows that SATree performs better than STree. The above suggests that utilizing self-attention mechanism between sibling nodes is crucial to boost the performance of rumor verification.

4.5 Case Study

Figure 3 presents a conversation correctly classified as a false rumor by CSATree. We can observe that our model learns higher attention weights from retweets that hold *deny* and *query* stances, which helps correctly classify this rumor. In addition, our model generates higher credibility to the tweets of the posting user with more followers and friends, or the tweets with more likes, which helps to propagate credible and authentic signals.

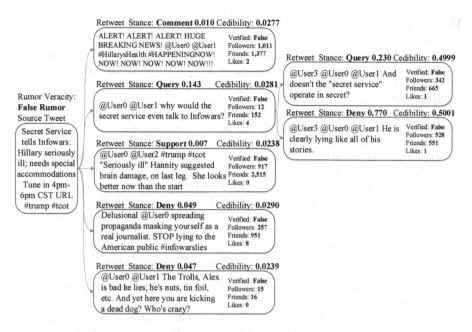

Fig. 3. A sample on testing sets of SemEval-2017 correctly classified as a false rumor by CSATree. We show the important tweets and omit other tweets in the conversation.

5   Conclusion

In this paper, we propose CSATree, a recursive tree model for rumor verification. To address the limitations of short retweets and fraud nodes, we employ a multi-head self-attention mechanism to capture the rich stance and semantic information between sibling nodes, and explore node credibility to enhance the aggregated representation of the rumor. We propose a multi-task learning approach that performs stance classification task and rumor verification task to incorporate stance-aware knowledge into CSATree. Experimental results on two public datasets demonstrate that CSATree effectively models the conversation tree and further improves the performance of rumor verification.

Acknowledgment. This work is supported by the National Key R&D Program of China under Grants (No. 2018YFB0204300).

References

1. Chen, Y., Hu, L., Sui, J.: Text-based fusion neural network for rumor detection. In: Douligeris, C., Karagiannis, D., Apostolou, D. (eds.) KSEM 2019. LNCS (LNAI), vol. 11776, pp. 105–109. Springer, Cham (2019). https://doi.org/10.1007/978-3-030-29563-9_11
2. Cho, K., Van Merriënboer, B., Bahdanau, D., Bengio, Y.: On the properties of neural machine translation: encoder-decoder approaches. arXiv preprint arXiv:1409.1259 (2014)
3. Derczynski, L., Bontcheva, K., Liakata, M., Procter, R., Hoi, G.W.S., Zubiaga, A.: Semeval-2017 task 8: Rumoureval: determining rumour veracity and support for rumours. arXiv preprint arXiv:1704.05972 (2017)
4. Kendall, A., Gal, Y., Cipolla, R.: Multi-task learning using uncertainty to weigh losses for scene geometry and semantics. In: Proceedings of the IEEE Conference on Computer Vision and Pattern Recognition, pp. 7482–7491 (2018)
5. Khoo, L.M.S., Chieu, H.L., Qian, Z., Jiang, J.: Interpretable rumor detection in microblogs by attending to user interactions. In: Proceedings of the AAAI Conference on Artificial Intelligence, vol. 34, pp. 8783–8790 (2020)
6. Kochkina, E., Liakata, M., Zubiaga, A.: All-in-one: multi-task learning for rumour verification. arXiv preprint arXiv:1806.03713 (2018)
7. Kumar, S., Carley, K.M.: Tree LSTMS with convolution units to predict stance and rumor veracity in social media conversations. In: Proceedings of the 57th Annual Meeting of the Association for Computational Linguistics, pp. 5047–5058 (2019)
8. Li, Q., Zhang, Q., Si, L.: Rumor detection by exploiting user credibility information, attention and multi-task learning. In: Proceedings of the 57th Annual Meeting of the Association for Computational Linguistics, pp. 1173–1179 (2019)
9. Ma, J., Gao, W.: Debunking rumors on twitter with tree transformer. In: ACL (2020)
10. Ma, J., Gao, W., Wong, K.F.: Detect rumor and stance jointly by neural multi-task learning. In: Companion Proceedings of the the Web Conference 2018, pp. 585–593 (2018)
11. Ma, J., Gao, W., Wong, K.F.: Rumor detection on twitter with tree-structured recursive neural networks. Association for Computational Linguistics (2018)
12. Mendoza, M., Poblete, B., Castillo, C.: Twitter under crisis: can we trust what we RT? In: Proceedings of the First Workshop on Social Media Analytics, pp. 71–79 (2010)
13. Pamungkas, E.W., Basile, V., Patti, V.: Stance classification for rumour analysis in twitter: Exploiting affective information and conversation structure. arXiv preprint arXiv:1901.01911 (2019)
14. Reimers, N., Gurevych, I.: Sentence-bert: sentence embeddings using siamese bert-networks. arXiv preprint arXiv:1908.10084 (2019)
15. Vaswani, A., et al.: Attention is all you need. arXiv preprint arXiv:1706.03762 (2017)
16. Veyseh, A.P.B., Ebrahimi, J., Dou, D., Lowd, D.: A temporal attentional model for rumor stance classification. In: Proceedings of the 2017 ACM on Conference on Information and Knowledge Management, pp. 2335–2338 (2017)
17. Wei, P., Xu, N., Mao, W.: Modeling conversation structure and temporal dynamics for jointly predicting rumor stance and veracity. arXiv preprint arXiv:1909.08211 (2019)

18. Yu, J., Jiang, J., Khoo, L.M.S., Chieu, H.L., Xia, R.: Coupled hierarchical transformer for stance-aware rumor verification in social media conversations. Association for Computational Linguistics (2020)
19. Zubiaga, A., Aker, A., Bontcheva, K., Liakata, M., Procter, R.: Detection and resolution of rumours in social media: a survey. ACM Comput. Surv. (CSUR) **51**(2), 1–36 (2018)
20. Zubiaga, A., Liakata, M., Procter, R., Wong Sak Hoi, G., Tolmie, P.: Analysing how people orient to and spread rumours in social media by looking at conversational threads. PloS One **11**(3), e0150989 (2016)

Aspect and Opinion Terms Co-extraction Using Position-Aware Attention and Auxiliary Labels

Chao Liu[1,2], Xintong Wei[1,2], Min Yu[1,2(✉)], Gang Li[3], Xiangmei Ma[1,2], Jianguo Jiang[1,2], and Weiqing Huang[1]

[1] Institute of Information Engineering, Chinese Academy of Sciences, Beijing, China
`yumin@iie.ac.cn`
[2] School of Cyber Security, University of Chinese Academy of Sciences, Beijing, China
[3] School of Information Technology, Deakin University, Geelong, Australia

Abstract. Aspect and opinion terms co-extraction is to extract what target is being discussed from the sentences and know what kind of emotion this target has. There are many studies about this task. To obtain the important context in the input sentences and improve the model's performance, recent studies use the attention mechanism. But the attention mechanism used in them does not take the distance into account when calculating the weight of words and ignores the important influence of their neighboring words. To solve this problem, we introduce an **A**spect and **O**pinion Terms Co-**E**xtraction model, AOExtractor, that utilizes position-aware attention to extract the local context features for each word from their neighboring words and utilizes BERT to extract the global context features. At the same time, auxiliary labels are introduced to solve the problem of subword tokenization imposed by BERT. Finally, we concatenate the local and global context features to extract aspect and opinion terms simultaneously. The experimental results on four SemEval datasets prove the effectiveness of AOExtractor. Compared with the baseline, our model improves F1 by about 2–5%.

Keywords: Position-aware attention · Auxiliary labels · Aspect term extraction · Opinion term extraction · Natural Language Processing

1 Introduction

With the increasing frequency of online communication, it is significant to know what target people are discussing and what kind of emotion this target has. This not only can be used for public opinion analysis to maintain social stability but also can be used for personalized product recommendation to achieve a win-win goal for businesses and consumers. At the same time, it can also be used in many other fields, such as election support and privacy protection [1]. What target people are discussing corresponds to the aspect terms in the sentences,

© Springer Nature Switzerland AG 2021
H. Qiu et al. (Eds.): KSEM 2021, LNAI 12817, pp. 162–173, 2021.
https://doi.org/10.1007/978-3-030-82153-1_14

and what kind of emotion this target has corresponds to the opinion terms. Aspect and opinion terms co-extraction can extract aspect terms and opinion terms simultaneously, so this task has an important role.

Aspect terms refer to the words which describe the attributes and features of entities, and opinion terms refer to the emotional words corresponding to the aspect terms and with subjective emotional expression [2]. For example, in the sentence "*The staff is accomodating, the food is absolutely delicious and the place is lovely*", the aspect terms are *staff, food* and *place*, and the opinion terms are *accomodating, delicious* and *lovely*. Our task aims to extract them simultaneously. There are many studies about the aspect or opinion terms extraction, and many methods have been proposed. These methods can be parted into three types: rule-based methods [3–5], feature engineering-based methods [6,7] and deep learning-based methods. The deep learning-based methods are the mainstream methods at present. For example, History Attention and Selective Transformation model (HAST) [8] captures important information from the input with attention mechanism, and constructs truncated history attention to extract opinion terms. Terms extraction tasks can be regarded as sequence labeling tasks, when words predict their labels, the neighboring words are important for them. Attention mechanism used in many existing methods, such as HAST, does not take the distance into account when calculating the weight of words, so they cannot pay more attention to the neighbors of each word.

In this paper, we propose a co-extraction model AOExtractor for aspect and opinion terms co-extraction task, which utilizes position-aware attention and BERT with auxiliary labels to obtain the local and global context features, and then utilizes the local and global context features to extract aspect and opinion terms simultaneously. First, we construct auxiliary labels to solve the problem of subword tokenization imposed by BERT and utilize BERT model as our embedding layer to obtain token-level representations, and then we utilize the representations as the global context features. Then, we utilize position-aware attention to extract local context features for each word from their neighboring words. Finally, we concatenate the global and local context features to co-extract aspect and opinion terms. Our contributions include:

1) We propose a co-extraction model, AOExtractor, which can extract the local and global context features to make full use of the input information to co-extract aspect and opinion terms.
2) We use position-aware attention and BERT with auxiliary labels to obtain the local and global context features, respectively. Position-aware attention can take the distance into account and extract the local context features from the neighboring words of each word. Auxiliary labels can solve the problem of subword tokenization imposed by BERT.
3) The experimental results on four SemEval datasets prove the effectiveness of AOExtractor. Compared with the baseline, our model improves F1 by about 2–5%.

The rest of the organizational structure of our paper is as follows: we introduce the previous work related to our task in Sect. 2. In Sect. 3, the methodology of AOExtractor is introduced. We analyze the experiment results of AOExtractor in Sect. 4. In Sect. 5, the conclusion is introduced.

2 Related Work

With the wide application of aspect and opinion terms in many fields, more and more aspect and opinion terms extraction methods have been proposed in recent years. According to the technology they use, existing methods can be parted into the following three types [9].

The first type is the rule-based methods, they manually design rules by analyzing the dependency structure and syntactic information of sentences, and then iteratively extract terms. For example, Hu and Liu [3] propose a method which can extract aspect terms with association mining technology and opinion terms with the extracting synonyms/antonyms method in WordNet. The second type is the feature engineering-based methods, they predict the labels of the input words by using the syntax and language information in the marked annotation corpus. For example, Li et al. [6] propose a machine learning framework based on the conditional random fields to solve this problem, and Jin and Ho [7] utilize hidden markov model to solve this problem.

The third type is the deep learning-based methods. The above two types of methods depend on the quality of the rules and require the manual design of complex feature engineering, so they are no longer suitable for today's tasks. Deep learning-based methods can solve the above-mentioned problems and become the mainstream method today. They usually use recurrent neural network [10], recursive neural network [11], convolution neural network [12], attention model [9], and other methods to extract terms. For example, Wang et al. [9] co-extract aspect and opinion terms by constructing pairs of attention. Li et al. [8] use LSTM and attention mechanism to construct truncated history attention to extract aspect terms. Li et al. [13] propose a novel unified model, and use the original opinion-enhanced target word detection component to extract opinion terms. Zhao et al. [2] use LSTM and BERT to extract aspect and opinion terms in pairs. Many deep learning-based methods use the attention mechanism to extract terms. Attention mechanism is a solution to solve the problem by imitating human attention and proposed by Treisman and Gelade [14]. With attention mechanism, the model can improve its performance by capturing important context in the input sentences.

From the paper [15], we know that when predicting the label of a word, the closer words contribute more, and the farther words contribute less. As the example in Sect. 1, *the, is* and *accomodating* have a positive effect on the prediction of the label of *staff*, but the farther words have no key effect. However, in many existing terms extraction methods, the attention mechanism they use does not take the distance into account and ignores the important influence of their neighboring words when predicting the label of each word. To solve this problem, we introduce position-aware attention that can make full use of the relative position information between words to extract the local context features of input sentences. The ablation study in Sect. 4.3 proves the effectiveness of position-aware attention.

3   Methodology

In this section, we introduce the implementation details of AOExtractor. First, we present the architecture of AOExtractor and introduce the problem definition and auxiliary labels. Then, we detail the BERT embedding layer and position-aware attention. Finally, we introduce the aspect and opinion terms extractor.

3.1   An Overview of AOExtractor

The architecture of AOExtractor is illustrated in Fig. 1. AOExtractor model consists of input, BERT embedding layer, position-aware attention and aspect and opinion terms extractor. In AOExtractor, the input is the input tokens and the output is the labels with auxiliary labels. The whole architecture includes three parts. The first part corresponds to the lower left part of Fig. 1. This part obtains the global context features with BERT (BERT-Global) so that the model can get the meaning of the different words in different sentences. The second part corresponds to the right part of Fig. 1. BERT embedding layer (BERT-Local) converts the input into vectors. Then, we use the position-aware attention to extract the local context features. The third part is the aspect and opinion terms extractor. To utilize the local and global context features, we concatenate them as the input of the extractor. In Fig. 1, $\{t_1, t_2, \ldots, t_n\}$ are the input tokens, t_1 is the [CLS] token, and t_n is the [SEP] token.

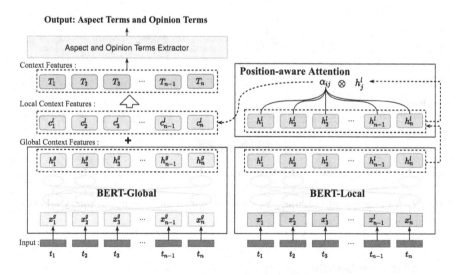

Fig. 1. The architecture of AOExtractor.

3.2   Problem Definition and Auxiliary Labels

Problem Definition. For a given sentence $S = \{w_1, w_2, w_3, \cdots, w_n\}$ with length n, our task is to extract all aspect terms $AT = \{at_1, at_2, \cdots, at_m\}$ and opinion terms $OT = \{ot_1, ot_2, \cdots, ot_t\}$ in sentence S at the same time, where m and t are not necessarily equal.

Auxiliary Labels. Aspect and opinion terms co-extraction can be regarded as a sequence labeling task, and the task often uses the BIO tagging scheme. We define seven different labels for our task, including five BIO labels: *B-AT* (beginning of AT), *I-AT* (inside of AT), *B-OT* (beginning of OT), *I-OT* (inside of OT) and O(others), and two special tokens of BERT tokenizer: [CLS] (beginning of the input tokens) and [SEP] (ending of the input tokens). Since we utilize BERT model as our embedding layer, BERT will tokenize input words into subwords as the input tokens, causing the problem of subword tokenization. If the subwords are not processed, it will cause the problem of mismatch between input tokens and output labels. As shown in Fig. 2. the opinion word *'lackluster'* is tokenized into three subwords: *'lack'*, *'##lus'* and *'##ter'*, the common word *'refund'* is tokenized into two subwords: *'ref'* and *'##und'*. Therefore, we introduce two auxiliary labels, X and Y, to handle the subwords. We keep the original label of the word for its first subword, and use the auxiliary label X to represent other subwords that belong to aspect terms or opinion terms, and use the auxiliary label Y to represent other subwords that are neither aspect terms nor opinion terms. Therefore, let $L = \{O, B\text{-}AT, I\text{-}AT, B\text{-}OT, I\text{-}OT\} \bigcup \{X, Y\} \bigcup \{[CLS], [SEP]\}$. After terms extraction, each token is classified as $y_i \in L$.

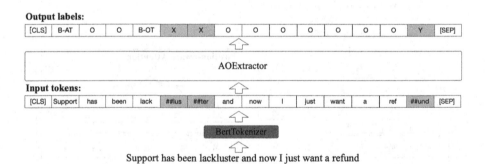

Fig. 2. An example of handling subwords tokenization by using auxiliary labels.

3.3   BERT Embedding Layer

The BERT model can not only capture long-term dependency in the input words, but also learn sufficient contextualized information, so we use the BERT model as our embedding layer and use it to obtain the hidden representation for each token. First, we concatenate the [CLS] token, the input tokens and the [SEP] token to generate input token sequences. Then, by summing the token, position, and segment embeddings, token t_i in the input token sequences is converted into input vector $\mathbf{x}_i$. The input vector $\mathbf{x}_i$ used to obtain global context features and local context features are regarded as $\mathbf{x}_i^g$ and $\mathbf{x}_i^l$, respectively. Finally, we utilize the BERT model to obtain the hidden representation for token t_i:

$$\mathbf{h}_i^g = BERT(\mathbf{x}_i^g) \tag{1}$$

$$\mathbf{h}_i^l = BERT(\mathbf{x}_i^l) \tag{2}$$

where $\mathbf{h}_i^l$ and $\mathbf{h}_i^g$ are the hidden representation of token t_i. The $\mathbf{h}_i^g$ of all tokens constitutes the global context features $\mathbf{h}^g$, and the $\mathbf{h}_i^l$ will be used in Sect. 3.4 to extract local context features.

3.4 Position-Aware Attention

Global context features can help AOExtractor better understand the dependency relationship between the input words at the sentence level, and get the meaning of the different words in different sentences. In terms extraction tasks, the neighboring words are important for each word to predict its label, which indicates that the closer words contribute more. In existing terms extraction methods, when calculating the weights of words, the attention mechanism they use does not take the distance into account, and ignores the influence of relative position information. Therefore, we introduce the position-aware attention, which can pay more attention to the neighboring words of a word, and we use it to obtain the local context features based on the BERT embedding layer. For position i, we first compute the weight of token t_j relative to token t_i:

$$\alpha_{ij} = \frac{exp(f(h_i^l, h_j^l))}{\sum_{t=1}^{n} exp(f(h_i^l, h_t^l))} \tag{3}$$

where n is the length of the input tokens, and $f(h_i^l, h_j^l)$ is the score function that can take the position information into account while calculating the weight of tokens. The score function is:

$$f(h_i^l, h_j^l) = d(t_i, t_j)(W_s[h_i^l, h_j^l] + b_s)v_s^T \tag{4}$$

where W_s, b_s and v_s^T are weight matrix. $d(t_i, t_j)$ calculates the weight decay rate for token t_j, which means that the farther the token t_j is, the smaller its weight will be. $d(t_i, t_j)$ is:

$$d(t_i, t_j) = \frac{1}{log_2(d+2)} \tag{5}$$

where d is the distance between token t_i and token t_j. Finally, we make a weighted sum of the hidden representations and obtain the context vector $\mathbf{c}_i^l$

of the token t_i, as shown in Eq. 6. Because the local context features represent the word and the context around the word, all context vector $\mathbf{c}_i^l$ constitutes the local context features $\mathbf{c}^l$.

$$\mathbf{c}_i^l = \sum_{j=1}^{n} \alpha_{ij} \mathbf{h}_j^l \tag{6}$$

3.5   Aspect and Opinion Terms Extractor

To utilize the global and local context features simultaneously, we concatenate them as the context features T_i of token t_i. And $T_i = [h_i^g; c_i^l]$, where h_i^g and c_i^l are the global and local context features of token t_i respectively. Our task can be regarded as a sequence labeling task. After obtaining the context features of tokens, we perform the classification for each token t_i:

$$y_i = \frac{exp(T_i)}{\sum_{k=1}^{l} exp(T_k)} \tag{7}$$

where y_i represents the label that the token t_i belongs to and l is the number of labels. In AOExtractor, we use cross-entropy as our loss function.

4   Experiments and Discussion

In this section, we introduce our datasets, hyperparameter, baselines, and the evaluation metric used in our experiment. And we analyze the results of our experiments and discuss the effectiveness of AOExtractor.

4.1   Experiments Settings

Dataset. We evaluate AOExtractor on 14lap, 14res, 15res, and 16res datasets, which are all from the laptop and restaurant domains of SemEval Challenges [16–18]. These four datasets are provided by the paper [19], where the aspect terms and opinion terms are labeled. It should be noted that a sentence may include multiple aspect terms and opinion terms. The following table shows the details of datasets (Table 1).

Table 1. Details of datasets. (#sen, #at, and #ot represent the number of input sentences, aspect terms, and opinion terms, respectively.)

Dataset	14lap			14res			15res			16res		
	#sen	#at	#ot	#sen	#at	#ot	#sen	#at	#ot	#sen	#at	#ot
Train	920	1283	1265	1300	2079	2145	593	834	923	842	1183	1289
Valid	228	317	337	323	530	524	148	225	238	210	291	316
Test	339	475	490	496	849	862	318	426	455	320	444	465

Hyperparameter Settings. AOExtractor is implemented with Pytorch. For the BERT embedding layer, we use the $BERT_{base}$ model[1]. The dimension of the hidden layer is 768, the number of heads of the multi-head attention mechanism is 12, and the layer number of transformer is 12. We use cross-entropy as our loss function and use AdamW optimizer. Other parameters are: $learning\_rate=2e\text{-}5$, $max\_sequence\_length=80$, $batch\_size=8$, $epoch=50$.

Baselines. To prove the effectiveness of AOExtractor, we compare AOExtractor with the following baseline models, and all of them use the same datasets as our experiment. Except for the results of BERT-BASE and HAST, other results are all from the published papers.

- **BERT-BASE** [20]: A basic BERT model with the same parameters as our model, and we adapt it to our task.
- **RINANTE** [21]: An approach that uses automatically mined rules to improve the accuracy of aspect and opinion terms extraction.
- **HAST** [8]: A framework that can extract aspect terms more accurately by using the aspect detection history and opinion summary.
- **Li-unified-R** [13]: A model that can adapt their original opinion-enhanced target word detection component to only extract opinion terms, and is a variant of Li-unified, where Li-unified is a novel unified model which can extract aspect terms and classify sentiment.
- **Peng H et al.** [19]: A two-stage model, which can extract aspects and opinion terms, and can also classify the aspect term sentiment.

Evaluation Metric. F1 is determined by the recall and the precision and can measure the performance of AOExtractor, so we use F1 as our evaluation metric. F1 is also the most commonly used evaluation metric on aspect and opinion terms extraction tasks.

4.2   Results and Discussion

The F1 of all baseline models and AOExtractor is shown in Table 2. In Table 2, AT represents the F1 of aspect terms extraction and OT represents the F1 of opinion terms extraction. AOExtractor-D means that two independent BERT embedding layers are used, and AOExtractor-S means that AOExtractor obtains the local and global context features sharing a BERT embedding layer.

As we can see from Table 2, AOExtractor has achieved the best results in all datasets, which proves the effectiveness of AOExtractor in aspect and opinion extraction tasks. Besides, we have the following observations. Firstly, the BERT-BASE model performs worst among all these methods. According to our ablation study, the main reason is the subword tokenization imposed by BERT, which leads to the mismatch between the input tokens and the output labels. Secondly,

---

[1] https://github.com/huggingface/pytorch-transformers.

Table 2. The performances (F1:%) of AOExtractor and all baselines.

Model	14lap		14res		15res		16res	
	AT	OT	AT	OT	AT	OT	AT	OT
BERT-BASE	60.46	57.05	64.04	62.60	56.54	56.43	62.68	62.26
RINANTE	60.50	69.60	73.00	76.29	60.39	65.70	60.60	54.10
HAST	79.17	–	82.12	–	78.59	–	81.04	–
Li-unified-R	–	75.70	–	82.13	–	77.44	–	83.16
Peng H et al.	–	74.84	–	82.45	–	78.02	–	83.73
AOExtractor-S	**83.96**	**78.84**	86.31	86.70	77.78	79.38	83.71	84.79
AOExtractor-D	83.82	78.48	**87.11**	**87.33**	**81.45**	79.71	**84.38**	**85.66**

on all datasets, the performance of AOExtractor-D is better than or almost equal to the performance of AOExtractor-S. This is because AOExtractor-D uses two independent BERT embedding layers, which will increase the parameters of the model and increase the resource consumption, but it can make our model perform better.

4.3 Ablation Study

AOExtractor includes three important components: position-aware attention (PAA), auxiliary labels (AL) and global context features (GCF). To prove their effectiveness, we conduct an ablation study by introducing three model variants. 'w/o AL' removes the auxiliary labels from the AOExtractor, 'w/o GCF' removes the global context features from the AOExtractor and 'w/o PAA' removes the position-aware attention from the AOExtractor. All experiments in the ablation study use two independent BERT embedding layers.

Table 3. The performance (F1:%) of AOExtractor's variants on four datasets.

Model	14lap		14res		15res		16res	
	AT	OT	AT	OT	AT	OT	AT	OT
AOExtractor	**83.82**	78.48	**87.11**	**87.33**	**81.45**	**79.71**	**84.38**	**85.66**
w/o AL	60.69	55.83	65.54	64.50	58.84	57.98	64.81	66.36
w/o GCF	83.06	79.58	85.79	86.44	79.64	79.59	83.95	84.77
w/o PAA	83.74	77.49	85.77	86.50	79.21	79.26	83.19	84.32

From Table 3, we can first observe that AL is an important component in AOExtractor, because removing it from AOExtractor will cause a serious decrease in F1 on all datasets. The reason is that BERT can cause the problem of subword tokenization, which leads to the problem of mismatch between the input tokens and the output labels during training.

Secondly, we can see that when PAA and GCF are removed from our model, the performance of AOExtractor also drops. The reason is that PAA can effectively extract the local context features around neighboring words, and GCF can extract the global context features in the input sentences to help our model understand the meaning of the different words in different sentences. Their removal leads to the loss of some information, which will have a certain impact on AOExtractor's performance. Besides, BERT-BASE in Table 2 is a basic BERT, which is equivalent to removing PAA component compared to AOExtractor w/o AL, and the results of AOExtractor w/o AL are better than BERT-BASE. The experimental results show that PAA plays an important role.

In addition, we find that on the 14lap dataset, after removing GCF, the performance of OT improves. Opinion terms are generally emotional words that describe aspect terms. Therefore, aspect terms are very important for opinion terms extraction. We guess that in the res datasets, there are some opinion terms and their corresponding aspect terms that are separated by other terms, so the words adjacent to opinion terms are no longer important words. Therefore, the global context features are important for opinion terms extraction on the res datasets.

4.4   Effectiveness of BERT Fine-Tuning in AOExtractor

BERT fine-tuning aims to update and optimize model's parameters during training. To explore the effect of the BERT fine-tuning on our task, we built a comparative experiment, the first group performs BERT fine-tuning during training, and the second group does not perform BERT fine-tuning. The figure below is the comparison results of whether BERT is fine-tuned in AOExtractor. The F1 of the first group is about 10–25% higher than the F1 of the second group. Therefore, it can be seen that the BERT fine-tuning are very important on our task.

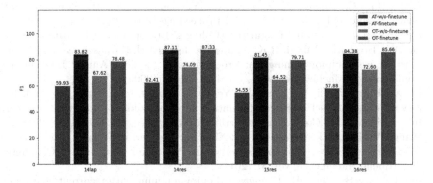

Fig. 3. The comparison results of whether BERT is fine-tuned in AOExtractor.

5 Conclusion

Aspect and opinion terms co-extraction refers to extracting aspect and opinion terms simultaneously. In our paper, we propose a co-extraction model AOExtractor. AOExtractor first utilizes BERT model to extract the global context features and utilizes auxiliary labels to solve the problem of subword tokenization imposed by BERT. Then, AOExtractor uses position-aware attention to obtain the local context features for each word from their neighboring words. Finally, the global and local context features are concatenated to extract aspect and opinion terms. The experimental results prove the effectiveness of AOExtractor. In the future, we will combine our task with aspect term sentiment classification task, and we will also explore the influence of opinion terms on aspect term sentiment classification task.

Acknowledgment. This work is supported by Youth Innovation Promotion Association CAS (No. 2021155).

References

1. Zhu, T., Li, G., Zhou, W., Xiong, P., Yuan, C.: Privacy-preserving topic model for tagging recommender systems. Knowl. Inf. Syst. **46**(1), 33–58 (2016)
2. Zhao, H., Huang, L., Zhang, R., Lu, Q., et al.: Spanmlt: a span-based multi-task learning framework for pair-wise aspect and opinion terms extraction. In: Proceedings of the 58th Annual Meeting of the Association for Computational Linguistics, pp. 3239–3248 (2020)
3. Hu, M., Liu, B.: Mining and summarizing customer reviews. In: Proceedings of the tenth ACM SIGKDD International Conference on Knowledge Discovery and Data Mining, pp. 168–177 (2004)
4. Hu, M., Liu, B.: Mining opinion features in customer reviews. In: AAAI, vol. 4, pp. 755–760 (2004)
5. Qiu, G., Liu, B., Bu, J., Chen, C.: Opinion word expansion and target extraction through double propagation. Comput. Linguist. **37**(1), 9–27 (2011)
6. Li, F., Han, C., Huang, M., Zhu, X., Xia, Y., Zhang, S., Yu, H.: Structure-aware review mining and summarization. In: Proceedings of the 23rd International Conference on Computational Linguistics (Coling 2010), pp. 653–661 (2010)
7. Jin, W., Ho, H.H., Srihari, R.K.: A novel lexicalized HMM-based learning framework for web opinion mining. In: Proceedings of the 26th Annual International Conference on Machine Learning, vol. 10. Citeseer (2009)
8. Li, X., Bing, L., Li, P., Lam, W., Yang, Z.: Aspect term extraction with history attention and selective transformation. In: Proceedings of the Twenty-Seventh International Joint Conference on Artificial Intelligence, pp. 4194–4200 (2018)
9. Wang, W., Pan, S.J., Dahlmeier, D., Xiao, X.: Coupled multi-layer attentions for co-extraction of aspect and opinion terms. In: Proceedings of the AAAI Conference on Artificial Intelligence, vol. 31 (2017)
10. Liu, P., Joty, S., Meng, H.: Fine-grained opinion mining with recurrent neural networks and word embeddings. In: Proceedings of the 2015 Conference on Empirical Methods in Natural Language Processing, pp. 1433–1443 (2015)

11. Wang, W., Pan, S.J., Dahlmeier, D., Xiao, X.: Recursive neural conditional random fields for aspect-based sentiment analysis. In: Proceedings of the 2016 Conference on Empirical Methods in Natural Language Processing, pp. 616–626 (2016)

12. Xu, H., Liu, B., Shu, L., Yu, P.S.: Double embeddings and CNN-based sequence labeling for aspect extraction. In: Proceedings of the 56th Annual Meeting of the Association for Computational Linguistics, pp. 592–598 (2018)

13. Li, X., Bing, L., Li, P., Lam, W.: A unified model for opinion target extraction and target sentiment prediction. In: Proceedings of the AAAI Conference on Artificial Intelligence, vol. 33, pp. 6714–6721 (2019)

14. Mnih, V., Heess, N., Graves, A., Kavukcuoglu, K.: Recurrent models of visual attention. In: Annual Conference on Neural Information Processing Systems 2014, Advances in Neural Information Processing Systems, vol. 27, pp. 2204–2212 (2014)

15. Ma, D., Li, S., Wu, F., Xie, X., Wang, H.: Exploring sequence-to-sequence learning in aspect term extraction. In: Proceedings of the 57th Annual Meeting of the Association for Computational Linguistics, pp. 3538–3547 (2019)

16. Pontiki, M., Galanis, D., Pavlopoulos, J., Papageorgiou, H., Androutsopoulos, I., Manandhar, S.: Semeval-2014 task 4: aaspect based sentiment analysis. In: Proceedings of the 8th International Workshop on Semantic Evaluation (SemEval 2014), pp. 27–35 (2014)

17. Pontiki, M., Galanis, D., Papageorgiou, H., Manandhar, S., Androutsopoulos, I.: Semeval-2015 task 12: aspect based sentiment analysis. In: Proceedings of the 9th International Workshop on Semantic Evaluation (SemEval 2015), pp. 486–495 (2015)

18. Pontiki, M., et al.: Semeval-2016 task 5: aspect based sentiment analysis. In: International Workshop on Semantic Evaluation, pp. 19–30 (2016)

19. Peng, H., Xu, L., Bing, L., Huang, F., Lu, W., Si, L.: Knowing what, how and why: a near complete solution for aspect-based sentiment analysis. In: Proceedings of the AAAI Conference on Artificial Intelligence, vol. 34, pp. 8600–8607 (2020)

20. Devlin, J., Chang, M.W., Lee, K., Toutanova, K.: Bert: Pre-training of deep bidirectional transformers for language understanding. In: Proceedings of the 2019 Conference of the North American Chapter of the Association for Computational Linguistics: Human Language Technologies, pp. 4171–4186 (2018)

21. Dai, H., Song, Y.: Neural aspect and opinion term extraction with mined rules as weak supervision, pp. 5268–5277 (2019)

Beyond Laplacian Smoothing
for Semi-supervised Community
Detection

Guoguo Ai[1], Hui Yan[1,2(✉)], Jian Yang[2], and Xin Li[3]

[1] School of Computer Science and Engineering,
Nanjing University of Science and Technology, Nanjing 210094, China
yanhui@njust.edu.cn
[2] The Key Laboratory of Intelligent Perception and Systems for High-Dimensional
Information of Ministry of Education, Nanjing 210094, China
[3] School of Internet of Things, Nanjing University of Posts and Telecommunications,
Nanjing 210003, China

Abstract. Graph Convolutional Networks (GCNs) have been proven
to be effective in various graph-related tasks, such as community detection. Essentially graph convolution is simply a special form of Laplacian smoothing, acting as a low-pass filter that makes the features of
nodes linked to each other similarly. For community detection, however, the similarity of intra-community nodes and the difference of inter-
community nodes are equally vital. To bridge the gap between GCNs
and community detection, we develop a novel Community-Centric Dual
Filter (CCDF) framework for community detection. The central idea is
that, besides of low-pass filter in GCN, we define network modularity
enhanced high-pass filter to separate the discriminative signals from the
raw features. In addition, we design a scheme to jointly optimize low-
frequency and high-frequency information extraction on statistical modeling of Markov Random Fields. Extensive experiments demonstrate that
the proposed CCDF model can consistently outperform or match state-
of-the-art baselines in terms of semi-supervised community detection.

Keywords: Graph Convolutional Networks · Community detection ·
Modularity · Markov Random Field

1 Introduction

Many complex systems in various fields (e.g., social science, genetic science, and
information science) are generally abstracted as networks, where nodes represent elements, and edges represent mutual interactions between elements in the
system, so networks also can be called graphs. One of the significant properties
of the network is community detection, which can help us discover objects with
the same function in the system, study the relationship between different communities, and so on. Community detection has been successfully used in many
applications, e.g., behavior prediction [16] and recommendation system [17].

© Springer Nature Switzerland AG 2021
H. Qiu et al. (Eds.): KSEM 2021, LNAI 12817, pp. 174–187, 2021.
https://doi.org/10.1007/978-3-030-82153-1_15

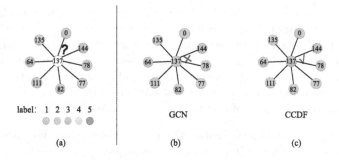

Fig. 1. Example of the wrongly-divided node in Texas

A large number of community detection algorithms based on various assumptions and techniques have been proposed, including modularity optimization [18], Markov dynamic algorithms [19], and GCN-based methods [5]. Among these methods, we would like to highlight GCNs, which leverage their representational power to provide state-of-the-art performance on community-finding tasks.

GCNs are constructed by stacking (graph) neural network layers, essentially recursively aggregate information from neighbors, which can be seen as a special form of Laplacian smoothing [11]. The smoothness of signals, i.e., low-frequency information, is the key to the success of graph neural networks (GNNs) [3,4,15].

However, off-the-shelf GCNs framework has two fundamental weaknesses which hinder their performance of community detection. Firstly, most of them seem to be tailor-made to work on assortative (homophilic) graphs [25], where nodes from the same community tend to form edges. In fact, nodes with distinct labels are more likely to link together in disassortative (heterophilic) networks [24]. If we force the representation of connected nodes to be similar by employing low-pass filter, obviously, those direct neighbors but belonging to the different communities inevitably tend to have a similar representation, leading to a blur inter-community distinction. Some researches [8] have further shown that exploring low-frequency signals is insufficient in different scenarios, like community detection. Secondly, it is well known that the node representation will become indistinguishable when we stack many GCN layers, causing over-smoothing [22]. These remind us that low-pass filter of current GCNs is far from optimal for real-world scenarios.

To remedy these two described weaknesses, we propose a dual graph filtering framework community-centric for community detection simply as CCDF. We first employ the theory of graph Laplacian and network modularity enhancement to formally define a high-pass filter to separate the high-frequency signals from the raw features, equipped to low-frequency signals extracted via GCN. Then we use Markov Random Fields (MRF) to integrate different types of signals adaptively. Figure 1 illustrates a sub-network in Texas, where each node's color denotes its community label. For the target node with id137 in Fig. 1(a), it is erroneously assigned to community 1 by GCN (Fig. 1(b)). The mistake is that most of its neighbors belong to community 1, which directly affects the target node's predicted label. In comparison, CCDF correctly assigns the target node to its correct community 3 (Fig. 1(c)). This is because CCDF refines the coarse results from GCN by pulling nodes belonging to different communities to be far away from each other in the process of message passing.

The main contributions of this paper are summarized as follows:

- We develop a Community-Centric Dual Filter framework. We cast GCN as a Laplacian smoothing filter to obtain low-frequency information and design network modularity enhanced filter, which can be viewed as Laplacian sharpening as the counterpart of Laplacian smoothing obtain high-frequency information. The learned low-frequency and high-frequency information capture the similarity of intra-community nodes and the difference of inter-community nodes, respectively.
- We propose a novel frequency adaptation method in a complete end-to-end deep network framework. On statistical modeling of MRF, our method simultaneously and adaptively exploits discriminative information from inter-community and intra-community. So it can flexibly enlarge the distance between different communities, while most existing GNNs cannot.
- Extensive experiments have demonstrated that the proposed method can outperform representative baselines on benchmark datasets. We also show that network modularity enhanced filter can significantly boost the performance of community detection.

2 Preliminaries

2.1 Notations and Problem Definition

A non-directed graph represents as $\mathcal{G} = (\mathcal{V}, \mathcal{E}, X)$, where $\mathcal{V} = \{v_1, v_2, \cdots, v_n\}$ consists of a set of nodes, and $\mathcal{E}$ is a set of edges between nodes. $X \in R^{n \times d}$ denotes the node attribute (feature) matrix, where X_i is the i-th row of attribute matrix X and X_{ij} is the j-th dimensional attribute of vertex v_i, respectively. The topological structure of graph $\mathcal{G}$ is represented by an adjacency matrix A, where $A_{ij} = 1$, if $(v_i, v_j) \in \mathcal{E}$, or 0 otherwise. And we define D as the diagonal degree matrix with $D_{ii} = \sum_j A_{ij}$. $\tilde{A}$ and $\tilde{D}$ stand for the adjacency matrix and diagonal degree matrix with added self-loops, respectively.

Given a graph $\mathcal{G}$, which partial nodes are labeled. The semi-supervised community detection task is then to label the rest unlabeled nodes in $\mathcal{G}$.

2.2 Graph Convolution Networks

Inspired by the successful applications of deep learning to the regular grid data (e.g., images and videos), researchers consider adopting the deep learning technique to process the irregular graph data (e.g. graphs or manifolds). GCNs generalize convolutional neural networks (CNNs) to graph-structured data. The core operation in GCNs is graph propagation, in which information is propagated from each node to its neighborhoods with some deterministic propagation rules. Spectral approaches apply the convolution operation directly to the spectrum of the graph (i.e., the singular values of graph Laplacian) by treating the node attributes as signals in the graph according to the spectral graph theory. However, it suffers the high computational complexity of singular value decomposition (SVD). Then, ChebNet [9] approximates the spectral filter with Chebyshev polynomials to solve the issue of too complicated calculation. After, [2] proposes GCN via a localized first-order approximation to ChebNet, which simplifies ChebNet. Since then, many methods attempt to advance this architecture, including GAT [12] proposes learning the importance of different neighbors for the central node via a self-attention mechanism, GMNN [20] combines GNNs with probabilistic graphical models, and MixHop [21] employs the mixed-order propagation, etc.

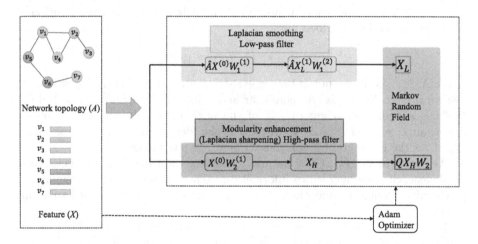

Fig. 2. Graphical representation of the proposed framework CCDF (Color figure online)

3 Our Proposed Model: CCDF

3.1 Overview

In this section, we design a novel Community-Centric Dual Filter (CCDF) framework for community detection which is shown in Fig. 2. We can observe that Fig. 2 consists of two parts: the left is a feature network with adjacency matrix A and node feature matrix X, the renormalized adjacent matrix $\hat{A}$ of A expressed as $\widetilde{D}^{-\frac{1}{2}}\widetilde{A}\widetilde{D}^{-\frac{1}{2}}$, which are used as the inputs of the neural network along with X. The right is CCDF's three major components. In the first component (the green box), the two convolutional layers of GCN can be interpreted as a special form of Laplacian smoothing that acts as low-pass filter to obtain low-frequency information retains the similarity of the intra-community nodes. The first layer is to learn a deep representation of the attributed network and the second layer is to derive node community membership. In addition, we design a network modularity enhancement that acts as high-pass filter to perform Laplacian sharpening, which learns high-frequency information captures the difference of inter-community nodes as the second component of CCDF (the red box). In the third component (the purple box), we leverage MRF to adaptively integrate the low-frequency and high-frequency information in a complete end-to-end deep network framework. The model CCDF is trained as a whole using the Adam optimizer [6].

3.2 Laplacian Smoothing

One of the key components in most GCN models is the graph convolutional layer, which can be described by:

$$X^{(m+1)} = \xi[(I - \widetilde{L})X^{(m)}W^{(m)}] \tag{1}$$

where $X^{(m+1)}$ is the output of the $(m+1)$-th layer, and $X^{(0)}$ is the input nodes' feature matrix X. $\xi(\cdot)$ is the nonlinear activation function Softmax or ReLU. $W^{(m)}$ is a trainable weight matrix of the m-th layer. The symmetric graph Laplacian $\widetilde{L} = I - \widetilde{D}^{-\frac{1}{2}}\widetilde{A}\widetilde{D}^{-\frac{1}{2}}$, where I is the identity matrix. The first term $(I - \widetilde{L})$ is the given graph Laplacian without the parameter.

As shown in Eq. (1), GCN naturally smooths the features in the neighborhoods as each node aggregates information from neighbors. This characteristic is related to Laplacian smoothing. The following is an explanation of Laplacian smoothing.

Regarding $X \in R^{n \times d}$ as a signal defined on graph with normalized Laplacian matrix $\widetilde{L}$, the signal smoothness over the graph can be calculated as:

$$trace(X^T\widetilde{L}X) = \sum_{i,j,k} A_{ij}\left(\frac{X_{ik}}{\sqrt{D_{ii}+1}} - \frac{X_{jk}}{\sqrt{D_{jj}+1}}\right)^2 \tag{2}$$

A smaller value of $trace(X^T\widetilde{L}X)$ indicates smoother graph signal [26], i.e., smaller signal difference between adjacent nodes.

Suppose that we are given a noisy graph signal X, we can adopt the following objective function to recover the low-frequency signal:

$$\arg\min_{X^*} g(X^*) = ||X^* - X||^2 + \beta trace(X^{*T}\widetilde{L}X^*) \tag{3}$$

Note that if we set $\beta = 1/2$, one-step gradient descent optimization of $g(X^*)$ in Eq. (3) equals to GCN convolutional operator [7], shown in Eq. (1).

3.3 Network Modularity Enhancement

The low-pass filter in GCNs mainly retains the commonality of node features, which inevitably ignores the difference, so that the learned representations of connected nodes become similar, and always utilizing low-pass filter will lead to the over-smoothing problem [28]. To alleviate the issue, we introduce network modularity, proposed in [23], applied to measure the significance of community structures. We define network modularity enhanced graph convolutional, which makes each node's feature farther away from the centroid of its neighbors from different communities. The new modularity Q of the community partition is expressed as:

$$Q(C) = \frac{1}{m} \sum_{i,j \in \mathcal{V}} (A_{ij} - \frac{\widetilde{D}_{ii}\widetilde{D}_{jj}}{2m})\delta(c_i, c_j) \tag{4}$$

where $C = (c_1, c_2, \ldots, c_n)$ be a partition of network $\mathcal{G}$, and c_i denotes the community label to which node i belongs to. m is the number of edges in the network. $\delta(\cdot, \cdot)$ is an indicator function, which is -1, if $c_i \neq c_j$, or 0 otherwise. Each element of modularity Q is shown as:

$$Q = \begin{cases} -(A_{ij} - \frac{(D_{ii}+1)(D_{jj}+1)}{2m}), & c_i \neq c_j \\ 0, & \text{otherwise} \end{cases} \tag{5}$$

From Eq. (5), we can see the modularity Q is defined as the difference between the number of edges with communities and the expected number of such edges over all pairs of nodes [27]. Unlike the definition of Kronecker delta in [23], Q here focuses on the pairwise nodes from different communities, while [23] emphasizes community partition based label consistency. Assume Q approaches the maximum, we have powerful high-frequency information hidden in the inter-community.

Connection to Laplacian Sharpening

Each element of Laplacian sharpening is described as:

$$I + \widetilde{L} = \begin{cases} -\frac{A_{ij}}{\sqrt{D_{ii}+1}\sqrt{D_{jj}+1}}, & i \neq j \\ 2, & \text{otherwise} \end{cases} \tag{6}$$

By comparing Eq. (5) with Eq. (6), we can learn that (1) Q has a consistent meaning with Laplacian sharpening. Q adopts the difference of both the degrees of nodes and edges as a discriminant criterion, while Laplacian sharpening adopts the quotient form. Therefore, network modularity enhanced graph convolutional can be viewed as a Laplacian sharpening as the counterpart of Laplacian smoothing. (2) Q captures the distinctive features from different communities by virtue of the known labels ignored by Laplacian sharpening.

3.4   Aggregation

Attention mechanism [12] is the most used strategy to learn the importance of different representations from multi-views or sources. For example, we can use two learnable coefficients to measure the proportion of low-frequency and high-frequency signals and aggregate them [8]. However, it would introduce more parameters to learn.

Alternatively, we resort to MRF as our aggregation strategy [5]. The essential ingredient of MRF is an objective (or energy) function consisting of the sum of unary potentials defined as $\phi\{c_i\}$ and pairwise potentials defined as $\theta\{c_i, c_j\}$:

$$E(C) = -\sum_i \phi\{c_i\} - \alpha \sum_{i,j} \theta\{c_i, c_j\} \tag{7}$$

where $\phi\{c_i\}$ for an individual i measures the cost that it has label c_i and $\theta\{c_i, c_j\}$ for i and j represents the cost that they have labels c_i and c_j, respectively. α is a parameter for balancing the unary and pairwise potentials.

In this work, we substitute low-frequency information learned X in Eq. (1) for the unary potential, and network modularity Q in Eq. (5), the sum of pairwise potentials for all node pairs of a given network, finally, we get community detection oriented energy function $E(C|A, X)$:

$$E(C|A, X) = -\sum_i X_i - \alpha \sum_{i,j} Q_{ij} \tag{8}$$

There is the property that the minimum of the energy function corresponds to the best possible community partition [1]. However, minimizing the energy function to yield the most probable community partition for a given network is intractable. The pairwise potentials are defined over a complete network rather than the sparse network. Next, we will use a mean filed approximately for MRF's inference [5] to solve the issue from Eq. (8).

The Gibbs distribution of $E(C|A, X)$ is

$$P(C|A, X) = \frac{1}{N}\exp\{-\sum E(C|A, X)\} \tag{9}$$

where N is a normalized constant.

The exact distribution $P(C|A, X)$ is difficult to compute. Thereby we replace the exact probability distribution with an approximate distribution $\hat{P}(C|A, X)$ which is decomposable, i.e.,

$$\hat{P}(C|A, X) = \prod \hat{P}_i(c_i|A, X) \tag{10}$$

Lemma 1 [5]. *Given $P(C|A, X)$ in Eq. (9) and its approximation $\hat{P}(C|A, X)$ in Eq. (10), we can derive the update equation of $\hat{P}_i(c_i|A, X)$ by minimizing the KL-divergence $D(P||\hat{P})$, we can derive*

$$\hat{P}_i(C|A, X) \leftarrow \frac{1}{N_i}\exp\{X + QX\} \tag{11}$$

3.5   The Whole Architecture

Based on the update Eq. (11), we transform the MRF's inference into a convolution process and formulate it as convolution operations to finalize the last component of the integrated end-to-end deep neural network. Here, we formally define the whole framework of CCDF, which has four steps:

$$X_L^{(1)} = \text{ReLU}(\hat{A}X^{(0)}W_1^{(1)}) \tag{12}$$

$$X_L = \text{Softmax}(\hat{A}X_L^{(1)}W_1^{(2)}) \tag{13}$$

$$X_H = \text{Softmax}(X^{(0)}W_2^{(1)}) \tag{14}$$

$$Z = \text{Softmax}(X_L + QX_HW_2) \tag{15}$$

where $X_L^{(1)}$, X_L and Z are defined as the outputs of the first, second and third convolution layer, X_H is a layer of nonlinear feature extraction. $W_1^{(1)}$, $W_1^{(2)}$, $W_2^{(1)}$ and W_2 are the corresponding weights, respectively.

CCDF can be trained by minimizing the cross entropy between the predicted and the (partial) ground-truth community labels under parameters $\theta = \{W_1^{(1)}, W_1^{(2)}, W_2^{(1)}, W_2\}$, i.e.,

$$\arg\min_{\theta} \mathscr{L}(Z, Y) = \arg\min_{\theta} \sum_{i \in V_l} \sum_{l=1}^{m} Y_{il} \ln Z_{il} \tag{16}$$

where V_l is the set of labeled nodes and m is the number of labels, Y_{il} is 1 if node v_i has label l, otherwise 0.

From Eq. (15), we can learn our method is to introduce a transformation of MRF model [5] and its inference to a convolutional layer to be added as the last layer of the whole framework.

Placing CCDF in the Context of Related Prior Work
It can be easily seen that GCN is a special case of our model. Specifically, when we ignore Eq. (14) and Eq. (15), the model becomes GCN. And in Eq. (15), we use the result of two-layer GCN (X_L) instead of nonlinear feature extraction (X_H) and then change the indicator function δ. Meanwhile, add the similarity matrix that derives from attributed space and force the balance coefficient to be positive. This model becomes MRFasGCN (MasG) which has been proposed by [5].

Experimental results (Fig. 4) show that GCN obtains a relatively coarse community result for both our method and MasG [5]. Then MasG further reinforces similar or nearby nodes to have compatible community labels. It offers smooth labeling among nearby nodes by shortening the distance between nodes from the same communities. The difference is that our model refines coarsely labeled communities by enlarging the distance between nodes from different communities. Compared with them, we find that most of GCNs prefer to aggregate the low-frequency information, which makes them inadequate for learning on disassortative graphs and suffers from over-smoothing seriously. Among the methods that differ from utilizing low-frequency information only, our method uses the MRF bridges the low-frequency and high-frequency information so able to integrate and train parameters in low-pass and high-pass extractors together to develop an end-to-end deep learning framework for community detection.

Table 1. The statistics of datasets

Datasets	#Nodes	#Edges	#Attributes	#Communities
Cora	2708	5429	1433	7
Citeseer	3327	4732	3703	6
Pubmed	19717	44338	500	3
Texas	183	328	1703	5
Wisconsin	262	530	1703	5
Cornell	195	304	1703	5
Washington	217	446	1703	5

4   Experiments

4.1   Datasets

We conduct experiments on seven widely-used benchmark datasets. We choose the commonly used citation graphs Cora, Citeseer and Pubmed for assortative datasets. We consider webpage graphs Texas, Wisconsin, Cornell, and Washington for disassortative datasets. We summarize the dataset statistics in Table 1.

Table 2. Comparison of prediction accuracy

Method	Cora	Citeseer	Pubmed	Texas	Wisconsin	Cornell	Washington
ChebNet [9]	81.20	69.80	74.40	64.13	53.43	38.77	47.70
JKNet [10]	80.20	68.70	78.00	64.21	55.72	51.02	*62.38*
IncepGCN [13]	77.60	69.30	77.70	63.04	54.96	*54.08*	60.55
SGC [11]	81.00	71.90	78.90	57.61	*56.49*	53.06	60.55
GAT [12]	83.00	*72.50*	79.00	64.18	48.85	47.96	46.79
DropEdge [13]	82.80	72.30	79.60	65.21	56.48	45.91	58.71
ALaGCN [14]	82.90	70.90	79.60	*68.48*	*56.49*	47.96	56.88
GraphHeat [15]	*83.70*	*72.50*	**80.50**	64.13	51.90	35.70	48.62
GCN [2]	81.50	70.30	79.00	63.04	54.96	47.96	56.88
CCDF	**84.10**	**73.70**	*80.10*	**77.17**	**62.59**	**61.22**	**70.64**

4.2   Experimental Setup

We aim to provide a rigorous and fair comparison between different methods on each dataset by using the same dataset splits and training procedure. For Cora, Citeseer and Pubmed, we use 20 nodes per class for training, 500 nodes for validation, and 1000 nodes for testing. There is no standard division for Texas, Wisconsin, Cornell and Washington. In order to verify the effectiveness and robustness, we use 20% for training, 30% for validation, and 50% for testing. We tune hyperparameters for all methods individually and the baseline results are essentially the same as their original reports. For CCDF, We tune the following hyper-parameters, in assortative datasets, the hyper-parameter set is: learning rate = 0.04, dropout = 0.8, weight decay in {2e−4, 6e−4, 4e−6}. In disassortative datasets, the hyper-parameter set is: learning rate = 0.05, dropout in {0.5, 0.6}, weight decay in {1e−3, 2e−3, 2e−4}. In training, we run 240 epochs, and the random seed is fixed. We adopt the widely-used Adam optimizer [6] and run experiments on Pytorch. Besides, we use Accuracy (ACC) as the metric to evaluate the performance of all methods. Our implementation is available online.[1]

4.3   Comparison with the Existing Methods

To comprehensively evaluate our method, we compare it with the following nine state-of-the-art semi-supervised methods, including ChebNet [9], JKNet [10], IncepGCN [13], SGC [11], GAT [12], DropEdge [13], ALaGCN [14], GraphHeat [15] and GCN [2].

As shown in Table 2, we can see our method CCDF improves upon GCN by a margin of 3.4%, 14.13% in Citeseer and Texas. CCDF improves 12.99% and 19.56% more accurately than GAT and SGC in Texas. In disassortative networks, CCDF much higher than other methods. Because nodes with distinct labels are more likely to link together in disassortative networks [24]. Only using low-pass filters is not suitable for disassortative networks. The experimental results show that our method CCDF performs the best on 8 of 9 methods, which demonstrates the effectiveness of CCDF.

4.4   Ablation Study

To validate the effectiveness of individual component in the proposed method CCDF, we compare CCDF with its five variants: 1) In our method, we ignore Eq. (14) and Eq. (15), which is equivalent to GCN. 2) The weight parameters W_2 in CCDF is set to 1 without training (as the most general way), namely CCDF without W_2. 3) Q in Eq. (5) is replaced by community structure embedding matrix, $max\{\log\frac{\tilde{A}_{ij}D}{d_id_j} - \log t, 0\}(t = 2)$, defined in [22], namely CCDF with C_{emb}. 4) Q is replaced by $I + D^{-\frac{1}{2}}AD^{-\frac{1}{2}}$, which is the initial first-order Chebyshev filter derived in GCN, namely CCDF with $S_{1-order}$. 5) In order to compare

---

[1] https://github.com/KSEM2021/CCDF.

network modularity enhancement and Laplacian sharpening, we replace Eq. (5) with Eq. (6), when $c_i \neq c_j$, namely CCDF with $\hat{A}$. The last configuration is the full proposed method CCDF.

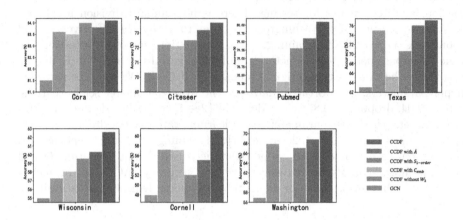

Fig. 3. Comparison of CCDF with its five variants

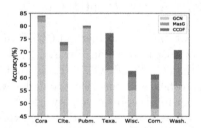

Fig. 4. Comparison experiment with GCN and MasG [5]

The results of the ablation study are shown in Fig. 3, from which we have the following two observations. First, all CCDF's variants with component changes witness clear performance drops compared to the full propose method, which indicates that the existence of W_2 and the Q in Eq. (5) have a certain influence on our method. Second, the experimental results of CCDF and its variants are significantly higher than GCN on six of seven datasets.

In order to compare with GCN and [5]'s method (MasG) which is stated in Sect. 3.5, we add one comparative experiment between GCN, MasG, and our method. The results show in Fig. 4.

5   Alleviating Over-Smoothing Problem

To verify whether CCDF can alleviate the over-smoothing problem, we compare the performance of GCN and CCDF at different model depths in Cora, Citeseer, Pubmed, and Texas. The results show in Fig. 5. We can see that GCN achieves the best performance at two layers. As the number of layers increases, the performance of GCN drops rapidly, which indicates that GCN suffers from over-smoothing seriously. On the contrary, the results of CCDF are relatively stable and higher than GCN, which indicates that CCDF has the ability to suppress over-smoothing. CCDF contains both low-frequency and high-frequency information, which can keep node representations from becoming indistinguishable.

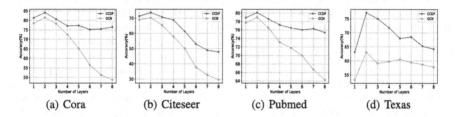

(a) Cora   (b) Citeseer   (c) Pubmed   (d) Texas

Fig. 5. Test accuracy with different model depth

6   Conclusion

In this paper, we develop a Community-Centric Dual Filter (CCDF) framework for semi-supervised community detection task. CCDF can simultaneously and adaptively exploit low-frequency and high-frequency information from intra-community and inter-community, respectively. Furthermore, we leverage MRF to adaptively integrate the low-frequency and high-frequency information in a complete end-to-end deep network framework. Extensive experiments validate the effectiveness of our proposed method and demonstrate that CCDF can outperform or match baseline on various datasets.

Acknowledgments. This work was supported by the National Natural Science Foundation of China (No. 61773215, 61802206).

References

1. Nowozin, S., Lampert, C.H.: Structured Learning and Prediction in Computer Vision. Now publishers Inc. (2011)
2. Kipf, T.N., Welling, M.: Semi-supervised classification with graph convolutional networks. arXiv preprint arXiv:1609.02907 (2016)

3. Nt, H., Maehara, T.: Revisiting graph neural networks: all we have is low-pass filters. arXiv preprint arXiv:1905.09550 (2019)
4. Li, Q., Wu, X.M., Liu, H., et al.: Label efficient semi-supervised learning via graph filtering. In: Proceedings of the IEEE/CVF Conference on Computer Vision and Pattern Recognition, pp. 9582–9591 (2019)
5. Jin, D., Liu, Z., Li, W., et al.: Graph convolutional networks meet Markov random fields: semi-supervised community detection in attribute networks. In: Proceedings of the AAAI Conference on Artificial Intelligence, vol. 33, no. 01, pp. 152–159 (2019)
6. Kingma, D.P., Ba, J.: Adam: a method for stochastic optimization. arXiv preprint arXiv:1412.6980 (2014)
7. Jin, W., Derr, T., Wang, Y., et al.: Node similarity preserving graph convolutional networks. Proceedings of the 14th ACM International Conference on Web Search and Data Mining, pp. 148–156 (2021)
8. Bo, D., Wang, X., Shi, C., Shen, H.: Beyond low-frequency information in graph convolutional networks. arXiv preprint arXiv:2101.00797 (2021)
9. Defferrard, M., Bresson, X., Vandergheynst, P.: Convolutional neural networks on graphs with fast localized spectral filtering. arXiv preprint arXiv:1606.09375 (2016)
10. Xu, K., Li, C., Tian, Y., et al.: Representation learning on graphs with jumping knowledge networks. In: International Conference on Machine Learning, pp. 5453–5462. PMLR (2018)
11. Wu, F., Souza, A., Zhang, T., et al.: Simplifying graph convolutional networks. International International Conference on Machine Learning, pp. 6861–6871. PMLR (2019)
12. Veličković, P., Cucurull, G., Casanova, A., et al.: Graph attention networks. arXiv preprint arXiv:1710.10903 (2017)
13. Rong, Y., Huang, W., Xu, T., et al.: DropEdge: towards deep graph convolutional networks on node classification. arXiv preprint arXiv:1907.10903 (2019)
14. Xie, Y., Li, S., Yang, C., et al.: When Do GNNs work: understanding and improving neighborhood aggregation. In: Proceedings of the Twenty-Ninth International Joint Conference on Artificial Intelligence, IJCAI (2020)
15. Xu, B., Shen, H., Cao, Q., et al.: Graph convolutional networks using heat kernel for semi-supervised learning. arXiv preprint arXiv:2007.16002 (2020)
16. Yin, H., Hu, Z., Zhou, X., et al.: Discovering interpretable geosocial communities for user behavior prediction. In: IEEE 32nd International Conference on Data Engineering (ICDE), pp. 942–953 (2016)
17. Bernardes, D., Diaby, M., Fournier, R., et al.: A social formalism and survey for recommender systems. ACM SIGKDD Explor. Newsl. 16(2), 20–37 (2015)
18. Blondel, V.D., Guillaume, J.L., Lambiotte, R., et al.: Fast unfolding of communities in large networks. J. Stat. Mech.: Theory Exp. P10008 (2008)
19. Jin, D., Yang, B., Baquero, C., et al.: A Markov random walk under constraint for discovering overlapping communities in complex networks. J. Stat. Mech.: Theory Exp. P05031 (2011)
20. Qu, M., Bengio, Y., Tang, J.: GMNN: Graph Markov neural networks. In: International Conference on Machine Learning. pp. 5241–5250. PMLR (2019)
21. Abu-El-Haija, S., Perozzi, B., Kapoor, A., et al.: MixHop: higher-order graph convolutional architectures via sparsified neighborhood mixing. In: International Conference on Machine Learning, pp. 21–29. PMLR (2019)
22. Li, Y., Sha, C., Huang, X., et al.: Community detection in attributed graphs: an embedding approach. In: Proceedings of the AAAI Conference on Artificial Intelligence (2018)

23. Newman, M.E., Girvan, M.: Finding and evaluating community structure in networks. Phys. Rev. E **69**(2), 026113 (2004)
24. Zhu, J., Yan, Y., Zhao, L., et al.: Generalizing graph neural networks beyond homophily. arXiv preprint arXiv:2006.11468 (2020)
25. Chien, E., Peng, J., Li, P., et al.: Adaptive universal generalized PageRank graph neural network. arXiv preprint arXiv:2006.07988 (2020)
26. Cui, G., Zhou, J., Yang, C., et al.: Adaptive graph encoder for attributed graph embedding. In: Proceedings of the 26th ACM SIGKDD International Conference on Knowledge Discovery and Data Mining (2020)
27. Newman, M.E.: Modularity and community structure in networks. Proc. Natl. Acad. Sci. U.S.A. **103**(23), 8577–8582 (2006)
28. Oono, K., Suzuki, T.: Graph neural networks exponentially lose expressive power for node classification. arXiv preprint arXiv:1905.10947 (2019)

Landscape-Enhanced Graph Attention Network for Rumor Detection

Jianguo Jiang[1,2], Qiang Liu[1,2], Min Yu[1,2(✉)], Gang Li[3], Mingqi Liu[1],
Chao Liu[1], and Weiqing Huang[1]

[1] Institute of Information Engineering, Chinese Academy of Sciences, Beijing, China
yumin@iie.ac.cn
[2] School of Cyber Security, University of Chinese Academy of Sciences,
Beijing, China
[3] School of Information Technology, Deakin University, Geelong, Australia

Abstract. Rumor detection aims to classify the truthfulness of content
on social media. Due to the rapid development of web-based social platforms, rumors are disseminated in an ever faster speed. Recently, this
problem is tackled as a graph classification problem instead of traditional text classification or time series classification problem, thanks to
the natural graph structure of social networks, i.e. content dissemination
network in rumor detection. However, we argue that the existing graph-
based methods have several defects. They deal with two uni-directional
networks separately, which restricts the interaction between nodes. Moreover, there is a gap between training and target representation, since they
only learn node-level embedding and simply use average or max pooling to obtain whole graph embedding. Hence, we explore a novel method
named L-GAT which solves the above drawbacks. Specifically, we employ
a unified graph attention network to aggregate information without splitting information stream. Besides, we enhance the original graph with
two virtual global nodes—landscape nodes—to capture global information, and train these global node embedding in an end-to-end style to
bridge the gap between training and target. Experiments show that our
proposed L-GAT is effective in improving the performance over all the
existing rumor detection methods.

Keywords: Rumor detection · Fake news detection · Graph neural
network · Graph representation learning · Social network

1 Introduction

Rumor is defined as unverified or intentionally false information that emerges
and spreads among people [8,28] with the rise of web service [25,26]. As the
rising amount of data is being generated day by day [6,9,36], automatic rumor
detection plays a more and more significant role in maintaining the security
and cleanliness of online environment. As indicated in [1,2], even a single rumor

© Springer Nature Switzerland AG 2021
H. Qiu et al. (Eds.): KSEM 2021, LNAI 12817, pp. 188–199, 2021.
https://doi.org/10.1007/978-3-030-82153-1_16

has the potential to cause a vast range of social and economic losses. Therefore, designing automatic methods to detect rumors online is demanded with an emergency.

Rumor detection, also known as fake news detection, attracts increasing attention both in real-world applications and the research community in recent years. However, how to detect rumors accurately is still an open and challenging problem. Conventional methods focus on utilizing text information, including post content and its comments. However, since the rumors are usually designed carefully by the primordial disseminator, and comments can also be manipulated, these methods using only text information may fail in reality. Recently, to make full use of abundant structural information such as retweeting behavior beyond text information, several studies have proposed their solution. For example, RvNN [23] uses recursive neural networks [34] to encode the tree-structured propagation network, while BiGCN [4] adapts graph convolutional networks [14] to do this job.

Nevertheless, we argue that the existing graph-based methods have two main defects. Firstly, they deal with two uni-directional networks, i.e. bottom-up (retweeting) and top-down (being retweeted) networks separately, which restricts the interaction between nodes, thus causes a bottleneck for model performance. Secondly, there is a gap between training and target representation, since they simply use average or max pooling to obtain whole graph embedding with the node-level embedding in hand.

In this work, we also focus on classifying rumors on Twitter considering both text and graph information. We explore a novel model named L-GAT which solves the above two drawbacks. Specifically, we see all edges as bi-directional, and use a unified graph attention network to aggregate information, without considering top-down or bottom-up information flow. Besides, we enhance the original graph with two landscape nodes to capture global information and train these global node embedding in an end-to-end style to bridge the gap between training and target.

Our contributions are summarized as follows:

1. To the best of our knowledge, we are the first to apply GAT in rumor detection problem.
2. We propose a novel and efficient method L-GAT, where three modifications are designed specifically for rumor detection problem based on vanilla GAT.
3. The results of the experiment on two Twitter datasets indicate that our proposed method reaches state-of-the-art performance.

The rest of this paper is organized as follows: Sect. 2 investigates the related works. Section 3 and Sect. 4 introduce the problem and our model respectively. Results of experiment are given in Sect. 5. We make a conclusion of our work in Sect. 6.

2 Related Work

2.1 Feature Engineering-Based Rumor Detection

Most of the traditional rumor detection methods rely on handcrafted features to learn a supervised classifier.

A few early research works [5,15,28,37,40] utilized feature engineering to extract text features such as lexical features, syntactic features and style features from rumor contents. Ma et al. [19] compared two content representation approaches, the Bag-of-Words (BOW) approach and the neural network approach, then showed that the BOW approach is more suitable for small-scale datasets in rumor detection task. Horne et al. [11] extracted the features of structure and proper nouns from news titles to distinguish between true and false news, they found that fake news try to establish mental relationship between entities and claims. Potthast et al. [27] classified hyperpartisan news by capturing writing style feature via Unmasking—a meta-learning-based method and found that the style of two extremely one-sided news have more in common than any of the two have with the mainstream.

In addition to text features, later researchers extract some other features such as diffusion features and user-interaction features [24,33,38,39]. Jin et al. [12] were inspired by epidemiological theory and employed an enhanced epidemiological model to characterize information relationship between twitter and events through recognizing skeptics, this strategy can be combined with other model such as content model to detect rumors. Shu et al. [32] crawled lots of user information from social networks and constructed datasets to help model the relationships between user profiles and fake news. Ma et al. [22] evaluated the structure-similarities between two propagation tree via building the kernel of propagation tree to detect rumors. These traditional methods not only have to extract complex features but also are heavily dependent on handcrafted feature sets.

2.2 Deep Learning-Based Rumor Detection

In recent years, the methods based on deep learning which can extract features from raw data without feature engineering have occupied the center stage of the machine learning domain. Thanks to the capacity to fit any functions of neural networks, deep learning-based methods are able to take more complex information into consideration.

Liu et al. [16] employed BERT to encode text contents in news and use extra information for making the model more robust. They divided classification tasks into two stages to deal with coarse-grained labels and fine-grained labels independently. Liu et al. [17] employed a GRU-based network and a CNN-based network to represent user-propagation path of time-series then concatenated them to detect rumors on Twitter. Different from other widely-used approaches, this approach utilizes only user characteristics particularly. Ma et al. [23] employed a tree-based Recursive Neural Network (RvNN) to catch both potential semantic information and propagation characteristics and combine the information in both top-down direction and bottom-up direction. These methods only refer to features of content or sequence and rarely catch graph-based features.

2.3   Graph Neural Network-Based Methods

Compared to the methods described in Sect. 2.2, graph neural network (GNN) can express graph data in a low dimensional space and aggregate information by connecting relationships, which makes GNN show excellent effects in solving various problems with graph data [3,7,10]. Likewise, GNN addresses rumor detection problem effectively.

Bian et al. [4] proposed Bi-directional Graph Convolutional Networks (Bi-GCN) dividing the propagation tree into bottom-up tree and top-down tree that aggregates latent features along all sub-trees with different levels and catches complex diffusion patterns respectively. Lu et al. [18] employed a hybrid model consisting of GCN, CNN and GRU to represent user interaction, retweet propagation and text contents, then modeled reasonable relevancy among them via co-attention mechanism. However, the methods considering two directions of information dispersion independently restrict the interaction between nodes which will cause a bottleneck for model performance. What's more, most previous works for rumor detection mainly focused on learning node-level embedding and simply used average or max pooling to obtain graph-level embedding which may generate a gap between training and target representation.

Table 1. Comparison of relevant works. Column notations: source story texts (ST), user characteristics (UC), propagation structure (PS), social network (SN), and graph-level embedding (GE). For the ST column, "S" and "L" indicates short and long text, respectively.

	ST	UC	PS	SN	GE
GRU-RNN [20]	✓(S)				
CSI [30]	✓(S)	✓			
RvNN [23]	✓(S)		✓	✓	
PPC [17]	✓(S)	✓	✓		
dEFEND [31]	✓(L)			✓	
BiGCN [4]	✓(S)		✓	✓	
Our work	✓(S)		✓	✓	✓

Table 2. Statistics of the datasets.

Statistic	Twitter15	Twitter16
# of posts	331,612	204,820
# of Users	276,663	173,487
# of events	1,490	818
# of True	374	205
# of False	370	205
# of Unverified	374	203
# of Non-rumor	372	205
Average # of posts per event	223	251
Maximum # of posts per event	1,768	2,765
Minimum # of posts per event	55	81

We compare some related rumor detection works and ours in Table 1. By the way, user characteristics are barely accessible due to privacy concerns. The uniqueness of our work are: suitable for short text, without the requirement of user characteristics and capable of learning graph-level representation.

3 Problem Definition

Suppose $\mathcal{C} = \{C_1, C_2, .., C_{|\mathcal{C}|}\}$ is a corpus consisting of multiple claims. Each claim C_i is represented by (V_i, E_i), where $V_i = \{r^i, v_1^i, v_2^i, .., v_{n_i-1}^i\}$ is a set of nodes representing posts or responses (e.g. comments, retweet posts, etc.), and E_i is a set of edges connecting the direct interaction between two nodes (e.g. commenting, retweeting, etc.). Each node in V_i may contain some attached features, such as TF-IDF feature if text content is available. It is worth noting that claim C_i is a special form of graph—tree—where r^i is the root post to judge whether it is a rumor or not. For each claim C_i, there is an associated label $y_i \in Y$, where Y is a discrete label set. The value of Y may vary under different scenario, e.g. {*Non-Rumor, False Rumor, True Rumor, Unverified Rumor*}. A claim is known to be a rumor when its label is *False*.

We define rumor detection as a graph classification problem. Given a corpus $\mathcal{C}$ and some labeled claims $\mathcal{C}_{train} = \{(C_i, y_i)|C_i \in \mathcal{C}, y_i \in Y\}$, our target is to learn a mapping $f : \mathcal{C} \to Y$ to predict the unlabeled claims in corpus.

4 Methodology

In this section, we will clarify the details of our proposed L-GAT method. We use graph attention network [35] as our backbone module. GAT is designed to tackle with graphs with both property and structural information. However, applying vanilla GAT to rumor detection directly will end up with failure. Therefore, we make three modifications based on GAT, i.e. virtual global nodes (landscape nodes), root feature enhancement, and data augmentation. And we name the modified method as L-GAT. The workflow overview of L-GAT is shown in Fig. 1.

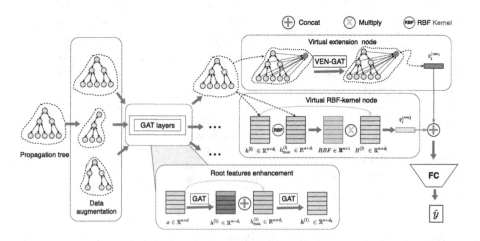

Fig. 1. The architecture of L-GAT model.

4.1   Landscape Nodes

Since GNNs learn node-level embedding but our goal in rumor detection is to classify graphs, the gap between training and target occurs when we use GNNs to detect rumor. Previous GNN-based works usually obtain graph-level embedding by max/mean pooling node embeddings. However, we argue that pooling is insufficient to fill the gap.

In this work, we enhance the original graph with two virtual landscape nodes termed virtual extension node (VEN) and virtual RBF-kernel node (VRN) respectively. Both landscape nodes enable L-GAT model to learn global node embedding in an end-to-end fashion.

With regard to VEN, we add an extra node to the graph by connecting it to all nodes of the original graph to construct the extended graph $\tilde{C}_i^{(ven)} = (V_i \cup \{v_i^{(ven)}\}, E_i \cup E_i^{(ven)})$, where $E_i^{(ven)} = \{v \rightarrow v_i^{(ven)} | v \in V_i\}$. It is worth noting that the edges in extra set $E_i^{(ven)}$ are uni-directional and from original nodes to the virtual extension node so as to avoid interfering between unrelated nodes during forward propagation.

In rumor detection, root node is a core target to predict. Intuitively, the smaller distance to root node, the more important a node is. To encode this prior knowledge into our method, we further construct a VRN where we aggregate information from all nodes with RBF-kernel. Therefore, the final virtual graph is $\tilde{C}_i = (V_i \cup \{v_i^{(ven)}, v_i^{(vrn)}\}, E_i \cup E_i^{(ven)} \cup E_i^{(vrn)})$, where $E_i^{(vrn)} = \{v \rightarrow v_i^{(vrn)} | v \in V_i\}$.

Then, we use L-GAT to encode the constructed virtual graph. For non-VRN nodes, the formulas are similar to GAT:

$$\alpha_{ij}^{(l)} = \frac{\exp\left(\text{LeakyReLU}\left(a^T[Wh_i^{(l-1)} \| Wh_j^{(l-1)}]\right)\right)}{\sum_{k \in \mathcal{N}_i} \exp\left(\text{LeakyReLU}\left(a^T[Wh_i^{(l-1)} \| Wh_k^{(l-1)}]\right)\right)}, \tag{1}$$

$$h_i^{(l)} = \sigma\left(\sum_{j \in \mathcal{N}_i} \alpha_{ij}^{(l)} Wh_j^{(l-1)}\right), \tag{2}$$

where a and W are learnable weights, $\mathcal{N}_i$ represents the neighbors of node v_i, and $h_i^{(l)}$ refers to the l-th layer embedding of node v_i. σ is a non-linear activation.

For VRN node i, attention weights are calculated by RBF-kernel:

$$\alpha_{ij}^{(l)} = \frac{\exp(-\frac{1}{2\delta^2}\|h_j^{(l-1)} - h_{root}^{(l-1)}\|^2)}{\sum_{k \in \mathcal{N}_i} \exp(-\frac{1}{2\delta^2}\|h_k^{(l-1)} - h_{root}^{(l-1)}\|^2)}, \tag{3}$$

where δ is a hyper parameter of RBF-kernel. Multi-head attention [35] is also used in our model. However, we omit the formula here for brevity.

We concatenate the embeddings of $v_i^{(ven)}$ and $v_i^{(vrn)}$ in the last layer as the final embedding of graph C_i for prediction.

4.2   Root Feature Enhancement

As indicated in [4], root node plays a vital role in rumor detection. Therefore, we employ root feature enhancement for L-GAT. Concretely, for the l-th layer of L-GAT, we concatenate all node embeddings with the representation of $(l-1)$-th layer of root node. Formally, we replace $h_j^{(l-1)}$ with $h_j^{(l-1)}||h_{\text{root}}^{(l-1)}$ in Eq. 1, 2 and 3.

4.3   Data Augmentation

For graph data, DropEdge [29] is usually adapted to augment training set. However, applying DropEdge under rumor detection will raise some problems because of the tree structure of content dissemination network. When we drop an edge of a tree, the tree will become two separated components. More components will be detached from root node when the number of dropped edges increase.

To tackle with this problem, we propose DropTree strategy, i.e. when drop nodes, we will drop the sub-trees rooted to them simultaneously. The strategy ensures that the rest of the trees are still a connected tree rooted by the original root node.

5   Experiment

In this section, we will illustrate the details of our experiments.

5.1   Datasets

For experimental evaluation, we use two real-world datasets *Twitter15* and *Twitter16*[1] released by [22]. Twitter is one of the most popular online social media platforms in the world. Each *Twitter* dataset provides a group of propagation trees in which root nodes refer to source story, other nodes refer to comment contents and edges represent retweet or being retweeted relationship. Each tree corresponds to one of four class labels, i.e. Non-rumor (N), False rumor (F), True rumor (T), and Unverified rumor (U), which are annotated according to the rumor tracking websites such as emergent.info. What's more, we extract top-5000 words in terms of the TF-IDF values as feature for each node. We show the statistics of the two datasets in Table 2.

5.2   Baselines

We comprehensively compared our method with the following listed baselines:

- **DTC** [5]: A Decision-Tree Classifier to assess the confidence of the information based on handcrafted features.

---

[1] https://www.dropbox.com/s/7ewzdrbelpmrnxu/rumdetect2017.zip?dl=0.

- **RFC** [15]: A Random Forest Classier utilizing a combination of handcraft characteristics of user, text and structure.
- **SVM-TS** [21]: A model based on Support Vector Machine (SVM) that utilizes time-series to model a set of handcraft news features.
- **SVM-TK** [22]: An SVM model that utilizes a Tree Kernel to model propagation structures.
- **GRU-RNN** [20]: A Recurrent Neural Network (RNN) -based model with GRU units that learns representation of user comments to detect rumors.
- **BU-RvNN and TD-RvNN** [23]: A tree-structured Recursive Neural Network with GRU units that captures rumor features via bi-directional propagation structure.
- **PPC** [17]: A fake news detection model that combines recurrent and convolutional networks to model user characteristics along with the propagation sequence.
- **BiGCN** [4]: A Graph Convolutional Network with root-enhancement mechanism that learns rumor representations via bi-directional propagation graph.

We implement feature engineering-based methods (i.e. DTC) with scikit-learn; GRU-RNN, PPC, RvNN and our model with Pytorch.

5.3   Evaluation Metrics

To ensure fairness, we randomly split the datasets into five parts, and conduct 5-fold cross-validation to obtain robust results. To make a comprehensive comparison, we calculate Accuracy (Acc.) over the four categories and F1 measure (F_1) on each one.

5.4   Loss Function and Hyper-parameters

We use cross-entropy loss and Adam optimizer [13] for all neural network based methods. The dimension of each node's hidden feature vectors is set to 64. The rate of dropout and the dropping rate of edge are 0.5 and 0.3 respectively. For training epoch, we will use early stop mechanism based on the evaluation metrics on the validation set to promise fully training. The δ of RBF-kernel is simply set to 1. In addition, we primarily use pytorch 1.5 and torch-geometric 1.6 to finish our experiments.

5.5   Results and Analysis

The results compared with all baselines are shown in Table 3. Obviously, our proposed method L-GAT achieves the best performance among all methods by most evaluation measures in the task of rumor detection on both *Twitter* datasets.

As we can see, deep learning-based methods perform better than traditional feature engineering-based methods. It makes sense since the deep learning-based methods are apt to learn high-level representations of rumors to capture effective features automatically. This is why deep learning surpasses machine learning in many tasks. In general, models based on more complex structures have better results. Sequence-based models (i.e. GRU-RNN, PPC) perform the worst, followed by tree-based models. Because RNN or CNN has no ability to process data with tree or graph structure which make sequence-based models get less structural features of information propagation.

Table 3. Result comparison in Accuracy and F1 measure (N: *Non-Rumor*; F: *False Rumor*; T: *True Rumor*; U: *Unverified Rumor*).

Twitter15					
Method	Acc.	N	F	T	U
		F_1	F_1	F_1	F_1
DTC	0.454	0.733	0.355	0.317	0.415
RFC	0.565	0.810	0.422	0.401	0.543
SVM-TS	0.544	0.796	0.472	0.404	0.483
SVM-TK	0.667	0.619	0.669	0.772	0.645
GRU-RNN	0.641	0.684	0.634	0.688	0.571
BU-RvNN	0.708	0.695	0.728	0.759	0.653
TD-RvNN	0.723	0.682	0.758	0.821	0.654
PPC_RNN+CNN	0.477	0.300	0.507	0.640	0.359
BiGCN	0.822	0.776	0.834	**0.878**	0.793
L-GAT	**0.851**	**0.812**	**0.844**	**0.878**	**0.815**
Twitter16					
Method	Acc.	N	F	T	U
		F_1	F_1	F_1	F_1
DTC	0.465	0.643	0.393	0.419	0.403
RFC	0.585	0.752	0.415	0.547	0.563
SVM-TS	0.574	0.755	0.420	0.571	0.526
SVM-TK	0.662	0.643	0.623	0.783	0.655
GRU-RNN	0.633	0.617	0.715	0.577	0.527
BU-RvNN	0.718	0.723	0.712	0.779	0.659
TD-RvNN	0.737	0.662	0.743	0.835	0.708
PPC_RNN+CNN	0.564	0.591	0.543	0.394	0.674
BiGCN	0.863	0.760	**0.870**	**0.931**	0.853
L-GAT	**0.883**	**0.764**	0.857	0.917	**0.863**

However, our proposed model L-GAT exceed BiGCN which restricts the interaction between nodes due to deal with two directions separately. Just like BiGCN, we employ the root feature enhancement mechanism to make texts of source story play a greater role. In addition, we employ an improved data augmentation method as described in Sect. 4 instead of dropping edges randomly (e.g. DropEdge). Most importantly, we put forward a efficient method for learning graph-level representation to bridge the gap between training and target.

5.6 Ablation Study

In order to investigate how each of L-GAT portion contributes, we design submodels "-R", "-E", "-V", by removing the virtual extension node, the virtual RBF-kernel node and both of them, respectively. Besides, we use two modes "Tone" and "Vanilla" that indicate whether the corresponding model is strengthened through root feature enhancement and data augmentation mechanisms. As shown in the Fig. 2, each component of our model helps in improving the accuracy to different extents. Especially for, VEN contribute the most largely due to the ability to learn graph-level representations automatically.

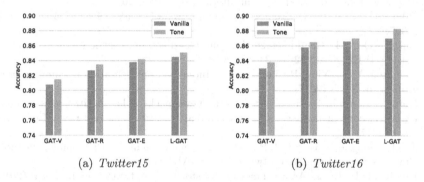

(a) *Twitter15*   (b) *Twitter16*

Fig. 2. L-GAT ablation analysis in accuracy.

6 Conclusion

In this paper, we focused on filling the gap between training and target and proposed a landscape-enhanced model L-GAT based on graph attention network founding on the fact that rumor detection should be defined as a graph classification problem in the current context. We chiefly designed VEN and VRN to obtain graph-level representation by aggregating global information. View of the occluded data, we employed an improved data augmentation method based on DropEdge. In addition, we utilized the root feature enhancement mechanism to strengthen bonds between root nodes and others. The experiment indicated L-GAT can detect rumors effectively. In the future, we will enable the model interpretable and hope for more comprehensive and practical datasets.

Acknowledgment. This work is supported by Youth Innovation Promotion Association CAS (No. 2021155).

References

1. Allport, G.W., Postman, L.: An analysis of rumor. Public Opin. Q. **10**(4), 501–517 (1946)
2. Allport, G.W., Postman, L.: The Psychology of Rumor. H. Holt and Company (1947)
3. Battaglia, P.W., Pascanu, R., Lai, M., Rezende, D., Kavukcuoglu, K.: Interaction networks for learning about objects, relations and physics. In: NIPS (2016)
4. Bian, T., et al.: Rumor detection on social media with bi-directional graph convolutional networks. In: AAAI, vol. 34 (2020)
5. Castillo, C., Mendoza, M., Poblete, B.: Information credibility on Twitter. In: WWW (2011)
6. Dai, W., Qiu, M., Qiu, L., Chen, L., Wu, A.: Who moved my data? Privacy protection in smartphones. IEEE Commun. Mag. **55**(1), 20–25 (2017)
7. Defferrard, M., Bresson, X., Vandergheynst, P.: Convolutional neural networks on graphs with fast localized spectral filtering. In: NIPS (2016)
8. DiFonzo, N., Bordia, P.: Rumor, gossip and urban legends. Diogenes **54**(1), 19–35 (2007)
9. Gai, K., Qiu, M.: Reinforcement learning-based content-centric services in mobile sensing. IEEE Netw. **32**(4), 34–39 (2018)
10. Hamilton, W.L., Ying, R., Leskovec, J.: Inductive representation learning on large graphs. In: NIPS (2017)
11. Horne, B., Adali, S.: This just in: fake news packs a lot in title, uses simpler, repetitive content in text body, more similar to satire than real news. In: AAAI, no. 1 (2017)
12. Jin, F., Dougherty, E., Saraf, P., Cao, Y., Ramakrishnan, N.: Epidemiological modeling of news and rumors on twitter. In: SNAKDD, pp. 1–9 (2013)
13. Kingma, D.P., Ba, J.: Adam: a method for stochastic optimization. In: ICLR (2015)
14. Kipf, T.N., Welling, M.: Semi-supervised classification with graph convolutional networks. In: ICLR (2017)
15. Kwon, S., Cha, M., Jung, K., Chen, W., Wang, Y.: Prominent features of rumor propagation in online social media. In: ICDM, pp. 1103–1108 (2013)
16. Liu, C., et al.: A two-stage model based on BERT for short fake news detection. In: Douligeris, C., Karagiannis, D., Apostolou, D. (eds.) KSEM 2019. LNCS (LNAI), vol. 11776, pp. 172–183. Springer, Cham (2019). https://doi.org/10.1007/978-3-030-29563-9_17
17. Liu, Y., Wu, Y.F.: Early detection of fake news on social media through propagation path classification with recurrent and convolutional networks. In: AAAI, vol. 1 (2018)
18. Lu, Y.J., Li, C.T.: GCAN: graph-aware co-attention networks for explainable fake news detection on social media. In: ACL (2020)
19. Ma, B., Lin, D., Cao, D.: Content representation for microblog rumor detection. In: Angelov, P., Gegov, A., Jayne, C., Shen, Q. (eds.) Advances in Computational Intelligence Systems. AISC, vol. 513, pp. 245–251. Springer, Cham (2017). https://doi.org/10.1007/978-3-319-46562-3_16
20. Ma, J., et al.: Detecting rumors from microblogs with recurrent neural networks (2016)
21. Ma, J., Gao, W., Wei, Z., Lu, Y., Wong, K.F.: Detect rumors using time series of social context information on microblogging websites. In: CIKM, pp. 1751–1754 (2015)

22. Ma, J., Gao, W., Wong, K.F.: Detect rumors in microblog posts using propagation structure via kernel learning. In: ACL (2017)
23. Ma, J., Gao, W., Wong, K.F.: Rumor detection on twitter with tree-structured recursive neural networks. In: ACL (2018)
24. Morris, M.R., Counts, S., Roseway, A., Hoff, A., Schwarz, J.: Tweeting is believing? Understanding microblog credibility perceptions. In: CSCW (2012)
25. Niu, W., Li, G., Tang, H., Zhou, X., Shi, Z.: CARSA: a context-aware reasoning-based service agent model for AI planning of web service composition. J. Netw. Comput. Appl. **34**(5), 1757–1770 (2011)
26. Niu, W., Li, G., Zhao, Z., Tang, H., Shi, Z.: Multi-granularity context model for dynamic web service composition. J. Netw. Comput. Appl. **34**(1), 312–326 (2011)
27. Potthast, M., Kiesel, J., Reinartz, K., Bevendorff, J., Stein, B.: A stylometric inquiry into hyperpartisan and fake news. In: ACL (2017)
28. Qazvinian, V., Rosengren, E., Radev, D., Mei, Q.: Rumor has it: identifying misinformation in microblogs. In: EMNLP, pp. 1589–1599 (2011)
29. Rong, Y., Huang, W., Xu, T., Huang, J.: DropEdge: towards deep graph convolutional networks on node classification. arXiv preprint arXiv:1907.10903 (2019)
30. Ruchansky, N., Seo, S., Liu, Y.: CSI: a hybrid deep model for fake news detection. In: CIKM, pp. 797–806 (2017)
31. Shu, K., Cui, L., Wang, S., Lee, D., Liu, H.: dEFEND: explainable fake news detection. In: KDD, pp. 395–405 (2019)
32. Shu, K., Wang, S., Liu, H.: Understanding user profiles on social media for fake news detection. In: MIPR, pp. 430–435 (2018)
33. Singh, M., Bansal, D., Sofat, S.: Detecting malicious users in twitter using classifiers. In: SIN (2014)
34. Socher, R., Lin, C.C.Y., Ng, A.Y., Manning, C.D.: Parsing natural scenes and natural language with recursive neural networks. In: ICML (2011)
35. Veličković, P., Cucurull, G., Casanova, A., Romero, A., Lio, P., Bengio, Y.: Graph attention networks. arXiv preprint arXiv:1710.10903 (2017)
36. Wang, X., Li, G., Jiang, G., Shi, Z.: Semantic trajectory-based event detection and event pattern mining. Knowl. Inf. Syst. **37**(2), 305–329 (2013)
37. Wu, K., Yang, S., Zhu, K.Q.: False rumors detection on sina weibo by propagation structures. In: ICDE (2015)
38. Yang, G., He, S., Shi, Z.: Leveraging crowdsourcing for efficient malicious users detection in large-scale social networks. IEEE Internet Things J. **4**(2), 330–339 (2016)
39. Zafarani, R., Liu, H.: 10 bits of surprise: detecting malicious users with minimum information. In: CIKM (2015)
40. Zhao, Z., Resnick, P., Mei, Q.: Enquiring minds: early detection of rumors in social media from enquiry posts. In: WWW (2015)

An Overview of Methods for Acquiring and Generating Decision Models

Vedavyas Etikala$^{(\boxtimes)}$ ⓘ and Jan Vanthienen ⓘ

Leuven Institute for Research on Information Systems (LIRIS),
KU Leuven, Leuven, Belgium
vedavyas.etikala@kuleuven.be

Abstract. Decisions are of significant value to organizations. Further-more, these business decisions are often represented in various knowledge sources, and manually modeling them is costly, tedious, and time-consuming. As decision modeling has seen a surge of interest since the introduction of the Decision Model and Notation (DMN) standard, research interest has also increased regarding automatically extracting decision models. This paper discusses an overview and classification of such techniques, including generating decision models from various knowledge sources such as natural language text, legacy code, other models, or event logs.

Keywords: Decision Model and Notation (DMN) · Business decision management · Decision modelling

1 Introduction

Efficient decision modeling adds significant value to organizations in managing their recurrent yet essential business decisions, such as granting a loan, determining credit card eligibility, or diagnosing a patient. In addition, representing business knowledge as decision models increases the interpretability of otherwise complex decision processes and paves the road towards automation of business decision management (BDM).

BDM, which concerns the entire process of modeling, managing, and enacting decisions present in the organization, has increased interest in recent years. Since the introduction of Decision Model and Notation (DMN) as a decision modeling standard by the Object Management Group (OMG) in 2015, modeling decision knowledge at a higher level of abstraction has been made possible and reliable [16,27,31].

Decision modeling with DMN finds its origin in decision tables [33], where rules for decision logic are represented in a structure of related tables. Each decision table maps combinations of input values to outcomes. Decision tables and the accompanying methodology have proven a powerful vehicle for acquiring the decision knowledge and for checking completeness, correctness, and consistency [13]. DMN builds upon these concepts, standardizes decision table formats in

ⓒ Springer Nature Switzerland AG 2021
H. Qiu et al. (Eds.): KSEM 2021, LNAI 12817, pp. 200–208, 2021.
https://doi.org/10.1007/978-3-030-82153-1_17

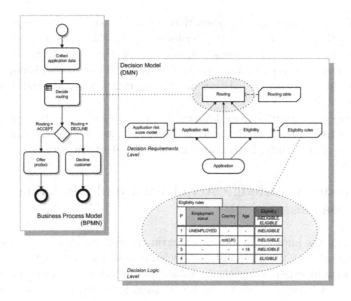

Fig. 1. Routing decision model (DMN) and its corresponding business process (BPMN)

use, standardizes the relations between decisions in a decision requirements diagram, and introduces a standard expression language (FEEL). An example of a DMN for a Routing decision is illustrated in Fig. 1.

Successful decision modeling requires a. good understanding of the business knowledge and learning the modeling technique [37] b. verification & validation of the modeled decisions. Both of these tasks are time-consuming if done by hand. As a result, there is a significant rise of interest in the direction of verification and validation of DMN models and application of DMN in various domains [10, 14,16,21,23,32]. Alongside, there is increasing research towards an automated or assisted generation of decision models with the main goal to minimize the manual labor in modeling decisions, which resulted in several approaches for automatic decision model discovery and generation. These approaches are not just aimed to decrease the time and cost of modeling but also to be inclusive of various data sources.

The following section gives a detailed overview of methods for generating business decision models based on multiple knowledge source formats, and their corresponding techniques are presented. The main contribution of this paper is an overview of classical and modern techniques focused on decision model generation using the DMN standard. These can be used to identify decision logic, dependencies, and concepts in a decision-making process. All the automated techniques are classified as single decision table generation (the result of the generation method is a single-decision table) or full-decision model generation (the result here is a full-decision model). This classification of the methods can help the knowledge engineers and decision modelers identify the appropriate method to build the decision generation method according to their available sources. Furthermore, most of the business decision knowledge is still stored and shared in textual documents [18,28], yet the research in the direction of NLP in the decision model extraction is elementary. Therefore, this paper is also intended to analyze various existing model generation methods and discuss the future directions.

This paper is structured as follows. First, we give a detailed overview of various generation methods in Sect. 2, In Sect. 3 we discuss the findings and implications of the study. Lastly, we conclude our study in Sect. 4.

2   Decision Knowledge Acquisition and Modeling Approaches

Depending on the knowledge source, operational decisions can be modeled using different strategies. Traditionally the decision modeler gathers the knowledge from the domain expert through discussions and models the decision manually. But there exist many sources to obtain decision knowledge, such as text, event logs, and historical case data. These knowledge sources have been studied to automatically extract model components such as information items, rules, and dependencies by identifying patterns in the data. The model generation methods in the literature can be broadly categorised into single decision table (Fig. 2) and full decision model generation methods (Fig. 3)

2.1   Single Decision Table Generation

In this class of methods, the output of the decision knowledge extracted is a single decision table.

Manual Modeling. Traditionally the modeling process starts from a decision description available in a text format as a policy, regulation, procedure, or law, and additional clarifications can be provided from a domain expert during the modeling process. In most cases, all relevant information items or rules are not available. The modeler and the domain expert gradually discover relevant criteria and outcomes in a dialogue mode and refine the table until a complete and consistent description of the decision logic is obtained. The decision table modeling guidelines are given in Vanthienen et al. [34]:

1. Define inputs (conditions) and outcomes of the decision situation.
2. Specify the problem in terms of decision rules.
3. Fill the decision table based on the rules.
4. If necessary, check the table for completeness, correctness, and contradictions.
5. Simplify the decision table and display it.

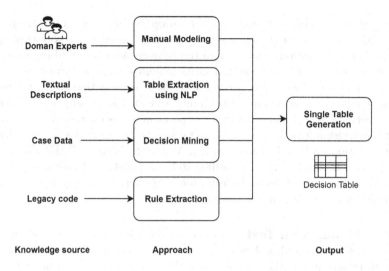

Fig. 2. Single table extraction

The verification step can be automated using tools like Prologa [3,11,33]. Table simplification can also be automated in multiple ways: reducing the number of rules by merging or reordering and splitting a table. Rule merging (table contraction) implies that rules with equal outcomes and complementary values for only one input item are joined together [24,33]. The number of rules can also be reduced by reordering the input information items (in combination with table contraction), which can be used to determine the order with the minimum number of rules. Finally, one decision table can (or should) be split into smaller tables if the table contains hidden dependencies. This process of reduction of the number of rules is called factoring, or normalization [35], similar to database normalization.

Along with the automation in verification and simplification steps, the following automated table generation methods were recently proposed in the literature to order to minimize the cost and time spent in manual modeling.

Decision Mining from Case Data. When historical data about case attributes and their outcome are available, using data mining or advanced business analytics, the decision rules can be discovered from the case data and transformed into a decision table [6,38]. Predictive models, based on past data, are widely used in both research and business [5,19,25]. Most research, however, focuses on improving the accuracy or precision of these models, and less research has been undertaken to increase their comprehensibility to the analyst or end-user. Even if comprehensibility is of a subjective nature, some representation formats are generally considered to be more easily interpretable than others, and decision tables score incredibly well here in terms of comprehensibility, ease of use, and confidence [20,26]. Usually, decision mining complements with business process mining, the discovery, monitoring, and improvement of business process knowledge from event logs that are readily available in modern information systems, e.g., audit trails, electronic patient records, or the transaction logs of an enterprise resource planning system [2]. Process mining can be used to discover models describing processes, monitor deviations, and check and improve business process performance. As decisions are an essential aspect of process models, it is clear that mining decisions are closely related to process mining. Mining decisions is not only about discovering the decision logic at a specific decision point in a process model. A decision is more than decision logic in one table, and it can be an entire decision model (see the later section on Full decision mining). Moreover, because DMN allows separating processes and decisions, according to the separation of concerns principle, the integrated mining of decisions and processes offers promising research topics (see the following section on full decision models).

Decision Mining from Text. As mentioned earlier, decision modeling starts from a law, text, manual, policy document, or procedure. The unavailability of a domain expert leaves the text as the only available source in most business cases. Automatic extraction of models from text has been researched in other standards, such as process models [17], rule models [7], etc. Mining decision logic from natural language descriptions, using pattern-based text mining approaches [4] and transforming these rules into a decision table is still in a novel stage.

2.2 Full Decision Model Generation

A complete decision model consists of two levels: the decision requirements level and the decision logic level. Approaches towards building decision models, therefore, will have to construct elements at both levels, showing both the dependencies between decisions and the logic of each decision [36].

Manual Decision Model Construction. When a business analyst or a domain expert builds a decision model from a problem specification (usually a text), multiple starting points are possible: one can start from the general structure (and build the DRD first), or one can start from the detailed decision logic of each decision and work upwards towards a top decision. Mixed forms are, of course, also possible and very common. And while building the requirements diagram, it is always an option to immediately specify the corresponding logic for a decision or postpone the detailed logic until the dependencies are completely specified. In reality, a mixture of all these approaches will be used. These strategies are similar to well-established modeling approaches in the BPM community, i.e., bottom-up, top-down, and combined modeling approaches, adapted to suit DMN modeling.

From Case Data. Case data can be a rich source for discovering decision rules. This can be in the form of a DMN decision table, but a more complex challenge is the mining of an entire decision model from (event and) data logs, including dependencies between decisions, based on the data relations between them [9,29]. Usually, however, this is in combination with process discovery from event logs (therefore, see the earlier section on decision mining from case data).

From Process Flows. A decision model can also be extracted from the process model when a business process model is available, based on split gateways. In these approaches, the decision points in a process model are identified, and the decision logic containing the data dependencies is derived from the process model, see [1, 8, 9, 12]. The result is a decision model, including the decision requirements diagram and decision logic. The process model has adapted accordingly, where the decision logic is now in the decision model and not hidden in the process model.

From Textual Descriptions. As discussed in earlier sections, mining decision rules from text, using text mining, and transforming these rules into a decision table is one thing [4]. It is even more challenging to mine dependencies between decisions and other elements of the requirements level [15].

From Other Knowledge. There have also been recent attempts made to extract or translate models from SVBR rules [22] and from UML and CMMN models [30].

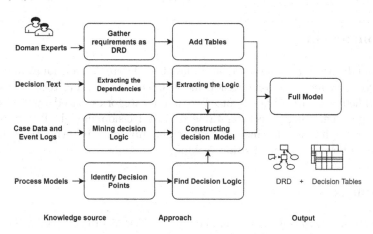

Fig. 3. Full model generation

3   Discussion and Future Work

Decision models make decision knowledge readily interpretable for all the business stakeholders by highlighting key concepts and relationships such as dependencies and decision-making logic. However, there is limited comprehensibility when the knowledge is contained as data logs or as a natural language text. Decision Model and Notation facilitate visualization of the domain knowledge and make the models executable. The research in generation decision models automatically from all the other knowledge sources will have great potential and added business value in the future. In this paper, we have presented the classification of single-decision table generation and full-decision table generation techniques. Single-decision table generation techniques are more suitable when the target model is just a standalone decision table representing the decision logic in the domain. Such content may not have dependencies on any other decisions. If they have any such dependencies, then the logic of sub-decisions is usually abstracted and considered only as an input. For example, Converting eligibility rules in a clinical domain with a single boolean decision output "Is eligible" could be written as a single decision table. On the other hand, a full-model generation approach can be used when the design goal is to generate the full decision model with multiple decision tables and with known dependencies. These methods are a better choice when the input knowledge source has all the information about the logic of the main and sub decisions and the dependencies between the various concepts in the model. For example, In loan-origination process consisting of multiple decisions, a text-based extraction method could be used if there is a policy written in natural language. Current automated extraction techniques, as listed in the Sect. 2, be it from textual data or from case logs, are still at an elemental stage. In the future, the research could move in the direction of advanced information extraction techniques like neural-networks-based lexical understanding for textual data or hybrid or ensemble approaches when there are multiple data sources available.

4   Conclusion

In this study, we have presented and classified different traditional and automated creation methods for decision models. Various existing techniques have been studied and are divided into two main categories based on the generated output, i.e., single decision table or full-decision model. The presented approaches are further classified into into eight subgroups in terms of the knowledge source format and acquisition technique.

References

1. van der Aa, H., Leopold, H., Batoulis, K., Weske, M., Reijers, H.A.: Integrated process and decision modeling for data-driven processes. In: Reichert, M., Reijers, H.A. (eds.) BPM 2015. LNBIP, vol. 256, pp. 405–417. Springer, Cham (2016). https://doi.org/10.1007/978-3-319-42887-1_33
2. Aalst, W.V.: Process Mining - Discovery, Conformance and Enhancement of Business Processes. Springer, Berlin (2011)
3. Antoniou, G., Harmelen, F.V., Plant, R., Vanthienen, J.: Verification and validation of knowledge-based systems: report on two 1997 events. AI Mag. **19**, 123–126 (1998)
4. Arco, L., Nápoles, G., Vanhoenshoven, F., Lara, A.L., Cardoso, G.C., Vanhoof, K.: Natural language techniques supporting decision modelers. Data Mining Knowl. Discov. **35**, 290–320 (2021)
5. Baesens, B., Mues, C., Martens, D., Vanthienen, J.: 50 years of data mining and or: upcoming trends and challenges. J. Oper. Res. Soc. **60**, S16–S23 (2009)
6. Baesens, B., Setiono, R., Mues, C., Vanthienen, J.: Using neural network rule extraction and decision tables for credit - risk evaluation. Manag. Sci. **49**, 312–329 (2003)

7. Bajwa, I.S., Lee, M., Bordbar, B.: SBVR business rules generation from natural language specification. In: AAAI Spring Symposium: AI for Business Agility (2011)
8. Batoulis, K., Meyer, A., Bazhenova, E., Decker, G., Weske, M.: Extracting decision logic from process models. In: Zdravkovic, J., Kirikova, M., Johannesson, P. (eds.) CAiSE 2015. LNCS, vol. 9097, pp. 349–366. Springer, Cham (2015). https://doi.org/10.1007/978-3-319-19069-3_22
9. Bazhenova, E., Weske, M.: Deriving decision models from process models by enhanced decision mining. In: Reichert, M., Reijers, H.A. (eds.) BPM 2015. LNBIP, vol. 256, pp. 444–457. Springer, Cham (2016). https://doi.org/10.1007/978-3-319-42887-1_36
10. Calvanese, D., Dumas, M., Laurson, Ü., Maggi, F.M., Montali, M., Teinemaa, I.: Semantics and analysis of DMN decision tables. In: La Rosa, M., Loos, P., Pastor, O. (eds.) BPM 2016. LNCS, vol. 9850, pp. 217–233. Springer, Cham (2016). https://doi.org/10.1007/978-3-319-45348-4_13
11. Calvanese, D., Dumas, M., Laurson, Ü., Maggi, F.M., Montali, M., Teinemaa, I.: Semantics, analysis and simplification of DMN decision tables. Inf. Syst. **78**, 112–125 (2018)
12. Campos, J., Richetti, P.H.P., Baião, F.A., Santoro, F.: Discovering business rules in knowledge-intensive processes through decision mining: an experimental study. In: Business Process Management Workshops (2017)
13. CODASYL: A modern appraisal of decision tables. a codasyl report. Technical report., Decision Table Task Group (1982)
14. Dasseville, I., Janssens, L., Janssens, G., Vanthienen, J., Denecker, M.: Combining DMN and the knowledge base paradigm for flexible decision enactment. In: Supplementary Proceedings of the RuleML 2016 Challenge 1620 (2016)
15. Etikala, V., Veldhoven, Z.V., Vanthienen, J.: Text2dec: extracting decision dependencies from natural language text for automated DMN decision modelling. In: Business Process Management Workshops (2020)
16. Figl, K., Mendling, J., Tokdemir, G., Vanthienen, J.: What we know and what we do not know about DMN. Enterp. Model. Inf. Syst. Archit. Int. J. Concept. Model. **13**(2), 1–16 (2018)
17. Friedrich, F., Mendling, J., Puhlmann, F.: Process model generation from natural language text. In: Mouratidis, H., Rolland, C. (eds.) Process model generation from natural language text. LNCS, vol. 6741, pp. 482–496. Springer, Heidelberg (2011). https://doi.org/10.1007/978-3-642-21640-4_36
18. Froelich, J., Ananyan, S.: Decision support via text mining. In: Handbook on Decision Support Systems (2008)
19. Gopal, R., Marsden, J.R., Vanthienen, J.: Information mining - reflections on recent advancements and the road ahead in data, text, and media mining. Decis. Support Syst. **51**, 727–731 (2011)
20. Huysmans, J., Dejaeger, K., Mues, C., Vanthienen, J., Baesens, B.: An empirical evaluation of the comprehensibility of decision table, tree and rule based predictive models. Decis. Support Syst. **51**, 141–154 (2011)
21. Janssens, L., De Smedt, J., Vanthienen, J.: Modeling and enacting enterprise decisions. In: Krogstie, J., Mouratidis, H., Su, J. (eds.) CAiSE 2016. LNBIP, vol. 249, pp. 169–180. Springer, Cham (2016). https://doi.org/10.1007/978-3-319-39564-7_17
22. Kluza, K., Honkisz, K.: From sbvr to bpmn and dmn models. proposal of translation from rules to process and decision models. In: ICAISC (2016)

23. Kluza, K., Honkisz, K.: From SBVR to BPMN and DMN models. proposal of translation from rules to process and decision models. In: Rutkowski, L., Korytkowski, M., Scherer, R., Tadeusiewicz, R., Zadeh, L.A., Zurada, J.M. (eds.) ICAISC 2016. LNCS (LNAI), vol. 9693, pp. 453–462. Springer, Cham (2016). https://doi.org/10.1007/978-3-319-39384-1_39

24. Laurson, Ü., Maggi, F.M.: A tool for the analysis of DMN decision tables. In: Proceedings of the BPM Demo Track 2016 Co-located with the 14th International Conference on Business Process Management (2016)

25. Liebowitz, J.: Big Data And Business Analytics. Auerbach Publications, Boca Raton (2016)

26. Martens, D., Baesens, B., Gestel, T.V., Vanthienen, J.: Comprehensible credit scoring models using rule extraction from support vector machines. Eur. J. Oper. Res. **183**, 1466–1476 (2007)

27. Post, R., Smit, K., Zoet, M.: Adoption and implementation of the decision model and notation standard (2020)

28. Silver, B.: DMN Method and Style. 2nd Edition: A Business Pracitioner's Guide to Decision Modeling. Cody-Cassidy Press (2018)

29. Smedt, J., Broucke, S.V., Obregon, J., Kim, A., Jung, J., Vanthienen, J.: Decision mining in a broader context: An overview of the current landscape and future directions. In: Business Process Management Workshops (2016)

30. Suchenia, A., Kluza, K., Wisniewski, P., Jobczyk, K., Ligeza, A.: Towards knowledge interoperability between the uml, dmn, bpmn and cmmn models (2019)

31. Taylor, J., Fish, A., Vanthienen, J., Vincent, P.: Emerging standards in decision modeling. In: Intelligent BPM Systems: Impact and Opportunity, pp. 133–146. BPM and Workflow Handbook series, iBPMS Expo (2013)

32. Valencia-Parra, Á., Parody, L., Varela-Vaca, Á.J., Caballero, I., Gómez-López, M.T.: DMN for data quality measurement and assessment. In: Di Francescomarino, C., Dijkman, R., Zdun, U. (eds.) DMN for data quality measurement and assessment. LNBIP, vol. 362, pp. 362–374. Springer, Cham (2019). https://doi.org/10.1007/978-3-030-37453-2_30

33. Vanthienen, J., Dries, E.: Illustration of a decision table tool for specifying and implementing knowledge based systems. Int. J. Artif. Intell. Tools **3**, 267–288 (1994)

34. Vanthienen, J., Mues, C., Aerts, A.: An illustration of verification and validation in the modelling phase of KBS development. Data Knowl. Eng. **27**(3), 337–352 (1998). https://www.sciencedirect.com/science/article/pii/S0169023X98800037

35. Vanthienen, J., Snoeck, M.: Knowledge factoring using normalization theory. In: International symposium on the management of industrial and corporate knowledge (1993)

36. Vanthienen, J.: Decisions, advice and explanation: an overview and research agenda, pp. 149–169. Edward Elgar Publishing, Cheltenham, UK (2021). https://www.elgaronline.com/view/edcoll/9781800370616/9781800370616.00016.xml

37. Vanthienen, J., Dries, E.: Illustration of a decision table tool for specifying and implementing knowledge based systems. Int. J. Artif. Intell. Tools **3**(2), 267–288 (1994)

38. Wets, G., Vanthienen, J., Timmermans, H.: Modelling decision tables from data. In: PAKDD (1998)

Fine-Grained Image Classification Based on Target Acquisition and Feature Fusion

Yan Chu[1(✉)], Zhengkui Wang[2(✉)], Lina Wang[1], Qingchao Zhao[1(✉)], and Wen Shan[3]

[1] Harbin Engineering University, Harbin, China
{chuyan,zhaoqc418}@hrbeu.edu.cn
[2] Singapore Institute of Technology, Singapore, Singapore
zhengkui.wang@singaporetech.edu.sg
[3] Singapore University of Social Sciences, Singapore, Singapore
viviensw@suss.edu.sg

Abstract. Fine-grained images classification aims to analyze visual objects from subordinate categories, e.g., models of cars or species of dogs, which is challenging due to the small inter-class variations and the large intra-class variations. Recent research has focused on extracting distinguishable local features via part-based model or attention networks to locate discriminative regions/parts, which highly relies on the part annotation, incurs high background noise and ignores the semantic information during the learning. In this paper, we present a fine-grained image classification model, RPN-SCA-BCNN (RSCAB), based on target acquisition and feature fusion. In RSCAB, we first adopt a new Soft-NMS enhanced Region Proposal Network (RPN) for weak supervised object detection to separate the distinguishable object and its background to remove the background noise and costly annotation requirement. Then, we provide a new attention mechanism Spatial-Channel Attention (SCA) to focus on the spatial discriminative parts of the image to reduce the feature redundancy. Based on SCA, we further construct a Bilinear Convolutional Neural Network (BCNN) to fuse the high and low dimensional features by leveraging two networks obtaining more abundant multi-dimensional attention features for classification. The experimental results show that the proposed RSCAB model achieves higher classification accuracy over the state-of-the-art algorithms.

Keywords: Deep learning · Weak supervision · Fine-grained classification · Attention mechanism · Bilinear convolutional neural network

1 Introduction

In generic image recognition, the target objects belong to coarse-grained meta-categories (e.g., cats, dogs and horses), which are quite different and easy to distinguish. Fine-grained image recognition (FGIR), however, aims to recognize images belonging to multiple subordinate categories of a super-category [5–7]. For example, it is to identify hundreds of sub-categories under the same basic category, such as different model of cars/ships/airplanes, or different species of animals/plants. Compared to generic image

© Springer Nature Switzerland AG 2021
H. Qiu et al. (Eds.): KSEM 2021, LNAI 12817, pp. 209–221, 2021.
https://doi.org/10.1007/978-3-030-82153-1_18

recognition, FGIR is a much more challenging and difficult problem, as the intra-class gaps and local differences are small. For example, to recognize different birds, there could be a slight difference only between the shape of the beak, the texture of the feathers or the color of the back [1, 2].

Conventional FGIR approaches first find the object (e.g., bird) and its local region (e.g., head, foot, wing, etc.), and then extract features from these regions [7–9]. They either use part-based models or resort to visual attentional networks to locate discriminative regions/parts to distinguish subtle differences. However, we have observed that existing approaches have several limitations: First, they do not separate the background and objects, which has potentially added a large amount of background noise. Second, the object or distinguishing part is identified by relying on the object or part annotation, which incurs high manpower overhead for labelling the data [10]. Third, on the other hand, the key factor to determine the accuracy of fine-grained image classification is the local detail feature extraction. The fusion between low-level and high-level features has widely used in improving the classification performance [11, 12]. Unfortunately, existing fusion approaches just simply integrate two-level features together that failed of mining the detailed semantic information or ignore the low-level feature information.

To tackle the above issues, in this paper, we propose a fine-grained image classification framework, RPN-SCA-BCNN (RSCAB), based on feature fusion. First, to avoid labeling and background interference, we propose an improved Region Proposal Network (RPN) by using Soft-NMS for weak supervised object detection and segmentation. The detector distinguishes the target object from the background and avoids the interference of background information in the subsequent image classification task. Second, we propose a new attention mechanism Spatial-Channel Attention (SCA) which focuses on the spatial response part and local feature channel in the feature map to reduce feature redundancy to improve the fine-grained feature learning ability. Third, based on the SCA, we further construct a spatial channel attention B-CNN model (SCA-BCNN). In SCA-BCNN, the high and low dimension attention features extracted by the two networks are fused to obtain more abundant multi-dimensional attention features and make final classification decisions.

The contribution of the paper is three-fold: 1) We propose a new target acquisition approach by using Soft-NMS to improve RPN to separate the target object and background in RSCAB, which highly removes the background noise. Meanwhile, our proposed approach only uses the image labels instead of the part annotations which avoids costly manual annotation overheads. 2) We propose a new attention mechanism Spatial-Channel Attention that focuses on the spatial discriminative parts of the image to reduce the feature redundancy, based on which we fuse the low and high dimensional features effectively. 3) We conduct extensive experiments on three widely used datasets and demonstrate the superiority of the proposed RSCAB framework over the leading fine-grained image classification methods.

The rest of this paper is organized as follows. Section 2 provides the related works. In Sect. 3, we provide the proposed fine-grained image classification algorithm. Section 4 and 5 provide the experimental evaluation and conclusion respectively.

2 Related Work

Deep learning shows strong ability in feature learning, and has made great progress in fine-grained image classification [8, 9, 13, 24, 25]. These methods can be categorized as classification method based on strong supervision and weak supervision.

Classification Methods Based on Strong Supervision. Part R-CNN uses R-CNN to generate candidate regions for the image, detect and score each local region to determine the final location of the distinguishing part [8]. Branson et al. [9] proposed pose normalized CNN algorithm, which aligns the position level image regions in the image. Different layer features are extracted from different level image blocks and are concatenated to generate the whole image representation in the CNN. Although these methods have achieved good results, they are sensitive to the detection accuracy of key points, and require annotation of objects and parts, which limits their application in real scenes.

Differently, we use the improved soft-NMS algorithm to optimize the RPN network, which can automatically detect the image to obtain the target area only based on the image category label, and distinguishes the target object of the image from the background to prevent the interference of background information.

Classification Methods Based on Weak Supervision. Compared with the strong supervision method, the weak supervision method is easier in data acquisition. For example, Xiao et al. [14] proposed a two-level attention algorithm, which focuses on the object level and the component level feature information, and uses the clustering algorithm to realize the classification task for local regions. Marcel Simon et al. [15] proposed a constellation algorithm to select the region with high response value in the feature map as the key point, and then extract the local region information. Zhang et al. [16] proposed a fine-grained image automatic classification method based on deep convolution filter. Liu et al. [17] proposed bilinear convolutional neural network, which cooperated with two sub networks to complete the task of region detection and feature extraction. Liu et al. [18] proposed full convolution attention network FCN attention, which was based on the full convolution attention location network of reinforcement learning, and could adaptively select the attention region driven by multi task. Zhao et al. [19] proposed a diversified visual attention network algorithm to locate the region of the input image, and then use convolutional neural network to learn its features. Recently, Jianlong Fu et al. [20] and Ming Sun et al. [22] proposed the multi-attention convolutional neural network and multi-attention multi-class constraint model to integrate the features from multi-channel features.

To improve the performance of image classification task, the above work tries to find the local region distinguishing features in the image. Differently, in this paper, we propose a more lightweight spatial channel attention mechanism SCA, which can effective extract important local features over the discriminative parts. Based on SCA, we adopt two improved B-CNN networks to fuse high and low dimensional attention features to enhance the feature representations.

3 RSCAB Framework

For the ease-of-understanding, we first provide an overview of the proposed fine-grained image classification model, RSCAB based on weak supervision feature fusion. Figure 1 shows the overall process of RSCAB image classification, which includes four main phases. In phase 1, to remove the influence of background noise, we adopt a target acquisition network for target detection and segmentation. After this phase, we completely distinguish the target object and the background which effectively remove the background noise and prevent over fitting. In phase 2, we extract the high and low dimensional features based on the target object image part, based on two improved ResNet-50 networks with SCA attention module. In phase 3, the weighted feature maps extracted from the previous two attention networks are pooled for bilinear feature fusion, and the bilinear feature vectors is then passed through signed square-root step, followed by normalization to obtain bilinear fusion features. In the last phase, the fused bilinear feature vector is input into the classifier and the classification result of the image is output.

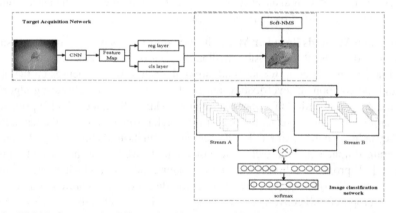

Fig. 1. RSCAB framework of fine-grained image classification model based on feature fusion.

3.1 Target Acquisition Network

In the process of extracting image features, RPN network uses the VGG-19 convolution network to extract the rough features of the detected image, and outputs a series of region of interest. In RSCAB, we use the improved soft-NMS to optimize the RPN network by selecting the target area with higher confidence to separate the target object and background. This can help remove the background noise and effectively prevents over fitting. The algorithm process is shown in Fig. 2.

The given image is passed into a CNN network, which outputs a 3 × 3 small network on the feature map output by the last convolutional layer. Each sliding window is mapped to a 256-d feature vector. In order to obtain a more accurate candidate area, it is necessary to optimize the preset area. We select anchors with 3 scales and 3 aspect ratios, so 9 anchors are finally generated. The output of the classification layer at each sliding window

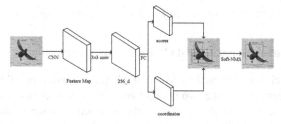

Fig. 2. An overview of approach for obtaining the target acquisition network.

position with 18 scores. The regression layer outputs the location information of 36 target regions of interest (ROI). Each anchor point will be marked as a positive label or a negative label to determine whether it is a target object. If the following two conditions are met, it is judged as a positive label: a label box has the highest intersection ratio; the label with an intersection ratio with any label box greater than 0.7. If the intersection ratio between a label box and all targets is less than 0.3, it is marked as a negative label. For the boundary regression of the target, the targets are parameterized according to the boundary coordinates according to below formula:

$$t_x = (x - x_a)/w_a, t_y = (y - y_a)/h_a \tag{1}$$

$$t_w = log(w/w_a), t_h = log(h/h_a) \tag{2}$$

$$t_x^* = (x^* - x_a)/w_a, t_y^* = (y^* - y_a)/h_a \tag{3}$$

$$t_w^* = log(w^*/w_a), t_h^* = log(h^*/h_a) \tag{4}$$

where x, y, w, h are the abscissa, ordinate, length and width of the center of the prediction matrix box respectively. t_i indicates parameterizing the boundary coordinates of the object. t_i^* indicates the label information associated with the positive anchor point. x_a, y_a, w_a, h_a indicate the horizontal and vertical coordinates, length and width of the anchor point box respectively, and x^*, y^*, w^*, h^* indicate the horizontal and vertical coordinates, length and width of the marked real position respectively.

The candidate boxes of RPN are highly overlapped. To reduce the redundancy, soft-NMS (Non-Maximum Suppression) algorithm is used according to the classification score of the region in RPN. The traditional NMS is a greedy algorithm, which takes the detection box with the largest score as the suppression box, and performs the intersection and union ratio (IOU) operation between the rest boxes and the suppression box to remove all IOU values higher than the preset threshold t. We use an improved soft-NMS to optimize RPN. When the regions overlap, the score of the detected box is multiplied by an attenuation function, which effectively reduces the probability of false negative and improves the detection accuracy. The specific calculation formula of the confidence score is as follows:

$$f_i = \begin{cases} f_i & f_i < t \\ f_i(1-f_i)^2 & f_i \geq t \end{cases} \tag{5}$$

where i is the index of detection boxes, f is a weight function and t is a threshold.

3.2 Bilinear Convolutional Neural Classification Model

The B-CNN model was proposed by Lin et al. [17]. The model includes two networks stream A and stream B, and the two parallel network structures both adopt VGG-Net. The function of the network A is to locate the local information of the object, while the network B is to extract the features of the detected local information. After bilinear combination and pooling of the features output by the two feature functions, the final bilinear feature vector is obtained. The two networks coordinate with each other to complete the task of fine-grained image classification.

The backbone network of the B-CNN model is composed of VGG-Net. As a general classification network, although VGG-Net has certain feature representation capabilities, it has certain limitations for the extraction of discriminative features in fine-grained image classification tasks. ResNet adopts a residual unit learning structure, which allows the original input information to be transmitted directly to the subsequent layers. The network only needs to learn $F(x) = H(x)$-x. ResNet effectively solves the problem of gradient dissipation, simplifies the learning goal, and reduces the amount of parameters. Compared with the VGG-Net, the ResNet has a deeper structure, which can learn deeper image features and improve the classification accuracy. We select ResNet-50 to replace the two-way VGG-Net in B-CNN as the feature extraction function of the improved model.

ResNet-50 contains five groups of convolution blocks (conv1–conv5) with 49 convolution layers and one fully connected layer. Compared with the original B-CNN model, it does not only improve the depth of the network, but also maintains the same output feature dimension, avoiding the doubling of feature dimension. In order to improve the feature extraction ability of B-CNN, the proposed attention block SCA is embedded between conv2, conv3 and conv4, conv5 of two-way networks (see Fig. 3). The improved B-CNN can focus on the contribution of each spatial and channel in the convolution layer.

The bilinear model B-CNN is composed of a four-tuple $B = F$ (f_A, f_B, P, C) where f_A is the first function to extract convolutional features in the B-CNN network; f_B is another function for extracting convolutional features in the B-CNN network, namely the following branch network. P is the bilinear pooling function, which fuses the features extracted by f_A and f_B. C is a classification function to classify the fused features.

The feature output of each position is combined using bilinear pooling. The bilinear pooling operation of the input image l at position I is defined as shown in the formula:

$$bilinear(l, I, f_A, f_B) = f_A(l, I)^T f_B(l, I) \qquad (6)$$

In order to further obtain the feature description of the image, the bilinear features of all positions are aggregated into one feature. All bilinear features are accumulated, namely:

$$x = \emptyset(I) = \sum\nolimits_{l \in L} bilinear(l, I, f_A, f_B) \qquad (7)$$

Bilinear fusion features can be obtained by square root and ℓ_2 normalization of bilinear feature vectors. Finally, the final representation vector z is input to the softmax classifier to complete the classification task.

$$y = sign(x)\sqrt{|x|} \tag{8}$$

$$z = \frac{y}{||y||_2} \tag{9}$$

3.3 Attention Module

After feature extraction of the backbone network, in order to further locate the discriminative local features, attention modules are added to the backbone network to extract the attention feature maps of spatial and channel dimensions respectively. And the integrated SCA attention modules are added to the first branch network conv2 and conv3 and the second branch network conv4 and conv5 convolution blocks to obtain different dimensions of attention characteristics.

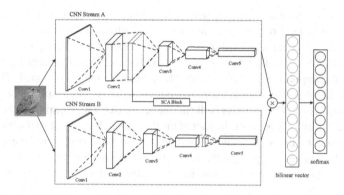

Fig. 3. B-CNN classification network based on SCA attention mechanism.

In this paper, we present a new spatial channel attention mechanism in RSCAB. It works as follows: The original features of the backbone network are projected to the spatial location information of the discriminative region. The focused features are mapped to the channel attention network. Then, the attention is focused on the feature channel containing the discriminative information, and gives a higher weight. The structure of SCA attention module is shown in Fig. 4.

Input the original feature map G, $G \in R^{w \times h \times c}$, where $w \times h$ is the 2-d spatial size of G, and c is the index of channels. The feature map F is generated by a 1×1 convolution, using global average pooling to reduce the dimensionality of F. It assigns weights through a fully connected layer with the parameter W_{fs}, and then compresses the feature map of $w \times h$ into a channel according to the direction of the channel through convolution operation. The sigmoid activation is used to generate the spatial attention

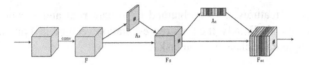

Fig. 4. SCA attention structure.

map A_s, $A_s \in R^{w \times h \times 1}$. The process of spatial attention extraction is as follows:

$$A_s(F) = \sigma(f^{7 \times 7}[\frac{1}{w \times h} \sum_{i,j}^{w,h} F_{i,j} \times W_{fc}]) \tag{10}$$

where $f^{7 \times 7}$ indicates the size of the convolution kernel, σ indicates the sigmoid activation, and W_{fs} indicates the fully connected layer with parameters.

Then, the spatial attention map A_s is fused with the original input G to get the point multiplication by element.

$$F_s = A_s \otimes G \tag{11}$$

Different from spatial attention, channel attention focuses on feature channels that contain discriminative local region information. Channel attention is to use effective network structure to establish the relationship between feature channels through squeezing and stimulating. It automatically learns the importance of each feature channel. By learning the weight, the importance of each channel to the feature map is obtained. The feature response on the important channel is enhanced, while the feature response on the unimportant channel is weakened. This results in a better model, which improves the accuracy of classification, and suppress the impact of invalid channels on the classification results. After processing by the SCA attention module, we can make decisions for each pixel in the image. We can finely highlight the most discriminative part of the image, instead of roughly extracting the attention region, to achieve the purpose of focusing attention.

4   Experiments

Datasets. We use three commonly used datasets in the evaluation, including CUB-200-2011 [2], Stanford cars [3], and Oxford flowers [4]. CUB-200–2011 contains 11788 images of 200 bird sub-categories, which is divided into 5994 images for training and 5794 images for testing. The Stanford cars dataset contains cars from different perspectives of 196 car sub-categories, which is divided into 8144 images for training and 8041 images for testing. The Oxford flowers dataset consists of 6149 training flower images and 2040 testing images.

Evaluation Metrics. We adopt two different evaluation metrics. The top-1 accuracy rate is the conventional accuracy, which means the model answer must be exactly the expected answer. To measure the accuracy of different categories, we also use the average accuracy rate to calculate the average accuracy among all the categories.

Baseline Algorithms. We have selected five the state-of-the-art fine-grained image classification algorithms as the baselines. 1) The mainstream weak supervised fine-grained image classification methods with two level attention model [14]. 2) NAC [15] algorithm uses convolution features to generate some key points, and based on these key points. The key areas in the original image are accurately located by calculating the gradient map. 3) B-CNN [17] extracts features from two convolutional neural networks, multiplies the features extracted by the two convolutional neural networks by outer product. The image descriptor obtained by pooling operation is taken as the final feature representation of the image. 4) MA-CNN [21] uses attention mechanism to obtain key features of multiple components of an image, and then predicts the category of each component feature. 5) RA-CNN [20] skillfully uses the attention mechanism to let the neural network learn how to locate the local area of the target, extract the key information and suppress the background information without using additional annotation. 6) MAMC [22] not only uses the multi attention mechanism, but also introduces the correlation of pairwise Attention Characteristics in the loss function by constructing the constraint of category and attention.

4.1 Experimental Results and Analysis

Feature Extraction Network Comparison: We compare various popular CNN, including AlexNet, VGG-16, Inception-v4 and ResNet-50, to select the backbone of feature extraction. As shown in Table 1, we list the results of four groups of comparative experiments and four popular CNN models. ResNet-50 has the highest accuracy on three datasets. Therefore, we select ResNet-50 as the feature extraction network of SCA-BCNN network.

Table 1. Performance comparison of feature extraction network.

Network	CUB-200–2011	Stanford cars	Oxford flowers
	Accuracy _top-1/%		
AlexNet	66.15%	76.23%	58.48%
VGG-16	75.03%	81.34%	68.21%
Inception-v4	81.21%	85.62%	82.73%
ResNet-50	**83.06%**	**88.33%**	**93.40%**

Bilinear Network Structures Comparison. To study the impact of different bilinear networks, the following bilinear network structures are compared on three datasets: (1) The original B-CNN model B-CNN; (2) The SCA attention module is only added between the conv2 and conv3 convolution blocks of the first network of the modified B-CNN; (3) The SCA attention module is only added between the conv4 and conv5 convolution blocks of the second network of the modified B-CNN; (4) The SCA attention module is added to the bilinear network of two feature functions.

Table 2. Comparison experiments of different bilinear network structures.

Network	CUB-200–2011	Stanford cars	Oxford flowers
(1) B-CNN (VGG-M + VGG-D) [14]	84.1%	91.3%	96.0%
(2) B-CNN (ResNet-50 × 2 + SCA_1)	85.3%	92.1%	96.6%
(3) B-CNN (ResNet-50 × 2 + SCA_2)	86.2%	92.3%	97.3%
(4) B-CNN (ResNet-50 × 2 + SCA × 2)	**86.7%**	**92.7%**	**98.0%**

Table 2 shows that compared with the original B-CNN model, the classification accuracy of the network with SCA attention module only added to one branch network and two-way network in CUB-200–2011 dataset is improved by 1.2%, 2.1% and 2.6% respectively, while that on Stanford cars dataset is improved by 0.8%, 1.0% and 1.4% respectively. Meanwhile, the classification accuracy of adding SCA attention module to the two-way networks is the highest. The results show that the proposed SCA attention module is effective, and the accuracy is improved on three datasets.

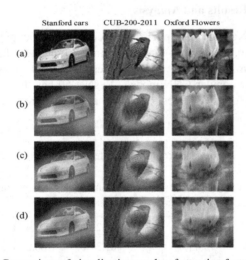

Fig. 5. Comparison of visualization results of attention feature maps.

Effectiveness of Attention. In order to further prove the effectiveness of the attention block SCA, the attention feature map extracted by the SCA-BCNN network model in the two-way feature function is visualized before the pooling and aggregation, and the heat map [23] generated by the last convolutional layer as shown in Fig. 5. For each dataset, (a) is the input original image; (b) is the heat map of the last convolution layer of ResNet-50 network; (c) is the heat map of the last convolution feature map of the original bilinear CNN; and (d) is the heat visualization result of adding the SCA attention block. From Fig. 5, we can see that the network after adding the SCA attention module focuses on discriminative regions on different datasets has better performance.

Performance Comparison. This experiment studies the overall performance of proposed RSCAB compared with other baseline algorithms. As shown in Table 3, RSCAB model achieves the classification accuracy of 86.9%, 93.4% and 98.3% respectively on three datasets, which are better than the classical weak supervision method in recent years. On CUB-200 and Stanford Cars datasets, compared with the original B-CNN model, it improves by 2.8% and 2.1% respectively. The results show that the improved RPN network and the RSCAB model with SCA attention module can focus on the discriminative regions in the image. It can improve the ability of extracting local important features, and achieve great classification accuracy on multiple datasets.

Ablation Experiment. In the ablation experiment, the effectiveness of the proposed target acquisition network and image classification network is verified. Therefore, in this experiment, the results of RSCAB model in the training process are verified through a variety of methods. The main comparative network structures contains: (1) B-CNN (basic) to denote the original bilinear network model; (2) Replacing the two-way network of the original B-CNN model with the modified ResNet-50; (3) After processing the input image through the modified RPN network, the model in (2) is input; (4) Adding SCA attention module to the two-way network feature function of the improved B-CNN; (5) The image is processed through RPN network and SCA attention modules are added to the modified B-CNN model.

Table 3. Comparative with state-of-the-art methods on different datasets.

Network	CUB-200–2011	Stanford cars	Oxford flowers
Two-level Attention [14]	77.9%	–	–
NAC [15]	81.0%	–	95.3%
B-CNN (VGG-M + VGG-D) [17]	84.1%	91.3%	–
MA-CNN [21]	86.5%	89.9%	89.9%
RA-CNN [20]	85.3%	92.5%	–
MAMC [22]	86.5%	93.0%	
RSCAB (ours)	**86.9%**	**93.4%**	**98.3%**

The results in Table 4 show that the top-1 accuracy of the original model B-CNN is improved by 1.5% and 2.1% only through improved RPN network processing or adding SCA attention module. The RSCAB model under the combined action of the two networks is 2.8% higher than the original B-CNN model, and the classification accuracy rate reaches the highest. The proposed RSCAB model has the advantage of the highest average accuracy and the lowest loss in performance.

Table 4. The ablation experiment on the CUB-200–2011 dataset.

Network	Accuracy _top-1/%	Accuracy/%	Loss
(1) B-CNN (VGG-M + VGG-D)	84.1%	85.2%	0.331
(2) B-CNN (ResNet-50 × 2)	84.8%	85.9%	0.326
(3) RPN+B-CNN (ResNet-50 × 2)	85.6%	86.8%	0.315
(4) B-CNN (ResNet-50 × 2 + SCA × 2)	86.2%	87.2%	0.297
(5) RPN+B-CNN (ResNet-50 × 2 + SCA × 2)	**86.9%**	**88.1%**	**0.262**

5 Conclusions

In this paper, we presented a new fine-grained image classification framework, RSCAB based on the target acquisition and feature fusion. Instead of directly extracting features from the images, we proposed a new target acquisition approach, a soft-NMS enhanced Region Proposal Network to detect the target object first, which highly reduces the background noise. The target acquisition approach does not require the parts of the image annotated that removes the manual labelling overheads. In addition, we proposed a new Spatial-Channel Attention mechanism that focuses on discriminative parts of the image. We fused the low and high dimensional features by two networks to improve the utilization of the low dimensional features for classification. Our extensive evaluation confirms that RSCAB outperforms the leading baselines over various datasets.

Acknowledgement. This research is supported by National Natural Science Foundation of China under Grant No. 61771155 and Singapore MOE TIF grant MOE2017-TIF-1-G018.

References

1. Luo, J., Wu, J.: A survey on fine-grained image categorization using deep convolutional features. Acta Automatica Sinica **43**(8), 1306–1318 (2017)
2. Wah, C., Branson, S., Welinder, P., Perona, P., Belongie, S.: The caltech-UCSD birds-200–2011 dataset (2011)
3. Krause, J., Stark, M., Deng, J., Fei-Fei, L.: 3D object representations for fine-grained categorization. In: ICCV, pp. 554–561 (2013)
4. Parkhi, O.M., Vedaldi, A., Zisserman, A., Jawahar, C.V.: Cats and dogs. In: CVPR, pp. 3498–3505 (2012)
5. Nilsback, M.E., Zisserman, A.: Automated flower classification over a large number of classes. In: ICVGIP, pp. 722–729 (2008)
6. Maji, S., Rahtu, E., Kannala, J., Blaschko, M., Vedaldi, A.: Fine-grained visual classification of aircraft. arXiv:1306.5151 (2013)
7. Ge, W., Lin, X., Yu, Y.: Weakly supervised complementary parts models for fine-grained image classification from the bottom up. In: CVPR, pp. 3034–3043 (2020)
8. Zhang, N., Donahue, J., Girshick, R., Darrell, T.: Part-based R-CNNs for fine-grained category detection. In: Fleet, D., Pajdla, T., Schiele, B., Tuytelaars, T. (eds.) ECCV 2014. LNCS, vol. 8689, pp. 834–849. Springer, Cham (2014). https://doi.org/10.1007/978-3-319-10590-1_54

9. Steve, B., Van Horn, G., Belongie, S., et al.: Bird species categorization using pose normalized deep convolutional nets. Eprint Arxiv, 68–77 (2014)
10. Krause, J., Jin, H., Yang, J., Fei-Fei, L.: Fine-grained recognition without part annotations. In: CVPR, pp. 5546–5555 (2015)
11. Liu, W., et al.: SSD: single shot MultiBox detector. In: Leibe, B., Matas, J., Sebe, N., Welling, M. (eds.) ECCV 2016. LNCS, vol. 9905, pp. 21–37. Springer, Cham (2016). https://doi.org/10.1007/978-3-319-46448-0_2
12. Lin, T.-Y., et al.: Feature pyramid networks for object detection. In: CVPR, pp. 2117–2125 (2017)
13. Ren, S., He, K., Girshick, R., et al.: Faster R-CNN: towards real-time object detection with region proposal networks. IEEE Trans. Pattern Anal. Mach. Intell. 39(6), 1137–1149 (2017)
14. Xiao, T., Xu, Y., et al.: The application of two-level attention models in deep convolutional neural network for fine-grained image classification. In: CVPR, pp. 842–850 (2015)
15. Simon, M., Rodner, E.: Neural activation constellations: Unsupervised part model discovery with convolutional networks. In: ICCV, pp. 1143–1151 (2015)
16. Zhang, X., Xiong, H., Zhou, W., et al.: Picking deep filter responses for fine-grained image recognition. In: CVPR, pp. 1134–1142 (2016)
17. Lin, T.-Y., Roychowdhury, A., Maji, S.: Bilinear CNNs for fine-grained visual recognition. arXiv:1504.07889 (2015)
18. Liu, X., Xia, T., Wang, J.: Fully convolutional attention localization networks: efficient attention localization for fine-grained recognition. arXiv:1603.06765 (2016)
19. Zhao, B., Wu, X., Feng, J., et al.: Diversified visual attention networks for fine-grained object classification. IEEE Trans. Multimed. 19(6), 1245–1256 (2017)
20. Fu, J., Zheng, H., Mei, T.: Look closer to see better: recurrent attention convolutional neural network for fine-grained image recognition. In: CVPR, pp. 4438–4446 (2017)
21. Fu, J., Zheng, H., Luo, J.: Learning multi-attention convolutional neural network for fine-grained image recognition. In: ICCV, pp. 5209–5217 (2017)
22. Sun, M., Yuan, Y., Zhou, F., Ding, E.: Multi-attention multi-class constraint for fine-grained image recognition. In: Ferrari, V., Hebert, M., Sminchisescu, C., Weiss, Y. (eds.) ECCV 2018. LNCS, vol. 11220, pp. 834–850. Springer, Cham (2018). https://doi.org/10.1007/978-3-030-01270-0_49
23. Selvaraju, R.R., Cogswell, M., Das, A., Vedantam, R., Parikh, D., Batra, D.: Grad-CAM: visual explanations from deep networks via gradient-based localization. Int. J. Comput. Vis. 128(2), 336–359 (2019). https://doi.org/10.1007/s11263-019-01228-7
24. Chu, Y., Yue, X., Wang, Q., Wang, Z.: SecureAS: a vulnerability as-sessment system for deep neural network based on adversarial examples. IEEE Access 8, 109156–109167 (2020)
25. Chu, Y., Yue, X., Yu, L., Sergei, M., Wang, Z.: Automatic image captioning based on ResNet50 and LSTM with soft attention. Wirel. Commun. Mob. Comput. 2020, 8909458 (2020)

LogAttn: Unsupervised Log Anomaly Detection with an AutoEncoder Based Attention Mechanism

Linming Zhang[1,2], Wenzhong Li[1(✉)] (iD), Zhijie Zhang[1], Qingning Lu[1], Ce Hou[1], Peng Hu[2], Tong Gui[2], and Sanglu Lu[1]

[1] State Key Laboratory for Novel Software Technology,
Nanjing University, Nanjing 210023, China
`lwz@nju.edu.cn`
[2] Huawei Nanjing Research Center, Nanjing 210012, China

Abstract. System logs produced by modern computer systems are valuable resources for detecting anomalies, debugging performance issues, and recovering application failures. With the increasing scale and complexity of the log data, manual log inspection is infeasible and man-power expensive. In this paper, we proposed LogAttn, an autoencoder model that combines an encoder-decoder structure with an attention mechanism for unsupervised log anomaly detection. The unstructured normal log data is proceeded by a log parser that uses a semantic analyse and clustering algorithm to parse log data into a sequence of event count vectors and semantic vectors. The encoder combines deep neural networks with an attention mechanism that learns the weights of different features to form a latent feature representation, which is further used by a decoder to reconstruct the log event sequence. If the reconstruction error is above a predefined threshold, it detects an anomaly in the log sequence and reports the result to the administrator. We conduct extensive experiments based on three real-world log datasets, which show that LogAttn achieves the best comprehensive performance compared to the state-of-the-art methods.

Keywords: Log anomaly detection · Sematic feature · AutoEncoder · Attention mechanism · Unsupervised learning

1 Introduction

System logs are universally produced by modern computer system to record operation states and critical events, which are valuable resources for detecting system anomalies, debugging performance issues, and recovering application failures [10,14,17]. With the increasing scale and complexity of computer systems, the number of logs could be millions, bringing the challenges for the administrators to fully understand the system status and detect anomalies efficiently. While manual log inspection is infeasible and man-power expensive, automated log anomaly detection has become an urgent task and a valuable research topic [24,28].

© Springer Nature Switzerland AG 2021
H. Qiu et al. (Eds.): KSEM 2021, LNAI 12817, pp. 222–235, 2021.
https://doi.org/10.1007/978-3-030-82153-1_19

In the recent years, many methods of automatic log anomaly detection have been proposed to mine abnormal events in logs through machine learning techniques [4,18,19]. Xu [28] proposed to detect anomalies in the log with a principal component analysis (PCA) approach. Lou [20] mined invariants in the log, where the change of invariants is considered as an anomaly in the system. Min et al. proposed DeepLog [6], deep model based on long short-term memory (LSTM) network to detect anomalies by analyzing the temporal information of the log sequence.

Despite that learning-based log anomaly detection has made great progress, it still confronts the following challenges. (1) Unstructured log parsing. Most log data are unstructured and they requires a parsing method to map unstructured log into structured format for data mining. Existing methods [27] [13] parse unstructured log into predefined log template, which require expert knowledge to define parsing rules and they are not extensible to new log events [16]. (2) Semantic feature extraction. Log data contain rich semantic information that are useful for understanding log anomalies. Previous works [6] intended to detect abnormal execution sequence from log data, and the semantic features has not been fully addressed. (3) Unsupervised anomaly detection. Since annotating log anomalies is complicated and man-power expensive, most log data are unlabeled. In practice, the detection of log anomalies is expected to be proceeded in an unsupervised way.

In order to address the above challenges, we proposed LogAttn, a log anomaly detection framework with an autoencoder based attention mechanism. We use deep learning method to embed log events and semantic features into latent vectors, and apply a clustering method to parse unstructured log data into pseudo labels. We propose an autoencoder model that combines an encoder-decoder structure with an attention mechanism for unsupervised log anomaly detection. The encoder uses an temporal convolutional network (TCN) to capture temporal semantic correlations and a deep neural network (DNN) to capture statistical correlations. The attention mechanism learns the weights of different features to form a latent feature representation, which is further used by a decoder to reconstruct the log event sequence. The overall model is trained with normal log data, and then executed online to detect anomaly events by comparing the reconstruction error with a predefined threshold. We conduct extensive experiments based on three real-world open system log datasets, which show that LogAttn has a better trade-off between precision and recall, and achieve the best comprehensive performance compared to the state-of-the-art methods.

2   Related Work

Log anomaly detection methods can be divided into two categories: supervised and unsupervised. Supervised log anomaly detection methods include SVM [12], LR [18], LOGROBUST [29], Decision Tree [5], etc. Due to the difficulties of annotating log data in reality, this paper only focuses on unsupervised log anomaly detection.

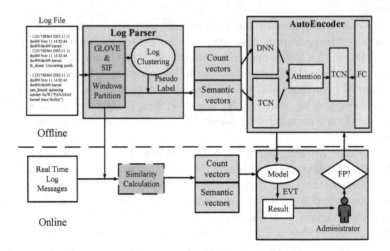

Fig. 1. The architecture of LogAttn.

Unsupervised log anomaly detection can be further divided into shallow learning based methods and deep learning based methods. Conventional unsupervised machine learning techniques were applied for log anomaly detection, which included PCA [28], IM [20]. Xu et al. [28] applied Principal Component Analysis (PCA) to generate the log normal and abnormal subspace, where the normal subspace is the first K principal components and the abnormal subspace is the rest of the dimensions. Lou et al. [20] applied an invariant mining (IM) algorithm to find the linear relationship maintained by the system under different inputs or loads. If any invariants are broken, the log sequence is considered an anomaly. Recently, deep learning techniques were introduced to unsupervised log anomaly detection. LogCluster [19] was a clustering based log anomaly detection method that groups similar log sequences by clustering them and detects anomaly if the nearest group is abnormal. Deeplog [6] was a deep learning based unsupervised log anomaly detection method that used Long Short-term Memory (LSTM) to detect abnormal log sequences. LogAnomaly [22] adopted a Template2Vec method to extract the semantic information hidden in the log template, and detected both continuous and quantitative log anomaly using a neural network.

Different from the existing unsupervised log anomaly detection methods that relied on predefined log templates, our work uses word embedding and clustering method to form log representations, and adopts a deep generative model combining with an attention mechanism for unsupervised log anomaly detection.

3   LogAttn Mechanism

3.1   Framework

We proposed an unsupervised framework called LogAttn for system log anomaly detection, which is illustrated in Fig. 1. The overall framework is divided into two parts: offline training and online detection.

During offline training, the unstructured normal log data is proceeded by a *log parser* to form formalized representations, which are used to train an *autoencoder (AE) model* to learn the normal execution pattern. The log parser uses a semantic analyse and clustering algorithm to parse log data into a sequence of event count vectors and semantic vectors. The autoencoder model is an encoder-decoder structure with an attention mechanism. The encoder uses an temporal convolutional network (TCN) to capture temporal semantic correlations and a deep neural network (DNN) to capture statistical correlations. The hidden layer of the encoder is connected to an *attention layer* to learn the weights of different features to form a latent feature representation, which is further used by a decoder to reconstruct the log event sequence. By training the AE model in an unsupervised way, it can reconstruct the normal log execution sequence effectively.

During online execution, the newly generated log sequence is proceeded by the log parser, and then fed to the well-trained AE model to reconstruct the input sequence. The error between the reconstructed log sequence and the original log sequence is calculated. If the log follows a normal pattern, it should be successfully reconstructed with very low error. If the reconstruction error is above a predefined threshold, it detects an anomaly in the log sequence and reports the result to the administrator.

3.2   Log Parsing Based on Semantic Analysis and Clustering

Log parsing is the first and indispensable part of log anomaly detection, which converts the log's text messages into a sequence of execution flows. Unlike traditional log parsers (such as LKE [9], LogSig [27], Drain [13], IPLoM [21], etc.) that used predefined templates to parse text messages, we propose a novel log parsing method that uses semantic analysis to embed log events into latent vectors, and applies clustering on the latent vectors to form their pseudo labels (represented by cluster IDs). The detailed process is described as follows.

(1) We first apply word embedding on the log sentence through Global Vectors for Word Representation (GloVe) [25]. GloVe is a word representation tool based on global word frequency statistics, which can convert a word into an embedding vector representation that captures semantic features among words, such as their similarity, analogy and so on.

(2) We then calculate the weighted coefficient of each word using Smooth Inverse Frequency (SIF) [1] to form sentence vectors. The lower the frequency of a word appears in a sentence, the more important it is in the sentence, corresponding to a larger weighted coefficient. Thereafter, we let each sentence vector subtracts its projection on the first principal component of the matrix composed of all sentence vectors, which can erase the common information of all sentences and increase the discrimination among the sentence embedding vectors.

(3) After obtaining the embedding vectors of the log events, we cluster them through the DBSCAN [8] algorithm, and use the cluster IDs to form the

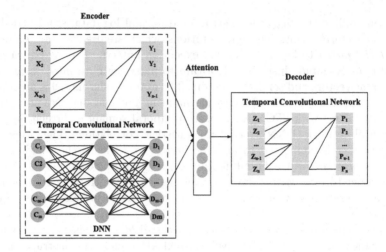

Fig. 2. The structure of encoder-decoder with an attention mechanism.

pseudo labels of the log events. By substituting the log events with the cluster IDs, we can parse the log text as a sequence of execution flow represented by pseudo labels.

(4) We further adopt a window-based partition to divide the log data into subsequences. A subsequence is a basic unit in our model to detect whether there is an anomaly. The log partition can be carried out with a sliding window or a session window. The sliding window partitions log data along time steps into overlapping subsequences (with moving forward a step size). The session window partitions log data based on session IDs where a unique session ID corresponds to a subsequence representing an execution flow of a session.

(5) Based on window partition and the embedding vector of each sentence, we form a sequence of *semantic vectors* for each log subsequence represented by the embedding vectors of the log events.

(6) Based on the pseudo labels and window partition, we form a sequence of *count vectors* for the log subsequences. A count vector is formed by calculating the occurrence frequency of each class of event in the log sequence, which represents the statistical pattern of a log subsequence.

3.3   Log Anomaly Detection Model

The proposed log anomaly detection model is illustrated in Fig. 2, which is the combination of an autoencoder and an attentional mechanism. The encoder uses a temporal convolutional network (TCN) to process the semantic vector sequence and a deep neural network (DNN) to process the corresponding event count sequence to form compact representations of both temporal and sematic features. An attention mechanism is assigned to learn the importance weights of sematic and statistical features. The decoder takes both attention weights and compact feature vectors as input to reconstruct the subsequence of log events. The overall model is trained offline with normal log data, and then executed online to detect anomaly events by comparing the reconstruction error with a predefined threshold. The detail process is explained in the following.

AutoEncoder. Anomaly detection based on dimensionality reduction assumes that the data have a certain degree of correlation and can be embedded into a lower latitude subspace [30]. After the original data is embedded in a lower latitude, the abnormal and normal data will be separated. Autoencoder is a powerful unsupervised learning technique for information compression, where an encoder is used to find a compressed representation of a given data, while a decoder is used to reconstruct the original input. During training, the decoder forces the encoder to select the feature with the most useful information, which is preserved in the compressed representation.

The encoder we used for log data contains a temporal convolutional network (TCN) [3]and a deep neural network (DNN), which are explained in the following.

The time convolution network (TCN) is a new type of neural network model derived from convolutional neural network (CNN). Unlike normal convolution, TCN uses the causal convolution and void convolution to extract features across time steps, which is powerful to capture the temporal dependencies of sequence data and provide a visual field for temporal modeling. In TCN, dilated causal convolutions are used to allow the filter to be applied to a region larger than the length of the filter itself by skipping part of the input, which are formulated by

$$a_{l,t} = \sum_{i=0}^{k_l^a - 1} f_l^a(i) \cdot a_{l-1,t-d_l^a \cdot i}, \tag{1}$$

where $a_{l,t}$ is the output of layer l at time t, and f_l^a, k_l^a, d_l^a are the filter, filter size and dilation factor of the layer respectively.

The deep neural network (DNN) used in our model is a three-layered fully-connected neural network, whose structure is illustrated in the left part of Fig. 2. It is used to capture the statistical characteristics of log event count sequence.

Attention Mechanism. The latent representations of the semantic features and statistical features generated from the encoder are connected to an attention layer [2] to fuse the heterogeneous features and learn the importance of different elements in the feature vectors. Therefore, the attention mechanism can be seen as an interface between the encoder and decoder, providing the decoder with the importance weights from the hidden stats. With this setup, the model can selectively focus on the useful parts of the input sequence to learn the "alignment" between them.

At time step t, denote the encoder's output by a vector of length s with elements $Y_t, Y_{t-1}, \ldots, Y_{t-s+1}$. The attention mechanism can be formally represented by

$$Z_t = \sum_{k=0}^{s-1} \alpha_{t,k} Y_{t-k} \tag{2}$$

$$\alpha_{t,k} = \frac{\exp(e_{t,k})}{\sum_{k=0}^{S-1} \exp(e_{t,k})} \tag{3}$$

$$e_{t,k} = P(Y_{t-k}) = v^T \tanh(W Y_{t-k} + b) \tag{4}$$

where $e_{t,k}$ is the importance of Y_{t-k}; $\alpha_{t,k}$ is the normalized value of the importance; and W, b and v are the model's parameters to be learned.

Loss Function. The decoder consists of a TCN network that has the same structure as the encoder, which is normalized by a softmax layer to reconstruct the input log subsequence. Multiple vectors in the reconstructed sequence represent the probability of the possible types of log events at the current time. We use *cross entropy* [11] as the loss function of the decoder, which is given by

$$\text{Loss} = -\sum_{i=1}^{l} \sum_{j=1}^{N} R_{i,j} \log P_{i,j}, \tag{5}$$

where l is the length of the log subsequence and N is the number of log events; $R_{i,j} \in \{0,1\}$ is an indicator, i.e., $R_{i,j} = 1$ if the i-th log event belongs to the j-th pseudo label, and $R_{i,j} = 0$ otherwise; and $P_{i,j}$ is the output of the decoder representing the probability that the i-th log event belongs to the j-th pseudo label.

3.4   Selection of Anomaly Threshold

After training the autoencoder, the reconstructed sequence of the log can be obtained, and the *reconstruction error* between the reconstructed sequence and the original sequence can be quantified using the Kullback–Leibler (KL) divergence [7], which is calculated by

$$D_{KL}(p\|q) = \sum_{i=1}^{N} [p(x_i) \log p(x_i) - p(x_i) \log q(x_i)], \tag{6}$$

where $p(\cdot)$ and $q(\cdot)$ are the reconstructed log events and the original log events accordingly, and N is the total number of log events in the subsequence.

If the reconstruction error exceeds a threshold, an anomaly is considered to be detected. Here we use the extreme value theory (EVT) [26] to derive the anomaly threshold. The goal of extreme value theory is to find the law of extreme events, which is generally considered to be different from the distribution of the whole data. Extreme value theory makes it possible to detect those extreme events without considering the complex distribution of the original data.The peak-over-threshold (POT) [26] in the extreme value theory uses Generalized Pareto distribution (GPD) to fit the extreme value beyond the threshold. We use the POT to learn the threshold of anomaly log with the following formulas.

$$\bar{F}_\tau(x) = \mathbb{P}(\tau - X > x \mid X < \tau) \underset{\tau \to \tau}{\sim} \left(1 + \frac{\gamma x}{\sigma(\tau)}\right)^{-\frac{1}{\gamma}}, \tag{7}$$

where σ and γ are the parameters of GPD, τ is the anomaly threshold, X is the difference value, and $\tau - X$ represents the part beyond the threshold τ.

The parameters δ and γ are estimated using maximum likelihood estimation (MLE). The estimated values $\hat{\sigma}$ and $\hat{\gamma}$ are used to calculate the quantile under a given anomaly probability q,

$$z_q \simeq \tau - \frac{\hat{\sigma}}{\hat{\gamma}} \left(\left(\frac{qn}{N_\tau}\right)^{-\hat{\gamma}} - 1\right), \tag{8}$$

where τ is the empirical threshold of anomaly detection, n is the total number of all observed values, and N_τ is the number of points less than τ.

4 Performance Evaluation

4.1 Experimental Environment

Implementation. We conduct experiments on a personal computer (CPU: Intel Core i7-8900U 1,8 GHz, Memory: 16 GB DDR4 2666 MHz, and OS: 64-bit Ubuntu 16.04). The default parameter settings are as follows. The TCN structure of our encoder and decoder are the same (a three-layer TCN network), and the DNN in our encoder is a three-layer fully connected network. The window size of the log sequence is 10. The anomalous proportion of EVT is set to 0.08.

Datasets. We use three open system log datasets to evaluate the algorithms, which are described in the following.

- **HDFS** [28]: The HDFS dataset was generated from a Hadoop cluster consisting of 200 amazon EC2 nodes. There were 11,197,954 log entries in the dataset, of which anomaly accounted for 2.9%. We split the log entries into different sessions using the identity character block_id. These sessions are flagged by Hadoop domain experts. We used 4,855 sessions as the training set, which was parsed from the previous 100,000 log entries. The remaining 553,366 normal sessions and 15,838 abnormal sessions were used as the test set.
- **BGL** [23]: The BGL dataset was collected from a Blue Gene/L supercomputer system deployed on Lawrence Livermore National Labs (LLNL). The dataset contains a total of 4,747,963 log entries, of which 348,460 are marked as anomaly. The BGL dataset uses the first 80% (based on the log timestamp) as the training set and the last 20% as the test set.

- **Thunderbird** [23]: The Thunderbird dataset was collected from a Thunderbird supercomputer system at Sandia National Labs (SNL) in Albuquerque, with 9,024 processors and 27,072GB of memory. The first four million log entries in the dataset were analyzed, with the first 80% (based on the timestamp of the log) as the training set and the last 20% as the test set.

Performance Metrics. We use the following standard performance metrics to evaluate the algorithms: Precision (P), Recall (R), and F1-score (F_1), given by

$$P = \frac{TP}{TP + FP}, \quad R = \frac{TP}{TP + FN}, \quad F_1 = 2 \times \frac{P \times R}{P + R}, \tag{9}$$

where TP is the True Positives, FP is the False Positives, and FN is the False Negatives.

Baseline Algorithms. We compare the proposed LogAttn algorithm with five unsupervised log anomaly detection methods: two shallow learning based methods *PCA* [28] and *IM* [20], and three deep learning based methods *LogCluster* [19], *Deeplog* [6], and *LogAnomaly* [22]. We implement LogAttn and DeepLog with the deep learning python library PyTorch. For PCA, IM, and LogCluster, we use their open source toolkit [15].

Table 1. Performance of log anomaly detection algorithms on different datasets (P means Precision; R means Recall; F1 means F1-score; '-' means unavailable)

Methods	HDFS			BGL			Thunderbird		
	P	R	F1	P	R	F1	P	R	F1
PCA	**0.98**	0.74	0.79	0.50	0.61	0.55	0.51	0.55	0.53
LogCluster	0.87	0.74	0.80	0.42	0.87	0.57	0.48	0.50	0.49
IM	0.88	0.95	0.91	0.83	**0.99**	0.91	0.73	0.81	0.77
DeepLog	0.95	0.96	0.96	0.90	0.95	0.93	0.88	0.92	0.90
LogAnomaly	0.97	0.94	0.96	**0.96**	0.94	0.95	-	-	-
LogAttn	0.95	**0.99**	**0.97**	**0.96**	0.98	**0.97**	**0.91**	**0.93**	**0.92**

4.2   Numerical Results

We perform comparative experiments between LogAttn and baselines on the above datasets. Table 1 are the experimental results on HDFS, BGL, and Thunderbird respectively. In general, LogAttn performed well in all three datasets, reaching the F1-score of 0.97,0.97 and 0.91.

    As can be seen from the experimental results, LogAttn, DeepLog and IM are the most effective log anomaly detection methods, while LogAttn has the best overall performance, reaching the F1-score of 0.97, 0.97, and 0.91 accordingly

Table 2. Performance of LogAttn with/without semantic analysis on BGL dataset (P means Precision; R means Recall; F1 means F1-score).

Template	w/o semantic analysis			w/ semantic analysis		
	P	R	F1	P	R	F1
T1	0.94	0.98	0.96	0.96	0.99	0.98
T2	0.90	0.98	0.94	0.96	0.98	0.97
T3	0.88	0.99	0.93	0.95	0.98	0.96

on the three datasets. PCA and LogCluster have poor performance, and their F1-scores on the three datasets are lower than 0.80.

In HDFS dataset, IM is less accurate, but has a recall rate of 0.95. DeepLog also had a recall rate of 0.96, but an accuracy rate of 0.95. LogAttn significantly improved the recall rate to 0.99 and F1-score to 0.97 while ensuring a high accuracy. The dramatic increase in recall rate means that almost all anomalies can be detected by LogAttn automatically, leading to a large saving of manpower, time and resources.

In the BGL dataset, IM and DeepLog all have good comprehensive performance. The recall rate of IM is as high as 0.99, but unfortunately the precision is only 0.83. This unbalanced experimental result means that although almost all the anomalies are detected, there are large amount of normal logs detected as anomalies. DeepLog also has a recall rate of 0.96 with an accuracy of 0.90, which is obviously a better trade-off than the other algorithms.

In the Thunderbird dataset, the experimental results are similar. The comprehensive performance of IM, DeepLog and LogAttn is above 0.80, while that of PCA and LogCluster is poor. The recall rate of DeepLog and LogAttn was 0.92, but the precision and F1-score of LogAttn are higher than that of DeepLog.

Ablation Study of Semantic Features. To show that the addition of semantic analysis can improve the robustness of the whole system, we conduct comparative experiments on the basis of three different number of template libraries T1, T2, T3 of BGL respectively, and the results of with/without semantic analysis are recorded. As shown in Table 2, with the same number of templates, log anomaly detection tasks perform better with semantic analysis. The difference in the number of templates will affect the experimental results. We can see that the comprehensive performance of three different templates stabilized above 0.96 in the case of semantic analysis, while the F1-score without semantic analysis 0.96, 0.94, 0.93 for T1, T2, T3 accordingly. With the same template, the performance of semantic analysis is better than that of non-semantic analysis. We can also see from Table 2 that the change in the number of templates has a small impact on performance when there is semantic analysis, while the performance fluctuation is larges when there is no semantic analysis.

Visualization of Attention Weights. Both semantic information and statistical information have different priorities for log anomaly detection, which are represented by their attention weights. The attention mechanism enables automatic selection and fusion of log characteristics. In order to evaluate the impact of the combination of semantic and statistical characteristics of the subsequence on the log anomaly detection task, we perform a visualization analysis on the attention weight for the HDFS, BGL, and Thunderbird dataset.

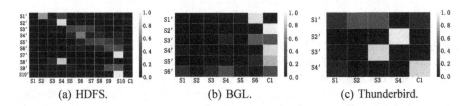

(a) HDFS.   (b) BGL.   (c) Thunderbird.

Fig. 3. Visualization of attention weights. It is shown that HDFS has larger weights on semantic features; BGL has larger weights on statistical features; Thunderbird has large weights on both.

As shown in Fig. 3(a), S1-S10 is the semantic vector sequences, and C1 is the count vector sequence. The concatenation of S1-S10 and C1 is taken as the input of the attention model, and S1'-S10' is the output. From the results, we can see that parts of the semantic features have much higher weights than the rest features. As shown in Fig. 3(b), S1-S6 is the sequential sequence of logs, and C1 is the quantitative sequence of logs, which shows that the statistical information in BGL have higher weights than that of the semantic information. Similar conclusion is found in Thunderbird (Fig. 3(c)).

5   Conclusion

Log anomaly detection is a valuable research topic for modern computer systems to debug performance issues and recover application failures. In this paper, we proposed an autoencoder model called LogAttn that combined an encoder-decoder structure with an attention mechanism for unsupervised log anomaly detection. It developed a log parser that used a semantic analyse and clustering algorithm to parse log data into a sequence of event count vectors and semantic vectors. The encoder combined neural networks with an attention mechanism to learn the weights of different features to form a latent feature representation, which was used by the decoder to reconstruct the log event sequence. If the reconstruction error was above a predefined threshold, an anomaly in the log sequence was detected and reported to the administrator. Extensive experiments based on three open log datasets showed that LogAttn outperformed the state-of-the-art methods.

Acknowledgment. This work was partially supported by the National Key R&D Program of China (Grant No. 2018YFB1004704), the National Natural Science Foundation of China (Grant Nos. 61972196, 61832008, 61832005), the Key R&D Program of Jiangsu Province, China (Grant No. BE2018116), the Collaborative Innovation Center of Novel Software Technology and Industrialization, and the Sino-German Institutes of Social Computing.

References

1. Arora, S., Liang, Y., Ma, T.: A simple but tough-to-beat baseline for sentence embeddings. In: International Conference on Learning Representations (ICLR 2017) (2017)
2. Bahdanau, D., Cho, K., Bengio, Y.: Neural machine translation by jointly learning to align and translate. arXiv preprint arXiv:1409.0473 (2014)
3. Bai, S., Kolter, J.Z., Koltun, V.: An empirical evaluation of generic convolutional and recurrent networks for sequence modeling. arXiv preprint arXiv:1803.01271 (2018)
4. Breier, J., Branišová, J.: Anomaly detection from log files using data mining techniques. In: Kim, Kuinam J. (ed.) Information Science and Applications. LNEE, vol. 339, pp. 449–457. Springer, Heidelberg (2015). https://doi.org/10.1007/978-3-662-46578-3_53
5. Chen, M., Zheng, A.X., Lloyd, J., Jordan, M.I., Brewer, E.: Failure diagnosis using decision trees. In: International Conference on Autonomic Computing (2004)
6. Du, M., Li, F., Zheng, G., Srikumar, V.: Deeplog: anomaly detection and diagnosis from system logs through deep learning. In: Proceedings of the 2017 ACM SIGSAC Conference on Computer and Communications Security, pp. 1285–1298 (2017)
7. Erven, T., Harremoës, P.: Rényi divergence and kullback-leibler divergence. IEEE Trans. Inf. Theory **60**, 3797–3820 (2014)
8. Ester, M., Kriegel, H., Sander, J., Xu, X.: A density-based algorithm for discovering clusters in large spatial databases with noise. In: Proceedings of the Second International Conference on Knowledge Discovery and Data Mining (KDD 1996) (1996)
9. Fu, Q., Lou, J.G., Wang, Y., Li, J.: Execution anomaly detection in distributed systems through unstructured log analysis. In: IEEE international conference on data mining (ICDM 2009), pp. 149–158. IEEE (2009)
10. Gai, K., Qiu, M., Zhao, H., Sun, X.: Resource management in sustainable cyberphysical systems using heterogeneous cloud computing. IEEE Trans. Sustain. Comput. **3**, 60–72 (2018)
11. Han, J., Kamber, M.: Data Mining: Concepts and Techniques. Morgan Kaufmann, Massachusetts (2011)
12. He, P., Zhu, J., He, S., Li, J., Lyu, M.R.: Towards automated log parsing for large-scale log data analysis. IEEE Trans. Dependable Secure Comput. **15**(6), 931–944 (2017)
13. He, P., Zhu, J., Zheng, Z., Lyu, M.R.: Drain: an online log parsing approach with fixed depth tree. In: IEEE International Conference on Web Services, pp. 33–40. IEEE (2017)

14. He, S., Lin, Q., Lou, J.G., Zhang, H., Lyu, M.R., Zhang, D.: Identifying impactful service system problems via log analysis. In: 26th ACM Joint Meeting on European Software Engineering Conference and Symposium on the Foundations of Software Engineering, pp. 60–70 (2018)

15. He, S., Zhu, J., He, P., Lyu, M.R.: Experience report: system log analysis for anomaly detection. In: IEEE 27th International Symposium on Software Reliability Engineering (ISSRE 2016), pp. 207–218. IEEE (2016)

16. Kabinna, S., Bezemer, C.-P., Shang, W., Syer, M.D., Hassan, A.E.: Examining the stability of logging statements. Empir. Softw. Eng. **23**(1), 290–333 (2017). https://doi.org/10.1007/s10664-017-9518-0

17. Khatuya, S., Ganguly, N., Basak, J., Bharde, M., Mitra, B.: Adele: anomaly detection from event log empiricism. In: IEEE Conference on Computer Communications (INFOCOM 2018), pp. 2114–2122. IEEE (2018)

18. Liang, Y., Zhang, Y., Xiong, H., Sahoo, R.: Failure prediction in ibm bluegene/l event logs. In: IEEE International Conference on Data Mining (ICDM 2007), pp. 583–588. IEEE (2007)

19. Lin, Q., Zhang, H., Lou, J.G., Zhang, Y., Chen, X.: Log clustering based problem identification for online service systems. In: IEEE/ACM 38th International Conference on Software Engineering Companion (ICSE-C 2016), pp. 102–111. IEEE (2016)

20. Lou, J.G., Fu, Q., Yang, S., Xu, Y., Li, J.: Mining invariants from console logs for system problem detection. In: USENIX Annual Technical Conference (ATC 2010), pp. 1–14 (2010)

21. Makanju, A.A., Zincir-Heywood, A.N., Milios, E.E.: Clustering event logs using iterative partitioning. In: Proceedings of the 15th ACM SIGKDD international conference on Knowledge discovery and data mining (KDD 2009), pp. 1255–1264 (2009)

22. Meng, W., Liu, Y., Zhu, Y., Zhang, S., Zhou, R.: Loganomaly: unsupervised detection of sequential and quantitative anomalies in unstructured logs. In: Twenty-Eighth International Joint Conference on Artificial Intelligence (IJCAI 2019) (2019)

23. Oliner, A., Stearley, J.: What supercomputers say: a study of five system logs. In: IEEE/IFIP 37th International Conference on Dependable Systems and Networks (DSN 2007), pp. 575–584. IEEE (2007)

24. Pecchia, A., Cotroneo, D., Kalbarczyk, Z., Iyer, R.K.: Improving log-based field failure data analysis of multi-node computing systems. In: IEEE/IFIP 41st International Conference on Dependable Systems & Networks (DSN 2011), pp. 97–108. IEEE (2011)

25. Pennington, J., Socher, R., Manning, C.D.: Glove: global vectors for word representation. In: Proceedings of the 2014 conference on empirical methods in natural language processing (EMNLP 2014), pp. 1532–1543 (2014)

26. Siffer, A., Fouque, P.A., Termier, A., Largouët, C.: Anomaly detection in streams with extreme value theory. In: Proceedings of the 23rd ACM SIGKDD International Conference on Knowledge Discovery and Data Mining (KDD 2017) (2017)

27. Tang, L., Li, T., Perng, C.S.: LogSig: generating system events from raw textual logs. In: Proceedings of the 20th ACM international conference on Information and knowledge management (CIKM 2011), pp. 785–794 (2011)

28. Xu, W., Huang, L., Fox, A., Patterson, D., Jordan, M.I.: Detecting large-scale system problems by mining console logs. In: Proceedings of the ACM SIGOPS 22nd symposium on Operating systems principles, pp. 117–132 (2009)

29. Zhang, X., Li, Z., Chen, J., He, X., Cheng, Q.: Robust log-based anomaly detection on unstable log data. In: Proceedings of the 27th ACM Joint Meeting on European Software Engineering Conference and Symposium on the Foundations of Software Engineering (2019)
30. Zhou, C., Paffenroth, R.C.: Anomaly detection with robust deep autoencoders. In: Proceedings of the 23rd ACM SIGKDD International Conference on Knowledge Discovery and Data Mining (KDD 2017), pp. 665–674 (2017)

DNEA: Dynamic Network Embedding Method for Anomaly Detection

Xuan Zang[1,2] , Bo Yang[1,2(✉)] , Xueyan Liu[1,2] , and Anchen Li[1,2]

[1] College of Computer Science and Technology, Jilin University,
Changchun 130012, China
ybo@jlu.edu.cn
[2] Key Laboratory of Symbolic Computation and Knowledge Engineering Attached
to the Ministry of Education, Jilin University, Changchun 130012, China

Abstract. Network embedding is a basic method for dynamic network analysis. Diverse dynamic network embedding methods have emerged in recent years, however, most existing works regard all observed information as true information, ignoring the anomalous edges in the dynamic networks. When the observed information is mixed with anomalous edges, the learned node embeddings cannot depict precise network properties effectively. Therefore, network embedding that can identify anomalous edges is a promising research topic. Inspired by this, we propose a novel end-to-end dynamic network embedding method called Dynamic Network Embedding for Anomaly Detection (DNEA), which can learn the robust node embeddings based on the neighborhood information and community structure in the dynamic networks. DNEA captures the dynamic characteristics of the network to reconstruct the network topology structure based on Stochastic Block Model (SBM), and detects anomalous edges from the perspective of reconstruction probability. In addition, DNEA utilizes negative sampling to handle the challenge of scarce anomaly labels. Experimental results on real-world datasets demonstrate DNEA can outperform the state-of-the-arts.

Keywords: Dynamic network · Network embedding · Anomaly detection · Graph convolutional network · Stochastic block model

1 Introduction

There are a wide variety of complex networks in the real world, such as social networks and traffic networks. Network embedding is a fundamental method for network analysis. At present, most of the network embedding methods [1–3] are oriented to static networks. However, a majority of real-world networks are continuously changing over time. For example, in social networks, new users are constantly appearing, and the following relationship among users is also time-varying. If we focus solely on static networks, much valuable information will be lost, including the changing rules of the network over time, as well as many new

© Springer Nature Switzerland AG 2021
H. Qiu et al. (Eds.): KSEM 2021, LNAI 12817, pp. 236–248, 2021.
https://doi.org/10.1007/978-3-030-82153-1_20

nodes and edges in the network. Therefore, it is of great significance to study dynamic networks and learn dynamic node representations.

There are often some anomalous edges mixed in dynamic networks that should never have appeared in the real network but were added by some users for malicious purposes [4]. These anomalous edges are likely to destroy the network information. For example, in order to improve the popularity and recommendation rankings of certain products in the e-commerce network, an attacker user may click on a product multiple times to increase its views, or click the product and other popular ones to make them as similar as possible. These anomalous edges are likely to influence the decision of other users. However, most of the methods for dynamic network analysis [5–9] cannot identify the anomalous information in the network. They simply consider that all observed information is true so that the network features mined by these approaches are not entirely accurate. Therefore, detecting anomalies in dynamic networks and improve the robustness of the network embedding is very important for network mining, and it is also meaningful for some practical applications including recommendation systems and data security. This study pays attention to identifying edges that do not correspond with the normal dynamic network pattern.

In recent years, plentiful anomaly detection methods [10–16] based on dynamic network embedding have emerged, which input time-varying network structures to learn dynamic node representation for anomaly detection tasks. However, existing studies still have some limitations. Many methods [13–16] learn node embeddings rely only on the neighborhood information ignoring the community structure so that the learned representation is not stable. In other words, they can perform well when the proportion of anomalies in the network is small, but the detection result drops sharply when the proportion of anomalies increases. Besides, some methods [14,16] define a metric to calculate the anomalous score of edges without explanation. As a result, they are not able to summarize the difference between anomalous edges and normal edges in a practical sense.

To solve the aforementioned problems, we propose a Dynamic Network Embedding algorithm for Anomalous edge detection named DNEA. Firstly, in order to improve the stability of the algorithm, the community structure as an important feature of complex networks is explored. Mining the community structure is based on the network structure and the aggregated neighbor information, and the global information and local information are balanced to comprehensively learn the node embedding. Then, the network structure is reconstructed based on the SBM [17] framework, and anomalous edges are identified by the reconstruction probability. Finally, the training process of DNEA employs the negative sampling method to deal with the problem of scarce anomaly labels. The contributions of this paper are summarized as follows:

– We propose a novel dynamic network embedding method for anomaly detection called DNEA, which can learn the temporal node representations and detect anomalous edges in the dynamic network.

- We capture the neighborhood structure and community structure of dynamic networks, which can combine the local and global information and help improve the stability of the model.
- We explain and identify anomalous edges from the perspective of reconstruction probability, reflecting the common feature of anomalous edges, i.e. the weaker reconstruction ability.
- We conduct anomaly detection experiments on three real-world dynamic datasets, DNEA outperforms state-of-the-arts in both dynamic and static settings. The superiority of DNEA can be proved by the experimental results.

2 Related Work

In this section, we introduce the existing work of dynamic network embedding and the development of anomaly detection in dynamic networks.

2.1 Dynamic Network Embedding

In recent years, the study of dynamic networks has attracted the attention of many researchers, and many dynamic network embedding methods have been raised. Dynamic network embedding aims to learn the time-varying vector representations of the nodes with the evolution of the network, and the learned node representations can serve as input for various dynamic network analysis tasks, such as link prediction, node classification, and community detection. Some methods [5,6] learn node embeddings based on matrix factorization, and then dynamically update node representation according to the smoothness of network evolution. With the development of deep learning, many researchers tend to carry out dynamic network embedding based on deep learning. The studies [7–9] apply graph deep learning including Graph Convolutional Network (GCN), Autoencoder, and Graph Attention Network (GAT) to learn node representations on each snapshot, and catch temporal features of dynamic networks based on the temporal neural network like Long Short-Term Memory (LSTM) or Recurrent Neural Network (RNN). These methods can capture the time-varying network topology structure to learn node representations. However, the anomalous information in the network is ignored so that the learned node representations are not robust, especially for networks with many anomalous edges.

2.2 Anomaly Detection in Dynamic Network

As a classic network analysis task, anomaly detection has been developed into dynamic networks. For example, Goutlier [10] introduces a probabilistic method to generate edges in the network, which determines the anomaly by abnormal connection. CM-Sketch [11] identifies outlier by incorporating local and global structure in each stream and approximates stream structure based on the sketch. As network embedding has gradually attracted the attention of researchers, more and more anomaly detection methods are based on network embedding. Sricharan et al. [12] combine changes in the graph structure and edge weight to detect anomalous relationships changing over time through commute-time embedding. Yu et al. [13] propose Netwalk in 2018, which learns the latent representation of nodes according to random walks in the dynamic network, and detects anomalies based on clustering technique. In addition, recent works [14–16] mostly combine graph neural network and temporal neural network to mine the varying network structure and learn network representation, then define the anomalous score to identify the anomalies. However, they only consider the neighborhood information in the network embedding ignoring the community structure, which results in poor model stability.

3   Method

In this section, we firstly introduce the problem definition, then illustrate the proposed model DNEA and its loss function in detail.

3.1   Problem Definition

Given an undirected dynamic network $\mathbb{G} = (\mathbb{V}, \mathbb{E})$, which can be divided into a series of snapshots G^t according to timestamp, i.e. $\mathbb{G} = \{G^t\}_{t=1}^{T}$, in which T represents the number of snapshots. For any snapshot t, $G^t = (V^t, E^t)$, V^t and E^t are node set and edge set, E^t can be characterized by the binary adjacency matrix $A^t \in \mathbb{R}^{n \times n}$ $\left(n = \left|\cup_{t=1}^{T} V^t\right|\right)$. DNEA is expected to identify anomalous edges by learning node embedding $X^t \in \mathbb{R}^{n \times k}$ in the dynamic network.

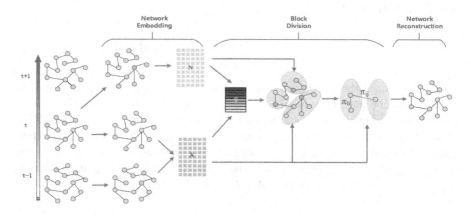

Fig. 1. Framework of DNEA.

3.2   DNEA Framework

Figure 1 demonstrates the overview of DNEA model. Firstly, for each snapshot t, the node embedding $X^t \in \mathbb{R}^{n \times k}$ and the neighbor embedding $N^t \in \mathbb{R}^{n \times k}$ are extracted from the network evolution and network structure. Then the intimacy score between them $c^t \in \mathbb{R}^n$ is calculated, which represents the ability of each node to express neighborhood information. According to the characteristics of network community structure, all nodes can be divided into k blocks[1]. Specifically, nodes with the $Topk$ intimacy score were selected as the center nodes of k blocks, and the block feature $B^t \in \mathbb{R}^{k \times k}$ is calculated through the embeddings of the center nodes. The block-block link probability $\Pi^t \in R^{k \times k}$ can be described by the similarity between block features. Based on SBM, the network structure can be reconstructed using node embedding X^t and block-block link probability Π^t, and the reconstruction probability of the edge is regarded as the metric to measure anomalous score. In the training process, anomalous edges are obtained through sampling, and the objective is to make the reconstruction ability of normal edges stronger and that of anomalous edges poorer.

Network Embedding. According to the smoothness of dynamic network evolution [18], the node embedding generally evolves smoothly between continuous snapshots. The transformation of node embedding is captured by a 2-layer Multilayer Perceptron (MLP) $x\,(\cdot)$ corresponding to the evolution of network structure. The initial node embedding is obtained by $X^0 = x\left(A^0\right)$, and the node embedding X^t is updated as:

$$X^t = X^{t-1} + x\left(A^t - A^{t-1}\right) \tag{1}$$

Then the neighborhood information of nodes is aggregated based on the Graph Convolutional Network (GCN). The adjacent matrix A^t and the node embedding X^t are the input, and the GCN $n\,(\cdot, \cdot)$ obtaining the neighbor embedding N^t is designed as:

$$N^t = n\left(A^t, X^t\right) = \frac{1}{R} \sum_{r=1}^{R} \left(\left(A_{nor}^t\right)^r X^t W_n^{(r)}\right) \tag{2}$$

where R denotes the maximum hop number of the aggregated neighbors. By adjusting R, the nodes can flexibly control the balance between global and local information. When R increases, the nodes aggregate neighbors with more global information; conversely, when R becomes smaller, the model pays more attention to the local information of the network. $W_n^{(r)}$ represents the parameters of aggregating R-hop neighbors. A_{nor} is the normalized adjacency matrix through $A_{nor} = \widetilde{D}^{-\frac{1}{2}} \widetilde{A} \widetilde{D}^{-\frac{1}{2}}$, in which $\widetilde{A} = A + I$, $\widetilde{D}$ is $\widetilde{A}$ degree matrix.

Block Division. The intimacy score c^t is calculated through X^t and N^t, which is used to describe the ability of the node to express the neighborhood information. The higher the intimacy of X_i^t and N_i^t, the stronger the ability of node i to express its neighborhood information. The intimacy score is designed as:

$$c\left(X^t, N^t\right) = \sigma(X^t W_c N^t + b_c) \tag{3}$$

---

[1] The terms block and community mentioned in this paper are interchangeable.

where W_c and b_c are trainable parameters, and σ is sigmoid activation function.

According to the obtained intimacy vector c^t, the node set $V_{topk}^t \subseteq V^t$ with the $Topk$ intimacy scores is selected as the center nodes of k blocks. The block feature B^t is formulated based on the selected block center node set V_{topk}^t as:

$$B^t = X_{topk}^t + c^t N_{topk}^t \tag{4}$$

X_{topk}^t and N_{topk}^t are obtained through concatenating the node embedding and the neighbor embedding of V_{topk}^t respectively.

The block-block link probability π_{ij}^t represents the probability that the node belonging to block i is connected to the node belonging to block j. According to the assumption that two blocks with higher similarity should be more closely related, π_{ij}^t can be calculated through the similarity between blocks as:

$$\pi_{ij}^t = 1 - \tanh\left(\left\|B_i^t - B_j^t\right\|_2^2\right) \tag{5}$$

X_{im}^t updated by Eq. 1 reflects the relationship between node i and block m, and it can be activated by the softmax layer to obtain the probability of node belonging to each block. We define Z^t as the block partition matrix, if node i is assigned to block m, then $z_{im}^t = 1$, otherwise $z_{im}^t = 0$. Z^t obeys a multinomial distribution with a parameter X^t:

$$Z^t \sim Mult\left(1, softmax\left(X^t\right)\right) \tag{6}$$

Network Reconstruction. Based on SBM, the network reconstruction process utilizes matrix Z^t and Π^t to obtain the connecting probability between nodes:

$$P\left(a_{ij}^t | Z^t, \Pi^t\right) = \prod_{g,l} \left(\pi_{gl}^{t^{a_{ij}^t}}\left(1 - \pi_{gl}^t\right)^{1-a_{ij}^t}\right)^{z_{ig}^t z_{jl}^t} \tag{7}$$

The probability is regarded as the parameter of Bernoulli distribution, and the adjacency matrix is reconstructed as:

$$A^t \sim Bern\left(\cdot | Z^t \Pi^t \left(Z^t\right)^T\right) \tag{8}$$

3.3 Negative Sampling and Loss Function

Since it can hardly obtain labeled anomalies, it is unrealistic to use labeled data for supervised learning, then negative sampling [19] is introduced. Assuming that all edges in the training datasets are normal, negative sampling is conducted for each positive edge $e_{ij}^t \in E^t$ to obtain a negative edge $e_{i'j'}^t$ as an anomalous edge. The goal is to make the anomalous score of the positive edge lower and that of the negative edge higher. In the test phase, the ability of anomalous edge detection of the model is verified with labeled data. The negative sampling process considers the degrees of the two linked nodes, i.e., the nodes with high degree are more likely to be replaced. Given a normal edge e_{ij}^t, the probability of node i being replaced is $\frac{d_i^t}{d_i^t + d_j^t}$, similarly, j is replaced with probability $\frac{d_j^t}{d_i^t + d_j^t}$.

The anomalous score of an edge is measured by the reconstruction probability, it is calculated as follows:

$$s\left(e_{ij}^t\right) = -\log P\left(a_{ij}^t | Z^t, \Pi^t\right) \tag{9}$$

The range of reconstruction probability is $[0, 1.0]$. The closer the reconstruction probability of e_{ij}^t is to 0, the more likely it is to be an anomalous edge.

Inspired by [20], the training process adopts the margin loss, and the loss function of the tth snapshot is:

$$L^t = \min \sum_{e_{ij}^t \in E^t} \sum_{e_{i'j'}^t \notin E^t} \max\left\{0, \gamma + s\left(e_{ij}^t\right) - s\left(e_{i'j'}^t\right)\right\} \tag{10}$$

The overall loss function of the model is the sum of the loss functions of each snapshot, i.e. $L = \sum_t L^t$. Note that all trainable parameters of DNEA are shared in each snapshot. The detailed training procedure is described in Algorithm 1.

Algorithm 1. DNEA

Input: $\{A^t\}_{t=1}^T$.
Parameter: k, R, γ.
Output: $\{X^t\}_{t=1}^T$.
 1: **repeat**
 2:     Let $L = 0$
 3:     **for** $t = 1$ to T **do**
 4:         Update X^t, N^t using Eq. 1, 2;
 5:         Calculate c^t, B^t, Π^t using Eq. 3, 4, 5;
 6:         Sample Z^t using Equation 6;
 7:         Reconstruct network using Eq. 8;
 8:         **for** all $e_{ij}^t \in E^t$ **do**
 9:             Sample $e_{i'j'}^t$;
10:         **end for**
11:         Calculate L^t using Eq. 10;
12:         $L = L + L^t$
13:     **end for**
14:     Minimize L
15: **until** Convergence;
16: **return** $\{X^t\}_{t=1}^T$.

---

4 Experiments

To test the effectiveness of the DNEA model, we conduct dynamic and static anomalous edge detection tasks in three real-world dynamic network datasets, and the superiority of the proposed model is verified by comparing it with the state-of-the-arts.

4.1 Datasets

Three real-world dynamic datasets are introduced, including CollegeMsg, Facebook-forum, and email-DNC, and the statistical data is shown in Table 1.

- **CollegeMsg**[2] is collected by the University of California on the social network Facebook. Nodes represent users on Facebook, and $a_{ij}^t = 1$ indicates that user i and user j exchanged at least one message at the tth snapshot.
- **Fb-Forum**[3] is also collected from the social network Facebook by the University of California. This dataset focuses on the activities on the Forum of Facebook, and the edge represents the interaction between two users.
- **Email-DNC**[4] is an email network collected from the Democratic National Committee of the United States (DNC) in 2016. Nodes represent users from DNC, and $a_{ij}^t = 1$ if there was one email sent between user i and j at the tth snapshot.

Table 1. Statistics of datasets.

Dataset	Nodes ($|V|$)	Edges ($|E|$)	Snapshots (T)
CollegeMsg	1,900	59,835	14
Facebook-Forum	900	33,720	17
Email-DNC	2,029	39,264	14

4.2 Baselines and Experimental Settings

To evaluate the performance of our proposed method, we compare the DNEA with three methods that can detect anomalous edges in the dynamic network based on network embedding.

- **Netwalk** [13] conducts random walk in the dynamic network, then learns the latent representation of nodes through the deep autoencoder, and finally detects anomalies based on clustering technique.
- **Addgraph** [14] combines GCN and GRU to capture long- and short-term patterns of dynamic networks to learn the node embeddings for anomaly detection, and introduces negative sampling to deal with the problem of insufficient labels.
- **DynAD** [15] utilizes GRU with pooling to improve GCN, and incorporates the attention mechanism to identify anomalies.

---

[2] http://snap.stanford.edu/data/CollegeMsg.html.
[3] http://networkrepository.com/fb-forum.php.
[4] http://networkrepository.com/email-dnc.php.

The anomalous edge detection tasks include dynamic and static settings. In both settings, the number of blocks k is set to 8, 4, and 8 for collegeMSG, Facebook-Forum, and Email-DNC, respectively, and the number of aggregated neighborhood hops $R = 2$, the margin parameter $\gamma = 0.5$. In the training process, for all baselines and DNEA, the learning rate is set to 0.001, and the maximum iteration is set to 300. AUC (area under ROC curve) is chosen as the evaluation metric, which is widely used in anomaly detection.

4.3 Dynamic Anomaly Detection

Firstly, the dynamic network is divided into snapshots according to the timestamp, in which 50% of snapshots are used for training, and the remaining 50% are used for testing. Note that each test snapshot is injected with 10% anomalous edges. The results for dynamic anomalous edge detection are shown in Fig. 2. It can be observed that the method we proposed is much better than baselines in the three datasets. In the training process, NetWalk only captures the normal pattern of the network by learning the dynamic node representation, without distinguishing between normal and anomalous edges during training. AddGraph, DynAD, and DNEA obtain some anomalous edges by negative sampling, and the optimization makes the score difference between normal and anomalous edges increase, which improves the robustness of the network embedding and overcomes the problem of scarce anomaly labels. With the increase of the number of time snapshots, the experimental effect of AddGraph algorithm decreases. Since the later snapshots emerge many nodes that rarely appear in the previous snapshots, AddGraph cannot well obtain the representation of these newly appearing nodes. However, DNEA aggregates the neighbor information and considers the community structure of the dynamic network when learning node representation, which is more conducive to learning the representation of newly emerged nodes with better quality, so DNEA can obtain stable effects in all snapshots. Besides, our proposed model DNEA can better perform anomaly detection, which proves that the reconstruction probability is effective to measure the anomalous edge.

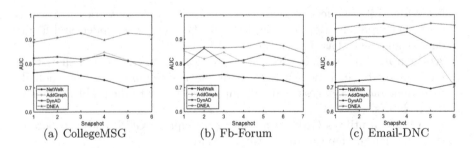

(a) CollegeMSG   (b) Fb-Forum   (c) Email-DNC

Fig. 2. AUC results for dynamic anomaly detection

4.4   Static Anomaly Detection

In the static settings, a simplified version of DNEA without the temporal transformation of the node embedding is conducted. All the data are divided into 50%
for training and the remaining 50% for testing, and 1%, 5%, and 10% of anomalous edges are injected respectively into test data. The result in the Table 2
shows that DNEA outperforms all the baselines in different settings for static
anomaly detection. Especially in the Email-DNC dataset, DNEA improves by
31%, 16%, and 13% on average compared to the three methods. Specifically, the
AUC of NetWalk decreased with the increase of anomaly percentage, and the
performance of AddGraph and DynAD with 10% anomaly is worse than with
1% anomaly. DNEA still can maintain a stable effect even if 10% of the anomalous edges are injected, which demonstrates that DNEA has good stability and
superiority.

Table 2. AUC results for static anomaly detection

Datasets	CollegeMSG			Fb-Forum			Email-DNC		
Anomaly percentage	1%	5%	10%	1%	5%	10%	1%	5%	10%
NetWalk	0.7758	0.7647	0.7226	0.7828	0.7667	0.7210	0.7328	0.7289	0.6927
AddGraph	0.8083	0.8090	0.7688	0.8465	0.8199	0.8091	0.8243	0.8200	0.8232
DynAD	0.8141	0.8368	0.8208	0.8464	0.8431	0.8138	0.8140	0.8604	0.8543
DNEA*	**0.8651**	**0.8634**	**0.9181**	**0.8625**	**0.8585**	**0.8725**	**0.9633**	**0.9599**	**0.9613**

4.5   Parameter Sensitivity

The training ratio generally has a great influence on the network embedding and
anomaly detection performance. We evaluate the effect of training ratio on the
Fb-Forum dataset with 10% anomalous edges in test datasets, and the training
ratio ranges from $\{10\%, 20\%, 30\%, 40\%, 50\%, 60\%\}$. We can observe from Fig. 3
that the average and maximum AUC increase gradually with the increase of
training ratio, reaching the peak when the ratio is 50%. And the difference
between the maximum and minimum AUC value decreases, indicating that the
increase of training data makes the model more stable. However, the AUC shows
a downward trend when the training ratio is 60%. Since there are no anomalies
in the training data, and a portion of anomalous edges obtained by negative
sampling may be normal. Too much training data will lead to the increase of the
error rate of sampling and the decrease of the model performance.

   In addition, we investigate the impact of parameter R on the three datasets,
in which the test data is the last snapshot with 10% of the anomalous edges. R is
the number of GCN layers and represents the maximum distance of aggregated
neighbors, ranging from $\{1, 2, 3\}$ in the experiment. It can be summarized from
Fig. 4 that the AUC is the best when $R = 2$ for various datasets. When $R = 1$,
the neighbor embedding N^t only considers one-hop neighbors, which cannot

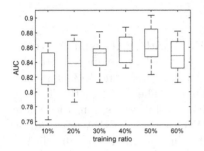 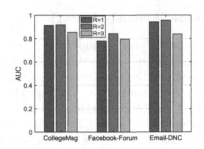

Fig. 3. Impact of training rate on DNEA. **Fig. 4.** Impact of parameter R on DNEA.

incorporate comprehensive neighborhood information. However, the embedding will absorb a lot of distant neighbor nodes when R continues to increase. These distant neighbors may provide some useless information, or even noise, which will confuse network embedding and degrade model performance. When $R = 2$, block center nodes can better express their neighborhood information and improve model performance by balancing global and local information, which helps to better mine community structure.

5   Conclusion

We present an end-to-end dynamic network embedding method for anomaly detection DNEA, which can learn robust node representation to detect anomalous edges in the dynamic network. DNEA selects nodes that can best express their neighborhood information as the block center nodes, and then the community structure is captured combining the global and local information, which improves the stability of the model. The topology structure is reconstructed, and the network reconstruction probability is utilized to define the anomalous edge, which better grasps the general feature of anomalous edges. Through anomalous edge detection tasks, the stability and superiority of DNEA are verified.

Acknowledgment. This research was funded by the National Natural Science Foundation of China under grant number 61876069; Jilin Province Key Scientific and Technological Research and Development project under grant numbers 20180201067GX, 20180201044GX; Jilin Province Natural Science Foundation under grant No. 20200201036JC.

References

1. Perozzi, B., Al-Rfou, R., Skiena, S.: DeepWalk: online learning of social representations. In: Proceedings of the 20th ACM SIGKDD International Conference on Knowledge Discovery and Data Mining, pp. 701–710 (2014)

2. Grover, A., Leskovec, J.: node2vec: scalable feature learning for networks. In: Proceedings of the 22nd ACM SIGKDD International Conference on Knowledge Discovery and Data Mining, pp. 855–864 (2016)
3. Kipf, T.N., Welling, M.: Semi-supervised classification with graph convolutional networks. In: 5th International Conference on Learning Representations (2017)
4. Noble, C.C., Cook, D.J.: Graph-based anomaly detection. In: Proceedings of the ninth ACM SIGKDD International Conference on Knowledge Discovery and Data Mining, pp. 631–636 (2003)
5. Li, J., Dani, H., Hu, X., Tang, J., Chang, Y., Liu, H.: Attributed network embedding for learning in a dynamic environment. In: Proceedings of the 2017 ACM on Conference on Information and Knowledge Management, pp. 387–396 (2017)
6. Zhu, D., Cui, P., Zhang, Z., Pei, J., Zhu, W.: High-order proximity preserved embedding for dynamic networks. IEEE Trans. Knowl. Data Eng. **30**(11), 2134–2144 (2018)
7. Goyal, P., Chhetri, S.R., Canedo, A.: dyngraph2vec: capturing network dynamics using dynamic graph representation learning. Knowl.-Based Syst. **187**, 104816 (2020)
8. Pareja, A., et al.: EvolveGCN: evolving graph convolutional networks for dynamic graphs. Proceedings of the AAAI Conference on Artificial Intelligence, vol. 34, pp. 5363–5370 (2020)
9. Sankar, A., Wu, Y., Gou, L., Zhang, W., Yang, H.: DySAT: deep neural representation learning on dynamic graphs via self-attention networks. In: Proceedings of the 13th International Conference on Web Search and Data Mining, pp. 519–527 (2020)
10. Aggarwal, C.C., Zhao, Y., Philip, S.Y.: Outlier detection in graph streams. In: 2011 IEEE 27th International Conference on Data Engineering, pp. 399–409. IEEE (2011)
11. Ranshous, S., Harenberg, S., Sharma, K., Samatova, N.F.: A scalable approach for outlier detection in edge streams using sketch-based approximations. In: Proceedings of the 2016 SIAM International Conference on Data Mining, pp. 189–197. SIAM (2016)
12. Sricharan, K., Das, K.: Localizing anomalous changes in time-evolving graphs. In: Proceedings of the 2014 ACM SIGMOD International conference on Management of Data, pp. 1347–1358 (2014)
13. Yu, W., Cheng, W., Aggarwal, C.C., Zhang, K., Chen, H., Wang, W.: NetWalk: a flexible deep embedding approach for anomaly detection in dynamic networks. In: Proceedings of the 24th ACM SIGKDD International Conference on Knowledge Discovery & Data Mining, pp. 2672–2681 (2018)
14. Zheng, L., Li, Z., Li, J., Li, Z., Gao, J.: AddGraph: anomaly detection in dynamic graph using attention-based temporal GCN. In: IJCAI, pp. 4419–4425 (2019)
15. Zhu, D., Ma, Y., Liu, Y.: A flexible attentive temporal graph networks for anomaly detection in dynamic networks. In: 2020 IEEE 19th International Conference on Trust, Security and Privacy in Computing and Communications (TrustCom), pp. 870–875. IEEE (2020)
16. Wang, B., Hayashi, T., Ohsawa, Y.: Hierarchical graph convolutional network for data evaluation of dynamic graphs. In: 2020 IEEE International Conference on Big Data (Big Data), pp. 4475–4481. IEEE (2020)
17. Holland, P.W., Laskey, K.B., Leinhardt, S.: Stochastic blockmodels: first steps. Social Netw. **5**(2), 109–137 (1983)

18. Chi, Y., Song, X., Zhou, D., Hino, K., Tseng, B.L.: Evolutionary spectral clustering by incorporating temporal smoothness. In: Proceedings of the 13th ACM SIGKDD International Conference on Knowledge Discovery and Data Mining, pp. 153–162 (2007)
19. Wang, Z., Zhang, J., Feng, J., Chen, Z.: Knowledge graph embedding by translating on hyperplanes. In: Proceedings of the AAAI Conference on Artificial Intelligence, vol. 28 (2014)
20. Lin, Y., Liu, Z., Sun, M., Liu, Y., Zhu, X.: Learning entity and relation embeddings for knowledge graph completion. In: Proceedings of the AAAI Conference on Artificial Intelligence, vol. 29 (2015)

Adversarial Constraint Evaluation on Biomedical Text Mining

Yashen Wang[(⊠)] and Huanhuan Zhang

National Engineering Laboratory for Risk Perception and Prevention (RPP), China
Academy of Electronics and Information Technology of CETC, Beijing, China
yswang@bit.edu.cn

Abstract. Language model pre-training has been shown to be effective for improving many NLP tasks, relying on its ability of representing complex context. The BERT language model (LM) has achieved remarkable results in standard performance indicators for tasks such as Named Entity Recognition (NER) and Semantic Text Similarity (STS), and has made significant progress in the field of biomedical natural language processing. This paper proposes a adversarial evaluation scheme for medical NER and medical STS. To this end, we propose three types of attack constraints, including semantics, grammaticality, and non-suspicion, as well as their corresponding automatic evaluation mechanisms. In these adversarial environments, the accuracy of the model drops significantly, and we quantify the extent of this performance loss. We also demonstrate that through adversarial training of each comparative model, the robustness of the model can be significantly improved.

Keywords: Adversarial examples · Adversarial constraint ·
Adversarial evaluation · Biomedical text mining

1 Introduction

As a critical step of text (structured) mining and understanding in biomedical literature, Biomedical Natural Language Processing (Biomedical NLP) in biomedical literature is presently one of the internationally concerned research question. Some applications of these technologies include drug-drug interaction, genetic disease technology, drug repurposing, new drug development, or automatic screening of biomedical documents [5, 6, 33]. With the exponential growth of digital biomedical literature, the application of natural language processing in decision-making is becoming more and more necessary [3].

Meanwhile, language model pre-training, such as ELMo [21] and BERT [7], has been shown to be effective for improving many NLP tasks, relying on its ability of representing complex context. These models have achieved remarkable results in standard performance indicators for tasks such as Named Entity Recognition (NER), Semantic Text Similarity (STS) and and Multi-label Classification, and has made significant progress in the field of biomedical NLP.

H. Qiu et al. (Eds.): KSEM 2021, LNAI 12817, pp. 249–261, 2021.
https://doi.org/10.1007/978-3-030-82153-1_21

A natural choice, therefore, is to apply these models to biomedical NLP [17]. However, despite the impressive results achieved by the NLP models mentioned above, in the domain of automated medical decision making, the robustness of the models used is more critical because they may affect the health of the patient. It's necessary to test the robustness of these models by using adversarial attacks in biomedical NLP tasks [9].

This work mainly focuses on the pre-trained BERT language model to operate an adversarial evaluation with three adversarial constraints on two biomedical text mining tasks. Especially, we present three adversarial constraints for biomedical adversarial examples, i.e., semantics, grammaticality, and non-suspicion, and moreover their corresponding automatic evaluation methods are discussed. Furthermore, this paper tests the strength of pre-trained BERT for medical tasks under these different constraints of adversarial attacks in medical Named Entity Recognition (NER) task by using [13] and medical Semantic Textual Similarity (STS) task by using [24]. From the experimental results, Finally, we demonstrate that the use of the proposed adversarial examples during training can increase the robustness of the model.

2   Related Work

An adversarial example is an input transformed by small perturbations that machine learning models consistently misclassify [28]. Recently they have been found vulnerable to adversarial examples that are legitimate inputs altered by small and often imperceptible perturbation [9]. This evaluation strategy shows that slight disturbances in the input may cause serious failures of the deep neural network [3]. E.g., the adversarial example is found to cheat the deep neural network for image classification task, e.g., two images that look exactly the same receive totally different predictions from the classifier. Most works make gradient-based perturbation on continuous input spaces. Previous research has proposed many kinds of adversarial attacks: (i) character substitution attack, which used character replacements to change a word into one that the model could not recognize [8,14]; (ii) word insertion/removal attack, which used heuristics to generate perturbed inputs by adding or removing important words [10,23]; (iii) synonym substitution attack ,which replaced important words from the input with synonyms [2,11]. Besides, [25] and [10] explored the creation of adversarial examples through concatenation of phrases to the input.

While existing works on adversarial examples have obtained success in the image and speech domains [1], it is still challenging to deal with text data in many applications of natural language processing (NLP) [28,29]. In most cases, the perturbation methods developed for images cannot be applied directly to text. Inspired by the approaches in computer vision, previous work has tested many NLP model's robustness by using adversarial attacks, showing that they are fragile under certain test conditions [11,31]. More recently, adversarial attacks have been applied to pre-trained models based on recurrent and transformer-based networks [11], involves applying intentional perturbations to the input sentences and testing whether they will make the model produce incorrect predictions.

This approach has shown that the models are still weak and have limited ability to generalize or understand the tasks they deal with [3,11]. On the other hand, by constructing high-quality opponents and including them in the training data, the robustness and generalization ability of the Machine Learning (ML) model can be improved [9].

Table 1. Adversarial examples with Semantics, Grammaticality and Non-Suspect adversarial constraints.

Adversarial Constraint	Adversarial Example	Description
Original	x: Avastin is targeted to treat breast cancers that carry a special genetic marker	–
→Semantic	x_{adv}: Avastin is targeted to treat udder cancers that carry a special genetic marker	replacing words in x with synonyms, aiming to create examples that preserve semantics
→Grammaticality	x_{adv}: Avastin is targeted to treat udder cancers that carries a special genetic marker	x is grammatically correct than x_{adv}, aiming to create examples that preserve grammaticality
→Non-Suspect	x_{adv}: Avastin is targeted to treat breast cancers that are gonna carry a special genetic marker	A human reader may suspect x_{adv} to have been modified, aiming to create examples that preserve non-suspect

3 Biomedical Adversarial Constraint Evaluation

Formally, this paper defines $\mathcal{F} : \mathcal{X} \to \mathcal{Y}$ as a predictive model, e.g., a deep neural network based NER model. Wherein, notation $\mathcal{X}$ denotes the input space and $\mathcal{Y}$ indicates the output space. Following [17], this paper focuses on adversarial perturbations which perturb a correctly predicted input, $x \in \mathcal{X}$, into an input which fools the model, x_{adv}.

3.1 Constraints on Adversarial Examples

We introduces three constraints on adversarial perturbations in biomedical natural language: semantics, grammatically, and non-suspicion. Also, we show examples of the adversarial attacks in Table 1.

(C1) **Semantics**: This constraint requires that semantics be preserved between x and x_{adv} [17]. A specific threat model for such adversarial examples is like deceptive plagiarism detection software. The attacker must preserve the semantics of the original document while avoiding detection. Many attacks contain semantic constraints to ensure that the ground-truth output is preserved. As long as the semantics of the input remain unchanged, the ground-truth output remains unchanged. But there are exceptions: it is conceivable that maintaining semantics does not necessarily maintain the task of outputting ground-truth.

(C2) **Grammaticality**: Note that, the grammatical constraints emphasized here, refer to descriptive grammars rather than prescriptive grammars. Under this constraint, the attacker is limited to the perturbation without introducing syntax errors. Because syntax errors do not necessarily change semantics. In the abovementioned plagiarism threat model, grammatical constraints apply.

(C3) **Non-suspect**: The non-suspect constraint specifies that x_{adv} must appear unmodified. Although the disturbance retains semantics and grammar, it switches between different writing types (e.g., modern English and ancient English, written-language and oral-language, as well as official documents and family letters etc.,), so readers may doubt it. Note that the definition of a non-suspect constraint depends on the context. Sentences that are not suspicious in kindergarten assignments may be suspicious in academic papers.

3.2   Adversarial Constraint Evaluation Method

A joint model for biomedical text is proposed here, which combine ScispaCy model [19] and TextFooler model [11]. Similar to [3], this paper utilizes ScispaCy models for processing texts to retrieve the medical and disease entities and terms of each sentence. We then leverage TextFooler Model to generate adversarial text. The TextFooler model claims that the created perturbations can retain semantics (related to C1), maintain grammaticality (related to C2), and comply with non-suspicion constraints (related to C3). Meanwhile, it reports high attack success rates, and attacks the most effective models, e.g., BERT. Besides, for Synonymy Adversaries, PyMedTermino [12] is utilized here, which uses the biomedical vocabulary of UMLS, to find the most similar or related words (synonyms) to the retrieved words [3].

(E1) **Automatic Evaluation of Semantics**: The STS benchmark is used as a general measurement method [17]. [16] studied the general evaluation measurements of machine translation (MT) task, such as BLEU, METEOR and chrF, as agents of semantic similarity in attack settings [22]. Although these n-gram-based methods have a small amount of calculation and can work well in a machine translation environment, they have *nothing* to do with human judgment and sentence coding. The sentence encoder encodes two sentences into a pair of fixed-length vectors, and then uses the cosine distance between the vectors as the similarity score. E.g., [11] utilized the Universal Sentence Encoder (USE) to evaluate semantic similarity and obtain a Pearson correlation score of 0.782 on the STS benchmark. Another evaluation option is BERT, with a score of 0.876 [7]. In addition, synonym substitution methods, e.g., [11] and [2], usually required that words can only be replaced with adjacent words in the corresponding embedding space, which aims to push synonyms together and separate antonyms.

(E2) **Automatic Evaluation of Grammaticality:** The easiest way to automatically evaluate grammar correctness is to use a rule-based grammar checker. Open-source grammar checking is available online in many languages. Following [17], LanguageTool [18], which is a popular and open-source checking tool, is utilized in this paper. LanguageTool provides thousands of human rules for English and a downloadable server interface for sentence analysis. Although there are other rule-based and some model-based syntax checker, the comparison between them is beyond the scope of this article.

(E3) **Automatic Evaluation of Non-suspect:** Automatic assessment can be used to guess if a hostile example is suspect. Models can be trained to classify articles as real or unstable, just like human judgment. For example, [27] trained sentence coders in real / false tasks as agents to assess language acceptability. Recently, [30] proved that GLOVER, a text generation model based on transformer, can classify the news articles generated by itself as human or machine written with high precision.

4   Biomedical Text Mining Tasks

Following [3], two tasks from the recently introduced BLUE benchmark [20] are discussed here.

(T1) **Biomedical Named Entity Recognition:** Named Entity Recognition (short as NER) is a classical subtask of information extraction. It tries to locate named entities in the given text and classify them into predefined medical categories (such as protein, cell type, chemical substance, disease, etc.). For this task, this paper introduces the BC5CDR dataset [13], consisting of 1,500 PubMed articles with 4,409 annotated chemicals and 5,818 diseases. They were selected from the CTD-Pfzer corpus that was used in the BioCreative V chemical-disease relation task. Given each word in a sentence, the goal of the model is to predict its label according to the BIO format. Two variants of the dataset are utilized here, one is related to disease and the other is related to chemical composition.

(T2) **Biomedical Semantic Textual Similarity:** Semantic Textual Similarity (STS) measures the equivalence of the underlying semantics of a pair of text fragments. This task aims at predicting the similarity between the given two medical sentences. We use the BioSSES dataset [24], which is a corpus of sentence pairs selected from the Biomedical Summarization Track. The goal of BioSSES is to use WordNet as a general domain ontology and Unified Medical Language System (UMLS) [15,32] as a biomedical domain ontology to calculate the similarity of biomedical sentences. The main task is to estimate the similarity score between a pair of sentences, which has been manually verified by doctors.

Table 2. Results from running the attack with Semantics, Grammaticality and Non-Suspect constraints in biomedical named entity recognition (NER) task.

Train Set	Model	Test Set	Precision	Recall	F-1
BC5CDR-Chemical	**BERT**	Original	**0.895**	**0.908**	**0.901**
		Semantics	0.737	0.755	0.746
		Grammaticality	0.741	0.690	0.715
		Non-Suspect	0.615	0.565	0.589
		Mixture (1:1:1)	0.625	0.546	0.583
	BiLSTM	Original	**0.894**	**0.853**	**0.873**
		Semantics	0.729	0.747	0.738
		Grammaticality	0.733	0.682	0.707
		Non-suspect	0.608	0.558	0.582
		Mixture(1:1:1)	0.618	0.540	0.577
BC5CDR-Disease	**BERT**	Original	**0.832**	**0.844**	**0.838**
		Semantics	0.340	0.394	0.365
		Grammaticality	0.548	0.281	0.371
		Non-Suspect	0.642	0.340	0.445
		Mixture (1:1:1)	0.533	0.276	0.364
	BiLSTM	Original	**0.825**	**0.842**	**0.834**
		Semantics	0.334	0.387	0.359
		Grammaticality	0.539	0.276	0.365
		Non-suspect	0.631	0.334	0.437
		Mixture(1:1:1)	0.524	0.271	0.357

Table 3. Results from running the attack with Semantics, Grammaticality and Non-Suspect constraints in biomedical semantic textual similarity (STS) task.

Train Set	Test Set	Pearson	Spearman
BioSSES	Original	0.829	**0.813**
	Semantics	**0.878**	0.672
	Grammaticality	0.767	0.613
	Non-suspect	0.773	0.782
	Mixture(1:1:1)	0.768	0.630

5   Experiments

5.1   Experimental Setup

Following [3], pre-trained BERT model and Bi-LSTM model are used here, because of their outstanding performance: (i) For pre-trained BERT model, we follow the fine-tuning procedure and evaluation metrics proposed on the

BLUE benchmark [20]. Especially, for the special choice of BERT, this paper uses BERT-base models pre-trained on PubMed dataset [20]. We use the original training set for each task to fine-tune the model, and use the original testing set and adversarial training set to evaluate the model. and (ii) For Bi-LSTM model, we follow the scheme of [26] for biomedical NER task, and adopt [4] for biomedical STS task.

In terms of measurement: (i) NER task utilizes F1 score for measurement; and (ii) STS task utilizes Pearson correlation coefficient for measurement.

5.2 Adversarial Evaluation for Biomedical Named Entity Recognition

Table 2 reports the NER results of the BC5CDR dataset on the original test set as well as our adversarial examples. Especially, we also mixture the test set with three kinds of adversarial examples with 1:1:1 and measure the combined effect of all the adversarial constraints. In this case, original test set is divided into three parts, and for each part, the corresponding examples are attacked by Semantic, Grammaticality and Non-Suspect respectively. We could conclude that the performance of BERT drops across all adversarial attacks. On dataset BC5CDR-Chemical, the F-1 performance drops 17.62% and 17.17% after Semantic attack and Grammaticality attack, and the drop is relatively slight; while the performance decreases more evidently after Non-Suspect attack and Mixture attack, with more than 30% (31.27% and 30.15% respectively).

Compared with dataset BC5CDR-Chemical, all the attack are more successful for dataset BC5CDR-Disease, and as shown in Table 2 the performance falls dramatically. The performance are almost below 0.5 after different kinds of attacks. This phenomenon may result from the fact that, the disease set contains more annotations and the number of annotated diseases is larger than the number of annotated chemicals. Moreover, different from former chemical set, the performance is most affected by Semantics attack with 59. 09% drop.

The adversarial attacks achieved similar performance on BERT model and BiLSTM model, and BERT is slightly more successful than BiLSTM according the anti-attack capability however is far more computationally expensive (as shown in Table 2).

5.3 Adversarial Evaluation for Biomedical Semantic Textual Similarity

Table 3 reports the results of the biomedical STS task tested in the BioSSES dataset. From the experimental results, we could find that, the Pearson of the model drops 7.53% and 6.80% under Grammaticality attack and Non-Suspect attack, respectively. While the performance of Pearson decreases dramatically in metric of Spearman, which reveals even more than 30.0% drop when adapting mixture attack. What's interesting is that, the results of Semantics adversarial constraint however show a different response for BERT. In other words, similar to the conclusion derived from [3], the Pearson coefficient with Semantics attack is higher than with the original test set.

5.4 Robustness Improvement with Adversarial Examples

This section investigates how to improve models robustness by introducing adversarial examples into training set.

For ease of description, we only discuss BERT model here. For both biomedical NER and STS tasks, we first fine-tune the model with two kinds of train set: (i) the overall original training set plus an adversarial version of the same set (with suffix of "(1:1)" in Table 4 and Table 5); (ii) remain randomly selected 50% of the original training set and replace the other half of it with adversarial examples (with suffix of "(0.5:0.5)"). Similarly, the test set are also processed as the train set. Like former experimental settings, all of types of adversarial constraints (i.e., Semantics, Grammaticality and Non-Suspect) are considered, to measure how the models perform under different attack.

Table 4 and Table 5 overview the experimental results for NER task of training with different kinds of adversarial constraints, and testing with the original test set compared with their respective adversaries. From the experimental results, we could see that semantics adversarial constraints have changed the models robustness most of all. Compared with baseline (first line in the table), training by adding adversarial constraints with proportion of 1:1 (with suffix of "(1:1)"), improves the robustness. Meanwhile, the suffix "(1:1)" defeats the suffix "(0.5:0.5)", and we argue that "(1:1)" provides more adversaries and hence more challenges to training the models ability. In the experimental table, "Mixture" also indicates the fusion of different adversarial constraints with proportion of 1/3:1/3:1/3, like the former experimental section, which aims at exploring How could the jointly of adversarial constraints boost the results. However, this mixture does not reveal the best improvement, wherein the observed fact is against our background expectation. Latter, we will discuss another mixture which is called "full mixture" here, and describe the comparison.

Table 5 shows the experimental results on BC5CDR-Disease dataset. The improvement of robustness by adding adversarial examples is more significant than former dataset, and Grammaticality, Non-Suspect and Mixture adversarial constraints all contribute to showing a performance boost, except for Semantics adversarial constraint. Besides, Non-Suspect adversarial constraint become the key rather than Semantics adversarial constraint, which reflects the fact that different types of text obtain different anti-attack capacity from different kinds of adversarial constraints. Similar to the previous experiment, suffix "(1:1)" also outperforms the suffix "(0.5:0.5)". With efforts above, we make Semantic and Non-Suspect constraints and more selective.

Table 4. Robustness improvement by adding Semantics, Grammaticality and Non-Suspect constraints into train set for BV5CDR-Chemical's biomedical named entity recognition (NER) task. The superscript † indicates the cases that outperforms the baseline (fist line) in metric of F-1 value, which reveals the robustness's improvement with help of adversarial examples.

Train Set	Test Set	Precision	Recall	F-1
Original	Original	0.895	0.908	0.901
+ Semantics(1:1)	Original	**0.903**	0.906	**0.904**[†]
	Semantics	0.876	**0.913**	0.894
+ Semantics(0.5:0.5)	Original	0.892	0.890	0.891
	Semantics	0.867	0.902	0.885
+ Grammaticality(1:1)	Original	0.893	0.906	0.899
	Grammaticality	0.854	0.796	0.824
+ Grammaticality(0.5:0.5)	Original	0.896	0.894	0.895
	Grammaticality	0.838	0.814	0.826
+ Non-Suspect(1:1)	Original	0.899	0.909	**0.904**[†]
	Non-Suspect	0.687	0.633	0.659
+ Non-Suspect(0.5:0.5)	Original	0.890	0.894	0.892
	Non-Suspect	0.671	0.613	0.641
+ Mixture(1:1)	Original	0.892	0.904	0.898
	Mixture	0.853	0.794	0.822
+ Mixture(0.5:0.5)	Original	0.889	0.893	0.891
	Mixture	0.670	0.612	0.640

For the biochemical STS task, we train the model with different adversaries and testing with different test sets, following the experimental setting as NER task. The comparative results are reported in Table 6. The results demonstrate that, training with adversarial examples could improves robustness of the original models to enhance the anti-attack ability. E.g., training with Grammaticality adversarial constraint improves the performance by 5.74% compared with the baseline which both trained and tested on the original dataset in metric of Pearson. We also see that, adding adversarial examples from different types of constraints has a negligible effect on the performance of metric Spearman, and there is no way to stop the loss. The effect of adding adversarial examples into train set on metric Pearson and metric Spearman presents a great imbalance. In other words, we think that, Spearman is not an ideal metric for measuring model's robustness.

Table 5. Robustness improvement by adding Semantics, Grammaticality and Non-Suspect constraints into train set for BV5CDR-Disease's biomedical named entity recognition (NER) task. The superscript † indicates the cases that outperforms the baseline (fist line) in metric of F-1 value, which reveals the robustness's improvement with help of adversarial examples. similarly, ‡ and § indicates the increase of Precision and Recall respectively, when comparing with the baseline (fist line).

Train Set	Test Set	Precision	Recall	F-1
Original	Original	0.832	0.844	0.838
+ Semantic(1:1)	Original	0.817	0.828	0.823
	Semantic	0.792	0.845	0.818
+ Semantic(0.5:0.5)	Original	0.809	0.810	0.810
	Semantic	0.790	0.836	0.812
+ Grammaticality(1:1)	Original	0.840‡	0.851§	0.846†
	Grammaticality	0.777	0.750	0.763
+ Grammaticality(0.5:0.5)	Original	0.830	0.835	0.833
	Grammaticality	0.749	0.740	0.744
+ Non-Suspect(1:1)	Original	**0.843‡**	**0.852§**	**0.848†**
	Non-Suspect	0.730	0.719	0.724
+ Non-Suspect(0.5:0.5)	Original	0.834‡	0.843	0.839†
	Non-Suspect	0.715	0.701	0.708
+ Mixture(1:1)	Original	0.837‡	0.843	0.840†
	Mixture	0.772	0.760	0.766
+ Mixture(0.5:0.5)	Original	0.826	0.831	0.829
	Mixture	0.765	0.740	0.753

5.5   Ablation Study

Adversarial attacks in natural language processing require appropriate ablation research, which provides the community with the relative performance of different adversarial attack mechanisms and adversarial constraint evaluation methods. This experimental section allow us to compare different attack strategies in a standardized environment, and could help researchers gauge model robustness against a variety of attacks.

We fine-tune the BERT model with the original train set plus: (i) a Semantics adversarial constraint version of the same set; (ii) a Grammaticality adversarial constraint version; and (iii) a Non-Suspect adversarial constraint version. Since we also use these adversarial constraint evaluation methods, we conduct an ablation study to understand which constraints the greatest impact on the reliability and of the augmented model. Then we carry out the pre-trained model on the original test set. Furthermore, we then reran three attack-enhanced training strategies (one for each constraint removed) on each of our NER and STS datasets. Table 7 shows attack results rate after individually removing each constraint. "Mixture", which trains the model on the original train set plus all the

Table 6. Robustness improvement by adding Semantics, Grammaticality and Non-Suspect constraints into train set for BioSSES's biomedical semantic textual similarity (STS) task. The superscript † indicates the cases that outperforms the baseline (fist line) in metric of Pearson value, which reveals the robustness's improvement with help of adversarial examples. similarly, ‡ indicates the increase of Spearman value, when comparing with the baseline (fist line).

Train Set	Test Set	Pearson	Spearman
Original	Original	0.829	0.813
+ Semantic(1:1)	Original	$0.837^\dagger$	0.565
	Semantic	$0.844^\dagger$	0.768
+ Semantic(0.5:0.5)	Original	0.766	0.662
	Semantic	0.787	0.607
+ Grammaticality(1:1)	Original	$\mathbf{0.877^\dagger}$	0.779
	Grammaticality	$0.836^\dagger$	0.662
+ Grammaticality(0.5:0.5)	Original	0.785	0.682
	Grammaticality	0.717	0.586
+ Non-Suspect(1:1)	Original	0.600	0.800
	Non-Suspect	$0.822^\dagger$	$\mathbf{0.844^\ddagger}$
+ Non-Suspect(0.5:0.5)	Original	0.656	0.607
	Non-Suspect	0.560	0.554
+ Mixture(1:1)	Original	0.651	0.774
	Mixture	$0.831^\dagger$	0.768
+ Mixture(0.5:0.5)	Original	0.767	0.670
	Mixture	0.783	0.606

Table 7. Ablation study of robustness improvement by adding Semantics, Grammaticality and Non-Suspect constraints into train set for NER task and STS task. The superscript ◇ indicates the invalid attack-enhanced training, respect to the condition that adding some adversarial constraint fails to leading performance's increasing.

Train Set	Test Set	BC5CDR-Chemical			BC5CDR-Disease			BioSSES	
		Precision	Recall	F-1	Precision	Recall	F-1	Pearson	Spearman
Original	Original	0.895	0.908	0.901	0.832	0.844	0.838	0.829	0.813
Mixture	Original	**0.911**	**0.924**	**0.918**	**0.847**	**0.859**	**0.853**	**0.844**	**0.828**
-Semantics	Original	0.897	0.910	0.904	0.834	0.846	0.840	$0.825^\diamond$	0.815
-Grammaticality	Original	0.910	0.923	0.917	$0.830^\diamond$	0.858	0.852	0.843	0.827
-Non-Suspect	Original	$0.891^\diamond$	0.921	0.915	0.844	0.857	0.850	0.841	0.825

three different adversarial constraint version of original train set, achieves the optimal results and become the best attack-enhanced strategy (compared with experimental results shown in Table 4, Table 5 and Table 6), which improves the average F-1 value by 1.79% in NER datasets. The Semantics constraint is the greatest inhibitor of attack performance.

6 Conclusion

This paper studies adversarial attacks against state-of-the-art biochemical NER task and STS task under three kinds of adversarial constraints. Extensive experiments demonstrate that it is necessary to add the adversarial examples into train set, so as to boost the model's robustness. Besides, It would be difficult to find a necessarily optimal constraint constraint set, for every attack scenario towards every types of dataset. expanding how to evaluate examples generated by multi-type of semantic composition, and how to evaluate semantic preservation in the condition that there is no original input for comparison, may become the future work direction.

Acknowledgements. We thank anonymous reviewers for valuable comments. This work is funded by: (i) the National Natural Science Foundation of China (No. U19B2026); (ii) the New Generation of Artificial Intelligence Special Action Project (No.AI20191125008); (iii) the National Integrated Big Data Center Pilot Project (No. 20500908, 17111001,17111002).

References

1. Akhtar, N., Mian, A.S.: Threat of adversarial attacks on deep learning in computer vision: a survey. IEEE Access **6**, 14410–14430 (2018)
2. Alzantot, M., Sharma, Y., Elgohary, A., Ho, B.J., Srivastava, M.B., Chang, K.W.: Generating natural language adversarial examples. ArXiv abs/1804.07998 (2018)
3. Araujo, V., Carvallo, A., Aspillaga, C., Parra, D.: On adversarial examples for biomedical nlp tasks. ArXiv abs/2004.11157 (2020)
4. Bao, W., Bao, W., Du, J., Yang, Y., Zhao, X.: Attentive siamese lstm network for semantic textual similarity measure. In: 2018 International Conference on Asian Language Processing (IALP), pp. 312–317 (2018)
5. Che, M., Yao, K., Che, C., Cao, Z., Kong, F.: Knowledge-graph-based drug repositioning against covid-19 by graph convolutional network with attention mechanism. Future Internet **13**, 13 (2021)
6. Dai, Y., Guo, C., Guo, W., Eickhoff, C.: Drug-drug interaction prediction with wasserstein adversarial autoencoder-based knowledge graph embeddings. Briefings in bioinformatics (2020)
7. Devlin, J., Chang, M.W., Lee, K., Toutanova, K.: Bert: Pre-training of deep bidirectional transformers for language understanding. ArXiv abs/1810.04805 (2019)
8. Ebrahimi, J., Rao, A., Lowd, D., Dou, D.: HotFlip: white-box adversarial examples for text classification. In: ACL (2018)
9. Goodfellow, I.J., Shlens, J., Szegedy, C.: Explaining and harnessing adversarial examples. CoRR abs/1412.6572 (2014)
10. Jia, R., Liang, P.: Adversarial examples for evaluating reading comprehension systems. In: EMNLP (2017)
11. Jin, D., Jin, Z., Zhou, J.T., Szolovits, P.: Is bert really robust? a strong baseline for natural language attack on text classification and entailment. arXiv: Computation and Language (2019)
12. Lamy, J.B., Venot, A., Duclos, C.: PyMedTermino: an open-source generic API for advanced terminology services. Stud. Health Technol. Inform. **210**, 924–8 (2015)

13. Li, J., et al.: Biocreative v cdr task corpus: a resource for chemical disease relation extraction. Database: The Journal of Biological Databases and Curation 2016 (2016)
14. Li, J., Ji, S., Du, T., Li, B., Wang, T.: Textbugger: Generating adversarial text against real-world applications. ArXiv abs/1812.05271 (2018)
15. Lindberg, D., Humphreys, B., McCray, A.: The unified medical language system. Methods Inf. Med. **32**(4), 281–91 (1993)
16. Michel, P., Li, X., Neubig, G., Pino, J.M.: On evaluation of adversarial perturbations for sequence-to-sequence models. In: NAACL-HLT (2019)
17. Morris, J.X., Lifland, E., Lanchantin, J., Ji, Y., Qi, Y.: Reevaluating adversarial examples in natural language. ArXiv abs/2004.14174 (2020)
18. Naber, D.: A rule-based style and grammar checker (2003)
19. Neumann, M., King, D., Beltagy, I., Ammar, W.: Scispacy: fast and robust models for biomedical natural language processing. In: BioNLP@ACL (2019)
20. Peng, Y., Yan, S., Lu, Z.: Transfer learning in biomedical natural language processing: an evaluation of bert and elmo on ten benchmarking datasets. In: BioNLP@ACL (2019)
21. Peters, M.E., et al.: Deep contextualized word representations. In: NAACL-HLT (2018)
22. Reiter, E.: A structured review of the validity of bleu. Comput. Linguist. **44**(3), 393–401 (2018)
23. Samanta, S., Mehta, S.: Towards crafting text adversarial samples. ArXiv abs/1707.02812 (2017)
24. Sogancioglu, G., Öztürk, H., Özgür, A.: Biosses: a semantic sentence similarity estimation system for the biomedical domain. Bioinformatics **33**, i49–i58 (2017)
25. Wallace, E., Feng, S., Kandpal, N., Gardner, M., Singh, S.: Universal adversarial triggers for attacking and analyzing nlp. In: EMNLP/IJCNLP (2019)
26. Wang, X., et al.: Cross-type biomedical named entity recognition with deep multitask learning. bioRxiv (2018)
27. Warstadt, A., Singh, A., Bowman, S.R.: Neural network acceptability judgments. Trans. Assoc. Comput. Linguist. **7**, 625–641 (2018)
28. Xu, Y., Zhong, X., Jimeno-Yepes, A., Lau, J.H.: Elephant in the room: An evaluation framework for assessing adversarial examples in nlp. ArXiv abs/2001.07820 (2020)
29. Yoo, J.Y., Morris, J.X., Lifland, E., Qi, Y.: Searching for a search method: Benchmarking search algorithms for generating nlp adversarial examples. ArXiv abs/2009.06368 (2020)
30. Zellers, R., et al.: Defending against neural fake news. In: NeurIPS (2019)
31. Zhang, W.E., Sheng, Q.Z., Alhazmi, A.A.F., Li, C.: Adversarial attacks on deep learning models in natural language processing: A survey. arXiv: Computation and Language (2019)
32. Zheng, L., et al.: A review of auditing techniques for the unified medical language system. J. Am. Med. Inform. Assoc. JAMIA **27**, 1625–1638 (2020)
33. Zhu, Y., Che, C., Jin, B., Zhang, N., Su, C., Wang, F.: Knowledge-driven drug repurposing using a comprehensive drug knowledge graph. Health Inform. J. **26**, 2737–2750 (2020)

Enhanced Self-node Weights Based Graph Convolutional Networks for Passenger Flow Prediction

Hao Liu[1], Fan Zhang[1], Yi Fan[1], Junyou Zhu[1], Zhen Wang[2], and Chao Gao[1,2(✉)]

[1] College of Computer and Information Science, Southwest University, Chongqing 400715, China
cgao@nwpu.edu.cn
[2] School of Artificial Intelligence, Optics, and Electronics (iOPEN), Northwestern Polytechnical University, Xi'an 710072, China

Abstract. Accurate and real-time passenger flow prediction is of great significance for realizing intelligent transportation systems. However, due to the complexity and unstable change of traffic network passenger flow data, passenger flow prediction remains a challenging problem in transportation research field. Moreover, the core problem is how to obtain the spatial and temporal characteristics efficiently. In this paper, we propose an Enhanced Self-node Weights Based Spatial-Temporal Graph Convolutional Networks (EST-GCN) model to capture the spatial and temporal characteristics. Specifically, in order to capture the spatial characteristics, we optimize the ability of Graph Convolutional of Network (GCN) in extracting the spatial characteristics of rail transit networks based on the difference maximization of aggregated information, hoping to solve the problem that GCN cannot fit peak value accurately. As for temporal characteristics, we leverage the Gate Recurrent Unit (GRU) model to obtain dynamic changes of passenger flow data to capture them. The EST-GCN model is a combination of these two models. Based on the Shanghai dataset, we use the proposed EST-GCN model for simulation experiments, and compare our proposed method with other mainstream passenger flow prediction algorithms. The experimental results demonstrate the superiority of our algorithm.

Keywords: Passenger flow prediction · Enhanced self-node weights based graph convolutional networks · Spatial and temporal characteristics

1 Introduction

Recently, with the economic development, city urbanization and population growth, metro has developed rapidly around the world due to its great power in relieving traffic congestion. Accurate passenger flow prediction helps managers to produce a reasonable operation plans in relieving traffic congestion, and provides traffic information for travelers selecting convenient travel routes [1].

© Springer Nature Switzerland AG 2021
H. Qiu et al. (Eds.): KSEM 2021, LNAI 12817, pp. 262–274, 2021.
https://doi.org/10.1007/978-3-030-82153-1_22

There are many traffic prediction methods, some of which consider temporal characteristics, such as the Autoregressive Integrated Moving Average model (ARIMA) [2], Kalman Filtering model [3] and Support Vector Regression Machine model (SVR) [4]. These methods effectively obtained the temporal characteristics of time series data, and realized the basic prediction of passenger flow. However, passenger flow data comes into existence between different stations at different times with complex spatial and temporal dependence [5]. Therefore, a good traffic prediction model should consider both temporal and spatial characteristics.

As deep learning develops rapidly, Convolutional Neural Networks model (CNN) has been widely applied in transportation field. However, CNN model is always used to process Euclidean data [6], such as images and regular grids. Therefore, many scholars are inclined to employ CNN method to model the spatial dependence of the traffic network through grid-based map segmentation. However, the metro system is a graph based structure whose spatial dependence cannot be described by CNN. Recently, Graph Convolutional Networks (GCNs) have shown great performance in processing graph structure data [7]. In addition, since the Recurrent Neural Network (RNN) as well as its variants Long and Short-term Memory (LSTM) and Gated Recurrent Unit (GRU) can effectively use the self-circulation mechanism, they can learn temporal characteristics well and achieve better prediction [3]. Therefore, Ling et al. [8] proposed a Temporal Graph Convolutional Network (T-GCN) model combining GRU and GCN, to capture spatial-temporal characteristics; He et al. [9], utilized a Deep Spatiotemporal Model (GC-LSTM) model, which combines GCN and LSTM, in order to predict passenger flow on high-speed rail networks. It's true that all these methods improve the prediction accuracy of the model. However, since the GCN model defines a smoothing filter in the Fourier domain, it cannot fit in with the peak passenger flow accurately.

To solve the problems above, this paper proposes an optimized deep learning framework named Enhanced Self-node Weights Based Spatial-Temporal Graph Convolutional Networks (EST-GCN) relying on difference maximization of aggregated information. This model offsets the average effect of smoothing filter and realizes the accurate prediction of peak value. The contributions can be listed as follows:

(1) The GCN model is optimized by increasing the node weight ratio on the diagonal of symmetric normalization matrix, which offsets the effect of smoothing filter and helps predict the peak passenger flow accurately.
(2) We evaluate our method on real-world traffic datasets(i.e., daily passenger flow of each station rail transit datasets in Shanghai, China). The results demonstrate that the EST-GCN model is superior in passenger flow prediction, especially for peak passenger flow prediction.

The rest of paper is organized as follows. In Sect. 2, we introduce the details of our methods including the problem definition and the overall architectures. In Sect. 3, we evaluate the predictive performance of EST-GCN by real metro traffic networks, including data description and experimental setup, evaluation metrics and baselines, and result analysis. Finally, we conclude this paper and discuss the future work in Sect. 4.

2   Methodology

2.1   Problem Definition

In this study, the aim is to predict the change of passenger flow during a period of time in the future, based on the historical passenger flow data in Shanghai rail transit.

Definition 1: The topological structure of metro network can be represented as a graph $G =< V, E >$, where V is the set of nodes representing the stations of metro with $V = \{v_i | i \in [1, N]\}$, and N is the number of stations. $E = \{e_{ij} = (v_i, v_j) | i, j \in [1, N], i \neq j\}$ represents a set of edges reflecting the physical connectivity between stations. There exists an edge between two nodes if the two nodes are adjacent, and $A \in \mathbb{R}^{N \times N}$ is used to describe the relationship between nodes. A_{ij} is 0 if there is no link between v_i and v_j, and 1 otherwise.

Definition 2: Feature matrix $X^{N \times F}$: the passenger flow is viewed as the attribute of nodes, denoted as $X \in \mathbb{R}^{N \times F}$, where F denotes the number of node attribute features, and X_t denotes the passenger flow on each station at time t.

In sum, the passenger flow prediction issue can be simply formulated as:

$$[P_{t+1}, P_{t+2}, ..., P_{t+T}] = \mathcal{F}(G; X_{t-i}, ..., X_{t-2}, X_{t-1}) \tag{1}$$

where $\mathcal{F}()$ is a constructed model, T is the length of predicted time series, and i is the length of given historical time series.

2.2   The Overall Architectures

The EST-GCN model consists of two parts, namely, the Enhanced Self-node Graph Convolutional Network (ES-GCN) and the Gated Recurrent Unit (GRU). As shown in Fig. 1(A), we first extract the network topology of the metro and passenger flow data of each station at different times as input data in the ES-GCN model. Then, we increase the weights of nodes on the diagonal of the symmetric normalized matrix to enhance the effect of spatial feature extraction. After that, in order to capture the temporal features, we input the obtained time series with spatial features into GRU model then the dynamic change is obtained by transmiting information between units in Fig. 1(B). Finally, the prediction results can be acquired from the fully connected layer.

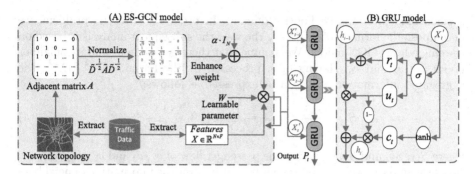

Fig. 1. The framework of EST-GCN. (A) ES-GCN: Enhanced Grpah Convolutional Network; (B) GRU: Gated Recurrent Unit.

Enhanced Graph Convolutional Network (ES-GCN): As we mentioned in Sect. 1, Convolutional Neural Networks model(CNN) is not suitable for processing graph structured data. Thus, researchers generalize CNN to GCN for optimization. The GCN model has been widely applied in various fields, such as unsupervised learning [10], document classification [11] and image classification [12]. The convolutional model in GCN can be divided into spatial and spectrum domain convolutions, and we adopt the latter one in our method. In spectrum graph analysis, a spectrum graph convolution is the multiplication of a graph signal and a smoothing filter in the Fourier domain of the graph. More specifically, the central node captures the spatial features between nodes through their corresponding first-order neighbors, and then GCN model can be built by stacking multiple convolutional layers, which can be definded as follows:

$$H^{(l+1)} = \sigma(\widetilde{D}^{-\frac{1}{2}} \widetilde{A} \widetilde{D}^{-\frac{1}{2}} H^l W^l) \qquad (2)$$

where H^l is the output of the l_{th} layer of GCN, when $l = 0$, $H^0 = X$. In $\widetilde{A} = A + I_N$, $\widetilde{A}$ represents the adjacency matrix added with self-connection information, I_N is the identify matrix. $\widetilde{D}$ is the diagonal node degree matrix of $\widetilde{A}$, and the node degree refers to the number of edges connected to the node. W^l denotes a learnable parameter matrix of the l_{th} layer and $\sigma(\cdot)$ denotes a non-linear activation function. Specifically, our model constructs the two-layer GCN model as follows:

$$X' = \sigma(\hat{A} \, ReLU(\hat{A}XW^{(0)})W^{(1)}) \qquad (3)$$

where $\hat{A} = \widetilde{D}^{-\frac{1}{2}} \widetilde{A} \widetilde{D}^{-\frac{1}{2}}$, and X' is the time series data with spatial features matrix output from 2-layer GCN model. $W^{(0)} \in \mathbb{R}^{F \times H}$ and $W^{(1)} \in \mathbb{R}^{H \times T}$ are weight matrices from the input to hidden layer and output layer, respectively. F is the length of the feature matrix, H is the number of hidden units, and T is the length of output. As described above, $X = H^{(0)}$ is a feature matrix as the input data of the first layer in GCN model, and $ReLU()$ is a non-linear activation function same as $\sigma(\cdot)$.

However, the GCN model cannot predict the peak passenger flow accurately when used in passenger flow prediction. It can be attributed to that GCN defines a smoothing filter in the Fourier domain. In order to solve the problem, we decompose the formula of GCN. By the way, the subsequent analysis is based on the single-layer GCN model. We assume that there is a node v_1 and its neighbor nodes are v_2 and v_5. Having been processed by the formula $\widetilde{D}^{-\frac{1}{2}}\widetilde{A}\widetilde{D}^{-\frac{1}{2}}$, the aggregated information of v_1 can be expressed as follows:

$$S'_{11} = \frac{1}{\sqrt{d_1^2}}S_{11} + \frac{1}{\sqrt{d_2 d_1}}S_{12} + \frac{1}{\sqrt{d_5 d_1}}S_{15} \tag{4}$$

where S_{11}, S_{12} and S_{15} represent the passenger flow of v_1, v_2 and v_5, respectively. S'_{11} is the updated value of passenger flow at v_1 after the information of neighbors being aggregated. d_1, d_2, and d_5 denote the degree of v_1, v_2 and v_5 respectively. In Eq. (4), we find that the updated value of v_1 is averaged by its neighbors through the smoothing filter, so its updated value is related to the degree of the node and its neighbor nodes. If $d_2, d_5 < d_1$, then $1/\sqrt{d_1^2} < 1/\sqrt{d_2 d_1}, 1/\sqrt{d_5 d_1}$, which means a greater degree of a node indicates smaller influence on itself. For metro networks, the high degree of node indicates the identity of transfer station and that a larger amount of passenger flow than other stations. The influence of itself should be enhanced to offset the averaged influence. Therefore, we add an identity matrix with coefficients to enhance the weight ratio of nodes on the diagonal of the symmetric normalized matrix, which can be formulated as:

$$En = \widetilde{D}^{-\frac{1}{2}}\widetilde{A}\widetilde{D}^{-\frac{1}{2}} + \alpha I_N \tag{5}$$

where α is the coefficient that enhances the weight ratio. $I_N \in \mathbb{R}^{N \times N}$ is the identity matrix.

Gate Recurrent Unit Model(GRU): GRU is a variant of RNN, which solves the defects of gradient disappearance and explosion of RNN [13]. In basic principles, GRU is similar to Long and Short-term Memory (LSTM), but GRU is renowned for its simpler structure, fewer parameters, and shorter training time. Thus, we choose GRU in our study.

Figure 1(B) illustrates the inner structure of an GRU unit. As shown in Fig. 1(B), there are two inputs fed into the structure. One is h_{t-1} which is the output from the previous GRU unit, and the other is X'_t that is the result of ES-GCN model at time t. GRU has two gate control units containing reset gate r_t and update gate u_t. For reset gate, it is used to control whether the value of candidate state c_t depends on the previous state h_{t-1}. For update gate, it is applied to control how much information the current state h_t needs to retain from the previous state h_{t-1} and how much information needs to be received from the candidate state c_t. In conclusion, the specific calculation process is shown below:

$$r_t = \sigma\left(W_r\left[X'_t, h_{t-1}\right] + b_r\right) \tag{6}$$

$$u_t = \sigma\left(W_u\left[X'_t, h_{t-1}\right] + b_u\right) \tag{7}$$

$$c_t = \tanh\left(W_c\left[X'_t, (r_t * h_{t-1})\right] + b_c\right) \tag{8}$$

$$h_t = u_t * h_{t-1} + (1 - u_t) * c_t \tag{9}$$

where X'_t is the output from ES-GCN model at time t. W and b denote the weights and biases in the training process, respectively.

As to loss function, we need to minimize errors between real and predicted passenger flow in each metro station. The loss function of EST-GCN is shown in Eq. (10):

$$loss = \left\| P_t - \widehat{P}_t \right\| + \lambda L_{reg} \tag{10}$$

where P_t and $\widehat{P}_t$ represent the real and predicted passenger flow, respectively. λ is a hyper-parameter, and λL_{reg} is the L2 regularization term to avoid overfitting.

In conclusion, we proposed the EST-GCN model that can predict the peak of passenger flow more accurately. More specifically, we optimize GCN to extract spatial characteristics of rail transit network by maximizing the difference of aggregated information. Moreover, the sequence data with spatial characteristics is used as the input of GRU to obtain temporal characteristics and then implement traffic prediction tasks eventually.

3   Experiments

3.1   Data Description and Experimental Setup

Data Desciption: The datasets used in this paper include Shanghai Metro datasets which contains (1) subway lines and stations; (2) subway smart card data. Based on these datasets, the passenger flow data of each metro station and the adjacency matrix data between stations can be extracted in above two datasets, respectively. Passenger flow data is a feature matrix, which describes the variation of the number of passenger flow on each station over time and the time interval is 15 mins. The details of Shanghai datasets are as follows: such datasets consist of passenger flow data in each station from 6th to 26th April 2015 and adjacency matrix data between 285 stations on 14 metro lines in Shanghai. The dimension of adjacency matrix is 285 × 285.

Experimental Setup: The proposed model is implemented based on Tensor-Flow framework. In our experiments, we refer to some literatures for parameter setting and initialization [14,15], so, we set 80% of data as the training set and the remaining 20% as the testing set. The hyperparameters used in EST-GCN model include batch size, learning rate, training epoch, hidden units and weight coefficient α. In this paper, we set the value of α as 0.6, and it will be discussed specifically in Sect. 3.3. According to the parameter settings in the T-GCN [8], we set batch size and the number of hidden units as 64 and learning rate as 0.001 in this paper. The iteration epoch is set as 2000 in the training phase.

3.2   Evaluation Metrics and Baselines

Evaluation Metrics: Five metrics are adopted to measure the performance of all methods. i.e. Mean Absolute Error (MAE), Root Mean Squared Errors

($RMSE$), Coefficient of Determination (R^2), Explained Variance Score (var) and Accuracy (Acc). In general, the smaller the $RMSE$ and MAE value, the better the effects of the model. Differently, higher R^2, var and Acc can help improve the performance of the model. The evaluation metrics are as follows:

(1) :Root Mean Squared Error ($RMSE$):

$$RMSE = \sqrt{\frac{1}{T_c N} \sum_{j=1}^{T_c} \sum_{i=1}^{N} \left(p_i^j - \widehat{p_i^j}\right)^2} \tag{11}$$

(2) :Mean Absolute Error (MAE):

$$MAE = \frac{1}{T_c N} \sum_{j=1}^{T_c} \sum_{i=1}^{N} \left|p_i^j - \widehat{p_i^j}\right| \tag{12}$$

(3) Accuracy (Acc):

$$Accuracy = 1 - \frac{\|P - \widehat{P}\|_F}{\|P\|_F} \tag{13}$$

(4) Coefficient of Determination (R^2):

$$R^2 = 1 - \frac{\sum_{j=1}^{T_c} \sum_{i=1}^{N} \left(p_i^j - \widehat{p_i^j}\right)^2}{\sum_{j=1}^{T_c} \sum_{i=1}^{N} \left(p_i^j - \bar{P}\right)^2} \tag{14}$$

(5) Explained Variance Score (var):

$$var = 1 - \frac{Var\{Y - \widehat{Y}\}}{Var\{Y\}} \tag{15}$$

where T_c is the number of time samples, and N is the number of metro stations. p_i^j and $\widehat{p_i^j}$ represent the real and predicted pedestrian flow data at the j_{th} time step in the i_{th} station, respectively. P and $\widehat{P}$ are the set of p_i^j and $\widehat{p_i^j}$. $\bar{P}$ is the average of P and $Var\{\}$ denotes the covariance.

Particularly, $RMSE$ and MAE are used to measure the prediction error. The smaller the value, the more accurate the prediction. Acc is used to measure the prediction accuracy. The higher the value, the better the performance of prediction. R^2 and var are used to calculate the correlation coefficient, which measures the correspondence of our prediction results with the real data. The value of Acc, R^2, var is proportionate to the prediction effects.

Baselines: We compare the performance of our model with the following five baselines include Historical Average method (HA) [3], Auto-Regressive Integrated Moving Average model (ARIMA) [2], Support Vector Regression model (SVR) [16], Gated Recurrent Unit network (GRU) [13], Attention Based Spatial-Temporal Graph Convolutional Network (ASTGCN) [17], A Temporal Graph Convolutional Network model (T-GCN) [8].

3.3 Experimental Analysis

Parameter Analysis: In Fig. 2, the prediction results of EST-GCN are dramatically improved in accuracy than other comparison algorithms, which indicates that the EST-GCN model can perform well in passenger flow prediction. There are two reasons why the EST-GCN model can achieve such great prediction effects. One is that it simultaneously obtains temporal and spatial character-

Table 1. The results of EST-GCN model and other baseline methods on Shanghai datasets. The ∗ indicates prediction effect of the model is poor and the bold denotes the best. The performance of EST-GCN model is the optimal.

T	model	metric				
		RMSE	MAE	Acc	R^2	var
15 min	HA	282.094	138.292	0.447	0.547	0.547
	ARIMA	246.116	157.955	0.327	∗	∗
	SVR	192.387	84.861	0.621	0.787	0.793
	GRU	150.123	79.072	0.652	0.786	0.804
	ASTGCN	127.258	**65.834**	0.689	0.853	0.857
	T-GCN	170.301	101.748	0.664	0.833	0.835
	EST-GCN	**114.905**	65.886	**0.774**	**0.924**	**0.924**
30 min	HA	282.094	138.292	0.447	0.547	0.547
	ARIMA	246.272	157.853	0.328	∗	∗
	SVR	182.235	84.405	0.643	0.811	0.812
	GRU	121.409	**53.813**	0.675	0.824	0.825
	ASTGCN	133.866	72.581	0.671	0.835	0.842
	T-GCN	127.808	76.802	0.750	0.907	0.907
	EST-GCN	**91.403**	56.849	**0.821**	**0.952**	**0.953**
45 min	HA	282.094	138.292	0.447	0.547	0.547
	ARIMA	246.437	157.760	0.328	∗	∗
	SVR	204.963	96.225	0.602	0.763	0.765
	GRU	122.809	**60.258**	0.681	0.825	0.826
	ASTGCN	130.182	70.561	0.678	0.842	0.848
	T-GCN	136.264	84.741	0.735	0.895	0.897
	EST-GCN	**96.841**	60.707	**0.812**	**0.947**	**0.948**
60 min	HA	282.094	138.292	0.447	0.547	0.547
	ARIMA	246.630	157.700	0.329	∗	∗
	SVR	219.703	102.668	0.576	0.731	0.732
	GRU	126.398	**59.541**	0.692	0.843	0.846
	ASTGCN	129.938	70.102	0.677	0.841	0.846
	T-GCN	137.752	84.560	0.735	0.894	0.895
	EST-GCN	**101.73**	63.572	**0.804**	**0.942**	**0.943**

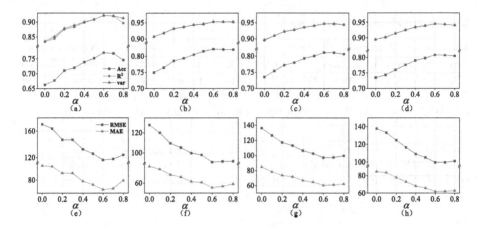

Fig. 2. Comparison of predicted performance under different parameter α based on Shanghai dataset. In (a)-(d), the Acc, R^2, var vary; in (e)-(h), the $RMSE$ and MAE change. Result shows that when $\alpha = 0.6$, the prediction effect is the best.

istics of the passenger flow data. More importantly, EST-GCN model increases the weight values of nodes on the diagonal of the adjacency matrix, which offsets the influence of smoothing filter on the results of spatial feature extraction, so that the predicted peak value of the model can still fit the real value.

In order to further explore the influence of increasing weight values of nodes on the diagonal of the adjacency matrix on experimental results, this section discusses this coefficient value. This paper designs a comparative experiment on the change of each passenger flow prediction and evaluation indicators under different value of cofficients. The experimental results are shown in Fig. 2. It indicates that when the coefficient α increases from 0.1 to 0.6, the values of $RMSE$ and MAE are constantly decreasing, which denotes that the prediction error is constantly decreasing, and the error declines fast. Moreover, the values of R^2, Acc and var are constantly increasing, which indicates that the accuracy of prediction is constantly improving with a dramatical rising trend. Having reached 0.7, however, the values of RMSE and MAE increase, and the upward trend of Acc, R^2 and var become flat. Therefore, a higher value of α does not always mean better performance. There is an optimal value that makes the ES-GCN model. Through comparative experimental analysis, when $\alpha = 0.6$, the prediction effect is the best, which also explains why we set $\alpha = 0.6$ in Sect. 3.1.

Moreover, it can be concluded that the coefficient α cannot increase indefinitely and it owns an optimal value. α is used to control the weight ratio of the self-node when capturing spatial feature information. The higher the α is, the more important the information is. For example, if it is a transfer station or a hub station that connects to several lines, it can attract more passengers. Meanwhile, increasing the influence of its own information can effectively offset the influence of the smoothing filter on the prediction results, thus improving the prediction effect. However, for other non-hub stations, such as neighboring stations of the transfer station, most of their passengers are transferred from other stations, and their own ability to attract passenger flow is limited. If α is increased at this time, the influence of neighboring sites will become smaller and smaller, which can reduce the ability of spatial feature extraction, thereby reducing the accuracy of prediction.

Result Analysis: Table 1 shows the prediction effects of HA, ARIMA, SVR, GRU, ASTGCN, T-GCN models and our proposed EST-GCN model. These results are based on different time granularities (i.e., 15 min (15 mins), 30 min (30 mins), 45 min (45 mins), 60 min (60 mins)). The passenger prediction effects are measured by the evaluation metrics shown in Sect. 3.2. The $*$ in Table 1 indicates that the passenger flow prediction effect calculated by the model using this evaluation metric is very small and can be ignored. The bold is the algorithm model with the best prediction effects under the same metrics.

Judging from Table 1, it can be found that methods based on neural networks and focusing on the importance of temporal features (including GRU, T-GCN, ASTGCN and EST-GCN models) generally have better prediction effects than other models. According to the results of all evaluation indicators, the proposed EST-GCN model has better passenger flow prediction effects at different time granularities in the future. The reason is that the EST-GCN model considers the extraction of spatio-temporal characteristics, and offsets the effect of the smoothing filter in the GCN model by enhancing the weight ratio of nodes on the diagonal of the symmetric normalized matrix.

Visualization of Results: In order to better reflect the superiority of our EST-GCN, this paper selects and visualizes the prediction results of all stations on April 26 at different times. Figures 3(a)-(d) show the comparison results of the real and predicted values of passenger flow at different time granularities at each station starting from 8 AM. In this paper, the Pearson correlation coefficient is calculated between the real and predicted values of passenger flow at different time granularities at each station, and the calculation results are 0.95 (15 mins), 0.91 (30 mins), 0.85 (45 mins), and 0.85 (60 mins), respectively. According to two-tailed significance test we get the conclusion that when the error ratio is less than 0.05, the real value of passenger flow and the predicted value of 4 time granularities are significantly correlated. From visualization results, we can see that there is a small gap between the real and predicted passenger flow for the minority of all sites, and more than 80% of real and predicted results in sites at different time granularities coincides with each other.

Figures 3(e)-(h) shows the comparison results of the real and predicted values of the passenger flow at different time granularities on the site. It can be seen from the visualization results that the two curves of the real and predicted value are basically consistent at the time granularity of 15 mins, 30 mins, 45 mins and 60 mins. In addition, since the proposed model offsets the influence of the smoothing filter in the GCN Fourier domain on the spatial feature extraction results by increasing the weight values of the nodes on the diagonal of the

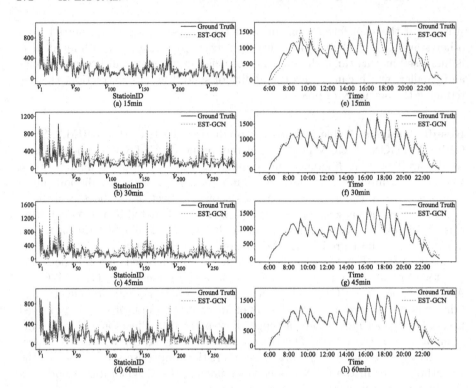

Fig. 3. (a)-(d) show comparison results of real and predicted passenger flow at different time granularities for each station. (e)-(h) display comparison of the real and predicted values of passenger flow at different time granularities on the v_3 station. The results show that our model can predict the passenger flow well, especially the peak value.

adjacency matrix, the model's prediction results for passenger flow peaks are excellent. It can detect the beginning and the end of peak hours, and make the prediction results correspond with the change trend of the actual rail transit station passenger flow. In order to further quantify the degree of fit between the real and predicted values of passenger flow at different time granularities, this paper uses the Pearson correlation coefficient to calculate the difference between the real and predicted passenger flow at different time granularities. The results are 0.92 (15 mins), 0.97 (30 mins), 0.98 (45 mins) and 0.98 (60 mins), respectively. Through the use of two-tailed significance test, it can be seen when the error ratio is less than 0.05, the real and predicted values of passenger flow at each time granularity are highly correlated, and they are fit to a high degree.

4   Conclusion

In this paper, an enhanced self-node weights based graph convolutional networks model (EST-GCN) is proposed and successfully applied to passenger flow prediction.This model can not only obtain the spatial and temporal characteristics of passenger flow, but offset the influence of defined smoothing filter in Fourier domain. Therefore, the predicted peak value of the model can still be consistent with the real data. Experiments on real-world datasets show that the prediction accuracy of the proposed model is higher than many state-of-the-art models, such as HA, ARIMA, SVR, GRU, ASTGCN and T-GCN model. In application, accurate passenger flow prediction can provide information for managers to ease traffic congestion by making reasonable operation plans in advance. In the future, we will further optimize the model architecture and parameter settings. Besides, we will take some external influencing factors, such as weather, accidents and social events, into account to further improve the prediction accuracy.

Acknowledgement. This work was supported by the National Key R&D Program of China (No. 2019YFB2102300), National Natural Science Foundation of China (Nos. 61976181, 11931015, 61762020), Key Technology Research and Development Program of Science and Technology Scientific and Technological Innovation Team of Shaanxi Province (No. 2020TD-013) and the Science and Technology Support Program of Guizhou (No. QKHZC2021YB531).

References

1. Gao, C., Fan, Y., Jiang, S., Deng, Y., Liu, J., Li, X.: Dynamic robustness analysis of a two-layer rail transit network model. IEEE Trans. Intell. Transp. Syst. 1–16 (2021). https://doi.org/10.1109/TITS.2021.3058185
2. Williams, B.M., Hoel, L.A.: Modeling and forecasting vehicular traffic flow as a seasonal arima process: theoretical basis and empirical results. J. Transp. Eng. **129**(6), 664–672 (2003)
3. Ye, J., Zhao, J., Xu, C.: How to build a graph-based deep learning architecture in traffic domain: a survey. IEEE Trans. Intell. Transp. Syst. **6**, 1–21 (2020). https://doi.org/10.1109/TITS.2020.3043250
4. Yao, Z.S., Shao, C.F.: Research on methods of short-term traffic forecasting based on support vector regression. J. Beijing Jiaotong Univ. **30**(3), 19–22 (2006)
5. Deng, Y., Gao, C., Li, X.: Assessing temporal-spatial characteristics of urban travel behaviors from multiday smart-card data. Phys. A **576**, 126058 (2021)
6. Wang, H., Gao, C., Liu, J.: Medication combination prediction using temporal attention mechanism and simple graph convolution. IEEE J. Biomed. Inform. 1–1 (2021). https://doi.org/10.1109/JBHI.2021.3082548
7. Yu, B., Yin, H., Zhu, Z.: Spatio-temporal graph convolutional networks: a deep learning framework for traffic forecasting. In: 27th International Joint Conference on Artificial Intelligence, pp. 3634–3640. IJCAI, Sweden (2018)
8. Zhao, L., Deng, M., Li, H.: T-GCN: a temporal graph convolutional network for traffic prediction. IEEE Trans. Intell. Transp. Syst. **21**(9), 3848–3858 (2020)
9. He, Y., Zhao, Y., Wang, H., Tsui, K.L.: GC-LSTM: a deep spatiotemporal model for passenger flow forecasting of high-speed rail network. In: 23rd International Conference on Intelligent Transportation Systems, pp. 1–6. IEEE, Rhodes (2020)
10. Kipf, T.N., Welling, M.: Semi-supervised classification with graph convolutional networks. In: 5th International Conference on Learning Representations, pp. 1–5. OpenReview, Toulon (2017)

11. Defferrard, M., Bresson, X., Vandergheynst, P.: Convolutional neural networks on graphs with fast localized spectral filtering. In: 29th Annual Conference on Neural Information Processing Systems, pp. 3844–3853. NIPS, Barcelona (2016)

12. Estrach, J.B., Zaremba, W., Szlam, A., LeCun, Y.: Spectral networks and deep locally connected networks on graphs. In: 2nd International Conference on Learning Representations, pp. 1–14. OpenReview, Banff (2014)

13. Fu, R., Zhang, Z., Li, L.: Using LSTM and GRU neural network methods for traffic flow prediction. In: 31st Youth Academic Annual Conference of Chinese Association of Automation, pp. 324–328. IEEE, Wuhan (2016)

14. Cao, W., Gao, J., Ming, Z., Cai, S.: Some tricks in parameter selection for extreme learning machine. In: IOP Conference Series: Materials Science and Engineering, p. 012002. IOP, Hawaii (2017)

15. Cao, W., Gao, J., Ming, Z., Cai, S., Zheng, H.: Impact of probability distribution selection on rvfl performance. In: 2nd International Conference on Smart Computing and Communication, pp. 114–124. Springer, Shenzhen (2017)

16. Smola, A.J., Schölkopf, B.: A tutorial on support vector regression. Statist. Comput. **14**(3), 199–222 (2004)

17. Guo, S., Lin, Y., Feng, N., Song, C., Wan, H.: Attention based spatial-temporal graph convolutional networks for traffic flow forecasting. In: 33rd AAAI Conference on Artificial Intelligence, pp. 922–929. AAAI, Honolulu (2019)

Interpretation of Learning-Based Automatic Source Code Vulnerability Detection Model Using LIME

Gaigai Tang[1,2], Long Zhang[2], Feng Yang[2], Lianxiao Meng[1,2], Weipeng Cao[3], Meikang Qiu[4], Shuangyin Ren[2], Lin Yang[2(✉)], and Huiqiang Wang[1(✉)]

[1] School of Computer Science and Technology, Harbin Engineering University, Harbin, China
[2] National Key Laboratory of Science and Technology on Information System Security, Institute of System Engineering, Chinese Academy of Military Science, Beijing, China
[3] College of Computer Science and Software Engineering, Shenzhen University, Shenzhen, China
[4] Department of Computer Science, Texas A&M University-Commerce, Commerce, TX 75428, USA

Abstract. The existing advanced automatic vulnerability detection methods based on source code are mainly learning-based, such as machine learning and deep learning. These models can capture the vulnerability pattern through learning, which is more automatic and intelligent. However, the outputs of many learning-based vulnerability detection models are unexplainable, even though they usually show high accuracy. It's meaningful to verify the credibility of the models so that we can better understand and use them in practice. To alleviate the above issue, we use an interpretation method called LIME to explain the learning-based automatic vulnerability detection model. For one thing, the preprocessing methods are all interpretable, including symbolization and vector representation, where the Bag of words model is chosen for source code vector representation. For another, the vulnerability detection models we select are based on Logistic Regression and Bi-LSTM. The former is interpretable, which is used to verify the effectiveness of LIME in the field of source code vulnerability detection. The latter is unexplained that is interpreted by LIME to its credibility on source code vulnerability detection. The experimental results show that LIME can effectively explain the learning-based automatic vulnerability detection model. Moreover, we find that under the condition of local interpretation, the predictions of the model based on Bi-LSTM are credible.

Keywords: Vulnerability detection · Machine learning · Logistic regression · Bi-LSTM · LIME · Model interpretation

© Springer Nature Switzerland AG 2021
H. Qiu et al. (Eds.): KSEM 2021, LNAI 12817, pp. 275–286, 2021.
https://doi.org/10.1007/978-3-030-82153-1_23

1 Introduction

Software vulnerabilities [14] are usually caused by the negligence or lack of professionalism of programmers. They promote the development of software security research [5,10,21]. With the development of software industry towards open-source, more software source code resources are available [26,29], and the security analysis work [12,27,30] based on source code benefits much. Meanwhile, the number of vulnerabilities is gradually increasing [17,20], vulnerability detection approaches have become more advanced corresponding, generally from the beginning of the rule-based method [2,6,7] to the popular learning-based method [3,16,28].

The most advanced learning-based models [11,13] are generally like black boxes, especially models based on deep learning [8,9], which are almost impossible to perceive their internal working state. This brings us the question of credibility: should I believe that some prediction of that model is correct? From the perspective of intuition, explaining the basic principles behind each independent prediction can make it easier for us to understand the prediction results, especially in the field of vulnerability detection, where is usually essential to make a reasonable predicate.

LIME (Local Interpretable Model-Agnostic Explanations) [22] is a method that can be used to explain the model that is unexplainable by learning an interpretable model locally around the prediction. For details, it is a method to explain models by presenting representative individual predictions and their explanations in a non-redundant way, framing the task as a submodular optimization problem. It has been successfully applied in the fields of image classification and text classification to explain the relevant learning-based models. These applications of LIME prompt us to apply it to interpret the learning-based source code automatic vulnerability detection model, which processes the source code as text sequence.

Our contributions mainly include two parts. Firstly, to verify if LIME can effectively interpret the model based on source code, we build an explainable vulnerability detection model based on Logical Regression. The validity of LIME is analyzed by comparing the predictions with Logical Regression. Secondly, to our best knowledge that based on processing the source code as text sequence, the vulnerability detection model based on Bi-directional Long-Short Term Memory (Bi-LSTM) [4] is the state-of-the-art model. The credibility of Bi-LSTM model on vulnerability detection is verified by interpreting the prediction results using LIME.

The rest of this paper is organized as follows. Section 2 discusses the work related to the automatic detection of software vulnerability and the interpretation model. Section 3 presents the construction of an interpretable vulnerability detection model based on Logistic Regression and interpretation of Bi-LSTM using LIME. In Sect. 4, we give the details of our experimental setting, results, and corresponding analysis. The conclusions and future works are discussed in Sect. 5.

2   Related Work

2.1   Learning-Based Automatic Source Code Vulnerability Detection Methods

From the perspective of development trend, the learning-based automatic source code vulnerability detection method can be split into machine learning and deep learning.

Bo Shuai and Haifeng Li [24] proposed a machine learning method based on Latent Dirichlet Allocation(LDA) model and Support Vector Machine (SVM), which can achieve faster and more stable classification. In Boris Chernis and Rakesh M. Verma [3], the text features including simple (character count, character diversity, if count, while count, and so on) and complex (character n-grams, word n-grams, and suffix trees) features are extracted from functions in C source code, then the Naive Bayes is used to analyze them. Jacob A. Harer and Louis Y. Kim [16] compare methods applied directly to source code with methods applied to artifacts extracted from the build process, finding that source-based models perform better.

Song Wang and Taiyue LiuA [28] proposed an algorithm based on deep learning for the semantic representation of programs from source code. They use deep trust network (DBN) to automatically learn semantic features from tag vectors extracted from program abstract syntax tree (AST). Zhen Li and Deqing Zou [19] presented a deep learning-based system for vulnerability detection called VulDeePecker. The features are obtained by first extracting code gadgets from the buggy programs, and then are transformed into vector representations, finally are fed to Bi-LSTM. VulDeePecker outperforms the other state-of-the-art code similarity-based vulnerability detection systems in terms of both accuracy and efficiency. Savchenko, A and Fokin, O [23] proposed DeeDP. It uses the AST representation of source code fragment, allows detection of vulnerabilities in C/C++ source code. Moreover, DeeDP uses deep learning method to organize rules to determine whether code fragments are vulnerable. Srikant,S.and Lesimple,N [25] proposed the Vulcan. It extracts contextual information about tokens in a line and inputs them as AST paths to a bi-directional LSTM with an attention mechanism.

2.2   The Methods for Interpreting Learning-Based Models

Alex Groce and Todd Kulesza [15] considered the problem of testing common machine learning programs when the only oracle is an end user, proposed a test selection method using the characteristics of classifiers. It can provide a good failure rate even for small test suite, and is independent of the algorithm. For performance analysis and debugging in modeling machine learning, Saleema Amershi and Max Chickering [1] introduced ModelTracker, an interactive visualization that includes a lot of traditional summary statistics and information contained in graphics. Moreover, it can show sample level performance, and support direct error checking and debugging. For the problem that how end users can effectively influence the predictions that machine learning systems make on their behalf, Todd Kulesza and Margaret M. Burnett [18] introduced interpretative debugging, a method for the system explains to the user how it makes each prediction, and then the user can explain to the learning system any necessary corrections. The evaluation shows that interpretative debugging improves the understanding of learning system by 52%, which makes the participants correct errors twice as efficient as those who use traditional learning system. MT Ribeiro and S Singh [22] proposed LIME, by learning an interpretable model around the prediction, the prediction of any classifier can be interpreted in an interpretable and faithful way. They also proposed a method to interpret the model by presenting the representative individual prediction and its interpretation in a non-redundant way, and to frame the task as a sub-module optimization problem. The flexibility of this method is proved by explaining different models of text (such as random forest) and image classification (such as neural network).

3   Interpretation for Learning-Based Vulnerability Detection Model Using LIME

In this section, we first introduce the interpretable source code preprocessing method, then introduce the construction of interpretable vulnerability detection model, and finally give details of interpreting Bi-LSTM-based vulnerability detection model using LIME.

3.1   Interpretable Source Code Preprocessing

Source code preprocessing methods we used include symbolic representation and vector representation. Symbolic representation is an interpretable abstract representation of source code. As for vector representation, we choose the BOW (Bag of words) model which is interpretable too.

In symbolization, vulnerability features (such as local variables, user-defined functions and data types) of each code widget are converted to symbolic representations, where the same features are mapped to the same symbolic representation. Among them, variable is symbolized as VN, user-defined function is symbolized as FN, and data with type of "string" is symbolized as S, where N is the index of the first occurrence of the feature. The symbolic results of the dataset can be used as the feature set for vectorization.

BOW puts all the words into a bag, regardless of their grammar, syntax and word order. It firstly segments words, then it gets the characteristics of the text by counting the number of times each word appears in the text, and finally it puts these words of each text sample together with the corresponding word frequency to complete vectorization. We use BOW to transform the symbolic results to sparse matrix vector only contains 0, 1, which are fed to the vulnerability detection model for training. Moreover, using symbolization can effectively reduce the total number of features represented by BOW, and can improve the quality of feature set.

3.2   Construction of Interpretable Vulnerability Detection Model

To better understand the interpretation results of LIME, we first build a source code vulnerability detection model based on interpretable model, that is, Logical Regression. It is selected because of its simple structure, and combine with BOW can make the output of the interpretation easier to be understood.

Linear Regression assumes that there is a linear correlation between the target value and the feature, that is, it satisfies a multiple linear equation. The Linear Regression model can be expressed as follows. Where $h(x)$ represents the target function, θ is the coefficient vector, x is the input vector.

$$h(x) = \theta^T x \tag{1}$$

The Sigmoid function can be expressed as follows. Where z represents input value, which is usually scalar data. The output of Sigmoid is in the range of (0, 1).

$$g(z) = \frac{1}{1 + e^{-z}} \tag{2}$$

By introducing Sigmoid function into the Linear Regression model, the continuous output value of the uncertainty range of Linear Regression is mapped to the range of (0,1). In this way, the Logistic Regression model is built. The essence of Logistic Regression is to assume that the data obeys a distribution, and then uses the maximum likelihood estimation to estimate the parameters. For each prediction, vulnerability detection model based on Logistic Regression can output the weight of all features participating in the prediction result.

$$h_s(x) = g(\theta^T x) = \frac{1}{1 + e^{-\theta^T x}} \tag{3}$$

3.3   Interpretation of Bi-LSTM-Based Vulnerability Detection Model Using LIME

The working principle of LIME to explain the Bi-LSTM-based Vulnerability Detection can be described as follows.

1. Train the Bi-LSTM model using the training dataset;
2. Select the concerned vulnerability sample, such as the one caused by memory leak as the concerned sample x;
3. Define the similarity calculation method and k features to be selected to explain, where we choose the *cosine similarity* here.
4. The disturbance sampling is carried out around the sample x, and the sample weights are given according to the distance from them to x;
5. The Bi-LSTM model is used to predict these samples, and the Linear Regression is trained to approximate the Bi-LSTM model near x.

Here gives the details of the above working principle as follows. LIME will generate a new dataset obtained by perturbing around the selected sample x.

The *cosine similarity* that is used for distance of x and the disturbance sample z can be expressed as follows.

$$\pi_x(z) = \frac{x \cdot z}{||x|| \times ||z||} \tag{4}$$

LIME then trains a Linear Regression model on the new dataset, and measures the difference between the two models by the following objective function:

$$\epsilon(x) = argminL(f, g, \pi_x) + \Omega(g) \tag{5}$$

Suppose that the original model f is an unexplained model that needs to be interpreted, and the interpretation model for instance x is model g. The proximity π_x defines the neighborhood size of sampling near instance x (i.e., the sample distance before and after disturbing x), $\Omega(g)$ is the complexity of the model g. We hope to minimize the loss L when the complexity $\Omega(g)$ of the interpretable model remains at a low level, that is, how close the interpretable model g is to the prediction of the original model f.

With the definition of similarity, the original objective function can be rewritten as follows. Where z is the sample after disturbance, $\pi_x(z)$ represents the similarity between x and z. $f(z)$ is the predicted value of the disturbance sample in the d-dimensional space (original feature) and takes the predicted value as the target, and $g(z')$ is the predicted value in the d-dimensional space (interpretable feature), and then takes the similarity as the weight. Therefore, the above objective function can be optimized by Linear Regression.

$$\epsilon(x) = \sum_{z',z \in Z} \pi_x(z)(f(z) - g(z'))^2 \tag{6}$$

4   Experiment Setting and Result Evaluation

Our experiments are mainly aimed at exploring three insights as follows.

1. Insight 1: Performance comparison of learning-based interpretable model and unexplained model in source code vulnerability detection.
2. Insight 2: The validation of the LIME used in the field of source code vulnerability detection.
3. Insight 3: The interpretation effect of LIME on Bi-LSTM-based vulnerability detection model.

4.1   Experiment Setting

Datasets. The datasets used in the experiment are from [19], which include three parts as follows. Each sample is a piece of source code with known vulnerabilities. Table 1 shows the number of samples (i.e., source code files) in each dataset.

Table 1. Number of samples in each dataset

Dataset	Description	Code Gadgets	Vulnerable code gadgets
BE-ALL	CWE-119	39753	10440
RM-ALL	CWE-399	21885	7285
HY-ALL	CWE-119& CWE-399	61638	17725

Evaluation Metrics. In our experiment, we adopt the commonly used indexes to evaluate the effectiveness of vulnerability detection model, that is, Accuracy(A) and F1-measure (F1). The value range of these four indicators is [0, 1]. For these two indicators, the closer their values are to 1, the better the performance of the model.

4.2 Result Evaluation

Insight 1. We evaluate the vulnerability detection performance of interpretable models and unexplainable models under interpretable features based on all datasets. The interpretable models are LR (Logic Regression), Tree (Decision Tree), where unexplainable models are SVM and Bi-LSTM.

Table 2. Effect of different learning-based models on vulnerability detection effectiveness

Dataset	Indicator	LR	Tree	SVM	Bi-LSTM
BE-ALL	A(%)	92.8	97.2	91.4	**98.1**
	F1(%)	88.6	95.6	86.2	**96.9**
RM-ALL	A(%)	81.7	80.1	79.8	**82.6**
	F1(%)	58.9	59.8	42.7	**65.0**
RM-ALL	A(%)	83.3	86.1	82.6	**90.2**
	F1(%)	67.2	74.3	63.8	**81.1**

From Table 2, we can find that the model based on deep learning (Bi-LSTM) performs better than the model based on machine learning on vulnerability detection for all datasets. This is because deep learning model can perform the strong fitting ability of neural network to achieve better generalization on large-scale datasets, while machine learning model is easy to be over-fit with too many features. Moreover, compared with BE-ALL, all learning-based models show poor performance on RM-ALL and HY-ALL. This may be because with the increasing size of the dataset, the number of features represented by BOW is increasing corresponding. Thus the quality of the feature set will decline, because it usually contains a lot of useless features, which affects the performance of the model. This is also the main reason why BOW model is replaced by distribution representation-based vectorization in recent years.

Insight 2. In consideration of the performance comparison results of Insight 1, we decided to select the dataset BE-ALL to analyze Insight 2. We choose two samples from BE-ALL to test the interpretation effect of the vulnerability detection model based on Logistic Regression, and to verify the interpretation effect of LIME on the vulnerability detection model. The number of features used to interpret the results is set to 10.

Figure 1 and Fig. 2 show the source code and symbolic representation results of the two samples. Both samples with ground-truth label of 1 (vulnerable). With symbolization, the length of the source code is simplified to a certain extent, which also makes the features of source code become more explicit.

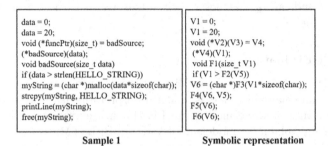

Fig. 1. Sample1 and its symbolization representation

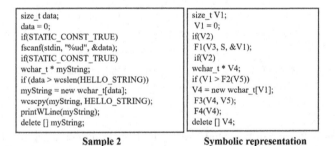

Fig. 2. Sample2 and its symbolization representation

For sample1, the LR model outputs the label of 1, LIME interprets the output of LR gets the label of 1 too. In Fig. 3, output interpretation of LR is shown on the left, while output interpretation of LR using LIME is shown on the right. From the 10 key feature sets that explain the prediction results of sample11, the results given by LIME are the same as those given by LR, and the positive feature sets that drive the prediction label to 1 are also the same. This shows

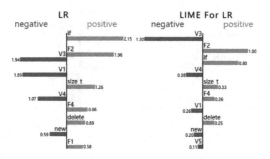

Fig. 3. Interpretation of LR for sample1

that LIME is accurate and effective on the prediction results interpretation for sample 1 output by LR.

For sample2, the LR model outputs the label of 0, LIME interprets the output of LR gets the label of 0 too. From the 10 key feature sets that explain the prediction results of sampel2, there is a deviation between the result given by LIME and that given by LR. Among them, the first four of the negative feature sets that drive the prediction label to 0 are the same, but one more feature given by LIME has little effect on the prediction result. This shows that LIME is also accurate and effective in the interpretation of LR to sample2.

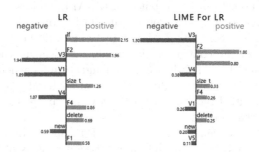

Fig. 4. Interpretation of LR for sample2

Generally speaking, prediction result interpretations of the two samples show that LIME can be effectively applied to the field of source code vulnerability detection.

Insight 3. The prediction labels of both samples output by Bi-LSTM are 1. Figure 5 shows the interpretation outputs by LIME for prediction results of Bi-LSTM. The interpretation result has some differences as to the result output by LR model. Sample 1 contains a vulnerability caused by the "free" function, which is symbolized as "F6". The interpretation feature set given by LR model

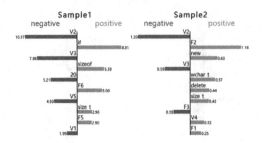

Fig. 5. Interpretation of Bi-LSTM using LIME for sample1 and sample2

for sample 1 with prediction label of 1 does not contain "F6", while the interpretation feature set given by Bi-LSTM model contains "F6", which shows a greater positive impact on prediction label of 1. Thus, it proves that the prediction result of Bi-LSTM model for this sample is credible. Sample 2 contains a vulnerability caused by memory leak. Usually, "new" and "delete" must appear in pairs to prevent memory leaks, which leads to that the "new" and "delete" should be the key features. In the interpretation feature set for sample 2 given by LR model, "delete" has a weak positive effect, while "new" has a negative effect, which lead to that LR gives the error label of 0. As for Bi-LSTM model, "new" and "delete" both have positive effects to output a prediction label of 1. Similarly, for sample 2, Bi-LSTM is more credible. In general, Bi-LSTM achieves a high vulnerability detection performance on BE-ALL, and the prediction results are credible. Moreover, we found some issues in the datasets we used. On the one hand, the samples containing "if" control blocks do not indicate the start and end positions of the control blocks, which may lead to the fact that only the features obtained from LIME are not enough to infer whether the decision results given by the model are credible. On the other hand, the sample containing multiple "if" control blocks, if LIME gives one "if" feature, we can't infer which "if" it is in the sample.

We also give the efficiency evaluation of LIME shown in Table 3. Here are two results of time cost, because the interpretation process of LIME including the classifier prediction. From the results we can find that, the time cost of extra interpretation is insignificant compared with the prediction time cost of Bi-LSTM. Thus, the LIME is also efficient.

Table 3. Efficiency of LIME on all datasets

Dataset	Number of features	Bi-LSTM time cost(s)	Total time cost(s)
BE-ALL	1284	3.97	4.35
RM-ALL	6058	14.87	16.64
HY-ALL	6947	18.00	20.95

5   Conclusion

Through experimental comparison and analysis, we found that the deep learning model performs better than the commonly used machine learning model on large-scale datasets. Also, LIME can be effectively applied to the field of source code vulnerability detection, especially the interpretation of deep learning model. With the explanation of LIME, we found that the prediction results of the Bi-LSTM-based vulnerability detection model are real and effective.

There is an obvious drawback of LIME, that is, it can't be extended to new samples. Moreover, we also found an interesting phenomenon, if there exists a sample containing multiple "if", LIME can not accurately locate the "if" used for interpretation. In the future, we will explore more applications of the latest interpretation models in the field of vulnerability detection.

References

1. Amershi, S., Chickering, et al.: Modeltracker: redesigning performance analysis tools for machine learning. In: Proceedings of the 33rd Annual ACM Conference on Human Factors in Computing Systems, pp. 337–346 (2015)
2. Checkmarx: In: https://www.checkmarx.com/
3. Chernis, B., Verma, R.: Machine learning methods for software vulnerability detection. In: Proceedings of the Fourth ACM International Workshop on Security and Privacy Analytics, pp. 31–39 (2018)
4. Cho, K., Van Merriënboer, B., Bahdanau, D., Bengio, Y.: On the properties of neural machine translation: Encoder-decoder approaches, pp. 103–111. Association for Computational Linguistics (2014). https://doi.org/10.3115/v1/W14-4012
5. Dai, W., Qiu, M., Qiu, L., Chen, L., Wu, A.: Who moved my data? privacy protection in smartphones. IEEE Commun. Mag. **55**(1), 20–25 (2017)
6. FlawFinder: In: http://www.dwheeler.com/flawfinder
7. Fortify, H.: In: https://www.hpfod.com/
8. Gai, K., Qiu, M.: Optimal resource allocation using reinforcement learning for iot content-centric services. Appl. Soft Comput. **70**, 12–21 (2018)
9. Gai, K., Qiu, M.: Reinforcement learning-based content-centric services in mobile sensing. IEEE Netw. **32**(4), 34–39 (2018)
10. Gai, K., Qiu, M., Zhao, H., Sun, X.: Resource management in sustainable cyber-physical systems using heterogeneous cloud computing. IEEE Transactions on Sustainable Computing, pp. 1–1 (2018)
11. Gai, K., Qiu, M., Elnagdy, S.A.: Security-aware information classifications using supervised learning for cloud-based cyber risk management in financial big data. In: 2016 IEEE 2nd International Conference on Big Data Security on Cloud, pp. 197–202. IEEE (2016)
12. Gai, K., Qiu, M., Sun, X., Zhao, H.: Security and privacy issues: a survey on fintech. In: International Conference on Smart Computing and Communication, pp. 236–247. Springer, Cham (2016)
13. Gai, K., Qiu, M., Zhao, H., Dai, W.: Anti-counterfeit scheme using monte carlo simulation for e-commerce in cloud systems. In: 2015 IEEE 2nd International Conference on Cyber Security and Cloud Computing, pp. 74–79. IEEE (2015)

14. Gai, K., Wu, Y., Zhu, L., Zhang, Z., Qiu, M.: Differential privacy-based blockchain for industrial internet-of-things. IEEE Trans. Ind. Inf. **16**(6), 4156–4165 (2019)
15. Groce, A., Kulesza, T., Zhang, et al.: You are the only possible oracle: effective test selection for end users of interactive machine learning systems. IEEE Trans. Softw. Eng.**40**(3), 307–323 (2013)
16. Harer, J.A., Kim, et al.: Automated software vulnerability detection with machine learning. CoRR abs/1803.04497 (2018)
17. Huang, T., Zhu, Y., Zhang, Qiu, M., et al.: An lof-based adaptive anomaly detection scheme for cloud computing. In: 2013 IEEE 37th Annual Computer Software and Applications Conference Workshops, pp. 206–211. IEEE (2013)
18. Kulesza, T., Burnett, M., Wong, W.K., Stumpf, S.: Principles of explanatory debugging to personalize interactive machine learning. In: Proceedings of the 20th international conference on intelligent user interfaces, pp. 126–137 (2015)
19. Li, Z., Zou, Deqing, A.O.: Vuldeepecker: a deep learning-based system for vulnerability detection. In: 25th Annual Network and Distributed System Security Symposium, NDSS 2018, San Diego, California, USA, 18–21 February 2018
20. Niu, J., Gao, Y., Qiu, M., Ming, Z.: Selecting proper wireless network interfaces for user experience enhancement with guaranteed probability. J. Parallel Distrib. Comput. **72**(12), 1565–1575 (2012)
21. Qiu, M., Ming, Z., Wang, J., Yang, L.T., Xiang, Y.: Enabling cloud computing in emergency management systems. IEEE Cloud Comput. **1**(4), 60–67 (2014)
22. Ribeiro, M.T., Singh, S., Guestrin, C.: "why should i trust you?" explaining the predictions of any classifier. In: Proceedings of the 22nd ACM SIGKDD international conference on knowledge discovery and data mining, pp. 1135–1144 (2016)
23. Savchenko, A., Fokin, O., Chernousov, A., Sinelnikova, O., Osadchyi, S.: Deedp: vulnerability detection and patching based on deep learning. Theor. Appl. Cybersecur. **2**(1), 1–7 (2020)
24. Shuai, B., Li, H., Li, et al.: Automatic classification for vulnerability based on machine learning. In: 2013 IEEE International Conference on Information and Automation (ICIA), pp. 312–318. IEEE (2013)
25. Srikant, S., Lesimple, N., O'Reilly, U.M.: Dependency-based neural representations for classifying lines of programs. CoRR abs/2004.10166 (2020)
26. Tao, L., Golikov, S., Gai, K., Qiu, M.: A reusable software component for integrated syntax and semantic validation for services computing. In: 2015 IEEE Symposium on Service-Oriented System Engineering, pp. 127–132. IEEE (2015)
27. Thakur, K., Qiu, M., Gai, K., Ali, M.L.: An investigation on cyber security threats and security models. In: 2015 IEEE 2nd International Conference on Cyber Security and Cloud Computing, pp. 307–311. IEEE (2015)
28. Wang, S., Liu, T., Tan, L.: Automatically learning semantic features for defect prediction. In: 2016 IEEE/ACM 38th International Conference on Software Engineering (ICSE), pp. 297–308. IEEE (2016)
29. Zhang, Q., Huang, T., Zhu, Y., Qiu, M.: A case study of sensor data collection and analysis in smart city: provenance in smart food supply chain. Int. J. Distrib. Sensor Netw. **9**(11), 382132 (2013)
30. Zhang, Z., Wu, J., Deng, J., Qiu, M.: Jamming ack attack to wireless networks and a mitigation approach. In: IEEE GLOBECOM 2008–2008 IEEE Global Telecommunications Conference, pp. 1–5. IEEE (2008)

Efficient Depth Completion Network Based on Dynamic Gated Fusion

Zhengyang Mu$^{(\boxtimes)}$ (ID), Qi Qi$^{(\boxtimes)}$ (ID), Jingyu Wang (ID), Haifeng Sun (ID), and Jianxin Liao (ID)

State Key Laboratory of Networking and Switching Technology,
Beijing University of Posts and Telecommunications, Beijing, China
{muzhengyang,qiqi8266}@bupt.edu.cn

Abstract. Depth completion aims to recover dense depth maps from sparse depth and RGB images. Current methods achieve high accuracy at the cost of large model size and huge computation complexity, which prevent them from wider applications. In this paper, we focus on making two key issues on depth completion – feature extraction and fusion – more efficient to achieve superior trade-off in model size and accuracy: (1) we propose efficient dual-branch encoder by exploring data characteristics of different modalities which can greatly reduce the model size and inference time; (2) we propose a dynamic gated fusion module, which is guided by input sparse depth to fuse information of both RGB and sparse depth feature more efficiently by generating dynamic fusing weights. Experiments on KITTI Depth Completion and NYU Depth v2 show that our method achieves 3.5x - 10x speedup against the state-of-art method, 9x param compressing and comparable accuracy compared with state-of-the-art methods, which shows our method achieves good trade-off between performance and speed.

Keywords: Depth completion · Feature fusion · Light-weighted model · Autonomous driving · Robotics

1 Introduction

Accurate and dense depth perception is the basic problem of computer vision, plays a vital role in many applications such as autonomous driving, augmented realities, and 3D object detection [7]. Although accurate depth information can be directly read from depth camera or LiDAR, they produce sparse depth maps with considerable missing data. For example: for outdoor scenes, only 5.9% pixels with valid depth in image plane can be detected even using high-cost Velodyne HDL-64e (64 layers) LiDAR; for indoor scenes, structured light-based devices (KINECT, Real Sense, etc.) obtain denser depth than LiDAR, but they have

This work was supported in part by the National Key R&D Program of China 2020YFB1807805, in part by the National Natural Science Foundation of China under Grants 62071067, 62001054, 61771068.

range limit and are sensitive to environment. Monocular depth estimation [22] and stereo matching algorithms can generate dense depth maps, but the former is an ill-conditioned problem and can only obtain imprecise or relative depths, while the latter is very sensitive to the quality of RGB features. Therefore, the problem of depth completion which combines two modalities is of great value for academic and industrial.

With the development of deep learning methods, more and more deep completion methods based on convolutional neural networks have been proposed, which has achieved a huge improvement compared to the traditional method [3,15,16]. A mainstream solution is to directly input the sparse depth map and RGB map into the encoder-decoder to generate depth, which is called early-fusion. These methods [1,12–14,19] use a single structure to process data with large domain gap, which increases the difficulty of network learning. In order to improve accuracy, such methods often use multi-task learning strategies. The normal map, confidence, segmentation and other results are also predicted while estimating the depth map, which further increases the learning difficulty of the backbone network. And always following complex post-processing processes to use these cues. Therefore, such methods often require large networks, such as ResNet34 even ResNet50 [6] with corresponding decoder. Although achieving good accuracy, the network size is too large for deployment and inference speed is slow. Another mainstream structure is to use a dual-branch encoder to process the RGB and sparse depth separately, then two modality features are fused and feed into decoder to generate depth map, which names late-fusion. This type of structure [9,10,20] enables different structure processing different modalities, making it possible to reduce model size and explore more complex feature interactions. However, current late fusion methods have two problems. First, the feature fusion strategy is relatively simple, mostly using channel-wise concatenation or element-wise addition. Second, the encoder structures are borrowed from image classification network, without exploring more efficient way to deal with RGB and sparse depth data to reducing model size and inference speed.

In this paper, we first design two lightweight encoders for RGB and sparse depth. For sparse depth, because the valid information is sparse and scattered, the shallow network for feature extraction is proposed, and the convolutions with larger kernel size are used to expand the receptive field, which can enable the subsequent convolutions to learn more meaningful features. For RGB, we used factorized convolution to build bottleneck block, which saves lots of parameters and computations with little performance drop. Secondly, we found that the valid points in the sparse depth map is not uniformly distributed, and sparsity of the same spatial area may vary per sample. In areas with more depth cues, the fusion weight of depth features should be higher than RGB features, we propose a dynamic gated feature fusion module (GFM) guided by sparse depth density distribution to handle this complexity for more powerful feature fusion. Ablation study shows that compared with the baseline method [20] (which is one of the SOTA methods which shares similar structure with us), our method only uses 2.68M parameters ($\frac{1}{10}$ of baseline model) and 5.8% accuracy improvement.

On two challenging public data sets KITTI Depth Completion and NYU depth v2, compared with the existing algorithm, our method uses few parameters to achieve comparable performance with state-of-the-art.

The major contributions and achievements of this paper are three-fold:

- We design a lightweight dual-branch encoder that fully explores the data characteristics to decrease parameters of depth completion pipeline.
- We propose a new feature fusion method called dynamic gated fusion module to increase the performance.
- Our compact network achieves good trade-off between accuracy and speed which enables our method to have wide range of applications even on embedded devices.

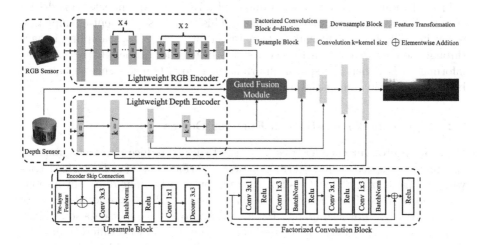

Fig. 1. The overall structure of our proposed network.

2 Method

2.1 Overall Architecture

Given sparse depth image sD made by projecting depth sensor readings onto the image plane the corresponding calibrated RGB image I, then depth completion network will predict a dense depth map by combining the information of two modalities. This problem is usually modeled as a per-pixel regression problem. Most of the existing works [12,20] use encoder-decoder structure, and some work uses two [5] or even multiple [14] encoder-decoder to perform model fusion and multi-stage processing. We adopt single encoder-decoder design for lightweight considerations. Based on the dual-branch late-fusion structure of DDP [20] (baseline), we redesign the encoder, skip-connections and feature fusion strategy, to form the network proposed in this paper. The specific structure is shown in Fig. 1.

Dual-branch encoder extracts the features of RGB and sparse depth, then uses the transformation layer to map features of two modalities into the same space for feature fusion. The dual-branch encoder design can reduce the learning difficulty which enables us to design lightweight networks according to each input's characteristic. The feature vectors generated by the two encoders are dynamically fused using the proposed dynamic gated feature fusion module, and feed into decoder made by stacked upsample block which composed of 3×3 convolution and deconvolution layers to perform dense depth regression. It is worth noticing that, unlike the previous work in which inputs are downsampled to $\frac{1}{16}$ resolution with 256 channels or even $\frac{1}{32}$ with 512 channels, we argue to use shallow network that inputs are downsampled to $\frac{1}{8}$ with 128 channels, which reduces the number of network parameters by 70%. In experiments, this design even leads to 7.5% accuracy improvement. This is because the depth completion is sensitive to spatial information loss. In the process of downsampling images through pooling or convolution with stride in encoder, although the semantic information is richer, the spatial information is lost. Our design well balanced between semantic and spatial information.

2.2   Lightweight Dual-Branch Encoder Design

RGB Branch. Our encoder uses three strategies to reduce parameter number and inference speed, while sacrifice little on performance: (1) Factorized convolution: factorizing 3×3 two-dim convolution into two one-dim convolutions with kernel sizes of 3×1 and 1×3 [17]; (2) using ResNet residual block [6] design; (3) early downsampling. To further improve the representation ability of network, we use stacked factorized convolution blocks with different dilation sizes to increase receptive field. The output of the encoder will be fed into 1×1 convolution for feature transformation.

Sparse Depth Branch. Current networks usually using redundant encoder for sparse depth, without fully explore the characteristics of it to make it efficient. The sparse depth input of depth completion contains little information due to depth sensor's hardware limit, so a shallow network is sufficient. In addition, the distribution of effective value points is always scattered, so the network should have large receptive field for extracting more meaningful information. Based on these two observations, we designed an encoder for sparse depth which consists of 5 convolution layers. Large convolution kernels (11,7,5) are used to rapidly expand the receptive field from conv1 to conv3, and 3×3 kernel convolution for detailed feature extraction. It also uses 1×1 convolution as transformation layer. BN is not used in this encoder because too much zero value at sparse depth will cause numerical disorder of BN and lead to bad training.

2.3 Dynamic Gated Fusion Module

After extracting RGB and sparse depth features, existing methods usually use additive fusion [14] or convolution fusion [12] for feature fusion:

$$X = E_{RGB}(I) + E_{sD}(D) \tag{1}$$

$$X = conv\,(E_{RGB}(I) \oplus E_{sD}(D)) \tag{2}$$

where X, E, I, D are fused feature, encoder of corresponding modality, RGB image and sparse depth input respectively; $Conv$ denotes 1×1 convolution and $\oplus$ is channel concatenation. Additive fusion (Eq. 1) combines the features of two modalities with equal weights, ignoring that depth feature should be allocated larger weight where depth cue is rich. For example, in areas where depth branch encodes sufficient information to predict dense map, if feature fusion is performed with equal weights, RGB features will distort the fusion. Convolutional fusion (Eq. 2) relies on a learnable convolution kernel as fusion weights of the two modalities. But the fusing weights may overfit the training set, it will lead false weight allocation when meeting unseen sparsity distribution. We will prove that in Sect. 3.3.

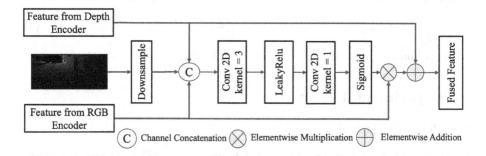

Fig. 2. Structure of proposed dynamic gated fusion module.

To better fuse the features, this paper proposes a dynamic gated feature fusion module (GFM). The structure is shown in Fig. 2. The two modality features generated by the encoder and the downsampled sparse depth map are concatenated in the channel dimension and sent to a small neural network to generate fusion weights in a per-sample aware way. The weights indicate which features at what locations in RGB features are suppressed or reserved. Then the weights are used to filter the RGB features, and finally adding to sparse depth features to complete and enhance depth feature. The small neural network is composed of two convolution layers with 3×3 and 1×1 kernel size and a LeakyRelu, sigmoid function is used to regularize the fusion weight. It can discover the confidence of each modality's features and generate dynamic fusion weights guided by each input's sparsity pattern. The module can be formulated as:

$$X = E_{sD}(D) + w \times E_{RGB}(I) \tag{3}$$

where $w = Net\left(E_{sD}(D), E_{RGB}(I), downsample(D)\right)$. Experiments show that this module brings large accuracy improvement by introducing few parameters, and it is suitable for different network architectures.

2.4 Loss Function

To better training the network, we combine l_1 and l_2 loss in our training phase. Each loss term is formulated as follow:

$$l_\rho\left(D^{gt}, D^{pred}\right) = \frac{1}{\|M\|} \sum_{x \in X} \sigma\left(d_x^{gt}\right) \times \left|d_x^{gt} - d_x^{pred}\right|^\rho \tag{4}$$

where D^{gt} is ground truth depth, D^{pred} is the depth map predicted by our network, d_x is the depth value at location x. For real-world data, the depth ground truth is often semi-dense, so we need function $\sigma(x)$ to filter invalid points. It will return 0 if depth value is invalid else 1. $\|M\|$ is total valid point number in the ground truth. The overall loss function can be expressed as:

$$L_{\text{train}} = \alpha \times l_1\left(D^{gt}, D^{\text{pred}}\right) + \beta \times l_2\left(D^{gt}, D^{\text{pred}}\right) \tag{5}$$

where α and β are the weights that control the ratio of the two loss items.

3   Experimental Results

3.1 Training Details

Our method is implemented using Pytorch, and is trained and tested on a workstation equipped with an NVIDIA Tesla M40 GPU. All models are optimized by Adam optimizer with $\beta_1 = 0.9; \beta_2 = 0.999$. Initial learning rate is set to 0.001 and reducing the learning rate by 0.5 when the loss does not decrease for 5 epochs, minimum learning rate is set to 5×10^{-5}. We set $\alpha = 1$ and $\beta = 1$ in loss for all experiments. Batch size is set to 32 for KITTI and 64 for NYU and trained about 50 epochs.

3.2 Dataset and Evaluation Metrics

KITTI Depth Completion [4] **(KITTI DC).** It consists of more than 90K RGB and LiDAR pairs of data and semi-dense depth ground truth for training and validation. In addition, the official also provides 1000 data with no ground truth for testing. In training, we crop all training data from 375×1242 to 256×1216, and use random horizontal flip as augmentation. We use official error metrics for evaluation: Root Mean Square Error (RMSE, in mm, main metric),

Mean Absolute Error (MAE, in mm) and their inverse depth version iRMSE (in 1/km) and iMAE (in 1/km).

NYU Depth v2 [16]. This data set consists of RGB images and depth images collected by Microsoft Kinect from 464 different indoor scenes. According to the official data split strategy, 249 scenes are used for training, and 654 labeled images are selected for evaluating the final performance. During training, we use similar augmentation strategy with [13] including color jitter, horizontal flip, rotation and center-crop to 304×228. Sparse depth maps are created by random sample 500 points from ground truth. We exploit RMSE, mean absolute relative error(REL in m), and the percentage of relative errors inside a certain threshold $(\delta_t, t \in \{1.25, 1.25^2, 1.25^3\})$ as evaluation metrics.

Table 1. Ablation study of our proposed designs on NYU Depth v2 validation set.

Exp.	Encoder Type	Feature size at Fusion	Feature Fusion	RMSE	REL	$\delta_{1.25}$	$\delta_{1.25^2}$	$\delta_{1.25^3}$	Param. (M)
1	Baseline	1/16*512	Add	0.1454	0.0203	99.1	99.8	99.9	28.44
2	Baseline	1/8*256	Add	0.1361	0.0195	99.3	99.9	99.9	7.01
3	Baseline	1/8*256	GFM	0.1307	0.0184	99.4	99.9	99.9	8.06
4	LDE	1/8*128	Add	0.1461	0.0226	99.2	99.8	99.9	2.37
5	LDE	1/8*128	Concat	0.1644	0.0267	98.7	99.8	99.9	2.56
6	LDE	1/8*128	GFM	0.1360	0.0193	99.3	99.9	100	2.68

3.3 Ablation Study

Here, we use reduced NYU dataset to conduct a series of experiments to verify the effectiveness of each design proposed in this paper. The experimental setup and results are shown in Table 1 where Exp. means experiments number. We use DDP [20] (share similar dual-branch and late-fusion structure with our method) as baseline. Its structure is shown in Exp.1: use ResNet18 (until Layer4) as encoder of two modalities, feature size sent to the decoder is $\frac{H}{16} \times \frac{W}{16} \times 512$, additive fusion is used for feature fusion.

The Effectiveness of Lightweight Dual-Branch Encoder (LDE). Exp.2 shows the effect of reducing the network's and depth and width: we use the output of layer3 in ResNet18 as the extracted features of two modalities, other settings same as Exp.1. The parameter number reduce significantly, and accuracy increased by 6.3%, which verifies our discussion in Sect. 2.1 that the depth completion task is sensitive to the loss of spatial information. In Exp.4, we replace baseline encoder with proposed lightweight dual-branch encoder and further decrease the network width. Comparing with Exp.1, our proposed lightweight structure compresses the parameter by 11x with little loss in accuracy. Comparing with Exp.2, parameter compressed by 2.7x with some accuracy loss, but this loss will be made up by our dynamic gated fusion module. The comparison shows that after adopting the lightweight design, the parameter number is reduced by 2.7 times, which only brings a slight loss of accuracy. These losses are compensated by our efficient GFM module. See the comparison between Exp. 2 and Exp. 6. The parameter number is reduced by 2.4 times without loss of accuracy.

The Effectiveness of Dynamic Gated Fusion Module (GFM). Comparing between Exp.4,5,6 prove the effectiveness of the proposed gated fusion module. Among them, the effect of convolution fusion is the worst, because the fusion weight of the 1×1 convolution used may not generalize well for unseen sparse depth distribution, during validation or testing, the weights are fixed for every sample. Additive fusion has better generalization effect than convolutional fusion because of equal weight fusion, and the accuracy is improved by 10.5%, and model size is reduced by 0.18M. Among all of them, our proposed GFM has the best accuracy, achieving 7.5% improvement in RMSE and 14.6% improvement in REL, only adding 0.3M parameters. Besides, we also apply GFM on baseline structure (Exp.2 vs Exp.3) and observe improvement in accuracy, shows our GFM can apply to different network design.

In short, compared with the baseline model (Exp.1 vs Exp.6), by carefully designing the dual-branch encoder and feature fusion method, our model achieves 6.5% improvement in RMSE and 5% improvement in REL with only using $\frac{1}{10}$ of the baseline model size.

Table 2. Quantitative results on test set of KITTI Depth Completion benchmark, for all metric, smaller is better.

Method	Param. (M)	RMSE	MAE	iRMSE	iMAE
TGV [3]	–	2761.29	1068.69	15.02	6.28
SparseConvs [18]	–	1601.33	481.27	4.94	1.78
MorphNet [2]	–	1045.45	310.49	3.84	1.57
Spade-RGBsD [9]	5.4	1035.29	248.32	2.6	0.98
HMSNet [8]	–	841.78	253.47	2.73	1.13
DDP [20](baseline)	28.4	832.94	203.96	2.1	0.85
Sparse2Dense [12]	42.82	814.73	249.95	2.8	1.21
PwP [19]	28.99	777.05	235.17	2.42	1.13
DeepLiDAR [14]	53.44	758.38	226.5	2.56	1.15
CSPN++ [1]	26.1	743.69	209.28	2.07	0.90
NLSPN [13]	25.84	741.68	199.59	1.99	0.84
Ours	2.68	790.13	226.10	2.49	1.03

3.4   Overall Performance

Quantitative Comparison. Table 2 shows the quantitative evaluation on KITTI test set ("-" indicates that the parameter information of the method

Table 3. Quantitative results on test set of NYU Depth v2 with setting of 500 sparse samples, RMSE and REL: smaller is better, δ_x: larger is better. Sample states the number of pixels were uniformly sampled from depth.

Method	#Samples	Param. (M)	RMSE	REL	$\delta_{1.25}$	$\delta_{1.25^2}$	$\delta_{1.25^3}$
Liao et al. [11]	225	27.85	0.442	0.104	87.8	96.4	98.9
Sparse2Dense [12]	200	42.82	0.230	0.044	97.1	99.4	99.8
Ours		2.68	0.170	0.020	99.1	99.8	99.9
Bilateral [16]		–	0.479	0.084	92.4	97.6	98.9
TGV [3]		–	0.635	0.123	81.9	93.0	96.8
Zhang et al. [21]		–	0.228	0.042	97.1	99.3	99.7
Sparse2Dense [12]	500	42.82	0.204	0.043	97.8	99.6	99.9
DeepLiDAR [14]		53.44	0.115	0.022	99.3	99.9	100.0
PwP [19]		28.99	0.112	0.018	99.5	99.9	100.0
NLSPN [13]		25.84	0.092	0.012	99.6	99.9	100.0
Ours		2.68	0.118	0.019	99.3	99.9	100.0

cannot be obtained). It is worth noting that DeepLiDAR [14] uses an additional 50K sets of rendered training data rendered to train the surface normal sub-network. The PwP [19] method uses additional normal vector labels for training. CSPN++ [1] and NLSPN [13] used complex post-processing methods, and the parameter number in Table 2 did not include the post-processing part. Our method uses only 2.68M parameters to achieve comparable accuracy. Compared with the Spade-RGBsD [9] method with similar model size level, our method significantly improves the accuracy through an efficient fusion method. Compared with DDP [20] (baseline) which shares similar structure with us but not has well-designed encoder and uses "Add fusion" to fuse two modalities, our model is 10x smaller than it and large RMSE accuracy improvement. Compared with PwP [19] and DeepLiDAR [14], our method does not use additional data and labels, and has achieved small improvement in MAE, iRMSE, and iMAE, and made huge model size compression. Table 4 shows the speed comparison, our method achieved superior inference speed. Figure 3 visualizes the trade-off between accuracy and model size of each method. It can be seen that our method has achieved better trade-off. For indoor scene, as shown in Table 3 and Fig. 3(b), it shares similar conclusions with the KITTI data set. For a very sparse input(200 samples), our method achieves best results. Overall, our method is the most efficient one by significantly reducing the model size while keeping comparable accuracy with SOTA methods on NYU dataset, and robust in very sparse input.

Table 4. Comparison of inference speed on KITTI, other method's speeds are borrowed from KITTI benchmark.

Method	DDP [20]	CSPN++ [1]	Sparse2Dense [12]	NLSPN [13]	DeepLiDAR [14]	Ours
Inference Time	0.08s	0.2s	0.08s	0.22s	0.07s	0.02s

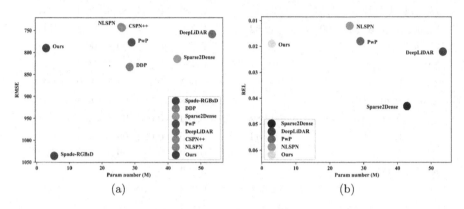

Fig. 3. Comparison of performance/parameter trade-off on (a) KITTI Depth Completion benchmark and (b) NYU Depth v2, best view in color and zoom.

Fig. 4. Qualitative comparation of our method against other mthods on KITTI DC test set. Best view in color and zoom.

Qualitative Comparison. Qualitative results in Fig. 4 demonstrate that our method has more accurate estimations in difficult scenes where input depth cues are sparse or lacking and difficult thin objects like poles. Specifically, in the left column, the sparse depth input of the car roof is lacking which leads to the failure prediction of the DDP [20] and sparse2dense [12]. But our method and

NLSPN can recover a more correct contour, while NLSPN's model size is 9x bigger than us. In the right column, due to our better feature fusion, the pole shape predicted by our method is more reasonable than others. In addition, even in areas with nearly no depth cues (the faraway car at the middle of right column sample), our method can also recover the right car shape, while other methods fail in this case.

4 Conclusion

This paper proposed an end-to-end efficient convolutional neural network for depth completion, which can recover the depth of each pixel in the image from sparse LiDAR data and dense RGB data. We first analyzed the data characteristics of each modality, and designed lightweight dual-branch encoder, which greatly reduced the model size and inference speed with little loss in accuracy. To further address the key issue of depth completion that how to exploit the observed spatial contexts from multi-modal data efficiently, gated fusion module (GFM) is proposed to dynamically generate fusion weights based on the input samples and the features extracted from two modalities. Comparing with other algorithms, our design significantly decreases model parameters (9x smaller or more) and inference speed (4x smaller or more) while keeping comparable accuracy with state-of-the-art, achieving good balance of speed and accuracy. This makes our method has wide range of application scenarios.

References

1. Cheng, X., Wang, P., Guan, C., Yang, R.: CSPN++: learning context and resource aware convolutional spatial propagation networks for depth completion. In: Proceedings of the AAAI Conference on Artificial Intelligence, vol. 34, pp. 10615–10622 (2020)
2. Dimitrievski, M., Veelaert, P., Philips, W.: Learning morphological operators for depth completion. In: Blanc-Talon, J., Helbert, D., Philips, W., Popescu, D., Scheunders, P. (eds.) ACIVS 2018. LNCS, vol. 11182, pp. 450–461. Springer, Cham (2018). https://doi.org/10.1007/978-3-030-01449-0_38
3. Ferstl, D., Reinbacher, C., Ranftl, R., Rüther, M., Bischof, H.: Image guided depth upsampling using anisotropic total generalized variation. In: Proceedings of the IEEE International Conference on Computer Vision, pp. 993–1000 (2013)
4. Geiger, A., Lenz, P., Urtasun, R.: Are we ready for autonomous driving? the KITTI vision benchmark suite. In: 2012 IEEE Conference on Computer Vision and Pattern Recognition, pp. 3354–3361. IEEE (2012)
5. Giannone, G., Chidlovskii, B.: Learning common representation from RGB and depth images. In: Proceedings of the IEEE/CVF Conference on Computer Vision and Pattern Recognition Workshops (2019)
6. He, K., Zhang, X., Ren, S., Sun, J.: Deep residual learning for image recognition. In: Proceedings of the IEEE conference on computer vision and pattern recognition, pp. 770–778 (2016)
7. Hou, J., Dai, A., Nießner, M.: Revealnet: seeing behind objects in RGB-D scans. In: Proceedings of the IEEE/CVF Conference on Computer Vision and Pattern Recognition, pp. 2098–2107 (2020)

8. Huang, Z., Fan, J., Cheng, S., Yi, S., Wang, X., Li, H.: HMS-Net: hierarchical multi-scale sparsity-invariant network for sparse depth completion. IEEE Trans. Image Process. **29**, 3429–3441 (2019)
9. Jaritz, M., De Charette, R., Wirbel, E., Perrotton, X., Nashashibi, F.: Sparse and dense data with cnns: depth completion and semantic segmentation. In: 2018 International Conference on 3D Vision (3DV), pp. 52–60. IEEE (2018)
10. Lee, B.U., Jeon, H.G., Im, S., Kweon, I.S.: Depth completion with deep geometry and context guidance. In: 2019 International Conference on Robotics and Automation (ICRA), pp. 3281–3287. IEEE (2019)
11. Liao, Y., Huang, L., Wang, Y., Kodagoda, S., Yu, Y., Liu, Y.: Parse geometry from a line: monocular depth estimation with partial laser observation. In: 2017 IEEE international conference on robotics and automation (ICRA), pp. 5059–5066 (2017)
12. Ma, F., Cavalheiro, G.V., Karaman, S.: Self-supervised sparse-to-dense: self-supervised depth completion from lidar and monocular camera. In: 2019 International Conference on Robotics and Automation (ICRA), pp. 3288–3295 (2019)
13. Park, J., Joo, K., Hu, Z., Liu, C.K., Kweon, I.S.: Non-local spatial propagation network for depth completion. In: ECCV (2020)
14. Qiu, J., et al.: Deeplidar: deep surface normal guided depth prediction for outdoor scene from sparse lidar data and single color image. In: Proceedings of the IEEE/CVF Conference on Computer Vision and Pattern Recognition, pp. 3313–3322 (2019)
15. Shao, W., Sheng, H., Li, C.: Segment-based depth estimation in light field using graph cut. In: Zhang, S., Wirsing, M., Zhang, Z. (eds.) KSEM 2015. LNCS (LNAI), vol. 9403, pp. 248–259. Springer, Cham (2015). https://doi.org/10.1007/978-3-319-25159-2_23
16. Silberman, N., Hoiem, D., Kohli, P., Fergus, R.: Indoor segmentation and support inference from RGBD images. In: Fitzgibbon, A., Lazebnik, S., Perona, P., Sato, Y., Schmid, C. (eds.) ECCV 2012. LNCS, vol. 7576, pp. 746–760. Springer, Heidelberg (2012). https://doi.org/10.1007/978-3-642-33715-4_54
17. Szegedy, C., Vanhoucke, V., Ioffe, S., Shlens, J., Wojna, Z.: Rethinking the inception architecture for computer vision. In: Proceedings of the IEEE conference on computer vision and pattern recognition, pp. 2818–2826 (2016)
18. Uhrig, J., Schneider, N., Schneider, L., Franke, U., Brox, T., Geiger, A.: Sparsity invariant cnns. In: 2017 international conference on 3D Vision (3DV), pp. 11–20. IEEE (2017)
19. Xu, Y., Zhu, X., Shi, J., Zhang, G., Bao, H., Li, H.: Depth completion from sparse lidar data with depth-normal constraints. In: Proceedings of the IEEE/CVF International Conference on Computer Vision, pp. 2811–2820 (2019)
20. Yang, Y., Wong, A., Soatto, S.: Dense depth posterior (DDP) from single image and sparse range. In: Proceedings of the IEEE/CVF Conference on Computer Vision and Pattern Recognition, pp. 3353–3362 (2019)
21. Zhang, Y., Funkhouser, T.: Deep depth completion of a single RGB-D image. In: Proceedings of the IEEE Conference on Computer Vision and Pattern Recognition, pp. 175–185 (2018)
22. Zhao, Yu., Jin, F., Wang, M., Wang, S.: Knowledge graphs meet geometry for semi-supervised monocular depth estimation. In: Li, G., Shen, H.T., Yuan, Y., Wang, X., Liu, H., Zhao, X. (eds.) KSEM 2020. LNCS (LNAI), vol. 12274, pp. 40–52. Springer, Cham (2020). https://doi.org/10.1007/978-3-030-55130-8_4

A Blockchain Based Framework for Smart Greenhouse Data Management

Chenkai Guo, Yapeng Zi, and Wei Ren[(⊠)]

School of Computer and Information Science, Southwest University, No. 2 Tiansheng Road, Beibei, Chongqing 400715, China

Abstract. The safe exchanging and storing of Internet of Things (IoT) data in greenhouse scenarios has intrigued researchers from both management and information science. The authentic and secure data is the key foundation of data analysis and decision making. On the other hand, the traditional centralized cloud computing system has a fatal failure that once the central server being successfully attacked, all the data will get lost. The backups will be difficult to retrieve and the system recovering will be time consuming. This paper introduces a double-chain based on IoT data storage system supporting knowledge management abilities of greenhouse scenario. The system collects data from Greenhouse sensors and store the data in Inter Planetary File System (IPFS) network, after the IPFS hash have been generated, the network again rehashes the values and upload onto the Ethereum chain for public queries. The distributed data storage improves the security of data, also supports the safe exchanging of information as well as the sharing of data between entities, improving the efficiency of knowledge management.

Keywords: Data management · Security · IoT · Blockchain · Agriculture · Greenhouse

1 Introduction

The exchanging and sharing safety of data knowledge has become an important issue in the field of knowledge management for researchers. On the other hand, the data security in smart greenhouse scenario intrigues attentions of researchers from both agriculture and information technology. The decision making on automatic collection of greenhouse data such as indoor temperature, light, water, fertilizer, air and many other factors, can achieve high yield and high economic benefits. However, smart greenhouse based on IoT faces the challenge of being attacked. For example, if the real time data of greenhouse are being tampered with, it will lead to the wrong calculation results of watering time and amount. And the investors will get nothing but a total loss.

Traditional IoT knowledge management techniques originated from cloud computing, which is a centralized technology and makes the data storage inflexible. Once the central server down, the operations of the entire IoT network will fall into chaos and important data will be lost. Also the probability of successful attacks will be higher. Cloud computing cannot play its role if we do not arrange fine allocation for cloud

© Springer Nature Switzerland AG 2021
H. Qiu et al. (Eds.): KSEM 2021, LNAI 12817, pp. 299–310, 2021.
https://doi.org/10.1007/978-3-030-82153-1_25

infrastructure resources [1]. And users will not be aware of data tampering [2]. Therefore, how to maintain the independence of knowledge data and realize the safe sharing of knowledge is the key to knowledge management.

For the safety management of intellectual property in data management, especially the storage and protection of real time data, we propose a solution based on both public blockchain and consortium blockchain. Compared with centralized cloud computing, our proposed solution maintains the transparency, dispersion and invariability of data to ensure its reliability.

The remaining structure of this paper is organized as follows. Section 2 presents the former works related to knowledge management technologies and the application of blockchain in diverse scenarios. The proposed blockchain based method and discussion on experiments are presented in Sect. 3. The concluding remarks are drawn in Sect. 4.

2   Related Works

Blockchain is a decentralized, distributed and often public digital ledger [3]. It consists of records called blocks that are used to record transactions on many computers. Therefore, it is impossible for any involved blocks to be changed retroactively without changing all subsequent blocks. Even if malicious users tamper or destroy the source data, other nodes can retrieve the complete and correct data before the attack, which reflects the openness and transparency of blockchain technology [4].

With the continuous development and fusion of various heterogeneous technologies [5], the IoT is also expanding rapidly, its functional aspects are unified and humans have the ability to control every object of the world through the Internet [6]. On its basis, an ecosystem of agricultural intelligent physical engineering networks has also been formed, but also inherits some security issues from the traditional network, such as wireless networks, wired networks, sensor networks, and with its continuous development, produces some new problems [7]. Data protection in the IoT system mainly lies in the control of data, take different means to protect data in the process of data transmission. But most of the technology used in the system is basically based on data encryption. There are many encryption protocols, but data protection requires more than encryption [8]. In this trend, mixed data protection methods become inevitable. Blockchain technology is suitable for IoT scenarios. The public blockchain model is more secure yet slow, while the consortium blockchain model can achieves much faster speed yet the nodes need authorization before adding into the network [9]. A secure hybrid industrial IoT framework using blockchain technology is proposed [10]. In this framework, the blockchain mechanism is used to extract information from the machine equipment and store the extracted records in the blockchain to maintain transparency for different users in different locations. The result showed an 89% success rate on user request time, forgery attacks, black hole attacks, and probability authentication scenarios.

The IEEE standard of blockchain-based IoT data management framework is proposed in [11], the standard applies not only to enterprise scenarios that use data management systems and data collected from IoT devices for internal business decisions, data sharing, and data transactions with external parties, but also serves as a block guide for building systems using blockchain and IoT technologies. The authors recommend using the Edge Cloud to access IoT devices and users, and then using its built-in blockchain for the autonomy and self-monitoring of the Edge Cloud [12]. The use of master node technology to introduce meta-devices and users into closed blockchain systems which extends the scope of blockchain to IoT-based DApps, but requires multiple layers of validation. A chain of trust is then proposed: Trust-Chain serves as a three-tier trust management framework that uses consortium blockchain to track interactions among supply chain participants and dynamically assigns trust and reputation ratings based on those interactions, but the supply chain supported by the IoT and consortium blockchain is separated in this project [13]. An RFID and blockchain-based agri-food supply chain traceability system is established, which includes the whole process of data collection and implements its security policy by blockchain [14].

In this paper, we propose a blockchain-based data protection mechanism, through the Inter Planetary File System (IPFS) protocol to encrypt data content and ensure the security of data transmission process. The main chain is on Ethereum, which stores an index of the IPFS hash value. The throughput and data security of the double-chain mechanism will be better than Ethereum alone.

3   System Structure

The system performance of public blockchain for transactions is very low, while consortium blockchain is "weakly centralized" in exchange for the optimization of efficiency and cost. To combine the advantages of public blockchain and consortium blockchain, a double-chain solution is proposed.

3.1   System Structure

The following is a double chain solution that combines blockchain technology with IoT sensor network to ensure data reliability. The System structure of double-chain solution as show in Fig. 1.

The IPFS [15] is the first level for sensors to upload data, IPFS uses content addressing to uniquely identify each file in the global namespace that connects all computing devices. Unlike the central server, IPFS is built around a distributed user operating system, which owns a part of all data and creates a flexible file storage and sharing system. This feature fits well with the decentralization of blockchain technology.

Then the IPFS hash values will be uploaded to Greenhouse Sample Data Chain (GSDC), which is on the second layer. In GSDC, each block will store more than one IPFS hash values and each block will be calculated an GSDC hash result, too. So only the IPFS hash values but not specific data will be stored in block. By this means, the GSDC chain will process much less data and easy to maintain with. The throughput and safety will be much higher. Finally, GSDC chain uploads the block hash to Ethereum for backup and public queries.

3.2   The Data Exchange Plan

In our double-blockchain solution, Ethereum's main chain and the greenhouse sample data chain involves designing the storage and transmission of hash values. The system

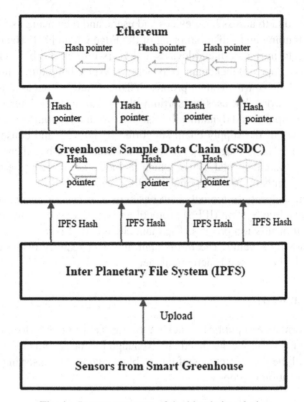

Fig. 1. System structure of double-chain solution.

also includes an IPFS network responsible for data formatting, receiving, storing, and hashing data. In the system, we design Greenhouse Sample Data Chain (GSDC) based on Ethereum technology. In GSDC, we create an account for each block data is distributed in the Merck Patricia Tree (MPT), where each data catalog has a unique object tree and a storage area.

As shown in Fig. 2, After perceiving external conditions, the sensor transmits the data to IPFS, IPFS stores the original data and the hashed fingers after the hash operation, then uploads the data hash to the GSDC chain, stores it in the account domain of the object tree, and finally uploads the block hash to Ethereum and saves it. On the GSDC chain, we use the poof of work (PoW) [16] as a consensus algorithm to maintain the GSDC chain and then upload the hash value generated by the block to Ethereum. In addition, we use Polkadot to validate the hash value of the generated block, use it to maintain the flow of data between the two chains, and store the block hash value on Ethereum, and the system can verify that the data whether has been tampered by changing the hash value on the Ethereum and GSDC chains.

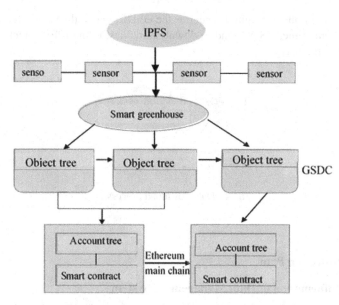

Fig. 2. Logical flow of double-chain solution.

The first layer of our system is IPFS. The advantage of IPFS is that it can identify the files connected to the device in the network, which can achieve wide access, this feature is suitable for agricultural systems, access to a variety of environmental parameters, such as sound, light, conducive to the user's query and final decision. when it accepts the original data, transfer it to as json format, and then uploaded to the GSDC for classification storage. Due to stored data transparent and open, users only need to access through the content, which improves the security of agricultural production.

The data flow is then as in Fig. 3, the sampled data is transmitted by sensor to IPFS network storage, then hashed blocks are stored from IPFS to GSDC, and the block format is constrained by smart contracts, and the block hash is eventually uploaded to Ethereum.

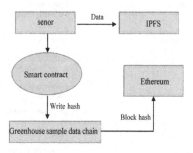

Fig. 3. Data upload process.

In Fig. 4, the public user initially queries the GSDC, which then sends the data hash back. At the same time, GSDC sends a download request to the IPFS, which sends the original data to the user.

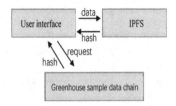

Fig. 4. Data download process.

3.3   Data Protection Plan

3.3.1   Key Information of Data Management System

There are many indicators and parameters to be monitored in smart greenhouse. With the traditional way, data are easy to be tampered with. We use blockchain technology to improve the data security of the IoT devices.

Table 1. Classification of key data information.

Subject information	Basic information	Operational type		Pre-operation environmental parameters	Post-operation environmental parameters	Trading information
Operator identification information	Crop type	Watering	Operation time	Temperature	Temperature	Operating costs
			Watering times			
			Water flow			
			Watering PH value			
			Watering EC value			
Planting license information	Sources of crop procurement	Fertilize		The relative humidity of the air	The relative humidity of the air	Current crop market price
Business license information	The purchase price of the crop	Pest control		Board temperature	Board temperature	
Contact information				The relative humidity of the substrate	The relative humidity of the substrate	
Greenhouse information				Substrate PH value	Substrate PH value	
				Substrate EC value	Substrate EC value	
				CO_2 concentration	CO_2 concentration	

To solve the above problems, this paper divides the key information involved in smart greenhouse into six categories: subject information, basic information, operation type, pre-operation environmental parameters, post-operation environmental parameters and transaction information. As shown in the Table 1, the subject information is divided into operator identity information, planting license information, business license information, contact information and greenhouse information. Basic information includes crop type, crop purchase source and crop purchase price. Operation types include many steps, such as watering, fertilization, pest control, etc. Here, aiming at typical watering operation examples, watering operation involves operation time, watering times, water flow, watering PH value and watering EC value. The environmental parameters before and after operation include air temperature, air relative humidity, substrate temperature, substrate relative humidity, substrate PH value, substrate EC value, carbon dioxide concentration and light intensity. Transaction information includes the operation cost and current crop market price.

The above classification can help manufacturers ensure which are open to the public and which are restricted. This requires asymmetric encryption of block- chain. In this paper SHA256 are used to encrypt information. The key data in this paper is classified and encrypted as follows [17]: the subject information, basic information and environmental parameters before and after operation are disclosed, the mode of directly transmitting data that is selected to the blockchain network.

3.3.2 The Designed Algorithms of System

The information related to the operation type is encrypted because this kind of information involves agricultural production secrets.

For these processes, we designed algorithms 1 to 5.

Algorithm 1 /*data upload*/

---

input: id of Greenhouse
           id of Product
output: return the result of upload
if (id of Greenhouse exists && id of Product exists)
    sample data {Subject information, Basic information, Operational type, Pre-operation environmental parameters, Post-operation environmental parameters, Trading information}
        if (data satisfy regulation)
            transfer data into json form
            encrypt specific data using SHA-256
            upload data to IPFS
            upload data to blockchain
            return success
        else
            return failure
else
        return failure

Algorithm 2 /*data validation*/
---

input: data
output: return true/ false
if (data does not meet production requirements)
     send error massage to producer
     return false
else
     return true

Algorithm 3 /* data query */
---

input: id of User
     id of Greenhouse
     id of Product
     level of User
output: return the result of inquire
if (id of Greenhouse exists && id of Product exists)
     if (level 2)
          get hash of data
          if (the operation result is different from the stored information)
               return failure
          else
               download data
               return success
     else if (level 1)
               download {subject information, basic information, pre-operation environmental parameters,
post-operation environmental parameters}
          else
               return failure
else
    return failure

Algorithm 4 /*data encryption*/

---

input: data
output: secret key
if (data exists)
    if (body information, basic information, environmental parameters before operation, environmental parameters after operation)
        upload {body information, basic information, environmental parameters before operation, environmental parameters after operation} to IPFS
          upload {body information, basic information, environmental parameters be- fore operation, environmental parameters after operation} to blockchain
      if (action information)
          invoke SHA-256 generate ciphertext and key,
            upload {action information} to IPFS upload {action information} to   blockchain
         return key
    else
      return null;

Algorithm 5/*authority management*/

---

input: node identity
output: level of node
if (node has normal rights)
      invoke the query module
    else
      if (node have advanced permission to inquire)
      get secret key
      invoke the query module

3.3.3 Discussion of System Safety

The double chain system involved in this paper is safer than traditional IoT that only one public chain or consortium chain. As mentioned in Introduction, the traditional IoT is based on cloud computing that is a centralized technology, and once the central server is broken, the data inside will be tampered and destroyed. Although the public chain is a completely decentralized technology, its upload and download performance is slow, which can't meet the throughput of large-scale data in smart greenhouses. At the same time, it is redundant for people who have nothing to do with the production process to participate in the consensus process. Although the uploading and downloading speed of the consortium chain is greatly improved compared with the public chain, the incomplete decentralization makes it constrained by the central node, and the network also has hidden dangers such as Sybil attack.

Figure 5 is the comparison results of IPFS storage of proposed solution, Ethereum only network storage and cloud storage. To compare the data upload and download time, we divide the data into five groups: 1M, 10M, 50M, 100M, 300M. As shown in Fig. 5 (a),

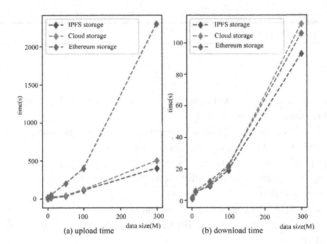

Fig. 5. Comparison of upload and download time in different systems.

the Ethereum network has the lowest speed of data upload. The storage speed of cloud storage is satisfactory, but the storage efficiency will still be affected by the downtime. The IPFS is nearly five times faster than blockchain and 21.6% faster than cloud storage in terms of storage speed. In Fig. 5 (b), the download speed of IPFS is outperformed than others. There are not much differences in the reading speed between cloud storage and Ethereum only storage. The reason is that the download speed of blockchain is not limited by the block size. Also, considering the network conditions and malicious attacks, the actual download speed of the network will be much slower in Ethereum network.

Double-chain structure, IPFS storage network, Polkadot and Ethereum technology have jointly built a more reliable smart greenhouse system. This is mainly because: (1) IPFS is based on distributed storage and sharing system. SHA256 is used for encryption. All transactions are recorded and stored in the immutable ledger of the blockchain, and linked with IPFS, so as to provide everyone with a high level of transparency and traceability in a safe, credible, reliable and efficient way. (2) IPFS hash values are uploaded to Ethereum, the information of block packing includes the operation time, which can offset the security vulnerability of replay attack caused by high delay to a certain extent. (3) The designed GSDC chain combines the public chain and consortium chain into a double-chain structure, which transmitted data through IPFS and applied to the agricultural IoT network. The hash value that transmitted by IPFS is stored in GSDC, Because of Polkadot's maintenance of the chain, the account tree is created on each GSDC block according to the category of the data, and the data information is stored as a content hash in the account tree. At this point, hash blocks on the GSDC are uploaded to Ethereum. As mentioned above, the two verify security by comparing hash values. (4) There are a large number of maintainers in Ethereum, and if an attacker wants to modify a data, it needs to modify both the hash values on the GSDC and Ethereum, which is more demanding and costly for the attacker. Table 2 is the comparison results between different systems.

Table 2. Comparison of different system performances.

	Double-chain solution	Consortium chain	Ethereum	Cloud file storage system
Upload	Medium	Medium	Low	Low
Download	Medium	Medium	Low	Low
Safety	High	Medium	High	High
Decentralization	High	Medium	High	High
Anti-tampered	High	Low	High	High
Network scale	Unlimited	Limited	Unlimited	Unlimited

4 Conclusions and Future Works

This paper proposed a double-blockchain based data security solution which aimed to maintain the confidentiality of important production data in smart greenhouse IoT data management. We designed a GSDC blockchain for recording data of the IoT devices. The IPFS network is applied for fast storage of raw data. Then IPFS network then generates hash values of these data and uploads to Ethereum for public data retrieval. The double-blockchain solution protected the data of being tampered while maintained a high speed of data storage. However, the solution is still under threats like the replay attacks when network latency is high. The fluctuating price of gas in Ethernet market will also cause uncertain cost. Besides, reasonable transaction speed, throughput, system load and other factors will be challenged when there are more and more new devices get connected.

Acknowledgements. This research was supported by the Capacity Development Foundation of Southwest University (Grants No. SWU116007).

References

1. Dai, W.Y., Qiu, L.F., Qiu, M.K.: Cloud infrastructure resource allocation for big data applications. IEEE Trans. Big Data **4**(3), 313–324 (2018)
2. Ren, W., Wan, X.T., Gan, P.C.: A double-blockchain solution for agricultural sampled data security in Internet of Things network. Future Gener. Comput. Syst. Int. J. Esci. **117**, 453–461 (2021)
3. https://en.wikipedia.org/wiki/Blockchain
4. Guo, Y.B., Zhu Ge, Q.F., Hu, J.T., Yi, J., Qiu, M.K.: Data placement and duplication for embedded multicore systems with scratch pad memory. IEEE Trans. Comput. Aided Des. Integr. Circuits Syst. **32**(6), 809–817 (2013)
5. Yin, D.L., Jiang, M.Y.: Teaching information resources integration based on heterogeneous data exchange and sharing of technology. In: 2008 International Symposium on Computer Science and Computational Technology, vol. 1, pp. 150–153 (2008)
6. Khanna, A., Kaur, A.: Evolution of Internet of Things (IoT) and its significant impact in the field of precision agriculture. Comput. Electron. Agric. **157**(2019), 218–231 (2019)

7. Hassija, V., Chamola, V., Saxena, V., Jain, D., Goyal, P., Sikdar, B.: A Survey on IoT security: application areas, security threats, and solution architectures. IEEE Access **7**, 82721–82743 (2019)
8. Babar, S., Stango, A., Prasad, N., Sen, J., Prasad, R.: Proposed embedded security framework for Internet of Things (IoT). In: International Conference on Wireless Communication IEEE (2011)
9. Dai, W.Y., Qiu, M.K., Qiu, L.F., Chen, L.B., Wu, A.N.: Who moved my data? Privacy protection in smartphones. IEEE Commun. Mag. **55**(1), 20–25 (2017)
10. Rathee, G., Sharma, A., Kumar, R., Iqbal, R.: A secure communicating things network framework for industrial IoT using blockchain technology. Ad Hoc Netw. (2019)
11. IEEE Standard for Framework of Blockchain-based Internet of Things (IoT) Data Management. https://doi.org/10.1109/IEEESTD.2021.9329260
12. Xu, J., Wang, S., Zhou, A., Yang, F.: A blockchain-enabled edge-computing platform for intelligent IoT-based dApps. China Commun. **17**(4), 78–87 (2020)
13. Malik, S., Dedeoglu, V., Kanhere, S. S., Jurdak, R.: TrustChain: trust management in blockchain and IoT supported supply chains. In: 2019 IEEE International Conference on Blockchain, pp. 184–193 (2019)
14. Feng, T.: An agri-food supply chain traceability system for China based on RFID & blockchain technology. In: 2016 13th International Conference on Service Systems and Service Management (ICSSSM), pp. 1–6 (2016)
15. Zheng, Q., Li, Y., Chen, P., Dong, X.: An innovative IPFS-based storage model for blockchain. In: 2018 IEEE/WIC/ACM International Conference on Web Intelligence (WI), pp. 704–708 (2018)
16. Keenan, T.P.: Alice in blockchains: surprising security pitfalls in PoW and PoS blockchain systems. In: 2017 15th Annual Conference on Privacy, Security and Trust (PST), pp. 400–4002 (2017)
17. Shifa, A., Asghar, M.N., Fleury, M.: Multimedia security perspectives in IoT. In: 2016 6th International Conference on Innovative Computing Technology (INTECH), Xplore, Dublin, Ireland, pp. 550–555. IEEE (2016)

Medication Combination Prediction via Attention Neural Networks with Prior Medical Knowledge

Haiqiang Wang[1], Xuyuan Dong[2], Zheng Luo[1], Junyou Zhu[1], Peican Zhu[3], and Chao Gao[1,3(✉)]

[1] College of Computer and Information Science, Southwest University, Chongqing 400715, China
[2] First Affiliated Hospital of Xi'an Jiaotong University, Xi'an 710072, China
[3] School of Artificial Intelligence, Optics, and Electronics (iOPEN), Northwestern Polytechnical University, Xi'an 710072, China
cgao@nwpu.edu.cn

Abstract. With the adoption of electronic health records (EHR), deep learning technologies have the potential to employ the EHR data to assist experts in better understanding the complex mechanisms underlying the health and disease. Existing studies have made progress on the research of medication combination prediction from the medical data, but few of them take into account the prior medical knowledge. This paper proposes a PKANet model that integrates the prior medical knowledge into the deep learning architecture to predict the medication combination. The prior medical knowledge is calculated from the mapping relation between diagnoses and medications hidden in the EHR data. It can provide the heuristic medications to help the PKANet model learn optimal parameters. In order to predict the possible medication combination, the PKANet model utilizes attention neural networks to obtain the relationship between different elements in the medical sequence data. The experiment results have demonstrated that the proposed PKANet model outperforms the state-of-the-art baselines on evaluation metrics.

Keywords: Electronic health records · Medication combination prediction · Prior medical knowledge · Attention neural networks

1 Introduction

Electronic health records (EHR) have detailedly recorded the treatment process of patients, such as diagnoses, treatment procedures and medications [4]. Such elements describe the changes of patients' health state over time. Based on the abundant EHR data, the deep learning technologies can predict the treatment medication combination according to the health state of patients [10,13,16]. It can assist experts to analyze a mass of medical data so that they can compile and replenish the clinical guidelines and expert rules of available tools (e.g., the

© Springer Nature Switzerland AG 2021
H. Qiu et al. (Eds.): KSEM 2021, LNAI 12817, pp. 311–322, 2021.
https://doi.org/10.1007/978-3-030-82153-1_26

medical expert system) [12]. Moreover, doctors have accumulated the prescribed experience over years, which is essential for the treatments of patients. It is necessary to leverage this kind of prior medical knowledge hidden in the EHR data to predict the medication combination based on deep learning technologies.

Previous studies have used the recurrent neural networks (RNN) to capture the temporal feature from EHR data [2,10,13,16]. However, the computation of hidden layers relies on the output of their previous hidden layers. It is inefficient in learning long sequences due to the sequential nature that prohibits the parallelized computing [11]. The multi-head attention provides a solving method for this shortcoming by learning features from different subspaces [15]. However, most existing studies focus on the inherent attributes of patients, such as diagnoses and treatment procedures, rather than the knowledge hidden in the medical records [4,10,13,16].

It has been proved that the prior medical knowledge can improve the performance of models [14]. For instance, the prior medical knowledge is incorporated into the deep learning model to promote the research of disease risk prediction [8]. The EHR data records the treatments of patients in the clinic, which contain the rich clinical experience of doctors. Such experience helps doctors decide which kind of medication is suitable for the recovery of patients. Thus, it is necessary to take into consideration such kind of prior medical knowledge in medication combination prediction.

In terms of above consideration, this paper proposes a deep learning model named PKANet, which combines the patient features and the prior medical knowledge. The PKANet model extracts the patient features from diagnosis sequences and treatment procedure sequences. Then, the prior medical knowledge is from the mapping relation between diagnoses and medications. It can provide the heuristic medication sequences according to the diagnostic results. The multi-head attention is used to obtain the relationship between different elements in the sequence data. It leverages multiple self-attention layers to learn the important features from different subspaces in parallel, and then concatenates such features to predict the medication combination. The contribution of this paper can be summarized as follows.

(1) The prior medical knowledge is from the mapping relation between diagnoses and medications in the EHR data to obtain heuristic medication features.
(2) The PKANet model combines patient features and heuristic medication features from prior medical knowledge to predict the medication combination.

In the following sections, we review the related works in Sect. 2. The framework of PKANet is shown in Sect. 3. Section 4 introduces our experiment. In the last, we conclude this work in Sect. 5.

2   Related Works

Prior Medical Knowledge. In recent years, the prior medical knowledge has shown great potential in clinical medicine. For instance, it can be used to process the medical image so that doctors can observe the lesions of patients clearly [3,6]. The integration of prior medical knowledge can improve the interpretability of neural networks [17], as well as promoting the performance of deep learning models [8]. In this paper, we use the prior medical knowledge to obtain heuristic medication features for the medication combination prediction.

Attention Neural Networks. Due to the outstanding performance, the attention mechanism is widely used to find the important elements [2,7,18]. The RNN-based attention mechanism is regarded as an effective method which captures the sequence feature [2]. However, it is still not able to process long sequences [11]. Another attention mechanism, the multi-head attention, has been applied in the natural language processing (NLP) to handle the long sequence data successfully [1]. The multi-head attention consists of several self-attention layers. On each layer, query, key and value vectors are defined to obtain the relationship between different elements [15]. In this work, we apply the multi-head attention to find the influential features from medical sequence data.

Medication Combination Prediction. Based on the electronic health records (EHR), many previous studies aim at the work of medication combination prediction. For example, Su et al. propose the graph-attention augmented temporal neural network to fuse the structure and temporal information [13]. Shang et al. construct a deep learning model to learn the medication knowledge using graph convolutional networks (GCN) [10]. Song et al. design the local-global memory neural network to remember the individual patterns of a patient and the group evidence of diseases [12]. He et al. treat the medical records of patients as multi-view data and leverage the multi-head attention to solve the issue of multi-view medical data learning [4]. These studies learn from the sequence data and predict the medication combination, but they pay little attention to the prior medical knowledge hidden in the EHR data. In our work, we attempt to obtain heuristic medication features from the prior medical knowledge, combining them with patient features to predict the medication combination.

3   The Framework of PKANet

In this section, we will introduce the proposed PKANet model detailedly. The framework of PKANet is shown in Fig. 1, including the prior medical knowledge module in Sect. 3.1, the medical information embedding module in Sect. 3.2, the feature representation learning module in Sect. 3.3 and the medication combination prediction module in Sect. 3.4.

3.1   Prior Medical Knowledge Module

The clinical events in EHR data contain the changing process of the health state of patients. It is recorded in a series of sequence data, such as the diagnosis sequence D_i, the procedure sequence P_i and the medication sequence M_i.

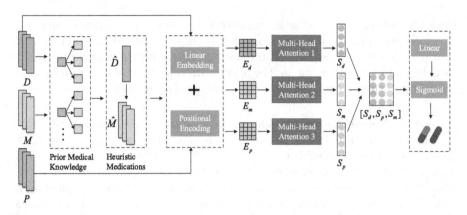

Fig. 1. The framework of PKANet. Firstly, the prior medical knowledge is calculated from the mapping relation between diagnoses D and medications M in the EHR data. Heuristic medications $\hat{M}$ are from the prior medical knowledge according to the diagnostic results $\hat{D}$. Then, the sequences of diagnoses D, treatment procedures P and heuristic medications $\hat{M}$ are translated into embedding vectors E_d, E_p and E_m respectively by the linear embedding and positional encoding. Such embedding vectors are input into different multi-head attention modules to obtain different attention vectors S_d, S_p and S_m. These attention vectors are concatenated as $[S_d, S_p, S_m]$ to integrate patient features and heuristic medication features. Lastly, $[S_d, S_p, S_m]$ is used to predict the medication combination with the sigmoid activation function.

The EHR data contains the prior medical knowledge in the clinical prescribed experience of doctors over years. In order to leverage such knowledge, we design a constraint rule for heuristic medications. More specifically, for each diagnosis in the medical records, we calculate the frequency of used medications. The higher the frequency of used medication is, the larger the possibility that the doctor uses such a medication for the certain diagnosis is. However, the occurrence frequency of a diagnosis varies widely from dozens to thousands. Therefore, we design a constraint rule to balance the occurrence number of different diagnoses. The constraint rule is as Eq. (1).

$$\hat{M} = \begin{cases} m, & \text{if } f_m \geqslant \eta f_d \\ \text{null}, & \text{if } f_m < \eta f_d \end{cases} \tag{1}$$

where f_d and f_m are the frequency of diagnosis d and corresponding medication m, respectively. If $f_m \geqslant \eta f_d$, it means that over η proportion of diagnoses have used such therapeutic medication. These medications, which can be formulated as $\hat{D} \rightarrow \hat{M}$ while representing the mapping relation between diagnoses and medications, are from the prior medical knowledge accumulated in the EHR data. Otherwise, if $f_m < \eta f_d$, such medication is not included according to the prior medical knowledge.

3.2   Medical Information Embedding Module

The medical information of the ith patient is formulated as $(D_i, P_i, \hat{M}_i)$. Diagnoses D_i and treatment procedures P_i are the inherent attributes of patients, which represent the health state feature of patients. While $\hat{M}_i$ is the heuristic medication from the prior medical knowledge. Therefore, $(D_i, P_i, \hat{M}_i)$ demonstrates the patient information and the heuristic medication. They are translated into linear embedding vectors (i.e., E'^i_d, E'^i_p and E'^i_m) as shown in Eq. (2), respectively.

$$\begin{cases} E'^i_d = W_d D_i \\ E'^i_p = W_p P_i \\ E'^i_m = W_m \hat{M}_i \end{cases} \tag{2}$$

where $W_d \in \mathbb{R}^{|D| \times d}$, $W_p \in \mathbb{R}^{|P| \times d}$ and $W_m \in \mathbb{R}^{|\hat{M}| \times d}$ are the embedding weight matrices, and d is the embedding dimension.

The recurrent feature of the sequence has been proved to be essential in the research of medication combination prediction [4]. However, the basic neural unit of multi-head attention is the self-attention mechanism instead of the recurrent neural networks (RNN). The positional encoding is applied in order to obtain such features [15]. The positional encoding is calculated as Eq. (3).

$$\begin{cases} PE(pos, 2j) = \sin(\dfrac{pos}{1000^{\frac{2j}{d}}}) \\ PE(pos, 2j+1) = \cos(\dfrac{pos}{1000^{\frac{2j+1}{d}}}) \end{cases} \tag{3}$$

where pos is the index of each item in the sequence, and the even and odd indexes of the embedding vector are denoted as $2j$ and $2j + 1$, respectively.

The final embedding vector is the sum of the linear embedding vector (i.e., E'^i_d, E'^i_p, E'^i_m) and the positional encoding vector (i.e., PE^i_d, PE^i_p, PE^i_m). The calculated processing is as Eq. (4).

$$\begin{cases} E^i_d = E'^i_d + PE^i_d \\ E^i_p = E'^i_p + PE^i_p \\ E^i_m = E'^i_m + PE^i_m \end{cases} \tag{4}$$

3.3   Feature Representation Learning Module

In order to extract the features from the sequence data, the multi-head attention, which consists of self-attention layers, is used to encode the embedding vectors of sequence data. The vectors learned by multi attention heads are concatenated to obtain the global feature. The self-attention mechanism needs a query vector and a pair of key-value vectors. The query vector Q and the key vector K are used to compute the weight matrix w, which is the dot product of these two vectors. All dot products are divided by $\sqrt{d}$ to counteract the effectiveness of dot products [15]. Then the attention vector is computed by the attention parameter and the value vector V as Eq. (5).

$$\text{Attention}(Q, K, V) = \text{softmax}(\frac{QK^T}{\sqrt{d}})V \tag{5}$$

In each self-attention mechanism, the query Q, key K and value V are the vectors from the same inputs used to capture the inter sequence feature [4]. Same as the previous study, it is beneficial to linearly project the aforementioned Q, K and V vectors for n times in order to obtain the linear projections [15], which are corresponding to n self-attention heads, respectively. Therefore, the translated parameter matrices W_Q, W_K and W_V work as Eq. (6).

$$\begin{cases} Q = E_* W_Q \\ K = E_* W_K \\ V = E_* W_V \end{cases} \tag{6}$$

where $W_Q \in \mathbb{R}^{d \times d}$, $W_K \in \mathbb{R}^{d \times d}$ and $W_V \in \mathbb{R}^{d \times d}$ are linearly translated parameter matrices. E_* is the embedding vector of the sequence data, referring to the diagnosis embedding vector E_d, the procedure embedding vector E_p and the heuristic medication embedding vector E_m.

The hth self-attention head is used to learn the Q_h, K_h, V_h vectors based on Eq. (4). Then the output vectors from n self-attention heads are concatenated together to represent the features of current sequence data as Eq. (7).

$$S_* = \text{MultiHead}(Q, K, V) = \text{Concat}(\text{head}_1, \text{head}_2, ..., \text{head}_n) \tag{7}$$

where $\text{head}_h = \text{Attention}(Q_h, K_h, V_h)$. S_* denotes the feature vectors of diagnosis S_d, the treatment procedure S_p and the heuristic medication S_m.

3.4 Medication Combination Prediction Module

For the patient at the t visit time, the vectors of diagnosis S_d^t, treatment procedure S_p^t and heuristic medication S_m^t are concatenated to obtain patient features and heuristic medication features. The concatenated vector (i.e., $[S_d^t, S_p^t, S_m^t]$) is translated into the linear vector to predict the medication combination. The sigmoid activation function is displayed as Eq. (8).

$$\hat{y}^t = \text{sigmoid}(\text{Linear}[S_d^t, S_p^t, S_m^t]) \tag{8}$$

In order to reduce the influence of drug labels, the loss function $\mathcal{L}$ is the combination of binary cross-entropy loss $\mathcal{L}_{\text{binary}}$ and multi-label margin loss $\mathcal{L}_{\text{multi}}$. The combined loss function $\mathcal{L}$ is defined as Eq. (9).

$$\begin{cases} \mathcal{L}_{\text{binary}} = -\sum_t^{T_o} \sum_i^{|y|} y_i^t \log \sigma\left(\hat{y}_i^t\right) + \left(1 - y_i^t\right) \log\left(1 - \sigma\left(\hat{y}_i^t\right)\right) \\ \\ \mathcal{L}_{\text{multi}} = \frac{1}{L} \sum_t^T \sum_i^{|y|} \sum_j^{|\hat{y}^t|} \max\left(0, 1 - \left(pos(\hat{y}_i^t) - pos(\hat{y}_j^t)\right)\right) \\ \\ \mathcal{L} = \lambda \mathcal{L}_{\text{binary}} + \gamma \mathcal{L}_{\text{multi}} \end{cases} \quad (9)$$

where $|y|$ and $|\hat{y}|$ denote the number of real medications y and predictive medications $\hat{y}$, respectively. T_o means the total visit times of the current patient, and L is the length of medication labels. At the tth visit, $pos(\hat{y}_i^t)$ and $pos(\hat{y}_j^t)$ stand for the predictive medication positions of the real medication set and predictive medication set, respectively. λ and γ are parameters which balance the binary cross-entropy loss and multi-label margin loss.

4 Experiments

4.1 Dataset

Our work is based on the MIMIC-III dataset[1], which provides the information of patients staying in intensive care units of the Beth Israel Deaconess Medical Center [5]. According to previous studies [4,10], we assume that all records in the MIMIC-III dataset are suitable for a certain disease and have been confirmed by professional doctors and researchers. The data processing follows the previous study [10]. The statistical information of the dataset is as Table 1.

Table 1. The statistical information of data

Statistical Items	Quantity
Diagnoses	1958
Treatment procedures	1426
Medications	145
Patients	6350
Clinical events	15016

4.2 Experiment Setup

The MIMIC-III dataset is divided into training, validation and test sets accounting for 2/3, 1/6 and 1/6, respectively. The embedding dimension of sequence data is 64 and the multi-head attention has 4 attention heads. We train the PKANet model for 15 epochs at the learning rate of 0.0002.

---

[1] https://mimic.physionet.org/.

In order to evaluate the predictive accuracy, this paper utilizes the frequently-used metrics in previous studies [4,10], such as the Jaccard similarity score (Jaccard), average F1 (F1) and precision-recall AUC (PRAUC). The higher the scores are, the greater the predictive accuracy of models is.

4.3   Experiment Results

In this subsection, we compare the performance of various models for medication combination prediction. Figure 2 displays the predictive precision of PKANet model and baselines on different evaluation metrics.

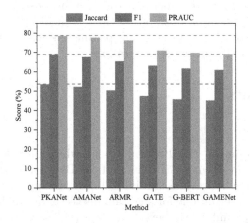

Fig. 2. The comparison of predictive accuracy between the PKANet and baselines.

As shown in Fig. 2, with the usage of multi-head attention, the PKANet model has an obvious improvement compared with ARMR [16], GATE [13] and GAMENet [10], which are based on the RNN. Such improvements are owing to the global feature preserved by PKANet model. More specifically, the recurrent structure of RNN determines that the current hidden state is generated from its previous state. Therefore, the RNN based model can learn the temporal feature of sequence data [13]. However, for such models, the initial patient features do not attract much attention with the time stamp increasing. In this case, the medical information of each time stamp should be considered across-the-board. Different from the RNN, the multi-head attention shows more powerful learning ability for the sequence data with the positional encoding [11]. The multi-head attention can combine the features from different subspaces with multiple attention layers. The positional encoding makes up for the shortcoming of position feature extraction compared with the RNN. Therefore, the PKANet model can obtain the global features from different subspaces and achieve a better performance.

Compared with the multi-head attention baseline model AMANet [4] and G-BERT [9], the PKANet obtains higher predictive scores. Diagnoses and treatment procedures are the inherent attributes of patients, and the PKANet also utilizes the prior medical knowledge which is from the statistical medication experience information. It can provide the prescribed experience for the PKANet model. Therefore, utilizing the prior medical knowledge, it is achievable to provide heuristic medications most suitable for patients according to the diagnosis results. The comparison result indicates that the prior medical knowledge can improve the predictive accuracy of medication combinations. The heuristic medications from the prior medical knowledge can help the PKANet model learn the optimal parameters.

4.4   Parameter Analysis

In this section, we examine the influence of parameter η in the prior medical knowledge and parameters λ and γ in the loss function. We fix the other parameters when focusing on one of them.

In order to analyze the impact of the prior medical knowledge, we examine the predictive accuracy of different evaluation metrics. As shown in Fig. 3, the values of parameter η range from 0 to 1. The similar variation tendency is shown in Fig. 3(a) and Fig. 3(b). For both Jaccard and F1, the PKANet model achieves the best performance when the parameter η is approximately 0.7. It indicates that the heuristic medication from the prior medical knowledge has been used by over 70% patients with the same diagnosis results. Although the variation tendency of PRAUC on Fig. 3(c) is different from the Jaccard and F1, it achieves the highest predictive accuracy as η approaches 0.7 as well. The difference may be that the accuracy calculation method of PRAUC relies on the Precision-Recall curve, rather than the precision value as the Jaccard and F1. Therefore, the PRAUC is less sensitive to the change of the parameter η. Whatever, the results illustrate that the best η is approximately 0.7 in the process of calculating the prior medical knowledge.

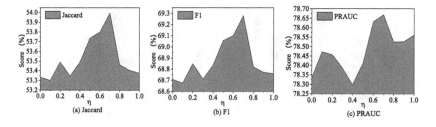

Fig. 3. The influence of parameter η on different evaluation metrics.

Figure 4 reports the predictive precision of different evaluation metrics on the parameters λ and γ. Firstly, we vary the value of λ from 0.1 to 1.0 and observe the change processing of Jaccard, F1 and PRAUC. As shown in Fig. 4 (a) Jaccard and Fig. 4 (b) F1, we find that the PKANet model achieves the best performance when $\lambda = 0.6$. Differently, the PKANet model obtains the highest score when $\lambda = 0.5$ as shown in Fig. 4(c) PRAUC. According to the analysis in Fig. 3, it is due to the different calculation methods. In order to make the PKANet perform better on different evaluation metrics as much as possible, $\lambda = 0.6$ may be a better choice. Secondly, we investigate the influence of γ by varying from 0.01 to 0.10 in Fig. 4. We can observe that the performance of PKANet model in all metrics decreases as γ increases from 0.01, because a larger γ may result in massive noises. It implies that $\gamma = 0.01$ is suitable for the PKANet model according to the experiment results.

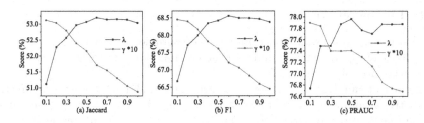

Fig. 4. The influence of parameter λ and γ on different evaluation metrics.

4.5 Case Study

The attention mechanism can extract some significant features that impact the current health state of patients mostly. It can distinguish the importance of sequence data at different visit times through attention weights and better represent the health state of patients. To show the influence of attention weights clearly, we randomly select a patient who has visited the hospital 6 times.

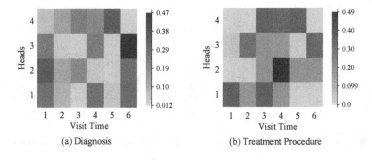

Fig. 5. The distribution of attention weights. (a) and (b) show the difference of attention weights in diagnoses and treatment procedures, respectively.

As shown in Fig. 5, on each attention head, the attention weights are distinguished in different visit times. For example, as shown in Fig. 5(a), the 6th visit is obviously more important than other visits. It indicates that the 6th diagnosis results impact the health state of this patient profoundly. However, in Fig. 5(b), it seems that the 4th treatment procedures have the largest attention weight. This phenomenon manifests that the 4th treatment procedures are more important than others. The distribution of the attention weight shows the process of extracting patient features, and then these distributional features are concatenated by the multi-head attention.

5   Conclusion

In this work, we proposed a PKANet model based on deep learning technologies to predict the medication combination, which combined the health state of patients and the prior medical knowledge. The diagnosis sequences and the treatment procedure sequences are used to represent the health state of patients. We calculate the prior medical knowledge from the mapping relation between diagnoses and medications. The heuristic medication sequences can be obtained by the prior medical knowledge according to the diagnostic results. Different attention modules are used to capture the features from the health state of patients and heuristic medication sequences to predict the medication combination. The experiment results show that the performance of PKANet exceeds the state-of-the-art baselines on different evaluation metrics. It is important for experts to design the clinic guidelines and expert systems for curing patients. Therefore, we expect that our model can help experts free from the redundant data analysis and better understand the conditions of patients.

Acknowledgements. This work was supported by the National Key R&D Program of China (No. 2020AAA0107700), National Natural Science Foundation of China (Nos. 61976181, 11931015), Key Technology Research and Development Program of Science and Technology Scientific and Technological Innovation Team of Shaanxi Province (No. 2020TD-013), the Science and Technology Support Program of Guizhou (No. QKHZC2021YB531) and Chongqing Graduate Student Research Innovation Project (No. CYS21115).

References

1. Cao, J., Zhao, H., Yu, K.: Cross aggregation of multi-head attention for neural machine translation. In: Proceedings of the 8th International Conference on Natural Language Processing and Chinese Computing, pp. 380–392 (2019)
2. Choi, E., Bahadori, M.T., Sun, J., et al.: RETAIN: an interpretable predictive model for healthcare using reverse time attention mechanism. In: Proceedings of the 30th Conference on Neural Information Processing Systems, pp. 3504–3512 (2016)
3. Grau, V., Mewes, A., Alcaniz, M., et al.: Improved watershed transform for medical image segmentation using prior information. IEEE Trans. Med. Imaging **23**(4), 447–458 (2004)

4. He, Y., Wang, C., Li, N., Zeng, Z.: Attention and memory-augmented networks for dual-view sequential learning. In: Proceedings of the 26th ACM SIGKDD International Conference on Knowledge Discovery & Data Mining, pp. 125–134 (2020)

5. Johnson, A.E., Pollard, T.J., Shen, L., et al.: MIMIC-III, a freely accessible critical care database. Sci. Data **3**(1), 1–9 (2016)

6. Kurrant, D., Baran, A., LoVetri, J., Fear, E.: Integrating prior information into microwave tomography part 1: impact of detail on image quality. Med. Phys. **44**(12), 6461–6481 (2017)

7. Lee, W., Park, S., Joo, W., Moon, I.C.: Diagnosis prediction via medical context attention networks using deep generative modeling. In: Proceedings of the 18th IEEE International Conference on Data Mining, pp. 1104–1109 (2018)

8. Ma, F., Gao, J., Suo, Q., et al.: Risk prediction on electronic health records with prior medical knowledge. In: Proceedings of the 24th ACM SIGKDD International Conference on Knowledge Discovery & Data Mining, pp. 1910–1919 (2018)

9. Shang, J., Ma, T., Xiao, C., Sun, J.: Pre-training of graph augmented transformers for medication recommendation. In: Proceedings of the 28th International Joint Conference on Artificial Intelligence, pp. 5953–5959 (2019)

10. Shang, J., Xiao, C., Ma, T., et al.: GAMENet: graph augmented memory networks for recommending medication combination. In: Proceedings of the 33rd AAAI Conference on Artificial Intelligence, pp. 1126–1133 (2019)

11. Song, H., Rajan, D., Thiagarajan, J.J., Spanias, A.: Attend and diagnose: clinical time series analysis using attention models. In: Proceedings of the 32nd AAAI Conference on Artificial Intelligence, pp. 4091–4098 (2018)

12. Song, J., Wang, Y., Tang, S., et al.: Local-global memory neural network for medication prediction. IEEE Trans. Neural Netw. Learn. Syst. **32**(4), 1723–1736 (2021)

13. Su, C., Gao, S., Li, S.: GATE: graph-attention augmented temporal neural network for medication recommendation. IEEE Access **8**, 125447–125458 (2020)

14. Tofighi, M., Guo, T., Vanamala, J.K., Monga, V.: Prior information guided regularized deep learning for cell nucleus detection. IEEE Trans. Med. Imaging **38**(9), 2047–2058 (2019)

15. Vaswani, A., Shazeer, N., Parmar, N., et al.: Attention is all you need. In: Proceedings of the 31st Conference on Neural Information Processing Systems, pp. 5998–6008 (2017)

16. Wang, Y., Chen, W., Pi, D., Yue, L.: Adversarially regularized medication recommendation model with multi-hop memory network. Knowl. Inf. Syst. **63**(1), 125–142 (2020). https://doi.org/10.1007/s10115-020-01513-9

17. Xiao, L., Zheng, C., Fan, X., et al.: Predicting ICU mortality from heterogeneous clinical events with prior medical knowledge. In: Proceedings of the 28th International Joint Conference on Artificial Intelligence, pp. 55–59 (2019)

18. Yin, M., Mou, C., Xiong, K., Ren, J.: Chinese clinical named entity recognition with radical-level feature and self-attention mechanism. J. Biomed. Inform. **98**, 103289 (2019)

CelebHair: A New Large-Scale Dataset for Hairstyle Recommendation Based on CelebA

Yutao Chen[1], Yuxuan Zhang[1], Zhongrui Huang[1], Zhenyao Luo[1], and Jinpeng Chen[1,2(✉)]

[1] School of Computer Science (National Pilot Software Engineering School), Beijing University of Posts and Telecommunications, Beijing, China
{chnyutao,zyuxuan,hzrngu,luozhenyao}@bupt.edu.cn
[2] Key Laboratory of Trustworthy Distributed Computing and Service, Beijing University of Posts and Telecommunications, Ministry of Education, Beijing, China
jpchen@bupt.edu.cn

Abstract. In efforts to build a hairstyle recommendation application, we are confronted with the lack of relevant hairstyle-related datasets. In this paper, we present a new large-scale dataset for hairstyle recommendation, CelebHair, based on the celebrity facial attributes dataset, CelebA. Our dataset inherited the majority of facial images along with some beauty-related facial attributes from CelebA. Additionally, we employed facial landmark detection techniques to extract extra features such as nose length and pupillary distance, and deep convolutional neural networks for face shape and hairstyle classification. Empirical comparison has demonstrated the superiority of our dataset to other existing hairstyle-related datasets regarding variety, veracity, and volume. Analysis and experiments have been conducted on the dataset in order to evaluate its robustness and usability.

Keywords: Hairstyle recommendation · CelebA · CNN · Classification · Dataset

1 Introduction

Hairstyles, together with other facial attributes, affect personal appearance significantly. With the appropriate hairstyle, one's beauty can be enhanced. However, most people and barbers have a very vague understanding of choosing one's suitable hairstyles. Therefore, it is necessary to build a hairstyle recommendation system to recommend the most suitable hairstyle for people, according to their face shapes and other facial attributes. However, the lack of relevant large-scale datasets with essential attributes for hairstyle recommendation has restricted the development of such a system. Satisfactory performance can not be attained based on a limited amount of data with incomplete facial attributes.

Y. Chen and Y. Zhang—Co-first authors with equal contribution.

© Springer Nature Switzerland AG 2021
H. Qiu et al. (Eds.): KSEM 2021, LNAI 12817, pp. 323–336, 2021.
https://doi.org/10.1007/978-3-030-82153-1_27

To address these problems, we present *CelebHair*, a new large-scale dataset for hairstyle recommendation based on CelebA [1]. It consists of 202,599 facial images with the corresponding hairstyles and a wide variety of facial attributes, such as face shape, nose length, and pupillary distance. Together, these attributes contribute to the exploration of the relationship between hairstyle, face shape, and other facial attributes.

CelebHair directly inherits around 200k facial images from the CelebA dataset, along with some hairstyle-related facial attributes. Apart from those, the attributes of our CelebHair dataset are collected from three sources:

- For extracting features like nose length and pupillary distance, we use a facial landmark detection algorithm, provided by Dlib [2], followed by algebraic computations to transform and discretize them;
- For face shape classification, we utilize a pre-trained network of YOLO v4 [3], which can be fine-tuned and customized into a face shape classifier, using an openly accessible face shape dataset on Kaggle [4];
- For hairstyle classification, we construct a deep convolutional neural network [5] with a spatial transformer [6] substructure for hairstyle classification, based on the training dataset Hairstyle30k [7].

To validate CelebHair's usability, we have built a hairstyle recommendation system with the Random Forests [8] algorithm as an example application of our dataset. The Random Forests algorithm tries to establish a mapping function from the dependent features like face shape, nose length, and pupillary distance, etc., to the target feature we want to predict – hairstyle. We have also shown a hairstyle try-on demo application using a combination of facial landmark detection, image rotation, and projection.

Our major contributions in this paper could be phrased as: 1) To the extent of our knowledge, CelebHair is the first robust, large-scale dataset containing hairstyles, face shapes, and a wide variety of facial attributes. 2) We have conducted exhaustive experiments around CelebHair and these experiments, in turn, have demonstrated the robustness and usability of this dataset. 3) We share our experience in dataset construction, from feature design to feature extraction.

The rest of this paper is structured as follows: in Sect. 2, we discuss related works around this paper; in Sect. 3, we elaborate on the collection of our dataset, especially hairstyle and face shape classification; in Sect. 4, we describe the dataset and compares it against other existing datasets; in Sect. 5, we showcased example applications for hairstyle recommendation & try-on.

2   Related Works

2.1   Hairstyle Datasets

We have found several datasets applicable to hairstyle-related tasks. The three most important of them, CelebA, Beauty e-Expert [9], and Hairstyle30k, are introduced here.

CelebA is a dataset of celebrities' facial images with labeled features, some of which, for instance, gender, age, and attractiveness, are considered helpful for our hairstyle recommendation task. CelebA has an advantage in its volume of approximately 200k images. However, only five facial landmarks: left eye, right eye, nose, left mouth, and right mouth, are available. The insufficiency of facial landmarks hinders the extraction of other in-depth facial attributes such as nose length, lip length, and eye width. Moreover, CelebA has very no hairstyle-related features besides hair's waviness and straightness.

Beauty e-Expert is another dataset specifically designed for beauty-related tasks, containing 1505 female photos with various attributes annotated with different discrete values. The Beauty e-Expert dataset covers face shape, facial landmarks, and some other features for clothing and makeup. Nevertheless, three fatal disadvantages have prevented us from adopting the dataset: the tiny volume, the absence of male figures, and the over-simplified hairstyle labels.

Hairstyle30k is a dataset entirely focused on one single attribute: hairstyle. The author has collected the data using keyword searching on online search engines, resulting in a slightly noisy dataset. The original dataset provides a complete variety of 64 hairstyles, with a simplified ten-kind version released afterward. However, no facial attributes other than the hairstyle are included in the dataset.

Domain expert knowledge has suggested that personal hairstyle choices can significantly depend on one's face shape, along with other less critical facial attributes. In a pursuit to build a hairstyle recommendation system, we came to realize the lack of such dataset: 1)that are large in volume; 2)that have labeled face shapes, and other detailed facial attributes; 3)that cover a wide variety in terms of race, gender, hairstyles, etc.

As all known datasets stated above are defective in at least one of these three aspects, we believe that a new large-scale hairstyle dataset is urgently needed.

2.2 Hairstyle Recommendation

Hansini and Dushyanthi [10] have built an end-to-end machine learning framework for hairstyle recommendation, starting from face detection, facial landmark extraction to hairstyle recommendation. However, the composition and source of the dataset involved in training seem unclear, and the features of the dataset seem relatively inadequate. Wisuwat and Kitsuchart have done a series of works [11,12] on the subject of hairstyle recommendation. Their dataset's volume seems quite restricted, and only female figures are available. Beauty e-Expert employs a tree-structured probabilistic graph model for hairstyle recommendation, trained upon their own Beauty e-Expert dataset. The model takes into account the relations between attributes from a probabilistic view.

2.3 Miscellaneous

In this paper, we use YOLO v4, an effective, optimized member of CNN for real-time object detection, to classify face shapes. For hairstyle recognition, we use a

CNN with a spatial transformer substructure as a hairstyle classifier. The spatial transformer network contains a localization network, which can be conveniently embedded between any two layers of a convolutional neural network. The spatial transformer network takes the input image, transforms it, and then feeds it forward into the next layer. Such transformations render CNNs immune to image translation, scale, rotation, and more generic warping.

Random Forests is an ensemble learning algorithm in which a multitude of decision trees together constitutes a forest. Each decision tree is trained on a subset sampled from the training dataset using the Bootstrap method, and each node in the decision tree may only consider a random subset of all available features to create diversity among base learners. When using random forests for classification, each decision tree in the forest produces a prediction individually. The base learners' predictions are then aggregated using majority voting or weighted voting to form the forest's classification result.

3   Data Collection

Previous discussions have shown that existing hairstyle-related datasets suffer from insufficiency in either volume or variety. Hence, we introduce CelebHair, a new large-scale dataset for hairstyle recommendation base on CelebA. CelebHair directly inherits around 200k images from CelebA, as well as some hairstyle-related attributes. Techniques including facial landmark detection and convolutional neural networks are also involved to append new facial attributes, for instance, face shape, nose length, and pupillary distance, to those already available in CelebA initially.

Features of the CelebHair dataset come from four sources:

1. Features including *eyebrow curve, eyeglasses, eye bags, cheekbone, age, chubby, gender, attractiveness,* and *beard* are directly inherited from the CelebA dataset;
2. Features including *forehead height, eyebrow length, eyebrow thickness, eye width, eye length, pupillary distance, nose length, nose-mouth distance, lip length, lip thickness,* and *jaw curve* are computed from the detected facial landmarks;
3. *Face shapes* are classified using YOLO v4;
4. *Hairstyles* are classified using a CNN with a spatial transformer network substructure.

A visual layout of our data collection framework is shown in Fig. 1. Note that the four substeps of data collection could be executed parallelly.

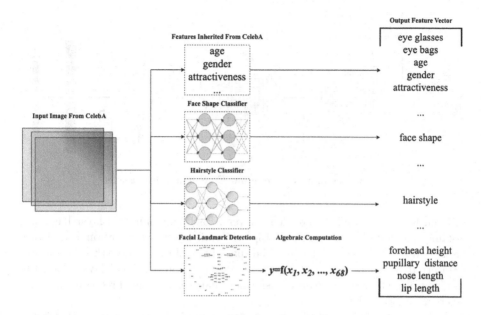

Fig. 1. The framework of CelebHair.

3.1 Hairstyle Classification

For hairstyle classification, the Hairstyle30k dataset, where ten kinds of most popular hairstyles are available as shown in Fig. 2, is used.

The architecture of the CNN hairstyle classifier is shown in Fig. 3. The input image comprises three channels (R, G, B) and is feed-forward into three convo-

Fig. 2. Ten classes of hairstyles available in the Hairstyle30k dataset.

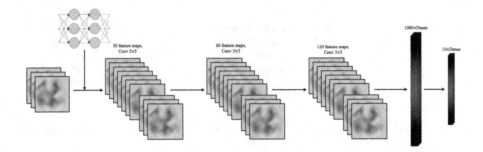

Fig. 3. The architecture of our CNN hairstyle classifier.

lutional layers followed by two dense layers. Each convolutional layer has max-pooling and batch normalization [13], while all layers, convolutional or dense, are activated by leaky ReLU [14]. The spatial transformer network substructure is inserted between the input layer and the first convolutional layers, and the localization net of the spatial transformer shares the same three convolutional layers as shown below.

The Hairstyle30k dataset, which contains 10,078 facial images with labeled hairstyles, is randomly shuffled and split into train/test/validation sets at a ratio of 85:10:5. A small validation set is incorporated for early stopping in case of overfitting. With the spatial transformer network (STN), the classification accuracy raises to 85.45% on the test set. A detailed comparison of the classification performance is given in Table 1.

Table 1. The accuracy of hairstyle classification models

	Train acc	Test acc
Without STN	53.58%	42.73%
With STN	88.62%	85.45%

However, the dimension of aligned images provided by Hairstyle30k is 128 × 128, which differs from the dimension of aligned images provided by CelebA, 178 × 218. The mismatch of dimensions has prevented us from feed CelebA facial images straightforwardly into the CNN hairstyle classifier as inputs. As a solution, we crop the CelebA images at the left-upper, left-lower, right-upper, right-lower, and center to retrieve five 128 × 128 images and run the hairstyle classifier on each of them. The results are then aggregated using majority voting to produce a hairstyle class for the corresponding CelebA image.

3.2   Face Shape Classification

To extract face shape attributes, we train a face shape classifier, using YOLO v4, an effective real-time object recognition algorithm. It split our image into cells, and each of them predicts several bounding boxes and the probability that there is an object in the bounding box. The face shape dataset we use comprises 5,000 images of female celebrities from all around the globe, categorized according to their face shapes, namely: heart, oblong, oval, round, and square, while each category consists of 1000 images. The training set of each class contains 800 images, whereas the testing set contains 200 images. We mark the bounding box for each of these images, for the original dataset does not include the bounding box of each face.

We train the model based on pre-trained weights with: *batch=64, subdivisions=16, max_batches = 10,000, steps $\in$ [8000,9000], width=416, height=416, classes=5.*

Five classes of face shapes and their recognition results are shown in Fig. 4. We evaluate the performance on the face shape classification results' precision as demonstrated in Table 2. Compared to existing work related to face shape classification, we have a much more extensive training size and higher accuracy, as shown in Table 3.

(a) heart   (b) oblong   (c) oval   (d) round   (e) square

Fig. 4. Five classes of face shapes and their classification results.

Table 2. Face shape classification results' precision

Label	True positives	False positives	Average precision[a]
Overall	931	151	95.73%[b]
Heart	186	17	98.16%
Oblong	194	24	98.46%
Oval	172	49	90.79%
Round	187	41	93.62%
Square	192	20	97.64%

[a] *For confidence threshold = 0.25, false negatives = 69, average IoU = 79.41%.*
[b] *IoU threshold = 50%, used area-under-curve for each unique recall.*

Table 3. Comparison with other approaches towards face shape classification

Approach	Training set size	Accuracy
SVM-Linear [11]	1,000	64.00%
SVM-RBF [11]	1,000	72.00%
MKL with descriptors [12]	500	70.30%
Our approach	**8,000**	**87.45%**

3.3 Facial Landmark Detection

We transform the image into the gray image based on OpenCV [15], then extract sixty-eight facial landmarks using Dlib, a toolkit containing machine learning algorithms and tools, as shown in Fig. 5(a) and Fig. 5(b). Arithmetic operations can be performed upon these facial landmarks to determine facial attributes, as shown in Fig. 5(c). Here we give a few examples in Table 4 on the calculation of such facial attributes, where $d(x,y)$ denotes the distance in pixels between landmark point x and y. The attributes, as continuous numerical values, are discretized using equal-width binning at the end.

Table 4. Examples for calculating facial attributes using facial landmarks

Attribute	Formula
Forehead height	$\dfrac{d(18,27)}{d(1,17)}$
Eye width	$\dfrac{d(37,40)+d(43,46)}{2\times d(1,17)}$
Pupillary distance	$\dfrac{d(42,48)}{d(1,17)}$
Nose length	$\dfrac{2\times d(28,34)}{d(22,9)+d(23,9)}$
Lip length	$\dfrac{d(51,53)+d(49,55)+d(59,57)}{3\times d(4,14)}$

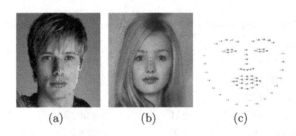

(a)   (b)   (c)

Fig. 5. Sixty-eight facial landmark points.

Table 5. Attributes and their variable options

Attribute	Options
Forehead height	Short(−1), tall(1)
Eyebrow curve	Straight(−1), curvy(1)
Eyebrow length	Short(−1), long(1)
Eyebrow thickness	Thin(−1), thick(1)
Eye width	Narrow(−1), wide(1)
Eye length	Short(−1), long(1)
Eyeglasses	None(−1), any(1)
Eye bags	None(−1), any(1)
Pupillary distance	Short(−1), long(1)
Cheekbone	Low(−1), high(1)
Nose length	Short(−1), long(1)
Nose-mouth distance	Short(−1), long(1)
Lip length	Short(−1), long(1)
Lip thickness	Thin(−1), thick(1)
Jaw curve	Straight(−1), curvy(1)
Age	Young(0), medium(1), old(2)
Chubby	No(−1), yes(1)
Gender	Female(−1), male(1)
Attractiveness	No(−1), yes(1)
Beard	None(−1), any(1)
Face shape	1–5, see Fig. 4
Hairstyle	1–10, see Fig. 2

4 Data Description

The CelebHair dataset currently contains 202,599 facial images (inherited from CelebA), and each of these images is labeled with 22 features: forehead height, eyebrow curve, eyebrow length, eyebrow thickness, eye width, eye length, eyeglasses, eye bags, pupillary distance, cheekbone, nose length, nose-mouth distance, lib length, lip thickness, jaw curve, age, chubby, gender, attractiveness, beard, face shape, and hairstyle. A complete list of viable options for each feature is given in Table 5.

In Fig. 6(a) and Fig. 6(b), we show the distribution of face shapes and hairstyles within the CelebHair dataset. We see that the majority of celebrity images in CelebA have a heart shape face. Also, undercut and spiky hair seem more popular, while bald and curtained hair seems less so.

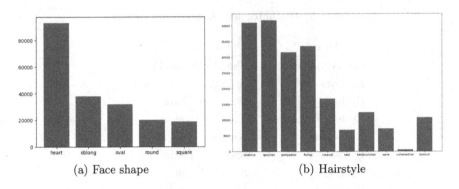

(a) Face shape   (b) Hairstyle

Fig. 6. The distribution of different face shapes & hairstyles in *CelebHair*.

We analyze various aspects of CelebHair to provide a deeper understanding of the dataset itself. Comparison with other similar datasets is also available. Table 6 shows statistics of CelebHair compared to other datasets, including CelebA, Face Shape Dataset, Hairstyle30k, Beauty e-Expert, AFAD [16], Adience [17], and UTKFace [18].

Table 6. Comparison between CelebHair and existing similar datasets

Name	Images	Hairstyle	Face shape	Featrues	Age	Gender	Landmarks
CelebA [1]	202,599	2	1	9	✓	✓	10
Face shape dataset [4]	1000	✗	✓	✗	✗	✗	✗
Hairstyle30k [7]	10,078	10	✗	✗	✗	✗	✗
Beauty e-Expert [9]	1,505	✓	3	✓	✗	✗	✗
AFAD [16]	164,432	✗	✗	✗	✓	✓	✗
Adience [17]	26,580	✗	✗	✗	✓	✓	✗
UTKFace [18]	23,708	✗	✗	✗	✓	✓	68
CelebHair	**202,599**	**10**	**5**	**17**	**✓**	**✓**	**68**

5   Application

5.1   Hairstyle Recommendation

For hairstyle recommendation, we have seen the Naive Bayes classification algorithm being used in previous work [10]. Given an adequate dataset with a proper amount of facial attributes and a labeled hairstyle feature, the problem of hairstyle recommendation can be reduced to classification, where a mapping function from the dependent facial attributes (as inputs) to the target hairstyle feature is established. Therefore, we use the Random Forests algorithm for hairstyle recommendation.

The CelebHair Dataset, which carries about 200k records, is shuffled and split into train/test sets at the ratio of 9:1. Then we fine-tune the Random Forests model concerning the number of trees (*n_estimators*) and the maximum depth of trees (*max_depth*). Results are shown in Table 7:

5.2 Hairstyle Try-On

There are currently two main methods to implement the integration of hairstyle and face, both of which require hairstyle templates. The first method uses simple image editing, superimposing the hairstyle on the face and manually adjusting the position of the hairstyle [19]. As an improvement on the first method, the second method uses a dual linear transformation procedure, in which 21 face contour points are adopted to calculate an affine transformation matrix between the hair template and the input face. Therefore, the second method can synthesize the visualized effect of hairstyle automatically. However, both approaches are limited by hair templates, for there are a limited number of hairstyle templates, but there are a variety of hairstyles on different people.

Table 7. Performance of random forests with different parameters

Hyper parameters	Train acc	Test acc
N_estimators=5, max_depth=3	37.68%	24.37%
N_estimators=10, max_depth=3	40.42%	29.65%
N_estimators=10, max_depth=5	54.39%	43.71%
N_estimators=20, max_depth=5	77.62%	75.43%
N_estimators=50, max_depth=5	89.12%	87.03%
N_estimators=100, max_depth=5	91.29%	86.63%

To address these problems above, we employ a novel approach to visualize the effect of hairstyle try-on and thus intuitively present the outcome of hairstyle recommendation that breaks through the limitations of hairstyle templates. In this approach, we migrate the recommended hairstyles to the input image of the face through face-swapping. We replace facial features on the template image of the face with a recommended hairstyle on it (Fig. 7(a)), with the facial features from the input face image (Fig. 7(b)), and the result (Fig. 7(c)) turns out well.

We implement the face swapping process using an algorithm [20] based on Dlib and OpenCV. A formal definition of the algorithm is given in Algorithm 1.

In Algorithm 1, firstly, we extract sixty-eight facial landmarks using Dlib, as shown in Fig. 5(c), to locate the part to be extracted from the input face image (Line 1). To make the result turns out well, we align the input image to fit the template image according to the facial landmarks detected (Line 2–Line 8). Then, we adjust the color balance in the input image to match the template image using OpenCV (Line 9). Finally, we transfer the facial features from the input face image to the template image (Line 10–Line 11).

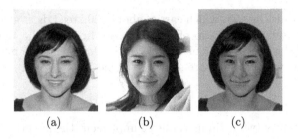

(a)   (b)   (c)

Fig. 7. The hairstyle try-on process.

Algorithm 1: Hairstyle Try-on Process

Input: Two images, one is the input face image, and the other is the template face image.

Output: The result of hairstyle try-on.

1: Extract facial landmarks from the input image and the template image using Dlib, which returns two 68*2 element matrices. Name matrices mentioned above as i_L and t_L;

2: Calculate the centroid from each of the point sets. Name them as i_C and t_C;

3: $i_L \leftarrow i_L - i_C$;

4: $t_L \leftarrow t_L - t_C$;

5: Calculate the standard deviation from each of the point sets. Name them as i_{SD} and t_{SD};

6: $i_L \leftarrow i_L/i_{SD}$;

7: $t_L \leftarrow t_L/t_{SD}$;

8: Calculate the rotation portion using the Singular Value. Decompose and return the complete transformation as an affine transformation matrix;

9: Change the colouring of the input image to match that of the template image by dividing the input image by a gaussian blur of the input image, and then multiplying by a gaussian blur of the template image;

10: Map the input image onto the template image;

11: Transfer the facial features from the input face image to the template image;

---

6   Conclusion

In this paper, we have introduced a new large-scale dataset, CelebHair. Compared with existing similar datasets, CelebHair has a larger volume and more varied features. Consequently, CelebHair provides sufficient support for models that require large-scale data, and should thus refine the performance of hairstyle recommendation models. Moreover, we give several possible applications to illustrate the usability of our dataset. In the future work, we would like to refine the hairstyle try-on experience for users by using Interface GAN.

Acknowledgments. This work is supported by Research Innovation Fund for College Students of Beijing University of Posts and Telecommunications, and National Natural Science Foundation of China under Grant No. 61702043.

References

1. Liu, Z., Luo, P., Wang, X., Tang, X.: Deep learning face attributes in the wild. In: Proceedings of the IEEE International Conference on Computer Vision, pp. 3730–3738 (2015)
2. King, D.E.: Dlib-ml: a machine learning toolkit. J. Mach. Learn. Res. **10**, 1755–1758 (2009)
3. Bochkovskiy, A., Wang, C.Y., Liao, H.Y.M.: Yolov4: Optimal speed and accuracy of object detection. arXiv preprint arXiv:2004.10934 (2020)
4. Lama, N.: Face shape dataset (2020). https://www.kaggle.com/niten19/face-shape-dataset
5. LeCun, Y., Haffner, P., Bottou, L., Bengio, Y.: Object recognition with gradient-based learning. Shape, Contour and Grouping in Computer Vision. LNCS, vol. 1681, pp. 319–345. Springer, Heidelberg (1999). https://doi.org/10.1007/3-540-46805-6_19
6. Jaderberg, M., Simonyan, K., Zisserman, A., Kavukcuoglu, K.: Spatial transformer networks. arXiv preprint arXiv:1506.02025 (2015)
7. Yin, W., Fu, Y., Ma, Y., Jiang, Y.G., Xiang, T., Xue, X.: Learning to generate and edit hairstyles. In: Proceedings of the 25th ACM International Conference on Multimedia, pp. 1627–1635 (2017)
8. Breiman, L.: Machine learning. Random Forest. **45**(1), 5–32 (2001)
9. Liu, L., Xing, J., Liu, S., Xu, H., Zhou, X., Yan, S.: Wow! you are so beautiful today!. ACM Tran. Multimedia Comput. Commun. Appl. (TOMM) **11**(1s), 1–22 (2014)
10. Weerasinghe, H., Vidanagama, D.: Machine learning approach for hairstyle recommendation. In: 2020 5th International Conference on Information Technology Research (ICITR), pp. 1–4. IEEE (2020)
11. Sunhem, W., Pasupa, K.: An approach to face shape classification for hairstyle recommendation. In: 2016 Eighth International Conference on Advanced Computational Intelligence (ICACI), pp. 390–394. IEEE (2016)
12. Pasupa, K., Sunhem, W., Loo, C.K.: A hybrid approach to building face shape classifier for hairstyle recommender system. Expert Syst. Appl. **120**, 14–32 (2019)
13. Ioffe, S., Szegedy, C.: Batch normalization: accelerating deep network training by reducing internal covariate shift. In: International conference on machine learning, pp. 448–456. PMLR (2015)
14. Maas, A.L., Hannun, A.Y., Ng, A.Y.: Rectifier nonlinearities improve neural network acoustic models. In: Proceedings of the International Conference on Machine Learning (ICML), vol. 30, p. 3. Citeseer (2013)
15. Bradski, G.: The opencv library. Dr Dobb's J. Softw. Tools **25**, 120–125 (2000)
16. Niu, Z., Zhou, M., Wang, L., Gao, X., Hua, G.: Ordinal regression with multiple output cnn for age estimation. In: Proceedings of the IEEE Conference on Computer Vision and Pattern Recognition, pp. 4920–4928 (2016)
17. Eidinger, E., Enbar, R., Hassner, T.: Age and gender estimation of unfiltered faces. IEEE Trans. Inf. Forensics Secur. **9**(12), 2170–2179 (2014)

18. Zhang, Z., Song, Y., Qi, H.: Age progression/regression by conditional adversarial autoencoder. In: IEEE Conference on Computer Vision and Pattern Recognition (CVPR). IEEE (2017)

19. Wang, W., Chen, Y., Kao, C.: Integrating augmented reality into female hairstyle try-on experience. In: 2011 Seventh International Conference on Natural Computation, vol. 4, pp. 2125–2127 (2011). https://doi.org/10.1109/ICNC.2011.6022427

20. Earl, M.: Switching eds: Face swapping with python, dlib, and opencv (2015). https://matthewearl.github.io/2015/07/28/switching-eds-with-python/

Image Super-Resolution Based on Residual Block Dense Connection

Juan Chen[1,2,3] (iD), Ang Gao[2], Siqi Liu[2], Haiyang Jia[1,2,3]($\boxtimes$) (iD), Yifan Shao[2],
and Wenxin Tang[2]

[1] College of Computer Science and Technology, Jilin University, Changchun 130012, China
jiahy@jlu.edu.cn
[2] College of Software, Jilin University, Changchun 130012, China
[3] Key Laboratory of Symbolic Computation and Knowledge
Engineering of Ministry of Education, Jilin University, Changchun 130012, China

Abstract. Image super-resolution models based on convolution neural networks are facing problems such as gradient disappearance, gradient explosion, and insufficient feature utilization. This paper proposes an image super-resolution model based on feature fusion of dense connection of residual blocks. The key contributions are as follows: (1) residual block mechanism, which can make full use of the hierarchical features extracted from the residual block to alleviate the shallow feature losing. (2) In order to extract more representative key features, the feature of each level extracted from residual blocks is input into subsequent residual blocks by dense connection mechanism. (3) local feature fusion is used in a single residual block, and global feature fusion is used in the tail of the model, so that the shallow key information can be transferred to the reconstruction layer as much as possible. Empirical experiment is deployed on four benchmark test sets (Set5, Set14, Urban100 and BSDS100), the results show that both the peak signal-to-noise ratio and structural similarity are improved. (Source code: https://github.com/brown-cats/SR_RFB).

Keywords: Image super-resolution reconstruction · Convolution neural network · Residual block · Dense connection · Feature fusion

1 Introduction

Image super-resolution (SR) refers to the technology of transforming low resolution (LR) image into high resolution (HR) image by calculation while retaining the original texture details of the image as much as possible [1]. Image SR methods are mainly divided into reconstruction-based (RB) [2, 3] and learning-based (LB) methods [4, 5].

The quality of image restoration based on reconstruction method is limited by LR image registration effect, parameter estimation and etc. While LB methods can mine more information of the original image, the quality of reconstructed images is better. Research shows that the performance of LB method can be improved with the increase of network width and layer number, but still facing a series of problems:

A. Gao and S. Liu—These authors contributed equally to this work.

© Springer Nature Switzerland AG 2021
H. Qiu et al. (Eds.): KSEM 2021, LNAI 12817, pp. 337–348, 2021.
https://doi.org/10.1007/978-3-030-82153-1_28

1. Increasing the depth or width of the neural network will lead to the problems of gradient disappearance, gradient explosion, and increase the number of parameters.
2. The sparse connections among residual blocks do not make full use of the shallow information, which results the incomplete information extraction.

An image SR model based on the feature fusion of residual block dense connection (RDFSR) is proposed. It mainly includes the following three mechanisms:

1) Residual Feature Block (RFB): A new residual module is proposed: its last convolution layer covers the features extracted from the first three convolution layers to reduce the training difficulty, and then the output feature maps of the four convolution layers are stacked in the depth direction. 1×1 convolution is used to fuse them to reduce the dimension and generate more representative image features.
2) Dense connection: Most image SR models based on convolution neural networks use sparse residual connection, which cannot take full advantages of residual connection. This paper introduces more connections between the RFBs.
3) Feature fusion: Local feature fusion is added in each RFB and global feature fusion is introduced at the reconstruction layer of RDFSR. Thus, fully retain the key features which lost in the transmission process of deep neural network.

The outline of this paper is as follows: Sect. 2 introduces the related work of image super-resolution method based on deep learning. Section 3 describes the proposed super-resolution algorithm in detail. Section 4 verifies the effectiveness of each mechanism of RDFSR through experiments. Section 5 summarizes the work of this paper and discusses future works.

2 Related Work

The process of image resolution magnification is also called up-sampling. According to the different phase of the up-sampling operation in the SR model, Wang [6] et al. divided the deep learning based SR model into pre up-sampling, post up-sampling, progressive up-sampling and iterative up and down sampling. This section details the advantages and limitations of these four frameworks.

2.1 Pre Up-Sampling SR

Pre up-sampling SR, as shown in Fig. 1(a), samples the LR image to the target size resolution firstly then refines the up-sampling image to get the target image through neural network, such as SRCNN [7], VDSR [8], ZSSR [9], etc. Pre up-sampling through the deep convolution network to refine the coarse-grained image, it greatly reduces the difficulty of network learning. However, most operations of the pre up-sampling method are performed in high-dimensional space, so the cost of time and space is much higher than other frameworks.

2.2 Post Up-Sampling SR

In order to solve the problem of high complexity of pre up-sampling SR, an end-to-end learnable post up-sampling SR is proposed, as shown in Fig. 1(b), such as ESPCN [10], FSRCNN [11], SRDenseNet [12]. Because the resolution of the image increases at the end of the model, the training and testing speed is improved. Therefore, the framework has been widely used in the field of SR.

2.3 Progressive Up-Sampling SR

Post up-sampling cannot learn the complex mapping from LR image to HR image, which leads poor effect in achieving large scales up-sampling (more than 8 times). Therefore, Lai [13] proposed a SR model based on progressive up-sampling, as shown in Fig. 1(c). For example, to achieve 8 times of up-sampling, LapSRN [13] completes three times of up-sampling operations, and each time the image is up sampled by deconvolution to 2 times of the original. The progressive up-sampling gradually predicts the residuals and optimizes the network. The learning deconvolution layer is used to replace the bicubic interpolation [4].

2.4 Iterative up and Down Sampling SR

The SR network with feedforward connection is difficult to represent the relationship between LR and HR, especially for large-scale amplification factor. In order to capture such relationship, iterative up-sampling and down-sampling SR is proposed, which iteratively calculates the reconstruction error, and then uses it to adjust the intensity of HR image, as shown in Fig. 1(d). Haris [14] et al. Used the iterative upper and lower sampling layers to connect the upper sampling layer and the lower sampling layer alternately, and used all the middle layer HR feature maps to reconstruct the final HR image.

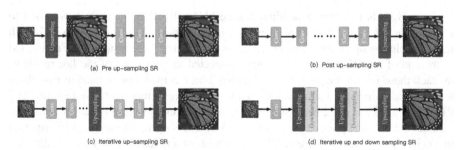

(a) Pre up-sampling SR

(b) Post up-sampling SR

(c) Iterative up-sampling SR

(d) Iterative up and down sampling SR

Fig. 1. Super-resolution model frameworks based on deep learning.

3 Proposed Method

This paper proposed an image SR model based on the feature fusion of residual block dense connection (RDFSR). This section will introduce the model in detail.

3.1 Residual Feature Block

In the task of image SR, residual connection can produce some important layered features from different aspects of the original LR image. Consider the case of several continuous residual block (Fig. 2). The features of the first residual block must travel a long path to reach the last block through repeated addition and convolution operations. Therefore, the residual features are difficult to be fully utilized, and only have impacts inside the residual block during the network learning process.

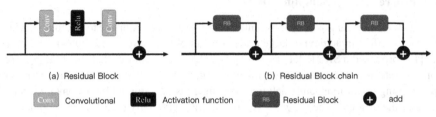

    (a) Residual Block   (b) Residual Block chain

Conv Convolutional   **Relu** Activation function   **RB** Residual Block   ⊕ add

Fig. 2. Structure of residual block (a) and residual block chain (b)

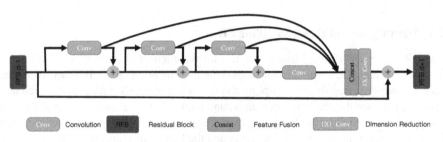

Conv Convolution   **RFB** Residual Block   **Concat** Feature Fusion   **1X1 Conv** Dimension Reduction

Fig. 3. Detailed structure of RFB module

    To solve this problem, a residual feature block (RFB) framework is proposed to make better use of local residual features. Figure 3 shows the details of an RFB with four convolution operations. Residual features of the first three residuals are connected to the end of the RFB directly and then connected to the output of the last residuals to stack these feature maps in series. Finally, 1×1 convolution is used to fuse these features and reduce the feature dimension to extract more representative features. The RFB framework can make better use of the residual feature than simply stacking multiple residual blocks. The previous residuals block contains useful hierarchical information that can be propagated to the end of the RFB without any loss or interference, allowing more discriminative features to be filtered out. At the same time, such structure realize the effect of learning and summarizing step by step. As shown in Fig. 3, after convolving the input at the first layer, the output will be transferred in two ways: one is directly to the tail of the block; the other will be added with the output of the previous layer, then the result will serve as the input of the subsequent layer. Such connection mode can summarize the features extracted from all previous convolution layers to realize information interaction between each layer, meanwhile avoid the problem of the loss of shallow layer feature information caused by excessive layers.

3.2 Dense Connection

Residual connection are used in DRCN [15] to connect the input data to the reconstruction layer in the SR model. RED [16] introduced multiple symmetric residual connection. Both methods can obtain better image SR results. Many experiments have proved that residual connection can effectively accelerate the speed of model training and improve the quality of reconstructed images. However, only one residual connection is used in DRCN, and only two symmetric layers are used in RED. The advantage of the residual connections are not fully used. Therefore, the dense connection between residual blocks is introduced, as shown in Fig. 4.

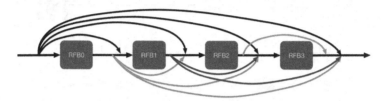

Fig. 4. Dense connection mechanism

In dense connections, the output of each RFB is input to all subsequent blocks via a residual connection, and the input of each block is a summary of the output of all previous blocks. Therefore, the output of layer i is calculated as follows:

$$O^i = \max(0, W^i * \sum_{j=1}^{i=1} O^j + b^i) \tag{1}$$

Dense connection mechanism increases the information exchanges and feature transmission of the network, thus alleviating the gradient disappearance. In addition, dense connection can realize feature multiplexing then reduce the number of parameters, thus result in higher performance with less memory and computation.

3.3 Feature Fusion

The local feature fusion is added inside the RFB, and the global feature fusion is added in the reconstruction layer. The structure of the feature fusion mechanism is shown in Fig. 5. Different from the adding operation in ResNet [17]; local feature fusion stacks the outputs of each layer inside the RFB in series, global feature fusion stacks the outputs of each RFB together.

Stacking feature maps have the following problems: (1) Information redundancy was caused, as feature maps of different layers may store the same features. (2) Stacking feature maps will cause dimension explosions. For example, each layer in the first four convolution layers will output 64 feature maps, if not handled properly, there will be an explosive increase in the dimension of the feature maps, and the amount of calculation for the network training increase sharply. Therefore, A 1 * 1 convolution layer is added after the stacked feature map. This convolution layer can eliminate redundant information in the previous convolution layer, then summarize all information to output more representative feature maps. The dimension of feature map can be reduced to prevent dimension explosion and reduce computation.

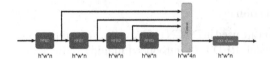

Fig. 5. Feature fusion mechanism

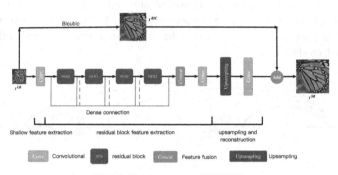

Fig. 6 The structure of RDFSR.

3.4 RDFSR

The proposed RDFSR model is mainly based on three mechanisms above. RDFSR includes three phases: shallow layer feature extraction, dense residual block feature extraction and nonlinear mapping, super resolution reconstruction. As shown in Fig. 6, the input and output of RDFSR network are I^{LR} and I^{SR} respectively. I^{LR} is obtained by subsampling images of the training set. Assume that the size of I^{LR} is H * W * C, then the size of I^{SR} is R^2 * (H * W) * C. Where H and W are the number of pixels in the vertical and horizontal sections of the image, R is the super-resolution multiple of the image, and C is the number of image channels. The algorithm flow of RDFSR is shown in Fig. 7.

Firstly, the I^{LR} is input into the network to extract shallow layer features through a convolution layer. The formula is:

$$F_0 = \text{Conv}\left(I^{LR}\right) = W_n * I^{LR} + b \tag{2}$$

Where W_n represents the convolution kernel matrix, used to extract the features of the input image, and b represents the bias matrix.

Secondly, the shallow feature F_0 is input into the densely connected RFBs to extract the deeper and more representative features. The formula is:

$$F_i = \text{RFB}(\sum_{j=0}^{i} F_j) = \text{Conv}_{1*1}(F_{\text{concat}}(F_{\text{Stack}}(C_1, C_2, C_3, C_4)) + F_{i-1}$$

$$C_i = \text{Conv}(\sum_{j=0}^{i-1} C_j) \tag{3}$$

RFB represents the calculation of one densely connected residuals block, F_{Concat} represents global feature fusion, F_{Stack} represents the recombination feature maps, $1 \leq i \leq 4$.

Finally, the I^{SR} is generated by sampling on the feature map and image reconstruction at the tail of the whole frame. The formula is as follows:

$$F_{RDFSR}\left(I^{LR}\right) = I^{SR} = UP(F_{Concat}(F_{Stack}(F_0, F_1, \ldots\ldots F_n)) + I^{BIC} \qquad (4)$$

$F_{RDFSR}(I^{LR})$ represents the SR image which is the final output of the model, F_i represents the output of each RFB and UP represents a subpixel up-sampling that enlarges the image to the target size. Finally, the I^{SR} is obtained by adding the reconstructed residual image with I^{BIC} which is obtained through bicubic interpolation of I^{LR}.

Algorithm 1 RDFSR framework
Input: I^{LR} Low-Resolution Image.
Output: I^{HR} High-Resolution Image.
Bicubic: Bicubic Interpolation.
F_{concat}: Feature Fusion.
Upsampling: Image up sampling
1: **function** RDFSR (I^{LR}, I^{Bic})
2:     $I^{HR} \leftarrow$ Bicubic (I^{LR})
3:     $j \leftarrow$ Conv (I^{LR})
4:     $i \leftarrow 0$
5:     **do**
6:         F_{concat} (j)
7:         j += RFB^i (j)
8:         i += 1
9:     **while** $i < 4$
10:    Res $\leftarrow$ Upsampling (F_{concat})
11:    I^{HR} += Res
12:    return I^{HR}
13: **end function**

Fig. 7. Algorithm of RDFSR

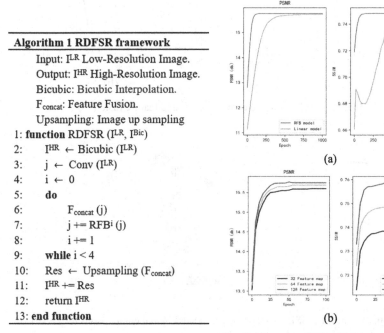

Fig. 8. Compare RFB with Linear model (a) and different number of feature maps (b)

4 Experiments

4.1 Settings

Div2K image data set [18–20] is selected as the training set; Set5 [21], Set14 [22], Urban100 [23] and BSDS100 [24] are selected as test sets.

There are 1000 images in the Div2K, data enhancement is deployed to increase the number of training samples, rotates the images in the Div2K by 90°, 180°, 270°, and flips horizontally and vertically, then cuts them into 50 * 50 image blocks. Finally, the training set are normalized, each pixel is divided by the maximum value 255.

When training the model, the size of the convolution kernel of all convolution layers is set as 3 * 3, and 64 feature maps are extracted from each convolution layer. In this paper, Mini-batch gradient descent algorithm is used to minimize the loss function. In this experiment, 500 epochs of training were carried out for each scale. The initial learning-rate is set as 0.001, which is halved every 100 epochs.

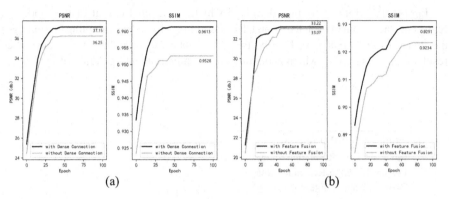

Fig. 9. Results of dense connection (a) and feature fusion (b)

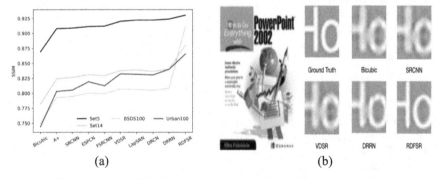

Fig. 10. The average SSIM on the test sets (a) and Visual comparisons for 2X (b)

4.2 Analysis of RFB

This section compares the RFB with the linear model of the same depth through experiments. The results, Fig. 8(a), proves the above assumption.

With same depth, the RFB is better than the linear model in PSNR (Peak signal-to-noise ratio) and SSIM (structural similarity). In terms of the convergence rate, RFB almost converges in 300 epochs, while linear model converges in 1000 epochs. The experimental results show that RFB can not only improve the quality of SR image, but also greatly reduce the training time.

The comparison on the dimensions of the output feature map of each convolution layer of RFB is also given. As shown in Fig. 8(b). It can be seen that increasing the output dimension of the feature map may enhance the results of reconstruction images. However, with the increase of the number of feature maps, the number of training parameters is also doubled. Therefore, considering the lightweight of the model, the economy of training time and the efficiency of result improvement, 64 feature maps are selected.

4.3 Analysis of Dense Connection

This section constructs a model with dense connections and a model without dense connections. The experimental results are shown in Fig. 9(a). After adding dense connections between RFBs, the PSNR of the test image increases by 0.9 db, and the SSIM increases by 0.0087. Therefore, adding dense connections between RFBs can improve the quality of image reconstruction.

4.4 Analysis of Feature Fusion

This section constructs a model with feature fusion and a model without feature fusion. The results are shown in Fig. 9(b). The model with feature fusion is better than the model without feature fusion in PSNR and SSIM. Feature fusion makes full use of the features extracted from the previous layers, which enhances the representation ability of deep neural network.

4.5 Comparing with Related Works

PSNR and SSIM are the main evaluation indexes in SR. Table 1 lists the results of RFBSR on the four test sets (Set5, Set14, Urban100 and BSDS100) comparing with the Bicubic [25], SRCNN [5], FSRCNN [11], ESPCN [26], VDSR [27], LapSRN [13], DRCN [28] and DRRN [29] at 2, 3 and 4 times respectively. Figure 10(a) gives the average SSIM values of different methods on the same test sets. PSNR and SSIM of RFBSR are better than the other methods on most test sets. Especially, the SSIM of RDFSR has a great improvement compared with related methods. The SR images reconstructed by RDFSR have better performance in texture and details, as shown in Fig. 10(b).

Table 1. PSNR/SSIM of RDFSR and mainstream methods.

Methods	Scale	Set5 PSNR/SSIM	Set14 PSNR/SSIM	BSDS00 PSNR/SSIM	Urban100 PSNR/SSIM
Bicubic	X2	33.66/0.9299	30.24/0.8688	29.56/0.8431	26.88/0.8403
SRCNN		36.66/0.9542	32.45/0.9067	31.36/0.8879	29.50/0.8946
ESPCN		37.00/0.9559	32.75/0.9098	31.51/0.8939	29.87/0.9065
FSRCNN		37.05/0.9560	32.66/0.9090	31.53/0.8920	29.88/0.9020
VDSR		37.53/0.9560	33.05/0.9130	31.90/0.8960	30.77/0.9140
LapSRN		37.52/0.9591	33.08/0.9130	31.08/0.8950	30.41/0.9112
DRCN		37.63/0.9588	33.04/0.9118	31.85/0.8942	30.75/0.9133
DRRN		**37.74**/0.9591	**33.23**/0.9136	32.05/0.8973	**31.23**/0.9188
RDFSR		37.15/**0.9613**	33.22/**0.9292**	**32.67/0.9471**	30.06/**0.9256**
Bicubic	X3	30.39/0.8682	27.55/0.7742	27.21/0.7385	24.46/0.7349
SRCNN		32.75/0.9090	29.30/0.8215	28.41/0.7863	26.24/0.7989
ESPCN		33.02/0.9135	29.49/0.8271	28.50/0.7937	26.41/0.8161
FSRCNN		33.18/0.9140	29.37/0.8240	28.53/0.7910	26.43/0.8080
VDSR		33.67/0.9210	29.78/0.8320	28.83/0.7990	27.14/0.8290
LapSRN		33.82/0.9227	29.87/0.8320	28.82/0.7980	27.07/0.8280
DRCN		33.82/0.9226	29.76/0.831	28.80/0.7963	27.15/0.8276
DRRN		**34.03**/0.9244	**29.96**/0.8349	28.95/0.8004	**27.53**/0.8378
RDFSR		32.64/**0.9258**	29.17/**0.8668**	**30.69/0.9094**	27.28/**0.8644**
Bicubic	X4	28.42/0.8104	26.00/0.7027	25.96/0.6675	23.14/0.6577
SRCNN		30.48/0.8628	27.50/0.7513	26.90/0.7101	24.52/0.7221
ESPCN		30.66/0.8646	27.71/0.7562	26.98/0.7124	24.60/0.7360
FSRCNN		30.72/0.8660	27.61/0.7550	26.98/0.7150	24.62/0.7280
VDSR		31.35/0.8830	28.02/0.7680	27.29/0.7260	25.18/0.7540
LapSRN		31.54/0.8850	28.19/0.7720	27.32/0.7270	25.21/0.7560
DRCN		31.53/0.8854	28.02/0.7670	27.23/0.7233	25.14/0.7510
DRRN		**31.68**/0.8888	28.21/0.7720	27.38/0.7284	**25.44**/0.7638
RDFSR		31.51/**0.9047**	**28.87/0.8446**	**29.40/0.8776**	24.53/**0.8066**

5 Conclusions and Future Works

The proposed RFB framework can effectively combine the residual blocks together, then take the full advantages of each layer features through local feature fusion. So the RDFSR model was proposed, which is based on RFB, dense connection and global feature fusion mechanism. The experimental results show that the RDFSR improves the quality of SR reconstruction. For the future works, the RDFSR can be improved in the following aspects:

(1) Network improvement and optimization. Propose new network connection methods and optimize the parameters to improve the perception and accuracy of SR images. Reduce the computation complexity while maintaining the good performance.
(2) Optimization of up-sampling scale. Due to the limitations of the up-sampling methods, the proposed model can only reconstruct the images with integer scale, but cannot reconstruct the images with fractional scale. And it is impossible to reconstruct images of different scales with one model. Therefore, how to build a SR model with variable and fractional scale is a subject worthy of further study.

Acknowledgement. This paper is supported by National Natural Science Foundation of China under Grant Nos. 61502198, 61472161, 61402195, 61103091, U19A2061 and the Science and Technology Development Plan of Jilin Province under Grant No. 20160520099JH, 20150101051JC, 20190302117GX, 20180101334JC, 2019C053-3.

References

1. Harris, J.L.: Diffraction and resolving power. J. Opt. Soc. Am. **54**, 931–936 (1964)
2. Tsai, R., Huang, T.: Multiframe image restoration and registration. Adv. Comput. Vis. Image Process 1 (1984)
3. Kim, S.P., Bose, N.K.: Recursive reconstruction of high resolution image from noisy undersampled multiframes. IEEE Trans. Acoustics Speech Signal Process. **38**, 1013–1027 (1990)
4. Dong, C., Loy, C.C., He, K., Tang, X.: Learning a Deep Convolutional Network for Image Super-Resolution. In: Fleet, D., Pajdla, T., Schiele, B., Tuytelaars, T. (eds.) ECCV 2014. LNCS, vol. 8692, pp. 184–199. Springer, Cham (2014). https://doi.org/10.1007/978-3-319-10593-2_13
5. Dong, C., Loy, C.C., He, K.M., Tang, X.O.: Image super-resolution using deep convolutional networks. IEEE Trans. Pattern Anal. Mach. Intell. **38**, 295–307 (2016)
6. Wang, Z., Chen, J., Hoi, S.: Deep learning for image super-resolution: a survey. IEEE Trans. Pattern Anal. Mach. Intell. (2020). https://doi.org/10.1109/TPAMI.2020.2982166
7. Dong, C., Loy, C.C., He, K., Tang, X.: Image super-resolution using deep convolutional networks. IEEE Trans. Pattern Anal. Mach. Intell. **38**, 295–307 (2016)
8. Kim, J., Lee, J.K., Lee, K.M.: Accurate Image Super-Resolution Using Very Deep Convolutional Networks (2016)
9. Shocher, A., Cohen, N., Irani, M., IEEE: "Zero-shot" super-resolution using deep internal learning. In: 2018 IEEE/CVF Conference on Computer Vision and Pattern Recognition, pp. 3118–3126 (2018)
10. Shi, W., Caballero, J., Huszár, F., Totz, J., Wang, Z.: Real-time single image and video super-resolution using an efficient sub-pixel convolutional neural network. In: 2016 IEEE Conference on Computer Vision and Pattern Recognition (CVPR) (2016)
11. Dong, C., Loy, C.C., Tang, X.: Accelerating the Super-Resolution Convolutional Neural Network. In: Leibe, B., Matas, J., Sebe, N., Welling, M. (eds.) ECCV 2016. LNCS, vol. 9906, pp. 391–407. Springer, Cham (2016). https://doi.org/10.1007/978-3-319-46475-6_25

12. Tong, T., Li, G., Liu, X., Gao, Q.: Image super-resolution using dense skip connections. In: IEEE International Conference on Computer Vision (2017)
13. Lai, W.-S., Huang, J.-B., Ahuja, N., Yang, M.-H., IEEE: Deep Laplacian pyramid networks for fast and accurate super-resolution. In: 30th IEEE Conference on Computer Vision and Pattern Recognition, pp. 5835–5843 (2017)
14. Haris, M., Shakhnarovich, G., Ukita, N.: Deep back-projection networks for single image super-resolution. IEEE Trans. Pattern Anal. Mach. Intell. (2020). https://doi.org/10.1109/TPAMI.2020.3002836
15. Kim, J., Lee, J.K., Lee, K.M.: Deeply-recursive convolutional network for image super-resolution. In: 2016 IEEE Conference on Computer Vision and Pattern Recognition (CVPR) (2016)
16. Mao, X.-J., Shen, C., Yang, Y.-B.: Image Restoration Using Convolutional Auto-encoders with Symmetric Skip Connections (2016)
17. He, K., Zhang, X., Ren, S., Sun, J.: Deep Residual Learning for Image Recognition (2016)
18. Dai, T., Cai, J., Zhang, Y., Xia, S.T., Zhang, L.: Second-order attention network for single image super-resolution. In: 2019 IEEE/CVF Conference on Computer Vision and Pattern Recognition (CVPR) (2019)
19. Zhang, Y., Li, K., Li, K., Wang, L., Zhong, B., Fu, Y.: Image Super-Resolution Using Very Deep Residual Channel Attention Networks. In: Ferrari, V., Hebert, M., Sminchisescu, C., Weiss, Y. (eds.) ECCV 2018. LNCS, vol. 11211, pp. 294–310. Springer, Cham (2018). https://doi.org/10.1007/978-3-030-01234-2_18
20. Zhang, Y., Tian, Y., Kong, Y., Zhong, B., Fu, Y.: Residual Dense Network for Image Super-Resolution. IEEE (2018)
21. Bevilacqua, M., Roumy, A., Guillemot, C., Alberi-Morel, M.-L.: Low-Complexity Single Image Super-Resolution Based on Nonnegative Neighbor Embedding (2012)
22. Zeyde, R., Elad, M., Protter, M.: On Single Image Scale-Up Using Sparse-Representations. In: Boissonnat, J.-D., et al. (eds.) Curves and Surfaces 2010. LNCS, vol. 6920, pp. 711–730. Springer, Heidelberg (2012). https://doi.org/10.1007/978-3-642-27413-8_47
23. Arbeláez, P., Maire, M., Fowlkes, C., Malik, J.: Contour detection and hierarchical image segmentation. IEEE Trans. Pattern Anal. Mach. Intell. 33, 898–916 (2011)
24. Huang, J.B., Singh, A., Ahuja, N.: Single image super-resolution from transformed self-exemplars. In: IEEE Conference on Computer Vision and Pattern Recognition (2015)
25. Zhang, X., Zheng, Z., Asanuma, I., Xu, Y.: A new kind of super-resolution reconstruction algorithm based on the ICM and the bicubic interpolation. Inform. Japan 16, 8027–8036 (2008)
26. Shi, W., et al., IEEE: Real-time single image and video super-resolution using an efficient sub-pixel convolutional neural network. In: 2016 IEEE Conference on Computer Vision and Pattern Recognition, pp. 1874–1883 (2016)
27. Kim, J., Lee, J.K., Lee, K.M., IEEE: Accurate image super-resolution using very deep convolutional networks. In: 2016 IEEE Conference on Computer Vision and Pattern Recognition, pp. 1646–1654 (2016)
28. Kim, J., Lee, J.K., Lee, K.M.: Deeply-Recursive Convolutional Network for Image Super-Resolution (2015)
29. Ledig, C., et al., IEEE: Photo-realistic single image super-resolution using a generative adversarial network. In: 30th Ieee Conference on Computer Vision and Pattern Recognition, pp. 105–114 (2017)

EGIM: Evolution Graph Based Interest Modeling for Click-Through Rate Prediction

Jian Hu, Qing Ding$^{(\boxtimes)}$, and Wenyu Zhang

School of Software Engineering, University of Science and Technology of China, Hefei, China
{hujian1,wenyuz}@mail.ustc.edu.cn, dingqing@ustc.edu.cn

Abstract. It is essential for the click-through rate prediction to learn informative representations. Some studies exploit user behavior data to learn user interest representation. These models usually integrate user historical data into the represented embedding without considering user relevance. Such an approach easily leads to suboptimal representations since it fails to capture the high-order collaboration signal. In this paper, we propose the Evolution Graph-based Interest Modeling (EGIM) to transform user behavior data into a dynamic structure. the user-item interaction is presented as an evolution graph. Graph Convolutional Network is applied as the interest extractor and the Long Short-Term Memory is adopted to learn the evolution of user interest. In the end, the relevance of the user interest sequence with the target item is introduced by the attention-based interest-aggregation layer. Extensive experimental results on three real-world datasets demonstrate that EGIM has significant improvements in terms of Recall@20 and NDCG@20 over several state-of-the-art models.

Keywords: CTR Prediction · Interest representation · User-item interaction · Evolution graph · Graph convolutional network · Deep learning

1 Introduction

Most of recommendation system applies click-through rate (CTR) prediction modeling to discover users interesting. In the early stage, The most common method is linear regression (LR) [10], which usually utilize the user's and the item's feature group to calculate the rate of user click. However, the traditional LR model does not consider the feature combination. In the last few years, some deep learning models have been proposed to learn sophisticated feature interactions in CTR predictions. For example, NCF [8] generates high-order features through deep neural networks. Deep&Cross Network (DCN) [12], DeepFM [5] and Wide&Deep [1] extend it for dividing features into low-order and high-order. These methods achieve good performance with the co-design of both the learning algorithm and serving system.

© Springer Nature Switzerland AG 2021
H. Qiu et al. (Eds.): KSEM 2021, LNAI 12817, pp. 349–360, 2021.
https://doi.org/10.1007/978-3-030-82153-1_29

In order to further improve the performance of CTR, DIN [19] conducts a more in-depth study on user historical interactions. By observing the collected data, researcher found that there are two characteristics in user behavior data. Specifically, firstly, DIN believes the interest shown by users is very diverse in the process of browsing websites. Secondly, due to the diversity, historical items are not consistent in determining whether the recommended item is clicked. Thus, DIN leverages an attention-based method to capture relative interests from the user behavior sequence with regard to the candidate item. However, it ignores the ordering of user behavior sequences. Practically, the ordering of items reflects the change process of user interests.

To solve this problem, DIEN [18] uses a specially designed GRU [2] structure to capture the user interest. The method applies GRU to modeling the sequence of the entire behavior data, considering the impact of previous interactions on subsequent interactions. DSIN [4] introduces a hierarchical view of behavior sequence by dividing items into sessions. However, the main focus of these methods is to model the correlation between historical items and candidate items. Most of these methods pay little attention to the correlation between users and fail to embed the crucial collaborative signal.

In this paper, we borrow ideas from the area of Graph Convolution Network (GCN) [3] and design a new modeling paradigm, which we name as Evolution Graph based Interest Modeling (EGIM). We discuss the evolution of user interests at the full user level. EGIM converts the historical interactions into the user-item interaction graph, where edges represent the interaction and the graph structure represents the collaborative signal. The evolution graph is represented as multiple snapshots. Each snapshot contains users' interaction information. Motivated by the dynamical network representation, we apply the GCN on each snapshot to update user representation and the Long Short-Term Memory (LSTM) [9] to model user representation sequence. More importantly, user representation in the current snapshot is computed dependently on the previous snapshots. After evolving-interest extractor layer, user interest sequence are fed into the attention-based interest-aggregation layer to obtain the user's final interest representation.

In summary, the contributions of this paper can be summarized as follows:

- We emphasize the importance of the collaboration signals in CTR prediction since it can reflect the fine-grained change of user interests.
- We propose the novel EGIM model based on the evolution graph for CTR prediction. The model applies GCN to capture the high-order collaboration signal and adopts LSTM to model the user representation sequence.
- We evaluate our model on three real-world datasets to demonstrate the effectiveness of the proposed method compared to several state-of-the-art baselines.

In the following part of the paper, we first introduce the related work in Sect. 2. Then, we define the problem and explain our model in Sect. 3. In Sect. 4, we verify the utility with experimental results. Finally, the conclusions and outlooks are presented in Sect. 5.

2   Related Work

Deep Neural Networks (DNN) based methods have achieved great success in CTR prediction task. Most works use a DNN to capture interactions between features from different fields so that engineers could get rid of boring feature engineering works [1,5,8,12]. There is also some work to study the user's historical data to model the user's interest [18,19]. To exploit the complex relations between users and items as well as their information at the same time, recently, recommendation method based on GCN start to attract research attention. The method based on GCN update the user or item embedding. NGCF [13] updates node embedding by using multi-hop neighborhood information. In order to realize lightweight computations, LightGCN [7] analyzed the information dissemination of interactive graphs and simplified the design of GCN to make it more concise and suitable for the recommendation. To supply more personalized recommendations, DiffNet [15] applies GCN for influence diffusion and tries to combine relations between users with user-item interactions in social recommendations. GC-SAN [16]connect all the items in the same session together to generate a homogeneous session graph for items and thus apply GCN for item attributes diffusion. Similarly, KGNN-LS [11] captures inter-item relatedness by mining their associated attributes on a knowledge graph built on item attributes by using the knowledge graph where edge information is external knowledge.

3   The Evolution Graph Based Interest Modeling

3.1   Problem Definition

In this article, we define the problem as to predict the probability that the user clicks at candidate items based on the feature representations. A set of users is denoted as $\mathcal{U} = \{u_1, u_2, \cdots, u_N\}$ and a set of items is denoted as $\mathcal{I} = \{i_1, i_2, \cdots, i_M\}$, where N and M denote the number of users and items. $G = (\mathcal{W}, \mathcal{E})$ is represented as the user-item interaction graph where $\mathcal{W}$ is the node sets. $\mathcal{W}$ is divided into two parts including user node $u_k \in \mathcal{W}_u, k = \{1, \ldots, N\}$ and item node $i_j \in \mathcal{W}_i, j = \{1, \ldots, M\}$. Edge $(u_k, i_j) \in \mathcal{E}$ is directed from a user node u_k to an item node i_j. We divide the user-item interaction graph into the set of graph snapshots, i.e., $G = \{G^1, G^2, \cdots, G^T\}$, where T denotes the number of snapshots. $G^t = (\mathcal{W}^t, \mathcal{E}^t)$ is the temporal graph as the graph of all edges occurring up to time t. We focus on modeling the multi-interests from the evolution of the user-item interaction graph and recommend a list of items that maximize the user's future needs.

3.2   Model Framework

In order to model the collaboration signals from the user behavior data directly, we propose the EGIM, as shown in Fig. 1. The basic idea of EGIM is to simulate the evolution of user interest and generate a final interest representation for each user. The details of each layer will be explained in the following sections.

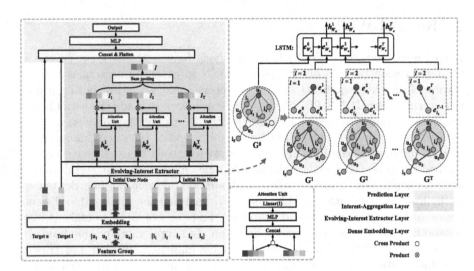

Fig. 1. The architecture of EGIM. Overall, from the bottom up, it can be divided into four layers: 1. Dense Embedding Layer, which projects sparse feature group into low-dimensional vectors. 2. Evolving-Interest Extractor Layer, which extracts interest sequence with the evolution embedding mechanism. 3. Interest-Aggregation Layer, which captures the relative interest with the target item. 4. Prediction Layer, which contains DNN to do CTR prediction.

Dense Embedding Layer. EGIM apply the same method as mainstream to parameterize the feature group into a holistic representation [5,12]. We divide the raw data into two groups: user feature group and item feature group. The embedding layer performs appropriate bucket transformation on continuous features and converts discrete features into one-hot or multi-hot encoding. After concatenating the continuous features and discrete features, FNN network [17] can be used to map the high-dimension vectors to low-dimension vectors. User (item) embedding vector is represented by $\mathbf{e}_{u_k} \in \mathbb{R}^d$ ($\mathbf{e}_{i_j} \in \mathbb{R}^d$), where d represents the embedding size. This method can be viewed as constructing a matrix as an embedded lookup table:

$$\mathbf{e}_\mathcal{W} = [\underbrace{\mathbf{e}_{u_1}, \cdots, \mathbf{e}_{u_N}}_{\mathbf{e}_{\mathcal{W}_u}}, \underbrace{\mathbf{e}_{i_1}, \cdots, \mathbf{e}_{i_M}}_{\mathbf{e}_{\mathcal{W}_i}}], \tag{1}$$

where $\mathbf{e}_{\mathcal{W}_u} \in \mathbb{R}^{N \times d}$ and $\mathbf{e}_{\mathcal{W}_i} \in \mathbb{R}^{M \times d}$. Since the process of producing embedding slow down the convergence speed of the entire work, we apply the pre-training procedure to complete embedding table. $\mathbf{E}^0$ will be used for the initial embedding of users and items on the first snapshot.

Evolving-Interest Extractor Layer. In this section, our goal is to simulate the user's evolving interest from the user-item interaction graph. To this end, we designed the Evolving-Interest Extractor Layer with aggregating neighbors and the evolution embedding mechanism.

Research has shown that the interacted items provide direct evidence about the user's interest [8]. Based on this, in EGIM, user embedding is related to user interest. As high-order collaborative signals can be extracted by GCN, we apply the aggregate function on snapshot to enrich the node's representation. Taking users $\mathcal{U}$ on the snapshot $G^t = (\mathcal{W}^t, \mathcal{E}^t)$ as an example, the l-th layer of GCN takes $(\mathbf{e}^t_{\mathcal{W}_u})^l$, the embedding of the user node, and $(\mathbf{e}^t_{\mathcal{W}_i})^l, \mathcal{W}_i \in N^t_u$, the embedding of the first-order neighbor, as input to update the node embedding $(\mathbf{e}^t_{\mathcal{W}_u})^{l+1}$. Mathematically write:

$$(\mathbf{e}^t_{\mathcal{W}_u})^{l+1} = \sigma \left((\mathbf{e}^t_{\mathcal{W}_u})^l + \sum_{\mathcal{W}_i \in N^t_u} \frac{1}{\sqrt{|N^t_u|}\sqrt{|N^t_i|}} (\mathbf{e}^t_{\mathcal{W}_i})^l \right), \tag{2}$$

where σ is the nonlinear activation function (typically ReLU) for all layer and the symmetric normalization term $\sum_{\mathcal{W}_i \in N^t_u} \frac{1}{\sqrt{|N^t_u|}\sqrt{|N^t_i|}}$ follows the design of standard GCN [6] to avoid the scale of embedding increasing. The initial embedding matrix comes from the embedded lookup table, i.e., $\mathbf{e}^0_{\mathcal{W}_u} \in \mathbf{E}^0$ ($\mathbf{e}^0_{\mathcal{W}_i} \in \mathbf{E}^0$). With reference to the studies [7,14], simple aggregation can improve the generalization ability of GCN model. We apply the sum aggregator function and discard feature transformation. So the number of parameters will not increase as the number of snapshots increases. After aggregation, EGIM incrementally builds the embedding of snapshot at time t from the embedding of snapshot at time $t-1$. The reason will be discussed further in Sect. 3.3. User embedding sequence $S = \{\mathbf{e}^0_{\mathcal{W}_u}, \mathbf{e}^1_{\mathcal{W}_u} \dots, \mathbf{e}^T_{\mathcal{W}_u}\}$ are acquired after multiple iterations on the set of graph snapshots.

When user interests change over time, we need to ensure that EGIM can simulate the change process. Our goal is to perform sequence learning from the user embedding sequence $S = \{\mathbf{e}^0_{\mathcal{W}_u}, \mathbf{e}^1_{\mathcal{W}_u} \dots, \mathbf{e}^T_{\mathcal{W}_u}\}$ obtained by Eq. 2. EGIM apply LSTM to match user embedding sequence and generates hidden states. The hidden state $\mathbf{h}^t_{\mathcal{W}_u}$, which refer to the user interest at time t, is described as follow:

$$\mathbf{h}^t_{\mathcal{W}_u} = LSTM \left(\mathbf{h}^{t-1}_{\mathcal{W}_u}, \mathbf{e}^t_{\mathcal{W}_u} \right), \tag{3}$$

where $\mathbf{h}^{t-1}_{\mathcal{W}_u}$ is the hidden state of previous LSTM cells, and $\mathbf{e}^t_{\mathcal{W}_u}$ is the the user embedding at time t, and $LSTM (,)$ is the combination function combining both sources of information. It is defined as follows:

$$\begin{aligned}
f_t &= \sigma \left(W_f \cdot \left[\mathbf{h}^{t-1}_{\mathcal{W}_u}, \mathbf{e}^t_{\mathcal{W}_u} \right] + b_f \right) \\
i_t &= \sigma \left(W_i \cdot \left[\mathbf{h}^{t-1}_{\mathcal{W}_u}, \mathbf{e}^t_{\mathcal{W}_u} \right] + b_i \right) \\
o_t &= \sigma \left(W_o \cdot \left[\mathbf{h}^{t-1}_{\mathcal{W}_u}, \mathbf{e}^t_{\mathcal{W}_u} \right] + b_o \right) \\
\tilde{C}_t &= \tanh \left(W_C \cdot \left[\mathbf{h}^{t-1}_{\mathcal{W}_u}, \mathbf{e}^t_{\mathcal{W}_u} \right] + b_C \right) \\
C_t &= f_t \circ C_{t-1} + i_t \circ \tilde{C}_t \\
\mathbf{h}^t_{\mathcal{W}_u} &= o_t \circ \tanh (C_t),
\end{aligned} \tag{4}$$

where W_f, W_i, W_o, W_C are the weight matrices. b_f, b_i, b_o, b_C are the bias, $\circ$ denotes the element-wise multiplication. At time $T+1$, the output of LSTM is considered as the user's interest sequence.

Interest-Aggregation Layer. Inspired by DIN [19], the attention unit can be used to capture the relevance of the user interest sequence with respect to the target item, as shown in the right bottom of Fig. 1. Thus, the user's final interest representation I can be formulated as:

$$I = \sum_{t=1}^{T} I_t = \sum_{t=1}^{T} w_t h_{\mathcal{W}_u}^t = \sum_{t=1}^{T} a\left(h_{\mathcal{W}_u}^t, e_{\mathcal{W}_i}^0\right) h_{\mathcal{W}_u}^t, \qquad (5)$$

where the attention unit, $a\,()$, takes the hidden state $h_{\mathcal{W}_u}^t$ and target item embedding $e_{\mathcal{W}_i}^0$ as input. They are concatenated and then transformed into a vector. Then we apply a cross-product to the concatenated vector. The result together with the original vector are fed into a fully-connected network. The final output is a scalar which indicates to what extent is the interest relevant to the target item.

Prediction Layer. In the end, we leverage a prediction layer where all the features vectors, $e_{\mathcal{W}_u}^0$, $e_{\mathcal{W}_i}^0$ and I are concatenated and fed into the MLP layer for final prediction. $\hat{y}_{ui}$ is the score which reflects the preference of user u for item i and it is defined as:

$$\hat{y}_{ui} = \sigma\left(W_l[e_{\mathcal{W}_u}^0, e_{\mathcal{W}_i}^0, I] + b_l\right), \qquad (6)$$

where W_l is the weight matrix. b_l is the bias.

3.3   Interest Propagation

User behavior data are divided into multiple snapshots. In the set of snapshots, the user's interaction will change over time. To deal with this interest transfer problem and model the collaboration signals, we introduce an interest propagation mechanism in which using the information processed by the previous snapshot as the initialization of the current snapshot. Now suppose that the depth of GCN is l and detailed analysis follows:

$$\begin{aligned}
E^t &= \sigma\left((E^{t-1})^l + A^{t-1} \cdot (E^{t-1})^l\right) \\
&= \sigma\left((E^{t-1})^l \cdot (I + A^{t-1})\right) \\
&= \sigma\left((E^{t-1})^l \cdot \tilde{A}^{t-1}\right) \\
&= \sigma\left(\sigma\left((E^{t-1})^{l-1} \cdot \tilde{A}^{t-1}\right) \cdot \tilde{A}^{t-1}\right),
\end{aligned} \qquad (7)$$

$$E^{t-1} = \sigma\left(\sigma\left((E^{t-2})^{l-1} \cdot \tilde{A}^{t-2}\right) \cdot \tilde{A}^{t-2}\right), \qquad (8)$$

where $\mathbf{A}^{t-1}$ and $\mathbf{A}^{t-2}$ ($\mathbf{A} \in R^{(M+N)*(M+N)}$) are the adjacency matrix of the snapshot $\mathcal{G}^{t-1}$ and $\mathcal{G}^{t-2}$. $\tilde{\mathbf{A}}^{t-1} = \mathbf{A}^{t-1}+\mathbf{I}$ and $\tilde{\mathbf{A}}^{t-2} = \mathbf{A}^{t-2}+\mathbf{I}$ are the adjacency matrix with self-connections, and $\mathbf{E}^{t-1}$ and $\mathbf{E}^{t-2}$ are embedded lookup table of nodes and the shape of $\mathbf{E}^{t-1}$ is $R^{(M+N)*d}$. For Eq. 7 and Eq. 8, in fact, it can be understood as time-sharing aggregation of item information, which essentially means that user embedding aggregates item information in chronological order:

$$\mathbf{e}_{\mathcal{W}_u}^T = \sum_{t=1}^{T} \sigma \left(\sum_{i \in N_u^t} \mathbf{e}_{\mathcal{W}_i}^t \right) \tag{9}$$

In each update process, the item embedding will contain the others information on the previous snapshot. So we objectively connect multiple snapshots to reflect the evolution of user interests and to capture high-order collaborative signals. The above derivation shows that propagating embedding on two adjacent snapshots is essentially equivalent to achieving interest propagation operations.

3.4 Network Learning

To learn the model parameters, we followed the cross-entropy loss function, which has been intensively used in CTR prediction. The loss function is as follows:

$$\text{Loss} = \sum_{u,i \in \mathcal{W}, j \in \mathcal{W}^{\circ}} - \ln \sigma \left(\hat{y}_{ui} - \hat{y}_{uj} \right) + \lambda \|\Theta\|_2^2, \tag{10}$$

where $\hat{y}_{ui}$ and $\hat{y}_{uj}$ represent the user's preference score over positive item i and negative item j, $\mathcal{W}^{\circ}$ represents a negative item set and Θ represents all of the model parameters while λ is the regularization terms to prevent over-fitting.

For the selection of negative samples, this is formed by the items that are more than 1 unit ($u_k - i_j$ or $i_j - u_k$, which is a unit distance) apart from the target user in the user-item interaction graph (this graph is built from the entire training data). The number is K. Then, we sort the item set in descending order according to the number. The sampling is based on the Zipfian distribution. For item i with index $index$, The probability to be sampled is as follows:

$$P(\text{ index }) = \frac{\ln(\text{index} + 2) - \ln(\text{index} + 1)}{\ln(K+1)}, \tag{11}$$

where the denominator is all the same and the numerators are decrease sequentially, i,e. $\ln(2/1)$, $\ln(3/2)$ ... $\ln(D + 1/D)$. The sum of $P(\text{ index })$ is 1. That means the higher the ranking, the greater the probability of being sampled.

4 Experiments

In this section, we conduct experiments on three real-world datasets to evaluate EGIM and aim to answer the following research questions:

- **RQ1:** How does EGIM perform as compared with the most advanced methods?
- **RQ2:** How do the interest propagation and the evolution embedding mechanisms perform?
- **RQ3:** How do hyperparameters affect the performance of EGIM?

4.1 Experimental Settings

Dataset. We use real-world data collected from three well-known websites. The basic statistics are listed in Table 1. The Debiasing dataset[1] is from KDDCUP 2020 competition. It is a user-click dataset. The MUBI dataset[2] was collected to predict the popularity of movies. The Cloud-Theme dataset[3] contains more than 1.3 million click data from 355 different topics. We exclude users whose number of historical interactions are less than 5, and items that only appear in the test set and validation set.

Baselines. We compare our model with the following competitive benchmark.

- **NCF** [8]: This method use deep learning to model the interaction between user and item features.
- **Deep&Cross** [12]: The method divide features into low-order and high-order to learn sophisticated feature interactions in CTR predictions.
- **NGCF** [13]: This method realizes the explicit representation of users and items by encoding high-level connectivity in the user-item interaction graph.
- **DIN** [19]: This method apply an attention-based method to capture relative interests from the user behavior sequence with regard to the candidate item.
- **DIEN** [18]: The method combines improved RNN method to model users' sequential actions and capture the user's dynamic interest.

Table 1. Datasets statistics.

Dataset	Users	Items	Interactions	Density
Debiasing	21049	44764	756637	0.00035
MUBI	12583	38538	401310	0.00031
Cloud-Theme	19879	68870	1389911	0.00106

Evaluation Indicators. In order to evaluate the performance of methods, we adopt two metrics widely used in the recommendation tasks: Recall@K and Normalized Discounted Cumulative Gain (NDCG@K).

---

[1] https://tianchi.aliyun.com/competition.

[2] https://www.kaggle.com/clementmsika/mubi-sqlite-database-for-movie-lovers.

[3] https://tianchi.aliyun.com/dataset/dataDetail?dataId=9716.

Parameter Settings. Each of datasets is divided into training sets (70% of data), validation sets (10% of data), and test sets (20% of data) in chronological order. For all models, the batch size is set to 200. The initial learning rate is set to 0.005, and adjust it in $\{0.001, 0.0025, 0.01, 0.05, 0.1\}$. The dimensions of the embedding is searched in $\{25, 50, 100, 150, 200\}$. The depth of GCN is searched in $\{1, 2, 3, 4\}$ and the number of snapshots will be adjusted in $\{35, 25, 50\}$. We cross-validated the number of hidden units for LSTM, and the performance is stable at about 100. Moreover, if Recall@20 on the validation sets does not increase for 10 epochs, we employ the early stopping strategy.

4.2 Comparison of Performance (RQ1)

We compare the performance of all model. Table 2 reports the overall performance of all models, where bold fonts represents the best result among all methods. From this table, we have the following observations:

Table 2. The overall performances of all models on three datasets.

Methods	Debiasing		MUBI		Cloud-Theme	
	NDCG@20	Recall@20	NDCG@20	Recall@20	NDCG@20	Recall@20
NCF	0.09629	0.09917	0.16214	0.17183	0.06215	0.06691
NGCF	0.12923	0.13751	0.18223	0.19481	0.09647	0.09816
Deep& Cross	0.18134	0.18992	0.19901	0.20882	0.13407	0.14001
DIN	0.19503	0.20078	0.20406	0.21250	0.15827	0.16217
DIEN	0.19563	0.20488	0.20601	0.21698	0.13797	0.14118
EGIM-L	0.16364	0.17268	0.19613	0.20688	0.12218	0.13123
EGIM-D	0.18743	0.19891	0.18501	0.19622	0.14242	0.15520
EGIM	**0.20741**	**0.21283**	**0.22826**	**0.22834**	**0.16044**	**0.16921**

Deep&Cross consistently achieve good performance than the CF-based methods (NCF and NGCF) across all cases. This shows that the CF based method will limit the performance when it uses random initialization for embedding without considering features. the performance of DIN is better than Deep&Cross. The reason is that DIN introduce the relative interests with regard to the candidate item and use candidate items to guide representation learning. RNN-based method (DIEN) is superior to DIN. This verifies the importance of LSTM to capture evolutionary signals in sequence learning.

Finally, the performance of our model EGIM outperforms all baselines on the three datasets. For instance, EGIM improves more than 3.8% in terms of recall@20 compared with the second-best method DIEN on the Debiasing. This indicates that simulating the evolution of user interest on the user-item graph is essentially simulating the evolution of the high-order collaboration signal, not on the interaction items. So the embedded evolution mechanism can capture the fine-grained change of user interests.

4.3 Influence of Mechanisms (RQ2)

In this section, to evaluate the contribution of interest representation mechanism, we compared EGIM with two different variants, i.e., EGIM-L and EGIM-D. EGIM-L uses node embedding in the last snapshot to represent the user's final representation, which means that evolutionary embedding mechanism is not considered. EGIM-D abandons initialization to connect adjacent snapshots, which means that the user's interest propagation is ignored. The results are shown in Table 2.

We can see that any changes of the model can degrade performance. Specifically, EGIM is superior to EGIM-L, w.r.t. recall@20 by 23.25%, 10.38%, and 28.94% in Debiasing, MUBI and Cloud-Theme, respectively. This improvement is due to LSTM capturing the evolution of users' overall tastes and the diversity of users' preferences. Next, due to the poor performance of EGIM-D, we think that EGIM-D lacks interest propagation mechanism, so it is unable to integrate user information. It is difficult for EGIM-D to model collaboration signals in user behavior data, which leads to poor representation.

4.4 Hyper-Parameter Influence (RQ3)

The Depth of the GCN. EGIM aggregates collaboration signal through GCN. Considering the depth of GCN may affect the ability to extract features from the interaction graph, we tune the depth of GCN in $\{1, 2, 3, 4\}$ to verify the impact on model performance. The result can be seen from Fig. 2.

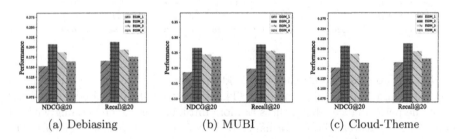

(a) Debiasing   (b) MUBI   (c) Cloud-Theme

Fig. 2. Influence of the depth of GCN

When using single layer, we find that the performance is significantly reduced. This implies the user with similar behavior are important for recommendations. Then, increasing the depth of GCN can improve the Recall@20 and NDCG@20, the evaluation indicators reaches the maximum value. However, when the propagation layers are stacked further, The performance of EGIM-3 and EGIM-4 began to decline. This might be due to the applying too deep architecture. As a result, the model seems to be over-fitting. Therefore, we set the optimal depth of GCN to 2 for our datasets.

The Number of Snapshots. We're also working on the effects of snapshots. In this experiment, the number of snapshots is from 1 to 70 for the training task. The results are shown in Fig. 3. We find that the performance of EGIM continues to improve, and then decreased. It can be summarized as the following reason: At the beginning, the number of snapshot sets used for training is small, which is equivalent to performing convolution operation on the whole user interaction data. So the sequence information is limited. With the increase of the number of snapshots, the performance of EGIM gradually increases. When the number of snapshots reaches a fixed value, the performance begins to decline, because the data is too sparse to aggregate domain information. So we set the snapshot number of three datasets to $\{35, 25, 50\}$, which can maximize the utilization of data information.

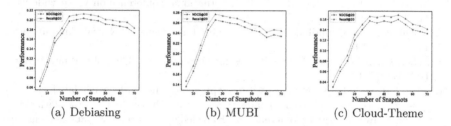

(a) Debiasing   (b) MUBI   (c) Cloud-Theme

Fig. 3. Influence of the number of snapshots.

5   Conclusion

In this paper, we proposed a new EGIM model based on the evolution of the user-item interaction graph. This model represents the user's historical interaction as evolution graph. The key of EGIM is to simulate the fine-grained change of user interests by modeling the user interest sequence. Extensive experiments on three real-world datasets demonstrate that EGIM has more accurate recommendations compared with several state-of-the-art models. In the future, we will plan to improve the processing of the evolution graph and convert the user-item interaction into an event-based continuous dynamic network. This will be beneficial to interpret the reasoning of user interaction behavior more effectively.

References

1. Cheng, H.T., et al.: Wide & deep learning for recommender systems. In: Proceedings of the 1st workshop on deep learning for recommender systems, pp. 7–10 (2016)
2. Cho, K., et al.: Learning phrase representations using rnn encoder-decoder for statistical machine translation. arXiv preprint arXiv:1406.1078 (2014)

3. Defferrard, M., Bresson, X., Vandergheynst, P.: Convolutional neural networks on graphs with fast localized spectral filtering. In: Advances in neural information processing systems, pp. 3844–3852 (2016)
4. Feng, Y., et al.: Deep session interest network for click-through rate prediction. arXiv preprint arXiv:1905.06482 (2019)
5. Guo, H., Tang, R., Ye, Y., Li, Z., He, X.: DeepFM: a factorization-machine based neural network for ctr prediction. arXiv preprint arXiv:1703.04247 (2017)
6. Hamilton, W., Ying, Z., Leskovec, J.: Inductive representation learning on large graphs. In: Advances in neural information processing systems, pp. 1024–1034 (2017)
7. He, X., Deng, K., Wang, X., Li, Y., Zhang, Y., Wang, M.: LightGCN: simplifying and powering graph convolution network for recommendation. arXiv preprint arXiv:2002.02126 (2020)
8. He, X., Liao, L., Zhang, H., Nie, L., Hu, X., Chua, T.S.: Neural collaborative filtering. In: Proceedings of the 26th international conference on world wide web, pp. 173–182 (2017)
9. Hochreiter, S., Schmidhuber, J.: Long short-term memory. Neural Comput. **9**(8), 1735–1780 (1997)
10. Seber, G.A., Lee, A.J.: Linear Regression Analysis, vol. 329. John Wiley & Sons, Hoboken (2012)
11. Wang, H., et al.: Knowledge-aware graph neural networks with label smoothness regularization for recommender systems. In: Proceedings of the 25th ACM SIGKDD International Conference on Knowledge Discovery & Data Mining, pp. 968–977 (2019)
12. Wang, R., Fu, B., Fu, G., Wang, M.: Deep & cross network for ad click predictions. In: Proceedings of the ADKDD 2017, pp. 1–7 (2017)
13. Wang, X., He, X., Wang, M., Feng, F., Chua, T.S.: Neural graph collaborative filtering. In: Proceedings of the 42nd international ACM SIGIR conference on Research and development in Information Retrieval, pp. 165–174 (2019)
14. Wu, F., Zhang, T., Souza, J.R.D., Fifty, C., Yu, T., Weinberger, K.Q.: Simplifying graph convolutional networks. arXiv preprint arXiv:1902.07153 (2019)
15. Wu, L., Sun, P., Fu, Y., Hong, R., Wang, X., Wang, M.: A neural influence diffusion model for social recommendation. In: Proceedings of the 42nd international ACM SIGIR conference on research and development in information retrieval, pp. 235–244 (2019)
16. Xu, C., et al.: Graph contextualized self-attention network for session-based recommendation. In: IJCAI, pp. 3940–3946 (2019)
17. Zhang, W., Du, T., Wang, J.: Deep learning over multi-field categorical data. In: Ferro, N., Crestani, F., Moens, M.-F., Mothe, J., Silvestri, F., Di Nunzio, G.M., Hauff, C., Silvello, G. (eds.) ECIR 2016. LNCS, vol. 9626, pp. 45–57. Springer, Cham (2016). https://doi.org/10.1007/978-3-319-30671-1_4
18. Zhou, G., et al.: Deep interest evolution network for click-through rate prediction. In: Proceedings of the AAAI conference on artificial intelligence, vol. 33, pp. 5941–5948 (2019)
19. Zhou, G., et al.: Deep interest network for click-through rate prediction. In: Proceedings of the 24th ACM SIGKDD International Conference on Knowledge Discovery & Data Mining, pp. 1059–1068 (2018)

Visualizing the Finer Cluster Structure of Large-Scale and High-Dimensional Data

Yu Liang$^{(\boxtimes)}$ (iD), Arin Chaudhuri (iD), and Haoyu Wang (iD)

IoT Analytics, SAS Inc., 701 SAS Campus Dr, Cary, NC 27513, USA
{yu.liang,Arin.Chaudhuri,haoyu.wang}@sas.com

Abstract. Dimension reduction and visualization of high-dimensional data have become very important research topics because of the rapid growth of large databases with high dimensions in data science. A successful dimension reduction and visualization method seeks to produce a low-dimensional representation of high-dimensional data that preserves both the global and local structure of the data. In this paper, we propose using a generalized sigmoid function to model the distance similarity in both high- and low-dimensional space. In particular, a single parameter v is introduced to the generalized sigmoid function in low-dimensional space, so that we can adjust the slope and the heaviness of the function tail by changing the value of the parameter easily. Using real-world data sets with different sample sizes and dimensions, we show that our proposed method can generate visualization results that are competitive with those of the state-of-the-art methods, such as uniform manifold approximation and projection (UMAP), t-distributed stochastic neighbor embedding (t-SNE), and related methods. In addition, by adjusting the value of v, our proposed method can preserve more of both the global and finer cluster structure of the data. Furthermore, like UMAP, our proposed method can easily scale to massive high-dimensional data. Finally, we use domain knowledge to demonstrate that the finer subclusters that are revealed with small values of v are meaningful.

Keywords: Data visualization · Manifold learning · Nonlinear dimension reduction · Cluster structure · Generalized sigmoid function

1 Introduction

Dimension reduction and visualization of high-dimensional data have become very important research topics in many scientific fields because of the rapid growth of data sets with large sample size and/or dimensions [6,8]. In the literature of dimension reduction and information visualization, linear methods such as principal component analysis (PCA) [10] and classical scaling [23] mainly focus on preserving the most significant structure or maximum variance in data; nonlinear methods such as multidimensional scaling [3], isomap [22], and curvilinear component analysis (CCA) [7] mainly focus on preserving the long or short

© Springer Nature Switzerland AG 2021
H. Qiu et al. (Eds.): KSEM 2021, LNAI 12817, pp. 361–372, 2021.
https://doi.org/10.1007/978-3-030-82153-1_30

distances in the high-dimensional space. They generally perform well in preserving the global structure of data but can fail to preserve the local structure. In recent years, the manifold learning methods, such as SNE [9], Laplacian eigenmaps [2], LINE [20], LARGEVIS [19], t-SNE and related methods [14,15,24], and UMAP [16], have gained popularity because of their ability to preserve both the local structure and some aspects of the global structure of data. These methods generally assume that data lie on a low-dimensional manifold of the high-dimensional input space. They attempt to find the manifold that preserves the intrinsic structure of the high-dimensional data.

Many of the manifold learning methods suffer from something called the "crowding problem" while preserving local distance of high-dimensional data in low-dimensional space. This means that if you want to describe small distances in high-dimensional space faithfully, the points with moderate or large distances between them in high-dimensional space are placed too far away from each other in low-dimensional space. Therefore, in the visualization, the points with small or moderate distances between them crash together. To solve this problem, UNI-SNE [5] adds a slight repulsion strength to any pair of points in low-dimensional space to prevent the points from moving too far away from each other. Alternatively, in low-dimensional space, t-SNE [15,24] uses Student's t-distribution, which has a heavy tail compared with the Gaussian distribution used in high-dimensional space. Kobak et al. [12] further extended the idea to use the t-distribution with one degree of freedom v. They show that for some data sets, setting $v < 1$ would reveal additional local structure of the data compared with Student's t-distribution with $v = 1$. However, these kinds of methods usually fail to preserve the global and topological structure of the data. To capture both the global and local structure of the data, UMAP uses a curve that is similar to the t-distribution but with two hyperparameters in low-dimensional space. By minimizing the cross entropy loss function, UMAP maintains both the global and local structure of the data.

Although the big success of UMAP in preserving the relevant structure of high-dimensional data, we found that, for some cases, the conventional UMAP might fail to reveal the finer cluster structure of the data. For instance, for Fashion-MNIST dataset, UMAP successfully classifies the data into four big categories (bags, footwear, trousers and other clothing). However, it fails in further differentiating the subclusters within footwear (boots, sneakers, and sandals), and subclusters within clothing (dresses, coats, and etc.). This motivates us to consider other function to model the distance similarity in high- and low-dimensional spaces. The function needs to keep certain repulsive strength even when the distance between two points is small, and thus helps us to represent the finer cluster structure of data. In the meantime, the function need to have small number of parameters which can be easily tuned.

In this work, we propose using a generalized sigmoid function [4] to model the membership strength of two points with distance x in the low-dimensional space. Specifically, we consider the following function

$$Q(x) = \frac{1.0}{\left[1.0 + (2^{1/v} - 1)x\right]^{v}} \tag{1}$$

Because parameter v controls the rate of the curve approaching 0 and 1, adjusting the value of v can affect the embeddings in low-dimensional space and the data visualization. To understand how the family of Eq. (1) behaves with varying v, we draw plots by setting $v = 0.5, 1, 2, 5, 10$. The results are summarized in Fig. 1.

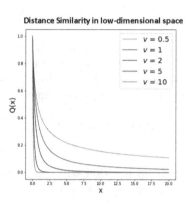

Fig. 1. The distance similarity in low-dimensional space is modeled by the function in Eq. (1). The graph shows the curve changes with $v = 0.5, 1, 2, 5, 10$.

We can see from the graph that the smaller the v value is, the more heavy-tailed the curve is. The heavy-tailed property of the curve can greatly alleviate the crowding problem. In addition, the smaller the v value is, the flatter the curve is. It means that when the distance between two points is small, there are still some repulsive strength to separate them. It thus provides more possibility of revealing the finer structure of the data. However, when the value of v approaches zero, the limit of the function is 0.5 when $x > 0$, and 1 when $x = 0$. Such a discontinuity will cause that each data point in the low-dimensional space becomes isolated. Therefore choosing a proper value for parameter v is important for a successful and meaningful embedding.

The advantages of our proposed method are in the following three aspects. First, we use a simple generalized sigmoid function to model the distance similarity in the low-dimensional space, which is indexed by a single parameter v. We can adjust the slope and heaviness of the function tail by changing the value of v directly. Second, we use real-world data sets to show that our proposed method can generate visualization results that are competitive with those of UMAP and t-SNE and its related methods. In addition, the value of v can be easily adjusted either to reveal the finer cluster structure of the data or to assist the visualization of data by increasing the continuity of neighbors. Third, for some data sets, decreasing the value of v can provide greater visibility of the intrinsic structure of the data that might not be visible using conventional UMAP or t-SNE. Furthermore, we use domain knowledge to demonstrate that the finer subclusters are meaningful.

The remainder of this paper is organized as follows. The algorithm of our proposed method is presented in Sect. 2. In Sect. 3, we illustrate the usage of our proposed method with different v values for various real data. The comparisons of our embeddings with other state-of-the-art methods are also presented in Sect. 3. Section 4 concludes the paper.

2   Methodology

Let $X = \{x_1, \ldots, x_N\}$ be N input data in high-dimensional space R^D, and let $d(x_i, x_j)$ be the distance between x_i and x_j under the metric $d : X \times X \to \mathbb{R}_{\geq 0}$. Let $N(x_i)$ be the k-nearest neighbors of x_i, and let ρ_i be the shortest distance from x_i to its k-nearest neighbors. Here ρ_i is defined as

$$\rho_i = \min\{d(x_i, x_j) | d(x_i, x_j) > 0, x_j \in N(x_i),$$
$$1 \leq j \leq k\}, \quad 1 \leq i \leq N$$

For each x_i, we use the sigmoid function with the parameter σ_i to model the distance similarity between points x_i and x_j, which is

$$P_{j|i} = \begin{cases} \dfrac{1.0}{1.0 + \frac{\max(0, d(x_i, x_j) - \rho_i)}{\sigma_i}} & \text{if } x_j \in N(x_i) \\ 0 & \text{otherwise} \end{cases}$$

Using the similar approach as UMAP, we can determine the value of σ_i by solving the following equation:

$$\sum_{j=1}^{k} P_{j|i} = \log_2(k)$$

For the simplicity of optimizing the loss function and also extracting more structure information in high-dimensional space, $P(j|i)$ is symmetrized as

$$P_{ij} = P_{j|i} + P_{i|j} - P_{i|j} \odot P_{j|i}$$

where $\odot$ stands for componentwise multiplication. In addition, let $P_{N \times N}$ denote the matrix of P_{ij}.

Let $Y = \{y_1, \ldots, y_N\}$ denote the representation of X in low-dimensional space R^d. We assume that the membership strength of y_i and y_j in the low-dimensional space can be modeled using the generalized sigmoid function (1). That is

$$Q(i, j) = \frac{1.0}{\left[1.0 + (2^{1/v} - 1)\|y_i - y_j\|_2\right]^v} \tag{2}$$

where $\|a\|_2$ is the L_2-norm of a vector a.

Algorithm 1

Input: Data set X, N, k, d, v
Output: Embedding Y in dimension R^d.

1: **for** $i = 1$ **to** N **do**
2:     Find the k-nearest neighbors for x_i in X.
3:     **for** $j = 1$ **to** k **do**
4:         Calculate $P_{j|i}$ for each x_j in the k-nearest neighbors of x_i.
5:     **end for**
6: **end for**
7: Calculate the symmetric matrix $P_{N \times N}$
8: Initialize embedding Y.
9: Optimize Y by minimizing the loss function using stochastic gradient descent algorithm with negative samplings.

As with the probabilistic model [19], the loss function can be written as

$$L = - \left(\sum_{(x_i, x_j) \in E} P_{ij} \log Q(i,j) + \sum_{(x_i, x_j) \notin E} \log(1 - Q(i,j)) \right) \tag{3}$$

where E is the collection of points (x_i, x_j) for which either $x_i \in N(x_j)$ or $x_j \in N(x_i)$. Using the negative sampling strategy proposed by [17], the loss function can be further written as

$$L = - \left(\sum_{(x_i, x_j) \in E} P_{ij} \log Q(i,j) + \sum_{k=1}^{M} \log(1 - Q(i,k)) \right) \tag{4}$$

where M is the number of negative samples for each vertex i. The gradient of the loss function can be written as

$$\frac{\partial L}{\partial y_i} = - \left(\sum_{(i,j) \in E} P_{ij} \frac{\partial Q(i,j)/\partial y_i}{Q(i,j)} - \sum_{k=1}^{M} \frac{\partial Q(i,k)/\partial y_i}{(1 - Q(i,k))} \right)$$

where

$$\partial Q(i,j)/\partial y_i = -v \left(1.0 + (2^{\frac{1}{v}} - 1)\|y_i - y_j\|_2 \right)^{-v-1} (2^{\frac{1}{v}} - 1)\|y_i - y_j\|_2^{-1}(y_i - y_j)$$

The stochastic gradient descent algorithm is used to optimize the loss function. The whole algorithm is illustrated in Algorithm 1.

3   Experimental Results

To study the embeddings generated using our proposed method with different v values, we consider the following real data sets with either large or small sample sizes:

- MNIST [13]: Data set includes 70,000 images of the handwritten digits 0–9. Each image is 28×28 pixels in size.
- Fashion-MNIST [25]: Data set includes 70,000 images of 10 classes of fashion items (clothing, footwear, and bags). Because the images are gray-scale images, 28×28 pixels in size, the feature dimension is 784.
- Epileptic Seizure Recognition data set [1]: Data set includes EEG recording at 178 time points for 11,500 subjects. The subjects can be classified into five categories. Only the subjects in category 1 have epileptic seizures. The main purpose of the study is to differentiate the patients with and without epileptic seizures.
- COIL-20 [18]: Data set includes 1,440 gray-scale images, 28×28 pixels in size, of 20 objects under 72 rotations spanning 360 degrees.
- Single-cell RNA-sequencing data [21]: The original data set from the reference consists of 23,822 single cells from two regions of an adult mouse cortex. Every data point includes the counts of RNA transcripts from each of 45,768 genes. According to the author, the genes can be classified into 133 transcriptomic types. Following [11] and [12], the data are preprocessed, and the 5,000 most significant genes are selected for analysis.

For all the data sets, we considered Euclidean distance. We set $k = 10$ (10 nearest neighbors) and vary v values from 1, 2, 5, to 10. The initial values of the embedding are set to be the eigenvectors of the normalized Laplacian. The visualizations are summarized in Fig. 2.

We can see from the graphs that when $v = 1$, the clusters for each data set have the greatest separation and the greatest distance. For example, all the digits are separated into distinct clusters in the MNIST data set when $v = 1$. With the increases in the value of v, the distances between different digits get smaller and smaller. Some digits, such as 4, 7, and 9, and 3, 5, and 8, join together eventually. Based on the embeddings, we use k-means to do classification and find that when $v = 1$ and $v = 2$, we get the smallest error, 4.4%.

For the Fashion-MNIST data set, with various v values, trousers (red) and bags (blue) always have the greatest distance from each other. In addition, shoes, bags, trousers, and other items (T-shirts, dresses, pullovers, shirts, and coats) are well separated when $v = 1$ or $v = 2$. When $v = 5$ and $v = 10$, bags and other items get much closer to each other. They are not distinct clusters anymore. It is also worth pointing out that when $v = 1$ or $v = 2$, we also see a few subclusters that are invisible when $v = 5$ or $v = 10$. For example, the majority of T-shirts (dark red) and dresses (orange) are separated from coats (yellow), pullovers (vermilion), and shirts (light green); sneakers (green), ankle boots (purple), and sandals (lemon) have some separation as well. In addition, sandals are now separated into two subclusters; one subcluster is close to sneakers, and the other is close to ankle boots. Furthermore, bags (blue) are separated into two subclusters as well.

To verify whether these subclusters are meaningful or not, we randomly sampled 100 images from each of the subclusters that we mentioned earlier and compared the images. We found that the separation of T-shirts and dresses from

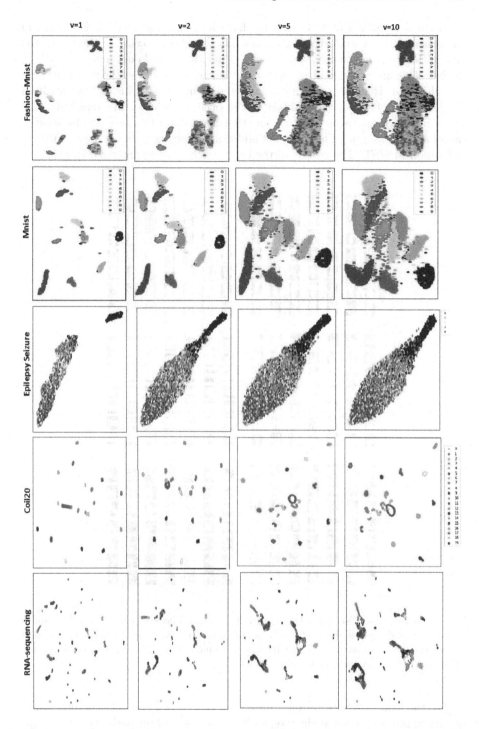

Fig. 2. Visualizations of real-world data sets with $v = 1, 2, 5,$ and 10, respectively. (Color figure online)

other clothing is due to whether they have long or short sleeves. For bags, in one subcluster, the majority of the bags have handles showing at the top of the image. However, in the other subcluster, either the bags do not have a handle or the handle is not showing at the top of the image. In addition, the images of sandals also show that the majority of the sandals in one subcluster have medium or high heels, whereas the sandals in the other subcluster are relatively flat. These image comparisons clearly show that the subclusters revealed by small v values are meaningful. They provide additional insights into the data structure of Fashion-MNIST. The results of the comparisons are summarized in Fig. 3.

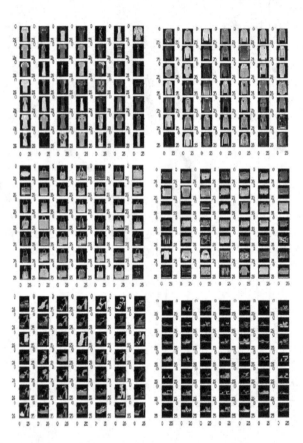

Fig. 3. Image comparisons for Fashion-MNIST data. The first row shows the cluster of T-shirts and dresses versus the cluster of coats, pullovers, and shirts. The second row shows the subclusters of bags with and without handles. The third row shows the subclusters of sandals with and without heels.

For the Epileptic Seizure Recognition data set, when $v = 1$, the embedding is separated into two isolated clusters, with the majority of the patients with epileptic seizures in one cluster and patients without epileptic seizures in the other.

With the increases in the value of v, the clear boundary between patients with and without epileptic seizures disappears, although a majority of the patients with epileptic seizures are still concentrated at the top of the graph.

For the COIL-20 data set, with different v values, the majority of the objects are well separated, except for cars (objects 3, 6, and 19), Anacin, and Tylenol. With the increases in the value of v, the between-class distance for different objects gets smaller and smaller, which can cause problems for data clustering. However, we can see more clearly the circular structure of each object with a higher value of v.

Similar findings can be seen in the single-cell RNA-sequencing data as well. When the v value is large, such as when $v = 5$ or $v = 10$, we can see four big clusters surrounded by some small clusters. The structure approximately agrees with the two-dimensional visualization plot generated using t-SNE [21], but it has a better global structure. Such graphs that are generated with large v values are helpful for studying the general relationship of different gene clusters. However, the overall number of clusters that can be identified is much less than suggested in [21]. (The paper suggests that there are 133 gene clusters.) When we further decrease the value of v, many clusters that were lumped together before are split into disconnected areas, helping us identify more gene clusters. For example, within the L6 gene clusters, there are 15 subclusters. Following [12], we draw the median point of each subcluster on the graphs of $v = 1$ and $v = 5$. On the graphs, those median points match either the isolated points or the small islands of the graphs well (Fig. 4). In addition, we can see that setting $v = 1$ can help us identify more L6 gene subclusters than setting $v = 5$.

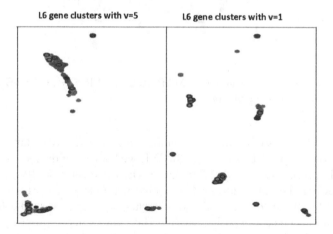

Fig. 4. Visualization of L6 gene subclusters based on $v = 1$ and $v = 5$. The circled points are the median point of each subcluster.

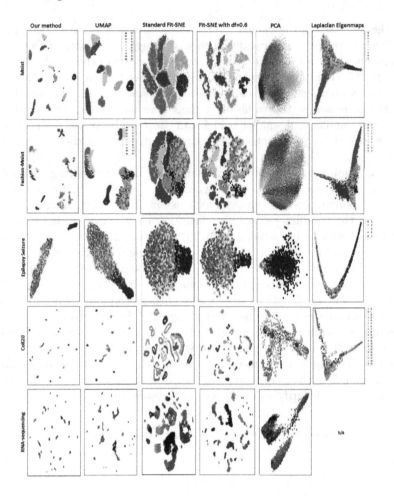

Fig. 5. Visualization comparison with UMAP, standard FIt-SNE, FIt-SNE with $df = 0.6$, PCA, and Laplacian eigenmaps.

In addition, we also compare our embeddings for the real data sets with UMAP, standard FIt-SNE ($df = 1$), FIt-SNE with variable degrees of freedom, PCA, and Laplacian eigenmaps. For our method, we set $k = 10$, $v = 1$, and epochs = 500 for the optimization. Other parameters are set to the default values. For UMAP, we study the embeddings when set min_dist to 0.0001, 0.001, 0.01, 0.1, and 1 while keeping other settings the same as in our proposed method. We found that the lower value of min_dist makes the embeddings in same cluster more densely packed together, and thus generates better separation among different clusters. However, when $min\_dist \leq 0.001$, further decreasing the value of min_dist does not change the embeddings much. So, we only present the results when $min\_dist = 0.001$. For FIt-SNE with variable degrees of freedom, we set $df = 0.6$. In order to get better visualization, we tune the learning rate for different data sets while keeping other parameters at the default values. The results can be seen in Fig. 5.

From the graph we can see that the quality of the embeddings generated using our method is competitive comparing with other methods. Both our method and UMAP has captured more global structure of the data comparing with standard FIt-SNE and FIt-SNE with $df = 0.6$ in the sense that data in different categories have greater distance than data in the same category. In addition, the isolation of different clusters helps the classification of the data. However, comparing with UMAP, our method separates more clusters that are similar to each other and reveal more subtle subclusters such as for Fashion-MNIST, MNIST, Epileptic Seizure Recognition, and single-cell RNA-sequencing data sets. In general, our methods reflects the data better in preserving both the global and finer data structures.

4   Conclusions

In this paper, we proposed using a generalized sigmoid function to model the distance similarity in both high-dimensional and low-dimensional spaces. In particular, the parameter v was introduced to the generalized sigmoid function in low-dimensional space. By changing the value of v, we can adjust the slope and the heaviness of the function tail. Using real data sets with different sample sizes and dimensions, we showed that decreasing the value of v can help reveal the finer cluster structure of the data while at the same time preserving the global structure of the data. Using visualization and domain knowledge, we showed that the subclusters in the MNIST, Fashion-MNIST, Epileptic Seizure Recognition, COIL-20, and single-cell RNA-sequencing data sets are meaningful. In practice, however, a very low value of v might result in the discovery of some clusters of random sampling noise, thus lead to spurious interpretation of the data structure. Practically, there is no unanimous choice of a criterion for selecting the v value. We suggest trying out different v values for data exploration to get a comprehensive understanding of the data.

References

1. Andrzejak, R.G., Lehnertz, K., Mormann, F., Rieke, C., David, P., Elger, C.E.: Indications of nonlinear deterministic and finite-dimensional structures in time series of brain electrical activity: dependence on recording region and brain state. Phys. Rev. E **64**(6) (2001)
2. Belkin, M., Niyogi, P.: Laplacian eigenmaps and spectral techniques for embedding and clustering. In: Advances in Neural Information Processing Systems, Cambridge, MA, pp. 585–591 (2002)
3. Borg, I., Groenen, P.J.: Modern Multidimensional Scaling: Theory and Applications. Springer, New York (2005)
4. Ceriotti, M., Tribello, G.A., Parrinello, M.: Simplifying the representation of complex free-energy landscapes using sketch-map. Proc. Natl. Acad. Sci. **108**(32), 13023–13028 (2011)

5. Cook, J., Sutskever, I., Mnih, A., Hinton, G.: Visualizing similarity data with a mixture of maps. In: Proceeding of the 11th International Conference on Artificial Intelligence and Statistics, San Juan, Puerto Rico, pp. 67–74 (2007)
6. Dai, W., Qiu, L., Wu, A., Qiu, M.: Cloud infrastructure resource allocation for big data applications. IEEE Trans. Big Data 4(3), 313–324 (2016)
7. Demartines, P., Hérault, J.: Curvilinear component analysis: a self-organizing neural network for nonlinear mapping of data sets. IEEE Trans. Neural Netw. 8(1), 148–154 (1997)
8. Gai, K., Qiu, M.: Reinforcement learning-based content-centric services in mobile sensing. IEEE Netw. 32(4), 34–39 (2018)
9. Hinton, G.E., Roweis, S.T.: Stochastic neighbor embedding. In: Advances in Neural Information Processing Systems, pp. 857–864. The MIT Press, Cambridge (2003)
10. Hotelling, H.: Analysis of a complex of statistical variables into principal components. J. Educ. Psychol. 24(6), 417 (1933)
11. Kobak, D., Berens, P.: The art of using t-SNE for single-cell transcriptomics. Nat. Commun. 10(1), 1–14 (2019)
12. Kobak, D., Linderman, G., Steinerberger, S., Kluger, Y., Berens, P.: Heavy-tailed kernels reveal a finer cluster structure in t-SNE visualisations. In: Brefeld, U., Fromont, E., Hotho, A., Knobbe, A., Maathuis, M., Robardet, C. (eds.) ECML PKDD 2019. LNCS (LNAI), vol. 11906, pp. 124–139. Springer, Cham (2020). https://doi.org/10.1007/978-3-030-46150-8_8
13. Lecun, Y., Cortes, C.: The MNIST database of handwritten digit images for machine learning research. IEEE Signal Process. Mag. 29(6), 141–142 (2012)
14. Linderman, G.C., Rachh, M., Hoskins, J.G., Steinerberger, S., Kluger, Y.: Fast interpolation-based t-SNE for improved visualization of single-cell RNA-seq data. Nat. Methods 16(3), 243–245 (2019)
15. Van der Maaten, L., Hinton, G.: Visualizing data using t-SNE. J. Mach. Learn. Res. 9(Nov), 2579–2605 (2008)
16. McInnes, L., Healy, J., Melville, J.: UMAP: uniform manifold approximation and projection for dimension reduction. arXiv preprint arXiv:1802.03426 (2018)
17. Mikolov, T., Sutskever, I., Chen, K., Corrado, G.S., Dean, J.: Distributed representations of words and phrases and their compositionality. In: Advances in Neural Information Processing Systems, pp. 3111–3119 (2013)
18. Nene, S.A., Nayar, S.K., Murase, H., et al.: Columbia object image library (coil-20) (1996)
19. Tang, J., Liu, J., Zhang, M., Mei, Q.: Visualizing large-scale and high-dimensional data. In: Proceedings of the 25th International Conference on World Wide Web, pp. 287–297 (2016)
20. Tang, J., Qu, M., Wang, M., Zhang, M., Yan, J., Mei, Q.: Line: large-scale information network embedding. In: Proceedings of the 24th International Conference on World Wide Web, pp. 1067–1077 (2015)
21. Tasic, B., et al.: Shared and distinct transcriptomic cell types across neocortical areas. Nature 563(7729), 72–78 (2018)
22. Tenenbaum, J.B., De Silva, V., Langford, J.C.: A global geometric framework for nonlinear dimensionality reduction. Science 290(5500), 2319–2323 (2000)
23. Torgerson, W.: The first major MDS breakthrough. Psychometrika 17, 401–419 (1952)
24. Van Der Maaten, L.: Accelerating t-SNE using tree-based algorithms. J. Mach. Learn. Res. 15(1), 3221–3245 (2014)
25. Xiao, H., Rasul, K., Vollgraf, R.: Fashion-MNIST: a novel image dataset for benchmarking machine learning algorithms. arXiv preprint arXiv:1708.07747 (2017)

Learning Resource Recommendation in E-Learning Systems Based on Online Learning Style

Lingyao Yan[1], Chuantao Yin[1(✉)], Hui Chen[2], Wenge Rong[2], Zhang Xiong[2], and Bertrand David[3]

[1] Sino-French Engineer School, Beihang University, Beijing 100191, China
{yanlingyao,chuantao.yin}@buaa.edu.cn
[2] School of Computer Science and Engineering, Beihang University, Beijing 100191, China
{chenhui,w.rong,xiongz}@buaa.edu.cn
[3] Echole Centrale de Lyon, 36 Avenue Guy de Collongue, 69134 Écully, France
bertrand.david@eclyon.fr

Abstract. With the development of the Internet, e-learning has become a new trend for education. However, unlike traditional learning that is face-to-face, e-learning systems construct an environment where learners control their learning process. Many issues have occurred in online learning systems, such as low efficiency, high dropout rates, poor grades and so on. One of the leading causes is students' low interest in e-learning content, and they cannot find attractive learning materials. Learning resource recommendations can solve this problem by recommending materials that learners may like. However, traditional recommendation methods omit that user's identity as a student and face underperformance. In this paper, a new learning resource recommendation method based on Online Learning Style is proposed. By integrating learning style characteristics into collaborative filtering algorithm with association rules mining, experimental results showed that the proposed method achieved 25% improvement compared to the method without learners' features.

Keywords: Online learning style · Online learning system · Clustering · Recommendation.

1 Introduction

E-learning systems have been widely used in course teaching. They have been developed and used in universities, schools, and even in business to manage the process of learning [3]. However, there exist problems in these e-learning systems. Massive learning resources and data in e-learning systems make it difficult for

Supported by National Natural Science Foundation of China (No. 61977003).

H. Qiu et al. (Eds.): KSEM 2021, LNAI 12817, pp. 373–385, 2021.
https://doi.org/10.1007/978-3-030-82153-1_31

learners to choose, and recommendation seems to be a good solution. Unfortunately, in most e-learning systems, learners are provided with almost the same learning resources. This homogenization of resources that learners are exposed to makes learning inefficient because many results from the system are useless for some learners. This problem is caused by the lack of personalization.

Recommender systems solve this problem by estimating users' preference on items and recommending what users might like to them proactively. Collaborative Filtering (CF) is one of the most successful technologies in recommender systems, and it has been developed and improved over the past years [2]. Data mining techniques have also been used to improve the process of recommendation, such as Association Rules Mining (ARM) and clustering [24]. However, current recommendation methods such as collaborative-filtering consider the student as users of a system but fail to capture features from the point of view that they are students.

Learning styles are designed to present an individual's preferences and priorities in the learning process. For instance, a student may have an excellent verbal ability when performing a task, but his or her visual ability may be weaker, so he or she prefers learning materials provided in verbal rather than visual form. Learning styles measure students' preferences for learning by analyzing their behavior during the learning process. Besides, if learning contents or learning materials were provided to learners without considering their preferences or learning styles, the learning process would be chaotic [1]. Therefore, this paper tends to integrate learning styles into the recommendation algorithm to improve the result of the recommendation. The Online Learning Style Model (OLSM) and Collaborative Filtering (CF) are utilized to recommend resources according to students' learning preferences. The contribution of this paper is as following: firstly, the recommendation algorithm is enhanced by getting more information from students based on Online Learning Style characteristics, which are designed especially for online learning; secondly, the method proposed is automatic, adaptive, and efficient without much expert knowledge; thirdly, with some feature engineering, the proposed method can be used in any e-learning systems for learning resource recommendation.

The rest of this paper is organized as follows: Sect. 2 introduces learning style models and e-learning recommendation systems. Section 3 portrays the proposed method. Section 4 shows the experimental results and analysis based on them. Section 5 concludes this paper and gives some discussions.

2   Related Work

2.1   Learning Style Models

For measuring a student's learning style, a Learning Style Model (LSM) is needed. During the last decades, researchers have proposed many learning style models. The Felder-Silverman Learning Style Model (FSLSM) [10] is one of the most popular LSMs [12]. It contains four dimensions: processing, perception, input, and understanding. For each dimension, there are two complementary categories. Felder et al. [11] also proposed a questionnaire assessment for FSLSM recognition called Index of Learning Styles (ILS). Besides, it is a refinement of some previous models such as the Dunn and Dunn learning style model [9], Myers-Briggs Type Indicator [21], Kolb's learning style model [13]. Thus, FSLSM has been widely used in many online learning systems, and ILS played an essential role in early research of learning style recognition [17]. Coffield et al. [8] analyzed 71 learning style models (LSMs). These learning style models are then classified into five categories.

However, these LSMs were proposed for traditional learning environments like in a classroom. The process of online learning and traditional learning are different. For instance, students in the classroom may have preferences for sound, light, and temperature conditions, while these conditions are hard to be measured in the online learning environment. Traditional learning is teacher-centered, where teachers are the main source of knowledge. On the contrary, online learning is student-centered, where the main elements are interactive web pages, students can decide how to learn. Therefore, to overcome traditional learning style models' problems, the online learning style model (OLSM) is proposed [16]. OLSM combines Entwistle's model [20], Felder-Silverman's model [10], Myers-Briggs model [21], and Kolb's model [13]. Besides, it adds a dimension that concerns the social characteristics of students. There are eight characteristics in OLS.

2.2   E-Learning Recommendation Systems

Soonthornphisaj et al. [25] proposed an intelligent e-learning system using a recommender system implemented by CF based on learners' ratings of materials. However, they did not mention the system's performance on the recommendation. Bourkoukou et al. [4] combined association pattern analysis (APA) and CF to recommend learning resources. They also used CF on rating data and then used APA to filter recommendation sequences obtained by CF. These works consider students as users but ignore that they are learners. Thus, they fail to use information associated with students.

Nafea et al. [23] pointed out this problem and introduced Felder-Silverman Learning Style Model (FSLSM) to extract information from learners through an Index of Learning Styles (ILS) [11] questionnaire. Results showed that information from students enhanced the performance of recommendation s. In another work [22], a recommender system is proposed, which considers students' learning styles based on the Felder-Silverman learning style model. The student vector which was represented as FSLSM's eight categories was obtained through the ILS questionnaire. These works integrate learning styles into e-learning recommender systems. However, there are several issues of using questionnaires: firstly, asking a learner to fill a questionnaire takes much time, especially in an adaptive learning system, to dynamically track the learner's learning style, this kind of recognition need to be done many times; secondly, filling a questionnaire is a kind of boring thing that a learner may fail to concentrate on, making the result not accurate; thirdly, learners may give ambiguous answers when filling a questionnaire, especially when they cannot understand the meaning behind those questions; last but not least, students may not have clear preferences, or they do not know what "learning style" they are so that they may tangle between choices of questions.

Lourenco et al. [19] combined Item-based CF and Association Rules Mining (ARM) to recommend products based on users' shopping history. The experimental results showed that the ARM algorithm could find patterns of frequently bought products by users.

Chen et al. [7] proposed a recommender system based on CF and ARM combined with clustering by OLSM. This work makes usage of learning style automatic. However, their system did not perform well on their dataset.

So far, most e-learning recommender systems use recommendation techniques on the interactive data between students and materials but lose information on students. Some works [22,23] try to integrate the learning style model into the recommendation, but the method of learning style recognition is inefficient. This paper proposes an automatic method to acquire students' learning style information without questionnaire filling. ARM is used for recommendation results filtering by Item-based CF, which is implemented within a cluster. The importance of the information extracted by the learning style model is demonstrated through the experiment in an e-learning recommender system.

3 Methodology

Characteristics in OLS are used to make clusters and recommend learning resources based on clustering results. Before clustering, a learner is represented as a vector $x_i = \{c_1, c_2, \ldots, c_8\}$ where c_i is the i-th characteristic in OLS, which is calculated as:

$$c_i = \sum_{j \in |r|} w_i N(x_i, r_j) \tag{1}$$

In Eq. 1, r_j represents the j-th resource in the learning system, $|r|$ represents the number of resources in the learning system, $N(x_i, r_j)$ represents the times that learner x_i clicks resource r_j. The architecture of the proposed method is shown in Fig. 1.

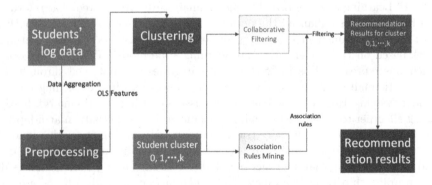

Fig. 1. The architechure of the proposed method.

3.1 Learner Clustering

K-means is selected for the clustering task for the following reasons: firstly, it is convenient for implementation; secondly, it is less time-consuming; thirdly, it has been widely used in many pieces of research.

A set of N learners is represented as $X = \{x_1, x_2, \ldots, x_N\}$, where x_i indicates the i-th learner in set X. One of the most critical hyperparameters in the K-means algorithm is the measurement of distance. In this paper, the Euclidian distance is selected, which is calculated as:

$$d(x_i, x_j) = \sqrt{\sum_{k=1}^{8} (c_{ik} - c_{jk})^2} \tag{2}$$

Where $d(x_i, x_j)$ represents the Euclidian distance between learners x_i and x_j, c_{ik} indicates learner x_i's character c_k. The procedure of K-means is to randomly select k cluster centers and to iterate until there are no changes in centers. During each iteration, the centers for different clusters are recalculated by learners' mean values in each cluster.

After clustering, learners are classified into k clusters which are represented as $\{C_1, C_2, \ldots, C_k\}$, where C_i indicates the i-th cluster.

3.2 Collaborative Filtering

Collaborative filtering (CF) is a basic recommendation algorithm that has been used in many pieces of research. Specifically, Item-based CF is selected where each learning resource is represented as a vector $r = \{t_1, t_2, \ldots, t_m\}$ in which t_i represents how many times learner x_i browses r and m indicates the total number of learners. Different from traditional Item-based CF, in this paper, CF is applied to learners in a particular cluster C_k. Similarities between learning resources are calculated through Euclidian distance:

$$sim(r_i, r_j | C_k) = \sqrt{\sum_{k=1}^{m} (t_{ik} - t_{jk})^2} \tag{3}$$

where t_{ik} represents the t_k of vector r_i. Then, for each learning resources r_i viewed by x_i, the score for the n most similar learning resources was calculated by:

$$score(r_j | C_k) = t_{ik} \times sim(r_i, r_j) \tag{4}$$

Finally, scores are sorted, and the top n results are considered as recommendations.

3.3 Learning Preferences Mining

Association Rules Mining is utilized to extract useful information from log files of learners. The association rules between learning resources are calculated. Furthermore, this process is conducted for each cluster of learners separately.

An association rule $R_i \rightarrow R_j$ indicates that the appearance of the learning resource set R_i will result in the appearance of the learning resource set R_j where R_i, R_j are subsets of the learning resources viewed by learners in a cluster. For learners in cluster C_k, The support of association rule $R_i \rightarrow R_j$ which indicates the ratio of learners who have clicked both r_i and r_j is calculated by:

$$sup(R_i \rightarrow R_j|C_k) = \frac{|S(R_i|C_k)|S(R_j|C_k)}{|C_k|} \tag{5}$$

Where $S(R_i|C_k)$ indicates the times R_i are viewed by students in C_k and $|C_k|$ indicates the number of students in C_k. For a subset of R noted as $R_s \subseteq R$, its support is calculated as:

$$sup(R_s|C_k) = \frac{|S(R_j|C_k)|}{|C_k|} \tag{6}$$

The confidence of an association rule indicates the reliability of the rule. It can be calculated by:

$$conf(R_i \rightarrow R_j|C_k) = \frac{sup(R_i \rightarrow R_j|C_k)}{sup(R_i|C_k)} \tag{7}$$

Subsets of learning resources are defined as frequency sets whose support exceeds a predefined support threshold. Association rules are obtained by the Apriori algorithm [18]. The above calculations are applied to learning resources that occur more than a threshold. These results are used for recommendation filtering after CF, which is described in detail in the next section.

3.4 Recommendation Results Filtering

For cluster C_k, learner x's degree of interest in learning resource r_m which is referred to as $P(x, r_m|C_k)$ is calculated by the similarity mentioned above:

$$P(x, r_m|C_k) = \sum_{r_n \in H(x) \cap S(r_m, L)} sim(r_m, r_n|C_k) \tag{8}$$

where H(x) represents the learning resources viewed by learner x, $S(r_m, L)$ indicates L learning resources that are most similar to r_m. After that, for cluster C_k, learner x's tendency of clicking learning resource r_m is calculated as:

$$T(x, r_m|C_k) = P(x, r_m|C_k) \times \sum_{R_i \in F(x)} conf(R_i \rightarrow \{r_m\}|C_k) \tag{9}$$

Where F(x) is the set of frequency sets in cluster C_k. To make the size of recommendation results adjustable, the threshold of tendency is defined as:

$$T_{th}(x, L|C_k) = \mu \times \frac{1}{N} \sum_{r_j \in R_{CF}(x_i, L)} T(x_i, r_j|C_k) \tag{10}$$

Where μ is a hyperparameter that is defined by the user, $R_{CF}(x, L)$ is recommendation results of length L on learner x generated by CF. Thus, for each recommendation result, its tendency is firstly calculated. The top N results are selected as candidates. The final results are candidates whose tendencies are above the threshold T_{th}. Through clustering, learners are divided into groups in which learners have similar learning behaviors and learning style features. Besides, the division of learners can reduce the computation complexity of CF.

4 Experimental Results and Analysis

To demonstrate the usability of the proposed method, its performance is evaluated through experiments on real data. This section is composed of five parts: data preparation and processing, metrics introduction, results of clustering, parameter tuning, and results analysis.

4.1 Dataset Preparation and Preprocessing

To make results more reliable, an open-source dataset is chosen for evaluation. OULAD (Open University Learning Analysis Dataset) [14] is an open-source dataset that records 32593 learners' interactions with a virtual learning environment composed of 22 modules. There are a total of 106552280 records in this dataset. In this paper, data associated with students' learning history are used. In this dataset, 20 kinds of learning resources are recorded. The relationships between learning resources and OLS characteristics are analyzed. The learning resources' descriptions and corresponding OLS characteristics are shown in Table 1, where '-' indicates no characteristic associated with this learning resource.

The process of data preparation is composed of two steps:

1) Data cleaning and aggregation: learners whose scores are below 60 are removed from the dataset. For each learner, each of his or her browsing logs is analyzed. Eventually, a table is conducted where each row represents a learner, each column represents a learning resource, and values are the clicking counts. After that, empirical parameters are selected to form learner vectors based on Eq. 1.
2) Outliers removal and scaling: outliers are detected and removed by the Local Outlier Factor algorithm. Then, MinMax scaling is applied to data, making each feature's value ranging from 0 to 1. Besides, L2 normalization is also used to make learner vectors normalized.

4.2 Evaluation Metrics

For clustering results evaluation, Calinski-Harabaz (CH) index [5] is selected. There is no fixed range of CH index's values, but the higher the value is, the closer the distance of the data within a cluster, the farther the distance of the

Table 1. Learning resources in OULAD and corresponding OLS characteristics

Learning resources	Description	OLS characteristics
Resource	PDF resources	Verbal
Url	Link to video resources	Visual
Glossary	Illustrations on terms in a course	–
utcontent	Brief introduction of a course	Global
Sharedsubpage	Information of multiple courses	–
Dualpane	Information and activities provision	Sensing
Ouelluminate	Live streaming of course	Visual
Ouwiki	Pages of Wikipedia	Intuitive, Verbal
Homepage	Homepage of a course	Motivational
Foruming	Service of forum	Communicational
Repeatactivity	Revision on course	Global
Questionnaire	Questions about course	–
Oucollaborate	Service of communication between assistants and learners	Communicational
Subpage	Content of chapters	Sequential
Folder	Files of a course	–
Page	Tips about a course	Global
Externalquiz	Tests for external websites	Motivational
Dataplus	Additional materials	–
Quiz	Test after course	Motivational
Htmlactivity	Interactive webpages containing learning resources	–

data between different clusters. Thus, a higher CH index value indicates better performance of a clustering algorithm.

To evaluate the recommendation algorithm's performance, three metrics are selected: Precision, Recall, and F1-score. Their definitions are as follows:

$$Precision = \frac{\sum_{x \in X} |R(x) \cap H(x)|}{\sum_{x \in X} |R(x)|} \tag{11}$$

$$Recall = \frac{\sum_{x \in X} |R(x) \cap H(x)|}{\sum_{x \in X} |H(x)|} \tag{12}$$

$$F1 = \frac{2 \times Precision \times Recall}{Precision + Recall} \tag{13}$$

Where x is a learner in a set of all learners X, R(x) represents the recommended learning resources for learner x, H(x) represents the learning resources viewed by learner x.

4.3   Clustering Results

One of the most critical parts of K-means is to find the best K. To do so, the preprocessed data are clustered with different values of K and their CH index values are calculated, as shown in Fig. 2(a). From Fig. 2(a), it can be seen that the CH score decreases as the k value decreases. Therefore, the best k value should be 2. After clustering learners into 2 clusters, Principal Components Analysis (PCA) is used to reduce learners' data into two dimensions. The result is shown in Fig. 2(b). In Fig. 2(b), learners' data from different clusters are shown in different colors. Data from different clusters are appropriately separated.

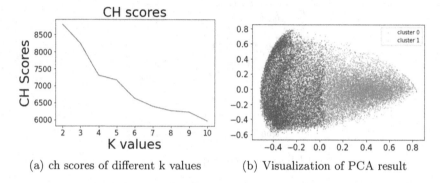

(a) ch scores of different k values   (b) Visualization of PCA result

Fig. 2. Clustering results

4.4   Hyperparameter Configuration

There are two hyperparameters in the proposed method: the minimum support threshold when generating frequency sets minSup and the ratio μ. Their default configurations are 0.07 and 0.1, respectively.

For support values ranging from 0.07 to 0.2, experiments are taken, and the numbers of rules extracted are shown in Fig. 3. Results on three metricsare shown in Fig. 4(a)–4(c).

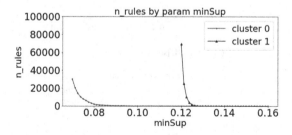

Fig. 3. Numbers of rules by minSup

In Fig. 4(a), for data in cluster 0, when minSup is greater than 0.115, the number of rules decreases to 0, while in cluster 1, when minSup is below 0.12, the number

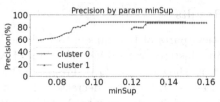

(a) Precision by minSup

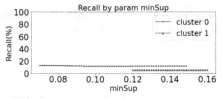

(b) Recall by minSup

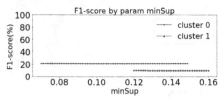

(c) F1-score by minSup

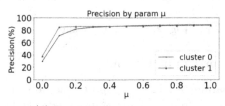

(d) Precision by μ

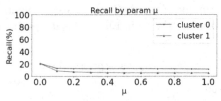

(e) Recall by μ

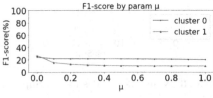

(f) F1-score by μ

Fig. 4. Parameters tuning results

of rules is too huge to be drawn in the figure. Thus, for metrics with different minSup values, the ranges of parameters in clusters 0 and 1 are 0.07 to 0.145 and 0.12 to 0.2, respectively.

From the results of Fig. 4(a)–4(c), for cluster 0, precision increases substantially while recall and f1-score changes little. Thus, the balance between complexity and performance is achieved for two clusters with minSup values of 0.1 and 0.13.

Then, results with different μ values ranging from 0 to 1 are obtained and shown in Fig. 4(d)–4(f). From Fig. 4(d)–4(f), when μ is between 0 and 0.4, the method's precision increases substantially, from 30%-40% to around 85%, while recall and f1-score decrease in varying degrees. For cluster 0, its recall and f1-score decrease slightly when μ is greater than 0.1, while its precision is still increasing. Thus, $\mu = 0.7$ is chosen for cluster 0. For cluster 1, its recall and f1-score decrease substantially when μ is between 0 to 0.4 and keep decreasing, while its precision barely increases after $\mu=0.1$. Thus, $\mu = 0.1$ is chosen for cluster 1.

4.5 Recommendation Results and Discussions

To demonstrate the effect of considering learning style features, Item-based CF with association rules mining (ARM) is implemented, and the parameters are tuned similarly. To be noted, the length of recommendation results is 10 for each method. The results are shown in Table 2. The results in Table 2 indicate that OLS features enhance the recommendation algorithm's performance in three metrics with a 25.8% improvement in precision. The only difference between the proposed method and CF with ARM is the clustering based on OLS characteristics. Thus, the integration of OLS characteristics helps to improve the performance of the recommendation algorithm.

Table 2. Results of different methods.

Methods	Precision	Recall	F1-score
The proposed method	86.47%	10.33%	18.42%
CF with ARM	68.74%	7.6%	13.74%

5 Conclusion and Future Work

In this paper, a method that integrates online learning style characteristics into the recommendation algorithm is proposed. The details of the proposed method are presented. Generally, it is composed of Collaborative Filtering (CF), Association Rules Mining (ARM), and Online Learning Style (OLS) characteristics.

Experiments were taken on real data, and the results show that OLS characteristics can make the recommendation algorithm more accurate and robust.

Although it is efficient, the proposed method relies heavily on the manual tuning of parameters, and the procedure of the proposed method is not end-to-end. Besides, cold start is still a problem to be solved. Some works may help to overcome the cold start problem [6,15,26]. In the future, more efforts will be made to propose an improved method that can also integrate learning style features and performs better than this current work.

References

1. Abrahamian, E., Weinberg, J.B., Grady, M., Stanton, C.M.: The effect of personality-aware computer-human interfaces on learning. J. Univers. Comput. Sci. **10**(1), 17–27 (2004)
2. Adomavicius, G., Tuzhilin, A.: Toward the next generation of recommender systems: a survey of the state-of-the-art and possible extensions. IEEE Trans. Knowl. Data Eng. **17**(6), 734–749 (2005)
3. Al-Fraihat, D., Joy, M., Sinclair, J., et al.: Evaluating e-learning systems success: an empirical study. Comput. Hum. Behav. **102**, 67–86 (2020)
4. Bourkoukou, O., El Bachari, E., El Adnani, M.: A recommender model in e-learning environment. Arab. J. Sci. Eng. **42**(2), 607–617 (2017)
5. Caliński, T., Harabasz, J.: A dendrite method for cluster analysis. Commun. Stat.-Theor. Methods **3**(1), 1–27 (1974)
6. Cao, W., Zhou, C., Wu, Y., Ming, Z., Xu, Z., Zhang, J.: Research progress of zero-shot learning beyond computer vision. In: Qiu, M. (ed.) ICA3PP 2020. LNCS, vol. 12453, pp. 538–551. Springer, Cham (2020). https://doi.org/10.1007/978-3-030-60239-0_36
7. Chen, H., Yin, C., Li, R., Rong, W., Xiong, Z., David, B.: Enhanced learning resource recommendation based on online learning style model. Tsinghua Sci. Technol. **25**(3), 348–356 (2019)
8. Coffield, F., et al.: Learning styles and pedagogy in post-16 learning: a systematic and critical review (2004)
9. Dunn, R., Griggs, S.A., Olson, J., Beasley, M., Gorman, B.S.: A meta-analytic validation of the Dunn and Dunn model of learning-style preferences. J. Educ. Res. **88**(6), 353–362 (1995)
10. Felder, R.M., Silverman, L.K., et al.: Learning and teaching styles in engineering education. Eng. Educ. **78**(7), 674–681 (1988)
11. Felder, R.M., Spurlin, J.: Applications, reliability and validity of the index of learning styles. Int. J. Eng. Educ. **21**(1), 103–112 (2005)
12. Giovannella, C.: What can we learn from long-time lasting measurements of felder-silverman's learning styles? In: 2012 IEEE 12th International Conference on Advanced Learning Technologies, pp. 647–649 (2012)
13. Kolb, A.Y.: The kolb learning style inventory-version 3.1 2005 technical specifications. Boston, MA: Hay Resource Direct **200**(72), 166–171 (2005)
14. Kuzilek, J., Hlosta, M., Zdrahal, Z.: Open university learning analytics dataset. Sci. Data **4**(1), 1–8 (2017)
15. Li, J., Jing, M., Lu, K., Zhu, L., Yang, Y., Huang, Z.: From zero-shot learning to cold-start recommendation. Proc. AAAI Conf. Artif. Intell. **33**, 4189–4196 (2019)

16. Li, R., Yin, C.: Analysis of online learning style model based on k-means algorithm. In: 3rd International Conference on Economics, Management, Law and Education (EMLE 2017), pp. 692–697 (2017)

17. Litzinger, T.A., Lee, S.H., Wise, J.C.: A study of the reliability and validity of the felder-soloman index of learning styles. In: Proceedings of the 2005 American Society for Education Annual Conference and Exposition, pp. 1–16 (2005)

18. Liu, Y.: Study on application of apriori algorithm in data mining. In: 2010 Second International Conference on Computer Modeling and Simulation, vol. 3, pp. 111–114 (2010)

19. Lourenco, J., Varde, A.S.: Item-based collaborative filtering and association rules for a baseline recommender in e-commerce. In: 2020 IEEE International Conference on Big Data (Big Data), pp. 4636–4645 (2020)

20. Marton, F., Hounsell, D., Entwistle, N.J.: The experience of learning: implications for teaching and studying in higher education (1997)

21. Myers, I.B.: A Guide to the Development and Use of the Myers-Briggs Type Indicator: Manual (1985)

22. Nafea, S.M., Siewe, F., He, Y.: A novel algorithm for course learning object recommendation based on student learning styles. In: 2019 International Conference on Innovative Trends in Computer Engineering (ITCE), pp. 192–201 (2019)

23. Nafea, S.M., Siewe, F., He, Y.: On recommendation of learning objects using felder-silverman learning style model. IEEE Access **7**, 163034–163048 (2019)

24. Obidallah, W.J., Raahemi, B., Ruhi, U.: Clustering and association rules for web service discovery and recommendation: a systematic literature review. SN Comput. Sci. **1**(1), 1–33 (2019). https://doi.org/10.1007/s42979-019-0026-8

25. Soonthornphisaj, N., Rojsattarat, E., Yim-ngam, S.: Smart e-learning using recommender system. In: Huang, D.-S., Li, K., Irwin, G.W. (eds.) ICIC 2006. LNCS (LNAI), vol. 4114, pp. 518–523. Springer, Heidelberg (2006). https://doi.org/10.1007/978-3-540-37275-2_63

26. Xie, Z., Cao, W., Ming, Z.: A further study on biologically inspired feature enhancement in zero-shot learning. Int. J. Mach. Learn. Cybern. **12**(1), 257–269 (2021)

Alignment-Based Graph Network for Judicial Examination Task

Jiaye Wu and Xudong Luo[✉]

Guangxi Key Lab of Multi-source Information Mining and Security College of
Computer Science and Information Engineering, Guangxi Normal University, Guilin,
Guangxi, China
luoxd@mailbox.gxnu.edu.cn

Abstract. The judicial examination task is to select the correct options
for a given question, which is a challenging task and is helpful for legal
assistant systems. We argue that by leveraging the potential semantic
information between question and option, we can enhance the model's
ability to understand the task's content and, therefore, propose an
Alignment-Based Graph Network (ABGN). Given a question-option pair,
ABGN first constructs semantic relation between question and option
with an alignment network and then uses a gated graph attention network to utilise all question-option pairs' global information. The experimental results show that our model achieves competitive performance
with standard methods on judicial examination task. Besides, with multi-
dimension analyses, we show the effectiveness of some components in our
full model.

Keywords: Open-domain question answering · Legal intelligence ·
Deep learning · Attention mechanism · Classification

1 Introduction

One of the most challenging examinations in China is the National Judicial
Examination, which is extremely important in a legal practitioner's career. Given
the difficulty of the judicial examination, we can use this task to test the ability
of AI models to analyse and understand the problem, and the research on this
task is beneficial to build a more useful and reliable AI system. The judicial
examination task is to give a computer system some questions and optional
answers to each question and let it choose the right answer to each question.

The judicial examination task is very similar to multi-choice Machine Reading Comprehension (MRC), such as SQuAD [19] and RACE [14]. Their goal is
to select the correct answer from a set of candidate answers based on the question given. Common approaches to machine reading comprehension are based on
sequence matching. For example, matching passage with the concatenated question and candidate answers sequence [33], or matching passage with the question
and then selecting a correct answer based on the matching result [37]. Moreover,

© Springer Nature Switzerland AG 2021
H. Qiu et al. (Eds.): KSEM 2021, LNAI 12817, pp. 386–400, 2021.
https://doi.org/10.1007/978-3-030-82153-1_32

Table 1. Example of concept-understanding questions (translated from Chinese)

Concept-understanding question: The basic principles of the constitution are mainly:

Option:

☑ The principle of popular sovereignty

☑ The principle of fundamental human rights

☑ The principle of power restriction

☑ The principle of the rule of law

Table 2. Example of case-analysis questions (translated from Chinese)

Case-analysis question: which of the following offenders are not eligible for parole under the penal code?

Option:

☑ Person a convicted of robbery and sentenced to 15 years' imprisonment

☒ Person B sentenced to 10 years' imprisonment for bribery

☒ Person C sentenced to life imprisonment for drug trafficking

☑ Person D sentenced to 7 years' imprisonment with a heavier penalty for being a recidivist

---

Wang et al. [26] propose the *co-matching* method, where passage, question, and candidate answers are matched one by one, and the correct answer is ultimately selected based on the matching.

However, we cannot use these methods directly for judicial examination tasks. As shown in Tables 1 and 2, different from the common multi-choice reading comprehension tasks, the judicial examination task does not directly provide a reference paragraph related to the question, and the number of correct answers is indeterminate. Besides, the judicial examination task is rich in types of questions involving both concept-understanding and case-analysis. The concept-understanding questions mainly examine the understanding of legal concepts and legal knowledge. In contrast, the case-analysis questions focus on analysing real legal cases, which requires the model we design to have good text comprehension and knowledge reasoning abilities and makes the judicial examination task difficult in natural language processing.

Therefore, the study of judicial examination tasks can help promote the development of judicial question answering systems [15,29] to provide professional advice to the ordinary person and help professionals be more efficient (*e.g.*, to give explanations, advice, or solutions to legal issues). In this paper, we consider enhancing the model's understanding of the text by explicitly establishing a connection between a question and its optional answers and utilising information between them at multiple levels to address the judicial examination task. At the same time, we propose to construct the judicial examination task's goal as an

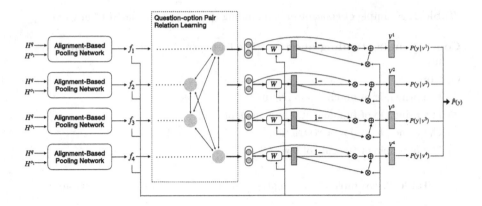

Fig. 1. Overall architecture of our model

option combination prediction problem (multi-class classification), allowing the model to be more flexible in dealing with multiple-choice questions (each question has one or more than one correct answer). The experimental results show that this method is more effective than the single classification method.

Based on the assumption that if there are opposing options, then the relationship between the options is beneficial to the answer choice, we propose an Alignment-Based Graph Network (ABGN). In particular, given a question-option pair, ABGN first explicitly establishes the relationship between each question-option pair with an alignment network. It then utilises a pooling network to fuse contextual knowledge further. Finally, it constructs a relation learning graph from all question-option pairs, which selectively propagate information along with the edge and get a more fine-grained representation for each node by a gated graph attention network.

Our main contributions are as follows. (1) We propose a novel DNN model ABGN for the judicial examination task. (2) We are the first to study the graph network in the judicial examination task. (3) The experimental results and analysis show that our proposed model is competitive with the baselines and demonstrates our model's strong effectiveness. (4) Given the commonality between the judicial examination task and the real-world MRC tasks, our approach is also instructive for a new solution to the real-world machine reading problems.

The rest of the paper is organised as follows. Section 2 details our model. Section 3 experimentally analyse our model. Section 4 examines the related work. Finally, Sect. 5 concludes the paper with future work.

2   Model Architecture

In this section, we present the details of each component in our ABGN. As shown in Fig. 1, ABGN first obtains the initial representation of question and options and then utilise Alignment-Based Pooling Network (ABPN) to get the corresponding enhanced semantic representations (Sects. 2.1 and 2.2). Finally,

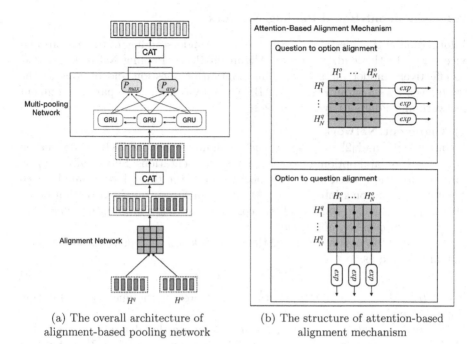

(a) The overall architecture of alignment-based pooling network

(b) The structure of attention-based alignment mechanism

Fig. 2. The architecture of alignment-based pooling network

a Gated Graph Attention Network (GGAN) is applied to model the question-option pair's relation and make the final prediction (Sect. 2.3).

2.1 Encoder

We initialise the input text representation by feeding the sequence of question and option to the pre-trained BERT model [7]. Specifically, given model a question-option pair, we transform them into corresponding tokens $\{Q = (q_1, ..., q_n), O^l = (o_1^l, ..., o_m^l)\}$ (with "[CLS]" and "[SEP]"), where n and m are the number of tokens in the question and option. We then use BERT to encode the tokens to get the high-level semantic token representation H^q and H^o, respectively. Therefore, each question-option pair $\{(Q, O^l) \mid 1 \leq l \leq 4\}$ is encoded as follows:

$$H^q = \text{BERT}(Q), \tag{1}$$

$$H^l = \text{BERT}(O^l). \tag{2}$$

The resulting matrix $H^q \in \mathbb{R}^{n \times d}$ and $H^l \in \mathbb{R}^{m \times d}$ are token representations of the question and l-th option, where d is the dimensionality of the token embeddings.

390 J. Wu and X. Luo

2.2 Alignment-Based Pooling Network

Information in the question contributes to our understanding of the options and vice versa. To this end, we use an Alignment-Based Pooling Network (ABPN) to effectively model the semantic information of question and options at the word level. As shown in Fig. 2(a), ABPN mainly contains two parts: Alignment Network and Pooling Layer (Sect. 2.2).

1) Alignment Network
Inspired by [13] and [2], we propose a novel alignment network to fuse information of the question and option into each other's representations. Specifically, we perform an attention-based alignment mechanism at the token level to model each question and option's interactions. As shown in Fig. 2(b), the attention-based alignment mechanism consists of two components: *question to option alignment* and *option to question alignment*.

For ease of discussion, we define the initial token-level representation of question and option as:

$$H_{1:n}^q, H_{1:m}^l \rightarrow Z^q, Z^l, \tag{3}$$

where $H_{1:n}^q \in \mathbb{R}^{N \times d}$ and $H_{1:m}^l \in \mathbb{R}^{M \times d}$ are represent the question and option tokens, respectively.

Question to option alignment. We first compute the alignment matrix $A \in R^{N \times M}$ that contains relevant scores for all pair of question token Z_i^q and option token Z_j^l via:

$$A = \mathrm{ReLU}(Z^q W)\mathrm{ReLU}(Z^l W)^{\mathrm{T}}, \tag{4}$$

where $W \in \mathbb{R}^{d \times d}$ is a trainable weight matrix. Then, for the i-th token in the question, we calculate its attention score with each token in the option to get attention matrix $A^{q \rightarrow l}$. The calculation formula is as follows:

$$\alpha_{i,j} = \frac{exp(A_{i,j})}{\sum_{k=1}^{M} exp(A_{i,k})}, \tag{5}$$

which is similar to [20]. Based on the attention score matrix $A^{q \rightarrow l}$, we can obtain the aligned option token representations by:

$$\tilde{Z}^l = A^{q \rightarrow l} Z^l. \tag{6}$$

Option to question alignment. Similar to *question to option alignment*, for j-th word in the option, we calculate its attention score with each word in the question to get attention matrix $A^{l \rightarrow q}$ by:

$$\alpha_{j,i} = \frac{exp(A_{i,j})}{\sum_{k=1}^{N} exp(A_{k,j})}. \tag{7}$$

Subsequently, we can obtain the aligned question token representations based on the attention matrix $A^{l \rightarrow q}$ by:

$$\tilde{Z}^q = A^{l \rightarrow q} Z^q. \tag{8}$$

2) Pooling Network

After alignment network, we first use a bi-directional GRU, with the output size of $\frac{1}{2}d$ for each direction, to learn a contextual-level representation P^l based on the concatenation of aligned question and option token representations:

$$\hat{Z}^l = [\tilde{Z}^q; \tilde{Z}^l], \tag{9}$$

$$P^l = \text{GRU}(\hat{Z}^l), \tag{10}$$

where $P^l \in \mathbb{R}^{(n+m) \times d}$ and $[;]$ is vector concatenation across row.

We choose to use GRU instead of LSTM because it performs similarly to LSTM but is more computationally efficient. Then we apply two pooling methods to utilise the above contextual information. We conduct max pooling and average pooling to get semantic features f_m^l and f_e^l, $i.e.$,

$$f_m^l = \text{MaxPooling}(P^l), \tag{11}$$

$$f_e^l = \text{AveragePooling}(P^l), \tag{12}$$

where f_m^l and $f_e^l \in \mathbb{R}^{1 \times d}$.

The final question-option pair representation is the concatenation of f_m^l and f_e^l:

$$f^l = [f_m^l; f_e^l]. \tag{13}$$

2.3 Gated Graph Attention Network

Inspired by [16], we design a Gated Graph Attention Network (GGAN) to provide enhanced prediction capability for judicial examination task by modelling global relations among question-option pairs. GGAN constructs a relation learning graph from question-option pairs where each question-option pair is treated as a node and then connect each pair of nodes to form a fully connected graph with $|\mathbb{O}|$ nodes.

In GGAN, we initialise the node representation v^l to the representation f^l returned by ABPN. For every node in the graph, we first use an attention mechanism that can attentively model the relation between nodes along the edges and learn the node's adjacent information. Then, we conduct a gated fusion function to update the node representation.

1) Node Level Attention

In the node level attention stage, we aggregate information from nodes adjacent to the node v^l. Followed by [36], the aggregation is done by a graph attention mechanism. It calculates the node weight $\beta^{l \to \bar{l}}$ of v^n according to adjacent $\bar{l}$-th node ($\bar{l} \in [1,4], l \neq \bar{l}$) as follows:

$$\beta^{l \to \bar{l}} = \text{softmax}(\text{MLP}([f^{\bar{l}}; f^l])), \tag{14}$$

where $f^{\bar{l}}$ and f^l are the initial representation of nodes $v^{\bar{l}}$ and v^l.

After that, we can obtain the adjacent information by computing a weighted sum of contiguous node representation as follows:

$$u^{l\to\bar{l}} = \sum_{\bar{l}\in[1,|O|],l\neq\bar{l}} (\beta^{l\to\bar{l}} \cdot f^l). \tag{15}$$

2) **Gated Fusion** Gated fusion function updates the node representation v^l by fusing the adjacent information and the initial node representation:

$$g = \sigma(W[u^{l\to\bar{l}}; f^l] + b), \tag{16}$$

$$v^l = g \odot f^l + (1 - g) \odot u^{l\to\bar{l}}, \tag{17}$$

where $\odot$ is the element-wise multiplication, σ is a sigmoid function, and g is a gating vector.

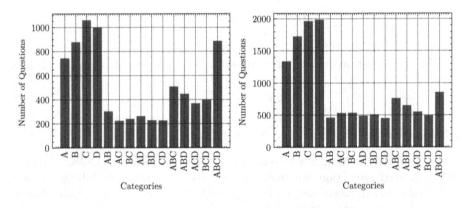

(a) The number distribution of categories in the concept-understanding questions

(b) The number distribution of categories in the case-analysis questions

Fig. 3. Number distributions of categories

Table 3. Statistics of datasets

Datasets	Concept-comprehension	Case-analysis
Train	6240	10617
Dev	1535	2680

2.4 Label Prediction

To improve the model's generalisability, we first compute the classification probability with each updated node representation, as each node obtains information from its neighbour nodes. The formula is described as follows:

$$P(y \mid v^l) = \text{softmax}(W_c^{\mathrm{T}} v^l + b), \tag{18}$$

where $W_c = \{w_j \mid 1 \leq j \leq C\} \in \mathbb{R}^{d \times C}$ denotes the weight matrix for classifier and b is the bias term. Then, all node prediction probabilities are combined to produce the final classification prediction:

$$\hat{P}(y) = \frac{1}{|\mathbb{O}|} \sum_{l=1}^{|\mathbb{O}|} P(y \mid v^l). \tag{19}$$

The model is trained end-to-end by minimising the cross entropy loss:

$$L = \text{CrossEntropy}(y^*, \hat{P}(y)), \tag{20}$$

where y^* is the ground truth label.

3 Experiments

This section presents the experimental analysis of our model.

3.1 Datasets

We use one publicly available dataset from the Chinese AI and Law challenge (CAIL 2020) [35] in this paper, i.e., sfks-train (the first and second stage data). The dataset contains two data files storing 7,775 (36.9%) concept-understanding questions and 13,297 (63.1%) case-analysis questions.

The training data consists of tuples (C, O, Q), where A is a list of correct options: $C = [c_1, \cdots, c_n], a_i \in \{A, B, C, D\}, c_i \neq a_j, 1 \leq n \leq 4\}$, O is a sets of options: $\{O^l \mid 1 \leq l \leq 4\}$, where O^l is a sequence of words, and Q is the question. Besides, some data items are incorrectly labelled, and we rectify them. The detailed statistics for the dataset and the dataset partition are shown in Fig. 3 and Table 3. In this paper, we use the results of the second stage of online testing as the model's performance on the test set. The test set consists of newly developed judicial exam questions written by professionals.

3.2 Baselines

The BERT [7] based baselines are our main object of comparison since they outperform previous baselines without fine-tuning. BERT is a model that contains a deep bidirectional Transformer [23] and has been pre-trained on the large-scaled unlabelled text dataset. BERT obtains state-of-the-art results in most natural language datasets. Based on BERT, we design BERT-Concat and BERT-Pair baselines, respectively. BERT-Concat considers question and option individually when processing input text, while BERT-Pair concatenates question-option pair together.

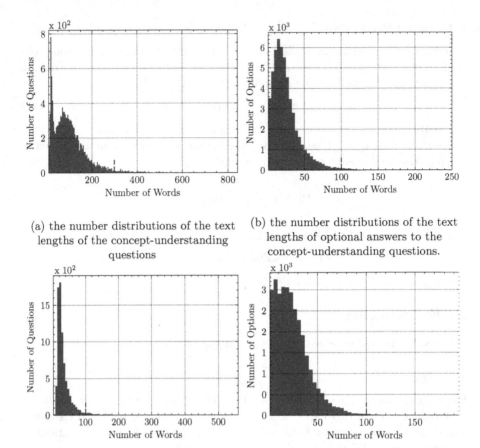

(a) the number distributions of the text lengths of the concept-understanding questions

(b) the number distributions of the text lengths of optional answers to the concept-understanding questions.

(c) the number distributions of the text lengths of the case-analysis questions, respectively

(d) the number distributions of the text lengths of optional answers to the case-analysis questions

Fig. 4. Number distribution of text length

3.3 Implementation Details

We use the Pytorch framework to construct our model, and the *bert-large* versions of BERT used in the experiment are from [3], where the model is pre-trained on Chinese Wikipedia using Whole Word Masking (WWM) strategy. Meanwhile, we set the maximum length of words in a question and an answer option as 300 and 100, respectively ([PAD] token padded when necessary) according to our observation on Fig. 4.

We used BertAdam as an optimiser during training and set the learning rate to 1e−04, warm-up proportion to 0.1. We train on a single Tesla V100 with a batch size of 16 and an accumulation step of 4. We use accuracy on the validation set to achieve early stopping for all experiments for a fair comparison.

Table 4. Main results. The numbers are marked in Bold and with * indicate the best results

Model	Dev			Test			Time consuming minutes per-epoch
	Concept	Case	Total	Concept	Case	Total	
BERT-concat	26.84	**31.90***	**30.06***	**37.93***	19.30	**22.0***	16
BERT-pair	**27.49***	30.78	29.58	31.03	18.71	20.5	45
Our full model	25.67	30.00	28.40	20.69	**20.47***	20.5	32

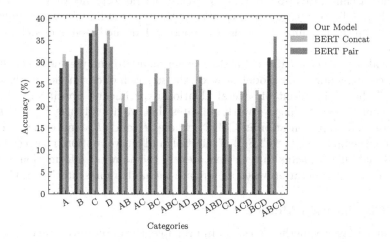

Fig. 5. The per-category performance

Table 5. Ablation tests on the dev and test set

Model	Test		
	Total	Concept	Case
Full model	**20.5**	20.69	**20.47**
w/o alignment-based pooling network	19.5	**27.59**	18.13
w/o gated fusion	19.0	20.69	18.71

3.4 Results

According to criteria *F1-score* and *Time-consuming* [5,8,9], we evaluate the performance of both our model and the baselines on the validation dataset. According to the *Accuracy* criterion, we evaluate the performance of our model on the test set. The results are shown in Table 4. From the table, we can see that our method underperforms the baselines overall on both concept-comprehension and case-analysis questions on the validation and test set. However, on the test set, our model achieves the best results on the case-analysis questions. Besides, we can observe that all methods' results are less desirable, which indicates the difficulty of the judicial examination task.

Table 6. The performance of the two classification methods

Model	Method	Dev
BERT-concat	Our method	**30.06**
	Another	22.42

To gain more insights into the difference in performance between our model and the baselines, we also report the per-category performance on the validation set in Fig. 5. In most categories, we can see that our model achieves competitive results with the baseline model and even better than the baseline model on some categories.

We also conduct a series of ablation experiments to analyse the effects of different components of our model to study the strength of our model on this task. Table 5 shows the result of several ablation experiments. Specifically, 1) w/o Alignment-Based Pooling Network indicates that we directly use H_0^q and H_0^l to initialise node representation in GGAN, where H_0^q and H_0^l denote the representation of the first token ("[CLS]") of question and answer option, respectively; 2) w/o Gated Fusion means that we concatenate the adjacent information and the initial node representation when we update the node representation in GGAN.

3.5   Classification Method

The output layer is method-specific. In principle, the order of the answer options is arbitrary. To some extent, ABD and ACD should be the same. Therefore, in order to explore the necessity of treating different answer option combinations as separate categories, we present another classification method based on the BERT-Concat baseline:

- After obtaining the representations of the problem and each option separately, we concatenate the representations of the problem and each option to obtain the vector representations of the four question-option pairs.
- Then, we use the representation of each question-option pair independently to make a prediction and determine whether the current option is correct or not (*i.e.*, to determine independently whether options A, B, C and D are the correct answers).
- Finally, the correct options for the problem based on the predictions of all question-option pairs.

We compare the method used in this paper with the method described above. As shown in Table 6, our method outperforms the other, meaning that modelling only the information of a single question-option pair is not sufficient to allow the model to make effective predictions in a judicial examination task.

4   Related Work

This section compares our work with related work to show how our work advances the state-of-art in the field.

4.1 Reading Comprehension

Reading comprehension as a fundamental and long-studied task in natural language comprehension has had many publicly available datasets for researchers, such as CNN/Daily Mail [12], RACE [14], SQuAD [19], and DuReader [11]. Thanks to these publicly available datasets, many research efforts on reading comprehension have emerged. Deep learning and attentional networks [4,20,21], for example, are used heavily on this task with good results. Besides, some studies use the *match* method [25,27,28] to solve machine reading comprehension tasks. In addition, based on the assumption that the proper use of external knowledge can help the model to understand the text better, many researchers [18,32] have recently started to improve the effectiveness of machine reading comprehension by using external knowledge. However, none of the above work has examined a dataset of multiple-choice questions like the judicial examination (the question may have multiple answers), and we focus on this kind of task and propose an effective method for it.

4.2 Graph Neural Network

Graph neural networks (GNNs) are first introduced in 2005 [10] and used to solve some strictly graph-theoretic problems. With the development of deep learning, GNNs have gained increasing popularity among scholars over the past many years [24,31], as they extend traditional deep learning networks from the Euclidean space to data that can be transformed into graph structures. Graph neural networks have been applied to many natural language processing tasks, such as sequence labelling [17], machine translation [1], and relation extraction [34]. They also have been shown successfully on question answering tasks [6,22,30]. The above studies assume that the model has a graph-structured input, as this assumption makes learning corresponding node embeddings convenient. To the best of our knowledge, we are the first to employ the graph network for the judicial examination task.

5 Conclusion

In this paper, we proposed an alignment-based graph network for judicial examination task. Our experiments showed that our proposed model achieves competitive performance. In the future, it is worth using domain knowledge to enhance our alignment-based graph network for judicial examination task. It is also interesting to study how to utilise the proposed architecture to solve problems of machine reading comprehension in other domains.

Acknowledgements. This work was supported by the National Natural Science Foundation of China (No. 61762016), and a research fund of Guangxi Key Lab of Multi-Source Information Mining & Security (No. 19-A-01-01).

References

1. Bastings, J., Titov, I., Aziz, W., Marcheggiani, D., Sima'an, K.: Graph convolutional encoders for syntax-aware neural machine translation. In: Proceedings of the 2017 Conference on Empirical Methods in Natural Language Processing, pp. 1957–1967 (2017)
2. Chen, Y., Wu, L., Zaki, M.J.: Reinforcement learning based graph-to-sequence model for natural question generation. In: 8th International Conference on Learning Representations (2020)
3. Cui, Y., Che, W., Liu, T., Qin, B., Wang, S., Hu, G.: Revisiting pre-trained models for Chinese natural language processing. In: Proceedings of the 2020 Conference on Empirical Methods in Natural Language Processing: Findings, pp. 657–668 (2020)
4. Cui, Y., Chen, Z., Wei, S., Wang, S., Liu, T., Hu, G.: Attention-over-Attention neural networks for reading comprehension. In: Proceedings of the 55th Annual Meeting of the Association for Computational Linguistics, vol. 1, pp. 593–602 (2017)
5. Dai, W., Qiu, L., Wu, A., Qiu, M.: Cloud infrastructure resource allocation for big data applications. IEEE Trans. Big Data 4(3), 313–324 (2018)
6. De Cao, N., Aziz, W., Titov, I.: Question answering by reasoning across documents with graph convolutional networks. In: Proceedings of the 2019 Conference of the North American Chapter of the Association for Computational Linguistics: Human Language Technologies, vol. 1, pp. 2306–2317 (2019)
7. Devlin, J., Chang, M.-W., Lee, K., Toutanova, K.: BERT: pre-training of deep bidirectional transformers for language understanding. arXiv preprint arXiv:1810.04805 (2018)
8. Gai, K., Qiu, M.: Reinforcement learning-based content-centric services in mobile sensing. IEEE Network 32(4), 34–39 (2018)
9. Gai, K., Qiu, M., Zhao, H., Sun, X.: Resource management in sustainable cyberphysical systems using heterogeneous cloud computing. IEEE Trans. Sustain. Comput. 3(2), 60–72 (2018)
10. Gori, M., Monfardini, G., Scarselli, F.: A new model for learning in graph domains. In: Proceedings of the 2005 IEEE International Joint Conference on Neural Networks, vol. 2, pp. 729–734 (2005)
11. He, W., et al.: Dureader: a chinese machine reading comprehension dataset from real-world applications. arXiv preprint arXiv:1711.05073 (2017)
12. Hermann, K.M., et al.: Teaching machines to read and comprehend In: Proceedings of the 28th International Conference on Neural Information Processing Systems, vol. 1, pp. 1693–1701 (2015)
13. Ji, L., Wei, Z., Hu, X., Liu, Y., Zhang, Q., Huang, X.-J.: Incorporating argument-level interactions for persuasion comments evaluation using co-attention model. In: Proceedings of the 27th International Conference on Computational Linguistics, pp. 3703–3714 (2018)
14. Lai, G., Xie, Q., Liu, H., Yang, Y., Hovy, E.: Race: large-scale reading comprehension dataset from examinations. In: Proceedings of the 2017 Conference on Empirical Methods in Natural Language Processing, pp. 785–794 (2017)
15. Liu, Y., Luo, X., Yang, X.: Semantics and structure based recommendation of similar legal cases. In: 2019 IEEE 14th International Conference on Intelligent Systems and Knowledge Engineering (ISKE), pp. 388–395 (2019)
16. Liu, Z., Xiong, C., Sun, M., Liu, Z.: Fine-grained fact verification with kernel graph attention network. In: Proceedings of the 58th Annual Meeting of the Association for Computational Linguistics, pp. 7342–7351 (2020)

17. Marcheggiani, D., Titov, I.: Encoding sentences with graph convolutional networks for semantic role labeling. In: Proceedings of the 2017 Conference on Empirical Methods in Natural Language Processing, pp. 1506–1515 (2017)
18. Mihaylov, T., Frank, A.: Knowledgeable reader: enhancing cloze-style reading comprehension with external commonsense knowledge. In: Proceedings of the 56th Annual Meeting of the Association for Computational Linguistics, vol. 1: Long Papers, pp. 821–832 (2018)
19. Rajpurkar, P., Zhang, J., Lopyrev, K., Liang, P.: Squad: 100,000+ questions for machine comprehension of text. In: Proceedings of the 2016 Conference on Empirical Methods in Natural Language Processing, pp. 2383–2392 (2016)
20. Seo, M., Kembhavi, A., Farhadi, A., Hajishirzi, H.: Bidirectional attention flow for machine comprehension. arXiv preprint arXiv:1611.01603 (2016)
21. Sordoni, A., Bachman, P., Trischler, A., Bengio, Y.: Iterative alternating neural attention for machine reading. arXiv preprint arXiv:1606.02245 (2016)
22. Sun, H., Dhingra, B., Zaheer, M., Mazaitis, K., Salakhutdinov, R., Cohen, W.: Open domain question answering using early fusion of knowledge bases and text. In: Proceedings of the 2018 Conference on Empirical Methods in Natural Language Processing, pp. 4231–4242 (2018)
23. Vaswani, A.: Attention is all you need. In: Proceedings of the 31st International Conference on Neural Information Processing Systems, pp. 6000–6010. Curran Associates Inc. (2017)
24. Velickovic, P., Cucurull, G., Casanova, A., Romero, A., Liò, P., Bengio, Y.: Graph attention networks. In: Proceedings of the 6th International Conference on Learning Representations, pp. 1–12 (2018)
25. Wang, S., Jiang, J.: Machine comprehension using match-LSTM and answer pointer. arXiv preprint arXiv:1608.07905 (2016)
26. Wang, S., Yu, M., Jiang, J., Chang, S.: A co-matching model for multi-choice reading comprehension. In: Proceedings of the 56th Annual Meeting of the Association for Computational Linguistics, vol. 2, pp. 746–751 (2018)
27. Wang, W., Yang, N., Wei, F., Chang, B., Zhou, M.: Gated self-matching networks for reading comprehension and question answering. In: Proceedings of the 55th Annual Meeting of the Association for Computational Linguistics, vol. 1, pp. 189–198 (2017)
28. Wang, W., Yang, N., Wei, F., Chang, B., Zhou, M.: R-NET: machine reading comprehension with self-matching networks. Tech. Rep. Nat. Lang. Comput. Group, Microsoft, Asia, Beijing, China, 5 (2017)
29. Wu, J., Liu, J., Luo, X.: Few-shot legal knowledge question answering system for COVID-19 epidemic. In: 2020 3rd International Conference on Algorithms, Computing and Artificial Intelligence, pp. 1–6 (2020)
30. Xu, K., Wu, L., Wang, Z., Feng, Y., Sheinin, V.: Sql-to-text generation with graph-to-sequence model. In: Proceedings of the 2018 Conference on Empirical Methods in Natural Language Processing, pp. 931–936, (2018)
31. Xu, K., Wu, L., Wang, Z., Feng, Y., Witbrock, M., Sheinin, V.: Graph2seq: graph to sequence learning with attention-based neural networks. arXiv preprint arXiv:1804.00823 (2018)
32. Yang, B., Mitchell, T.: Leveraging knowledge bases in LSTMs for improving machine reading. arXiv preprint arXiv:1902.09091 (2019)
33. Yin, W., Ebert, S., Schütze, H.: Attention-based convolutional neural network for machine comprehension. In: Proceedings of the Workshop on Human-Computer Question Answering, pp. 15–21 (2016)

34. Zhang, Y., Qi, P., Manning, C.D.: Graph convolution over pruned dependency trees improves relation extraction. In: Proceedings of the 2018 Conference on Empirical Methods in Natural Language Processing, pp. 2205–2215. Association for Computational Linguistics (2018)
35. Zhong, H., Xiao, C., Tu, C., Zhang, T., Liu, Z., Sun, M.: JEC-QA: a legal-domain question answering dataset. arXiv preprint arXiv:1911.12011 (2019)
36. Zhou, J., et al.:.Gear: graph-based evidence aggregating and reasoning for fact verification. In: Proceedings of the 57th Annual Meeting of the Association for Computational Linguistics, pp. 892–901 (2019)
37. Zhu, H., Wei, F., Qin, B., Liu, T.: Hierarchical attention flow for multiple-choice reading comprehension. In: Proceedings of the 32nd AAAI Conference on Artificial Intelligence, pp. 6077–6085 (2018)

Embedding-Based Network Alignment Using Neural Tensor Networks

Qiuyue Li, Nianwen Ning, Bin Wu[✉], and Wenying Guo

Beijing Key Laboratory of Intelligent Telecommunications Software and Multimedia, Beijing, China
{qiuyueli,nianwenning,wubin,gwy}@bupt.edu.cn

Abstract. Network alignment plays a significant role in network analysis and benefits a wide range of applications. However, existing methods are sensitive to structural noises and do not consider the one-to-one constraint on the anchor links. In this paper, to tackle this problem, we propose a novel framework called embedding-based network Alignment using Neural Tensor Networks (AlignNTN). It considers the one-to-one constraint and uses the neural tensor networks to learn the relationship between nodes in two networks. The proposed method provides a powerful way to learn the relationship between nodes and does not necessarily rely on demographic features. What is more, our model can easily incorporate with node attributes to improve the effectiveness of network alignment. Extensive experiments have been conducted on four real-world datasets, and the results demonstrate that the proposed method outperforms state-of-the-art methods by a significant margin.

Keywords: Network embedding · Network alignment · Neural tensor networks

1 Introduction

Network alignment aims to find the correspondence of nodes (anchor links) across two or more networks. Recent years have drawn more attention due to its potential for multiple concrete real-world applications ranging from cross-network recommendation [11] to link prediction [3].

Recently, network alignment has been widely studied. There are two methods to handle the network alignment problem: spectral methods and network representation learning methods. Spectral methods align two networks based on the operation of the adjacency matrices. It is a direct way to perform alignment between two networks [17]. In general, spectral alignment techniques (REGAL [6], FINAL [22], IsoRank [15]) hold the assumption of structural consistency, which indicates that a node tends to have a consistent connectivity structure across different networks. However, such techniques are sensitive to structural noises when networks do not follow the structure consistency principle. Network representation learning methods (MGCN [1], DANA [7], DeepLink [24], PALE

© Springer Nature Switzerland AG 2021
H. Qiu et al. (Eds.): KSEM 2021, LNAI 12817, pp. 401–413, 2021.
https://doi.org/10.1007/978-3-030-82153-1_33

[12], IONE [10]) solve the network alignment problem leveraging advances in graph embedding. It involves two stages which are embedding and matching. The first stage is to embed each network into a low-dimensional space to learn node representation, and the second stage is to learn a mapping function by the low-dimensional representations of nodes. It maps two networks to a common space and then measures the similarity of the two nodes from two networks. However, such mapping functions do not take into account the one-to-one constraint on the anchor links. Due to the one-to-one constraint on the anchor links, among all the potential anchor links incident to each node, only one of them will be positive, and the remaining ones will be all negative, where the existing anchor links as the positive instances and non-existing ones as the negative instances.

To solve those problems, we propose a novel supervised model called embedding-based network Alignment using Neural Tensor Networks (Align-NTN) to tackle the network alignment problem. This model contains two stages, namely, embedding and matching. Given two networks for predicting their anchor links, the first stage embed each network into a low-dimensional space to learn node representation. It can capture the main structural regularity of each network and filter the insignificant noise. In the matching stage, we model relational information leveraging a powerful neural tensor networks [16]. Furthermore, we rely on the one-to-one constraint on the anchor links. What is more, if nodes have demographic features (e.g., location, gender or user name), our model can easily incorporate those features to improve the accuracy of network alignment. The main contributions of our work are:

1. AlignNTN explore the potential of neural tensor networks in network alignment task, It can capture more powerful relational information.
2. We highlight the importance of the one-to-one constraint on the anchor links for network alignment task.
3. We evaluate the proposed models with detailed experiments on four real-world network datasets. The experiment results demonstrate our model can outperform state-of-the-art methods.

2 Related Work

2.1 Network Embedding

Network embedding methods embed node information into a low-dimensional latent space. Many network embedding methods have been proposed in the past few decades.

Inspired by the skip-gram model [13] in natural language processing, Deep-Walk [14] learns structural regularities present within short random walks. LINE [18] extends DeepWalk with an objective function to preserve both the first-order and second-order proximities in the large-scale networks. Node2vec [4] proposes two sampling strategies for generating neighborhood sets from the perspective of DFS and BFS.

Recently, some researchers have exploited Convolutional Neural Networks (CNN) and spectral graph theory to learn network embedding. GCN [8] defines convolutional kernels on graph-structured data to learn node embeddings by aggregating information passed from its neighborhood. GraphSAGE [5] learns a function that generates embeddings by sampling and aggregating features from the local neighborhood of nodes. GAT [21] takes advantage of the attention mechanism to compute the hidden embeddings of each node in the graph. DGCN [25] uses two convolutional networks to capture local and global consistency respectively and adopts an unsupervised loss to ensemble them. At the first step of AlignNTN framework, the node representations are learned independently to preserve specific structural regularities.

2.2 Network Alignment

Spectral Approaches. Many spectral approaches leverage matrix factorization to compute the alignment matrix directly. The IsoRank [15] simultaneously handles node and network similarity with structural consistency over the network, which holds the idea that two nodes from two networks are similar if their neighborhoods are similar as well. FINAL [22] considers network structure, node feature and edge feature to tackle alignment problem on attributed networks. REGAL [6] models alignment matrix by structure and attribute information then employs low-rank matrix approximation to speed up calculation.

However, these methods struggle to scale up to large networks due to the adjacency matrices' high sparsity. In addition, these methods are sensitive to structural noises, as networks do not follow the structure consistency principle.

Embedding-Based Approaches. The emergency of network embedding techniques has brought network alignment to a new era. They first learn the embeddings of node in each network via a single network structure and then learn the mapping function from one embedding space into another based on known anchor links. PALE [12] learns network embeddings by maximizing the co-occurrence likelihood of connected nodes and then applies linear or multi-layer perceptron (MLP) as the mapping function. IONE [10] learns the embedding of nodes with second-order node similarity. DeepLink [24] employs a random walk to generate node embeddings and then an auto-encoder to learn the mapping function. DALAUP [2] applies active learning to learn network embeddings, but its scalability is limited since the active learning schemes can be time-consuming on large-scale networks. MGCN [1] learn network embeddings with the local and hypergraph level graph convolutions and then uses linear as the mapping function. Our approach is similar to the PALE algorithm in the network embedding step. However, we use neural tensor networks to learn the relationship between the nodes in two networks under the one-to-one constraint on the anchor links in the mapping step.

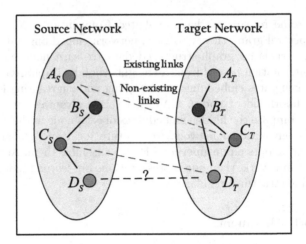

Fig. 1. Example of one-to-one constraint.

3   Model

3.1   Problem Definition

Let $G = \{V, E\}$ denote the network, where V and E are the set of nodes and edges, respectively. The alignment problem in this paper is to find hidden anchor links in two different networks with some known anchor links. Without loss of generality, given two networks, we choose one network as source network G^s, and the other as target network G^t. We aim to identify the corresponding node in the target network for each node in the source network. The formulation of the network alignment problem is as follows:

Network Alignment: Given two different networks $G^s = \{V^s, E^s\}$, $G^t = \{V^t, E^t\}$ and a set of observed anchor links $T = \{(u, v)|v \in V^s, u \in V^t\}$, our goal is to predict unobserved anchor links across G^s and G^t.

One-to-One Constraint: The one-to-one constraint on the anchor links means that only one of them will be positive, and the remaining ones will be all negative among all the potential anchor links incident to a node. In Fig. 1, we show an example of the application of the one-to-one constraint on the anchor links. Given a set of existing anchor links of two networks, we can determine a set of non-existing anchor links between them. These links can be served as the training set. The existing anchor links are positive instances, and non-existing ones are the negative instances. Formally, we can denote $\{(A_S, A_T), (C_S, C_T)\}$ as a set of positive instances, and $\{(A_S, C_T), (C_S, D_T), \dots\}$ as a set of negative instances.

3.2   Model Overview

To predict anchor links, we propose a novel embedding-based network Alignment model called AlignNTN. Figure 2 is an illustration of our proposed AlignNTN

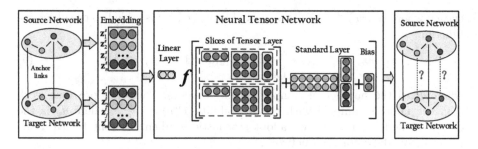

Fig. 2. Framework of our model AlignNTN.

framework, which contains two stages. We firstly embed the source and target networks into low-dimensional spaces, denoted as Z^s and Z^t respectively, where $Z^s \in \mathbb{R}^{|V^s| \times d}$, $Z^t \in \mathbb{R}^{|V^t| \times d}$, and d is the embedding size. After obtaining the node embeddings, taking the low-dimensional embeddings of nodes as features, we use Neural Tensor Networks to predict whether an anchor link exists between nodes from two networks with the application of one-to-one constraint on the observed anchor links.

3.3 Network Embedding

Since the networks are embedded independently, for convenience, we describe the embedding on network $G = \{V, E\}$ without distinguishing the source and the target network. For each pair of nodes $(v_i, v_j) \in E$, the goal is to maximize their co-occurrence probability:

$$\prod_{(v_i,v_j) \in E} p(v_i, v_j) \tag{1}$$

To reduce the computation complexity, we maximize the log-likelihood:

$$\sum_{(v_i,v_j) \in E} \log p(v_i, v_j) \tag{2}$$

where $p(v_i, v_j)$ can be defined using the Sigmoid function as in the skip-gram model [13]:

$$p(v_i, v_j) = \sigma(z_i^T \cdot z_j) = \frac{1}{1 + e^{-z_i^T \cdot z_j}} \tag{3}$$

leading to the maximize objective:

$$\sum_{(v_i,v_j) \in E} \log \sigma(z_i^T \cdot z_j) \tag{4}$$

Since we only model the observed edges, It exists a trivial solution $z_i^T \cdot z_j = \infty$. To avoid the trivial solution, for each observed edge (v_i, v_j), the nodes v_k are chosen where $(v_i, v_k) \notin E$, and the probability $p(v_i, v_k)$ is added to the objective function:

$$\log \sigma(z_i^T \cdot z_j) + \sum_{k=1}^{K} E_{v_k \propto P(v)}[\log(1 - \sigma(z_i^T \cdot z_k))] \tag{5}$$

where K is the number of sampled negative edges. Following previous work [13], the node is sampled with the probability $P(v) \sim d_v^{0.75}$ where d_v is the degree of node v. Finally, we adopt stochastic gradient descent to learn the latent embeddings for each network.

3.4   Network Alignment

Given the embeddings Z^s and Z^t of two networks produced by the previous stage and anchor links $(v_i^s, u_n^t) \in T$, For a pair of nodes (v_i^s, u_j^t), we denote z_i^s and z_j^t are the embedding of node v_i^s and u_j^t respectively. The goal of our approach is to predict whether a pair of nodes (v_i^s, u_j^t) is an anchor link and with what certainty, a simple way to model their relation is to take the inner product of their node embeddings. However, It can lead to insufficient or weak interaction between nodes. Following [16], we use Neural Tensor Networks (NTN) to model the relation between node embeddings (z_i^s, z_j^t), which is simplified as (z_i, z_j):

$$g(z_i, z_j) = U^T f(z_i^T W^{[1:k]} z_j + V \begin{bmatrix} z_i \\ z_j \end{bmatrix} + b) \tag{6}$$

The model computes a score indicate the probability that a pair of nodes (v_i^s, u_j^t) is an anchor links, where $W^{[1:k]} \in \mathbb{R}^{d \times d \times k}$ is a tensor, k is the number of slice, $U \in \mathbb{R}^k$ and $V \in \mathbb{R}^{k \times 2d}$ are weight vector, $b \in \mathbb{R}^k$ is a bias vector, and $f(\cdot) = tanh$ is an activation function.

The model is trained with the contrastive max-margin objective function [16]. The main idea is that the existing anchor links $T = (z_u^s, z_v^t)$ should receive a higher score than the non-existing ones $T_c = (z_u^s, z_c^t)$, where our model sampled non-existing nodes with the application of one-to-one constraint on the observed anchor links. Let $\Omega = \{U, W, V, b\}$ denote the set of NTN parameters. We minimize the following objective:

$$J(\Omega) = \sum_{i=1}^{N} \sum_{c=1}^{C} \max\left(0, 1 - g\left(T^{(i)}\right) + g\left(T_c^{(i)}\right)\right) + \lambda \|\Omega\|_2^2 \tag{7}$$

where N is the number of training observed anchor links and we score the anchor link higher than the non-existing one up to a margin of 1. For each existing anchor link, we sample C non-existing anchor links. We use standard L_2 regularization of all the parameters, weighted by the hyperparameter λ. The parameters are updated to minimize the objective function $J(\Omega)$ using the Adam optimization.

4 Experiment

In this section, we present the datasets and the performance of our proposed model, then examine the effectiveness of our model on four real-world datasets of eight networks.

Table 1. Descriptive statistics of datasets

Datasets	Network	Nodes	Edges	Attribute	Anchors
Douban	Douban online	3906	8164	538	1118
	Douban offline	1118	1511		
Allmv-Tmdb	Allmovie	6011	124709	14	5176
	Tmdb	5713	119073		
Fb-Tw	Facebook	17359	112381	0	1998
	Twitter	20024	114999		
Fq-Tw	Foursquare	17355	132208	0	3602
	Twitter	20417	236882		

4.1 Datasets

The statistical description of our datasets is presented in Table 1.

Douban Online - Douban Offline (Douban): The dataset contains two networks collected from Douban social network by [23]. The node represents users and the edge indicates the friendships of users. The location of the users is treated node attribute.

Allmovie-Tmdb (Allmv-Tmdb): The dataset contains two networks constructed from Rotten Tomatoes and Tmdb website by [19]. Two films have an edge connecting them if they have at least one common actor. The genres of the films are used to present node attributes. The identity of the film constructs the alignment groundtruth.

Facebook-Twitter (Fb-Tw): The dataset is gathered from Singapore-based Facebook and Twitter accounts by [20]. Users' short description determines the alignment groundtruth on their Twitter account that declares their Facebook account. Node attributes are not provided in this dataset.

Foursquare-Twitter (Fq-Tw): The dataset is also collected from Singaporean-based Foursquare and Twitter accounts as Facebook-Twitter by [20]. Node attributes are also not provided in this dataset.

4.2 Baseline Methods

We compare our approach against the following baselines:

- **IONE** [10]: IONE is a representation learning-based method that preserves the second-order proximity to learn node embeddings.
- **PALE-L** [12]: PALE-L is an embedding-based approach that learns nodes embedding by maximizing the co-occurrence likelihood of edge's vertices and then leverages linear as the mapping function.
- **PALE-M** [12]: A variant of PALE-L adopts multi-layer perceptron (MLP) to construct mapping function.
- **REGAL** [6]: REGAL is an unsupervised factorization-based alignment method. It leverages the power of automatically learning node embeddings to match nodes across different networks.
- **DeepLink** [24]: DeepLink is an embedding-based technique. It learns node embeddings via the skip-gram model and then uses auto-encoder and MLP to construct mapping function.
- **CENALP** [3]: CENALP is an embedding-based method. It unifies network alignment and link prediction tasks.
- **GAlign** [19]: GAlign is an unsupervised network alignment framework based on a multi-order embedding model and designs a data augmentation method and a refinement mechanism to adapt to consistency violations and noise.

4.3 Metrics

To evaluate the performance of the algorithms, we use three metrics: Accuracy (*Acc*), Mean Average Precision (*MAP*), and Precision@k (*Pre@k*).

Accuracy. We apply a heuristic greedy matching algorithm [9] on the similarity matrix. It is a post-processing step to get one-to-one alignments between the two networks and then compute the alignment accuracy on the groundtruth. The accuracy is calculated as $Acc = \frac{c}{g}$, where c is the correctly identified node pairs and g is the groundtruth node pairs.

MAP. MAP can be computed $MAP = mean(\frac{1}{ra})$ where ra is the rank position of positive matching node in the sequence of sorted candidates.

Pre@k. The metric measures whether the positive matching identity occurs in the top-k candidate list. $Pre@k$ is defined as $Pre@k = \frac{t}{g}$, where t is the times that target node in top k and g is the groundtruth node pairs.

4.4 Experiment Setting

We conducted our experiment on the no-attribute model, which only contains the structure of the network. A random 10-dimensional attribute is generated when the method requires attribute information. The dimension d of the embedding is set to 300. The number of slices k of W is set to 4. The number of negative sample C is set to 40. During training, We use a batch size of 64 and apply Adam

Table 2. *Acc* score with different training ratios (best performance in bold)

Dataset	Ratio	AlignNTN	GAlign	CENALP	DeepLink	REGAL	PALE-L	PALE-M	IONE
Douban	20%	**0.3430**	0.0011	0.2436	0.0670	0.0161	0.2257	0.2626	0.1061
	50%	**0.6064**	0.0018	0.3542	0.1753	0.0161	0.4150	0.4401	0.0751
	80%	**0.7098**	0.0045	0.5179	0.2054	0.0161	0.4554	0.5313	0.0670
Allmv-Tmdb	20%	**0.8215**	0.0002	0.1773	0.5673	0.0769	0.8145	0.7706	0.6181
	50%	**0.8377**	0.0000	0.6123	0.7883	0.0769	0.8215	0.8243	0.5542
	80%	**0.8508**	0.0010	0.8174	0.8275	0.0769	0.8391	0.8488	0.5770
Fb-Tw	20%	**0.0338**	0.0000	0.0013	0.0044	0.0010	0.0119	0.0213	0.0188
	50%	**0.1210**	0.0000	0.0040	0.0090	0.0010	0.0370	0.0290	0.0420
	80%	**0.1646**	0.0000	0.0050	0.0075	0.0010	0.0532	0.0481	0.0326
Fq-Tw	20%	**0.1607**	0.0000	0.0045	0.0076	0.0000	0.0902	0.0753	0.0440
	50%	**0.2593**	0.0000	0.0128	0.0272	0.0000	0.1677	0.1099	0.0650
	80%	**0.3093**	0.0000	0.0222	0.0583	0.0000	0.1942	0.1207	0.0457

optimizer with a learning rate of 0.001. The λ is set to 5e−4. The baselines are implemented according to the original papers. All experiments, including the sampling, are executed five times and report the average results.

4.5   Experimental Results

Effectiveness Analysis. In this section, we compare the performance of Align-NTN with baselines on four real-world datasets. The experiment results of *Acc* (training ratio = {20%, 50%, 80%}) are presented in Table 2. We tabulate *MAP*, *Pre*@10, and *Pre*@30 comparison on real-word datasets when the training ratio is 20% in Table 3.

From Table 2, we can observe that AlignNTN significantly outperforms all baselines in terms of *Acc* on four benchmark datasets and different training ratios. It demonstrates the efficacy of the proposed AlignNTN framework. Specifically, compared with the most competitive baseline on *Acc* under different training ratios, AlignNTN achieves an improvement of 8.04%, 16.63%, and 17.85%

Table 3. *MAP*, *Pre*@10, and *Pre*@30 comparison on real-world datasets when training ratio is 20% (best performance in bold)

Dataset	Metric	AlignNTN	GAlign	CENALP	DeepLink	REGAL	PALE-L	PALE-M	IONE
Douban	MAP	0.3470	0.0079	**0.4061**	0.1408	0.1005	0.2741	0.2577	0.2467
	Pre@10	**0.6849**	0.0067	0.6715	0.3486	0.2030	0.5799	0.6134	0.4715
	Pre@30	**0.8313**	0.0257	0.7799	0.5106	0.3739	0.6950	0.7542	0.6346
Allmv-Tmdb	MAP	**0.7966**	0.0021	0.2639	0.2830	0.1887	0.7956	0.7226	0.6937
	Pre@10	**0.9193**	0.0027	0.4362	0.6370	0.3868	0.9073	0.8889	0.8081
	Pre@30	**0.9517**	0.0068	0.6525	0.7812	0.6049	0.9459	0.9321	0.8608
Fb-Tw	MAP	**0.0410**	0.0010	0.0163	0.0069	0.0021	0.0198	0.0242	0.0258
	Pre@10	**0.1007**	0.0013	0.0244	0.0156	0.0025	0.0494	0.0657	0.0550
	Pre@30	**0.1887**	0.0050	0.0569	0.0294	0.0070	0.1082	0.1326	0.0969
Fq-Tw	MAP	**0.1730**	0.0010	0.0194	0.0146	0.0033	0.0978	0.0859	0.0627
	Pre@10	**0.3473**	0.0014	0.0330	0.0409	0.0053	0.2346	0.2283	0.1273
	Pre@30	**0.5049**	0.0049	0.0704	0.0784	0.0147	0.3761	0.3681	0.2273

on Douban, 0.7%, 1.34%, and 0.2% on Allmv-Tmdb, 1.25%, 7.90%, and 11.14% on Fb-Tw, and 7.05%, 9.16%, and 11.51% on Fq-Tw, respectively.

REGAL, GAlign, and CENALP do not perform well with only using the structural information since they heavily rely on the initialization of the embedding. REGAL, GAlign, and CENALP can perform better when they are initialized with privilege information. Whereas benefiting from the adopted network embedding technique, AlignNTN is robust to the initialization and focuses on exploring only the structural information to facilitate the alignment.

Although DeepLink, PALE, and IONE utilize the embedding approach to learn network representation, its alignment method is based on learning mapping functions between two networks. The function focuses more on preserving proximity inside each network while lacking awareness of one-to-one constraint on the anchor links.

Parameter Analysis. We compare three main parameters, including d, k, and C. The parameters are set by default to be $d = 300$, $k = 4$, $C = 40$ and the training ratio is 20%. The variation of parameters can reflect the importance of factors affecting the model.

For parameter d, Fig. 3(a) shows that *Acc* scores first increase with the number of dimensions and then tend to decrease. When the embedding dimension reaches a certain level, AlignNTN can capture enough essential information. If the embedding dimension continues to increase, it may contain some meaningless and redundant information.

For parameters k and C, Fig. 3(b) and Fig. 3(c) reveal that the performance of AlignNTN first increases with the number of slices k of W slightly, and then tends to stabilize. When the number of slices k of W reaches a certain level, the critical information related to the alignment task has been saved.

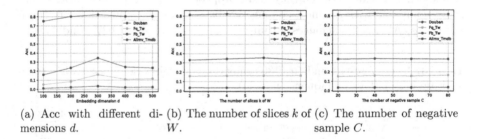

(a) Acc with different dimensions d.
(b) The number of slices k of W.
(c) The number of negative sample C.

Fig. 3. Parameter analysis on d, k, C

Table 4. Performance of whether model uses attributes.

Metric	Model	Douban			Allmv-Tmdb		
		20%	50%	80%	20%	50%	80%
Acc	AlignNTN	0.3430	0.6064	0.7098	0.8215	0.8377	0.8508
	AlignNTN$^+$	**0.3542**	**0.6655**	**0.7455**	**0.9317**	**0.9416**	**0.9438**
MAP	AlignNTN	0.3470	0.5918	0.7365	0.7966	0.8217	0.8162
	AlignNTN$^+$	**0.3661**	**0.6770**	**0.7764**	**0.9121**	**0.9235**	**0.9273**

Discussion on Attributes. We add an extended experiment. When the nodes in the network have attributes, we can easily combine the node structure information and attribute information to improve the performance of the algorithm. After the embedding stage, we normalize the node's attribute information, concatenate it behind the embedding, and then proceed to the matching stage. We call this model AlignNTN$^+$. Table 4 shows results of AlignNTN and AlignNTN$^+$ on Douban and Allmv-Tmdb datasets.

5 Conclusion

In this paper, we proposed AlignNTN to predict anchor links. It can incorporate the one-to-one constraint and use the neural tensor networks to learn the relationship between nodes in two networks. We evaluate our model with detailed experiments on four real-world network datasets. The experiment results demonstrate the superiority of our framework in comparison with other state-of-the-art approaches. As future works, we will exploit some parallel and distributed techniques to handle large-scale networks.

Acknowledgements. This work is supported by the National Natural Science Foundation of China under Grant (No. 61972047) and the NSFC-General Technology Basic Research Joint Funds under Grant (No. U1936220).

References

1. Chen, H., Yin, H., Sun, X., et al.: Multi-level graph convolutional networks for cross-platform anchor link prediction. In: Proceedings of the 26th ACM SIGKDD International Conference on Knowledge Discovery & Data Mining, pp. 1503–1511. Association for Computing Machinery, New York (2020)
2. Cheng, A., Zhou, C., Yang, H., et al.: Deep active learning for anchor user prediction. In: Proceedings of the Twenty-Eighth International Joint Conference on Artificial Intelligence, IJCAI-19, pp. 2151–2157. International Joint Conferences on Artificial Intelligence Organization, July 2019
3. Du, X., Yan, J., Zha, H.: Joint link prediction and network alignment via cross-graph embedding. In: Proceedings of the Twenty-Eighth International Joint Conference on Artificial Intelligence, IJCAI-19, pp. 2251–2257. International Joint Conferences on Artificial Intelligence Organization, July 2019

4. Grover, A., Leskovec, J.: Node2vec: scalable feature learning for networks. In: Proceedings of the 22nd ACM SIGKDD International Conference on Knowledge Discovery and Data Mining, KDD 2016, pp. 855–864. Association for Computing Machinery, New York (2016)

5. Hamilton, W., Ying, Z., Leskovec, J.: Inductive representation learning on large graphs. In: Guyon, I., et al. (eds.) Advances in Neural Information Processing Systems, vol. 30, pp. 1024–1034. Curran Associates, Inc. (2017)

6. Heimann, M., Shen, H., Safavi, T., et al.: REGAL: representation learning-based graph alignment. In: Proceedings of the 27th ACM International Conference on Information and Knowledge Management, CIKM 2018, pp. 117–126. Association for Computing Machinery, New York (2018)

7. Hong, H., Li, X., Pan, Y., Tsang, I.: Domain-adversarial network alignment. IEEE Trans. Knowl. Data Eng. (2020)

8. Kipf, T.N., Welling, M.: Semi-supervised classification with graph convolutional networks. In: 5th International Conference on Learning Representations, ICLR, Toulon, 24–26 April 2017, Conference Track Proceedings. OpenReview.net (2017)

9. Kollias, G., Mohammadi, S., Grama, A.: Network similarity decomposition (NSD): a fast and scalable approach to network alignment. IEEE Trans. Knowl. Data Eng. **24**(12), 2232–2243 (2012)

10. Liu, L., Cheung, W.K., Li, X., et al.: Aligning users across social networks using network embedding. In: Kambhampati, S. (ed.) Proceedings of the Twenty-Fifth International Joint Conference on Artificial Intelligence, IJCAI 2016, New York, NY, USA, 9–15 July 2016, pp. 1774–1780. IJCAI/AAAI Press (2016)

11. Man, T., Shen, H., Jin, X., et al.: Cross-domain recommendation: an embedding and mapping approach. In: Proceedings of the Twenty-Sixth International Joint Conference on Artificial Intelligence, IJCAI-17, pp. 2464–2470 (2017)

12. Man, T., Shen, H., Liu, S., et al.: Predict anchor links across social networks via an embedding approach. In: Kambhampati, S. (ed.) Proceedings of the Twenty-Fifth International Joint Conference on Artificial Intelligence, IJCAI 2016, New York, NY, USA, 9–15 July 2016, pp. 1823–1829. IJCAI/AAAI Press (2016)

13. Mikolov, T., Sutskever, I., Chen, K., et al.: Distributed representations of words and phrases and their compositionality. In: Burges, C.J.C., Bottou, L., Welling, M., Ghahramani, Z., Weinberger, K.Q. (eds.) Advances in Neural Information Processing Systems, vol. 26, pp. 3111–3119. Curran Associates, Inc. (2013)

14. Perozzi, B., Al-Rfou, R., Skiena, S.: DeepWalk: online learning of social representations. In: Proceedings of the 20th ACM SIGKDD International Conference on Knowledge Discovery and Data Mining, KDD 2014, pp. 701–710. Association for Computing Machinery, New York (2014)

15. Singh, R., Xu, J., Berger, B.: Global alignment of multiple protein interaction networks with application to functional orthology detection. Proc. Natl. Acad. Sci. U.S.A. **105**(35), 12763–12768 (2008)

16. Socher, R., Chen, D., Manning, C.D., et al.: Reasoning with neural tensor networks for knowledge base completion. In: Burges, C.J.C., Bottou, L., Welling, M., Ghahramani, Z., Weinberger, K.Q. (eds.) Advances in Neural Information Processing Systems, vol. 26, pp. 926–934. Curran Associates, Inc. (2013)

17. Tan, S., Guan, Z., Cai, D., et al.: Mapping users across networks by manifold alignment on hypergraph. In: Brodley, C.E., Stone, P. (eds.) Proceedings of the Twenty-Eighth AAAI Conference on Artificial Intelligence, 27–31 July 2014, Québec City, Québec, Canada, pp. 159–165. AAAI Press (2014)

18. Tang, J., Qu, M., Wang, M., et al.: LINE: large-scale information network embedding, pp. 1067–1077. International World Wide Web Conferences Steering Committee, Republic and Canton of Geneva, CHE (2015)
19. Trung, H.T., Van Vinh, T., Tam, N.T., et al.: Adaptive network alignment with unsupervised and multi-order convolutional networks. In: 2020 IEEE 36th International Conference on Data Engineering (ICDE), pp. 85–96 (2020)
20. Trung, H.T., Toan, N.T., Vinh, T.V., et al.: A comparative study on network alignment techniques. Expert Syst. Appl. **140**, 112883 (2020)
21. Velickovic, P., Cucurull, G., Casanova, A., et al.: Graph attention networks. In: International Conference on Learning Representations, ICLR 2018, Vancouver, Canada, 30 April–3 May 2018, Conference Track Proceedings. OpenReview.net (2018)
22. Zhang, S., Tong, H.: FINAL: fast attributed network alignment. In: International Conference on Knowledge Discovery and Data Mining, pp. 1345–1354. Association for Computing Machinery, New York (2016)
23. Zhong, E., Fan, W., Wang, J., Xiao, L., Li, Y.: ComSoc: adaptive transfer of user behaviors over composite social network, pp. 696–704. Association for Computing Machinery, New York (2012)
24. Zhou, F., Liu, L., Zhang, K., Trajcevski, G., et al.: DeepLink: a deep learning approach for user identity linkage. In: IEEE INFOCOM 2018 - IEEE Conference on Computer Communications, pp. 1313–1321 (2018)
25. Zhuang, C., Ma, Q.: Dual graph convolutional networks for graph-based semi-supervised classification, pp. 499–508. International World Wide Web Conferences Steering Committee, Republic and Canton of Geneva, CHE (2018)

Detecting Parkinson's Disease According to Gender Using Speech Signals

Rania Khaskhoussy[(✉)] and Yassine Ben Ayed

MIRACL: Multimedia Information System and Advanced Computing Laboratory,
Sfax University, Sfax, Tunisia
rania.khaskhoussy@enis.tn

Abstract. Parkinson's Disease (PD) is a progressive neurodegenerative disorder that mainly affects the central nervous system causing cognitive, emotional and language disorders. Speech impairment is one of the earliest PD symptoms, and may be used for an automatic assessment to support the diagnosis and the evaluation of the disease severity, in the two biological sexes (male and female). This study investigates the processing of voice signals for measuring the incidence of Parkinson's disease in women and men. The approach evaluates the use of several extracted features and two learning techniques Support Vector Machines (SVM) and Long Short-Term Memory (LSTM) to classify data obtained from four databases. Each database contains different data to each other and in a different language. The audio tasks were recorded using six different microphone. The results reveal cases of Parkinson's disease appear more in men than in women.

Keywords: Parkinson's disease · Signal processing · Feature extraction · LSTM · SVM · Gender

1 Introduction

Recently, The estimates of the World Health Organization (WHO) showed that neurodegenerative diseases as one of the most significant threats to public health. Hundreds of millions of people around the world suffer from neurological disorders, about 6.8 million people die each year from this affliction and the total number of people affected are expected to reach 82 million in 2030 and 152 million in 2050. Other than this, cost of neurological disorders for the economy is rising, according to WHO and ICM (Institute of Brain and Spinal Cord) in Europe, the cost was estimated at some €139 billion in 2004 and €800 billion in 2010. WHO estimates that by 2030, the worldwide scale cost will reach $2.000 billion annually. Among the most common disorders are Parkinson's disease (PD), Alzheimer, Epilepsy, Stroke, Headaches, Brain trauma, Neuroinfections, Multiple sclerosis and other diseases.

The Carenity social network reveals that Parkinson disease expected to exceed cancer disease in second rank of mortality around the year 2040. This

© Springer Nature Switzerland AG 2021
H. Qiu et al. (Eds.): KSEM 2021, LNAI 12817, pp. 414–425, 2021.
https://doi.org/10.1007/978-3-030-82153-1_34

mental disorder have human, social and financial effects, both at personal, professional and social level. Even patients are considered on the road to death because this disease characterized by a progressive loss of mental and physical capacities, leading to isolation of individuals from their families, society and health institutions. Human and social dimensions considered as the main source of contribution for this work. In fact determine which the most category infected by PD could reduce the effects, win a time to control the disease evolution and focus more on the group that is a lot affected, in order to provide them with the necessary precautions. Moreover the rising of financial problems of Parkinson disease which was estimated by [1] range from €2620 to €9820 per patient, also motivate the interest and the need for contributions that may reduce the load at the different levels of society.

Parkinson's disease was first described in 1817 under the term **trembling paralysis** in a book by the doctor James Parkinson entitled **Essay on shaking palsy**. PD affects the central nervous system causing a progressive and irreversible loss of neurons from the dopaminergic system which is found in the substantia nigra of the human brain, it's the system responsible for the manufacture, release of dopamine and controlling the execution of motor plans [2].

The causes of dopamine deficiency remains unknown in most cases [3], but scientists agree that a set of genetic and environmental factors play a part in the onset of PD like the age, family history, head trauma and even contact with some pesticides. This cognitive dysfunction affects several motor activities among these activities, speech production [4] such as slower or more irregular speech patterns, difficulty to finding action word, identification and production of action verb.

In this paper, a methodology to detect the most category infected by PD between women and men through speech analysis is proposed. The methodology uses signal processing techniques to extract various type of features from four databases, integrated with two learning technique to classify samples sustained phonation and speech tasks recorded with six different microphone.

The remainder of this paper is organized as follows. Section 2 reviews the most important contributions related with the detection of PD. Section 3 describes the adopted methodology. In Sect. 4 the discussion of the results is presented and Sect. 5 states the main conclusions and outlines future work.

2   Related Work

In 1998, it was proved that the voice is the primary deficit, most often affected in the early stages of PD [5]. Several studies describe approaches based on speech analysis for detecting PD. [6] Evaluate the performance metrics of two type of features, cepstral and phonetic extract from the signal voice, followed by an hybridization of the two to distinguish healthy subjects from PD patients. The study concluded that the best accuracy 98% was obtained by using the phonation features.

Statistical comparison of several types of jitter and shimmer features were used in [7] to assess the difference between two categories of voice samples. The analysis performed shows that the parameters of the two groups are uncorrelated and independent, and some variants of jitter and shimmer did not follow normal distribution for PD patients.

[8] Define a methodology to monitor speech symptoms in PD. The proposed approach uses a set of 13 features selected from three measurement type cepstral, spectral and F0 variability. The study concluded the best performance (92% accuracy) was obtained using the SVM classifier.

[9] Proposes a new algorithm based on combination of genetic algorithm and SVM for detecting the PD through voice. Twenty two linear and non-linear features are extracted from the signals which 14 features are based on fundamental frequency F0 (pitch), jitter, shimmer and noise to harmonics ratio (NHR). Four optimal features: maximum vocal fundamental frequency, highest vocal fundamental frequency, jitter (RAP) and shimmer (APQ5) are selected by the genetic algorithm to giving an accuracy rate of 94.50%.

[10] Illustrated the detection of PD using acoustic and phonetic characteristics present in portuguese speech. In regard to phonetic characteristics the authors extract and analysis the first and second formant frequencies (F1 and F2) of PD patients and healthy subjects. For the acoustic analysis the authors extract the mel frequency cepstral coefficients and its derived features, such as the gaussian mixture model and openSMILE toolkit characteristics. The paper concluded that the detection of PD disorders can be achieved through a small number of acoustic features. Furthermore the results demonstrated that F1 and F2 exhibited differences in central vowels for patients at later stages of the PD.

[11] Specified a methodology to discriminate between healthy people and people with PD using two types of Artificial Neural Networks (ANN) and Adaptive Neuro-Fuzzy Classifier (ANFC), as a method for selection of features and classification. The study use 23 features of different types as input to the different classifier. Four optimal features are selected by The ANFC and giving high accuracy (training 95.38% and testing 94.72%) to classify PD and healthy people.

Considering the articulatory features for plosive consonants [12] looked into the differences between these features in PD patients and healthy controls, using a sequential backward feature selection to find an optimal feature subset, and Support Vector Machine (SVM) for classification.

More recently, [13] described an optimization of 3 machine learning (ML) algorithms to detect early signs of PD through speech analysis in an uncontrolled environment. In another approach a new feature was proposed and extracted from mel-frequency cepstral coefficient (MFCC) features, named IMFCC for PD prediction from speech signal using ML algorithms [14]. We can also mention [15] which showed through speech analysis that PD patients with repetitive speech disorders had worse motor, cognitive, and speech functions than those without repetitive speech disorders. In the same way [16] use PD speech analysis and proved that PD Patients who have speech disorder having a higher dopaminergic deficit than PD patients which haven't speech disorders.

In all these works, there is common agreement that speech analysis show the best potential towards the detection of PD. In this paper we applies two learning techniques: SVM and LSTM to develop predictive models and explores several parameters extract from voice recordings of PD patients and healthy people, in order to measure the incidence of Parkinson's disease in women and men.

3   Methodology

For measuring the incidence of Parkinson's disease in women and men, the proposed approach is based on motor symptoms explicitly related to voice. Figure 1 shows the diagram describing the steps followed in this approach.

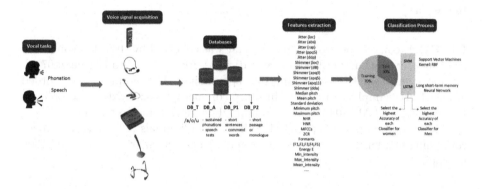

Fig. 1. Diagram of the proposed approach has 5 steps: (1) The voice examination begins; (2) Voice signal acquisitions equipment; (3) Create databases (4) Features extraction from speech samples; (5) training the data using two classifiers and evaluate the results.

3.1   Data Acquisition

DB_T. Collected by [17] and used in [18], DB_T contains two data subsets for train and test. For the training set, it consists of 20 PD patients (6 women and 14 men) who have been suffering from PD for 0 to 6 years with ages varying between 43 and 77 years, and 20 healthy people (10 women and 10 men) aged between 45 and 83. For all subjects three types of sustained vowels (/ a /, / o / and / u /) and other words were recorded.

For the testing set, it consists of 28 PD patients aged between 39 and 79 years and have been suffering from PD for 0 to 13 years. Each subject's record contains two sustained vowels / a / and / o / repeated three times.

All voice recordings are saved in WAV format and made with a Trust MC-1500 microphone with a frequency range 50 Hz and 13 kHz. The microphone is set at 96 kHz, 30 dB and placed 15 cm away from subjects.

DB_A. Consist of 195 sustained vowel phonation from 23 patients with PD (7 women and 16 men) and 8 healthy people (5 women and 3 men). The time since diagnosis ranged from 0 to 28 years, and the ages of the subjects ranged from 46 to 85 years (mean 65.8, standard deviation 9.8). Averages of six phonation were recorded from each subjects of the 31 participants (23 PD and 8 healthy), ranging from 1 to 36 s in length. All voice recordings are taken by a head-mounted microphone (AKG C420) positioned at 8 cm from the patient's lips and sampled at 44.1 kHz with 16 bit resolution (UCI Machine Learning Repository).

In order to validate the result obtained by the dataset already mentioned, we used another dataset contains 50 audio recordings of sustained phonation from 42 people with PD (14 women and 28 men) as a test data. The age range is from 36 to 85 (mean 64.4, standard deviation 9.24) and all the recordings were automatically captured in the patient's homes (UCI Machine Learning Repository).

DB_P1. It consists of two corpus, the first was collected by [10]. It is composed of 22 speakers with PD (12 women and 10 men), from ages 44 to 79 (mean 67.18, standard deviation 9.4), containing 1002 speech lines. The samples were recorded at a 44.1 kHz sampling rate with three type of microphone: desktop microphone; Plantronics, an EMU4040 system and an Olympus WS memo recorder.

The second corpus composed of 20 healthy individuals (10 women, 10 men) containing the sustained vowels (a, o and u) and taken by a Trust MC-1500 microphone.

DB_P2. Was gathered by [19], it is composed of 64 patients with PD (34 women and 30 men) and 35 healthy people (24 women and 11 men). The health state of PD patients was evaluated at stages 1–2.5 according to Hoehn and Yahr [20] and the mean age is 61.5 years for PD patients and 41.8 years for healthy subjects.

Three repetitions of two vocal tasks; phonation (sustained vowel /a/) and speech was recorded from each subjects with a duration of 5 s. All the audio tasks are recorded using two channels from acoustic cardioid (AKG Perception 220, frequency range 20–20,000 Hz) and a smartphone (an internal microphone of Samsung Galaxy Note 3) and sampled at 44.1 kHz with 16-bit resolution. As well the microphone was positioned at about 10 cm distance from the subjects.

3.2   Features Extraction

The features to be used in the process of building the classifier are different types. Table 1 describe the different features extracted from each database. All the features are extracted by different method and tools as Python and Praat. We then use it as input vectors to the different learning techniques for the classification process.

Table 1. Speech features used for the classification process.

Database	Features	Process
DB_T	MFCCs, ZCR, Formants (F1,F2,F3,F4,F5) Energy E, min_intensity, max_intensity mean_intensity, jitter, jitter(loc, abs, rap, ppq5, ddp) shimmer, shimmer(loc, dB, apq3, apq5, apq11, dda) pitch(Median, Mean, Minimum, Maximum) Standard deviation, NHR, HNR	SVM + LSTM
DB_A	jitter, jitter(loc, abs, rap, ppq5, ddp) shimmer, shimmer(loc, dB, apq3, apq5, apq11, dda) NHR, HNR, RPDE, PPE, DFA	SVM + LSTM
DB_P1	MFCCs, ZCR, Formants (F1,F2,F3,F4,F5) Energy E, min_intensity, max_intensity mean_intensity, jitter, jitter(loc, abs, rap, ppq5, ddp) shimmer, shimmer(loc, dB, apq3, apq5, apq11, dda) pitch(Median, Mean, Minimum, Maximum) Standard deviation, NHR, HNR	SVM + LSTM
DB_P2	jitter, jitter(loc, abs, rap, ppq5, ddp) Energy E, MFCCs shimmer, shimmer(loc, dB, apq3, apq5, apq11, dda) pitch(Median, Mean, Minimum, Maximum) min_intensity, max_intensity mean_intensity	SVM + LSTM

3.3 Classification Process

Support Vector Machine. First proposed by [21], SVMs are supervised learning models with associated learning algorithms that analyze data used for binary or multiclass classification. Their principle is simple: they aim to separate the data into classes using a boundary in such a way that the distance between the different data groups and the boundary between them is maximum. This distance appointed margin.

SVMs are often based on the use of kernels if the data is not linearly separable. These mathematical functions make it possible to separate the data by projecting them into a vector space of greater dimension than the intial space, in order to find the hyperplane that maximizes the margin between the classes [22,23].

The classification function f associated with the optimal hyperplane separator His given by:

$$f : \mathbb{R}^N \to \mathbb{R}; \ x \mapsto f(x) = w^t x + b \tag{1}$$

where x is an instance vector, w and b are respectively the weights and bias vector estimated during the training stage. For a given test instance x_t, the classification is based on the sign of the function of hyperplane separator f:

$$Clas(x_t) : sign(f(x_t) = w^t x_t + b) \tag{2}$$

In our work we use SVM as binary classifier with the most recognized kernels lineair, sigmoid and gaussian (RBF).

Long Short-Term Memory. Is a concept first described by [24]. LSTM is a special kind of RNN (recurrent neural network), capable of learning long-term dependencies and overcoming the vanishing gradient problem. In LSTM architecture the outputs depend on the present and previous inputs, and, for this reason, they are very suitable for modeling temporal sequences, as speech.

Sequential learning based on the LSTM architecture has become one of the most popular models for processing with sequential data. Suppose an input sequence of length t, $X = (x_1, ..., x_t)$ and an output sequence $Y = (y_1, ..., y_t)$ of the same length. A single-layer LSTM can be characterized by these two equations [25]:

$$h_t = \sigma_h(W^{hx}x_t + W^{hh}h_{t-1}) \tag{3}$$

$$y_t = \sigma_y(W^{yh}h_t) \tag{4}$$

Where σ_h and σ_y are activation functions. The hidden vector, h_t, is the cell state of a LSTM at time t, illustrating the memory stored in the model. The matrices W^{ij} indicate the transformations from a vector of type i to a vector of type j. The superscripts x, h and y stand for the types of input, hidden and output vectors, respectively.

4 Results and Discussion

Here we present the results achieved by LSTM and SVM on the four data sets generated by different feature extracted. Based on the data, we select the best configuration of each classifier.

After a series of experiments performed on the DB_A data set, we used three SVM kernels: Linear, Sigmoid and Gaussian and we have found that a soft margin support vector machine with gaussian kernel present the best result to detect the most category infected by PD. For long short-term memory we have chosen a four-layer composite architecture: input layer, two hidden layer and output layer (Fig. 2). Then we vary the number of neurons in the hidden layers depending on the number of features in each data set.

4.1 Validation

From one validation sample to another, the validation performance of the model may vary. Cross-validation makes it possible to draw several validation sets from the same database and thus obtain a more robust estimate, with bias and variance, of the validation performance of the model. A five-fold cross-validation scheme was used for the four data sets for the classification experiment, i.e., 70% of the data are used to train the models and the remaining 30% are considered to test the system. At the end of the procedure of each data sets we

Input features

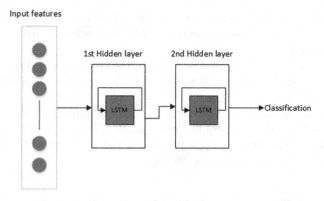

Fig. 2. Long Short-Term Memory architecture.

obtain 3 performance scores, one per block. The mean and standard deviation of the 3 performance scores are calculated to estimate the bias and variance of the validation performed.

4.2   Evaluation Metrics

To perform an evaluation of our proposed approach for detecting the incidence of Parkinson's disease in women and men, three metrics of evaluations were used: Precision (P), Recall (R) and F-score (F).

The Precision formula defined as:

$$P = (\frac{TP}{TP + FP}) \tag{5}$$

Recall defined as follow:

$$R = (\frac{TP}{TP + FN}) \tag{6}$$

The F-score formula is:

$$F = 2(\frac{P.R}{P + R}) \tag{7}$$

Where:

TP = True Positives,
TN = True Negative,
FP = False Positives,
FN = False Negative.

4.3   Experiment

The intent is to obtain a classifier that presents the best F-score (F). We have subdivided each data set into two groups Women and Men and looking forward to getting who is the most category present the highest F-score result, we proposed to use two different learning technique: SVM for machine learning and LSTM for deep learning.

Table 2, 3, 4, 5 and 6 shows the results of the two performed systems on the different data sets. We observe that the best F-score (F) is constantly given by the LSTM classifier.

By analyzing the results presented in the different tables we can conclude that in most cases the highest values of Precision, Recall and F-score were obtained with the male group. Our results confirm that the incidence of Parkinson's disease is higher in men than women [26–28].

Table 2. Classification results on the DB_A Database.

DB_A	LSTM			SVM (RBF)		
	P (%)	R (%)	F (%)	P (%)	R (%)	F (%)
WOMEN	95.00	100	98.00	91.00	95.00	93.00
MEN	99.00	100	99.00	97.00	99.00	98.00

Table 3. Classification results on the DB_P1 Database.

DB_P1	LSTM			SVM (RBF)		
	P (%)	R (%)	F (%)	P (%)	R (%)	F (%)
WOMEN	97.00	100	98.00	94.00	97.00	95.00
MEN	98.00	100	99.00	96.00	98.00	97.00

Table 4. Classification results on the DB_P2 Database using acoustic cardioid (AC) Microphone.

DB_P2 (AC)	LSTM			SVM (RBF)		
	P (%)	R (%)	F (%)	P (%)	R (%)	F (%)
WOMEN	84.00	61.00	76.00	68.00	72.00	66.00
MEN	69.00	98.00	81.00	68.00	74.00	68.00

Table 5. Classification results on the DB_P2 Database using Smart Phone (SP) Microphone.

DB_P2 (SP)	LSTM			SVM (RBF)		
	P (%)	R (%)	F (%)	P (%)	R (%)	F (%)
WOMEN	87.00	80.00	82.00	68.00	72.00	65.00
MEN	76.00	93.00	83.00	69.00	73.00	66.00

Table 6. Classification results on the DB_T Database.

DB_T	LSTM			SVM (RBF)		
	P (%)	R (%)	F (%)	P (%)	R (%)	F (%)
WOMEN	85.00	98.00	91.00	73.00	71.00	65.00
MEN	88.00	99.00	94.00	73.00	75.00	69.00

Figure 3 brings two illustrative curves showing the F-score of the four data sets using LSTM and SVM. It can be concluded that the figures confirm the same conclusion as given above as Parkinson's disease (PD) is found more frequently in men than in women.

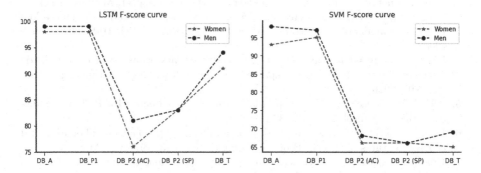

Fig. 3. Curves of classification results using LSTM and SVM.

The primary goal of the present work is to detect the most category infected by PD between women and men in order, to focus more on the most infecting category to accelerate the process of diagnosis of PD, thus, allowing patients to start treatment as soon as possible.

Our approach is precise and essential because it takes the study of four different databases, with a view to overcome any doubts that may intercept us and to properly check the results found. Also through the results found it is possible to use this approach with a smartphone collected data since it has many advantages such as the portability and accessibility [29].

5   Conclusion

In this study, we presented an approach based on speech signal analysis to detect the category most infected with Parkinson's disease between women and men. We used several sets of different features extracted from four databases, then we applied two learning techniques: SVM for machine learning and LSTM for deep learning and evaluated the results in terms of Precision, Recall, and F-score.

The obtained results in our proposed approach showed that there is a significant and evident difference between the results of male group and female group, thus supporting the idea that PD is found more frequently in men than in women.

In Future work, we will refine some feature sets to improve the performance, thus we think to use a method for feature selection which allows to represent the patient's condition properly. Finally, we suggest using other learning techniques for the classification step, which will help in improving the result.

References

1. von Campenhausen, S.: Costs of illness and care in Parkinson's disease: an evaluation in six countries. Eur. Neuropsychopharmacol. **21**, 180–191 (2011)
2. Goetz Christopher, G.: The history of Parkinson's disease: early clinical descriptions and neurological therapies. Cold Spring Harbor Perspect. Med. **1** (2011)
3. Smith, P.D.: Cyclin-dependent kinase 5 is a mediator of dopaminergic neuron loss in a mouse model of Parkinson's disease. Proc. Natl. Acad. Sci. **100**, 13650–13655 (2003)
4. Pinto, S.: La dysarthrie au cours de la maladie de Parkinson. Histoire naturelle de ses composantes: dysphonie, dysprosodie et dysarthrie. Revue neurologique **166**, 800–810 (2010)
5. Aileen, H.: Speech impairment in a large sample of patients with Parkinson's disease. Behav. Neurol. **11**, 131–137 (1998)
6. Upadhya, S.S.: Discriminating Parkinson and healthy people using phonation and cepstral features of speech. Procedia Comput. Sci. **143**, 197–202 (2018)
7. Upadhya Savitha, S.: Statistical comparison of jitter and shimmer voice features for healthy and Parkinson affected persons. In: Second International Conference on Electrical, Computer and Communication Technologies (ICECCT), pp. 1–6 (2017)
8. Taha, K.: Classification of speech intelligibility in Parkinson's disease. Biocybern. Biomed. Eng. **34**, 35–45 (2014)
9. Mohammad, S.: Speech analysis for diagnosis of Parkinson's disease using genetic algorithm and support vector machine. J. Biomed. Sci. Eng. **7**, 147–156 (2014)
10. Proença, J., Veiga, A., Candeias, S., Lemos, J., Januário, C., Perdigão, F.: Characterizing Parkinson's disease speech by acoustic and phonetic features. In: Baptista, J., Mamede, N., Candeias, S., Paraboni, I., Pardo, T.A.S., Volpe Nunes, M.G. (eds.) PROPOR 2014. LNCS (LNAI), vol. 8775, pp. 24–35. Springer, Cham (2014). https://doi.org/10.1007/978-3-319-09761-9_3
11. Mehmet, C.: Automatic recognition of Parkinson's disease from sustained phonation tests using ANN and adaptive neuro-fuzzy classifier. J. Eng. Sci. Des. **1**, 59–64 (2010)
12. David, M.: A Diadochokinesis-based expert system considering articulatory features of plosive consonants for early detection of Parkinson's disease. Comput. Methods Programs Biomed. **154**, 89–97 (2018)
13. Diogo, B.: Automatic detection of Parkinson's disease based on acoustic analysis of speech. Eng. Appl. Artif. Intell. **77**, 148–158 (2019)
14. Biswajit, K.: Parkinson disease prediction using intrinsic mode function based features from speech signal. Biocybern. Biomed. Eng. **40**, 249–264 (2020)
15. Takashi, T.: Clinical correlates of repetitive speech disorders in Parkinson's disease. J. Neurol. Sci. **401**, 67–71 (2019)
16. Sotirios, P.: Speech difficulties in early de novo patients with Parkinson's disease. Parkinsonism Relat. Disord. **64**, 256–261 (2019)
17. Betul, S.: Collection and analysis of a Parkinson speech dataset with multiple types of sound recordings. IEEE J. Biomed. Health Inform. **17**, 828–834 (2013)
18. Khaskhoussy, R., Ayed, Y.B.: Automatic detection of Parkinson's disease from speech using acoustic, prosodic and phonetic features. In: Abraham, A., Siarry, P., Ma, K., Kaklauskas, A. (eds.) ISDA 2019. AISC, vol. 1181, pp. 80–89. Springer, Cham (2021). https://doi.org/10.1007/978-3-030-49342-4_8
19. Evaldas, V.: Detecting Parkinson's disease from sustained phonation and speech signals. PLoS ONE **12**, 1–16 (2017)

20. Fahn, S.: Unified Parkinson's disease rating scale. Recent developments in Parkinson's disease volume II. Macmillan Healthcare Inf. **2**, 153–163 (1987)
21. Bernhard, B.: A training algorithm for optimal margin classifiers. In: Proceedings of the Fifth Annual Workshop on Computational Learning Theory, pp. 144–152 (1992)
22. Frank, D.: Recognizing emotion in speech. In: Proceeding of Fourth International Conference on Spoken Language Processing, ICSLP 1996, vol. 3, pp. 1970–1973 (1996)
23. Saloni, R.K.: Detection of Parkinson disease using clinical voice data mining. Int. J. Circuits Syst. Signal Process. **9**, 320–326 (2015)
24. Sepp, H.: Long short-term memory. Neural Comput. **9**, 1735–1780 (1997)
25. Huang, C.-W.: Attention assisted discovery of sub-utterance structure in speech emotion recognition. In: INTERSPEECH, pp. 1387–1391 (2016)
26. Miller, I.N.: Gender differences in Parkinson's disease: clinical characteristics and cognition. Mov. Disord. **25**, 2695–2703 (2010)
27. Gillies, G.E.: Sex differences in Parkinson's disease. Front. Neuroendocrinol. **35**, 370–384 (2014)
28. Podcasy, J.L.: Considering sex and gender in Alzheimer disease and other dementias. Dialogues Clin. Neurosci. **18**, 437 (2016)
29. Gai, K.: Reinforcement learning-based content-centric services in mobile sensing. IEEE Netw. **32**, 34–39 (2018)

Theoretical Study of Exponential Best-Fit: Modeling hCG for Gestational Trophoblastic Disease

Arpad Kerestely[1]([✉]), Catherine Costigan[2], Finbarr Holland[3],
and Sabin Tabirca[1,3]

[1] Transilvania University, Brasov, Romania
{arpad.kerestely,marius-sabin.tabirca}@unitbv.ro
[2] McAfee, Cork, Ireland
[3] University College Cork, Cork, Ireland
f.holland@ucc.ie,s.tabirca@cs.ucc.ie

Abstract. With the removal of the hydatidiform mole it has been shown that the human chorionic gonadotropin (hCG) hormone levels drop exponentially in women diagnosed with Gestational Trophoblastic Disease (GTD). This papers aims to introduce a new method at forecasting the decrease of the hCG levels as this could reduce the number of weekly blood test that a patient would require throughout the one year of monitoring. The hCG levels are modeled as a vertically shifted exponential curve, and this paper proposes and demonstrates a mathematical solution to finding the best parameters for this model. The method is validated using synthetic data as well as real data, and the results show that it is reliable, with decent accuracy and speed.

Keywords: Data mining · Exponential curve fit · Least squares · Mathematical modeling

1 Introduction

Gestational Trophoblastic Disease (GTD) is a term used to describe a range of illnesses which arise from trophoblastic tissue including complete and partial hydatidiform moles [19]. GTD causes the hormone human chorionic gonadotropin (hCG) to be very high but once the hydatidiform mole has been removed the hCG levels should drop exponentially [11]. In most cases the hCG levels will drop to normal with no further treatment but it has been shown that in the U.K. 15% of women with a complete hydatidiform mole will require chemotherapy [12].

It has been shown in [17,18] that the hCG levels in women with GTD drop according to the model

$$hCG(t) = Ae^{-\alpha t} + B \tag{1}$$

once the mole has been removed. Being able to make predictions about hCG levels in these women would be beneficial to healthcare professionals. Currently

© Springer Nature Switzerland AG 2021
H. Qiu et al. (Eds.): KSEM 2021, LNAI 12817, pp. 426–438, 2021.
https://doi.org/10.1007/978-3-030-82153-1_35

these women require weekly blood tests to monitor hCG levels for up to a year. By making accurate predictions of the hCG levels, women at risk of needing chemotherapy could be monitored more carefully and women not at risk might need fewer blood tests which would benefit both them and the hospitals staff.

The aim of this study is to use the method of least squares to fit the data to the model 1. The next two sections will present and demonstrate the proposed method. The following three sections will discuss implementation details and experimental results on simulated and real data. The last section concludes the paper.

2   Methods

The method of least squares is a model fitting method in which the best possible parameters to fit a model to data are calculated. Of the several methods used to fit a model to data, the least squares method in the most commonly used [6].

When fitting data with n data points to a model with k parameters to be calculated, then the least squares method can be used when $n > k$. In the case when $n < k$ the problem is underdetermined and the best fit parameters are not unique. Interpolation is a special case of this method and arises when $n = k$ [6].

Definition 1. *Given the points $(x_i, y_i)_{i=0}^{n-1}$ and the model $f(x)$ that has been fit to the data points. The residuals are the values*

$$r_i = y_i - f(x_i) \tag{2}$$

for each value of $i \in \{1, \ldots, n\}$.

The method of least squares minimizes the sum of the squares of the residuals in order to find the best parameters to fit the model to the data. When using the least squares method to fit a model, say $f(a_1, a_2, ..., a_k, x)$, where $a_1, a_2, ..., a_k$ are the parameters to be estimated, to a set of data $\{x_i, y_i\}_{i=0}^{n-1}$ the aim is to minimize the sum of the squares of the residuals

$$\phi(a_1, a_2, ..., a_k) = \sum_{i=0}^{n-1} (f(a_1, a_2, ..., a_k, x_i) - y_i)^2. \tag{3}$$

Usually, when using this method ϕ is minimised by solving the system of equations

$$\begin{aligned} \frac{\partial \phi}{\partial a_1}(a_1, \ldots, a_k) &= 0 \\ \frac{\partial \phi}{\partial a_2}(a_1, \ldots, a_k) &= 0 \\ &\vdots \\ \frac{\partial \phi}{\partial a_k}(a_1, \ldots, a_k) &= 0 \end{aligned} \tag{4}$$

for $a_1, a_2, ..., a_k$.

Proposition 1. *Given a set of data* $\{x_i, y_i\}_{i=0}^{n-1}$ *and a model*

$$m(t) = Ae^{-\alpha t} + B.$$ (5)

the best value for α *can be found by finding a root to the equation*

$$\frac{g_1(\alpha)f_0(\alpha) - g_0(\alpha)f_1(\alpha)}{f_0(\alpha)f_2(\alpha) - f_1^2(\alpha)} h_2(\alpha) + \frac{g_0(\alpha)f_2(\alpha) - g_1(\alpha)f_1(\alpha)}{f_0(\alpha)f_2(\alpha) - f_1^2(\alpha)} h_1(\alpha) = l_1(\alpha).$$ (6)

and then using this value of α *the best values of* A *and* B *are found using the equations*

$$A = \frac{g_1(\alpha)f_0(\alpha) - g_0(\alpha)f_1(\alpha)}{f_0(\alpha)f_2(\alpha) - f_1^2(\alpha)},$$ (7)

$$B = \frac{g_0(\alpha)f_2(\alpha) - g_1(\alpha)f_1(\alpha)}{f_0(\alpha)f_2(\alpha) - f_1^2(\alpha)}.$$ (8)

where the functions f, g, h *and* l *are defined as follows*

$$\begin{aligned} f_k(\alpha) &= \sum_{i=0}^{n-1} e^{-k\alpha x_i} \\ g_k(\alpha) &= \sum_{i=0}^{n-1} y_i e^{-k\alpha x_i} \\ h_k(\alpha) &= \sum_{i=0}^{n-1} x_i e^{-k\alpha x_i} \\ l_k(\alpha) &= \sum_{i=0}^{n-1} x_i y_i e^{-k\alpha x_i} \end{aligned}$$ (9)

Proof. In this case the function ϕ is defined to be

$$\phi(A, B, \alpha) = \sum_{i=0}^{n-1} (Ae^{-\alpha x_i} + B - y_i)^2$$ (10)

In order to minimise $\phi(A, B, \alpha)$, solve

$$\begin{aligned} \tfrac{\partial \phi}{\partial A}(A, B, \alpha) &= 0 \\ \tfrac{\partial \phi}{\partial B}(A, B, \alpha) &= 0 \\ \tfrac{\partial \phi}{\partial \alpha}(A, B, \alpha) &= 0. \end{aligned}$$ (11)

Using the functions 9 to simplify the problem the problem becomes

$$\begin{aligned} 2Af_2(\alpha) + 2Bf_1(\alpha) &= 2g_1(\alpha) \\ 2Af_1(\alpha) + 2Bf_0(\alpha) &= 2g_0(\alpha) \\ 2A^2 h_2(\alpha) + 2ABh_1(\alpha) &= 2Al_1(\alpha) \end{aligned}$$ (12)

Using Cramer's Rule

$$A = \frac{\Delta_1}{\Delta} = \frac{g_1(\alpha)f_0(\alpha) - g_0(\alpha)f_1(\alpha)}{f_0(\alpha)f_2(\alpha) - f_1^2(\alpha)},$$

$$B = \frac{\Delta_2}{\Delta} = \frac{g_0(\alpha)f_2(\alpha) - g_1(\alpha)f_1(\alpha)}{f_0(\alpha)f_2(\alpha) - f_1^2(\alpha)}.$$ (13)

as required. So
$$Ah_2(\alpha) + Bh_1(\alpha) = l_1(\alpha) \tag{14}$$

becomes
$$\frac{g_1(\alpha)f_0(\alpha) - g_0(\alpha)f_1(\alpha)}{f_0(\alpha)f_2(\alpha) - f_1^2(\alpha)}h_2(\alpha) + \frac{g_0(\alpha)f_2(\alpha) - g_1(\alpha)f_1(\alpha)}{f_0(\alpha)f_2(\alpha) - f_1^2(\alpha)}h_1(\alpha) = l_1(\alpha) \tag{15}$$

A root of this equation can be found in order to find the best value for α.

3   Properties of the Coefficients

Proposition 2. *The parameter A is always positive.*

Proof. In order to show this, the Cauchy-Schwartz inequality and Chebyshev inequality are used. The Cauch-Schwartz inequality says that for two sequences $\{x_i\}_{i=1}^n$ and $\{y_i\}_{i=1}^n$,

$$\left|\sum_{i=1}^n x_i \bar{y}_i\right|^2 \leq \sum_{j=1}^n |x_j|^2 \sum_{k=1}^n |y_k|^2. \tag{16}$$

And the Chebyshev inequality says that, given two sequences $\{x_i\}_{i=1}^n$ and $\{y_i\}_{i=1}^n$, which are both monotonic with the same monotonicity, then

$$\frac{\sum_{i=1}^n x_i}{n}\frac{\sum_{i=1}^n y_i}{n} \leq \frac{\sum_{i=1}^n x_i y_i}{n}. \tag{17}$$

From Eqs. 7 and 8
$$A = \frac{\Delta_1}{\Delta} = \frac{g_1(\alpha)f_0(\alpha) - g_0(\alpha)f_1(\alpha)}{f_0(\alpha)f_2(\alpha) - f_1^2(\alpha)} \tag{18}$$

Looking at the numerator by the Cauchy-Schwartz inequality

$$
\begin{aligned}
& g_1(\alpha)f_0(\alpha) - g_0(\alpha)f_1(\alpha) \\
= \quad & n\sum_{i=0}^{n-1} e^{-2\alpha x_i} - \left(\sum_{i=0}^{n-1} e^{-\alpha x_i}\right)^2 \\
= \quad & \sum_{i=0}^{n-1} 1^2 \sum_{i=0}^{n-1} e^{-2\alpha x_i} - \left(\sum_{i=0}^{n-1} 1 e^{-\alpha x_i}\right)^2 \\
\geq \quad & 0
\end{aligned} \tag{19}
$$

and at the denominator by the Chebyshev inequality

$$
\begin{aligned}
& f_0(\alpha)f_2(\alpha) - f_1^2(\alpha) \\
= \quad & n\sum_{i=0}^{n-1} y_i e^{-\alpha x_i} - \sum_{i=0}^{n-1} y_i \sum_{i=0}^{n-1} e^{-\alpha x_i} \\
= \quad & n^2\left[\frac{\sum_{i=0}^{n-1} y_i e^{-\alpha x_i}}{n} - \frac{\sum_{i=0}^{n-1} y_i \sum_{i=0}^{n-1} e^{-\alpha x_i}}{n \quad n}\right] \\
\geq \quad & 0
\end{aligned} \tag{20}
$$

Both the numerator and denominator are positive so $A \geq 0$.

Proposition 3. *If the data follows the model 1 the negative of the first derivative is between 0 and 1.*

Proof. In order to show this, it is assumed that the sequence in decreasing, so $y_0 > y_1 > \ldots > y_{n-1}$. This means that $\{e^{-\alpha x_i}\}_{i=0}^{n-1}$ is decreasing, so $\alpha > 0$.

The first derivative can be numerically estimated to be

$$\frac{y_{i+2} - 2y_{i+1} + y_i}{y_{i+1} - y_i} \tag{21}$$

The first derivative is definitely negative since the sequence is decreasing, this means the negative of the first derivative is positive.

$$
\begin{aligned}
0 &\leq & -\frac{\frac{y_{i+2}-2y_{i+1}+y_i}{y_{i+1}-y_i}}{} \\
&=& -\frac{\frac{e^{-\alpha(i+2)}-2e^{-\alpha(i+1)}+e^{-\alpha i}}{e^{-\alpha(i+1)}-e^{-\alpha i}}}{} \\
&=& -\frac{\frac{e^{-2\alpha}-2e^{-\alpha}+1}{e^{-\alpha}-1}}{} \\
&=& \frac{\left(e^{-\alpha}-1\right)^2}{1-e^{-\alpha}} \\
&=& 1 - e^{-\alpha} < 1
\end{aligned} \tag{22}
$$

This was tested on the real data. For each set of 3 consecutive points in the data, a test was carried out to check if the negative of Eq. 21 was greater than 0 and less than 1. It was found that the data mostly agreed with this with a few exceptions, were the hCG measurements didn't decrease with time.

Proposition 4. *Equation 6 can be rewritten as a polynomial by making the substitution $e^{-\alpha} = t$.*

Proof. In order to prove this statement, two assumptions are made:

1. $x_i = i$ for all i
2. $\sum_{i=1}^{n} y_i = 0$

Assumption 1 just means that the time steps may be relabeled so that they are consecutive integers and Assumption 2 means that all the data points must be translated so that the sum of the measurements is 0. In order to meet this condition the translated data points, $\{z_i\}_{i=0}^{n-1}$, will be

$$z_i = y_i - \frac{1}{n}\sum_{i=1}^{n} y_i \tag{23}$$

As before, in order to simplify the problem, a substitution is made. This time the functions $f(t)$ and $h(t)$ are defined to be

$$
\begin{aligned}
f(t) &= \sum_{k=1}^{n} y_k t^k \\
h(t) &= n\sum_{k=1}^{n} t^{2k} - \left(\sum_{k=1}^{n} t^k\right)^2.
\end{aligned} \tag{24}
$$

Taking the derivatives of these functions gives

$$f'(t) = \sum_{k=1}^{n} k y_k t^{k-1}$$
$$h'(t) = \frac{2}{t}\left(n\sum_{k=1}^{n} k t^{2k} - \sum_{k=1}^{n} k t^k \sum_{k=1}^{n} t^k\right). \tag{25}$$

Using these equations and the Assumptions 1 and 2, Eq. 6 can be written as the polynomial $p(t)$

$$p(t) = h(t) t f'(t) - \frac{1}{2} t h'(t) f(t) \tag{26}$$

Remark 1. A finite positive value of α makes $0 < t < 1$.

Proof. Since

$$t = e^{-\alpha}$$
$$\alpha = -\log t \tag{27}$$

If $\alpha > 0$ then $-\log t > 0$ so $\log t < 0$. This makes $0 < t < 1$.

Proposition 5. *Given a set of data points $(i, y_i)_{i=1}^{n}$ which is decreasing so that $y_1 > y_2 > \ldots > y_n$ and concave up so that $2y_{i+1} < y_i + y_{i+2}$. The polynomial 26 outlined in Proposition 4 has a root between 0 and 1.*

Proof. In order to write the polynomial 26, the following substitution is made

$$f(t) = \sum_{k=1}^{n} y_k t^k$$
$$h(t) = n\sum_{k=1}^{n} t^{2k} - \left(\sum_{k=1}^{n} t^k\right)^2. \tag{28}$$

$h(t)$ has two roots at 0 and two roots at 1

$$h(t) = t^2(1-t)^2 H(t) \quad \text{with} \quad H(1) \neq 0 \tag{29}$$

$f(t)$ has a single root at 1

$$f(t) = (1-t)F(t) = F(t) - tF(t) \tag{30}$$

Now looking at $f'(t)$ when $t = 1$ gives

$$f'(1) = -F(1)$$
$$\implies F(1) = -f'(1) = -\sum_{i=1}^{n} k y_k \tag{31}$$

Putting this into the polynomial 26 gives

$$p(t) = h(t) t f'(t) - \frac{1}{2} t h'(t) f'(t)$$
$$= t^2(1-t)^2 H(t) t f'(t) - \frac{1}{2} t h'(t)(1-t)F(t) \tag{32}$$

and using $h'(t)$, $\frac{1}{2} t h'(t)(1-t)$ can be written as

$$\frac{1}{2} t h'(t)(1-t) = \frac{t^2(1-t)^2}{2}\left(2(1-2t)H(T) + t(1-t)H'(t)\right) \tag{33}$$

In order to show that there is a root for polynomial 26 between 0 and 1, it will be shown that the polynomial has a positive value at $t = 0$ and a negative value at $t = 1$. Finding the Taylor expansion about $t = 0$ for the functions in $p(t)$ up to $O(t^3)$ and subbing these into $p(t)$ gives

$$f(t) = y_1 t + y_2 t^2 + y_3 t^3 + O(t^4)$$
$$h'(t) = (2n - 2)t - 6t^2 + O(t^3) \tag{34}$$

and

$$\tfrac{1}{2} t h'(t) f(t) = t^3 \left((n-1)y_1 + (ny_2 - y_2 - 3y_1)t \right) + O(t^5)$$
$$h(t) t f'(t) = t^3 \left((n-1)y_1 + (2(n-1)y_2 - 2y_1)t \right) + O(t^5) \tag{35}$$

so

$$p(t) = t^4 \left((n-1)y_2 - y_1 \right) + O(t^5) \tag{36}$$

Since the sequence $(y_i)_{i=1}^n$ is decreasing and $\sum_{i=1}^n y_i = 0$

$$(n-1)y_2 + y_1 \geq \sum_{\substack{i=1 \\ = 0}}^n y_i \tag{37}$$

So at $t = 0$, $p(t) > 0$.

At $t = 1$, expanding $h(t)$, $f(t)$ and looking at their derivatives, gives

$$h(t) = \frac{1}{12}(n^4 - n^2)(t-1)^2 + \frac{1}{12}(n^5 - n^3)(t-1)^3 +$$
$$\frac{1}{360}(8n^2 + 15n^3 - 24n^4 - 15n^5 + 17n^6)(t-1)^4 + O\big((t-1)^5\big) \tag{38}$$

$$h'(t) = \frac{1}{6}(n^4 - n^2)(t-1) + \frac{1}{4}(n^5 - n^3)(t-1)^2 +$$
$$\frac{1}{90}(8n^2 + 15n^3 - 25n^4 - 15n^5 + 17n^6)(t-1)^3 + O\big((t-1)^4\big) \tag{39}$$

$$f(t) = \sum_{k=1}^n k y_k (t-1) + \frac{1}{2} \left(\sum_{k=1}^n k(k-1)y_k \right)(t-1)62 +$$
$$\frac{1}{6} \left(\sum_{k=1}^n k(k-1)(k-2)y_k \right)(t-1)^3 + O\big((t-1)^4\big) \tag{40}$$

$$f'(t) = \sum_{k=1}^n + \left(\sum_{k=1}^n k(k-1)y_k \right)(t-1) + \frac{1}{2} \left(\sum_{k=1}^n k(k-1)(k-2)y_k \right)(t-1)^2 +$$
$$\frac{1}{6} \left(\sum_{k=1}^n k(k-1)(k-2)(k-3)y_k \right)(t-1)^3 + O\big(t-1)^4\big) \tag{41}$$

Using these to find $h(t)tf'(t)$ and $\frac{1}{2}th'(t)f(t)$ gives

$$h(t)tf'(t) = \frac{(t-1)^2 t}{12}\left((n^4 - n^2)\sum_{k=1}^{n} ky_k + \right.$$

$$\left(\left(n^4 - n^2\right)\sum_{k=1}^{n} k(k-1)y_k + (n^5 - n^3)\sum_{k=1}^{n} ky_k\right)(t-1)\right) + O\left((t-1)^4\right)\ (42)$$

and

$$\frac{1}{2}th'(t)f(t) = \frac{t(t-1)^2}{2}\left(\frac{(n^4 - n^2)}{6}\sum_{k=1}^{n} ky_k + \right.$$

$$\left(\frac{1}{12}(n^4 - n^2)\sum_{k=1}^{n} k(k-1)y_k + \frac{(n^5 - n^3)}{4}\sum_{k=1}^{n} ky_k\right)(t-1)\right) + O\left((t-1)^4\right)\ (43)$$

And so $p(t)$ can be written as

$$p(t) = \frac{t(t-1)^3}{24}\left(n^2(n+1)(n-1)\sum_{k=1}^{n} k^2 y_k - \right.$$

$$\left. n^2(n-1)(n+1)^2\sum_{k=1}^{n} ky_k\right) + O\left((t-1)^4\right)\quad (44)$$

In order to show that at $t = 1$ $p(t)$ is negative it must be shown that

$$n^2(n+1)(n-1)\sum_{k=1}^{n} k^2 y_k - n^2(n-1)(n+1)^2\sum_{k=1}^{n} ky_k > 0\qquad (45)$$

Factorizing out the positive factor $n^2(n^2 - 1)$ it remains to show that

$$\sum_{k=1}^{n} \left(k^2 y_k - (n-1)ky_k\right) > 0\qquad (46)$$

Using the assumption that $\sum_{k=1}^{n} y_k = 0$ and the fact that $2y_k < y_{k-1} + y_{k+1}$

$$\sum_{k=2}^{n-1}(n-k)(k-1)y_k < 0.\qquad (47)$$

Splitting each y_k so that a number a_k is taken from each

$$\sum_{k=2}^{n-1}(n-k)(k-1)y_k = \sum_{k=2}^{n-1}2a_ky_k + \sum_{k=2}^{n-1}\left((k-k)(k-1) - 2a_k\right)y_k$$

$$< \sum_{k=2}^{n-1}a_ky_{k-1} + \sum_{k=2}^{n-1}a_ky_{k+1} + \sum_{k=2}^{n-1}\left((k-k)(k-1) - 2a_k\right)y_k$$

$$= \sum_{k=1}^{n-2}a_{k+1}y_k + \sum_{k=3}^{n}a_{k-1}y_k + \sum_{k=2}^{n-1}\left((n-k)(k-1) - 2a_k\right)y_k$$

$$= a_2y_1 + \left((n-2) - 2a_2 + a_3\right)y_2 + \left((n-2) - 2a_{n-1} + a_{n-2}\right)y_{n-1}$$

$$+ a_{n-1}y_n + \sum_{k=3}^{n-2}\left((n-k)(k-1) - 2a_k + a_{k+1} + a_{k-1}\right)y_k$$

Claim that there exists a sequence $(a_i)_{i=1}^{n}$ with

$$a_1 = a_2 = a_{n-1} = a_n = 0 \qquad \text{and}$$
$$(n-k)(k-1) - 2a_k + a_{k+1} + a_{k-1} = C > 0 \quad \forall k \in \{2, 3, \ldots, n-1\}.$$

If this claim is true, the sum becomes

$$\sum_{k=2}^{n-1}Cy_k. \tag{48}$$

Using the fact that $2y_k < y_{k+1} + y_{k-1}$ it can be shown that $y_1 + y_n > 0$. This also means that $\sum_{k=2}^{n-1} < 0$, so

$$\sum_{k=2}^{n-1}Cy_k < 0. \tag{49}$$

In order to show that this sequence exists, firstly the value for C is calculated.

$$\sum_{k=2}^{n-1}\left((n-k)(k-1) + a_{k-1} - 2a_k + a_{k+1}\right) = (n-2)C \tag{50}$$

and from this, it can be shown that

$$C = \frac{1}{n-2}\sum_{k=2}^{n-1}(n-k)(k-1) = \frac{1}{6}(n^2 - n) > 0 \tag{51}$$

and the values for the a_k's can be found using the recursive equation stated in the assumptions

$$a_{k+1} - 2a_k + a_{k+1} = \frac{1}{6}(n^2 - n) - (n-k)(k-1) \tag{52}$$

Solving this equation gives

$$a_k = \frac{1}{12} \left((k-1)(k-2)(k-n+1)(k-n) \right) \tag{53}$$

It is known that $k, n \in \mathbb{Z}$ and that $k \geq 0, n > 1, k \leq n$. It is clear from the form of a_k in Eq. 53 that $a_k = 0$ for $k = 1, k = 2, k = n-1$ and $k = n$ and that for $2, k, n-1, a_k > 0$. This means that the sequence of a_k that was claimed to exist really exists, so Eq. 47 holds true and at $t = 1$, $p(t) < 0$.

It has been shown that the polynomial $p(t)$ in Eq. 26 is positive at $t = 0$ and negative at $t = 1$ meaning that the polynomial has a root between 0 and 1.

4   Implementing the Nonlinear Least Squares Method

The method described in Proposition 1 was implemented in order to fit the data to the model 1. Implementation details can be seen in [8] as well as at the following GitHub page: https://github.com/akerestely/nonlinearBestFit. The Bisection [4] method was used to find a root of Eq. 6. Newton's Method and Broyden's Method as well as some other root finding methods were tested first but they did not work, even though they are known to converge to the root of an equation faster. The Bisection method worked well, and even for small n, a good approximation for the parameters A, B and α was found.

Algorithm 1. Finding A, B and α using the nonlinear least squares method

---

input: $(x_i, y_i)_{i=0}^{n-1}$
α = bisection(equation 6) {using the bisection method on equation 6}
A = findA(α) {find A using equation 7}
B = findB(α) {find B using equation 8}
output: A, B, α

---

5   Testing on Simulated Data

In order to test the methods for estimating A, B and α some test data was created $\{x_i, y_i\}_{i=0}^{n-1}$ where x was a random number between 0 and 100 and $y = Ae^{-\alpha x} + B$. In Fig. 1, A, B and α were given the values 1000, 3 and 0.01 respectively.

The model was then fit to the data to see if the method for estimating the parameters could find parameters close to the original ones. As it can be seen in Fig. 1, the algorithm found the parameters that were used for generating the data.

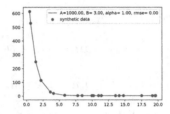

Fig. 1. The curve generated by the found parameters matches the data perfectly.

6 Testing on Real Data

Firstly three data points are used to calculate the best values for A, B and α for Eq. 1 using the technique described in Proposition 1. Using the values of the coefficients in Eq. 1 the fourth point is predicted. This value is then compared to the actual value for the hCG measurement. The error is the difference between the actual value and the predicted value.

Next, the first four measurements are used to calculate the best values for the parameters in the model, the fifth point is predicted and the error is calculated. This procedure continues until all the hCG measurements have been predicted. This is then repeated for every other patients data in order to test how well the method works for predicting the hCG measurements.

The algorithm presented in this paper can work as an extrapolation, forecasting method. If we feed at least 3 data points to the algorithm, it can learn a model, which we can use to generate future data points i.e. to forecast the normal devolution of the disease. To test the effectiveness of the algorithm on the extrapolation, we used a dataset with all it's points to find the model and calculate the rmse. Next we used the same dataset but used only the first few points to find the model and again we used all the points to calculate the rmse. Looking at the rmse values we can see how close the extrapolation is from the

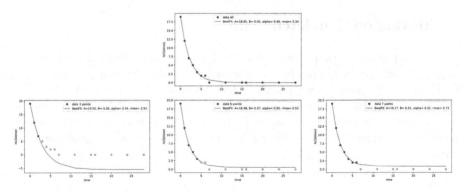

Fig. 2. Fitting the curve on the same dataset with different number of training data points (blue dots). (Color figure online)

actual values and we can also see how is the quality of the prediction affected by adding new points to the model fitting. Results can be seen in Fig. 2.

The result were compared against the results given by *scipy's curve_fit* method which uses *Levenberg-Marquardt* algorithm for fitting. Although there were no notable differences between the results, the method proposed in this paper converged faster.

7   Conclusions

In this study the method of least squares was used to fit a vertically shifted exponential curve to clinical data sampled periodically from women diagnosed with Gestational Trophoblastic Disease. The proposed method was proven mathematically. Experiments were conducted using synthetic data as well as real data, and the results show that the proposed method is fast and reliable both at detecting anomalies in a patients hCG levels and at forecasting them.

References

1. Almufti, R., et al.: A critical review of the analytical approaches for circulating tumor biomarker kinetics during treatment. Ann. Oncol. **25**(1), 41–56 (2014)
2. Ammar, G., Dayawansa, W., Martin, C.: Exponential interpolation: theory and numerical algorithms. Appl. Math. Comput. **41**(3), 189–232 (1991)
3. Costigan, C., Tabirca, S., Coulter, J.: Mathematically modelling hCG in women with gestational trophoblastic disease using logarithmic transformations. In: 2016 UKSim-AMSS 18th International Conference on Computer Modelling and Simulation (UKSim), pp. 55–59. IEEE (2016)
4. Ehiwario, J., Aghamie, S.: Comparative study of bisection, Newton-Raphson and secant methods of root-finding problems. IOSR J. Eng. **4**(04), 01–07 (2014)
5. Enderling, H., Chaplain, M.A.J.: Mathematical modeling of tumor growth and treatment. Curr. Pharm. Des. **20**(30), 4934–4940 (2014)
6. Forsythe, G.E.: Computer methods for mathematical computations. Prentice-Hall Ser. Autom. Comput. **259** (1977)
7. Huang, S.J., Huang, C.L.: Control of an inverted pendulum using grey prediction model. IEEE Trans. Ind. Appl. **36**(2), 452–458 (2000)
8. Kerestely, A., Costigan, C., Tabirca, S.: Vertically shifted exponential best-fit. In: Proceedings of the 35th International Business Information Management Association (IBIMA), Seville, Spain, pp. 13855–13868 (2020)
9. Phillips, G.M.: Interpolation and Approximation by Polynomials, vol. 14. Springer, Heidelberg (2003)
10. Pisal, N., Tidy, J., Hancock, B.: Gestational trophoblastic disease: is intensive follow up essential in all women? BJOG: Int. J. Obstet. Gynaecol. **111**(12), 1449–1451 (2004)
11. Schoeberl, M.R.: A model for the behavior of β-hCG after evacuation of hydatidiform moles. Gynecol. Oncol. **105**(3), 776–779 (2007)
12. Seckl, M.J., Sebire, N.J., Berkowitz, R.S.: Gestational trophoblastic disease. Lancet **376**(9742), 717–729 (2010)

13. Soper, J.T.: Gestational trophoblastic disease. Obstet. Gynecol. **108**(1), 176–187 (2006)
14. Szidarovszky, F., Yakowitz, S.J.: Principles and Procedures of Numerical Analysis, vol. 14. Springer, Heidelberg (2013)
15. Van Trommel, N., Massuger, L., Schijf, C., Sweep, C., Thomas, C., et al.: Early identification of persistent trophoblastic disease with serum hCG concentration ratios. Int. J. Gynecol. Cancer **18**(2), 318–323 (2008)
16. Xiao, X., White, E.P., Hooten, M.B., Durham, S.L.: On the use of log-transformation vs. nonlinear regression for analyzing biological power laws. Ecology **92**(10), 1887–1894 (2011)
17. You, B., et al.: Early prediction of treatment resistance in low-risk gestational trophoblastic neoplasia using population kinetic modelling of hCG measurements. Br. J. Cancer **108**(9), 1810–1816 (2013)
18. You, B., et al.: Predictive values of hCG clearance for risk of methotrexate resistance in low-risk gestational trophoblastic neoplasias. Ann. Oncol. **21**(8), 1643–1650 (2010)
19. Young, T., Coleman, R., Hancock, B., Drew, D., Wilson, P., Tidy, J., et al.: Predicting gestational trophoblastic neoplasia (GTN): is urine hCG the answer? Gynecol. Oncol. **122**(3), 595–599 (2011)
20. Zwietering, M., Jongenburger, I., Rombouts, F., Van't Riet, K.: Modeling of the bacterial growth curve. Appl. Environ. Microbiol. **56**(6), 1875–1881 (1990)

Lane Keeping Algorithm for Autonomous Driving via Safe Reinforcement Learning

Qi Kong[1], Liangliang Zhang[1], and Xin Xu[2(✉)]

[1] Autonomous Driving Division, JD.com American Technologies Corporation,
Mountain View, CA 94043, USA
{qi.kong,liangliang.zhang}@jd.com
[2] Autonomous Driving Division, JD.com, Beijing, China
xuxin178@jd.com

Abstract. Autonomous driving can possibly facilitate the load and change the methods for transportation in our everyday life. Work is being done to create algorithms of decision making and motion control in Autonomous driving. Recently, reinforcement learning has been a predominant strategy applied for this purpose. But, problems of using reinforcement learning for autonomous driving is that the actions taken while exploration can be unsafe, and the convergence can be too slow. Therefore, before making an actual vehicle learn driving through reinforcement learning, there is an urgent need to solve the safety issue. The significance of this paper is that, it introduces Safe Reinforcement Learning (SRL) into the field of autonomous driving. Safe reinforcement learning is the method of adding constraints to ensure the safe exploration. This paper explores the Constrained Policy Optimization (CPO) algorithm. The principle is to introduce constraints in the cost function. CPO is based on the framework of the Actor-Critic algorithm where the space that is explored during the policy update process is enforced by setting tough constraints which reduces the size of policy update. A comparison is also made with typical reinforcement learning algorithms to prove its advantages in learning efficiency and safety.

1 Introduction

Autonomous driving has the potential to ease the load and change the means of transportation in our daily life. A lot of work is being done to develop coordinated function of decision making and motion control in Autonomous driving. In recent years, reinforcement learning has been a prevailing method applied for this purpose [5,11]. In the task of Reinforcement Learning (RL), the agent is able to perceive the state of environment and take action to maximize the long-term rewards based on real value returns. The agent optimizes the policy based on the trial and error method without given [10,14]. Therefore, RL prospects a huge advantage in the field of autonomous driving.

Safe RL is defined as the process of learning policies that maximize the expectation of the long term reward, ensure reasonable system performance and

© Springer Nature Switzerland AG 2021
H. Qiu et al. (Eds.): KSEM 2021, LNAI 12817, pp. 439–450, 2021.
https://doi.org/10.1007/978-3-030-82153-1_36

respect safety constraints during the learning or deployment processes [2,7,15]. Some did modifications in optimization criterion and others in exploration process. The optimization criterion is depicted by various terms in the published work in the field of RL, including the expected sum of rewards, expected return, cumulative discounted reward or return. The optimization criteria is not always risk free, it can be unsafe in many dangerous tasks [9]. From the published literature there are 4 major methods of optimization criterion including the worst-case criterion, the risksensitive criterion [12], the constrained criterion, and other optimization criteria [13]. Methods in the optimization criteria can sometimes become excessively negative or at the occasions they can be unmanageable. In modifying the exploration have numerous approaches to overcome the problems where exploratory activities may have serious outcomes. From the literature there are mainly two approaches of modifying the exploration process to avoid consequences through the incorporation of external knowledge [3,6] and through the use of a risk-directed exploration [4,8,16]. These approaches have drawback of not being generally dependable in every situation due to their failure to distinguish unsafe situations sometimes.

Putting deep insight into previous work in the field of safe RL, we can observe that most of them are not used in autonomous driving. Although, autonomous driving is in dire need of safe exploration while learning. The purpose of this paper is to introduce Constrained Policy Optimization (CPO) in the field of autonomous driving. In this paper, constrained policy optimization is used for lane keeping function. The purpose is to always ensure the safe policy during learning process and policy update, and at the same time improve the convergence speed. while designing an algorithm, we consider safety, stability guarantees, satisfaction at each iteration and high dimensional control while maintaining the performance.

2   The Proposed Method

In order to ensure the safety of the learning process, this paper chooses to explore an algorithm of safe reinforcement learning called the constrained policy optimization (CPO) [1]. CPO algorithm ensures the safety of the policy by modifying the policy update.

2.1   Lane Keeping Based on Constrained Policy Optimization Algorithm

The safety requirements in RL process are particularly important for autonomous driving. This paper attempts to use the CPO algorithm. It is used in autonomous driving, and it takes a step to make it possible to get out of the lab and apply it to real cars. We have chosen to apply CPO implementation in autonomous driving for the lane keeping problem.

Markov Modeling of Lane Keeping Problems. Based on the introduction in the second chapter to RL, this paper carried out the autonomous driving task of lane keeping. In Markov decision process modeling, the core components include: state space, action space, reward function and cost function.

As shown in Fig. 1, during this paper, different lane maps are set up, each map consists of a series of points. Each point information include following details: The information point number k, the abscissa x, the ordinate y, and the tangential direction θ. Each information point is recorded as a tuple $[k, x, y, \theta]$. The position of the vehicle is determined by the horizontal and vertical coordinates, and thus the point closest to the vehicle on the centerline of the lane is deter-

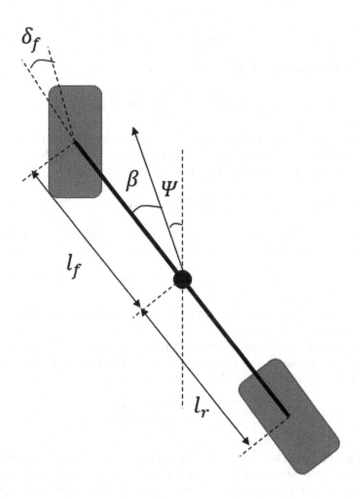

Fig. 1. Vehicle two-degree-of-freedom kinematics model

mined. This is done by calculating the distance d from the centerline of the target lane, and the angle between the body orientation angle and the centerline direction. Therefore, one state of the car is recorded as $[d, \psi]$. The vehicle maintains a constant speed during driving and adjusts the direction of advancement by free car steering. The steering operation of the vehicle is indicated by the steering angle of the front wheel, so an action of the vehicle is recorded as $[\delta_f]$.

(1) State space: Tuple $[k, x, y, \theta]$ (Information of a point) $[d, \psi]$ (One state of vehicle).
(2) Action: $[\delta_f]$

$$
\begin{aligned}
x_{t+1} &= x_t + v_t \cos\left(\psi_t + \beta\right) \cdot dt, \\
y_{t+1} &= y_t + v_t \sin\left(\psi_t + \beta\right) \cdot dt, \\
\psi_{t+1} &= \psi_t + \frac{v_t}{l_r} \sin(\beta) \cdot dt.
\end{aligned}
\tag{1}
$$

Vehicle Beta can be calculated by following formula:

$$
\beta = \tan^{-1}\left[\frac{l_r}{l_f + l_r} \tan\left(\delta_f\right)\right],
\tag{2}
$$

where l_f and l_r are the front and rear axle lengths of the car model.
(3) Reward function: The design of the reward function refers to the quadratic objective function in the optimal control problem,

$$
J = \frac{1}{2}\left[x^t Q x + u^t R u\right].
\tag{3}
$$

Taking into account the current state, the impact of the action, the action taken under the state s, a reward value is set as:

$$
r(s, a) = \frac{1}{2}\left[s^t Q s + a^t R a\right],
\tag{4}
$$

where Q and R are diagonal matrices and they are the state weight matrix and the action weight matrix.
(4) Cost function: The design of the cost function relative to the reward function is usually very simple, for this paper. For the lane keeping problem, the cost function is a step function about state:

$$
c(d) = \begin{cases} 0, |d| < \text{bound}, \\ 100, |d| \geq \text{bound}. \end{cases}
\tag{5}
$$

Approximate Solution of CPO Algorithm. For policy learning with high dimensional space (such as neural networks), the direct solution will bring a lot of computational cost, which is very unrealistic in solving the actual problem. Because In this paper, the solution of CPO adopts an approximate solution method, and may be introduced after considering the approximation. The error has tightened the original constraint range. The specific approximation is as follows:

For a small policy learning update step size δ, both the objective function and the constrained cost function can be linearized around the policy πk, the constraint of KL divergence can be approximated very well by second-order expansion (here at $\pi = \pi k$, the KL divergence and its first derivative are both zero). Using g to represent the gradient of the objective function, and b_i to represent the gradient of constraint i, for the KL divergence, the Hessian matrix is represented by H, and by defining:

$$c_i = j_{C_i}(\pi k) - di, \tag{6}$$

the original problem can be approximated as:

$$\theta_{k+1} = \arg \max_{\theta} g^T (\theta - \theta_k),$$

$$\text{s.t. } c_i + b_i^T (\theta - \theta_k) \leq d \quad \forall i, \tag{7}$$

$$\frac{1}{2} (\theta - \theta_k)^T H (\theta - \theta_k) \leq \delta.$$

Because the Fisher Information Matrix (FIM) H is always positive semi-definite. The above problem is a convex problem, so when the problem is feasible, it can be efficiently solved using the dual method. We have

$$B = [b_1, b_2, b_3, \ldots, b_m] \text{ and } c = [c_1, c_2, c_3, \ldots, c_m]^T. \tag{8}$$

By definition, the dual problem of the above problem can be expressed as:

$$\max_{\substack{\lambda \geq 0 \\ v \geq 0}} -\frac{1}{2\lambda} \left(g^T Hg - 2r^T v + v^T Sc\right) + v^T c - \frac{\lambda \delta}{2}, \tag{9}$$

where $r = g^T H^{-1} B$ and $S = B^T H^{-1} B$. It is a convex problem with the number of variables as $m + 1$, when the number of constraints is small in comparison to the policy network parameter θ, and solving the above dual problem is very simple. If λ^* and v^* are the solutions to the duality problem, then the solution to the original problem becomes:

$$\theta_{k+1} = \theta_k + \frac{1}{\lambda^*} H^{-1} (g - Bv^*). \tag{10}$$

Here is the derivation part of specific solution of the linear quadratic constraint programming problem. Consider the linear quadratic constraint programming problem is:

$$p^* = \min_{x} g^T x,$$

$$\text{s.t. } b^T x + c \leq 0, \tag{11}$$

$$x^T Hx \leq \delta,$$

where $g, b, x \in \mathbb{R}^n, c, \delta \in \mathbb{R}, \delta > 0, H \in S^n$. When the solution is feasible, then the optimal solution x^* is:

$$x^* = -\frac{1}{\lambda^*} H^{-1} (g + v^* b). \tag{12}$$

Given that the Fisher information matrix H in the original problem is always positive, so the optimization problem is a convex optimization problem. Therefore, when there is a feasible solution, the optimal solution is obtained efficiently by the coupling, and the optimal solution of the dual problem and the optimal solution of the original optimization problem is equivalent.

Here we need to construct a new optimization problem based on the original optimization problem with inequality constraints, and the generalized Lagrangian function is given as:

$$
\begin{aligned}
\min_{x \in R^n} \max_{\lambda \in R^m} &\mathcal{L}(\theta, \lambda, v) \\
= &- g^T (\theta - \theta_k) \\
&+ \lambda \left[\frac{1}{2} (\theta - \theta_k)^T H (\theta - \theta_k) - \delta \right] \\
&+ v \left[c + b (\theta - \theta_k) \right],
\end{aligned}
\tag{13}
$$

where $\lambda \geq 0, v \geq 0, v$ is the Langrange multiplier.

Substituting the condition

$$
\frac{\partial \mathcal{L}}{\partial \theta} = -g + \lambda H (\theta - \theta_k) + vb = 0,
\tag{14}
$$

and the Langrangian function can be rewritten as:

$$
\mathcal{L}(\lambda, v) = -\tfrac{1}{2\lambda} \left(q - 2r^T v + v^T S v \right) + vc - \lambda \delta,
\tag{15}
$$

where

$$
r = g^T H^{-1} b,
\tag{16}
$$

$$
S = b^T H^{-1} b,
\tag{17}
$$

$$
\frac{\partial \mathcal{L}}{\partial v} - \frac{S}{\lambda} v + \left(c + \frac{r}{\lambda} \right),
\tag{18}
$$

$$
\frac{\partial \mathcal{L}}{\partial \lambda} = \frac{1}{2\lambda^2} \left(q - 2r^T v + v^T S v \right) - \delta,
\tag{19}
$$

when

$$
\frac{\partial \mathcal{L}}{\partial v} = 0,
\tag{20}
$$

$$
v = \frac{\lambda c + r}{S}.
\tag{21}
$$

Substituting above formula into the partial derivative of the Langrangian function, we have

$$
\frac{\partial \mathcal{L}}{\partial \lambda} = \frac{1}{2\lambda^2} \left(q + \frac{r^2}{s} \right) + \frac{c^2}{2S} - \delta = \frac{1}{2} \left(\frac{A}{\lambda^2} - B \right),
\tag{22}
$$

where

$$A = q - \frac{r^2}{s},\tag{23}$$

$$B = 2\delta - \frac{c^2}{s}.\tag{24}$$

Also keep in mind $\lambda_{\text{mid}} = -\frac{r}{c}, \lambda_a = \frac{\sqrt{A}}{B}, \lambda_b = \frac{\sqrt{q}}{2\delta}$, and the optimal solution to the problem is given below:

– If $\lambda_{\text{mid}} > 0$:
  • $c < 0$:

$$\because v \geq 0, \mathcal{L} \text{ decreases monotonically},\tag{25}$$

$$\therefore v^* = \to \lambda_a > \lambda_{mid}, \text{ then } \lambda_1^* = \lambda_{mid};\tag{26}$$

$$\lambda_{mid} > \lambda_a, \text{ then } \lambda_1^* = \lambda_a;\tag{27}$$

$$\mathcal{L}_{mid} = \tfrac{1}{2}\left(\tfrac{qc}{r} + \tfrac{2\delta r}{c}\right), \mathcal{L}_a = -\sqrt{2\delta q};\tag{28}$$

$$\mathcal{L}_b > \mathcal{L}_{mid}, \text{ then } \lambda^* = \lambda_b;\tag{29}$$

$$\mathcal{L}_{mid} > \mathcal{L}_b, \text{ then } \lambda^* = \lambda_{\text{mid}};\tag{30}$$

$$v^* = \max\left(0, c\lambda^* - r\right).\tag{31}$$

  • $c > 0$:

$$\because \frac{\lambda c + r}{S} > 0,\tag{32}$$

$$\therefore v \in \left(0, \frac{\lambda c + r}{s}\right), \text{ then } \mathcal{L} \text{ Increases monotonically};\tag{33}$$

$$v \in \left(\frac{\lambda c + r}{s}, \infty\right), \text{ then } \mathcal{L} \text{ Decreases monotonically};\tag{34}$$

$$\lambda_a < \lambda_{\text{mid}}, \text{ then } \lambda_1^* = \lambda_{\text{mid}}; \quad \lambda_a > \lambda_{\text{mid}}, \text{ then } \lambda_1^* = \lambda_a;\tag{35}$$

$$\lambda_{\text{mid}} < \lambda_b, \text{ then } \lambda_2^* = \lambda_{\text{mid}}; \quad \lambda_{\text{mid}} > \lambda_b, \text{ then } \lambda_2^* = \lambda_b;\tag{36}$$

$$L_{\lambda_1} > \mathcal{L}_{\lambda_2}, \text{ then } \lambda^* = \lambda_1^*;\tag{37}$$

$$\mathcal{L}_{\lambda_1} > \mathcal{L}_{\lambda_2}, \text{ then } \lambda^* = \lambda_2^*.\tag{38}$$

– If $\lambda_{\text{mid}} > 0$:
  • $c < 0$:

$$\lambda^* = \lambda_b.\tag{39}$$

  • $c > 0$:

$$\lambda^* = \lambda_a,\tag{40}$$

$$v^* = \max\left(0, c\lambda^* - r\right).\tag{41}$$

3   Experiments

There are some parameters which are fixed for experiments performed. They are mentioned below:

- Discount factor γ is set to 0.95;
- KL delta δ_{KL} is set to 0.00001;
- Safety constraint i.e. $d = 2$;
- Learning rate of 0.001.

In the experiment, the policy network is designed in such a manner that the vehicle gets started form a range of random initial positions throughout the process and gradually learns the optimal policy. The cost network is directly loaded as mentioned above in Sect. 2. The value network is initialized and it assigns value to the state by calculating an expected cumulative reward for the current state s. Every state passes through the value network. The states having more value in the network are those which are expected to get more reward.

We trained the CPO algorithm with the most basic Actor-Critic algorithm, the difference between RL and SRL is the setting of constraints, and the change in policy search. The constraints in CPO are the safety constraints that is the distance from the centerline of the target lane. The comparison below is made on straight road.

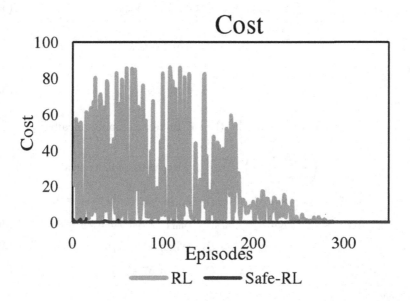

Fig. 2. Cost comparison RL vs safe RL.

Figure 2 is the cost curve of the two algorithms the actor critic and CPO actor critic. As it can be seen from the curve comparison chart, safe reinforcement learning has a very fast speed of learning (converges to a stable, optimal policy quickly) as compared to simple actor critic algorithm. The cost of safe reinforcement learning as compared to actor critic is negligible. This mainly is because the CPO imposes constraints on the extent of policy updates when the algorithm is in the process of optimizing. For the CPO, each update has the best step size and therefore convergences faster.

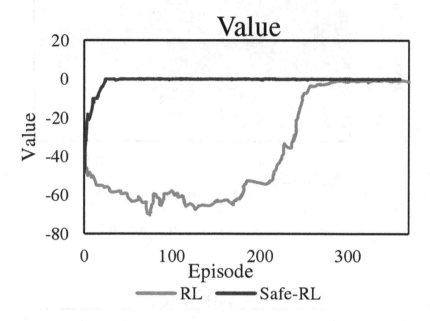

Fig. 3. Value comparison RL vs safe RL.

Figure 3 is the comparison of the value curve, and it shows the same behavior and confirms the fast convergence as mentioned above. Figure 4 confirms the safety of the CPO algorithm as compared to Actor Critic RL. The CPO algorithm safely completes the path of the task from start to finish, and the distance from the center line of the target lane is always in the safe zone that is below the bound. Normal RL algorithms go through the process of trial and error exploration, and continue to enter unsafe states.

Figure 5 shows the variance curves of two algorithms off centerline. One of the most important aspects for evaluating lane keeping the indicator here is the smoothness of the trajectory. It can be clearly observed from Fig. 5 that the variance of CPO is much lower in the initial stage. The variance of the AC algorithm, has remained at a very high state throughout the learning process. Even after the policy optimization the variance of the AC algorithm is not reduced to the same level as the CPO. It can be seen that the training results of the CPO algorithm has a more stable effect than that of the traditional method.

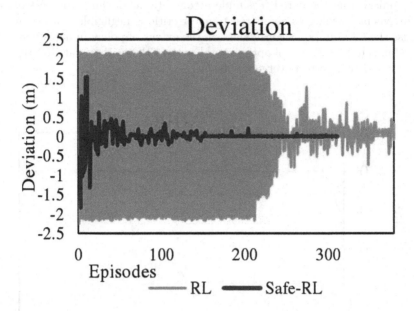

Fig. 4. Deviation comparison RL vs Safe RL.

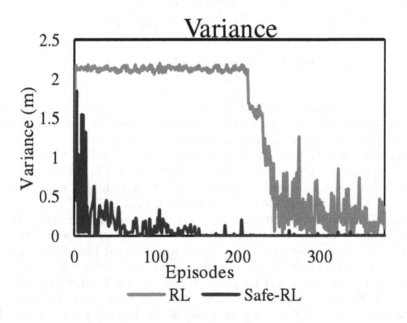

Fig. 5. Variance comparison RL vs Safe RL.

4   Conclusion

In this paper, we built up a method called CPO enhanced safe RL, a method where vehicle explores the space without going out of the lane. Constrained Policy Optimization (CPO), the principal general-purpose policy search algorithm, is with surety for close requirement fulfillment at every iteration. This strategy permits to train neural network policy for high-dimensional control while making sure about policy behavior all through learning. Assurances depend on another hypothetical outcome, which is of independent interest. In future, we would try to use some other techniques that can be used to make the learning safe.

References

1. Achiam, J., Held, D., Tamar, A., Abbeel, P.: Constrained policy optimization. In: International Conference on Machine Learning, pp. 22–31. PMLR (2017)
2. Alshiekh, M., Bloem, R., Ehlers, R., Könighofer, B., Niekum, S., Topcu, U.: Safe reinforcement learning via shielding. In: Proceedings of the AAAI Conference on Artificial Intelligence, vol. 32 (2018)
3. Baheri, A., Nageshrao, S., Kolmanovsky, I., Girard, A., Tseng, H.E., Filev, D.: Deep q-learning with dynamically-learned safety module: a case study in autonomous driving. In: Neural Information Processing Systems (NeurIPS 2019) (2019)
4. Baheri, A., Nageshrao, S., Tseng, H.E., Kolmanovsky, I., Girard, A., Filev, D.: Deep reinforcement learning with enhanced safety for autonomous highway driving. In: 2020 IEEE Intelligent Vehicles Symposium (IV), pp. 1550–1555. IEEE (2019)
5. Chen, J., Tang, C., Xin, L., Li, S.E., Tomizuka, M.: Continuous decision making for on-road autonomous driving under uncertain and interactive environments. In: 2018 IEEE Intelligent Vehicles Symposium (IV) (2018)
6. Driessens, K., Džeroski, S.: Integrating guidance into relational reinforcement learning. Mach. Learn. **57**(3), 271–304 (2004)
7. Garcıa, J., Fernández, F.: A comprehensive survey on safe reinforcement learning. J. Mach. Learn. Res. **16**(1), 1437–1480 (2015)
8. Gehring, C., Precup, D.: Smart exploration in reinforcement learning using absolute temporal difference errors. In: Proceedings of the 2013 International Conference on Autonomous Agents and Multi-agent Systems, pp. 1037–1044 (2013)
9. Geibel, P., Wysotzki, F.: Risk-sensitive reinforcement learning applied to control under constraints. J. Artif. Intell. Res. **24**, 81–108 (2005)
10. Hafner, R., Riedmiller, M.: Reinforcement learning in feedback control. Mach. Learn. **84**, 137–169 (2011)
11. Hoel, C.J., Wolff, K., Laine, L.: Tactical decision-making in autonomous driving by reinforcement learning with uncertainty estimation. In: 2020 IEEE Intelligent Vehicles Symposium (IV), pp. 1563–1569. IEEE (2020)
12. Howard, R.A., Matheson, J.E.: Risk-sensitive Markov decision processes. Manag. Sci. **18**(7), 356–369 (1972)
13. Konda, V.R., Tsitsiklis, J.N.: Actor-critic algorithms. In: Advances in Neural Information Processing Systems, pp. 1008–1014. Citeseer (2000)
14. Li, M.G., et al.: DBUS: human driving behavior understanding system. In: 2019 IEEE/CVF International Conference on Computer Vision Workshop (ICCVW), pp. 2436–2444. IEEE (2019)

15. Thananjeyan, B., et al.: Recovery RL: safe reinforcement learning with learned recovery zones. IEEE Robot. Autom. Lett. **6**(3), 4915–4922 (2021)
16. Wen, L., Duan, J., Li, S.E., Xu, S., Peng, H.: Safe reinforcement learning for autonomous vehicles through parallel constrained policy optimization. In: 2020 IEEE 23rd International Conference on Intelligent Transportation Systems (ITSC), pp. 1–7. IEEE (2020)

BS-KGS: Blockchain Sharding Empowered Knowledge Graph Storage

Yue Zhang[1], Keke Gai[2(✉)] [iD], Yihang Wei[1], and Liehuang Zhu[2]

[1] School of Computer Science and Technology, Beijing Institute of Technology,
Beijing 100081, China
{3220201017,3120201079}@bit.edu.cn
[2] School of Cyberspace Science and Technology, Beijing Institute of Technology,
Beijing 100081, China
{gaikeke,liehuangz}@bit.edu.cn

Abstract. Utilizing blockchain-based storage in knowledge graph construction is considered an alternative to ensure both security and traceability of files. Sharding is a promising solution to improve blockchain throughput by concurrently processing transactions. However, there are two key challenges in sharding, namely, difficulties in generating transaction allocation strategy and security threats. This paper addresses above issues and proposes a blockchain sharding-empowered knowledge graph storage (BS-KGS) scheme. To achieve optimal transaction sharding strategies, we construct a dynamic programming algorithm that considers multiple resource constraints. Moreover, our approach guarantees transaction security via implementing several methods, including *Verifiable Random Function* (VRF), asset mortgage, and *Practical Byzantine Fault Tolerance* (PBFT) consensus. Evaluation results have demonstrated that our method is efficient in transaction sharding.

Keywords: Blockchain · Transaction sharding · Knowledge graph storage · Dynamic programming · Performance optimization

1 Introduction

Knowledge graphs have been paid widespread attentions along with the prosperous growth of artificial intelligence. Lu et al. [12] proposed a thoroughly study on big knowledge and its engineering issues with several applications. During knowledge graph construction, process files are easy to be maliciously tampered and forged, which results in deviations in inference results [16,18]. Blockchain is transparent and tamper-resistant, which has enabled broad prospects in the process of building knowledge graphs [2]. Qiu et al. built a dynamic scalable blockchain based communication architecture for IoT [14]. Wang et al. [17] have proposed a scheme of process file storage and traceability of knowledge graph based on blockchain and distributed file storage system. Process files can be obtained from blockchain on demand when reasoning errors or file security issues

© Springer Nature Switzerland AG 2021
H. Qiu et al. (Eds.): KSEM 2021, LNAI 12817, pp. 451–462, 2021.
https://doi.org/10.1007/978-3-030-82153-1_37

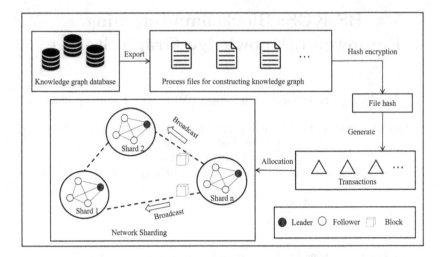

Fig. 1. High level architecture of the proposed BS-KGS scheme.

take place. In this way, repetitive work, such as rebuilding knowledge graph, can be avoided. However, the throughput of blockchain system is far lower than that of traditional centralized systems [5,6].

Sharding is a chain-based solution to improve blockchain scalability. The basic idea of sharding is dividing network nodes into several independent partitions. Transactions are processed in parallel by different shards to improve the throughput of the system [1]. Parallel transaction processing is considered to be a major advantage of implementing sharding, concerning efficiency improvement.

Based on our investigation, there are at least two critical challenges in sharding-based optimization. The first challenge is improper transaction allocation may result in heavy communication overhead and even reduce system performance [4,7]. Specifically, frequent cross-shard communication may occupy much bandwidth and increase transaction confirmation time, ultimately reducing the throughput of blockchain system [11]. The other challenge is transaction security threats in sharding, such as double spending, *Distributed Denial of Service* (DDoS) attacks, etc. [19]. It is necessary to ensure most nodes are honest in each shard.

Many prior studies have investigated transaction sharding in blockchain [9,20]. Two major methods are account/balance and UTXO models [19]. In the account/balance model, a transaction is usually assigned to a shard in terms of sender's address. Using this method can easily detect double spending transactions without cross-shard communication [13] but fails in defending DDoS attacks [10]. When an attacker initiates a large number of transactions by using the same address, these transactions will be allocated to the same shard and cause the depletion of fragment resources.

In order to address the security issue of knowledge graph construction, this paper proposes a *Blockchain Sharding-empowered Knowledge Graph Stor-*

age (BS-KGS) scheme. Since different transactions (composed of hash value of knowledge graph files) are varied in size, our approach aims to maximize benefits of each shard by considering computation costs, storage space, and communications. The proposed problem has been proved a NP-hard problem (refer to Sect. 2).

Figure 1 illustrates the high level architecture of the proposed BS-KGS scheme. First, we export the constructed knowledge graph from database and perform hash encryption on the exported process files. After the hash value of the file is packaged and signed, a transaction is generated and sent to the blockchain network. Second, network sharding needs to be completed before transaction sharding, and a leader node is elected in each shard to complete special tasks. The leader node pre-evaluates the resource consumption of each transaction and decide which transactions to process. The selected transactions are sent to follower nodes in this shard. Third, all nodes participate in consensus process through a series of operations, including verification, processing transactions, and generating blocks. The generated block in one shard will be broadcasted to leader nodes of all the other shards for verification to prevent double spending. Finally, valid blocks are added to the blockchain ledger.

Main contributions of this work are twofold:

1. This paper proposes a BS-KGS scheme, which solves the problem of safe storage and traceability of knowledge graph construction files. Under the condition of multiple constraints, the optimal transaction allocation plan is given to complete efficient and reasonable transaction sharding.
2. We propose a novel block checking and confirmation mechanism to prevent double-spending attacks specifically targeting different shards. In addition, this work creatively combines VRF, asset mortgage and improved PBFT consensus mechanism, which prevents malicious behavior of nodes and guarantees transaction security in the sharding.

The remainder of this paper is organized as follows. First, the proposed model is described in Sect. 2 and the problem is formally defined. Next, Sect. 3 presents algorithms used in the proposed method. Experimental results and analysis are given in Sect. 4. Finally, Sect. 5 draws conclusions of this work.

2 Concepts and the Proposed Model

2.1 Model Design

Transaction Generation and Sharding. The key application of knowledge graph lies in the query and reasoning of knowledge, so that its modeling stage is extremely important. In the BS-KGS model, process files for constructing the knowledge graph are stored in the blockchain. On one hand, the security of files is guaranteed; on the other hand, repetitive work can be avoided by querying the blockchain ledger. The specific process is to export process files of the knowledge graph from the database and perform hash encryption. Then use the hash value to generate a transaction and send it to the blockchain network.

Network sharding is the basis of transaction sharding. In network sharding, nodes are divided into several sub-networks to verify transactions at the same time, which improves the parallel processing capability of the system. It is necessary to ensure that the number of malicious nodes in each shard is small enough, so that randomness should be guaranteed when assigning nodes. In the model, VRF is used to randomly select nodes to join shards, so as to prevent malicious nodes from occupying a partition. Each node generates a pair of keys *(SK, PK)*, where *SK* represents the private key and *PK* represents the public key. The node calculate *result* and *proof* according to Eq. (1) and Eq. (2). The node is assigned to a network shard according to last few bits of *result*. Other nodes in the network can verify that *result* is calculated correctly through *PK* and *proof*. The advantages of the VRF lottery mechanism are as follows.

$$result = VRF\_AVL(SK, info) \tag{1}$$

$$proof = VRF\_PROVE(SK, info) \tag{2}$$

- The input *info* is publicly recognized, and the *result* of the VRF_AVL function for the same *info* is fixed, so that it is impossible to change the lottery result by trying multiple times.
- When the node receives lottery information of other nodes, it can use the attached *proof* to verify the identity of *SK* owner and the correctness of *result*. Therefore, the result of this draw cannot be forged.

Each shard needs to elect a leader node to complete special tasks, such as selecting transactions, generating blocks, and verifying blocks from other shards. The leader node needs to mortgage part of assets as a deposit, which will be confiscated when it is found to be malicious. A *Shard Routing Table* (SRT) is maintained in the network to record the leader routing information of each shard. When a transaction is generated, the leader node of each shard will determine whether to process the transaction according to the resource constraints. When a transaction is accepted for processing by one shard, the other shards will be notified. The leader node in each shard maintains a *Transaction Sharding Table* (TST) to record which shard the transaction is processed in.

Block Generation and Synchronization. Transactions are executed in different shards, and each shard performs consensus independently. Figure 2 shows the basic workflow of transaction sharding, which is divided into three phases.

- **Phase I** (corresponding to steps 1 to 4 in Fig. 2). First, the leader evaluate the transaction overhead, such as calculation cost, storage space, and communication consumption, to determine whether to process it. Second, the leader sorts collected transactions and stores them in the transaction list, which is broadcasted to all followers in the shard. After receiving the transaction list, followers verify and simulate the execution of these transactions. Then, based on simulation execution results, the hash summary of the new block is calculated and broadcasted to other nodes of the shard. Suppose that there are

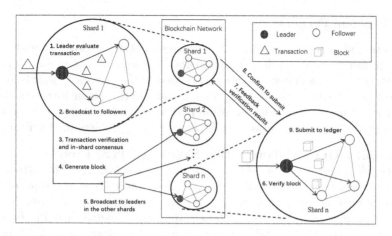

Fig. 2. The basic workflow of transaction sharding.

f Byzantine nodes in the network partition. When a node receives the same digest from $2f$ other nodes, it broadcasts a commit message. Finally, when a node receives $(2f+1)$ commit messages, it temporarily puts the new block (not verified by other shards) into buffer. During the procedure, once followers discover that the leader forges messages, the leader's mortgage deposit will be confiscated. The shard selects a new leader and change the view, which ensures that the leader in each shard is honest.

- **Phase II** (corresponding to steps 5 to 6 in Fig. 2). Since transactions are dynamically allocated to different shards for consensus, it is necessary to communicate between shards to prevent double spending. Once a shard produces a block, it needs to be broadcasted to leaders of all the other network shards. After receiving blocks from other fragments, the leader puts them into a buffer. The leader checks the legitimacy of the block structure, and then traverses all transactions in the block to check the legitimacy of transactions. In particular, the leader checks whether there is a double-spend transaction based on the TST.

- **Phase III** (corresponding to steps 7 to 9 in Fig. 2). When the block is valid, a signed confirmation is sent to the leader that generated the block. After receiving confirmation message from other shards, the leader notifies nodes in the shard to add the block to ledger. Then, $(shard\_id, block\_id, ack, sig)$ messages are sent to leaders of all the other shards. Among them, $shard\_id$ is the shard number, $block\_id$ is the block number, ack is the confirmation flag, and sig is the signature of the leader in $shard\_id$. The leader that receives the ack message broadcasts the block (numbered $block\_id$) in the buffer to other nodes in the shard, so that the block will be added to the local ledger. Once the leader node in other shards returns a conflict message, all shards are notified to delete the invalid block in the buffer.

2.2   Problem Formulation

Computing resources, storage space, and communication costs required by different transactions are varied. The benefits of processing transactions are also various. Hence, transaction allocation is related to the revenue of shards and the performance of entire system. The problem posed in this paper is that the leader finds the optimal transaction allocation plan to maximize the revenue of shard. We define the *Optimal Transaction Sharding* (OTS) problem in Definition 1.

Definition 1 Optimal Transaction Sharding (OTS) Problem:
Inputs: *A transaction list (TL) containing transaction ID. The attribute of each transaction is a four-tuple $\langle C_i, S_i, T_i, F_i \rangle$, where C_i is the required computing resource of transaction i, S_i is the occupied storage space, and T_i is the communication consumption. The benefit that can be obtained is F_i. In sharding, the upper limit of computing resources is C^c, the storage limit is S^c, and the network bandwidth limit is T^c. As shown in Eq. (3), we define a binary function $s(Tran_i)$. A value of 1 indicates that the $Tran_i$ is selected, and a value of 0 indicates that the $Tran_i$ is not selected.*
Output: *A transaction allocation plan in the sharding.*
Proposed Problem: *In transaction sharding, find a set of transactions that gives the sharding the maximum benefit F within resource constraints.*

$$s(Tran_i) = \begin{cases} 0 & \text{if } Tran_i \text{ is not selected,} \\ 1 & \text{if } Tran_i \text{ is selected.} \end{cases} \tag{3}$$

This problem can be formally described as follows:

$$F = Max\left[\sum_{s(Tran_i)=1} F(Tran_i) \right]. \tag{4}$$

$$C = \sum_{s(Tran_i)=1} C(Tran_i). \tag{5}$$

$$S = \sum_{s(Tran_i)=1} S(Tran_i). \tag{6}$$

$$T = \sum_{s(Tran_i)=1} T(Tran_i). \tag{7}$$

Find the value of F, under constraint $0 \leq C \leq C^c$, $0 \leq S \leq S^c$, $0 \leq T \leq T^c$.
In Eq. (4), $Max\left[\sum_{s(Tran_i)=1} F(Tran_i) \right]$ represents the maximum payoff for all trading options in the shard. The total computing resource consumption C is the sum of computing resources of transactions selected by the leader node in the shard, expressed in Eq. (5). Similarly, Eq. (6) and Eq. (7) calculate the sum of storage space consumption S and the sum of cross-shard communication consumption T, respectively. Theorem 1 demonstrates the proposed OTS problem is a NP-hard problem, and the proof is given as follows.

Theorem 1. $\exists$ *a set of transactions* $\{TL_i\}$ *with I transactions, where* $i \in N, 0 \le i \le I$. $\forall Tran_i \in \{TL_i\}$, $\exists$ *computing consumption* C_{Tran_i}, *storage occupation* S_{Tran_i}, *communication cost* T_{Tran_i}, *and the gain* F_{Tran_i}. *Resource constraints of the shard are* $C^c, S^c,$ *and* T^c, *respectively. Then the OTSP is a NP-hard problem.*

Proof. The problem described in Theorem 1 can be reduced to a *Multi-dimensional Cost Knapsack* (MCK) problem. The leader node in each sharding selects transactions from *TL*, which is equivalent to the process of loading items into the knapsack. Each selection of an item needs to pay three kinds of costs, and the final reward is the value of the selected item. Constraints on the three dimensions of the knapsack are C^c, S^c, and T^c. F[i][C][S][T] represents the maximum value that the first i items can obtain at the cost of three dimensions (computing resource C, storage space S, and communication cost T). $\therefore$ $OTS \le$ MCK.

$\because$ MCK problem has be proved as a NP-hard problem [8] and $OTS \le$ MCK. $\therefore OTS$ problem is also a NP-hard problem. Proved.

3   Algorithms

The *Optimal Transaction Sharding Allocation* (OTSA) algorithm is a selection algorithm that runs on the leader node in each shard. The OTSA algorithm is based on an optimized dynamic programming algorithm [15] to solve OTS problem, which gives the optimal transaction choice under the constraints of the existing resources of the sharding. The main function of the algorithm is to give the optimal selection plan and the maximum benefit that can be obtained by sharding. Pseudo codes of OTSA algorithm are shown in Algorithm 1.

One input of the OTSA algorithm is a transaction list (**TL**). The transaction in the list includes four attributes, that is, the calculation resource required to process the transaction *TL.calculation*, the space occupied by the transaction *TL.storage*, the communication cost needed to verify the transaction *TL.communication*, and the processing fee provided by the transaction *TL.feedback*. Another input is resource constraints of the shard, including the upper limit of computing resources C^c, the upper limit of storage resources S^c, and the upper limit of network bandwidth T^c. The output of the OTSA algorithm is **F-Table** and **P-Table**, among which, **F-Table** stores the maximum profit that can be obtained by sharding, and **P-Table** stores the optimal transaction selection plan. Next, we introduce main phases of OTSA algorithm.

1. Initialize **P-Table** and **F-Table**. Set all the attributes of **P-Table** and **F-Table** to 0 to perform the initial calculation of the optimal plan.
2. Traverse the transactions in **TL**. When considering the strategy of the *i-th* transaction (selected or not), it can be transformed into the problem only related to the first (*i-1*) transactions. We use a set of temporary variables (including cal, sto, com, and fee) to save transaction attributes at (*i-1*). F[i][j][k][l] is related to F[i-1][j][k][l] and F[i-1][j-cal][k-sto][l- com], so that

---

Algorithm 1. Optimal Transaction Sharding Allocation Algorithm

---

Require: A transaction list **TL**, computing resource limit $\mathbf{C^c}$ in sharding, storage space limitation $\mathbf{S^c}$ in sharding, communication resource limit $\mathbf{T^c}$ in sharding

Ensure: The maximum benefit **F-Table** can be obtained in the sharding, and the optimal selection plan table **P-Table**

1: $\{TL.length$ is the number of optional transactions$\}$
2: **for** i ← 0 to $TL.length$ **do**
3:     P[i] ← 0 {Initialize **P-Table**}
4: **end for**
5: **for** j ← 0 to C^c **do**
6:     **for** k ← 0 to S^c **do**
7:         **for** l ← 0 to T^c **do**
8:             F[j][k][l] ← 0 {Initialize **F-Table** }
9:         **end for**
10:     **end for**
11: **end for**
12: **for** i ← 1 to $TL.length$ **do**
13:     cal ← TL[i-1].calculation, sto ← TL[i-1].storage
14:     com ← TL[i-1].communication, fee ← TL[i-1].feedback
15:     **for** j ← C^c to cal **do**
16:         **for** k ← S^c to sto **do**
17:             **for** l ← T^c to com **do**
18:                 **if** F[j][k][l] <F[j-cal][k-sto][l-com] + fee **then**
19:                     F[j][k][l] ← F[j-cal][k-sto][l-com] + fee
20:                     P[i] ← 1 {Mark the selected transaction}
21:                 **end if**
22:             **end for**
23:         **end for**
24:     **end for**
25: **end for**
26: **return F-Table, P-Table**

---

the three-dimensional array $F[C^c][S^c][T^c]$ is used to save the status of the previous $(i\text{-}1)$ transactions.

3. Traverse $C^c, S^c, and \ T^c$ in reverse order. Compare the profit when the $i\text{-}th$ transaction is selected with that when it is not, and then adopt the larger value. If the transaction is selected, mark it accordingly in **P-Table**.

4. Execute the loop until all transactions in the **TL** are processed, and the optimal transaction selection plan is obtained.

Theorem 2. *The transaction selection plan generated by OTSA algorithm is an optimal solution to the shard under local resource constraints.*

Proof. When there is only one transaction to be selected and the transaction cost does not exceed the sharding resource limits, the maximum benefit is the transaction fee, that is, F-Table[0]. Assume that F-Table[i-1] is the optimal solution consisting of the first $(i\text{-}1)$ transactions. When deciding whether to choose the $i\text{-}th$ transaction, the algorithm will compare with the previous state to ensure that the current state has the highest processing fee (within the resource limits). Due to mathematical induction, F-Table[i] is still the optimal solution consisting of the first i transactions. Proved.

Time complexity analysis: we give a brief analysis of the time complexity of Algorithm 1. Assuming that there are N transactions to be selected in total. Three dimensional constraints are C^c, S^c and T^c. For each transaction to be selected, the number of times we need to calculate is proportional to $C^c \times S^c \times T^c$. Therefore, the time complexity of Algorithm 1 is $O(NC^cS^cT^c)$.

4 Experiment Evaluations

We use a set of experiments to evaluate our proposed model, which focuses on accuracy and efficiency. Section 4.1 presents the experimental configurations and Sect. 4.2 shows partial experimental results as well as the brief discussion.

4.1 Experimental Configuration

We develop a simulator based on Python 3.6, which supports other approaches for comparison. The hardware configuration used in our experimental evaluations include a PC with Windows 10, Intel Core i5-7200U CPU and 8G RAM. As shown in Table 1, we configure different parameters to design a group of experimental settings. The configured parameters include the number of transactions N and the constraints of the sharding (computing resource limit C^c, storage resource limit S^c, and communication resource limit T^c).

We compare our OTSA algorithm with the *Heuristic Algorithm* (HA) [3] and two greedy algorithms to evaluate the performance of BS-KGS scheme. Specifically, *Greedy Algorithm One* (GAO) always chooses the high-return transaction first, within the total resource constraints of the sharding. *Greedy Algorithm Two* (GAT) selects the current optimal transaction by calculating the "cost-effectiveness" (that is, the revenue divided by the cost in each dimension) of each transaction. We compare the differences between the theoretical optimal benefits and outputs of the four methods to evaluate the accuracy.

In Eq. (8), $Output_i$ is the profit of the i-th output of the algorithm, TOV_i represents the theoretical optimal value. If the value of $Error_i$ is 0, it means that the algorithm gives the optimal solution. We define the Average Hit Rate in Eq. (9), where $\sum_{c(Error_i)=0} r(Error_i)$ represents the number of times the optimal solution is given, and R_{total} represents the total number of test rounds. In order to estimate the efficiency of four algorithms, the actual time consumption is also analyzed. There are 50 rounds of tests for each parameter configuration.

$$c(Error_i) = Output_i - TOV_i = \begin{cases} 0 & Output_i \text{ is optimal solution,} \\ else & Output_i \text{ is local optimal solution.} \end{cases} \quad (8)$$

$$AHR = \frac{\sum\limits_{c(Error_i)=0} r(Error_i)}{R_{total}}. \quad (9)$$

Table 1. Parameter settings in the evaluations

Settings	N	C^c	S^c	T^c
1	10	100	100	50
2	20	200	200	80
3	40	500	500	200

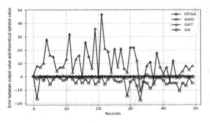

(a) Error comparison under Setting 1.

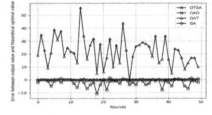

(b) Error comparison under Setting 2.

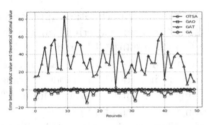

(c) Error comparison under Setting 3.

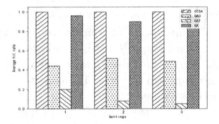

(d) AHR under three settings.

Fig. 3. Error comparison of four algorithms under different settings.

4.2 Experiment Results

Figure 3 shows the error comparison of four algorithms under different settings. Comparing (a)–(c) in Fig. 3, we find that our method has stable performance when the number of optional transactions for each shard increases. In addition, the *Error* of our method is 0 under all settings, indicating that the optimal solution can always be obtained. For other schemes, the range of *Error* fluctuations increases as N (the number of transactions) increases. Figure 3 (d) intuitively indicates *AHR* comparison of four algorithms under three settings. For instance, under Setting 1, the AHR of GAO, GAT and GA are 0.44, 0.2, and 0.96, respectively. The AHR of OTSA algorithm is always 100% under different settings. It is observed that GAO and GAT lack stability and are easy to obtain local optimal solutions. In addition, GAT deviates much more than GAO.

The running time comparison of four algorithms under different settings is shown in Fig. 4. Under the same setting, the running time of each algorithm is around a certain value, so that a relatively smooth waveform can be seen. Both greedy algorithms (GAO and GAT) execute fast, and the running time is

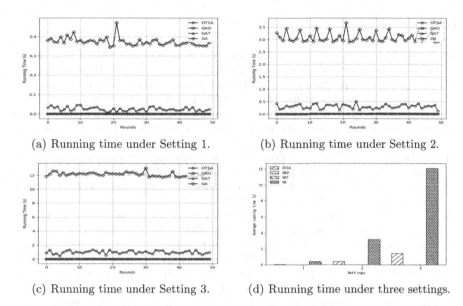

(a) Running time under Setting 1.   (b) Running time under Setting 2.

(c) Running time under Setting 3.   (d) Running time under three settings.

Fig. 4. Running time comparison of four algorithms under different settings.

almost negligible. Our method has a shorter running time than GA. Comparing (a)–(c) in Fig. 4, it can be found that when the transaction number N increases, the execution time growth rate of the four algorithms is quite different. The running time of two greedy algorithms is almost unchanged, and still remains at a negligible level. The running time of OTSA increases slightly with the increase of N, while the execution time of GA increases significantly. In general, two greedy algorithms perform fast but easily fall into local optimal solutions. Although the GA has a high AHR, its performance declines rapidly as the number of transactions increases, which cannot meet the demand for efficient transaction processing in sharding. Our algorithm can obtain the optimal solution under different settings and has a relatively stable performance.

5   Conclusions

We proposed the BS-KGS scheme to solve the storage security problem of knowledge graph, in which the optimal transaction allocation plan was given. In addition, two critical challenges in transaction sharding, namely, overhead and security, were addressed in this paper. Our experimental evaluation proved that our method was superior in improving the performance of blockchain system.

Acknowledgements. This work is partially supported by National Natural Science Foundation of China (Grant No. 61972034), Natural Science Foundation of Shandong Province (Grant Nos. ZR2019ZD10, ZR2020ZD01), Natural Science Foundation of Beijing Municipality (Grant No. 4202068), Ministry of Education - China Mobile Research Fund Project (Grant No. MCM20180401).

References

1. Amiri, M.J., Agrawal, D., Abbadi, A.E.: On sharding permissioned blockchains. In: IEEE International Conference on Blockchain, pp. 282–285. IEEE, July 2019
2. Cong, X., Zi, L.: Blockchain applications, challenges and evaluation: a survey. Discret. Math. Algorithms Appl. **12**(4), 2030001:1–2030001:21 (2020)
3. Foster, J.D., Berry, A.M., Boland, N., Waterer, H.: Comparison of mixed-integer programming and genetic algorithm methods for distributed generation planning. IEEE Trans. Power Syst. **29**(2), 833–843 (2013)
4. Gai, K., Qiu, M.: Optimal resource allocation using reinforcement learning for IoT content-centric services. Appl. Soft Comput. **70**, 12–21 (2018)
5. Gai, K., Qiu, M.: Reinforcement learning-based content-centric services in mobile sensing. IEEE Netw. **32**(4), 34–39 (2018)
6. Gai, K., Wu, Y., Zhu, L., Qiu, M., Shen, M.: Privacy-preserving energy trading using consortium blockchain in smart grid. IEEE TII **15**(6), 3548–3558 (2019)
7. Gai, K., et al.: Resource management in sustainable cyber-physical systems using heterogeneous cloud computing. IEEE Trans. Sustain. Comput. **3**(2), 60–72 (2018)
8. Gokce, E.I., Wilhelm, W.E.: Valid inequalities for the multi-dimensional multiple-choice 0–1 Knapsack problem. Discret. Optim. **17**, 25–54 (2015)
9. Gupta, H., Janakiram, D.: CDAG: a serialized blockdag for permissioned blockchain. arXiv preprint arXiv:1910.08547 (2019)
10. Lee, D.R., Jang, Y., Kim, H.: Poster. In: Proceedings of the 2019 ACM SIGSAC Conference on Computer and Communications Security. ACM, November 2019
11. Liu, Y., Liu, J., Yin, J., Li, G., Yu, H., Wu, Q.: Cross-shard transaction processing in sharding blockchains. In: Qiu, M. (ed.) ICA3PP 2020. LNCS, vol. 12454, pp. 324–339. Springer, Cham (2020). https://doi.org/10.1007/978-3-030-60248-2_22
12. Lu, R., Jin, X., Zhang, S., Qiu, M., Wu, X.: A study on big knowledge and its engineering issues. IEEE Trans. Knowl. Data Eng. **31**(9), 1630–1644 (2018)
13. Manuskin, A., Mirkin, M., Eyal, I.: Ostraka: secure blockchain scaling by node sharding. In: 2020 IEEE EuroS&PW. IEEE, September 2020
14. Qiu, H., Qiu, M., Memmi, G., Ming, Z., Liu, M.: A dynamic scalable blockchain based communication architecture for IoT. In: Qiu, M. (ed.) SmartBlock 2018. LNCS, vol. 11373, pp. 159–166. Springer, Cham (2018). https://doi.org/10.1007/978-3-030-05764-0_17
15. Shao, Z., et al.: Real-time dynamic voltage loop scheduling for multi-core embedded systems. IEEE Trans. Circuits Syst. II **54**(5), 445–449 (2007)
16. Wang, S., Huang, C., Li, J., Yuan, Y., Wang, F.: Decentralized construction of knowledge graphs for deep recommender systems based on blockchain-powered smart contracts. IEEE Access **7**, 136951–136961 (2019)
17. Wang, Y., Yin, X., Zhu, H., Hei, X.: A blockchain based distributed storage system for knowledge graph security. In: Sun, X., Wang, J., Bertino, E. (eds.) ICAIS 2020. LNCS, vol. 12240, pp. 318–327. Springer, Cham (2020). https://doi.org/10.1007/978-3-030-57881-7_29
18. Yao, Y., Kshirsagar, M., Vaidya, G., Ducrée, J., Ryan, C.: Convergence of blockchain, autonomous agents, and knowledge graph to share electronic health records. Front. Blockchain **4**, 661238 (2021)
19. Zamani, M., Movahedi, M., Raykova, M.: RapidChain: scaling blockchain via full sharding. In: ACM CCS, pp. 931–948 (2018)
20. Zilliqa: Zilliqa (2021). https://www.zilliqa.com/

Faster Nonlocal UNet for Cell Segmentation in Microscopy Images

Xuhao Lin[1,2] and Shengsheng Wang[1,2(✉)]

[1] College of Computer Science and Technology, Jilin University,
Changchun 130012, China
wss@jlu.edu.cn
[2] Key Laboratory of Symbolic Computation and Knowledge Engineering of Ministry
of Education, Jilin University, Changchun 130012, China

Abstract. Deep neural networks have shown great potential in medical image segmentation fields. Most of the current methods are based on UNet, which generates long-range dependence step by step by stacking a large number of local operations. However, global information cannot be effectively aggregated using only local operations. The nonlocal module is an effective method for obtaining global information, but the nonlocal block is always criticized for its exorbitant computation and GPU consumption. For the purpose of solving this problem, a faster nonlocal UNet (FN-UNet) is proposed for obtaining the long-range dependency of biomedical images through a more effective and efficient method. Inspired by the recently introduced nonlocal U-Nets and asymmetric nonlocal neural networks, we integrate the asymmetric fusion nonlocal block (AFNB) and asymmetric pyramid nonlocal block (APNB) into the proposed network. Additionally, thorough experiments are performed on the cell segmentation dataset of the ISBI Challenge. The results show that compared with the typical nonlocal UNet network, the proposed network can obtain better results on the basis of occupying less GPU memory and computation.

Keywords: Deep learning · Nonlocal UNet · Semantic segmentation · Fully convolution network · Cell segmentation

1 Introduction

Cell segmentation is a significant portion of microscopic image analysis, and it plays a significant role in cell morphology to determine the shape, structure and size of cells. In addition, there have been tremendous advances in cell segmentation in recent years. Such progress is inseparable from the emergence of excellent deep learning methods, such as ResNet [5] and UNet [16]. In particular, UNet is the most prominent on the cell segmentation task, and it is composed of an encoder that extracts features from the input image and a decoder that restores the feature map to its original size, accompanied by skip connections between

© Springer Nature Switzerland AG 2021
H. Qiu et al. (Eds.): KSEM 2021, LNAI 12817, pp. 463–474, 2021.
https://doi.org/10.1007/978-3-030-82153-1_38

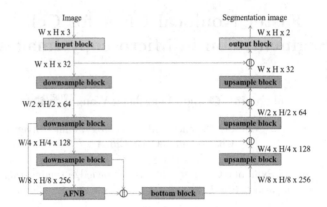

Fig. 1. The structure of our proposed faster nonlocal UNet.

them. Currently, there are many innovative networks based on UNet in the field
of biological segmentation, such as residual symmetric UNet [10] and the residual deconvolutional network [3]. Although UNet performs very well, it only uses
local operations, such as convolution and downsampling operations, which do not
effectively aggregate long-range dependencies. To obtain long-range dependence,
the convolutional layer should be applied repeatedly. However, there are several
limitations to do this, such as computational inefficiencies [19] and optimization
difficulties [5].

Wang et al. [19] proposed the nonlocal module, which was inspired by [1,18].
Compared with local operations, the greatest advantage of nonlocal operations
is that they can directly calculate the relationship between each location of
the feature map, thus obtaining the dependence of long distances instead of
repeatedly stacking local operations.

Furthermore, they [20] also integrated the nonlocal module [19] into UNet [16]
to obtain long-range dependence. In nonlocal UNet [20], the nonlocal block [19]
is applied in the bottom block and the upsampling block of UNet to obtain the
long-range dependence, and the global information is also employed to help the
upsampling block recover the spatial information. For the purpose of reducing
the parameters of the network, the downsampling block is only used twice. However, it is possible that due to limitations of computing and the GPU memory,
nonlocal UNet only adopts the nonlocal blocks in the bottom block and the first
upsampling block. Even so, nonlocal UNet has difficulty achieving results when
high-resolution images are input, while microscopic images usually feature high
resolution. To address the above problems, some improvements are made to our
proposed network. First, the nonlocal module requires many computations and
GPU memories, while the nonlocal UNet applies multiple nonlocal operations,
which inevitably requires too much computation and many GPU memories. To
address this problem, the APNB block proposed in [24] was used instead of a
typical nonlocal operation, which incorporates spatial pyramid pooling [4] into
nonlocal operations, thus significantly reducing computation while having no

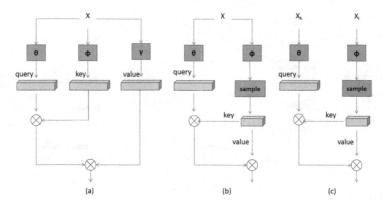

Fig. 2. Here, we show the structure of the typical nonlocal block (a). (b) and (c) are the APNB block and the AFNB block, respectively, where paths for keys and values are combined, and space pyramid pooling is adopted to reduce the consumption of computing resources.

effect on performance. Additionally, due to the reduced number of calculations, the APNB module is adopted in each upsampling block and bottom block of the proposed network. Second, the downsampling operation inevitably leads to the loss of spatial information. For the purpose of solving this problem, in our proposed network, the AFNB proposed in [24] was applied for feature fusion at different scales to aggregate spatial information and detailed information of images. In summary, the efficiency of nonlocal UNet will be improved, and at the same time, fewer computations and fewer GPU memories will be used during training.

Our major contributions are summarized as follows:

- By combining the advantages of nonlocal UNet, AFNB and APNB, it was proposed that faster nonlocal UNet can effectively reduce the computation and GPU memory;
- To improve the capacity of the model to recognize boundary pixels, a boundary enhancement cross entropy loss(BE loss) is proposed;
- To demonstrate the effectiveness of our proposed approach, experiments on the cell segmentation dataset of the ISBI Challenge were performed.

2 Related Work

2.1 Nonlocal UNet

Many studies [19,23] have shown that the use of long-distance dependency is of great importance for semantic segmentation, and UNet commonly used in biological image segmentation gathers global information through multiple downsampling layers and convolutional layers. However, downsampling and convolution

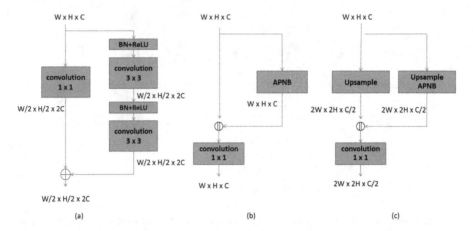

Fig. 3. The figure above shows the module structure used in our proposed network. (a) is the downsampling block, in which a residual structure is adopted. (b) and (c) are the structures of the bottom block and the upsampling block, respectively, where the APNB block is applied, and the 1×1 convolutional layer is finally used to maintain the number of channels. Where, + indicates the addition operation on the channel, and ∥ indicates the concatenation operation on the channel.

are local operations and rely only on local operations, which has shown limited ability to capture these long-range dependencies. Furthermore, using the down-sampling layer will also lose spatial information. To address the above problem, nonlocal UNet [20] introduces the nonlocal block into UNet [16] and changes the original four downsamplings to two.

2.2 AFNB and APNB

The nonlocal block is always criticized by its exorbitant computations and GPU consumption. To address the above problem, [24] proposed the AFNB block and the APNB block. According to their experiment, most of the calculation amounts of nonlocal blocks are matrix multiplication. In this case, space pyramidal pooling [4] is embedded in the nonlocal block, which reduces the calculation amount of matrix operation to a great extent. At the same time, spatial pyramid pooling [4] provides sufficient feature statistics of global information to compensate for the performance degradation caused by reduced computation.

3   Methodology

The goal of our work is to obtain the semantic segmentation of cell images by building neural network models. Inspired by nonlocal UNet [20] and asymmetric nonlocal neural networks [24], a new network named faster nonlocal UNet (FN-UNet) is proposed for cell segmentation tasks. In the network, the advantages of the asymmetrical pyramid nonlocal block [24] and nonlocal UNet [20] architecture are combined.

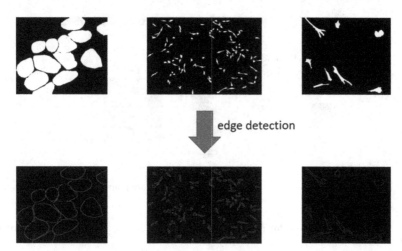

Fig. 4. An example of three datasets: (a) DIC-C2DH-HELa, (b) PHC-C2DL-PSC and (c) Fluo-C2DL-MSC. We use boundary detection to obtain the corresponding boundary map on the three datasets and adopt the boundary graph to generate the weight map of the loss function used in our method.

3.1 Overall Network Architecture

Inspired by nonlocal UNet [20] and asymmetric nonlocal neural networks [24], a new network named faster nonlocal UNet (FN-UNet) is proposed for cell segmentation tasks. For the baseline network, our proposed network adopts UNet [16] with an encoder-decoder structure. However, our proposed network only downsamples 3 times. The network structure is given in Fig. 1.

According to the nonlocal neural network [19], the nonlocal block can facilitate the performance of segmentation networks. Hence, the proposed network applies nonlocal blocks to the bottom block and the upsampling block of the network, similar to nonlocal UNet [20], to obtain global information and use global information to help the upsampling block recover spatial information. However, in the proposed network, APNB blocks [24] instead of typical nonlocal blocks are employed because of the excessive computing and GPU occupancy of typical nonlocal blocks. Typical nonlocal blocks and APNB blocks are shown in Fig. 2 (a) and (b), respectively. As Fig. 2(a) shows, $Q = \theta(x)$, $K = \phi(x)$ and $V = \gamma(x)$, where x is input feature, θ, ϕ and γ are 1×1 convolution layers that reduce the dimensionality of the channels. Q, K and V are embeddings transformed from X when $Q \in R^{C' \times W \times H}$, $K \in R^{C' \times W \times H}$ and $V \in R^{C' \times W \times H}$.

In addition, fusion features of different scales can effectively promote semantic segmentation, as hinted at in [9,11,12,21,22]. Therefore, AFNB blocks were used to combine the shallow feature maps with deep feature maps to utilize high-level semantics and low-level image details. The AFNB block is shown in Fig. 2 (c), which receives both the high-resolution feature map X_h and the low-resolution feature map X_l.

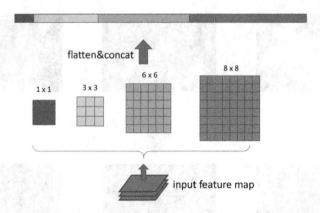

Fig. 5. The spatial pyramidal pooling structure used in our proposed faster nonlocal UNet.

Additionally, a residual connection is adopted to connect the output of AFNP and APNB to their input to avoid AFNB and APNB failing to produce accurate features that reduce overall performance, especially at the beginning of training. After that, He et al. [5] has proven that the residual connection can effectively assist in the training and performance of the deep neural network. Therefore, the residual connection is used in our proposed network, as shown in Fig. 3.

3.2 Loss Function

In biomedical image segmentation, the segmentation of cell boundaries is of great significance, but usually, the boundary information is often blurred in the segmentation of cell boundaries, resulting in lower segmentation results than expected. On the one hand, the main reason for this situation is the imbalance of categories. The pixels of the boundary category are far fewer than those of other categories. Thus, the network pays little attention to the boundary category. On the other hand, each boundary pixel is mixed with other classes of pixels, which makes segmentation networks difficult to distinguish the boundary pixel. Therefore, the segmentation network will perform well when the pixel is far away from the boundary but will perform worse as the pixel is closer to the boundary.

To deal with the problem mentioned above, inspired by [14], we propose the boundary enhancement cross entropy loss (BE loss). Then, it is assumed that the size of the input image x is $s \times s$ and the total number of categories is C when $\vec{P} = \{p_{i1}, p_{i2}, \cdots, p_{iC}\}$ is set as the probability vector, where i represents the ith pixel of the image. In addition, it is also assumed that the ith pixel is labeled as l_i. Our proposed BE loss can be formalized as:

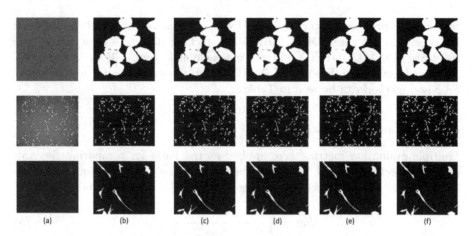

Fig. 6. Some of the segmentation results of our test set (a) images, (b) ground truth, (c) our network, (d) nonlocal UNet, (e) UNet, and (f) DeepLabv3+.

$$Loss = -\frac{1}{s^2}\sum_{i=1}^{s^2} \omega_i \, log \, p_{il_i} \qquad (1)$$

where ω_i is the weight of BE loss, which can be formalized as:

$$\omega_i = \omega_c + \gamma \sum_{j \in B} \frac{1}{\sigma\sqrt{2\pi}} e^{-\frac{(x_i - x_j)^2 + (y_i - y_j)^2}{2\sigma^2}} \qquad (2)$$

where ω_c is the weight map that addresses class imbalance in the image, γ is a penalty parameter, B is the set of boundary pixels, the final part of the equation is the Gaussian weighted Euclidean distance weight presented in [14], and hyperparameter σ determines the range of influence of the boundary pixel. It should be noted that the Gaussian weighted Euclidean distance weight calculates the Euclidean distance between each pixel and all boundary pixels and improves the segmentation network's capacity to differentiate boundaries. To calculate the Euclidean distance from each pixel to all edge pixels, edge detection is used to obtain the edge image (see Fig. 4 for the effect).

4   Experiment

4.1   Dataset

In this section, in order to evaluate the effectiveness of our network, our proposed network is compared with several typical SOTA approaches on the open datasets of ISBI cell segmentation challenges [13,17]. In addition, its task is to automatically segment the microscopic images into cell regions and background regions. Our proposed faster nonlocal UNet performs well on the three datasets: HeLa cells on flat glass (DIC-C2DH-HeLa), picking stem cells on a polystyrene substrate (PhC-C2DL-PSC) and rat mesenchymal stem cells on a flat poly-acrylamide substrate (Fluo-C2DL-MSC). Then, the experimental results of our proposed method can be seen in Table 1.

4.2   Evaluation Metrics

Multiple evaluation metrics were applied as the basis for comparing the proposed method with other SOTA methods, including the Dice similarity coefficient (Dice) and the intersection over union (IoU). These can be formulated as:

$$dice = \frac{2 \times TP}{FP + FN + 2 \times TP} \tag{3}$$

$$IoU = \frac{TP}{TP + FP + FN} \tag{4}$$

4.3   Data Preprocessing

First, we group the data sets into training sets (60%), validation sets (20%) and testing sets (20%). As the training data of the dataset used are very small, the training data of DIC-C2DH-HeLa and Fluo-C2DL-MSC are even less than 100. A deep neural network with sufficient generalization ability cannot be trained with so little training data. To solve the problem mentioned above, data augmentation was used to obtain more training data on the training set. In our proposed method, random rotation, mirror symmetry transformation and random elastic deformation are conducted to avoid overfitting of the model. Finally, the processed images were randomly cropped to 256×256 images.

4.4   Implementation Details

The PyTorch framework [15] is the basis for our proposed FN-UNet, and FN-UNet is run on the NVIDIA GeForce GTX 1080Ti GPU when ReLU is the activation function that we use. In addition, to avoid overfitting, BatchNorm was employed to fine-tune our model [6]. For the gradient descent algorithm, Adam optimizers [7] were used to train the model with a batch size of 4 and an initial learning rate of 0.0004. Moreover, the learning rate decay [8] was employed to accelerate the convergence speed. The hyperparameters γ and σ of BE loss are set as 10 and 15,

For APNB, to obtain a much smaller number of matrix multiplication calculations, it embeds spatial pyramid pooling [4] into nonlocal blocks. As shown in Fig. 5, in our method, four parallel pooling layers were used in spatial pyramid pooling [4] to obtain outputs of 1×1, 3×3, 6×6 and 8×8.

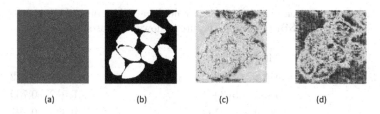

(a)   (b)   (c)   (d)

Fig. 7. Heatmap of feature maps in our proposed network: (a) original picture, (b) ground truth, and (c) and (d) are the corresponding heatmaps.

4.5 Model Efficiency

In practical applications, the efficiency of the model is also an important criterion to evaluate the model. In this part, we compare our FN-UNet with other SOTA methods in three aspects: FLOPs, GPU memory, and parameters. Since we crop the size of the image to 256×256 during data processing, we used $3 \times 256 \times 256$ images with batch size 1 as the input for each network in comparison. Table 2 shows the comparison results. We can see in Table 2 that deeplabv3+ [2] has higher parameters and computations than UNet [16] due to its deeper network structure. Nonlocal UNet [20] uses the traditional nonlocal module twice in the network, so its GPU memory footprint is much higher than other methods. Under the comprehensive evaluation of these three indicators, our proposed FN-UNet achieves the best performance. First, because our FN-UNet refers to the network structure of nonlocal UNet [20], we reduce the number of downsampling times and the number of downsampling channels in the network, so the parameters are greatly reduced compared with UNet [16] and DeepLabv3+ [2]. In addition, as we use the APNB module [24] to replace the traditional nonlocal module, the computation amount of matrix multiplication in nonlocal operation is greatly reduced, so the network's dependence on computation amount and GPU memory is greatly reduced.

4.6 Experiment Result

In this part, to appraise the capability of our model, our network is compared with other SOTA methods, including UNet [16], deeplabv3+ [2], nonlocal UNet [20], and some methods that have good performance in the ISBI tracking challenge. Table 1 shows the comparison results of our experiments. The FN-UNet proposed by us has a competitive performance in all indicators of the three datasets. In these three datasets, our FN-UNet obtained 0.902 and 0.844, 0.808 and 0.695, 0.763 and 0.627, respectively, in Dice and IoU. Table 1 shows that when we use AFNB, we obtain better results than UNet because we use AFNB to aggregate the spatial information and the detailed information of the image, which alleviates the loss of spatial information caused by downsampling. Later, when we used AFNB and BE loss simultaneously, the IoU rose again by approximately 2%. This is because BE loss forces the network to spend more attention

Table 1. The experimental results of faster nonlocal UNet on the three cell segmentation datasets of the ISBI Challenge. Figure 1 shows our baseline.

Dataset	Method	Dice	IoU
DIC-C2DH-HeLa	UNet	0.801	0.742
	DeepLabv3+	0.812	0.739
	Nonlocal UNet	0.855	0.791
	Ours(+AFNB)	0.819	0.752
	Ours(+BELoss+AFNB)	0.832	0.771
	FN-UNet(+BELoss+AFNB+APNB)	**0.902**	**0.844**
PhC-C2DL-PSC	UNet	0.698	0.562
	DeepLabv3+	0.712	0.582
	Nonlocal UNet	0.766	0.663
	Ours(+AFNB)	0.702	0.581
	Ours(+BELoss+AFNB)	0.711	0.611
	FN-UNet(+BELoss+AFNB+APNB)	**0.808**	**0.695**
Fluo-C2DL-MSC	UNet	0.701	0.543
	DeepLabv3+	0.716	0.557
	Nonlocal UNet	0.747	0.607
	Ours(+AFNB)	0.713	0.558
	Ours(+BELoss+AFNB)	0.722	0.582
	FN-UNet(+BELoss+AFNB+APNB)	**0.763**	**0.627**

on the cell boundary, which enables us to obtain a more accurate cell boundary. The heatmap is shown in Fig. 7. Finally, when we add APNB, our index increased by approximately 6% again. This is because, unlike nonlocal UNet [20], we used nonlocal operations for each upsampling in the network. Therefore, FN-UNet could obtain more accurate segmentation results after upsampling.

As shown in Table 2, not only are common evaluation indicators including IoU and Dice compared, but GFLOPs and GPU memories are also compared for comprehensive evaluation. Compared with UNet [16] and deeplabv3+ [2], our method yields better results, while compared with nonlocal UNet [20], our proposed network not only achieves better results but is also much better in terms of computation and GPU memories. Therefore, when considering all the indicators, our FN-UNet obtains the most ideal result. Our segmentation results are shown in Fig. 6. Then, it should be noted that one sample on each of the three datasets was chosen to show our segmentation results. It shows that our proposed approach is competitive with the SOTA approach, and our network shows good generalization and robustness in these three datasets. In addition, our proposed BE loss forces the network to spend more attention on boundary pixels, as shown in Fig. 7. Additionally, our approach improves the network's ability to recognize contact cells to some extent.

Table 2. The comparison of parameters and GPU memories based on the whole network; during the test, a batch size of 1 was used.

Model	Input size	FLOPs(G)	GPU Mem	Parameters(M)
UNet	$3 \times 256 \times 256$	48.39	1895	28.96
DeepLab v3+	$3 \times 256 \times 256$	63.48	1281	58.04
Nonlocal UNet	$3 \times 256 \times 256$	41.46	3087	1.01
Ours	$3 \times 256 \times 256$	5.9	1194	2.18

5 Conclusion

In this work, the faster nonlocal UNet were proposed for cell segmentation. Furthermore, our core contribution is to combine the advantages of nonlocal UNet, AFNB and APNB to propose a faster nonlocal UNet. Specifically, this method significantly reduces the computational resources required for training, while it maintains competitive performance with the SOTA method. Of course, BE loss was also proposed. In this case, the performance of the network is enhanced to distinguish boundary pixels and the ability to segment touch cells, and at the same time, the problem of category imbalance is also improved. Then, our approach was also evaluated on the three cell segmentation datasets of the ISBI Challenge, and results that could compete with the SOTA approach were obtained.

Acknowledgment. This work is supported by the Innovation Capacity Construction Project of Jilin Province Development and Reform Commission (2019C053-3), the Science & Technology Development Project of Jilin Province, China (20190302117GX) and the National Key Research and Development Program of China (No. 2020YFA0714 103).

References

1. Buades, A., Coll, B., Morel, J.M.: A non-local algorithm for image denoising. In: 2005 IEEE Computer Society Conference on Computer Vision and Pattern Recognition (CVPR 2005), vol. 2, pp. 60–65. IEEE (2005)
2. Chen, L.C., Papandreou, G., Kokkinos, I., Murphy, K., Yuille, A.L.: DeepLab: semantic image segmentation with deep convolutional nets, atrous convolution, and fully connected CRFs. IEEE Trans. Pattern Anal. Mach. Intell. **40**(4), 834–848 (2017)
3. Fakhry, A., Zeng, T., Ji, S.: Residual deconvolutional networks for brain electron microscopy image segmentation. IEEE Trans. Med. Imaging **36**(2), 447–456 (2016)
4. He, K., Zhang, X., Ren, S., Sun, J.: Spatial pyramid pooling in deep convolutional networks for visual recognition. IEEE Trans. Pattern Anal. Mach. Intell. **37**(9), 1904–1916 (2015)
5. He, K., Zhang, X., Ren, S., Sun, J.: Deep residual learning for image recognition. In: Proceedings of the IEEE Conference on Computer Vision and Pattern Recognition, pp. 770–778 (2016)

6. Ioffe, S., Szegedy, C.: Batch normalization: accelerating deep network training by reducing internal covariate shift, pp. 448–456 (2015)
7. Kingma, D.P., Ba, J.: Adam: a method for stochastic optimization. arXiv preprint arXiv:1412.6980 (2014)
8. Krogh, A., Hertz, J.A.: A simple weight decay can improve generalization, pp. 950–957 (1992)
9. Lazebnik, S., Schmid, C., Ponce, J.: Beyond bags of features: spatial pyramid matching for recognizing natural scene categories. In: 2006 IEEE Computer Society Conference on Computer Vision and Pattern Recognition (CVPR 2006), vol. 2, pp. 2169–2178. IEEE (2006)
10. Lee, K., Zung, J., Li, P., Jain, V., Seung, H.S.: Superhuman accuracy on the SNEMI3D connectomics challenge. arXiv preprint arXiv:1706.00120 (2017)
11. Lin, G., Milan, A., Shen, C., Reid, I.: RefineNet: multi-path refinement networks for high-resolution semantic segmentation, pp. 1925–1934 (2017)
12. Liu, W., Rabinovich, A., Berg, A.C.: ParseNet: looking wider to see better. arXiv preprint arXiv:1506.04579 (2015)
13. Maška, M., et al.: A benchmark for comparison of cell tracking algorithms. Bioinformatics **30**(11), 1609–1617 (2014)
14. Miao, Z., Fu, K., Sun, H., Sun, X., Yan, M.: Automatic water-body segmentation from high-resolution satellite images via deep networks. IEEE Geosci. Remote Sens. Lett. **15**(4), 602–606 (2018)
15. Paszke, A., et al.: Automatic differentiation in pytorch (2017)
16. Ronneberger, O., Fischer, P., Brox, T.: U-net: convolutional networks for biomedical image segmentation, pp. 234–241 (2015)
17. Ulman, V., et al.: An objective comparison of cell-tracking algorithms. Nat. Methods **14**(12), 1141–1152 (2017)
18. Vaswani, A., et al.: Attention is all you need. arXiv preprint arXiv:1706.03762 (2017)
19. Wang, X., Girshick, R., Gupta, A., He, K.: Non-local neural networks, pp. 7794–7803 (2018)
20. Wang, Z., Zou, N., Shen, D., Ji, S.: Non-local U-nets for biomedical image segmentation, vol. 34, no. 04, pp. 6315–6322 (2020)
21. Yu, F., Wang, D., Shelhamer, E., Darrell, T.: Deep layer aggregation, pp. 2403–2412 (2018)
22. Zhang, Z., Zhang, X., Peng, C., Xue, X., Sun, J.: ExFuse: enhancing feature fusion for semantic segmentation, pp. 269–284 (2018)
23. Zhao, H., Shi, J., Qi, X., Wang, X., Jia, J.: Pyramid scene parsing network, pp. 2881–2890 (2017)
24. Zhu, Z., Xu, M., Bai, S., Huang, T., Bai, X.: Asymmetric non-local neural networks for semantic segmentation. In: Proceedings of the IEEE/CVF International Conference on Computer Vision, pp. 593–602 (2019)

An Improved YOLO Algorithm
for Object Detection in All Day Scenarios

Junhao Wang[✉] (iD)

School of Computer Engineering and Science, Shanghai University, Shanghai, China
chess333@shu.edu.cn

Abstract. Object detection is one of the widest studies in computer vision. And there are many useful algorithms for this task. Though most of the studies are effective in the daytime or dark scene, they are not applicable in some special cases that need to carry out object detection in the scenarios for both daytime as well as night such as rescue scenarios in serious disasters of earthquake, landslide, mountain torrent, flood and on. To solve this issue, we attend to study the object detection algorithm in the scenarios for both daytime as well as dark scene. Considering the high efficiency of the YOLO algorithm under sufficient light conditions as well as the needs of object detection under poor light, this paper proposes an improved end-to-end YOLOv3 network under dark conditions. The main idea is to integrate the YOLOv3 object detection network and the Retinex image enhancement network to ensure that the image be easier to perform feature extraction and object recognition. Extensive experiments were conducted on several public datasets. The results show that compared with the traditional YOLOv3 object detection model, the proposed algorithm can improve the mean average precision from 53.23% to 59.79% in the object detection task with poor light.

Keywords: YOLOv3 · Retinex · Object detection · Deep learning · Image enhancement

1 Introduction

Object detection under normal light conditions has more mature technologies, while under dark conditions it is more difficult. For some special extreme situations, such as earthquake, landslide, mining accident and other disasters that causes the light source and power supply to be cut off and rescue has to be done in poor light or even total black scenarios, object detection accuracy and recall rate may be significantly reduced. This may has great impact on the all day rescue efforts in turn. As the rescue work requires higher robustness of object detection algorithms to adapt to variable environmental factors, this brings great challenges for this task in such special area. In this kind of work, the traditional object algorithms with sufficient light sources are not enough to solve the problem as most of them are trained with normal images. So it is important to study object detection under dark conditions.

© Springer Nature Switzerland AG 2021
H. Qiu et al. (Eds.): KSEM 2021, LNAI 12817, pp. 475–486, 2021.
https://doi.org/10.1007/978-3-030-82153-1_39

At present, a lot of studies on noise removal, blur removal, image enhancement and other technologies have been done. However, for object detection in the extreme environments, the effectiveness of these technologies is limited. To solve this problem, there are two possible ways. One is to directly use the traditional image enhancement algorithms, and the other is to exploit neural networks based on deep learning. For the former, they can improve the image brightness to some extent, but they also introduce more noises at the same time. These noises disturb the observable information of the image, which is not conducive to the image feature extraction. For the latter, although the dark image object detection algorithm based on deep learning has certain advantages in accuracy and speed, it may affect the detection effect of normal image object and cannot implement the all day object detection task.

As mentioned above, both traditional pattern recognition or image detection algorithms and deep learning object detection algorithms such as YOLO have poor detection performances for objects with low background brightness, complex blur, compact density and high overlap. To solve this problem, based on the deep learning object detection algorithm YOLOv3 and Retinex image enhancement network, an all day RS-YOLOv3 object detection network is put forward. It makes it easier to extract and recognize the features of low illumination images. In addition, the algorithm in this paper is not only suitable for the task of object detection in low illumination images, but also has good effects on object detection in normal-brightness images, which solves the problem of all day object detection to a large extent.

2   Related Work

Object detection algorithms can be roughly divided into two categories: traditional manual features based algorithms and convolutional neural network based algorithms. In the past, traditional manual features based object detection algorithms were used, mainly through ViolaJones (VJ) detector or the sliding window method to traversal the image and then detect. Then a linear support vector machine (SVM) is used as a classifier.

The emergence of convolutional neural network has an epochal significance for the field of object detection. Girshick et al. proposed Regions with CNN Features (R-CNN) object detection framework in 2014 [4]. The idea of this method is to find out the Region Proposal, and select a small number of windows based on the edge, texture, color and other information in the picture, so as to achieve a higher recall rate. Meanwhile, R-CNN maintains the traditional object detection method, using the anchor box for object detection. Spatial Pyramid Pooling Networks (SPPNET) designed and proposed by He et al. in 2014 is used to solve the problem that the input image size is required to be fixed when extracting features from R-CNN network. In 2015, Girshick et al. improved on the basis of R-CNN and SPPNET and proposed Fast R-CNN object detection algorithm. The main feature of Fast R-CNN is that it performs in a multi-task learning manner, which realizes the synchronous training of object classification and bounding box regression while finetuning the network. The speed of the model training part is 9 times that of R-CNN, and the detection speed is 200 times that of R-CNN. Subsequently, Girshick et al. proposed the Faster RCNN algorithm [12]. This algorithm achieves the end-to-end object detection based on deep learning, and also realizes the real-time object detection. Joseph et al. proposed the You Only Look Once (YOLO) object detection algorithm [9]. The main principle is to input the image into the multi-layer convolutional neural network to extract the image features, and then directly return the coordinates of the object box and its category in the output layer, and finally remove the overlapping object box through NMS processing. Faster-RCNN, on the other hand, uses candidate boxes to scan the feature images to find objects after extracting the feature images. Then it uses two subnetworks for regression and classification, one is used to add offset and scale the candidate box to return to object coordinates, and the other is used for object classification. With the continuous update of technology, YOLOv3, YOLOv4 and YOLOv5 also came out one after another. The main improvements lie in the increase of positive samples, flexible configuration of parameters and the application of built-in over-parameter optimization strategy. Besides, they improve the detection accuracy of small objects. After the deep learning based object detection algorithm becomes the mainstream. Generally, algorithms in object detection field are divided into single-stage and two-stage algorithms. YOLO is the representative algorithm of the former, while Faster R-CNN is the representative algorithm of the latter.

There are few researches in the field of object detection under dark conditions. This kind of work mainly focuses on image denoising and enhancement preprocessing and network structure. Xuan et al. proposed an image and video enhancement technique [2]. The principle of the algorithm is to deconvolve the input low-light video first, and then apply the optimized image dehazing algorithm on the deconvolution video. Liu et al. proposed a fast denoising method, which is able to get the clean image out of a lot of noise images [7]. Since the low illumination image can produce more noise after the enhancement processing, this method has a better effect on the noise reduction of the enhanced images. The above two methods have good effect on general noise images, but the effect is poor if the brightness is extremely low. Chen et al. proposed a data-driven approach to solve the problem of rapid imaging systems in extremely low light conditions. The deep neural network is trained to learn the image processing techniques of raw data under low light conditions, including color conversion, demosaic, noise reduction and image enhancement, etc. The end-to-end training method is then used to avoid noise amplification and to characterize the cumulative errors of traditional camera processing in this environment [1]. Yukihiro proposed a Domain Adaption generation model based on knowledge distillation, reused datasets to create potential features to train Glue layers, and then applied this to object detection under low light conditions [13]. The above two low illumination object detection algorithms based on deep learning are only for pure dark conditions, and the detection effect of images with normal brightness is poor. Therefore, there are still limitations to all day object detection.

3   RS-YOLOv3 Objection Detection

In the dark, the images with low illumination do not have enough features for visual processing, resulting in a significant decrease of object detection accuracy. For example, Fig. 1 shows a sample from the dark image dataset LOL dataset [15]. The brightness of this image is very low. After the direct object detection test, it can be seen that the classification accuracy is not as so good. Besides, some objects on the right of this image also fail to be detected and the recall rate is very low.

(a)   (b)

Fig. 1. Object detection for dark image and simple image enhancement processing.

This paper uses the basic pixel transform algorithm at first, through simple enhancement processing, the objects in Fig. 1(a) are clearer as shown in Fig. 1(b), which can be distinguished by eye. However, this operation has also increased a lot of noise. The image has become more blurred, which makes feature extraction be more difficult.

The main idea of this algorithm is to integrate the YOLOv3 object detection network with Retinex image enhancement network, which is more conducive to low illumination image feature extraction.

3.1   YOLOv3 Network Architecture

YOLOv3 uses Darknet53 as the backbone feature extraction network. Darknet53 contains 53 convolutional layers, which is combined with Resnet network so that it can alleviate the problem of gradient disappearance in deep network training. In order to enhance the detection accuracy of the network on objects of different scales, YOLOv3 adopts a method similar to FPN, which integrates the feature layer at the lower level containing more fine-grained information with the feature layer at the higher level containing more semantic information. There are two feature fusion processes in YOLOv3, forming three detection layers of different scales, corresponding to the detection of large-scale objects, medium-scale objects and small-scale objects respectively. Feature layers of different scales are divided into SS grids, each grid generates 3 prior boxes, and a total of 10647 prior box are generated. Each prior box is a vector of (B + C + N) dimension, where B represents 4 bounding box offsets, C represents the reliability of object prediction and N represents the total number of categories that need to be predicted.

The Loss function of YOLOv3 consists of object box position loss $Loss_{loc}$, object confidence loss $Loss_{onf}$ and object class loss $Loss_{cls}$. Among them, the object box position loss includes BCE Loss generated by the center point X and Y and MSE Loss generated by the length and width of the predicted box W and H. Object class Loss refers to several BCE Loss of the category brought by classification. The total loss function is defined as follows:

$$Loss = Loss_{conf} + loss_{loc} + Loss_{cls} \qquad (1)$$

3.2   Retinex Image Enhancement

Image enhancement techniques based on Retinex theory have made great progress in the past 20 years. Retinex theory is one of the models describing how the visual system senses the surface reflectivity of a scene to explain the color vision of the human eye [6]. The main goal of the theory is to try to decompose a given image I into two different images: the physical reflectivity image R and the light image L. That is to say, for the coordinate point(x,y), there is:

$$I(x,y) = R(x,y) \times L(x,y) \qquad (2)$$

Through this decomposition, Retinex theory attempts to eliminate or suppress light images in order to explain the visual system's preference for physical reflectivity image R. In Retinex theory, the elimination or suppression of ambient illumination exactly meets the requirement of adjusting the dynamic range of illumination for image enhancement under non-uniform illumination environment.

Early techniques of image enhancement algorithms based on Retinex theory eliminate light images directly by using a low-pass filter and leave only physical reflectivity images as the result. These approaches often introduce large distortion in terms of image fidelity. Based on the assumption of different illumination prior information, the subsequent algorithms adopt diffusion equation or optimization theory, and establish the structural information constraint items of the illumination image to estimate the illumination image.

As can be seen from Fig. 2, the input image I is obtained through the illumination estimation module. After the illumination image L is obtained, the physical reflectivity image R can be calculated by Eq. (2). Then the illumination image is adjusted and multiplied by the physical reflectivity image again to obtain the enhanced result I_E.

In this process, the light image is first estimated, and then the physical reflectivity is calculated. This is also the basic idea used by most image enhancement algorithms based on Retinex theory [8] at present.

Estimating the illumination image according to Equation (2) is to essentially solve a mathematical problem, which requires certain assumptions about illumination. For example, a common assumption is that illumination is locally slow in space. This assumption is more from the perspective of physical modeling than from the perspective of perception. Considering that the visual system has a perceptual preference for the physical reflectivity of the scene, this assumption may lead to discrepancies between the results and the real perception.

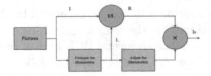

Fig. 2. Basic flow of image enhancement algorithm based on Retinex theory.

Studies have shown that the visual system is more sensitive to the relative changes in light and shade in a scene, but less sensitive to the absolute intensity of the light [5]. Therefore, the change of light and shade in the scene stimulates the visual system to produce the corresponding neural response, and visual contrast can be considered as an approximate description.

3.3   RS-YOLOv3 Object Detection Algorithm

Before the dataset is input into the network, a selection function is used to calculate the average pixel of the image. If the pixel is lower than the value α, the low-illumination image is input into the Retinex image enhancement module of the input layer of the neural network. After being enhanced by Retinex, it is input into the YOLOv3 neural network for training. The Retinex image enhancement detection algorithm MSR is shown in Algorithm 1.

Algorithm1: MSR

Input: weight, scales_size, h, w
Output: gray scale
log_R zeros((h, w))
for i : range(scales_size)
img min(data[nonzero(img)])
L_blur min(data[GaussianBlur(img)])
dst_Img,dst_Lblur calculating logarithm(img and L_blur)
dst_Ixl multiply(dst_Img, dst_Lblur)
log_R weight * subtract(dst_Img, dst_Ixl) + log_R
End

In order to improve the efficiency of feature extraction of enhanced low-illuminating small object images in the network, this paper uses two subsampled feature maps in Darknet53, and adds a conversion module between Darknet53 network and the first predictive feature layer to realize up-sampling of the feature fusion map at the third scale in YOLOv3 network. After that the results are then fused with the 2 subsampled feature maps in Darknet 53 and fed into the detection layer for prediction.

Besides, in order to improve the accuracy of detection of small objects with low illumination and reduce the amount of calculation, the prediction layers with the scale of 1313 and 2626 in the original network are deleted. After images are input into the detector, the vector output from the network is processed to obtain the classification and location information of the detected objects. In addition, the whole network adopts the method of feature pyramid, so that different objects can be detected at different scales. Compared with the original YOLOv3 algorithm, which predicts on three scales, the improved RS-YOLOv3 algorithm only needs to predict on two scales, so it can detect small objects with low illumination in the image faster. The whole network architecture can be seen in Fig. 3.

Appropriate initial frame can not only speed up the training process of the network, but also increase the accuracy of the recognition algorithm. In this paper, according to the characteristics of objects under dark conditions, K-means clustering algorithm is adopted to generate the most similar initial frame of various objects. The objective function of clustering is:

$$min \sum_{i=0} \sum_{j=0} [1 - IOU(Box[i], Box[j])] \qquad (3)$$

where IOU represents the crossover ratio between the clustering result $Box[i]$ and the real value $Box[j]$ [16].

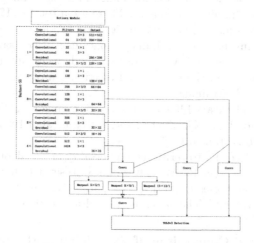

Fig. 3. RS-YOLOv3 network structure diagram.

4   Experiments and Results Analysis

In this paper, based on the traditional YOLOv3 object detection network, a module based on Retinex image enhancement algorithm is added to the input layer, and then a conversion module is added between Darknet53 network and the first predictive feature layer to realize up-sampling of the feature fusion graph at the third scale in the YOLOv3 network, which ensures that the low illumination image is easier to feature extraction and recognition. In order to increase the applicability and versatility of the algorithm, namely all-day object detection, three experiments are carried out in this paper:

The dataset used in Experiment 1 is composed of normal images and low illumination images. This dataset comes from network resources. In order to improve the practicability of the detection model, the dataset is preprocessed to make the dark image and the normal image have a clear boundary. There are 21 object categories.

The dataset used in Experiment 2 is the dark image dataset with low illumination. The dataset is partly derived from the Dark image dataset of the See-in-the-Dark Dataset [1] and some from self-labeled dark images. The dataset used in Experiment 3 is Pascal VOC dataset [3] with normal illumination.

4.1   Experimental Settings and Datasets

In this experiment, the operating system is 64bit Windows 10. The deep learning framework is Pytorch 1.4.0, using Anaconda environment and Python 3.6 language. The initial learning rate lr is 0.001 and the batch size is 8. By test comparison, the average pixel value α of low-illumination images is set as 60.

Experiment 1: During the training, this paper takes 6441 images as the training set, including 1669 low-illumination images, and 6001 images as the test set, including 1178 low-illumination images. There are a total of 12,442 images. The epoch is set as 30. Finally, 1000 new images are randomly selected as the test set. Despite some invalid data, each image contains nearly 6 samples on average. Due to the large gap between types, most of the datasets are images aggregated by a single category, and the unbalanced distribution of samples also increases the difficulty of model training.

Experiment 2: There are 1469 low-illumination images in the training set and 516 low-illumination images in the test set, with a total of 1985 low-illumination images. The epoch is trained for 30 times.

Experiment 3: In order to verify the universality of the algorithm, the dataset used in Experiment 3 is the Pascal VOC public dataset with normal illumination, and there are 20 categories in total. Other parameters are the same as those in the previous experiments. The epoch is trained for 30 times.

4.2   Analysis and Comparison of Experimental Results

The algorithm proposed in this paper is the improvement of YOLOv3. In order to compare the performance differences between the two algorithms, the metric changes in the training process are given for comparison.

Experiment 1 Results and Analysis. The traditional YOLOv3 object detection algorithm and the improved object detection algorithm are trained with epoch of 30 times respectively, and two weight files are obtained. Then, several low-illumination pictures are randomly selected from the test set, and the two algorithms are applied for comparative analysis, as shown in Fig. 4. Figure 4 (a, c, e) are the results of the traditional YOLOv3 algorithm, and Fig. 4 (b, d, f) are the results of the RS-YOLOv3 object detection algorithm.

Through the experimental samples, it can be clearly found that the Fig. 4(a) in the first line of object detection cannot detect any object by traditional algorithm. In the Fig. 4(c, e), traditional algorithms miss some of the objects and

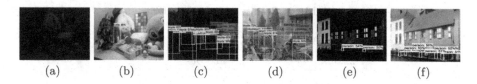

(a)   (b)   (c)   (d)   (e)   (f)

Fig. 4. The results of YOLOv3 and RS-YOLOv3

have relatively low recall rates. However, the RS-YOLOv3 object detection algorithm can enhance the image brightness better and the detection accuracy is better. It can also be seen that the low illumination condition has a particularly obvious influence on the detection of small objects, while the influence on large objects is relatively slight. After training with epoch for 30 times, the model gradually decreases the value of the loss function through continuous learning in the training process.

The deep learning algorithm uses the YOLOv3 object detection algorithm and the improved YOLOv3 object detection algorithm in this paper. The training results are shown in Table 1.

Table 1. The accuracies of two algorithms.

Object detection algorithm	mAP@[IoU = 0.5:0.95]
YOLOv3	53.23%
RS-YOLOv3	59.79%

Experiment 2 and Results Analysis. In order to improve the universality of the algorithm, a small dataset with all low-illumination images (the average pixels are all less than $\alpha = 60$) is also made in this paper. The accuracy is shown in Table 2.

It can be seen from the results that due to the small experimental dataset and the limitations of YOLO algorithm itself, the algorithm in this paper still has a great space for development in the detection of small objects with low illumination, but the effect is acceptable for large objects. Moreover, it has a good effect on object detection in all low illumination images. A sample comparison before and after object detection is shown in Fig. 5.

Fig. 5. Object image before and after detection.

Table 2. Results of Experiment 2.

mAP@[IoU = 0.5:0.95]	mAP@[IoU = 0.5:1]
22.02%	40.85%

Experiment 3 and Results Analysis. This algorithm is for all day object detection, so it still needs good effect for normal illumination image. As can be seen from the experimental results, for normal illumination images, the accuracy of this algorithm is close to that of the traditional object detection algorithm, reaching more than 70%, and the detection accuracy and recall rate are both high, reaching the practical level. Multi-objects are also shown in the experimental sample diagram, and the algorithm can still accurately detect objects in the case of high coincidence degree of detection boundary box. Therefore, the algorithm in this paper has a good detection effect for all-day oriented objects, which is of great practical significance. Sample diagram of experimental results is shown in Fig. 6, and comparison of accuracy of experimental results is shown in Table 3.

Fig. 6. Test results of Experiment 3.

Table 3. Results of Experiment 2.

Object detection algorithm	mAP@[IoU = 0.5]
YOLOv2 [10]	57.90%
YOLOv3 [11]	73.43%
RCNN [4]	59.20%
Faster-RCNN [12]	76.80%
RPN [14]	70.4%
RS-YOLOv3	73.68%

5   Conclusion

In this paper, an improved RS-YOLOv3 object detection algorithm is established by deep learning method. Aiming at all-day oriented object detection task, it is superior to the traditional image detection algorithm to a certain extent and achieves the purpose of detecting objects in dark and daytime conditions. Pascal

VOC dataset and the Dark image dataset of the See-in-the-Dark Dataset is used
to carry out weight training on the improved YOLOv3 deep neural network, and
different performance is obtained by adjusting the hyperparameters of the algorithm. The recall rate and accuracy of the algorithm can meet the requirement
of all-day oriented object detection operation, which indicates that the proposed
method has certain application value. The results of three different data sets
show that the detection effect of the proposed algorithm is good. This is a significant attempt for the application of object detection algorithm. The accuracy
of the detection model can be further improved in the future when more dark
image data and more training time are obtained, so as to realize all-day object
detection.

Acknowledgements. As an undergraduate, it is the first time for me to present my
results in KSEM2021. I cannot express my excitement. First of all, I'd like to thank my
supervisor, Professor Peng Junjie. He is knowledgeable and rigorous in his scholarship.
He gave me good suggestions on the general direction of my thesis and carefully guided
my thesis writing. At the same time, I also want to thank my senior male Yuan Haochen
and senior female Wu Ting, who gave me a lot of help in revising the paper. Finally, I
would like to express my heartfelt thanks to my teachers and the people who care and
support me.

References

1. Chen, C., Chen, Q., Xu, J., Koltun, V.: Learning to see in the dark. In: Proceedings
   of the IEEE Conference on Computer Vision and Pattern Recognition, pp. 3291–
   3300 (2018)
2. Dong, X., et al.: Fast efficient algorithm for enhancement of low lighting video.
   In: 2011 IEEE International Conference on Multimedia and Expo, pp. 1–6. IEEE
   (2011)
3. Everingham, M., Eslami, S., Gool, L.V., Williams, C., Winn, J., Zisserman, A.:
   The pascal visual object classes challenge: a retrospective. Int. J. Comput. Vis.
   111(1), 98–136 (2015)
4. Girshick, R.: Fast R-CNN. In: Proceedings of the IEEE International Conference
   on Computer Vision, pp. 1440–1448 (2015)
5. Jobson, D.J., Rahman, Z.U., Woodell, G.A.: A multiscale retinex for bridging the
   gap between color images and the human observation of scenes. IEEE Trans. Image
   Process. **6**(7), 965–976 (1997)
6. Li, Z., Song, X., Chen, C., Wang, C.: Brightness level image enhancement algorithm
   based on retinex algorithm. J. Data Acquisit. Process. 41–49 (2019)
7. Liu, Z., Lu, Y., Tang, X., Uyttendaele, M., Jian, S.: Fast burst images denoising.
   ACM Trans. Graph. **33**(6CD), 232.1-232.9 (2014)
8. Pu, T., Zhang, Z., Peng, Z.: Enhancing uneven lighting images with naturalness
   preserved retinex algorithm. J. Data Acquisit. Process. **36**, 76–84 (2021)
9. Redmon, J., Divvala, S., Girshick, R., Farhadi, A.: You only look once: unified,
   real-time object detection. In: Proceedings of the IEEE Conference on Computer
   Vision and Pattern Recognition, pp. 779–788 (2016)
10. Redmon, J., Farhadi, A.: Yolo9000: better, faster, stronger. In: IEEE Conference
    on Computer Vision & Pattern Recognition, pp. 6517–6525 (2017)

11. Redmon, J., Farhadi, A.: Yolov3: an incremental improvement. CoRR abs/1804.02767 (2018), http://arxiv.org/abs/1804.02767
12. Ren, S., He, K., Girshick, R., Sun, J.: Faster R-CNN: towards real-time object detection with region proposal networks. IEEE Trans. Pattern Anal. Mach. Intell. **39**(6), 1137–1149 (2017)
13. Sasagawa, Y., Nagahara, H.: YOLO in the dark - domain adaptation method for merging multiple models. In: Vedaldi, A., Bischof, H., Brox, T., Frahm, J.-M. (eds.) ECCV 2020. LNCS, vol. 12366, pp. 345–359. Springer, Cham (2020). https://doi.org/10.1007/978-3-030-58589-1_21
14. Wang, J., Chen, K., Yang, S., Loy, C.C., Lin, D.: Region proposal by guided anchoring. In: Proceedings of the IEEE/CVF Conference on Computer Vision and Pattern Recognition, pp. 2965–2974 (2019)
15. Wei, C., Wang, W., Yang, W., Liu, J.: Deep retinex decomposition for low-light enhancement. arXiv preprint arXiv:1808.04560 (2018)
16. Xu, J., Dou, Y., Zheng, Y.: Underwater target recognition and tracking method based on YOLO-V3 algorithm. J. Chin. Inertial Technol. **28**, 129–133 (2020)

EMRM: Enhanced Multi-source Review-Based Model for Rating Prediction

Xiaochen Wang[1,2], Tingsong Xiao[2], and Jie Shao[2,3(✉)]

[1] Guizhou Provincial Key Laboratory of Public Big Data, Guizhou University,
Guiyang 550025, China
[2] Center for Future Media, School of Computer Science and Engineering,
University of Electronic Science and Technology of China, Chengdu 611731, China
{wangxiaochen,xiaotingsong}@std.uestc.edu.cn, shaojie@uestc.edu.cn
[3] Sichuan Artificial Intelligence Research Institute, Yibin 644000, China

Abstract. Rating prediction, whose goal is to predict user preference
for unconsumed items, has become one of the core tasks in recommendation systems. Recently, many deep learning-based methods have been
applied to the field of recommendation systems and have achieved great
performance, especially when user reviews are available. User reviews
usually contain rich semantic information and can reflect the preferences
of users. However, user reviews are usually sparse. To alleviate this problem, we propose a method called EMRM, which stands for **E**nhanced
Multi-source **R**eview-based **M**odel for rating prediction, to collect multi-
source auxiliary reviews for each user. EMRM not only collects multi-
source auxiliary reviews from nearest neighbors but also from farthest
neighbors who have dissimilar consuming behaviors and historical rating
records, so it can improve both the accuracy and diversity of recommendations. Our method extracts useful semantic information from user
reviews and multi-source auxiliary reviews by applying Ordered-Neurons
Long Short-Term Memory (ON-LSTM). Experimental results demonstrate that EMRM achieves better rating prediction accuracy than other
baselines on three real-world datasets.

Keywords: Recommendation systems · Rating prediction · ON-LSTM

1 Introduction

In this era of "information overload", more than 10 million messages were viewed
by users on Facebook in one minute. While people enjoy the convenience brought
by the Internet, a large number of multi-structured data are produced. If these
data are not resolved properly, it will be difficult for people to find useful information. The recommendation system is one of the most effective ways to solve
the "information overload" problem, which can provide technical support for
users of recommending items that they might like. It helps users find products

H. Qiu et al. (Eds.): KSEM 2021, LNAI 12817, pp. 487–499, 2021.
https://doi.org/10.1007/978-3-030-82153-1_40

or services based on their historical purchasing behavior, thus improving the user experience and user stickiness. In many online platforms such as online shopping and video-streaming providers, recommendation systems play a pivotal role in increasing revenue.

The most widely used algorithm in the recommendation system is based on Collaborative Filtering (CF) [18], whose core concept is "birds of a feather flock together". The CF-based methods usually mine users' historical purchasing behavior data to extract user interests and recommend items that users might like. Although the CF-based methods achieve great performance on rating prediction accuracy, the data density is usually less than one millionth, so the CF-based methods are difficult to fully learn the preferences of users and the attributes of items.

For alleviating the data sparsity problem, the recommendation system based on user reviews [2,6] not only fetches information from user-item rating records but also extracts user preferences and item attributes from user review text. Many review-based recommender methods achieve better rating prediction accuracy than the baselines that do not use user reviews. Although rich semantic information implied in user reviews can improve the rating prediction accuracy of recommendation systems, user reviews also have the data sparsity problem. This is because only a few users are willing to spend time on writing reviews. In order to alleviate the data sparsity problem in user reviews, PARL [14] and MRMRP [13] use two different algorithms to supplement user reviews by collecting reviews written by similar users and have achieved promising results.

In this paper, we propose a deep learning-based model, named Enhanced Multi-source Review-based Model (EMRM), to fully learn user preferences and item attributes by modeling user review text. Holding the view that reviews written by both nearest neighbors and farthest neighbors can contribute to the final rating prediction, EMRM constructs two user auxiliary review documents for each user. It extracts user preferences and item attributes from user review document (aggregation of reviews written by the user), item review document (aggregation of reviews written for the item), and two user auxiliary review documents (aggregation of reviews written by nearest neighbors and farthest neighbors) with four parallel neural networks. After extracting latent features from four review documents by ON-LSTM [10], we use the Multi-Layer Perceptron (MLP) to compute the final rating prediction. Overall, our key contributions can be summarized as follows:

- To alleviate the data sparsity problem and improve the accuracy and diversity of recommendations, we construct a similar auxiliary review document and a similar auxiliary review document for each user by collecting user reviews written by nearest neighbors and farthest neighbors.
- We apply ON-LSTM to extract user preferences and item attributes from four review documents and apply the filtering layer to control the flow of information. ON-LSTM achieves great performance on obtaining latent semantic features from textual information.

- The experiments conducted on three real-world datasets demonstrate that our EMRM method achieves better rating prediction performance than other baselines.

The rest of this paper is organized as follows: Sect. 2 states related work, Sect. 3 formulates our approach. Section 4 presents our experiments, and finally, Sect. 5 concludes our work.

2   Related Work

In this section, we give a brief review of two different categories of studies related to review-based recommender methods: techniques based on topic, and techniques based on deep learning.

In the early stage, researchers have made a lot of efforts to extract semantic features from user review text using topic modeling techniques. They integrate latent semantic topics into latent factor models. For example, Rating-Boosted Latent Topics (RBLT) [11] uses linear discriminant analysis to extract topic features from rating-boost review documents as latent factors by repeating the review r times in the corpus if it was rated r, so that features in higher-rated reviews will dominate the topics. Collaborative Deep Learning (CDL) [12] uses the Stacked De-noising Auto Encoder (SDAE) to learn latent features of items from user review text, which is then fed into a click-through rate prediction model for predicting the ratings. However, these methods based on bag-of-words (BOW) usually do not pay much attention to the word order and lose much contextual information.

The recent research trend of recommendation systems is to use deep learning. Many works focus on utilizing Convolutional Neural Network (CNN), Long Short-Term Memory (LSTM), and their variants to obtain better latent semantic features from textual information by considering the word order and the local context. For instance, Deep Cooperative Neural Networks (DeepCoNN) [17] employs two parallel CNN networks to learn latent factors for users and items from the user review document and the item review document respectively. Then, it obtains the final rating prediction by coupling the two latent factors into Factorization Machines (FM). MRMRP [13] collects supplementary reviews written by users who have similar consuming behaviors and historical rating records, thus extracting extra user features from user reviews from similar users. It has been proven in [1,15] that dissimilar users can also contribute to both the accuracy and diversity of recommendations. Holding the view that the method MRMRP collecting the supplementary reviews ignores the information implied in reviews written by dissimilar users, we propose a new method.

In this paper, we propose the EMRM model for rating prediction. The proposed EMRM model differs significantly from the above models in several aspects. Firstly, we introduce a more reasonable algorithm to supplement user profiles, which constructs two user auxiliary review documents for each user by collecting user reviews written by nearest neighbors and farthest neighbors.

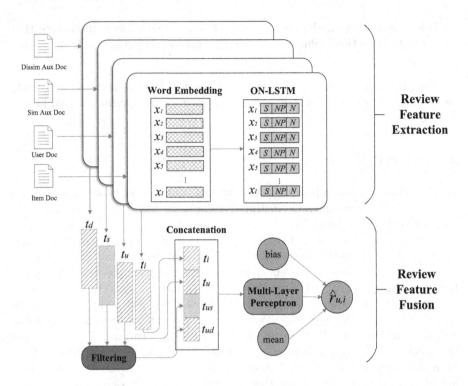

Fig. 1. Architecture of the EMRM model.

Secondly, we extract user preferences and item attributes from four review documents with the ON-LSTM. ON-LSTM achieves great performance on obtaining latent semantic features from textual information by integrating tree structures into LSTM to express richer information. Our proposed model can alleviate the data sparsity problem of user reviews and improve the rating prediction performance.

3   Our Model

In this section, we present the proposed EMRM model. Figure 1 illustrates its overall architecture.

3.1   Construction of Two User Auxiliary Review Documents

As previously mentioned, we construct two user auxiliary review documents for each user. The two user auxiliary review documents respectively refer to the aggregation of reviews written by nearest neighbors and farthest neighbors. Here, nearest neighbors refer to users who give similar ratings to the same item and have the highest similarity with the specified user and farthest neighbors mean users who give dissimilar ratings to the same item and have the lowest similarity. According to each historical consuming record, we find out the most similar and the most dissimilar users for the specified user and put their reviews on the specified item into similar auxiliary review document and dissimilar auxiliary review document respectively. On the one hand, if two users have high similarity, their interests and hobbies are likely to be similar in theory. Therefore, their reviews on an item might complement each other. On the other hand, reviews written by the most dissimilar users can also complement the profiles of the users. To some extent, reviews written by the most dissimilar user may express something that the user dislikes. Given a target user u, we show the details of the construction process of similar auxiliary review document and dissimilar auxiliary review document in Algorithm 1.

The similar auxiliary review document is the aggregation of reviews written by nearest neighbors who have high similarity scores with user u. In turn, the dissimilar auxiliary review document is the aggregation of reviews written by farthest neighbors who have low similarity scores with user u. These users have consumed at least one same item with user u. We design a formula to compute the similarity score between two users, which is an extension of the Pearson correlation coefficient. Equation 1 gives the definition of our similarity formula:

$$S(x,y) = e^{|I_x \cap I_y|/|I_x|+|I_y|} \frac{\sum_{i \in I_x \cap I_y}(x_i - \bar{x})(y_i - \bar{y})}{\sqrt{\sum_{i \in I_x}(x_i - \bar{x})^2}\sqrt{\sum_{i \in I_y}(y_i - \bar{y})^2}}, \tag{1}$$

where x and y are two different users, I_x and I_y represent the collection of items consumed by user x and user y respectively. $I_x \cap I_y$ is the collection of items that both user x and user y have consumed. x_i and y_i are the ratings given by user x and user y on item i respectively, $\bar{x}$ and $\bar{y}$ are the average value of all ratings given by user x and user y, and $|I_x \cap I_y|$ are the number of items that user x and user y have both consumed. Besides, the data sparsity problem is usually serious when the size of the dataset is large. Thus, two users who have consumed many same items are very likely to have common habits, and we introduce the multiplier $e^{|I_x \cap I_y|/|I_x|+|I_y|}$ to make such two neighbors get a larger similarity score.

In training data, for each item i consumed by user u, we will first select all the samples containing item i. Considering that different users have different scoring habits, we select all the samples in which the rating on item i differs from the rating given by user u by no more than 1 as similar neighbors. In turn, all samples in which rating on item i differ from the rating given by user u by more than 1 are considered as dissimilar neighbors. Then, we calculate the similarity score between each similar/dissimilar neighbor and user u according to the historical rating records. At last, we select the review written by the user who has the highest similarity score with user u and add it into the similar auxiliary review document. In addition, we select the review written by the user

---

Algorithm 1: Construction of two auxiliary review documents.

Input: identification of user u

Output: similar auxiliary review document and dissimilar auxiliary review
document of user u

   // get user $u's$ consuming record in training data

1 $record = get\_record(u)$;

   // initialize review document written by similar users and dissimilar users

2 $similar\_auxiliary\_doc = None$;

3 $dissimilar\_auxiliary\_doc = None$;

4 **for** item i in record **do**

     // get user $u's$ rating of item i

5     $rate = get\_rate(u, i)$;

     // get identifications of users who have consumed item i

6     $user\_set = seek\_user(i)$;

     // get identifications of users who score item i between $[rate-1, rate+1]$

7     $similar\_user\_set = seek\_similar\_user(i, rate)$;

8   **for** item i in similar_user_set **do**

       // compute similarity score of users in similar_user_set with user u

9       $users\_similarity = compute\_user\_similarity(u, similar\_user\_set)$;

       // get the identification of the user who is most similar with user u

10      $u\_selected = max(users\_similarity)$;

11   **if** $u\_selected \neq Null$ **then**

12        $review = review_{u\_selected,i}$;

13   **else**

14        $review = None$;

15      $similar\_auxiliary\_doc+ = review$;

    // get identifications of users who score item i not between $[rate-1, rate+1]$

16     $dissimilar\_user\_set = user\_set - similar\_user\_set$;

17   **for** item i in dissimilar_user_set **do**

       // compute similarity score of users in dissimilar_user_set with user u

18       $users\_similarity = compute\_user\_similarity(u, dissimilar\_user\_set)$;

       // get the identification of the user who is most dissimilar with user u

19      $u\_selected = min(users\_similarity)$;

20   **if** $u\_selected \neq Null$ **then**

21        $review = review_{u\_selected,i}$;

22   **else**

23        $review = None$;

24      $dissimilar\_auxiliary\_doc+ = review$;

25 $return$ $similar\_auxiliary\_doc$ and $dissimilar\_auxiliary\_doc$;

---

who has the lowest similarity score with user u and add it into the dissimilar
auxiliary review document.

3.2 ON-LSTMs for Processing Reviews

As shown in Fig. 1, EMRM uses four parallel neural networks to obtain useful
features from the user review document, the similar user auxiliary document, the
dissimilar user auxiliary document, and the item review document. Specifically,
four ON-LSTM networks are used to extract semantic information in different
aspects covered by the four review documents. After obtaining latent features of
four review documents, we first introduce them into the filtering layers to filter
them and then fuse them by MLP for the final rating prediction.

At first, we process the review document using the same method as many
baselines, such as PARL and MRMRP. To be specific, for each review document
$D = (w_1, w_2, ..., w_l)$, we use an embedding layer to convert each word to its corresponding embedding vector $x_i \in \mathbb{R}^n$. Then, we concatenate these embedding
vectors according to their order in the review document. Finally, we obtain a
review document matrix $D \in \mathbb{R}^{n \times l}$:

$$D = [x_1, x_2, ..., x_l], \tag{2}$$

where l is the number of words in the review document, n is the dimension of
the embedding vector and x_i represents the word embedding vector of the $i-th$
word in the review document D.

After obtaining the review document matrix D, we encode it with ON-LSTM.
ON-LSTM sorts the neurons in a specific order, thus allowing the hierarchical
structure to be integrated into the LSTM to express richer information. In other
words, high-hierarchy information means that it should be kept longer in the
corresponding coding interval of the high-hierarchy (not easily filtered out by
the forget gate), while low-hierarchy information means that it is easier to be
forgotten in the corresponding interval. The formula of ON-LSTM is as follows:

$$
\begin{aligned}
f_t &= \alpha(W_f x_t + U_f h_{t-1} + b_f), \\
i_t &= \alpha(W_i x_t + U_i h_{t-1} + b_i), \\
o_t &= \alpha(W_o x_t + U_o h_{t-1} + b_o), \\
\widehat{c_t} &= tanh(W_c x_t + U_c h_{t-1} + b_c), \\
\widetilde{f_t} &= \overrightarrow{cs}(softmax(W_{\widetilde{f}} x_t + U_{\widetilde{f}} h_{t-1} + b_{\widetilde{f}})), \\
\widetilde{i_t} &= \overleftarrow{cs}(softmax(W_{\widetilde{i}} x_t + U_{\widetilde{i}} h_{t-1} + b_{\widetilde{i}})), \\
w_t &= \widetilde{f_t} \circ \widetilde{i_t}, \\
c_t &= w_t \circ (f_t \circ c_{t-1} + i_t \circ \widehat{c_t}) \\
&\quad + (\widetilde{f_t} - w_t) \circ c_{t-1} + (\widetilde{i_t} - w_t) \circ \widehat{c_t}, \\
h_t &= o_t \circ tanh(c_t). \tag{3}
\end{aligned}
$$

The gate structure and output structure of ON-LSTM are similar to LSTM.
As in LSTM, f_t, i_t, o_t, c_t and h_t are forget gate, input gate, output gate, final
memory cell and output at time t respectively. The difference is that the update
mechanism from $\widehat{c_t}$ to c_t. $\widetilde{f_t}$ and $\widetilde{i_t}$ are master forget gate and master input

gate respectively. $\overrightarrow{cs}$ and $\overleftarrow{cs}$ are right and left cumsum operations. w_t gives a vector whose intersection part is 1, and the rest are all 0. $\circ$ denotes the dot product operation. Therefore, high-hierarchy information can be kept longer in the corresponding coding interval while low-hierarchy information would be easier to be forgotten. By allowing the hierarchical structure to be integrated into the LSTM, we can extract richer semantic information from the review document matrix D.

3.3 MLP for Feature Fusion

After adopting the above operation steps on the user review document, the item review document, the similar auxiliary review document and the dissimilar user auxiliary review document, we can get four vectors: t_u, t_i, t_s and t_d. These vectors are the latent features of their corresponding review documents. The similar user auxiliary review document and dissimilar user auxiliary review document serve as supplementary documents to the user review document while the data sparsity problem is serious.

Reviews in the two auxiliary review documents are additional information that may help to make rating prediction. However, they are written by different users. Therefore, we define a filtering layer to filter out t_s and t_d as follows:

$$g_1 = tanh(W_{g1} * t_u + b_{g_1}),$$
$$t_{us} = g_1 \odot t_s,$$
$$g_2 = tanh(W_{g2} * t_u + b_{g_2}),$$
$$t_{ud} = g_2 \odot t_d, \tag{4}$$

where W_{g1} and W_{g2} are the weight vectors, and b_{g_1} and b_{g_2} are the biases. g_1 and g_2 are filtering gates that control the flow of information in t_s and t_d respectively.

MLP is an effective method to deal with low-dimensional dense embedding vectors. After obtaining four vectors t_u, t_i, t_{us} and t_{ud}, we concatenate them as a^0 and feed it into the MLP to predict the rating of user u upon item i as follows:

$$a^0 = [t_u, t_i, t_{us}, t_{ud}],$$
$$a^{l+1} = f(W_l * a^l + b_l), \tag{5}$$

where l is the hidden layer number in MLP. a^l, W_l and b_l are the output, weight vector and bias at the l-th hidden layer. Then, the scalar is generated and input into the addition method for the final rating prediction.

What needs special attention is that the user rating behavior has subjective individuality, which is the so-called *personality*. According to our analysis of samples in the training data, some users tend to give high ratings and some tend to give low ratings. User bias and item bias can also influence the performance of rating prediction. We encapsulate these factors into the final prediction as follows:

$$\widehat{r}_{u,i} = \widehat{b}_{u,i} + \mu + b_u + b_i, \tag{6}$$

where μ is the mean value of all ratings in training data, and b_u and b_i are the biases for user u and item i.

3.4   Optimization Objective

We take the square loss as the objective function for parameter optimization:

$$L = \frac{1}{M} \sum_{i=1}^{M}(r_{u,i} - \widehat{r}_{u,i})^2, \tag{7}$$

where M is the number of instances in the training data, $\widehat{r}_{u,i}$ denotes the prediction rating value and $r_{u,i}$ is the true rating value.

4   Experiments

In this section, we conduct extensive experiments on three real-world datasets from two different resources. We also carried out ablation experiments to verify that different components have a positive impact on the overall performance of EMRM. For every experiment, grid search is performed to tune the hyper-parameters, and we evaluate its performance over 5 runs on the testing set.

4.1   Datasets and Evaluation Metric

Our experiments are conducted on three publicly accessible datasets that contain review text. The three datasets include Amazon-5cores datasets[1] (Musical Instruments and Office Products) and a Beer dataset provided by the RateBeer website [8]. 5-core means that each user and each item in the dataset have no less than 5 reviews.

Table 1. Statistics of three evaluated datasets.

Datasets	#users	#items	#ratings	#w_u	#w_i	#w_s	#w_d	density
Musical instruments	1429	900	10261	141.32	200.12	182.33	153.10	0.798%
Office products	405	2420	53227	197.93	229.52	239.81	144.32	0.448%
Beer	7725	21976	66625	34.06	103.20	78.01	40.03	0.039%

We conducted the same preprocessing operations mentioned in [5] to preprocess reviews in three datasets. Table 1 summarizes the statistics of three datasets after preprocessing. In Table 1, w_u means the number of words per user review document, w_i represents the number of words per item review document, w_s means the number of words per user similar auxiliary document and w_d means the number of words per user dissimilar auxiliary document. For each dataset, we

---

[1] http://jmcauley.ucsd.edu/data/amazon/.

randomly select 20% of it as the testing data, 72% of it as the training data, and the remaining data as the validation data. Moreover, each user and each item have at least one sample in the training data. Similar with prior work [13,14], the performance of our proposed algorithm is judged by Mean Squared Error (MSE) metric:

$$MSE = \frac{1}{N} \sum_{i=1}^{N} (r_{u,i} - \widehat{r}_{u,i})^2, \tag{8}$$

where $\widehat{r}_{u,i}$ denotes the prediction rating value, $r_{u,i}$ is the true rating value and N is the number of instances in the testing data.

4.2 Baselines

- **PMF:** Probabilistic Matrix Factorization (PMF) is a classical Matrix Factorization (MF) based method [9].
- **RBLT:** Rating-Boosted Latent Topics (RBLT) extract user feature and item feature in the shared topic space and subsequently introduce them into the MF model to make the final rating prediction [11].
- **CMLE:** Collaborative Multi-Level Embedding (CMLE) extracts user features and item features from both reviews and user-item interactions by combining the word embedding method with the MF model [16].
- **DeepCoNN:** Deep Cooperative Neural Networks (DeepCoNN) employs two parallel CNN networks to learn user preferences and item attributes and use the FM model to make the final prediction [17].
- **TransNets:** TransNets is an extension of the DeepCoNN model [3] by adding a neural network to model the target user-item review.
- **TARMF:** TARMF models user features and item features from both user reviews and user-item interactions by employing the attention-based recurrent neural network (RNN) and the MF model [7].
- **ANR:** ANR imports the attention mechanism to conduct aspect-based feature learning for users and items [4].
- **PARL:** PARL collects a user auxiliary review document for each user by collecting user reviews written by friends thus addressing the sparsity problem of user reviews [14].
- **CARP:** CARP proposes a sentiment capsule architecture to learn the informative logic unit and the sentiment-based representations in user-item level for the rating prediction [6].
- **MRMRP:** MRMRP supplements user reviews by collecting reviews written by nearest neighbors [13]. It employs three parallel CNN networks to learn latent factors for users and items and obtains the final rating prediction by coupling the three latent factors into MLP.

Table 2. MSE Performance comparison on four real-world datasets. Our results are highlighted in boldface, and the best results of baselines are highlighted in underline. † means that the variation in achieving the best result is statistically significant at the 0.05 level.

Datasets	Musical instruments	Office products	Beer
PMF [9]	$1.398^{\dagger}$	$1.092^{\dagger}$	$1.641^{\dagger}$
RBLT [11]	$0.815^{\dagger}$	$0.759^{\dagger}$	$0.576^{\dagger}$
CMLE [16]	$0.817^{\dagger}$	$0.759^{\dagger}$	$0.605^{\dagger}$
DeepCoNN [17]	$0.814^{\dagger}$	$0.860^{\dagger}$	$0.618^{\dagger}$
TransNets [3]	$0.798^{\dagger}$	$0.759^{\dagger}$	$0.581^{\dagger}$
TARMF [7]	$0.943^{\dagger}$	$0.789^{\dagger}$	$0.912^{\dagger}$
ANR [4]	$0.795^{\dagger}$	$0.742^{\dagger}$	$0.590^{\dagger}$
PARL [14]	0.782	0.731	0.561
CARP [6]	0.773	0.719	0.556
MRMRP [13]	<u>0.715</u>	<u>0.711</u>	<u>0.546</u>
EMRM	**0.692**	**0.701**	**0.532**

Table 3. Effect of different components in EMRM.

Methods	Musical instruments	Office products	Beer
DeepCoNN	0.814	0.860	0.617
+Similar document	0.745	0.729	0.559
FM → MLP	0.715	0.711	0.546
CNN → ON-LSTM	0.705	0.705	0.540
+Dissimilar document	0.692	0.701	0.532

4.3   Model Comparison and Ablation Study

Table 2 compares the performance of our method and baselines on the two Amazon-5cores datasets and the Beer dataset. We can observe that the review-based method achieves better performance on rating prediction. All models using user review text are better than PMF on all datasets. This shows that the rich semantic information hidden in the user review text can improve the rating prediction performance. In addition, since deep neural networks have the capacity of powerful data representations, deep learning-based methods, such as PARL and MRMRP, get better performance than shallow methods such as PMF and CMLE.

+Similar Document denotes that we import similar auxiliary review document into DeepCoNN, and experimental results in Table 3 demonstrate that similar auxiliary review document can improve recommendation performance. FM → MLP means that we replace FM in DeepCoNN with MLP to conduct the final rating prediction, and experimental results in Table 3 show that MLP is more effective in fusing latent features extracted from the review documents. CNN → ON-LSTM denotes that we replace CNN in MRMRP with ON-LSTM to extract latent features from user reviews. +Dissimilar Document denotes that dissimilar auxiliary review document is imported to enrich user profiles. From the results of the last two lines in Table 3, we can see the contribution of ON-LSTM and dissimilar auxiliary review document.

5   Conclusion

In this paper, the EMRM method is proposed to alleviate the data sparsity problem in user reviews. EMRM enriches user profiles by collecting reviews from nearest neighbors and farthest neighbors. In our proposed model, we use ON-LSTM to extract features and use MLP to conduct the final rating prediction. From the results of the ablation study, it can be seen that the accuracy of rating prediction can be improved by using reviews of nearest neighbors and farthest neighbors. In addition, experiments on three real-world datasets show that our EMRM model outperforms many baselines in recommendation systems. In the future, we would like to import the attention mechanism to explore the interpretability of the EMRM model.

Acknowledgments. This work was supported by Major Scientific and Technological Special Project of Guizhou Province (No. 20183002) and Sichuan Science and Technology Program (No. 2019YFG0535).

References

1. Anelli, V.W., Noia, T.D., Sciascio, E.D., Ragone, A., Trotta, J.: The importance of being dissimilar in recommendation. In: SAC, pp. 816–821 (2019)
2. Bao, Y., Fang, H., Zhang, J.: TopicMF: simultaneously exploiting ratings and reviews for recommendation. In: AAAI, pp. 2–8 (2014)
3. Catherine, R., Cohen, W.W.: TransNets: learning to transform for recommendation. In: RecSys, pp. 288–296 (2017)
4. Chin, J.Y., Zhao, K., Joty, S.R., Cong, G.: ANR: aspect-based neural recommender. In: CIKM, pp. 147–156 (2018)
5. Kim, D.H., Park, C., Oh, J., Lee, S., Yu, H.: Convolutional matrix factorization for document context-aware recommendation. In: RecSys, pp. 233–240 (2016)
6. Li, C., Quan, C., Peng, L., Qi, Y., Deng, Y., Wu, L.: A capsule network for recommendation and explaining what you like and dislike. In: SIGIR, pp. 275–284 (2019)
7. Lu, Y., Dong, R., Smyth, B.: Coevolutionary recommendation model: mutual learning between ratings and reviews. In: WWW, pp. 773–782 (2018)
8. McAuley, J.J., Leskovec, J., Jurafsky, D.: Learning attitudes and attributes from multi-aspect reviews. In: ICDM, pp. 1020–1025 (2012)
9. Salakhutdinov, R., Mnih, A.: Probabilistic matrix factorization. In: NIPS, pp. 1257–1264 (2007)
10. Shen, Y., Tan, S., Sordoni, A., Courville, A.C.: Ordered neurons: integrating tree structures into recurrent neural networks. In: ICLR (2019)

11. Tan, Y., Zhang, M., Liu, Y., Ma, S.: Rating-boosted latent topics: understanding users and items with ratings and reviews. In: IJCAI, pp. 2640–2646 (2016)
12. Wang, H., Wang, N., Yeung, D.: Collaborative deep learning for recommender systems. In: KDD, pp. 1235–1244 (2015)
13. Wang, X., Xiao, T., Tang, J., Ouyang, D., Shao, J.: MRMRP: multi-source review-based model for rating prediction. In: DASFAA (2), pp. 20–35 (2020)
14. Wu, L., Quan, C., Li, C., Ji, D.: PARL: let strangers speak out what you like. In: CIKM, pp. 677–686 (2018)
15. Zeng, W., Shang, M.S., Zhang, Q.M., Lu, L., Zhou, T.: Can dissimilar users contribute to accuracy and diversity of personalized recommendation? Int. J. Mod. Phys. C **21**(10), 1217–1227 (2010)
16. Zhang, W., Yuan, Q., Han, J., Wang, J.: Collaborative multi-level embedding learning from reviews for rating prediction. In: IJCAI, pp. 2986–2992 (2016)
17. Zheng, L., Noroozi, V., Yu, P.S.: Joint deep modeling of users and items using reviews for recommendation. In: WSDM, pp. 425–434 (2017)
18. Zhou, G., et al.: Deep interest evolution network for click-through rate prediction. In: AAAI, pp. 5941–5948 (2019)

Blockchain-as-a-Service Powered Knowledge Graph Construction

Yuwen Li[1], Hao Yin[1], Keke Gai[2(✉)] (iD), Liehuang Zhu[2], and Qing Wang[3]

[1] School of Computer Science and Technology, Beijing Institute of Technology,
Beijing 100081, China
{3120191092,yinhao}@bit.edu.cn
[2] School of Cyberspace Science and Technology, Beijing Institute of Technology,
Beijing 100081, China
{gaikeke,liehuangz}@bit.edu.cn
[3] Research Institute of China Mobile Communications Group Co., Ltd.,
Beijing, China
wangqingyjy@chinamobile.com

Abstract. The growing interest in the knowledge graph has attracted a great attention from both academia and the industry. Blockchain-based knowledge construction is deemed to be an alternative by adopting smart contract. However, the complexity of blockchain technology is an obstacle to apply blockchain solutions in practical scenarios. In this paper, we propose a Blockchain-as-a-Service (BaaS) approach to address the complexity issue. Through our BaaS system, developers can focus on knowledge graph constructions instead of struggling for mastering blockchain technology. We have implemented our BaaS system and measured the performance.

Keywords: Blockchain · Knowledge graph · Blockchain-as-a-service · Smart contract · Cloud computing

1 Introduction

Research on knowledge graph has received attentions from both academia and industry over decades. Knowledge graph contains semantically structured human knowledge from multiple data sources [5] and plays an important role in processing human knowledge in many applications, such as question answering, recommender system, and some domains-specific applications (e.g. medicine and education) [29]. For example, Lu et al. [13] proposed a thoroughly study on big knowledge and its engineering issues with several applications.

Considerable attention has been paid to the construction of knowledge graph. Qiu et al. [20] used data flow and knowledge graph with Gaussian distribution execution time for heterogeneous systems to minimize the total cost. They also [18] proposed a topological graph convolutional network to predict urban traffic flow and density. Wang et al. [23] proposed a smart contract based decentralized

© Springer Nature Switzerland AG 2021
H. Qiu et al. (Eds.): KSEM 2021, LNAI 12817, pp. 500–511, 2021.
https://doi.org/10.1007/978-3-030-82153-1_41

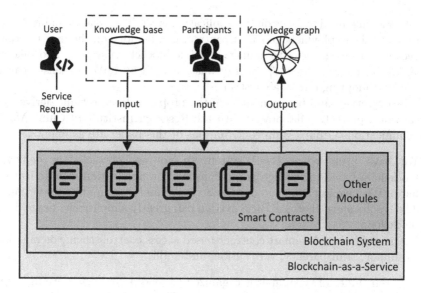

Fig. 1. A BaaS based knowledge graph construction model.

crowd sourcing scheme to construct knowledge graphs for deep recommender system. In their work, blockchain offers a trust-worthy, tamper-resistant and auditable crowd sourcing platform. Another work [24] proposed a scheme to protect knowledge graph from tampering and offer traceability by introducing blockchain. Zhang et al. [27] proposed a blockchain-based semantic knowledge sharing mechanism to achieve decentralized semantic knowledge sharing between different organizations.

Although blockchain-based knowledge graph construction has many attractive features, there are still some obstacles in practice. First, it is costly to run a decentralized application in a public blockchain [3,6,8]. For instance, Ethereum uses a Proof-of-Work (POW) consensus, in which costs miners a large volume of resources (e.g., energy or finance) to maintain consensus as well as smart contracts. Second, technical obstacles exist as running a blockchain system requires heavy technological supports [17]. Finally, managing multiple blockchain systems is difficult. Each permissioned participate node can access to the ledger; therefore, multiple blockchain access control mechanisms are needed.

In this paper, we propose a *Blockchain-as-a-Service* (BaaS) approach to address obstacles in blockchain-based application deployment. Figure 1 shows a blockchain-based knowledge graph crowd sourcing construction model. BaaS users are developers who can focus on knowledge graph constructions when obtaining services from the BaaS. Participants of crowd sourcing can contribute to knowledge graph by invoking smart contracts. The construction process of the smart contract can be guaranteed due to the auditability offered by blockchain.

BaaS is a cloud-based technology that provides a full lifecycle service of the blockchain (e.g., creation, deployment, and management). The knowledge graph researchers only need to focus on the application layer. The creation of blockchain system and the deployment of smart contract can be done on the user interface. Moreover, it is much easier to manage multiple blockchain systems and take full advantage of cloud service [7]. Energy waste caused by PoW consensus can be avoided by adopting our BaaS system.

The objectives and functionalities of the proposed BaaS scheme derive from a real-world project, collaborated with the Research Institute of China Mobile Communications Group. Main contributions of this paper are as follows.

1. We have proposed a BaaS system to address obstacles in deploying blockchain-based knowledge graph construction application in practical scenario. We have implemented our BaaS system and measured its performance. The results show that our BaaS system can greatly simplify the usage of the blockchain.
2. We have developed a smart contract-based access control scheme on our BaaS to support transparency, verification, and audit.

The remainder of this paper is organized as follows. In Sect. 2, we introduce the background knowledge about blockchain. The system design and evaluation results are described in Sects. 3 and 4, respectively. Finally, we conclude our work and discuss future work in Sect. 5.

2   Background

Knowledge graph is a graph structured collection of real world entities and properties linked by semantic relationships. Different from traditional database scheme, knowledge graph organize knowledge through semantic of knowledge and reason about knowledge. Thus, the knowledge graph can be used for inferring new knowledge and answering questions. The knowledge graph is deemed to be an important tool for artificial intelligence and has been used in many applications such as search engine, AI assistant and knowledge base.

Since nakamoto satoshi proposed bitcoin (a decentralized cryptocurrency) in 2008 [15], blockchain has experienced rapid development, as the underlying technology of bitcoin. Blockchain contains a decentralized ledger, which can maintain consistency and availability without a trusted party in a Peer-to-Peer (P2P) network through the consensus protocol and cryptographic algorithm. Due to its transparency, traceability, tamper-proof, and immutability characteristics, blockchain has achieved great success in the economy and cryptocurrency fields.

The emerging of smart contract supported blockchains such as Ethereum and HyperLedger Fabric has brought more possibility to the blockchain. By supporting turing-complete smart contract, blockchain has changed from a distributed ledger to a distributed computing platform. The idea of running user-defined programs on the blockchain has further broaden the application scenarios of blockchain. Blockchain has been widely used in many applications such as supply chain management [11], food safety management [4] and smart grid [10].

Though there are many different blockchain systems, they share some of the same characteristics.

First, every blockchain system has a chained data structure. As the name of the blockchain suggests, the ledger of blockchain is stored in a chain of blocks. Every valid transaction will be packed in a block, and blocks will be organized as a continuous chain. The blocks are connected by hash pointer, which means every block (except the genesis block) saves the hash of the previous block. The length of chain will grow when a new block is committed through the consensus protocol and appended to chain. This data structure ensures that blockchain is append-only with immutable past [28].

Second, a blockchain system has consensus protocol. As a decentralized system, nodes of the blockchain system need consensus protocol to reach a consensus and maintain the consistency of distributed ledger [26]. What makes the consensus protocol in the blockchain so special is that consensus protocol needs to provide trustworthy consensus result among a group of mutually distrustful participants [25].

Finally, blockchain is a distributed system. The nodes of the blockchain run in a peer-to-peer network without a centralized infrastructure, which avoids the risk of single point of failure and enhances the robustness of the system [28].

The concept of smart contract was proposed as a set of digital form promises and protocols which performed on these promises [22]. And this concept was widely used in practical until the emergence of blockchain technology. In general, a smart contract is a computer program having self-verifying, self-executing, tamper-resistant properties [14]. Smart contracts are automatically executable and enforceable. The execution process of smart contract cannot be influenced or manipulated by any arbitrator nor need any trusted party with the support of blockchain. The result of smart contract is traceable and verifiable. The emergence of smart contracts has greatly enhanced the flexibility of the blockchain system, expanded the application range of blockchain.

3 System Design

3.1 Design Objective

The major goal of our BaaS system is to simplify the difficulty of creating, maintaining, and using of a blockchain system, reduce the obstacles in the deployment of smart contracts and blockchain powered applications. The system should hide the complex configuration process of blockchain and provide user with a concise graphical user interface. User should be able to create a custom structured blockchain within a few minutes, check the state of the blockchain, deploy and invoke smart contracts through the graphical user interface. The specific design objectives are as follows:

- **Functionality:** The BaaS system should have sufficient functionality to provide full lifecycle management for blockchain system and smart contract. User can create, configure, and monitor a custom structured blockchain system.

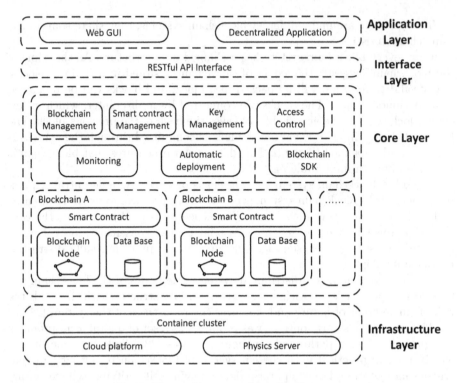

Fig. 2. The architecture of our BaaS system.

Subsequently, user can deploy and invoke the smart contract in the blockchain system. Moreover, these functionalities should be provided through a user-friendly interface.

- **Security:** The BaaS system should have trust-worthy and secure access control ability to protect the resources in BaaS system. The process of access control should be hard to manipulation and auditable [9].
- **Efficiency:** The BaaS system should be able to deploy the blockchain efficiently. A blockchain with reasonable number of nodes should be created in a few minutes.

3.2 Architecture Overview

The architecture of our BaaS system divides into four layers, as shown in Fig. 2. The lowest level is the infrastructure layer which provides the physical infrastructure for baas system. The nodes of blockchain will run in this layer as a container cluster in remote server or on-premise server.

The layer above is the core layer which as its name shows, is the core of the whole BaaS system. The core layer will implement most of functional features of BaaS system. The modules of the core layer can be divided into three categories.

The operation and maintenance category contains monitoring and automatic deployment module, which is responsible for managing container and execution environment of container. The SDK category will package the software development kit of the underlying blockchain for other core layer modules and upper layer to interact with blockchain system. The management category will process and manage blockchain and related information in BaaS system through monitoring, automatic deployment and SDK module to provide every core function of BaaS system.

The interface layer is above the core layer. Our BaaS system adopts the design idea of separates the front-end and the back-end. The presentation logic is independent of the back-end. All of the functions and features of our BaaS system are provided through a set of RESTful API interface which brings exceptional versatility to our BaaS system.

The application layer includes the applications who use the service of our BaaS system through the interface layer. We developed a web GUI as the front end of BaaS system. The user can create, manage and interact with the blockchain in our BaaS system through this web GUI. User can also deploy and invoke smart contract to running user developed blockchain application through the web GUI. Moreover, user can develop own application to interact with smart contract through the interface layer to implement a powerful distributed application.

Our BaaS system support HyperLedger fabric blockchain. HyperLedger Fabric is an open-source blockchain platform which is funded by the Linux Foundation. The project of HyperLedger Fabric aims to propose a resiliency, flexibility, scalability, confidentiality blockchain architecture and Fabric is designed as a modular and extensible general-purpose blockchain [1]. Unlike other blockchains, HyperLedger fabric has a unique characteristic called channel. This characteristic allows user to create multiple ledger in one blockchain system. Moreover, HyperLedger Fabric uses byzantine-fault tolerant consensus instead of Proof-of-Work, which greatly reduces the waste of computing power, makes it a great platform to deploy distributed applications.

3.3   Major Components

Monitoring and Automatic Deployment Modules: These two modules are designed to interact and manage containers in the infrastructure layer. The container is an emerging light-weight virtualization concept. It is used to achieve elasticity of large-scale resource sharing as traditional virtual machines, but less resource and time-consuming, which is a promising solution for delivering applications to the cloud [16]. Therefore, we use container to deploy and run the blockchain system as shown in Fig. 3.

Every node of the blockchain will run in a separate container. The nodes of blockchain can be efficiently deployed to remote or on-premise server through the container technology. The automatic deployment module is responsible for deploying and managing the containers in the remote or on-premise server. Moreover, the automatic deployment module is also responsible for managing the

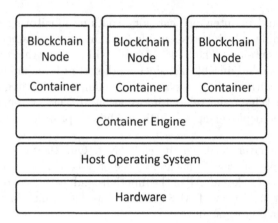

Fig. 3. The structure of container-based virtualization.

network of containers. The nodes of different blockchains need to be isolated in separate networks to ensure the security of blockchains. The monitoring module is another module that interacts with containers directly. It will monitor the status of containers and record containers logs. Information gathered by the monitoring module will be offered to modules in core layer and users.

Blockchain Management Module: Blockchain management module manages the information of blockchains and performs operations related to blockchains. The full lifecycle management of blockchain is provided by this module. The process of creating a blockchain system is as follows. First, this module will parse the blockchain creating request sent through the interface layer. After parsing the structure and configuration of the requested blockchain, the blockchain management module will create the necessary configuration files and generate certificates for every nodes through key management module. Finally, the blockchain management module will create and start nodes in blockchains with the help of the automatic deployment module. Apart from creating blockchain, blockchain management module is also responsible for channel management. User can create new channel or adding nodes to channel dynamically in blockchains.

Smart Contract Management Module: Smart contract management module manages smart contracts in blockchains. In order to run smart contract in blockchain, user needs to upload and install smart contract to blockchain. When user sends the request of installing the smart contract, the smart contract management module will distribute the code of smart contract to the nodes of blockchain. After smart contract is installed, user can instantiate the contract in the blockchain. In the process of instantiation, the storage space of contract will be created on the blockchain and parameters may be inputted to initialize the smart contract. Since instantiation, the contract is successfully deployed on blockchain and user can invoke the contract.

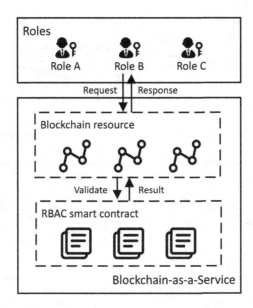

Fig. 4. The blockchain-based RBAC model.

Our BaaS system also supports smart contract upgrade. When there is need to upgrade, user can install the new version of smart contract, then upgrade the smart contract through smart contract management module.

Key Management Module: Blockchain system needs secure key generation and management service to achieve its security promise, since it is a technology highly dependent on cryptography. Every node of blockchains needs certificates to prove its identity, ensure the integrity of information, and communicate with other nodes securely. Key management module is developed in order to generate keys and certificates for entities in blockchain. This module will generate standard X.509 certificates required by the blockchain system.

Access Control Module: The access control module is responsible for managing the user of our blockchain system and offering access control for resources in BaaS system. Using cloud platform will bring a lot of convenience, however, concerns about security is also raised which brings the demand for secure access control [12,19]. In our BaaS system, we proposed a blockchain based access control scheme. In traditional cloud platform, the lack of transparency is one of users' concerns. The user does not know the access control rules which been enforced nor know the actual processing flow of the access control [2]. The transparency, immutability, and auditability characteristics of blockchain makes it an ideal solution for access control.

We adopt a *Role-Based Access Control* (RBAC) strategy in our access control module. In RBAC model, permissions are associated with roles, and users are assigned to appropriate roles [21]. The usage of RBAC simplifies the allocation of user permissions, reduces the operating overhead of the access control system. Our access control model is shown in Fig. 4. The processing flow of access

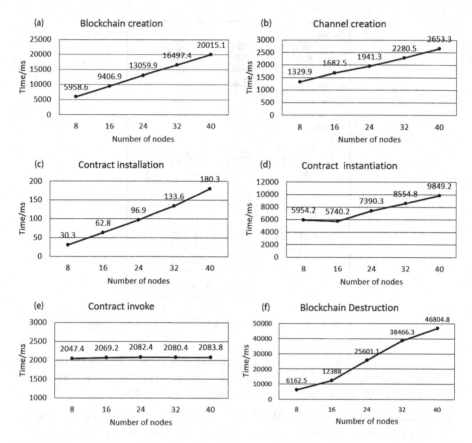

Fig. 5. The evaluation result of our BaaS system, (a) the blockchain creation time, (b) the channel creation time, (c) the contract installation time, (d) the contract instantiation time, (e) the contract invoke time, (f) the blockchain destruction time.

control is implemented in smart contract. When user access the resources in BaaS system, the access control smart contract will be automatically executed. The access control contract will check the user's role and permission assignment information stored in the blockchain to determine whether the user has permission to access a specific resource. Subsequently, the BaaS system will authorize the access depend on the output of the access control smart contract. Users can trust the access control provided by the BaaS system, because the permission assignment and the logic of access control smart contract are public due to the transparency of the blockchain system.

4   Experiment Evaluations

4.1   Experiment Configuration

We chose Hyperledge Fabric 1.4 as the underlying blockchain system, used golang as the programming language, docker as the container engine to

Table 1. Test environment

Environment	Version	Notes
Ubuntu	18.04LTS	Operating system
HyperLedger Fabric	1.4	Blockchain system
Golang	v1.14.4 linux/amd64fa	Complier
Docker	v19.03.11	Open source container engine

implement our BaaS system and tested it in on-premise server. The testing system had an intel core i7-9700 CPU, 32 GB memory with Ubuntu operating system. The version of the dependent software is shown in Table 1.

4.2 Evaluation Results

There are 6 types of main operations in our BaaS system which is important to the performance of our BaaS system, they are blockchain creation, channel creation, contract installation, contract instantiation, contract invoke and blockchain destruction. The time complexity of contract invoke is $O(1)$ to the scale of the blockchain system since the latency of contract invoke is the time that contract execute plus a fixed block time (the time of a new block been add to the blockchain). The time complexity of other operations is $O(n)$ in which n is the number of nodes in the blockchain system. Because for every operation, the BaaS system have to process information related to n nodes and operate on every node which cost $O(n)$ time. And the time spend by blockchain node is unrelated to the number of nodes. Thus, the time complexity is $O(n) + n * O(1) = O(n)$.

Because the number of organizations and nodes in a blockchain system has impact on performance, we tested the performance of our BaaS system with different organization numbers and node numbers. In our test case, each organization has four nodes and we changed the number of nodes as independent variable. To improve the accuracy of the test, each test had been run multiple times and averaged.

The test result shows in Fig. 5. We had measured the time spent of some typical operations in the usage of BaaS system under different numbers of organizations and nodes. The result proves our time complexity analysis and shows that operations such as blockchain creation, channel creation, contract installation, contract instantiation, and blockchain destruction have linear time complexity to the number of nodes in blockchains. And the time spent in contract invoke remains stable when nodes of blockchain increase.

5   Conclusions

In this paper, we developed a BaaS system to support blockchain-powered knowledge graph construction schemes. The proposed system had four advantages: 1) It makes the development of blockchain-powered knowledge graph construction scheme much easier. The researcher could focus on the knowledge graph instead of the underlying detail of blockchain. 2) Creating a new blockchain in BaaS system only cost a few minutes, which greatly saves time. 3) It is much easier to manage multiple blockchain system for different domain specific knowledge graph which can improve the performance. 4) We proposed a blockchain based access control scheme in our BaaS system, which is transparent and trustworthy.

In the future, our work can be extended in aspects as follow: 1) Supporting more different blockchain such as private Ethereum and EOS. 2) Improving the performance of the BaaS system in high concurrency scenarios. 3) Researching the model of supporting cross-chain interaction.

Acknowledgments. This work is supported by Ministry of Education - China Mobile Research Fund Project (Grant No. MCM20180401) and is partially supported by National Natural Science Foundation of China (Grant No. 61972034), Natural Science Foundation of Beijing Municipality (Grant No. 4202068), and Natural Science Foundation of Shandong Province (Grant No. ZR2019ZD10, ZR2020ZD01).

References

1. Androulaki, E., et al.: Hyperledger fabric: a distributed operating system for permissioned blockchains. In: Proceedings of the Thirteenth EuroSys Conference, pp. 1–15 (2018)
2. Charanya, R., Aramudhan, M.: Survey on access control issues in cloud computing. In: 2016 International Conference on Emerging Trends in Engineering, Technology and Science (ICETETS), pp. 1–4. IEEE (2016)
3. Dai, W., Qiu, M., Qiu, L., Chen, L., Wu, A.: Who moved my data? Privacy protection in smartphones. IEEE Commun. Mag. **55**(1), 20–25 (2017)
4. Fang, Z., Gai, K., Zhu, L., Xu, L.: LNBFSM: a food safety management system using blockchain and lightning network. In: Qiu, M. (ed.) ICA3PP 2020. LNCS, vol. 12454, pp. 19–34. Springer, Cham (2020). https://doi.org/10.1007/978-3-030-60248-2_2
5. Fensel, D., et al.: Introduction: what is a knowledge graph? In: Knowledge Graphs, pp. 1–10. Springer, Cham (2020). https://doi.org/10.1007/978-3-030-37439-6_1
6. Gai, K., Guo, J., Zhu, L., Yu, S.: Blockchain meets cloud computing: a survey. IEEE Commun. Surv. Tutor. **22**(3), 2009–2030 (2020)
7. Gai, K., Qiu, M.: Reinforcement learning-based content-centric services in mobile sensing. IEEE Netw. **32**(4), 34–39 (2018)
8. Gai, K., Wu, Y., Zhu, L., Qiu, M., Shen, M.: Privacy-preserving energy trading using consortium blockchain in smart grid. IEEE Trans. Ind. Inf. **15**(6), 3548–3558 (2019)
9. Gai, K., Wu, Y., Zhu, L., Zhang, Z., Qiu, M.: Differential privacy-based blockchain for industrial internet-of-things. IEEE Trans. Ind. Inform. **16**(6), 4156–4165 (2019)
10. Gai, K., Wu, Y., Zhu, L., Xu, L., Zhang, Y.: Permissioned blockchain and edge computing empowered privacy-preserving smart grid networks. IEEE Internet Things J. **6**(5), 7992–8004 (2019)
11. Li, H., Gai, K., Zhu, L., Jiang, P., Qiu, M.: Reputation-based trustworthy supply chain management using smart contract. In: Qiu, M. (ed.) ICA3PP 2020. LNCS, vol. 12454, pp. 35–49. Springer, Cham (2020). https://doi.org/10.1007/978-3-030-60248-2_3

12. Li, Y., Gai, K., Qiu, L., Qiu, M., Zhao, H.: Intelligent cryptography approach for secure distributed big data storage in cloud computing. Inf. Sci. **387**, 103–115 (2017)
13. Lu, R., Jin, X., Zhang, S., Qiu, M., Wu, X.: A study on big knowledge and its engineering issues. IEEE Trans. Knowl. Data Eng. **31**(9), 1630–1644 (2018)
14. Mohanta, B.K., Panda, S.S., Jena, D.: An overview of smart contract and use cases in blockchain technology. In: IEEE 9th International Conference on Computing, Communication and Networking Technologies (ICCCNT), pp. 1–4 (2018)
15. Nakamoto, S., Bitcoin, A.: A peer-to-peer electronic cash system. Bitcoin, p. 4 (2008). https://bitcoin.org/bitcoin.pdf
16. Pahl, C.: Containerization and the PaaS cloud. IEEE Cloud Comput. **2**(3), 24–31 (2015)
17. Qiu, H., Qiu, M., Memmi, G., Ming, Z., Liu, M.: A dynamic scalable blockchain based communication architecture for IoT. In: Qiu, M. (ed.) SmartBlock 2018. LNCS, vol. 11373, pp. 159–166. Springer, Cham (2018). https://doi.org/10.1007/978-3-030-05764-0_17
18. Qiu, H., Zheng, Q., Msahli, M., Memmi, G., Qiu, M., Lu, J.: Topological graph convolutional network-based urban traffic flow and density prediction. IEEE Trans. Intell. Trans. Syst. **99**, 1–10 (2020)
19. Qiu, M., Gai, K., Xiong, Z.: Privacy-preserving wireless communications using bipartite matching in social big data. Future Gener. Comput. Syst. **87**, 772–781 (2018)
20. Qiu, M., Jiang, Y., Dai, W.: Cost minimization for heterogeneous systems with Gaussian distribution execution time. In: IEEE 17th International Conference on High Performance Computing and Communications (HPCC) (2015)
21. Sandhu, R.S.: Role-based access control. In: Advances in Computers, vol. 46, pp. 237–286. Elsevier (1998)
22. Szabo, N.: Smart contracts: building blocks for digital markets. EXTROPY: J. Transhumanist Thought, (16) 18(2) (1996)
23. Wang, S., Huang, C., Li, J., Yuan, Y., Wang, F.Y.: Decentralized construction of knowledge graphs for deep recommender systems based on blockchain-powered smart contracts. IEEE Access **7**, 136951–136961 (2019)
24. Wang, Y., Yin, X., Zhu, H., Hei, X.: A blockchain based distributed storage system for knowledge graph security. In: Sun, X., Wang, J., Bertino, E. (eds.) ICAIS 2020. LNCS, vol. 12240, pp. 318–327. Springer, Cham (2020). https://doi.org/10.1007/978-3-030-57881-7_29
25. Xiao, Y., Zhang, N., Lou, W., Hou, Y.T.: A survey of distributed consensus protocols for blockchain networks. IEEE Commun. Surv. Tutor. **22**(2), 1432–1465 (2020)
26. Yin, H., Wei, Y., Li, Y., Zhu, L., Shi, J., Gai, K.: Consensus in lens of consortium blockchain: an empirical study. In: Qiu, M. (ed.) ICA3PP 2020. LNCS, vol. 12454, pp. 282–296. Springer, Cham (2020). https://doi.org/10.1007/978-3-030-60248-2_19
27. Zhang, B., Li, X., Ren, H., Gu, J.: Semantic knowledge sharing mechanism based on blockchain. In: Liu, Y., Wang, L., Zhao, L., Yu, Z. (eds.) ICNC-FSKD 2019. AISC, vol. 1075, pp. 115–127. Springer, Cham (2020). https://doi.org/10.1007/978-3-030-32591-6_13
28. Zheng, Z., Xie, S., Dai, H.N., Chen, X., Wang, H.: Blockchain challenges and opportunities: a survey. Int. J. Web Grid Serv. **14**(4), 352–375 (2018)
29. Zou, X.: A survey on application of knowledge graph. J. Phys: Conf. Ser. **1487**(1), 012016 (2020)

Finetuned YOLOv3 for Getting Four Times the Detection Speed

Xin Liu and Jun Wu[✉]

School of Computer Science, Hubei University of Technology, Wuhan, China
201910756@hbut.edu.cn, wujun@whut.edu.cn

Abstract. Object detection is an exciting research area in computer vision, widely used in autonomous driving, face recognition, and drones. Due to the limitation of mobile devices, the size of object detection models is limited, and it is not easy to achieve the ideal balance between detection accuracy and detection speed. So reducing the model size and increasing the model detection speed becomes a trendy research topic. The Slice-Concat structure proposed in this paper does not require too many changes to YOLOv3 and YOLOv3-SPP, and the four times improvement in detection speed is obtained only by changing the width and height of the input feature map. While getting a 4-fold FPS improvement, the network model parameters remain essentially unchanged, and the computational effort becomes a quarter of that of the original network. The improved YOLO model can also obtain a larger batch size with the same image size, providing an excellent solution for training models on hardware-constrained devices.

Keywords: Object detection · YOLOv3 · YOLOv3-SPP · Lightweight · Real-time detection

1 Introduction

Object detection has become the fundamental of many other computer vision tasks, such as segmentation, image detection, object tracking, etc. The primary mission of object detection is to answer the two questions of the object in the picture or video and where it is in the photo or video. As image data becomes more and more abundant, traditional machine learning-based object detection methods such as Viola-Jones Detectors [1, 2], Histogram of Oriented Gradients (HOG) detectors [3], and Deformable Part-based Model (DPM) [4–6] has been unable to achieve ideal results in massive data sets. In 2012, Alex et al. [7] proposed the AlexNet, which won the championship by far surpassing second place in the ImageNet competition. Furthermore, the AlexNet made neural networks, and even deep learning regained widespread attention. Since then, convolutional neural networks and deep learning have become mainstream in the field of object detection.

Currently, widely used object detection methods based on convolutional neural networks can be roughly divided into two categories. One is based on two-stage target detection methods. The other is based on one-stage target detection methods. Two-stage

© Springer Nature Switzerland AG 2021
H. Qiu et al. (Eds.): KSEM 2021, LNAI 12817, pp. 512–521, 2021.
https://doi.org/10.1007/978-3-030-82153-1_42

will first use the corresponding Region Proposal algorithm (either a traditional algorithm or a neural network) to generate suggested object candidate regions from the input image, and then send all the candidate regions to a classifier for classification, such as RCNN [8], SPPNet [9], Fast R-CNN [10], Faster R-CNN [11, 12], FPN [13], Mask R-CNN [14], etc. One-stage directly extracts features from the network to predict object classification and location, such as YOLO [15–18], SSD [19], RetinaNet [20], etc. The One-stage target detection algorithm represented by YOLO combines the generation of the candidate frame and the classification and regression of the object into one step, which dramatically improves the detection speed of the algorithm. With the development of the YOLO network model, the accuracy of the network model has been effectively improved, and the corresponding network model parameters have also become complicated. This paper proposes a Slice-Concat network structure that allows YOLOv3 and YOLOv3-SPP to significantly increase network model detection speed and reduce the amount of network model calculations while the model parameters are unchanged.

The main contribution of this paper is to propose a novel approach to model lightweight. Without modifying the original network much, a quadruple detection speedup is obtained by replacing the first convolutional layer with a Slice-Concat structure or by modifying the stride size of the first convolutional layer only. In addition, the above improvement method can use a larger batch size with the same input feature map size, thus accelerating the convergence speed of the network model and the stability of the model training.

The rest of the paper is organized as follows. Section 2 describes the relevant work in the research area and the specific details of the Slice-Concat structure proposed in this paper. Section 3 describes how the baseline network can be enhanced. Section 4 describes the running environment of the experiments, the setting of Hyper-Parameters in experiments, the introduction of the data set, and the evaluation metrics. Then the experimental results are described and analyzed. Finally, Sect. 5 concludes the paper.

2 Related Work

Li, YD et al. [21] proposed YOLOv3-Lite in 2019. This method combines deep separable convolution, feature pyramid, and YOLOv3. It uses deep separable convolution to reduce the parameters in the feature extraction process, meanwhile using feature pyramids enriched with semantic features to improve accuracy. Mao, QC et al. [22] proposed mini-YOLOv3, which uses deep separable convolution and point-by-point grouping convolution to reduce network parameters based on Darknet-53 and uses feature pyramids to maintain model accuracy. Ma, HJ et al. [23] proposed to replace the Darknet53 feature extraction network of YOLOv3 with a lightweight convolutional neural network ShuffleNet v2, which is used to lighten the YOLOv3 and use the new loss function GIoU for prediction.

2.1 Slice-Concat Structure

The network optimization proposed by the researchers, as mentioned above, has dramatically changed the overall structure of the YOLO, and the Slice-Concat structure

514   X. Liu and J. Wu

proposed in this article only needs to finetune the original network to achieve the desired performance improvement. This paper proposes the Slice-Concat structure, which is shown in Fig. 1. The structure will perform the following operations:

- Firstly, perform a slice operation on the picture, and take a value for every other pixel in an image, so that four images can be obtained, and the content of these four pictures is complementary, and no information is lost;
- Then the four parts are spliced together so that the width and height information is concentrated in the channel space, and the input channel is expanded by four times;
- Finally, the obtained new picture is passed through the convolutional layer to get two times down-sampled feature map without information loss.

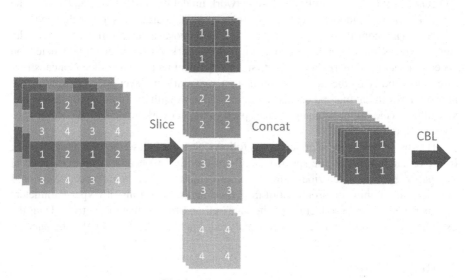

Fig. 1. Slice-Concat structure

In object detection tasks, FLOPs are usually used to measure the complexity of algorithms and models. The unit of large models is usually G. The unit of small models is usually M. This paper defines FLOPs as considering only the number of multiplication and addition operations of parameter layers such as convolutional layers and fully connected layers, ignoring the BN layers and ReLU layers. At the same time, the convolutional layer and the fully connected layer will also ignore the calculation amount of only addition operations, such as bias addition and shortcut residual addition. The definition of FLOPs is shown in the formula (1), where k is the size of the convolution kernel, H_{out} is the height of the output feature maps, W_{out} is the width of the output feature maps, C_{in} is the number of channels of the input feature maps, and C_{out} is the number of channels of the output feature maps.

$$FLOPs = k^2 * H_{out} * W_{out} * C_{in} * C_{out} \tag{1}$$

3   Model Design

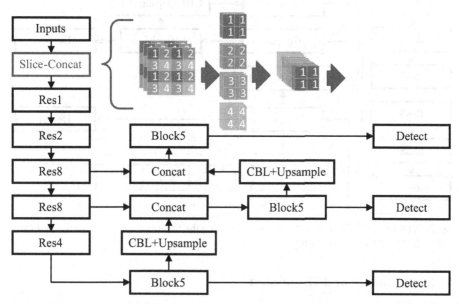

Fig. 2. YOLOv3-SC network structure. Replacing the first convolutional layer of YOLOv3 with a Slice-Concat structure

This paper replaces the first convolutional layer of YOLOv3 and YOLOv3-SPP Backbone with the Slice-Concat structure to obtain YOLOv3-SC and YOLOv3-SPP-SC. Other structures remain unchanged. The network structures of YOLOv3-SC and YOLOv3-SPP-SC are shown in Fig. 2 and Fig. 3. The CBL module is a basic convolution module composed of a normal convolution layer, a Batch Normalization layer, and a Leaky ReLu activation function. The ResX module is a residual structure composed of a CBL module and a residual structure. Its main function is to enhance the ability of feature extraction. The X in the ResX module represents the number of repetitions of the residual structure. For example, Res1 means that the residual structure appears once, and Res8 means that the residual structure is repeated eight times. The Block 5 module consists of five CBL modules with different convolution kernel sizes. The sizes of the convolution kernel of the five CBL modules are 1 * 1, 3 * 3, 1 * 1, 3 * 3, 1 * 1. The convolution kernel of the first convolutional layer of YOLOv3 and YOLOv3-SPP is 3 * 3, the stride is 1, and the number of output channels is 32. The convolutional layer will not change the height and width of the feature maps. After the picture is inputted into the Slice-Concat structure, the height and width of the output feature map become half of the original, so the height and width of the feature maps of YOLOv3-SC and YOLOv3-SPP-SC are half of YOLOv3 and YOLOv3-SPP. According to Eq. (1). YOLOv3-SC and YOLOv3-SPP-SC are a quarter of the computational effort of YOLOv3 and YOLOv3-SPP.

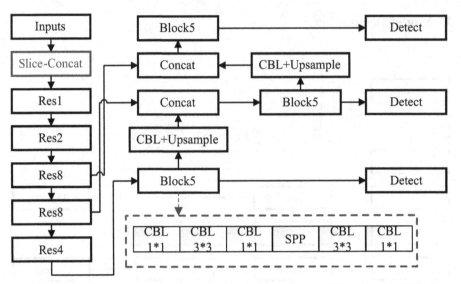

Fig. 3. YOLOv3-SPP-SC network structure, replacing the first convolutional layer of YOLOv3-SPP with a Slice-Concat structure

4   Experiments and Discussion

This section evaluates the performance of each network model on the Pascal VOC dataset. The purpose of these experiments is to demonstrate that the Slice-Concat structure proposed has an enhanced effect on the detection speed of YOLOv3.

4.1   Experiments Settings and Dataset

Hardware Platform. The CPU is Intel(R) Xeon(R) CPU E5–2678 v3 @ 2.50GHz, the GPU is NVIDIA GTX 1070Ti, the OS is Ubuntu 16.04, the development language is Python 3.8, and the training framework is Pytorch 1.8.0.

Dataset. The dataset used in this experiment is PASCAL VOC2012 [24], which contains 20 categories of objects. Each picture is labelled with 20 categories, including people, animals (such as cats, dogs, birds, etc.), vehicles (such as cars, boats, and aeroplanes, etc.), and furniture (such as chairs, tables, sofas, etc.), with an average of 2.4 targets per picture. The training and validation sets used in the experiment are all images corresponding to the years 2008–2011 in the PASCAL VOC 2012 dataset, which contains 11540 images with 27450 objects. There are 5717 images in the training set and 5823 images in the validation set. The test set is the official test set of PASCAL VOC 2007, with 4952 images (Tables 1 and 2).

Evaluation Metrics. This experiment uses mAP, a standard evaluation metric for object detection, to measure the precision of these models. FPS is used to measure the detection speed of these models. The higher the value of FPS, the faster the model detection speed.

Table 1. Statistics of 20 category instances in the PASCAL VOC 2012 dataset

Category	Training set	Validation set	Testing set
Aeroplane	432	433	285
Bicycle	353	358	337
Bird	560	559	459
Boat	426	424	263
Bottle	629	630	469
Bus	292	301	213
Car	1013	1004	1201
Cat	605	612	358
Chair	1178	1176	756
Cow	290	298	244
Diningtable	304	305	206
Dog	756	759	489
Horse	350	360	348
Motorbike	357	356	325
Person	4194	4372	4528
Pottedplant	484	489	480
Sheep	400	413	242
Sofa	281	285	239
Train	313	315	282
Tvmonitor	392	392	308
Sum	13609	13841	12032

Parameters are used to measure the size of these models, and the smaller its value, the more lightweight the model is. Moreover, GFLOPs is used to measure the computational effort of these models. The smaller its value, the smaller the computational effort required by the model and the lower the hardware performance needed.

4.2 Results and Discussion

First, in this section, YOLOv3 and YOLOv3-SPP are used as the baseline for this experiment, while YOLOv3-SC and YOLOv3-SPP-SC are improved models of the Slice-Concat structure proposed in this paper. Then the baseline and our models are compared in four dimensions: mAP, FPS, Parameters, and GFLOPs. S2 in YOLOv3-S2 in Table 3 and Table 4 means that the stride of the first convolution layer is 2. SC3 in YOLOv3-SC3 means that the convolution kernel size of the Slice-Concat structure is 3*3, and SC1 in YOLOv3-SC1 means that the convolution kernel size of the Slice-Concat structure is 1*1. YOLOv3- SPP is changed as above.

Table 2. Hyper-parameters in experiments.

Hyper-parameters	Value
Learning rate	0.0032
Cosine annealing hyperparameter	0.12
Momentum	0.843
Weight decay parameter	0.00036
Epochs of warmup	2
Momentum of warmup	0.5
Bounding box loss parameter	0.0296
Classification loss parameter	0.243
Object loss parameter	0.301
IoU threshold	0.6

Table 3. Results of our proposed YOLOv3-SC and YOLOv3-SPP-SC against baseline on mAP and FPS

Model	Image size	mAP	FPS
YOLOv3 [18] (Baseline)	640	81.9	28.7
YOLOv3-S2	640	**85.9**	**128.2**
YOLOv3-SC3	640	82.9	103.1
YOLOv3-SC1	640	84.5	**128.2**
YOLOv3-SPP (Baseline)	640	82.8	27
YOLOv3-SPP-S2	640	**84.7**	**133.3**
YOLOv3-SPP-SC3	640	83.2	99
YOLOv3-SPP-SC1	640	**84.7**	**133.3**

From Table 3, we have the following observations: (1) As expected, the FPS of YOLOv3-SC1 and YOLOv3-S2 is about four times higher than that of baseline, and the FPS of YOLOv3-SC3 is slightly lower than that of YOLOv3-SC1 and YOLOv3-S2. (2) After setting the stride of the first convolutional layer to 2, the YOLOv3-S2 model has a vast improvement in mAP, about 4%. YOLOv3-SC3 and YOLOv3-SC1 also receive a 1% and 2.6% improvement in mAP, respectively. (3) Slice-Concat structure also works on YOLOv3-SPP. The mAP is improved compared to baseline, and FPS increases to about four times baseline.

From Table 4, we have the following observations: (1) Whether the stride is modified or the convolutional layer is replaced with a Slice-Concat structure, the Parameters remain essentially the same. (2) When stride is set to 2 or after finetuning the baseline with Slice-Concat, each layer's feature map size after finetuning is one-fourth of the size before finetuning. According to Eq. (1), the GFLOPs of the model will be a quarter of the baseline size after finetuning.

Table 4. Results of our proposed YOLOv3-SC and YOLOv3-SPP-SC against baseline on parameters and GFLOPs

Model	Image size	Parameters	GFLOPs
YOLOv3 [18] (Baseline)	640	61.6M	155.2
YOLOv3-S2	640	61.5M	38.8
YOLOv3-SC3	640	61.6M	39.3
YOLOv3-SC1	640	61.6M	**38.7**
YOLOv3-SPP (Baseline)	640	62.6M	156.1
YOLOv3-SPP-S2	640	62.6M	39
YOLOv3-SPP-SC3	640	62.6M	39.5
YOLOv3-SPP-SC1	640	62.6M	**38.9**

Since the improvement method proposed in this paper is to change the width and height of the input feature map to half of the original one, which in turn improves the detection speed of the model. The question naturally arises, if we directly change the image size to half of the original one, can we achieve the same effect? From Table 5, we can see that for the same network model and the same device, the larger the image size is, the smaller the batch size is. And the larger the batch size is, the shorter the training time of the model and the distribution of the weights normalized by the BN layer is closer to the distribution of the data itself, which makes the model training more effective. The improved model in this paper can increase the value of batch size with the same image size. This allows devices with insufficient video memory to get better training results and shorten the training time of the model.

5   Conclusion

In this paper, the Slice-Concat structure we proposed changes the feature map size of the input image to one-fourth of the original size after downsampling the input image. It also combined the width and height information of the feature map into the channel space so that the width and height information of the feature map could be retained more. At the same time, this paper also found that modifying only the stride of the first convolutional layer of the network can achieve the same effect as the Slice-Concat structure. The above operation increased the detection accuracy, significantly improved the model detection speed, dramatically reduced the model computation, and increased the batch size during network training with almost no increase in model parameters. This paper verifies the effectiveness of the above operation on the YOLOv3 model. Meanwhile, the same results were obtained on the YOLOv3-SPP model. The improved method proposed in this paper shows excellent robustness in the YOLO series model.

Table 5. The batch size results with different image sizes and the convergence time and epoch of the model.

Model	Image size	Batch size	Time/h	Epoch
YOLOv3	320	12	9.689	120
YOLOv3	640	3	36.645	120
YOLOv3-S2 (Ours)	640	**16**	4.618	80
YOLOv3-SC3 (Ours)	640	**16**	**4.412**	80
YOLOv3-SC1 (Ours)	640	**16**	4.529	80
YOLOv3-SPP	320	12	9.833	120
YOLOv3-SPP	640	3	36.954	120
YOLOv3-SPP-S2 (Ours)	640	**16**	**4.446**	80
YOLOv3-SPP-SC3 (Ours)	640	**16**	4.536	80
YOLOv3-SPP-SC1 (Ours)	640	**16**	4.528	80

This provides a reference for better training of network models for devices with smaller memory capacity and also provides an idea for model lightweight. Since we have only verified the effectiveness of this scheme on YOLO-related networks, it will be the future research direction of our group whether it has good robustness on other models.

Acknowledgements. This work is supported by the National Natural Science Foundation of China (Grant No. 61602161,61772180), Hubei Province Science and Technology Support Project (Grant No: 2020BAB012), The Fundamental Research Funds for the Research Fund of Key Lab of Traffic and Internet of Things (WUT: 2015III015-A03).

References

1. Viola, P., Jones, M.: Rapid object detection using a boosted cascade of simple features[C]. In: Proceedings of the 2001 IEEE Computer Society Conference on Computer Vision and Pattern Recognition. CVPR 2001: IEEE (2001)
2. Girshick, R., et al.: Region-based convolutional networks for accurate object detection and segmentation. IEEE Trans. Pattern Anal. Mach. Intell. **38**(1), 142–158 (2015)
3. Dalal, N., Triggs, B.: Histograms of oriented gradients for human detection[C]. In: 2005 IEEE Computer Society Conference on Computer Vision and Pattern Recognition (cvpr'05): IEEE, pp. 886–893 (2005)
4. Felzenszwalb, P.F., et al.: Object detection with discriminatively trained part-based models. IEEE Trans. Pattern Anal. Mach. Intell. **32**(9), 1627–1645 (2009)
5. Felzenszwalb, P., McAllester, D., Ramanan, D.: A discriminatively trained, multiscale, deformable part model[C]. In: 2008 IEEE Conference on Computer Vision and Pattern Recognition: IEEE, pp. 1–8 (2008)
6. Felzenszwalb, P.F., Girshick, R.B., McAllester, D.: Cascade object detection with deformable part models[C]. In: 2010 IEEE Computer Society Conference on Computer Vision and Pattern Recognition: IEEE, pp. 2241–2248 (2010)

7. Krizhevsky, A., Sutskever, I., Hinton, G.E.: Imagenet classification with deep convolutional neural networks. Commun. ACM **60**(6), 84–90 (2017)
8. Girshick, R., et al. Rich feature hierarchies for accurate object detection and semantic segmentation[C]. In: Proceedings of the IEEE Conference on Computer Vision and Pattern Recognition, pp. 580–587 (2014)
9. He, K., Zhang, X., Ren, S., et al.: Spatial pyramid pooling in deep convolutional networks for visual recognition. IEEE Trans. Pattern Anal. Mach. Intell. **37**(9), 1904–1916 (2015)
10. Girshick, R.. Fast R-cnn[C]. In: Proceedings of the IEEE International Conference on Computer Vision, pp. 1440–1448 (2015)
11. Faster R-CNN: Towards Real-Time Object Detection with Region Proposal Networks.
12. Ren, S., et al.: Faster R-CNN: towards real-time object detection with region proposal networks. IEEE Trans. Pattern Anal. Mach. Intell. **39**(6), 1137–1149 (2016)
13. Lin, T., et al.: Feature pyramid networks for object detection[C]. In: Proceedings of the IEEE Conference on Computer Vision and Pattern Recognition, pp. 2117–2125 (2017)
14. He, K., et al.: Mask R-cnn[C]. In: Proceedings of the IEEE International Conference on Computer Vision, pp. 2961–2969 (2017)
15. Redmon, J., et al.: You only look once: unified, real-time object detection. In: Proceedings of the IEEE Conference on Computer Vision and Pattern Recognition, pp. 779–788 (2016)
16. Bochkovskiy, A., Wang, C., Liao, H.M.: Yolov4: Optimal Speed and Accuracy of Object Detection[J]. arXiv:2004.10934 (2020)
17. Redmon, J., Farhadi, A.: Yolo9000: better, faster, stronger. In: Proceedings of the IEEE Conference on Computer Vision and Pattern Recognition, pp. 7263–7271 (2017)
18. Redmon, J., Farhadi, A.: Yolov3: an incremental improvement. arXiv:1804.02767 (2018)
19. Liu, W., et al.: SSD: single shot multibox detector. In: Leibe, B., Matas, J., Sebe, N., Welling, M. (eds.) Computer Vision – ECCV 2016: 14th European Conference, Amsterdam, The Netherlands, October 11–14, 2016, Proceedings, Part I, pp. 21–37. Springer International Publishing, Cham (2016). https://doi.org/10.1007/978-3-319-46448-0_2
20. Lin, T., et al.: Focal loss for dense object detection. In: Proceedings of the IEEE International Conference on Computer Vision, pp. 2980–2988 (2017)
21. Li, Y., et al.: Yolov3-lite: a lightweight crack detection network for aircraft structure based on depthwise separable convolutions. Appl. Sci. **9**(18), 3781 (2019)
22. Mao, Q., et al.: Mini-yolov3: real-time object detector for embedded applications. Ieee Access **7**, 133529–133538 (2019)
23. Ma, H., Liu, Y., Ren, Y., et al.: Detection of collapsed buildings in post-earthquake remote sensing images based on the improved Yolov3. Rem. Sens. **12**(1), 44 (2020)
24. Everingham, M., et al.: The pascal visual object classes challenge: a retrospective. Int. J. Comput. Vision **111**(1), 98–136 (2015)

A Systematic Approach for Maintainable Business Process Models

Hajer Ben Haj Ayech[1]([✉]), Emna Ammar Elhadjamor[2]([✉]),
and Sonia Ayachi Ghannouchi[1,2]([✉])

[1] ISG Sousse, Sousse University, Sousse, Tunisia
s.ayachi@coselearn.org
[2] RIADI Laboratory-ENSI, Manouba University, Manouba, Tunisia

Abstract. The BPM lifecycle brings incremental improvement to business process models. In this paper, we propose a systematic approach to promote the maintainability of business process models, which stimulates the ease of their modifications and reduces the difficulties of maintenance. The proposed approach is based on a new extension of the BPM lifecycle. In this regard, we considered a set of the maintainability metrics for business processes models. Particularly, these metrics are classified into two main categories: static maintainability metrics and dynamic maintainability metrics. We evaluate the static maintainability metrics in the modeling phase and the dynamic maintainability metrics in the execution phase in the BPM lifecycle. After both assessments, a set of recommendations is given to allow the designer to improve the maintainability of the considered models and facilitate maintenance tasks in the future. These phases are illustrated and validated through a case study from the health care sector.

Keywords: Approach for maintainable BPMN · BP maintainability · BPM lifecycle · Maintenance lifecycle · Metrics · Recommendations

1 Introduction

According to the IEEE Standard 1219 [1], the software maintenance is the modification of a software product after its delivery. It is used for several functions such as correct errors, improve the design, make improvements to better support the needs of users, adapt the system to various changes (for example changes to government rules, make changes to files or databases, etc.).

Nowadays, the business process is a very important concept in the information systems field. Business process management (BPM) brings incremental improvement to business processes using several methodologies, techniques, and tools, in order to guarantee the organization's competitive position in the market [2].

Based on the similarity between the software and the business process, the maintenance task presents the different modifications and changes that can be applied in the business process models [3]. In fact, it ensures the continuity of use of the process model, their continuous improvement, the adaptation of the model to changes in the environment, and the satisfaction of different customer requests. The ease of maintenance is

© Springer Nature Switzerland AG 2021
H. Qiu et al. (Eds.): KSEM 2021, LNAI 12817, pp. 522–531, 2021.
https://doi.org/10.1007/978-3-030-82153-1_43

dependent on the evaluation of the characteristic "maintainability". For that, it is necessary to have business process models that are easy to maintain. According to Oktay [4] the business process maintainability is "the ease with which a single or a collection of business processes can be modified to correct faults, improve performance or other attributes, or adapt to a changing environment". Rolon et al. [5] suggests that the maintainability facilitates the maintenance task of business process models and it reduces their modification efforts. In fact, more maintainable models guarantee their simplicity and their understandability as they evolve. Besides, the authors add that business process metrics provide useful information about the level of maintainability of these models.

However, the software as well as the business process maintenance are characterized by their huge costs and time-consuming implementation. In reality, the business process lifecycles do not explicitly present the notion of maintenance. In this sense, we thought to propose an approach that integrates the concept of maintenance in the BPM lifecycle, which can be a solution to decrease the costs and the time necessary to carry out the changes and to obtain maintainable models (easily adapted to changes). The remainder of this paper is organized as follows. Section 2 summarizes recent related work based on similar concepts. Section 3 describes in detail our approach. Section 4 describes the application of our approach in the emergency care case study. Section 5 presents a discussion for comparing our approach to related work. The last section gives a brief conclusion.

2   Related Work

To ensure the continuity of using business process models in a dynamic environment, they must be scalable, adapting to different changes, and be easily modified. For this reason, maintainability is important to the business process model. In addition, the modeling phase of the business process lifecycle plays a key role in obtaining a maintainable model with fewer errors and costs. Rolon and Sadowska [6] assess the complexity of the business process model of BPMN notation. The result of the analysis experience includes 13 metrics related to the understandability and 6 metrics related to the modifiability of business process models. In addition, Gruhn and Laue [7] adapt software complexity metrics to assess the complexity of the process. The purpose of evaluating these indicators is to indicate whether the model is structured and easy to understand and to check whether the model is divided into small modules. Lamghari et al. [8] propose a new method, based on the BPM lifecycle, to improve the quality of business processes to achieve acceptable performance levels. The work presented by Dumas et al. [9] focuses on the redesign phase in the BPM lifecycle by proposing four dimensions (duration, cost, quality, and flexibility) to quantify the performance of the designed model. To assess the structural complexity of BPMN. Aguilar et al. [10] adapted the framework (FMESP-Framework for the Modeling and Evaluation of Software Processes) for business process models. The goal of this framework is to select the easiest way to maintain models. BPMN-CM (Business Process Modeling Notation Change Management) is another tool developed in [11] to manage the evolution of business process models. By analyzing the impact of changes, it allows checking the consistency of the model after each change. The work objective proposed by Sadowska [19] is to determine a set of indicators and thresholds indicating the quality level of the BPMN model by focusing on the four main quality characteristics namely: Modifiability, understandability, complexity, and correctness. The contribution of Abdul et al. [12] aims to adapt the complexity metrics of software programs to evaluate the complexity of business process models. To improve the quality of business process models, Kahloun and Ghannouchi [2] defined a set of recommendations for the modeler which appear after a comparison between the values of the quality metrics and the threshold values. The SIG (Software Improvement Group) maintainability model is another method to evaluate the quality of software based on the maintainability characteristic. In fact, Oktay, [4] adapts the SIG model of software maintenance to a collection of interrelated business process models. Always based on the similarity between the software and the business process, the author adapted a set of software maintainability metrics for evaluating business process models regarding for example coupling, duplication, volume, unit size, and unit complexity.

3 Proposed Approach

Our approach allows maintenance to be considered during the BPM lifecycle. In our work, the maintainability assessment includes two phases (redesign and execution) of the BPM lifecycle. These evaluations are based on a comparison of maintainability indicators with thresholds selected from the literature. If the value of the maintainability metric exceeds the threshold, one or more suggestions will be generated to improve the BPMN model, the ease of change, and to favor their maintainability. Concretely, we have created a new extension of the BPM lifecycle (Fig. 1).

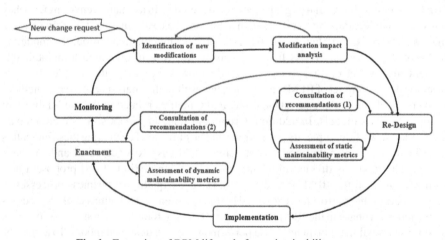

Fig. 1. Extension of BPM lifecycle for maintainability support

In fact, we proposed to add two sub-cycles for evaluating maintainability metrics. The first sub-cycle is for the design phase, and the second one is for the execution (enactment) phase. Then, based on the maintenance lifecycle proposed by IEEE, we have included the two new phases "identification of new modifications" and "modification impact analysis" to consider the maintenance tasks for business process models.

3.1 Assessment of Static Maintainability Metrics

Several metrics were selected. For this reason, we divide them into two categories, namely complexity indicators and coupling indicators. For the complexity category, we have selected the following metrics:

- NOA (Number Of Activities) and NOAJS (Number of Activities, Joins, and Slipts): Vanderfeesten et al. [3] adapted this metric for the business process models and they proposed the metric NOA and NOAJS.
- CFC (Control-Flow Complexity): Cardoso [19] proposed a metric for measuring the complexity of the control flow in the business process model. CFC assesses the complexity of the process introduced by gateways such as "XOR-Split", "OR-Split" and "AND-Split".
- HPC (Halsted-based Process Complexity): Vanderfeesten et al. [3] proposed the HPC (Halsted-based Process Complexity) metric for the assessment process: length, difficulty, and volume.
- IC (Interface Complexity): Vanderfeesten et al. [3] proposed the IC for evaluating the complexity of processes.
- Modularity (M): Modularity presents the degree of decomposition of the model into sub-processes [7].

In this category, Mendling proposed also a set of structural metrics to assess the models of business processes. Later, from this set, Sadowska et al. [13] selected the metrics of modifiability and understandability for the BPMN. In our solution, we used Sn(G) metric to calculate the number of structural nodes in a model. For the evaluation of the complexity of a graphic (G), Mendling defines CNC (G) (Coefficient of network complexity) metric for evaluating the complexity of a graph G. Rolon and Sadowska, [6] have approved a set of metrics of modifiability of business process models. Based on these related work, we have used for the complexity metrics: The TNG (Total Number of Gateways) which counts the number of gateways in the model. In fact, the higher gateway heterogeneity is, the more difficult modification in the model becomes; the TNDO (Total Number of Data Objects) which represents the sum of the number of input and output data objects; and the TNE (Total Number of Events) which counts the number of events used in the process model.

For the coupling metrics: we have chosen the following metrics.

- Coupling: for measuring the number of interconnections between the modules of the model [3].
- ICP (Imported Coupling) and ECP (Exported Coupling): ICP counts the number of messages or sequence flows sent by the activities of the process or by the sub-process for each activity. ECP counts the number of message flows received by the activity or sub-process for each activity [14].
- RFP: Response For a Process metric is used to calculate the coupling in terms of control flows [14].
- CLP and CLA: CLP (Connectivity Level Between Pools) and CLA (Connectivity Level Between Activities) deal with the modifiability of the model [6].

3.2 Consultation of Recommendations (1)

Recommendations are at this stage mainly related to complexity metrics and coupling metrics. Recommendations of the complexity metrics include for example:

- CFC: Minimize gateways such as: OR-split-join to reduce the complexity of the control flow in order to have a more understandable process, and avoid using the OR Gateway whenever possible.
- NOA: Create sub-processes and reduce the number of tasks.
- NOAJ: Reduce the number of activities or gateways (joins/splits) and create subprocesses.

    Recommendations of the coupling metrics include for example:

- CP: Reduce the number of interconnections between activities in a process model. In fact, the higher the coupling value is, the more the change is difficult.
- ICP: Create processes/sub processes with a limited number of control flows and incoming message flows to reduce the likelihood of error, and to reduce service time and modification costs.

3.3 Assessment of Dynamic Maintainability Metrics

After the execution of the BPMN models, the dynamic metrics are compared with threshold values. If there are unacceptable values, a set of recommendations is given to the expert to correct and modify the model. The dynamic maintainability metrics are the following:

- Process Duration (MIN, MAX, AVG): This metric has three measures such as: Minimal process execution time (MIN), Maximal process execution time (MAX), Average process execution time (AVG).
- Activity duration: This metric count the average duration of an activity.
- Activity waiting time: This metric allows measuring the waiting time to execute an activity.
- Total duration for 2 (or more) activities without waiting time: This metric counts the sum of the average execution time for a fragment without taking into account the time lost between two activities or between three activities (or more).
- Waiting time for 2 (or more) activities: This metric counts the average of the waiting time between two or more executed activities (fragment).
- Total duration for 2 (or more) activities with waiting time: This metric counts the sum of the average execution times between two or more activities while taking into account the waiting time between them.
- Number of resources: The resources can be either human or material resources. This metric counts the resources used by one activity. For a fragment, it allows to count the average number of resources used by this fragment.

3.4 Consultation of Recommendations (2)

These guidelines can directly affect the third phase of the BPM lifecycle, but in some cases, they also require a return to the "Re-Design" phase to make modifications in the BPMN model. After applying the modifications and obtaining a process with good maintainability, the monitoring phase is performed.

3.5 Identification of New Modifications

This phase is initiated by the arrival of a new modification request from outside the organization. This request can be either a demand for change coming from a customer or an innovation in the environment for example a new technology that appears. Similarly, this stage can be initiated by a modification recommended through the monitoring phase.

3.6 Modification Impact Analysis

The analysis of impact determines the positive and negative effects of the modification request. Based on the analysis of the impacts of the proposed changes, an expert defines the costs of the modification request. Then s/he decides whether this request is accepted or refused.

4 Developed Plugin and Experimentation

To verify our solution, we chose Visual Paradigm as a tool for modeling business processes expressed in BPMN notation. To be more precise, we adapted a plug-in to enable us to implement our solution. This plugin is open source, developed by Sadowska [15] using Java, and adapted by Kbaier and Ghannouchi [16] to evaluate the quality of the BPMN models. We extended this plugin to evaluate the maintainability of a given BPMN model. Figure 2 summarizes how our plugin extension works. As a case study, we selected the medical field and evaluated the emergency care process introduced in [17]. The emergency care process includes six main activities: Registration, Sorting, Delayed emergency in case of not urgent patient, Consultation inbox, Shock treatment and the lying waiting. In this activity, there are two situations: transferring the patient to another department (hospitalization/special consultation) to ensure the continuity of care or the patient needs long-term treatment (during shock treatment activities).

First after the design of the BPMN model, the modeler can evaluate the static maintainability metrics. For example, there are two metrics, CFC and CLA, with unacceptable values colored in red and there are a set of recommendations (Fig. 3): "Minimize gateways such-as OR-split-joins to reduce the complexity of control flow", and "Be away from OR routing every time it is possible". Next, based on these recommendations, we have tried to improve the emergency care model. Indeed, we have applied the first recommendation of the CFC metric. To reduce the number of gateways, we have removed a XOR gateway while keeping the same model logic of the emergency care process. After these modifications, we obtained an improved model of the emergency care process with a good level of maintainability (Fig. 4).

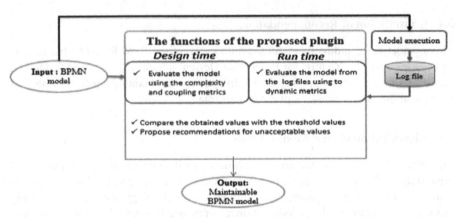

Fig. 2. The proposed plugin

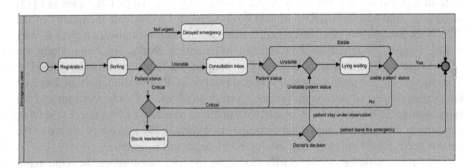

Fig. 3. Recommendations of static maintainability metrics

Fig. 4. The new model of the emergency care process

After that, we included a set of dynamic metrics where their evaluation is based on the execution of one hundred instances of the considered emergency care process. If there are unacceptable values (which exceed the threshold values), we have proposed a set of recommendations. For example, to decrease the execution time for the sorting activity, we have chosen to apply the recommendation "Add a new resource" (Fig. 5):

- Add a new nursing assistant who diagnoses the patient's condition in order to complete the sorting task and reduce the waiting time between the two activities (recording and sorting).
- Another proposal is to add a new agent for the "registration" activity to wait for the same objective and decrease the waiting time.

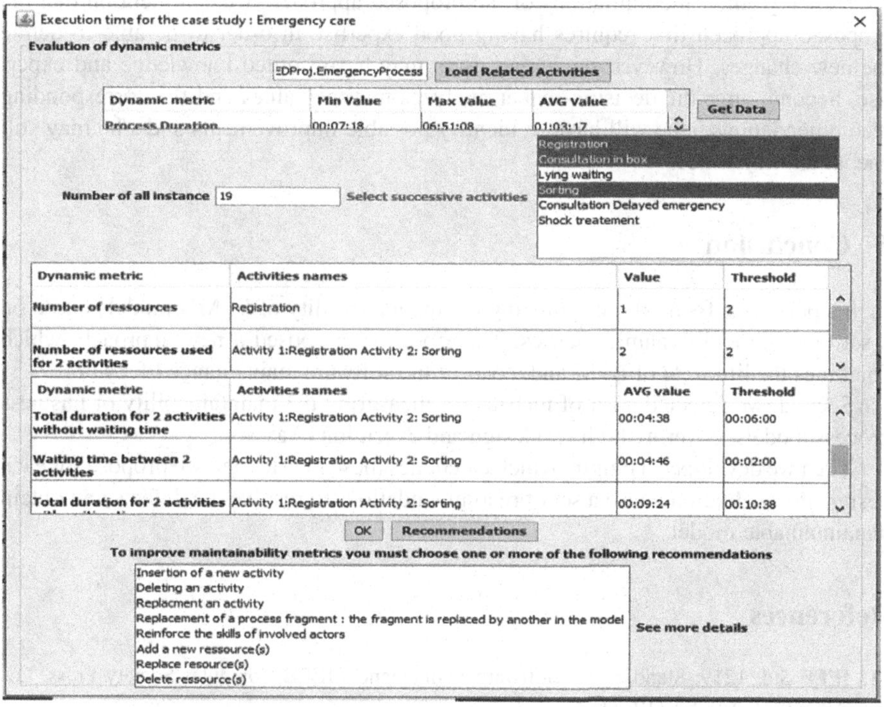

Fig. 5. Recommendations of dynamic metrics of maintainability of emergency care model

5 Discussion

After studying several research papers, in this section, we try to discuss the differences between our proposed approach and other related works summarized in Sect. 2. More precisely, we have identified a set of metrics that allow the maintainability of the business process model under evaluation to foster its modification. In addition, we propose a set of recommendation. The advantage of these recommendations is that they ensure, on the one hand, the ease of application of the modifications and on the other hand, they ensure the quality of the BPMN model. In addition, none of methods proposed in the literature takes into account the static and dynamic evaluation, at the same time, based on the criterion of maintainability of BPMN models. Moreover, we have enriched our work with new dynamic recommendations that are standard and adaptable for other processes.

Through the approach proposed in this paper, we benefit from (i) the identification of static and dynamic metrics with real values to be extracted from event logs generated by the enactment of Business Processes, (ii) the definition of a set of recommendations related to business process evaluation, (iii) the explicit integration of the maintenance into process engineering. To evaluate the proposed approach, we choose the "emergency care" process, in the medical field, because it is rather complex, and requires continuous improvement.

Now regarding the limitations of the proposed approach, we can mention that the proposed approach first requires having good expertise in order to be able to define the new changes. However, our target users may have limited knowledge and expertise. Second, after the decision-maker analyzes metrics values and the corresponding recommendations, s/he will have to identify possible improvements and s/he may still encounter difficulties.

6 Conclusion

In this paper, we focused on evaluating the maintainability of BPMN models based on a set of static and dynamic metrics. Therefore, we proposed a new approach, which combines the lifecycle of BPM and a part of the software maintenance lifecycle.

Second, we selected a set of metrics for measuring the maintainability of business process models, covering both (re)design and execution phases.

Then we developed a plugin, which calculates these metrics and we propose for each design and evaluation phase a set of recommendations to resolve the defects and obtain a maintainable model.

References

1. IEEE Std. 1219: Standard for Software Maintenance. IEEE Computer Society Press, Los Alamitos CA, USA (1993)
2. Kahloun, F., Ghannouchi Ayachi, S.: Improvement of quality for business process modeling driven by guidelines. In: International Conference on Knowledge Based and Intelligent Information and Engineering Systems (2018)
3. Vanderfeesten, I., Cardoso, J., Mendling, J., Reijers, H.A., van der Aalst, W.: Quality metrics for business process models. BPM Workflow Handbook **144**, 179–190 (2007)
4. Oktay, T.: Towards a maintainability model for business processes adapting a software maintainability model (position paper). In: IEEE 1st International Workshop on Communicating Business Process and Software Models Quality, Understandability, and Maintainability (CPSM) (2013)
5. Rolon, E., Ruiz, F., García, F., Piattini, M.: Applying software metrics to evaluate business process models. CLEI Electron. J. **9**(1), 5 (2006)
6. Rolon, E., Sadowska, M.: Prediction models for BPMN usability and maintainability. In: IEEE Conference on Commerce and Enterprise Computing (2009)
7. Gruhn, V., Laue, R.: Complexity metrics for business process models. In: 9th International Conference on Business Information Systems (BIS), Lecture Notes in Informatics, pp. 1–12 (2006)

8. Lamghari, Z., Radgui, M., Saidi, R., Rahmani, M.D.: A set of indicators for BPM life cycle improvement. In: International Conference on Intelligent Systems and Computer Vision (ISCV) (2018)
9. Dumas, M., Mendling, J., La Rosa, M., Reijers, H.: Introduction to business process management. In: Fundamentals of Business Process Management. Springer-Verlag, NY (2013)
10. Aguilar, E., Ruiz, F., García, F., Piattini, M.: Evaluation measures for business process models. In: Proceedings of the 2006 ACM symposium on Applied computing, pp. 1567–1568 (2006)
11. Kherbouche, M.: Contribution à la gestion de l'évolution des processus métiers. PhD thesis, Littoral Côte d'Opale University (2013)
12. Abdul, A., Koh, T., Wong, P.: Complexity metrics for measuring the understandability and maintainability of business process models using goal-question-metric (GQM). Int. J. Comput. Sci. Netw. Sec. **8**(5) (2008)
13. Sánchez-González, L., García, F., Mendling, J., Ruiz, F.: Quality assessment of business process models based on thresholds. In: Meersman, R., Dillon, T., Herrero, P. (eds.) OTM 2010. LNCS, vol. 6426, pp. 78–95. Springer, Heidelberg (2010). https://doi.org/10.1007/978-3-642-16934-2_9
14. Khlif, W., Zaaboub, N., Ben-Abdallah, H.: Coupling metrics for business process modeling. WSEAS Trans. Comput. **9**(1), 31–41 (2010)
15. Sadowska, M.: An approach to assessing the quality of business process models expressed in BPMN. e-Informatica Softw. Eng. J. **9**(1) (2015)
16. Kbaier, W., Ghannouchi Ayachi, S.: Determining the threshold values of quality metrics in BPMN process models using data mining technique. Proc. Comput. Sci. **164**, 113–119 (2019)
17. Elhajamor Ammar, E., Ghannouchi Ayachi, S.: Towards KPI-Based Health Care Process Improvement, In: HCist - International Conference on Health and Social Care Information Systems and Technologies, CENTERIS / ProjMAN / HCist 2017, Barcelona, Spain. Published by Elsevier in Journal Procedia Computer Science, **121**(C), January 2017, pp. 767–774 (2017)
18. Cardoso, J.: Evaluating the process control-flow complexity measure. In: IEEE International Conference on Web Services (ICWS'05) (2005)
19. Sadowska, M.: Quality of business models expressed in BPMN. Master Thesis (2013)

Improved Evolution Algorithm that Guides the Direction of Individual Mutation for Influence Maximization in Social Networks

Xiaoqin Tang$^{(\boxtimes)}$ and Xuxing Liu

College of Computer and Information Science, Southwest University, Chongqing 400715, China

Abstract. The purpose of influence maximization in social networks is to find K nodes as the spread source to activate as many nodes as possible. To improve the efficiency and effectiveness of the classic genetic algorithm in large social networks, the diffusion evaluation function is first proposed to estimate the impact range of seed nodes. Then the individuals are initialized based on the diffusion degree centrality of the node. Adapted a crossover strategy is used to help the evolution algorithm to achieve the purpose of local search. Besides, a direction vector is designed to guide the individual's mutation. Through experiments on real social networks, the improved evolution algorithm can approximate the state-of-the-art greedy algorithm in the final result while also significantly improving time efficiency.

Keywords: Influence maximization · Evolution algorithm · Diffusion evaluation function · Crossover strategy · Direction vector

1 Introduction

In recent years, many large-scale social network platforms, such as Weibo, Douban, Facebook, have developed rapidly, the dissemination behavior among people has been studied. As a result, it promoted the development of viral marketing [1], rumor control [2, 3], user recommendation [4, 5], infectious disease prediction [6].

However, if some firms want to make full use of social networks as a means of marketing and information dissemination, they must face many challenges. For example, one firm needs to promote its products on social networks, and because of its limited budget, it can only find a small number of users to use its products for free and then form a "word-of-mouth" effect to promote product sales. In social networks, there are many essential Key Opinion Leaders. Therefore, if one firm can find out the most influential nodes from the networks and make them the initial spread source, the information will be thoroughly disseminated.

To solve this problem, we simplify the social network to a network structure composed of nodes and edges $G(V, E)$. Nodes $v \in V$ represent the users in the network and edges $(v, u) \in E$ represent the relationship between users. The p on the edges represents the possibility that users will be affected by each other.

© Springer Nature Switzerland AG 2021
H. Qiu et al. (Eds.): KSEM 2021, LNAI 12817, pp. 532–545, 2021.
https://doi.org/10.1007/978-3-030-82153-1_44

The purpose of influence maximization in social networks is to find K nodes, then activate them to spread freely in the network. This random spreading is represented by the function $\sigma()$. The process is formulated as follows:

$$S^* = \frac{\arg\max}{S \subseteq V, |S| = K}\sigma(S) \tag{1}$$

Domingos and Richardson [7, 8] are the first to study influence maximization. Subsequently, Kempe et al. [9] simplified the influence maximization into a discrete optimization problem. Meanwhile, Kempe et al. [10] proved that influence maximization in social networks is NP-hard. They simplified information diffusion in the network into two propagation models, Independent Cascade Model (IC) and Linear Threshold Model (LT). Kempe initially proposed a greedy algorithm to solve this problem and gave an approximate guarantee close to the optimal solution (1 − 1/e). However, the greedy algorithm does not have good scalability, resulting in low time efficiency.

To decline the time complexity of the greedy algorithm, improved algorithms based on the greedy algorithm began to appear. Leskovec et al. [11] proposed the CELF algorithm using the submodularity of the influence maximization function. Subsequently, to improve that the greedy algorithm is a quadratic algorithm on the number of nodes, Goyal et al. [12] proposed the CELF++ algorithm to improve the algorithm's efficiency further.

However, when its improved algorithms face large social networks, they still have a high time complexity. As a result, some heuristic algorithms based on the network structure be used to solve the problem, such as the Degree algorithm [13], Pagerank algorithm [14, 15]. However, most of these algorithms do not consider the impact overlap of nodes. Usually, the accuracy of the algorithm is not too high.

In social networks, there are many different communities because users have the same hobbies, occupations, and other attributes. Wang et al. [16] proposed CGA algorithm based on community classification to improve the efficiency of greedy algorithm. Some studies [17] considered the differences in the diffusion of seed nodes between and within communities and proposed a Two-phases diffusion model to estimate the impact of seed nodes.

In recent years, various intelligent optimization algorithms have begun to be used to solve the problem of influence maximization. Jiang et al. [18] used an Expected Diffusion Value to replace the Monte-Carlo simulation and used the simulated annealing algorithm to search for the most influential k nodes. Some studies [19] used a simple genetic algorithm to solve influence maximization within a feasible running time. However, the optimal solution and time efficiency of the algorithm cannot be guaranteed because of the blind mutation search of the genetic algorithm. In 2017, Gong et al. [20] used the discrete particle swarm algorithm to solve the problem. They extended the impact diffusion estimation range of the seed node-set based on the Three Degree Theory [21]. In the Two-Hop area, a LIE function is proposed to replace Monte-Carlo simulation to evaluate the impact of seed nodes.

It can be seen from the above that, so far, there are mainly the following ways to solve influence maximization: (1) Based on the improvement of the greedy algorithm. (2) Heuristic algorithm based on network structure. (3) Algorithm based on community classification. (4) Intelligent optimization algorithms. However, most algorithms still have the problem of time-consuming Monte-Carlo simulation and low effectiveness.

In this article, an improved evolution algorithm will be proposed. The main contributions are as follows: (1) Considering the impact diffusion of the seed node-set outside its Two-Hop area, a theoretically more accurate LIEEX function is proposed. (2) In the crossover process of the evolution algorithm, a crossover strategy for individuals is designed. (3) A direction vector is designed to help the algorithm find the optimal global solution and accelerate the convergence speed.

The rest of this paper is organized as follows. Section 2 introduces the impact diffusion evaluation function and algorithm details. Section 3 presents experimental procedure and results. Section 4 concludes this paper.

2 Model and Algorithm

In this part, an impact diffusion evaluation function will be introduced and the specific details of the algorithm will be given. Finally, the time complexity of the algorithm will be analyzed.

2.1 Impact Diffusion Evaluation Function

Usually, algorithms use Monte-Carlo simulations to estimate the impact of seed nodes. This kind of behavior will reduce the algorithm's efficiency. Jiang et al. [18] proposed an Expected Diffusion Value (EDV) to replace the Monte-Carlo simulation, but the EDV only calculates the impact estimate of the seed node-set in the range of its neighbors, called the One-Hop area. To improve this situation, Gong et al. [20] based on the Three Degree Theory [21], extended the impact scope of the seed node set to the range of its neighbors' neighbors, called the Two-Hop area, and proposed LIE (Local Influence Estimation) function to approximate the global influence of the seed node-set.

In the independent cascade model, each active node will independently activate its inactive neighbor nodes at the next moment. Therefore, considering the possibility that the seed node-set will diffuse outside the Two-Hop area, a new LIEEX (LIE EXTENSION) function is proposed. The function formula is as follows:

$$\sigma_1(S) = \sigma_0(S) + \sigma_1^*(S)$$

$$= k + \sum_{i \in N_S^{(1)} \setminus S} \left(1 - \prod_{(i,j) \in E, j \in S} (1 - p_{ij}) \right) \tag{2}$$

$$LIEEX(S) = \sigma_0(S) + \sigma_1^*(S) + \sigma_2^*(S)^+$$

$$= k + \sigma_1^*(S) + \frac{\sigma_1^*(S)}{\left| N_S^{(1)} \setminus S \right|} \left(\sum_{u \in N_S^{(2)} \setminus S} pd_u^* + \sum_{u \in N_S^{(2)} \setminus S} pd_u^{out} \right) \tag{3}$$

In the above formulas (2) and (3), where S represents the Seed node-set, $N_S^{(1)}$ and $N_S^{(2)}$ are One-hop area and Two-hop area of the seed node. The parameter d_u^* represents the number of edges of node u within $N_S^{(1)}$ and $N_S^{(2)}$, and The parameter d_u^{out} represents the number of edges of node u outside $N_S^{(2)}$.

Finally, the influence maximization problem is simplified. The best solution can be obtained by finding the seed node set with the largest LIEEX function value.

2.2 The Main Framework of the Proposed Algorithm

Algorithm 1 Main framework of improved evolution Algorithm

Input: Graph $G = (N, E)$, seed set scale k, the number of individuals m, Crossover probability P_c, Mutation probability P_m, the number of iterations g, the inertia weight ω, the learn factors c_1 and c_2.

Output: Set of seed set $|S| = k$

1. Initialize Population $X_i(x_{i1}, x_{i2}, ..., x_{ik}) \leftarrow dd(G, m, k)$ $(i = 1, ..., m)$
2. Initialize the local optimal individual $Ipbest \leftarrow argmax(|LIEEX(X_i)|)$
3. Initialize the global optimal individual $Gpbest \leftarrow argmax(|LIEEX(X_i)|)$
4. while Termination Condition g do
5.   for half of Population$(m/2)$ do
6.   if Random $R_c < P_c$ then
7.   Random select two individuals X_i, X_t
8.   Crossover operator: $X_i \leftrightarrow X_t$
9.   end if
10.   end for
11.   for each individual do
12.   if Random $R_m < P_m$ then
13.   update $D_i \leftarrow F(Gpbest, Ipbest, c_1, c_2, \omega)$
14.   Mutation operator: $X_i' \leftarrow X_i + D_i$
15.   end if
16.   end for
17.   update $Ipbest \leftarrow argmax(|LIEEX(X_i)|)$
18.   update $Gpbest \leftarrow max(Gpbest, Ipbest)$
19.   update Population $X_i(x_{i1}, x_{i2}, ..., x_{ik}) \leftarrow roulette\_select(LIEEX(X_i), X_i, m)$
20. end while
21. return $S = Gpbest$

In the Algorithm 1, the population $X_i(x_{i1}, x_{i2}, \ldots, x_{ik})$ are initialized based on the diffusion degree centrality of the node. Based on the proposed LIEEX function, the impact diffusion value of individuals is evaluated. The individual with the largest impact diffusion value is found and used to initialize the contemporary optimal individual $Ipbest$ and the global optimal individual $Gpbest$ (line 2–3). There are two significant operations in the evolution algorithm, namely crossover operation (line 8) and mutation operation (line 14). For each individual $X_i(x_{i1}, x_{i2}, \ldots, x_{ik})$, this paper designs a direction vector $D_i(d_{i1}, d_{i2}, \ldots, d_{ik})$ to guide the mutation of the individuals. When each iteration is completed, the algorithm will update the $Ipbest$ and $Gpbest$ (line 17–18). Finally, the roulette algorithm selects m individuals as the initial population for the next iteration.

Next, in the Sect. 2.3, 2.4, and 2.5, a detailed description of the initialization operation, the crossover operation, and the mutation operation will be given.

2.3 Initialization of Individuals

In order to speed up the evolution algorithm convergence, a heuristic method based on the diffusion degree centrality of the node is used to initialize the individuals, as shown in Algorithm 2:

Algorithm 2 $dd(G, m, k)$ based on the diffusion degree
Input: Graph $G = (N, E, p)$, the number of individuals m, seed set scale k
Output: Population $X_i(x_{i1}, x_{i2}, ..., x_{ik})$ $(i = 1, ..., m)$
1. for each node v do
2.   compute its DiffusionDegree dd_v
3. end for
4. *Candidate_nodes* ← select$(G, N, 2\%)$
5. for $i \leq m$ do
6. X_i ← *Random(Candidate_nodes, k)*
7. end for
8. return Population group $X_i(x_{i1}, x_{i2}, ..., x_{ik})$ $(i = 1, ..., m)$

Firstly, according to the diffusion degree centrality of node proposed by Kundu et al. [13], the diffusion degree ranking of the nodes in the network is calculated (line 2). The diffusion degree formula is as follows

$$C_{DD}(v) = C'_{DD}(v) + C''_{DD}(v)$$
$$= p * C_D(v) + \sum_{i \in neighbors(v)} C'_{DD}(i) \tag{4}$$

Then select the rank top 2% nodes of the diffusion degree as the candidate nodes-set (line 4), and randomly select k nodes from the candidate nodes-set to initialize the individual X_i each time. It can be seen that the diffusion degree based on the node can easily initialize the individuals.

2.4 Crossover Operation of Individuals

In order to gather the gene nodes with better impact diffusion value in the parent as much as possible in the offsprings, the LIEEX function first evaluates the gene node $x_{ih}, x_{th}(h \in [1, k])$ of the individual X_i, X_t, and the marginal revenue value of each node is calculated by gradually increasing the gene nodes. The impact diffusion value of the gene node is represented by $\sigma(x_{ih})$. Then, based on the $\sigma(x_{ih})$, the gene nodes x_{ih}, x_{th} in X_i, X_t are arranged in ascending and descending order, respectively. It can be seen from Fig. 1, and the evolution algorithm produces a crossover position $flag = random(1, k)$, finally all gene nodes on the left of the flag gene node in the two parents X_i, X_t will cross-swap to get an elite offspring X_c and a suboptimal offspring X_d.

As above, this kind of crossover operation can find the optimal local solution better. The crossover operation is specifically shown in Algorithm 3:

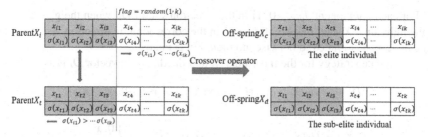

Fig. 1. Crossover operation of individuals

Algorithm 3 Crossover Operation
Input: parent X_i, X_t
Output: offspring X_c, X_d
1. for each gene node x_{ih} do
2.   Compute $\sigma(x_{ih}) = \sigma(x_{i1}, x_{i2}, ..., x_{ih}) - \sigma(x_{i1}, x_{i2}, ..., x_{ih-1})$
3. end for
4. Sort X_i by ascending by $\sigma(x_{ih})$
5. for each gene node x_{th} do
6.   Compute $\sigma(x_{th}) = \sigma(x_{t1}, x_{t2}, ..., x_{th}) - \sigma(x_{t1}, x_{t2}, ..., x_{th-1})$
7. end for
8. Sort X_t by descending by $\sigma(x_{th})$
9. for range(1, $flag = random(1, k)$) do
10. $x_{ih} \in X_i, x_{th} \in X_t$
11.   if $x_{ih} \notin X_t \& x_{th} \notin X_i$ then
12. $x_{ih} \leftrightarrow x_{th}$
13.   end if
14. end for
15. return X_c, X_d

2.5 Mutation Operation of Individuals

In the classical genetic algorithm, the mutation behaviors of the individuals are usually random, it can help the algorithm jump out of the optimal local solution and achieve the purpose of global search. However, when the algorithm faces large social networks, this kind of blind mutation search often leads to a significant reduction in the search efficiency. Therefore, in order to improve the random mutation behavior of the individuals, this paper combines the discrete particle swarm algorithm [20] idea and designs a direction vector D_i to guide the mutation of the individuals, so as to achieve the overall situation Optimization.

The direction vector of the design is as follows:

$$D_i = (d_{i1}, d_{i2}, ..., d_{ik}) \quad (i = 1, ..., m) \tag{5}$$

For each component $d_{ih} \in \{0, 1\}$ in the direction vector D_i, when the gene node x_{ih} in the individual X_i will mutate, if $d_{ih} = 1$ in the corresponding direction vector D_i, the gene node x_{ih} is mutated; otherwise, no mutation is made.

The update strategy for the individual X_i and the direction vector D_i is as follows:

$$D_i \leftarrow F(\omega D_i + c_1 r_1 (IPbest \cap X_i) + c_2 r_2 (GPbest \cap X_i)) \tag{6}$$

$$F(X_i) = (f_1(x_{i1}), f_2(x_{i2}), ..., f_k(x_{ik})) \quad f_j(x_{ij}) = \begin{cases} 0, x_{ij} < 2 \\ 1, x_{ij} \geq 2 \end{cases} \tag{7}$$

$$X_i \leftarrow X_i + D_i \tag{8}$$

In formula (6), the individual X_i and $Ipbest$, $Gpbest$ do intersection operations. As shown in Fig. 2, D_i^{Ipbest} and D_i^{Gpbest} can be obtained, respectively. Assuming $X_i = (6, 1, 8, 15, 9, 7, 23)$, $Ipbest = (6, 8, 3, 2, 5, 10, 23)$ and $Gpbest = (15, 5, 1, 3, 2, 6, 23)$. It can be seen from Fig. 2 that the X_i and the $Ipbest$ are intersected, $(6, 8, 23)$ can be obtained, then the components of the corresponding positions of the nodes $6, 8, 23$ in D_i^{Ipbest} are 0, it means that these gene nodes have relative advantages and should be preserved. On the contrary, for the $1, 15, 9, 7$ gene nodes in the X_i, the components of the corresponding position in D_i^{Ipbest} are 1, indicating that these gene nodes are not better and should be mutated and discarded. Finally, $D_i^{Ipbest} = (0, 1, 0, 1, 1, 1, 0)$. The operations for the individual X_i and the $Gpbest$ are similar.

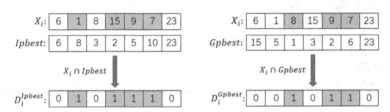

Fig. 2. Update of direction vector D_i

After calculating D_i^{Ipbest} and D_i^{Gpbest}, the direction vector D_i can be obtained by formula (6). The function F() in formula (6) is a threshold function, and its operation method is shown in formula (7). Finally, according to formula (8), the mutation operation is performed on the individual X_i. Assuming $X_i + D_i = X_i' \left(x_{i1}', x_{i2}', \ldots, x_{ik}' \right)$, the mutation rules of gene nodes in X_i are as follows:

$$x_{ih}' = \begin{cases} x_{ih}, & if\ d_{ih} = 0 \\ Random(N, x_{ih}), & if\ d_{ih} = 1 \end{cases} \tag{9}$$

The mutation operation of individuals is specifically shown in Algorithm 4:

Algorithm 4 Mutation operator

Input: Individual $X_i(x_{i1}, x_{i2}, ..., x_{ik})$, Graph $G = (N, E)$
Output: Individual $X_i'(x_{i1}', x_{i2}', ..., x_{ik}')$
1. for each gene node x_{ih} in X_i do
2.   if $d_{ih} = 1$ in D_i then
3.   Select one node from Graph $G = (N, E)$
4.   end if
5. end for
6. return $X_i'(x_{i1}', x_{i2}', ..., x_{ik}')$

2.6 Time Complexity Analysis

When the algorithm initializes the population, it needs to calculate the diffusion degree of all nodes and initialize m individuals from the top 2% nodes, so the time complexity is $O(n) + O(mk)$. Where n represents the number of nodes. Because $mk \ll n$, the time complexity of this step is $O(n)$; In the crossover process, the time complexity required to calculate the evaluation value of the gene nodes is $O(k)$, the time required to sort the nodes is $O(klog_2^k)$, and in the worst-case $flag = k/2$, so the time complexity of the crossover operation is $O(klog_2^k)$. When the number of iterations is g and the population size is m, the time complexity of the crossover operation is $O(gmklog_2^k)$, and the time complexity of the mutation operation is $O(gmk)$. The total time complexity is $O(n) + O(gmklog_2^k) + O(gmk)$. In addition, the time complexity of the LIEEX function is $O(k\bar{D}^2)$, $\bar{D}$ is the average degree of nodes in the network, the total time complexity of the algorithm is $O(gmk^2\bar{D}^2log_2^k)$.

3 Experimental Results and Analysis

In this part, we compare improved evolution algorithm (namely the GA-PSO) with CELF [11] algorithm, Degree algorithm, Random algorithm, classic genetic algorithm (GA) [19], simulated annealing algorithm (SAEDV) [18], discrete particle swarm optimization algorithm (DPSO) [20]. Experiments were done on four actual social network data. We compare the effectiveness and time efficiency of the algorithm on the independent cascade model, respectively. In particular, GA-PSO, SAEDV, and DPSO search for seed nodes according to their respective impact diffusion evaluation functions. The classic genetic algorithm GA uses the LIEEX function proposed in this paper. Finally, when calculating the influence of the selected seed nodes, the Monte-Carlo simulation method is used uniformly. The specific details are as follows.

3.1 Experimental Data Sets and Algorithm Parameter Settings

In the four actual networks, p2p-Gnutella08 is a peer-to-peer file-sharing directed network, node i and node j represent the host, and the edge represents the file-sharing connection. Ca-GrQc (General Relativity and Quantum Universe), Ca-CondMat (Condensed Matter Physics) and Ca-HepTh (High Energy Physics) are author collaboration networks of journals. If author i and author j co-authored a paper, then the network contains undirected edges from i to j. The above three real networks are all captured from the electronic journal Arxiv. Other statistical characteristics of the four social networks as following in Table 1:

Table 1. Statistical characteristics of four real social networks

Network	$|N|$(Nodes)	$|E|$(Edges)	$\bar{D}$(Average degree)
p2p-Gnutella08	6301	20777	6.59
Ca-GrQc	5242	14496	5.53
Ca-CondMat	23133	93497	8.08
Ca-HepTh	9877	25998	5.26

Before starting the experiment, some parameters of the SAEDV, DPSO, GA, and GA-PSO need to be set. In this experiment, the parameters of the SAEDV algorithm are set as follows, the initial temperature $T_0 = 1000000$, after each iteration the temperature drop $\Delta T = 2000$, the number of inner loop $q = 300$, and the final temperature $T_f = 200000$; The parameters of the DPSO algorithm are provided by the literature [20]; The parameters of the GA algorithm refer to the literature [19], population size $m = 100$, crossover probability $p_c = 0.9$, mutation probability $p_m = 0.1$, the iteration number $g = 1500$; the parameters of GA-PSO algorithm are set as follows, population size $m = 100$, crossover probability $p_c = 0.9$, mutation probability $p_m = 0.2$, and the iteration number $g = 100$. The parameters in the direction vector D_i refer to the literature [20], the learning factor $c_1 = 1$, $c_2 = 2$, $r_1, r_2 \in [0, 1]$, and the inertia coefficient $\omega = 0.8$.

Finally, all algorithms are written in python 3.7, and the comparison experiment is run on the pc configured with Intel(R) Core(TM) i5-7400 CPU @ 3.00GHZ, 8G memory.

3.2 Experiments for the Designed Direction Vector

In this part, we will verify the role of the direction vector in guiding the mutation. The GA-NPSO algorithm represents the situation that the direction vector is removed.

When the number of target seeds $k = 35$ and the number of iteration $g = 200$, we compare the speed of convergence between GA-PSO and its variant version GA-NPSO, and the final result is obtained by Monte-Carlo simulation.

It can be seen from Fig. 3 that due to the guidance of the direction vector, the GA-PSO algorithm can reach convergence after about 60 iterations in the p2p-Gnutella08 and Ca-GrQc networks. In CondMat and HepTh networks, convergence can be reached after about 80 iterations. However, the GA-NPSO algorithm is difficult to converge to the optimal global solution within 200 iterations.

It can be known from the experimental results, the direction vector designed in this paper can help the evolution algorithm to perform global search better.

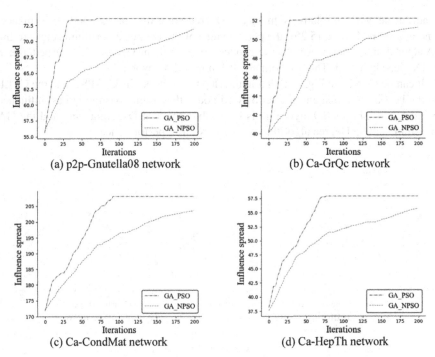

Fig. 3. Comparison of GA-PSO algorithm and GA-NPSO algorithm performance

3.3 Comparisons for the Influence Spread

In this part, seven algorithms will run on an independent cascade model with $p = 0.01$, and the final result is obtained by uniformly using Monte-Carlo simulation. This paper tests the result of each algorithm under the seed node $k \in [5, 50]$.

As shown in Fig. 4(a), the GA-PSO algorithm and the CELF algorithm are similarly the same in the final influence spread. Among seed nodes $k \in [35, 50]$, GA-PSO is slightly better than the CELF algorithm. In the p2p-Gnutella08 network, the DPSO algorithm and the SAEDV algorithm are very close to the CELF algorithm. The GA algorithm is better than the Degree algorithm but worse than the SAEDV algorithm. Since k seed nodes are randomly selected each time, Random is obviously the worst algorithm.

In the GrQc network, as shown in Fig. 4(b), among the seed nodes $k \in [5, 35]$, GA-PSO, CELF, DPSO, and SAEDV have the better impact propagation effect. Among seed nodes $k \in [40, 50]$, the GA-PSO is slightly worse than the CELF, DPSO and SAEDV algorithm. For the Degree algorithm, when the number of seed nodes k is small, the algorithm has good performance. However, as the number of seed nodes increases, the Degree algorithm becomes significantly worse because the influence range between nodes usually overlaps. The GA algorithm is better than the Degree algorithm in this network and far better than the Random algorithm.

In the large-scale CondMat network, as shown in Fig. 4(c), GA-PSO, CELF, DPSO, and SAEDV are the best four algorithms. Because the average degree of nodes in the

CondMat network is relatively high, the Degree algorithm has a good performance. Among seed nodes k ∈ [5,25], the performance of the Degree algorithm is close to the GA algorithm. However, Among seed nodes k ∈ [30,50], the GA algorithm is better than the Degree algorithm. The Random algorithm is still the worst.

It can be seen from Fig. 4(d) that in the HepTh network, the GA-PSO and the CELF are the best algorithms, and the set of seed nodes they found has the largest influence spread range. The DPSO algorithm is better than the SAEDV algorithm, and the GA algorithm and the Degree algorithm have a very close performance.

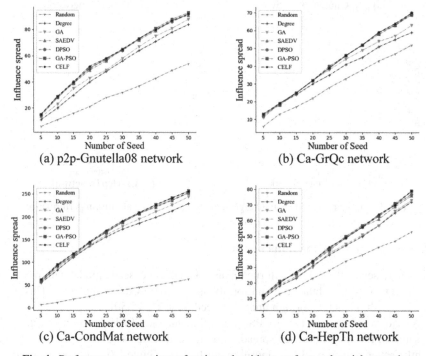

(a) p2p-Gnutella08 network

(b) Ca-GrQc network

(c) Ca-CondMat network

(d) Ca-HepTh network

Fig. 4. Performance comparison of various algorithms on four real social networks

From the experimental data above, it can be known that the GA-PSO algorithm has greatly improved premature convergence of the classic GA algorithm. The GA-PSO algorithm can achieve the same effect as the CELF algorithm in the final results. Besides, the LIEEX function enables the GA-PSO algorithm higher accuracy to estimate the impact propagation of the seed node-set.

3.4 Comparison for Algorithm Time Efficiency

In this part, the number of seed nodes is set to 35, and the time efficiency of each algorithm is tested on four actual social network data. Because the Random algorithm has no reference significance in time efficiency, so this article cancels the Random algorithm in the comparison experiment.

It can be seen from Fig. 5, the CELF algorithm is the least computationally efficient. In p2p-Gnutella08, GrQc, and HepTh, the running time of the CELF algorithm is relatively close. However, as the network scale increases, the running time of the CELF algorithm increases rapidly. In the CondMat network, the CELF algorithm takes several hours. For the other four intelligent optimization algorithms, the running time consumption of the SAEDV algorithm is the largest. The running time of the GA algorithm is also significantly higher than that of the DPSO and GA-PSO algorithms. From the experimental data, the GA-PSO algorithm has reduced the running time of the four networks by approximately 65%, 67%, 68%, 63% compared with the GA algorithm. Simultaneously, the GA-PSO algorithm has relatively closer time consumption among the four networks and is less affected by network scale changes. The Degree is the fastest algorithm, usually only tens of milliseconds. However, it is greatly affected by the network structure.

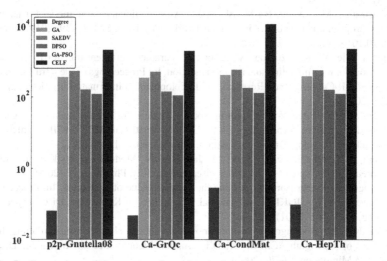

Fig. 5. Comparison of the running time of each algorithm on four real social networks

4   Conclusions

In this paper, we studied the influence maximization problem in social networks. The proposed LIEEX function takes into account the impact of the seed node-set outside its Two-Hop area. It can be seen from the experimental results that the LIEEX function has higher accuracy. Simultaneously, when initializing the individuals, a method based on diffusion degree centrality was used, which provides an excellent performance guarantee for the evolution algorithm at the beginning of evolution. Also, thanks to the unique strategy of the GA-PSO algorithm in the crossover of individuals, the excellent genes in the parent individuals can be better gathered in the offspring individuals after each round of iteration. Finally, the designed direction vector avoids the premature phenomenon of classic genetic algorithms. In terms of the final effect, the GA-PSO algorithm is close to the state-of-art CELF algorithm, and in some social networks, it is even better than the CELF algorithm. At the same time, GA-PSO has good scalability when facing large social networks.

However, due to the limitation of computing resources, this article does not focus on the study of vast networks. In future work, we will study parallel search on algorithms to solve influence maximization in vast social networks.

References

1. Bhattacharya, S., Gaurav, K., Ghosh, S.: Viral marketing on social networks: an epidemiological perspective. Physica A **525**, 478–490 (2019)
2. Ding, L., Ping, H., Guan, Zhi-Hong., Li, T.: An efficient hybrid control strategy for restraining rumor spreading. IEEE Trans. Syst. Man Cybernet.: Syst. (2020). https://doi.org/10.1109/TSMC.2019.2963418
3. Askarizadeh, M., Ladani, B., Manshaei, M.: An evolutionary game model for analysis of rumor propagation and control in social networks. Physica A **523**, 21–39 (2019). https://doi.org/10.1016/j.physa.2019.01.147
4. Yuan, F., He, X., Karatzoglou, A., Zhang, L.: Parameter-efficient transfer from sequential behaviors for user modeling and recommendation. In: Proceedings of the 43rd Internat-ional ACM SIGIR Conference on Research and Development in Information Retrieval, pp. 1469–1478 (2020)
5. Ye, M., Liu, X., Lee, W-C.: Exploring social influence for recommendation: a generative model approach. In: Proceedings of the 35th international ACM SIGIR Conference on Research and Development in Information Retrieval, pp. 671–680 (2012)
6. Husein, I., Noerjoedianto, D., Sakti, M., Jabbar, A.H.: Modeling of epidemic transmission and predicting the spread of infectious disease. Syst. Rev. Pharmacy 11 (2020)
7. Domingos, P., Richardson, M.: Mining the network value of customers. In: Proceedings of the Seventh ACM SIGKDD International Conference on Knowledge Discovery and Data Mining, pp. 57–66 (2001)
8. Richardson, M., Domingos, P.: Mining knowledge-sharing sites for viral marketing. In: Proceedings of the Eighth ACM SIGKDD International Conference on Knowledge Discovery and Data Mining, pp. 61–70 (2002)
9. Kempe, D., Kleinberg, J., Tardos, É.: Maximizing the spreadof influence through a social network. In: Proceedings of the Ninth ACM SIGKDD International Conference on Knowledge Discovery and Data Mining, pp. 137–146 (2003)
10. Kempe, D., Kleinberg, J., Tardos, Éva.: Influential nodes in a diffusion model for social networks. In: Caires, Luís., Italiano, Giuseppe F., Monteiro, Luís., Palamidessi, Catuscia, Yung, Moti (eds.) ICALP 2005. LNCS, vol. 3580, pp. 1127–1138. Springer, Heidelberg (2005). https://doi.org/10.1007/11523468_91
11. Leskovec, J., Krause, A., Guestrin, C., Faloutsos, C., VanBriesen, J., Glance, N.: Cost-effective outbreak detection in networks. In: Proceedings of the 13th ACM SIGKDD International Conference on Knowledge Discovery and Data Mining, pp. 420–429 (2007)
12. Goyal, A., Lu, W., Lakshmanan, L.V.: Celf++ optimizing thegreedy algorithm for influence maximization in social networks. In: Proceedings of the 20th International Conference Companion on World Wide Web, pp. 47–48 (2011)
13. Kundu, S., Murthy, C.A., Pal, S.K.: A new centrality measure for influence maximization in social networks. In: Kuznetsov, S.O., Mandal, D.P., Kundu, M.K., Pal, S.K. (eds.) PReMI 2011. LNCS, vol. 6744, pp. 242–247. Springer, Heidelberg (2011). https://doi.org/10.1007/978-3-642-21786-9_40

14. Chen, S., He, K.: Influence maximization on signed social networks with integrated pagerank. In: 2015 IEEE International Conferenceon Smart City/SocialCom/ SustainCom (SmartCity). IEEE, pp. 289–292 (2015)
15. Yin, X., Hu, X., Chen, Y., Yuan, X., Li, B.: Signed-PageRank: an efficient influence maximization framework for signed social networks. IEEE Trans. Knowl. Data Eng. (2019). https://doi.org/10.1109/TKDE.2019.2947421
16. Wang, Y., Cong, G., Song, G., Xie, K.: Community-based greedy algorithm for mining top-k influential nodes in mobile social networks. In: Proceedings of the 16th ACM SIGKDD International Conference on Knowledge Discovery and Data Mining, pp. 1039–1048 (2010)
17. Shang, J., Zhou, S., Li, X., Liu, L., Wu, H.: CoFIM: a community-based framework for influence maximization on large-scale networks. Knowl.-Based Syst. **117**, 88–100 (2017)
18. Jiang, Q., Song, G., Gao, C., Wang, Y., Si, W., Xie, K.: Simulated annealing based influence maximization in social networks. In: Proceedings of the AAAI Conference on Artificial Intelligence (2011)
19. Bucur, D., Iacca, G.: Influence maximization in social networks with genetic algorithms. In: Squillero, G., Burelli, P. (eds.) EvoApplications 2016. LNCS, vol. 9597, pp. 379–392. Springer, Cham (2016). https://doi.org/10.1007/978-3-319-31204-0_25
20. Gong, M., Yan, J., Shen, B., Ma, L., Cai, Q.: Influence maximization in social networks based on discrete particle swarm optimization. Inf. Sci. **367**, 600–614 (2016)
21. Christakis, N.A., Fowler, J.H.: Connected: The Surprising Power of Our Social Networks and How They Shape Our Lives. Little, Brown Spark (2009)

Incorporating Common Knowledge and Specific Entity Linking Knowledge for Machine Reading Comprehension

Shoukang Han[1,3], Neng Gao[1], Xiaobo Guo[2,3(✉)], and Yiwei Shan[1]

[1] State Key Laboratory of Information Security, Institute of Information Engineering, CAS, Beijing, China
{hanshoukang,gaoneng,shanyiwei}@iie.ac.cn
[2] Institute of Information Engineering, Chinese Academy of Sciences, Beijing, China
guoxiaobo@iie.ac.cn
[3] School of Cyber Security, University of Chinese Academy of Sciences, Beijing, China

Abstract. Machine comprehension of texts often requires external common knowledge and coreference resolution in the passage. However, most current machine reading comprehension models only incorporate external common knowledge. We propose CoSp model, which incorporates both common knowledge and specific entity linking knowledge for machine reading comprehension. It employs an attention mechanism to adaptively select relevant commonsense and lexical common knowledge from knowledge bases, then it leverages the relational-GCN for reasoning on the entity graph, which is constructed by the entity coreference and co-occurrence for each passage. Hence we obtain knowledge-aware and coreference-aware contextual word representation for answer prediction. Experimental results indicate that CoSp model offers significant and consistent improvements over BERT, outperforming competitive knowledge-aware models on ReCoRD and SQuAD1.1 benchmarks.

Keywords: Machine reading comprehension · Knowledge-aware question answering · Entity graph · Graph convolutional network · Knowledge base

1 Introduction

Machine reading comprehension (MRC) aims to teach machines to read and understand human language text so as to answer related questions. It can be naturally used to evaluate natural language understanding (NLU) ability, and also be widely applied to QA applications, search engines, as well as dialogue systems [10]. Nowadays, with the development of deep learning [11], increasing computing power [5,9] and the availability of large-scale datasets [12,23,34], MRC has achieved remarkable advances [25,35]. Recently, pre-trained language models (PLMs) such as BERT [7], GPT [21] and T5 [22], have greatly boosted

© Springer Nature Switzerland AG 2021
H. Qiu et al. (Eds.): KSEM 2021, LNAI 12817, pp. 546–558, 2021.
https://doi.org/10.1007/978-3-030-82153-1_45

MRC, and exceeded human-level performance on some MRC datasets. They are pre-trained on unlabeled text and then fine-tuned on downstream NLU tasks, including MRC. Among these PLMs, BERT has attracted widespread attention, which uses Transformer encoder [27] and trains a bidirectional masked LM. Due to the large amounts of unlabeled data and the sufficiently deep architectures, BERT is able to capture complex linguistic phenomena, understanding language better [15].

Apparently, reading comprehension requires not only language understanding, but also *background knowledge* that supports sophisticated reasoning [8,31]. Linguistic knowledge bases like WordNet [19] and commonsense knowledge bases like DBPedia [14] and NELL [2] can provide a large amount of available background common knowledge. Therefore, some works [8,31,32] are proposed to leverage external knowledge bases (KBs) to further improve BERT for MRC. KT-NET [31] uses attention-based desired knowledge selection from KBs, and then fuses selected knowledge with BERT to enable context-aware and knowledge-aware predictions. However, a study [15] has shown that BERT can not well capture entity linking information, which is indispensable for answering entity-centric questions.

Passage: A year that began in uncertainty for <u>Roger Federer</u> ended with a historic title for the 17-time grand slam champion and his country. When <u>Federer</u> defeated <u>Richard Gasquet</u> of France 6-4 6-2 6-2 [...]. <u>Switzerland</u> had never before won team tennis' most prestigious event, playing in one previous final in 1992 when <u>Federer</u> was merely 11 [...]	**Passage**: <u>Zoe Ball</u> made a desperate, grovelling call to husband <u>Fatboy Slim</u> in an attempt to explain [...]. Ball [...] who was said to be 'furious', and embarrassed by widely-published images of the mother of his two children with her arms wrapped around pop singer <u>TayTay Starhz</u> [...]. <u>Fatboy Slim</u>, 52, whose real name is <u>Norman Cook</u>, is thought to [...]
Question: "You saw how well <u>Roger</u> was playing, how he just killed **XXX** today" said <u>Wawrinka</u>.	**Question**: A friend told the newspaper that **XXX** [...] has no fears for their 16-year marriage [...]
BERT Prediction: Olympics **Prediction with knowledge**: Richard Gasquet	**BERT Prediction**: Fabtboy Slim **Prediction with knowledge**: Norman Cook
Common knowledge: NELL: (Roger Federer, athlete-plays-sport, tennis) NELL: (Richard Gasquet, athlete-plays-sport, tennis) WordNet: (kill, same-synset-with, defeat)	**Common knowledge**: NELL: (husband, same-synset-with, marriage)
Specific entity linking knowledge: Roger Federer <--> Federer <--> Roger	**Specific entity linking knowledge**: Fatboy Slim <--> Norman Cook

Fig. 1. Motivating examples from ReCoRD

Intuitively, both external common knowledge and internal passage-specific entity linking knowledge are conducive to improving the reading comprehension ability of the MRC model. Figure 1 has shown two motivating examples from ReCoRD dataset. The left passage describes Roger Federer's big victory over Richard Gasquet in the Davis Cup, and the question is who did Federer kill. BERT gives a wrong answer "Olympics". It fails on this case as it doesn't know "kill" has the meaning "defeat". After introducing the lexical knowledge that "kill and defeat are synonymous", the right answer "Richard Gasquet" can be reasonably inferred. The right passage describes Norman Cook's wife Zoe Ball went into a scandal with a singer, and the question is who had no fears for the marriage with Zoe. BERT gives a wrong answer "Fatboy Slim". It fails on this case as it doesn't know "Norman Cook" and "Norman Cook" are the same person. By explicitly introducing entity linking information, we can accurately infer that the answer is "Norman Cook". In short, these two examples illustrate the necessity and importance of incorporating common knowledge and specific entity linking knowledge for MRC.

To the best of our knowledge, this is the first study to use both external common knowledge and internal specific entity linking knowledge to improve the accuracy of reading comprehension. In this paper, we propose CoSp model (abbr. incorporating Common knowledge and Specific entity linking knowledge for MRC). It not only integrates commonsense and lexical common knowledge from KBs, but also integrates specific entity linking knowledge in the given passage. For common knowledge fusion, CoSp retrieves relevant KB entities from WordNet and NELL for each word, and select the most relevant KB embeddings to integrate. For specific knowledge fusion, we heuristically construct an entity graph for each passage based on the entity coreference in the same passage and entity co-occurrence in the same sentence. Then R-GCN is used to learn the deep linking relationship among entities. We evaluate the effectiveness of the proposed model on two datasets, ReCoRD and SQuAD1.1. The experimental results show that the CoSp has made great improvements on the basis of BERT, and surpasses several representative MRC models. Through ablation experiments, we have further proved that the fusion of common knowledge and the fusion of specific entity linking knowledge can improve reading comprehension respectively. What's more, taking consideration of two kinds of knowledge simultaneously can bring much more improvements.

The contributions of this paper are as follows: 1. We investigate the necessity and feasibility of integrating common knowledge and specific entity linking knowledge simultaneously in MRC tasks. 2. We design a new MRC approach called CoSp. It outperforms BERT and representative MRC models on ReCoRD and SQuAD1.1.

The rest of this paper is organized as follows. Section 2 presents the details of the preprocessing and our model. Section 3 presents the experimental results and some analysis. Section 4 reviews related works. Finally, we conclude the paper in Sect. 5.

2   Our Approach

Given a passage $P = \{p_1, \ldots, p_n\}$ and a relevant question $Q = \{q_1, \ldots, q_m\}$, the extractive MRC is to predict an answer A which is a span in the passage, i.e., $A = \{p_i, \ldots, p_j\}$, i and j indicate the start and end positions.

We propose CoSp model, which is to enhance BERT with commonsense and lexical common knowledge from knowledge bases and specific entity linking knowledge from the given passage. To fuse commonsense and lexical common knowledge, we adopt knowledge graph embedding [33]. Given passage P and question Q, a set of potentially relevant KB entities $E(w)$ is retrieved for each token $w \in P \bigcup Q$, and each entity $e \in E(w)$ is associated with a learned embedding **e**. Then we employ an attention mechanism to select the most relevant KB embeddings, and integrates them with contextual representations. To fuse specific entity linking knowledge, the passage is transformed into an entity graph where nodes are entities or entity mentions, and edges are relations between them. Then we use R-GCN for information aggregation in the graph. Details about the KB embeddings retrieval from external KBs and the entity graph construction for a passage are given in Sect. 2.1.

As depicted in Fig. 2, based on retrieved relevant KB embeddings and the constructed entity graph of the passage, given a question and passage, CoSp model proceeds as follows: (1) a *BERT encoding layer* computes contextual representations for the question and passage; (2) a *common knowledge fusion layer* employs an attention mechanism to select the most relevant KB embeddings, and integrates them with contextual representations; (3) a *specific knowledge fusion layer* uses R-GCN to aggregates information among entities in the graph to obtain coreference-aware representations; (4) a *self-matching layer* further fuses common and specific knowledge into contextual word representation; and (5) an *output layer* predicts the final answer.

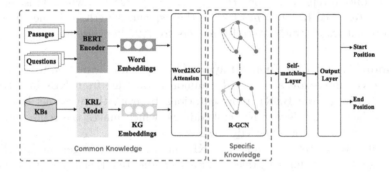

Fig. 2. Framework of CoSp model

2.1   KB Embeddings Retrieval and Entity Graph Construction

KB Embeddings Retrieval. We use two KBs: WordNet and NELL. Each triple consists of a subject entity, a relation, and an object entity. WordNet stores lexical relation between word synsets, e.g., (*location, hypernym_of, city*). NELL stores beliefs about entities, where the subject entity is usually real-world entities and the object entity can be either entities or concept categories, e.g., (*New York, located_in, United States*). In this work, we refer to the synsets in WordNet and the concept categories in NELL as *KB entities*. Instead of symbolic facts, we choose KB embeddings. We adopt the BILINEAR model which measure the validity via a bilinear function (refer to [33] for details).

For WordNet, we retrieve its synsets as relevant KB entities for each word in a passage and question. For NELL, we first recognize named entities and their coreference in the passage and question with off-the-shelf NER and coreference resolution tools, and then retrieve relevant NELL entities by string matching. After this retrieval process, we obtain a set of potentially relevant KB entities for each word, where each KB entity is associated with a KB embedding.

Entity Graph Construction. Because coreference resolution introduces both additional useful and erroneous link, we find out entity nodes in an entity graph via simple string matching for a given passage instead. Undirected edges are defined according to positional properties of each entity pair as: (1) sentence-level edge for every pair of entities appearing in the same sentence; (2) entity-level edge for every mention text of an entity.

2.2   CoSp Model

BERT Encoding Layer. This layer takes as input the passage P and the question Q, and uses BERT to computes the contextual representation for each token.

Specifically, we concatenate the question Q and the passage P, and pass the resulting sequence $S = [[CLS], Q, [SEP], P, [SEP]]$ to a pre-trained BERT model to obtain representations $\mathbf{H} = [\mathbf{h}_1, \ldots, \mathbf{h}_L] \in \mathbb{R}^{L \times d_1}$, where $\mathbf{H}$ is the final hidden states of BERT, $L = m+n+3$ is the sequence length, d_1 is the dimension of contextual embeddings. We refer readers to [7,27] for details.

Common Knowledge Fusion Layer. This layer uses attention to adaptively integrate commonsense and lexical common knowledge from KBs into BERT. It takes as input the BERT representations $\mathbf{h}_i$ from the previous layer, and enriches them with relevant KB embeddings, which makes the representations both context-aware and knowledge-aware.

Specifically, we retrieve candidate KB entities $E(s_i)$ and get the BERT representation $\mathbf{h}_i \in \mathbb{R}^{d_1}$ for each token s_i. Each candidate KB entity e_j is associated with a KB embedding $\mathbf{e}_j \in R^{d_2}$, where d_2 is the dimension of KB embeddings. Then we employ an attention mechanism to adaptively select the most relevant KB entities. We compute an attention weight α_{ij} for entity e_j via a bilinear operation as:

$$\alpha_{ij} \propto \exp(\mathbf{e}_j^T \mathbf{W} \mathbf{h}_i)$$

where $\mathbf{W} \in \mathbb{R}^{d_2 \times d_1}$ is a weight parameter to be learned.

Note that the candidate KB entities sometimes are misleading and unnecessary, we follow [32] to further introduce a knowledge sentinel vector $\hat{\mathbf{e}} \in \mathbb{R}^{d_2}$. The attention weight on the sentinel is calculated as:

$$\beta_i \propto \exp(\hat{\mathbf{e}}^T \mathbf{W} \mathbf{h}_i)$$

The retrieved KB embeddings $\mathbf{e}_j$ and the sentinel vector $\hat{\mathbf{e}}$ are then aligned and aggregated via their corresponding attention weights as:

$$\mathbf{k}_i = \sum_j \alpha_{ij} \mathbf{e}_j + \beta_i \hat{\mathbf{e}}$$

Where $\sum_j \alpha_{ij} + \beta_i = 1$, $\mathbf{k}_i$ can be viewed as a knowledge state vector that encodes external KB knowledge with respect to the current token. We concatenate $\mathbf{k}_i$ with the BERT representation $\mathbf{h}_i$ to obtain context-aware and knowledge-aware representation $\mathbf{t}_i = [\mathbf{h}_i, \mathbf{k}_i] \in \mathbb{R}^{d_1 + d_2}$.

R-GCN Based Specific Knowledge Fusion Layer. This layer aims to integrate specific entity linking knowledge from the given passage. To achieve it, we uses a Relational Graph Convolutional Network (R-GCN) [24] to aggregate information across different entity nodes in the entity graph.

Since each entity is recognized by a named entity recognition (NER) tool, entity node vectors are computed with the associated text span for each entity. Therefore, we construct a binary entity-token mapping matrix $\mathbf{M}$, where $\mathbf{M}_{ij}$ is 1 if j-th token in the passage is within the span of the i-th entity. We use $\mathbf{M}$ to select the text span associated with an entity, and these knowledge-aware token vectors are passed into a mean pooling to calculate the entity node vector $\mathbf{m}_i \in \mathbb{R}^{d_1 + d_2}$.

After obtaining entity node vectors, the R-GCN is employed to make use of different edge types and propagate entity information to their neighbors. At l-th layer, given the entity node vector $\mathbf{m}_i^l \in \mathbb{R}^{d_1 + d_2}$ of entity node i, its different types of relations R_i and corresponding relation-specific neighbors $\mathbf{m}_j^l \in \mathbb{R}^{d_1 + d_2}$, $j \in \{N_{R_i}\}$, the update vector $\mathbf{u}_i^l$ can be obtained via

$$\mathbf{u}_i^l = \sum_{r \in R_i} \sum_{j \in N_{R_i}} \mathbf{W}_r^l \mathbf{m}_j^l + \mathbf{W}_0^l \mathbf{m}_i^l$$

where $\mathbf{W}_r^l$ stands a relation-specific weight matrix and $\mathbf{W}_0^l$ stands a general weight.

Similar to Entity-GCN [6], we concatenate update vector $\mathbf{u}_i^l$ and entity node vector $\mathbf{m}_i^l$ of current entity, and apply a gate on it by a linear transformation f_s:

$$\mathbf{g}_i^l = \sigma(f_s([\mathbf{u}_i^l, \mathbf{m}_i^l]))$$

Then it will be used for updating weights to obtain the entity node vector $\mathbf{e}_i^{l+1}$ for the same entity in the next layer:

$$\mathbf{m}_i^{l+1} = \mathbf{g}_i^l \odot \tanh(\mathbf{u}_i^l) + (1 - \mathbf{g}_i^l) \odot \mathbf{m}_i^l$$

We stack such layers for L hops in which all parameters are shared. The information of each entity will be propagated up to L-entity distance away, generating coreference-aware representation of entity nodes.

After the fusion of specific entity linking knowledge with R-GCN, we use the same entity-token mapping matrix $\mathbf{M}$ to make information flowing from entities back to tokens, and we get coreference-aware representation $\mathbf{n}_i \in \mathbb{R}^{2d_1 + 2d_2}$ for each token by concatenating previous knowledge-aware token embeddings $\mathbf{t}_i$ with associated entity node vectors $\mathbf{m}_i^L$ corresponding to the token.

Self-matching Layer. This layer takes the knowledge-aware and coreference-aware token representation $\mathbf{n}_i$ as input, and employs a self-attention mechanism to further enable interactions. Given two tokens p_i and p_j along with their representations $\mathbf{n}_i$ and $\mathbf{n}_j$, we use a trilinear function [25] to compute their similarity:

$$s_{ij} = \mathbf{w}^T[\mathbf{n}_i, \mathbf{n}_j, \mathbf{n}_i \odot \mathbf{n}_j],$$

where $\mathbf{w} \in \mathbb{R}^{6d_1 + 6d_2}$ is trainable weight parameters. And we obtain a similarity matrix $\mathbf{S}$ with s_{ij} being the ij-th entry. Then we apply a row-wise softmax operation on $\mathbf{S}$ to get the self-attention weight matrix $\mathbf{A}$, and the attended vector $\mathbf{v}_i$ for each token s_i is calculated as:

$$a_{ij} = \frac{\exp(s_{ij})}{\sum_j \exp(s_{ij})},$$

$$\mathbf{v}_i = \sum_j a_{ij}\mathbf{n}_j$$

where a_{ij} is the ij-th entry of $\mathbf{A}$. Finally, we build the output for each token by a concatenation $\mathbf{o}_i = [\mathbf{n}_i, \mathbf{v}_i, \mathbf{n}_i - \mathbf{v}_i, \mathbf{n}_i \odot \mathbf{v}_i] \in \mathbb{R}^{8d_1 + 8d_2}$

Output Layer. We simply use a linear output layer and a standard softmax operation, to predict answer boundaries. The probability of each token p_i being selected as the start or end position of the answer span is independently calculated as:

$$p_i^1 = \frac{\exp(\mathbf{w}_1^T\mathbf{o}_i)}{\sum_j \exp(\mathbf{w}_1^T\mathbf{o}_j)}, \quad p_i^2 = \frac{\exp(\mathbf{w}_2^T\mathbf{o}_i)}{\sum_j \exp(\mathbf{w}_2^T\mathbf{o}_j)}$$

where $\mathbf{w}_1, \mathbf{w}_2 \in \mathbb{R}^{8d_1 + 8d_2}$ are trainable parameters. The training loss is the negative log-likelihood of the true start and end position:

$$L = -\frac{1}{N}\sum_{j=1}^{N}(\log p_{y_j^1}^1 + \log p_{y_j^2}^2)$$

where N is the number of examples in the dataset, and y_j^1, y_j^2 are the true start and end positions of the j-th example, respectively. At inference time, the span (i, j) where $i \leq j$ with maximum $p_i^1 p_j^2$ is chosen as the predicted answer.

3 Experiments

3.1 Datasets

We evaluate our model on two datasets: SQuAD1.1 and ReCoRD. SQuAD1.1 [23] is a popular extractive machine reading comprehension dataset consisting of 100,000+ questions created by crowd workers on 536 Wikipedia articles. Each context is a paragraph from an article and the answer to each question is guaranteed to be a span in the context. ReCoRD [36] is a large-scale machine reading

Table 1. Statistics of datasets

Dataset	Train	Dev	Test
SQuAD1.1	87,599	10,570	9533
ReCoRD	100,730	10,000	10,000

comprehension dataset requiring commonsense reasoning. It is collected from CNN and Daily Mail news articles. In each example, the passage is formed by the first few paragraphs of a news article, with named entities recognized and marked. The question is a sentence from the rest of the article, with a missing entity specified as the golden answer.

Table 1 provides the statistics of ReCoRD and SQuAD1.1. On both datasets, the training and development (dev) sets are publicly available, but the test set is hidden. One has to submit the code to retrieve the final test score. Both datasets use Exact Match (EM) and (macro-averaged) F1 as the evaluation metrics.

3.2 Experimental Settings

Data Preprocessing. We use WordNet and NELL to incorporate common-sense and lexical common knowledge, and use pre-trained KB embeddings provided by [32]. For WordNet, KB embeddings are trained using the preprocessed data provided by [1] which contains 151,442 triples with 40,943 synsets and 18 relations. For NELL, KB embeddings are trained on a subset consisting of 180,107 entities and 258 concepts. Both KB embeddings are 100-dimension.

Then we retrieve relevant knowledge from the two KBs using the resource provided by [31], and construct entity graphs only for passages. For WordNet, text is tokenized by the BasicTokenizer of BERT, and synsets for each word are retrieved using NLTK [17], returned as candidate KB entities for the word. For NELL, entity mentions are given as answer candidates on ReCoRD, and recognized by Stanford CoreNLP [18] on SQuAD1.1, then associated entities or concepts are retrieved as candidate KB entities. For entity graph construction, the maximum number of entities in a graph is set to be 80.

Finally, we use the BERT FullTokenizer to tokenizer all passages and questions. The maximum question length is set to 64, questions longer than that are truncated. The maximum input length is set to 384, input sequences longer than that are segmented into chunks with a stride of 128. The maximum answer length at inference time is set to 30.

Training Details. We initialize parameters of the BERT encoding layer with pre-trained models officially released by Google. We empirically find that the cased, large model performs the best on both datasets. Throughout our experiments, we use this setting unless specified otherwise. The R-GCN layer number L is set as 3, and dropout with rate 0.2 was applied before R-GCN layer. Other trainable parameters are randomly initialized. We use the Adam optimizer [13] with an initial learning rate of 3e−5. During training, the KB embeddings are fixed, and the pre-trained BERT encoder is fine-tuned.

3.3   Results and Analysis

Main Results. We compare our CoSp with baseline models on ReCoRD and SQuAD1.1. The results are given in Table 2 and Table 3 respectively.

On ReCoRD (Table 2), we compare our model with the following baselines: (1) DocQA [3], SAN [16], and DocQA with ELMo [20] are official baselines, re-implemented by the dataset creators [36]; (2) GraphBert, DCReader+BERT and SKG-BERT are three MRC models on the leaderboard (unpublished); (3) [31] implements the knowledge-aware model KT-NET and an BERT baseline.

On SQuAD (Table 3), we compare our CoSp model with the following baselines: (1) QANet is a well performing MRC model proposed by [35]; (2) MARS and nlnet are two unpublished competitive models on the leaderboard; (3) [31] implements a BERT baseline and knowledge-aware model KT-NET.

Table 2. Results on ReCoRD

Model	Dev		Test	
	EM	F1	EM	F1
Human	91.28	91.64	91.31	91.69
DocQA	36.59	37.89	38.52	39.76
SAN	38.14	39.09	39.77	40.72
DocQA w/ELMo	44.12	45.39	45.44	46.65
GraphBert	–	–	60.80	62.99
DCReader+BERT	–	–	70.49	71.98
SKG-BERT	–	–	72.24	72.78
BERT	70.22	72.16	–	–
KT-NET	71.60	73.61	73.01	74.76
Ours	**72.58**	**74.93**	**74.13**	**75.97**

Table 3. Results on SQuAD1.1

Model	Dev		Test	
	EM	F1	EM	F1
Human	80.3	90.5	82.30	91.22
QANet	–	–	82.47	89.31
MARS	–	–	83.19	89.55
nlnet	–	–	83.47	90.13
BERT	84.41	91.24	–	–
KT-NET	85.15	91.70	85.94	92.43
Ours	**85.67**	**92.34**	**86.73**	**92.69**

Our CoSp model significantly outperforms BERT baseline on both ReCoRD and SQuAD1.1 datasets, with F1 score 75.97% on the ReCoRD test set and 92.69% on the SQuAD1.1 test set. It implies that leveraging commonsense and lexical common knowledge from KBs and specific entity linking knowledge in the passage is necessary. Besides, our CoSp also outperforms the competitive knowledge-aware KT-NET model, indicating that R-GCN based specific entity linking knowledge fusion plays an effective role.

Table 4. Ablation results on the ReCoRD dev set

Models	F1
w/o Common Knowledge	73.51
w/o Specific Knowledge	73.59
w/o R-GCN edge type	73.88
Full Model	74.93

Table 5. Results of R-GCN with Different Hops

R-GCN Hops	F1
2	74.81
3	74.93
4	74.78

Ablation Study. To evaluate the performance of different components in our model, We perform an ablation study on ReCoRD dev set. As shown in Table 4, once we remove the common knowledge fusion layer, it shows significant performance drop with more than 1.4%, proving the intuition that the commonsense and lexical common knowledge from KBs is necessary. Besides, removing R-GCN based specific knowledge fusion layer causes noticeable accuracy loss about 1.3%, it indicates that specific entity linking knowledge is equally important. Additionally, if we remove edge types, which makes R-GCN degraded to vanilla GCN, the accuracy drops about 1%, and it again illustrates the importance of entity coreference and co-occurrence.

Hops Analysis of R-GCN Layer. Moreover, we also evaluate the impacts of different R-GCN reasoning hops, the results are given in Table 5. We empirically find that R-GCN layer with 3 hops performs the best.

4   Related Work

The research of machine reading comprehension has attracted great interest with the creation of a variety of datasets, including SQuAD [23], TriviaQA [12], HotpotQA [34] etc. Early neural MRC models have similar architectures, focusing on attention-based interaction between the passage and the question, such as BiDAF [25], DocQA [3], SAN [16], and QANet [35]. DocQA [3] uses BiDAF-like bi-directional attention for interaction and shared-normalization objective across multiple paragraphs. QANet [35] uses CNN for local interaction and self-attention for global interaction, instead of recurrent networks. Recently, pre-trained LMs, like GPT [21], BERT [7], T5 [22], etc., have dominated the encoder design for MRC owing to their effective knowledge transfer, even in the zero-shot setting [29,30]. And we use BERT encoder in this paper.

Meanwhile, Several MRC datasets that require external knowledge have been created, such as ReCoRD [36], CommonsenseQA [26], ARC [4] and so on. ReCoRD is an extractive MRC dataset, and the latter two are multi-choice MRC datasets, with relatively smaller size than ReCoRD. In addition, some MRC models incorporating external knowledge have been proposed. TriAN [28] uses ConceptNet KB to determine the relationship between each document word and the word in the question and the optional answer, but it uses randomly initialized relation vectors as input feature, which only contain the local information in a given document. KT-NET [31] uses KG embedding pre-trained on the whole KB, which contains global KG information, and then uses the attention mechanism to select and integrate relevant knowledge. None of the above work takes into account specific knowledge of entity linking knowledge in a given passage, which is important for entity-centric questions.

5   Conclusion

We proposed CoSp, which incorporates common knowledge and specific entity linking knowledge for reading comprehension. Specifically, we first adaptively selects relevant KB embeddings from WordNet and NELL to enhance BERT with commonsense and lexical common knowledge. Then we construct an entity graph for the given passage based on entity coreference and co-occurrence, and leverage R-GCN for reasoning to enhance BERT's coreference ability. Finally, we use attention-based self-matching layer to obtain knowledge-aware and coreference-aware contextual word representation for answer prediction. Our model achieves significant improvements over BERT and outperforms competitive knowledge-aware models. In the future, instead of the simple and heuristic method for entity graph construction, we may incorporate new advances in building the entity graph to further enhance our model.

Acknowledgment. This work is partly supported by the Youth Innovation Promotion Association, Chinese Academy of Sciences (No. 2017213).

References

1. Bordes, A., Usunier, N., Garcia-Duran, A., Weston, J., Yakhnenko, O.: Translating embeddings for modeling multi-relational data. In: Advances in Neural Information Processing Systems (2013)
2. Carlson, A., Betteridge, J., Kisiel, B., Settles, B., Hruschka, E.R., Mitchell, T.M.: Toward an architecture for never-ending language learning. In: Twenty-Fourth AAAI Conference on Artificial Intelligence (2010)
3. Clark, C., Gardner, M.: Simple and effective multi-paragraph reading comprehension. arXiv preprint arXiv:1710.10723 (2017)
4. Clark, P., et al.: Think you have solved question answering? Try ARC, the AI2 reasoning challenge. arXiv preprint arXiv:1803.05457 (2018)
5. Dai, W., Qiu, L., Wu, A., Qiu, M.: Cloud infrastructure resource allocation for big data applications. IEEE Trans. Big Data 4(3), 313–324 (2016)
6. De Cao, N., Aziz, W., Titov, I.: Question answering by reasoning across documents with graph convolutional networks. arXiv preprint arXiv:1808.09920 (2018)
7. Devlin, J., Chang, M.W., Lee, K., Toutanova, K.: BERT: pre-training of deep bidirectional transformers for language understanding. arXiv preprint arXiv:1810.04805 (2018)

8. Feng, Y., Chen, X., Lin, B.Y., Wang, P., Yan, J., Ren, X.: Scalable multi-hop relational reasoning for knowledge-aware question answering. In: Proceedings of the 2020 Conference on Empirical Methods in Natural Language Processing (2020)
9. Gai, K., Qiu, M., Zhao, H., Sun, X.: Resource management in sustainable cyber-physical systems using heterogeneous cloud computing. IEEE Trans. Sustain. Comput. $3(2)$, 60–72 (2017)
10. Gao, J., Galley, M., Li, L., et al.: Neural approaches to conversational AI. Found. Trends® Inf. Retriev. $13(2$–$3)$ (2019)
11. Goodfellow, I., Bengio, Y., Courville, A.: Deep Learning. MIT Press, Cambridge (2016)
12. Joshi, M., Choi, E., Weld, D.S., Zettlemoyer, L.: Triviaqa: a large scale distantly supervised challenge dataset for reading comprehension. arXiv preprint arXiv:1705.03551 (2017)
13. Kingma, D.P., Ba, J.: Adam: a method for stochastic optimization. arXiv preprint arXiv:1412.6980 (2014)
14. Lehmann, J., et al.: Dbpedia-a large-scale, multilingual knowledge base extracted from wikipedia. Semant. Web $6(2)$, 167–195 (2015)
15. Liu, N.F., Gardner, M., Belinkov, Y., Peters, M., Smith, N.A.: Linguistic knowledge and transferability of contextual representations. arXiv preprint arXiv:1903.08855 (2019)
16. Liu, X., Shen, Y., Duh, K., Gao, J.: Stochastic answer networks for machine reading comprehension. arXiv preprint arXiv:1712.03556 (2017)
17. Loper, E., Bird, S.: NLTK: the natural language toolkit. In: Proceedings of the ACL-02 Workshop on Effective Tools and Methodologies for Teaching Natural Language Processing and Computational Linguistics (2002)
18. Manning, C.D., Surdeanu, M., Bauer, J., Finkel, J.R., Bethard, S., McClosky, D.: The Stanford CoreNLP natural language processing toolkit. In: Proceedings of 52nd Annual Meeting of the Association for Computational Linguistics (2014)
19. Miller, G.A.: WordNet: a lexical database for English. Commun. ACM $38(11)$, 39–41 (1995)
20. Peters, M.E., et al.: Deep contextualized word representations. arXiv preprint arXiv:1802.05365 (2018)
21. Radford, A., Narasimhan, K., Salimans, T., Sutskever, I.: Improving language understanding by generative pre-training (2018)
22. Raffel, C., et al.: Exploring the limits of transfer learning with a unified text-to-text transformer. J. Mach. Learn. Res. 21 (2020)
23. Rajpurkar, P., Zhang, J., Lopyrev, K., Liang, P.: Squad: 100,000+ questions for machine comprehension of text. arXiv preprint arXiv:1606.05250 (2016)
24. Schlichtkrull, M., Kipf, T.N., Bloem, P., van den Berg, R., Titov, I., Welling, M.: Modeling relational data with graph convolutional networks. In: Gangemi, A., et al. (eds.) ESWC 2018. LNCS, vol. 10843, pp. 593–607. Springer, Cham (2018). https://doi.org/10.1007/978-3-319-93417-4_38
25. Seo, M., Kembhavi, A., Farhadi, A., Hajishirzi, H.: Bidirectional attention flow for machine comprehension. arXiv preprint arXiv:1611.01603 (2016)
26. Talmor, A., Herzig, J., Lourie, N., Berant, J.: CommonsenseQA: a question answering challenge targeting commonsense knowledge. arXiv preprint arXiv:1811.00937 (2018)
27. Vaswani, A., et al.: Attention is all you need. In: Advances in Neural Information Processing Systems (2017)

28. Wang, L., Sun, M., Zhao, W., Shen, K., Liu, J.: Yuanfudao at SemEval-2018 task 11: three-way attention and relational knowledge for commonsense machine comprehension. arXiv preprint arXiv:1803.00191 (2018)
29. Xie, Z., Cao, W., Ming, Z.: A further study on biologically inspired feature enhancement in zero-shot learning. Int. J. Mach. Learn. Cybern. **12**(1), 257–269 (2021). https://doi.org/10.1007/s13042-020-01170-y
30. Xie, Z., Cao, W., Wang, X., Ming, Z., Zhang, J., Zhang, J.: A biologically inspired feature enhancement framework for zero-shot learning. In: 2020 7th IEEE International Conference on Cyber Security and Cloud Computing/2020 6th IEEE International Conference on Edge Computing and Scalable Cloud. IEEE (2020)
31. Yang, A., et al.: Enhancing pre-trained language representations with rich knowledge for machine reading comprehension. In: Proceedings of the 57th Annual Meeting of the Association for Computational Linguistics (2019)
32. Yang, B., Mitchell, T.: Leveraging knowledge bases in LSTMs for improving machine reading. In: Proceedings of the 55th Annual Meeting of the Association for Computational Linguistics (2017)
33. Yang, B., Yih, W.T., He, X., Gao, J., Deng, L.: Embedding entities and relations for learning and inference in knowledge bases. arXiv preprint arXiv:1412.6575 (2014)
34. Yang, Z., et al.: HotpotQA: a dataset for diverse, explainable multi-hop question answering. In: Proceedings of the 2018 Conference on Empirical Methods in Natural Language Processing (2018)
35. Yu, A.W., et al.: QANet: combining local convolution with global self-attention for reading comprehension. arXiv preprint arXiv:1804.09541 (2018)
36. Zhang, S., Liu, X., Liu, J., Gao, J., Duh, K., Van Durme, B.: Record: bridging the gap between human and machine commonsense reading comprehension. arXiv preprint arXiv:1810.12885 (2018)

Readmission Prediction with Knowledge Graph Attention and RNN-Based Ordinary Differential Equations

Su Pei[1], Ke Niu[1(✉)], Xueping Peng[2], and Jingni Zeng[1]

[1] Beijing Information Science and Technology University, Beijing, China
{peisu1128,niuke,zjn981223}@bistu.edu.cn
[2] Australian Artificial Intelligence Institute, Faculty of Engineering and Information
Technology, University of Technology Sydney, Ultimo, Australia
xueping.peng@uts.edu.au

Abstract. Predicting the readmission risk within 30 days on the Electronic Health Record (EHR) has been proven crucial for predictive analytics in healthcare domain. Deep-learning-based models are recently utilized to address this task since those models can relatively improve prediction performance and work as decision aids, which helps reduce unnecessary readmission and recurrence risk. However, existing prediction models, limited by fuzzy relevance of patient data, are unable to get higher prediction accuracy due to data noise generated by patients with different disease types. To solve this problem, we propose an end-to-end model called GROM, which integrates knowledge graph to alleviate the interference of data noise generated in the processing of irregularity dynamic clinical data with neural ordinary differential equation (ODE). The experimental results show that our model achieved the highest average precision and proved that the graph attention mechanism is suitable to improve performance of predicting the risk of readmission within 30 days.

Keywords: Deep learning · Knowledge graph · Electronic health record · ICU Readmission Prediction

1 Introduction

In recent years, with the continuous development and advancement of medical informatization technology, a large quantity of electronic data, such as Electronic Health Record (EHR) [17], have been generated. How to effectively utilize the valuable information hidden behind these data to benefit a large number of patients has raised the attentions from both researchers and practitioners [10–12]. One of the numerous analytical tasks is to predict the future readmission [18] based on a patient's historical EHR data. Readmission prediction can assist doctors to make clinical decisions, reduce the cost of readmission and the risk of

© Springer Nature Switzerland AG 2021
H. Qiu et al. (Eds.): KSEM 2021, LNAI 12817, pp. 559–570, 2021.
https://doi.org/10.1007/978-3-030-82153-1_46

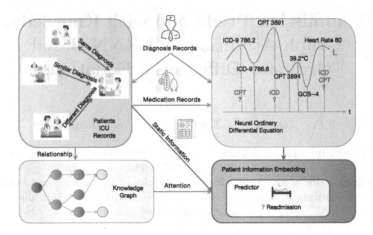

Fig. 1. How to use the relationship between patients' condition to predict the accuracy of readmission.

relapse after discharge. According to previous research [5], about 10% of the critically ill patients may re-enter ICU, which is a negative indicator to therapeutic effect. Therefore, building predictive models with ICU-related data to provide doctors with auxiliary diagnosis is an important issue of high application value. In this paper, we apply deep learning techniques to ICU readmission prediction.

With the development of deep learning technology, the research on the prediction of ICU readmission continue to develop. As shown on the upper right of Fig. 1, some researches utilized discrete data with irregular time intervals, such as physiological measurements and procedure codes. The absence of these data at certain time points made it impossible to directly use them to represent the complete patient treatment process. To solve this problems, some researchers represented timestamp codes by adding time-related information("embedding") to digital vectors, and modified the internal workings of recursive cell method with ordinary differential equations [4]. However, the model was still insufficient in predicting. When using electronic health records to predict, the interaction between static variables and the nonlinear correlation between static variables and predicted risks were not considered [1]. As shown on the left of Fig. 1, existing readmission researches lacked effective treatment of the relationship between patients with different disease types and could not obtain reliable representation of the relationship between patients. Given the correlation between nonlinear static variables, researchers often rely on additional information provided by experts in the hierarchical information of diagnostic codes to construct knowledge graphs to strengthen the connections between data. Current researches together show that when the data quantity is limited, graph attention model uses figure of the parent-child relationship to learn robust representation [3,9], connecting different patients' health information, enhancing the influence of each other, and finally improving the forecasting accuracy under the conditions of using similar disease information.

Considering that we need to use static data to interact with each other, graph attention can use ontological information related to data volumes to determine the specificity of medical concepts. When there were fewer medical concepts observed in the data, their ancestors would gain more weight and thus be able to understand the data more accurately and to provide general (coarse-grained) information about their children. It could be seen that this method was suitable for us to make up the existing defects. Therefore, as shown in Fig. 1, in order to solve the problems existing in previous algorithms, we proposed an end-to-end approach called GROM (**G**raph Attention and **R**NN-based Neural **O**rdinary Differential Equations **M**odel), which integrates RNN-based ODE model with graph-based attention mechanism to improve prediction performance. The proposed model constructs a knowledge graph through the diagnostic code scoring mechanism, strengthens the relationship between patients, and provides help for prediction and patient information to readjust similar diagnostic results.

In order to verify whether the effect of our model on ICU readmission meets our expectations, we used Medical Information Mart for Intensive Care III (MIMIC-III) data sets [6] in experiments. Through experimental comparison, our model can solve the lack of data correlation in the original research well, and achieve better prediction accuracy using the graph attention mechanism. Our main contributions are summarized as follows:

- We investigate the relationship among patient conditions to predict the accuracy of readmission according to patient's static and dynamic data.
- We propose GROM, an end-to-end, robust model to accurately predict patients' future readmission with mutual integration of medical knowledge graph and RNN-based ODE.
- We evaluate the proposed model on a real-world data set, while demonstrates that the GROM is superior to all the comparative methods.

The remainder of this paper is organized as follows. Details about our model are presented in Sect. 2. And next, in Sect. 3, we demonstrate the experimental results conducted on real-world dataset. Lastly, we conclude our work in Sect. 4.

2   Method

In our research, GROM, a model we proposed based on graph attention with RNN-based ODE, is used to predict the risk of readmission within 30 days in ICU. The RNN-based ODE is the basis model which uses multilayers of the network to process time series associated with patient information in prediction. And graph attention mechanism is utilized in this model to learn the knowledge graph of patient diagnostic code to improve the accuracy of model predictions. The overall architecture of the proposed model is shown in Fig. 2, the left part of the model is the graph attention module. The knowledge graph obtained from the input data according to the Clinical Classifications Software (CCS) classification standard [15] is embedded into the graph matrix, and then the graph attention matrix is embedded into the right RNN sequence. In this section, we will describe

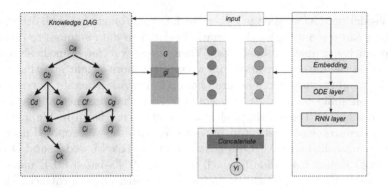

Fig. 2. The graph attention matrix G operates on all entities with diagnostic code and is fully joined to the ODE&RNN model.

each layer of the model in detail and Algorithm 1 describes the overall training procedure of the proposed GROM.

2.1   RNN-Based ODE Layer

There are a large volume of irregular sampling to obtain patient-related time information, including diagnostic and procedural codes, as well as medication and vital sign codes, which are mapped to the corresponding "embeddings". Diagnoses&procedures and medication&vital signs are processed separately, as they are measured on different time scales [13]. It is difficult for such information to be directly applied to the neural network, so we use the Shen Chang differential equation model proposed by Chen [2], which is very attractive to the processing of time series. In ODEs, the continuously defined dynamic information can be naturally incorporated into any data arriving at any given time [1]. So, we calculate the time-aware code embedded in the ODE dynamic simulation, and neural nodes are used to simulate the dynamic process of embedding.

To make better use of the data's timestamp information and be able to make predictions at any point in time, the neural ODE models the time series as a continuous trajectory of change. Each trajectory is determined by the local initial state S_{t_0} and the potential dynamic global set shared by all time series. Given observation t_0, t_1, ..., t_n and initial state S_{t_0}, an ODE solver produces S_{t_1}, ..., S_{t_n}, which describe the latent state at each observation. We define this generative model formally through a sampling procedure:

$$s_{t_0} \sim p(s_{t_0})$$
$$s_{t_1}, s_{t_2}, ..., s_{t_N} = \texttt{ODESlove}(s_{t_0}, f, \theta f, t_0, ..., t_N)$$
$$each x_{t_i} \sim p(x|s_{t_i}, \theta x) \tag{1}$$

Function f is a time-invariant function that takes the value s at the current time step and outputs the gradient: $\partial s(t)/\partial t = f(s(t), \theta f)$. This function is parametrized using a neural network. Because f is time-invariant, given any latent state s(t), the entire latent trajectory is uniquely defined. Extrapolating this latent trajectory lets us make predictions arbitrarily far forwards or backwards in time.

In GROM, we, using adjunction sensitivity to calculate gradients, treat the ODE approximately as a black box layer to process an irregularly sampled time series in the data. After the ODE layer processes the time information, the processed information is passed to the RNN layer for further processing. Bidirectional RNN is used to overcome the drawback that the prediction accuracy decreases with the increase of sequence length, and to deal with the gradient disappearance.

2.2   Graph Attention Layer

In GROM, we implement a layer based on graph attention mechanism. Graph attention layer is introduced into GROM as a layer, and the result is splicing with the result vector generated by the ODE layer to produce the output after further processing.

To make better use of patients' limited treatment information, the graph attention layer was introduced in this study. In robust representation of medical code, the embedded sequences of the relationship among the medical ontology encoding, hierarchical clinical constructs and medical concepts are usually of arbitrary length and need to be integrated into a fixed-size vector for further processing. Therefore, for the directed acyclic graph with ICD-9 [14] relation obtained by CCS classification, each medical concept node is assigned a basic embedding vector E_I, and the basic embedding is combined with its ancestor nodes through graph-based attention mechanism to obtain the final embedding vector M_I of the i-th medical code. Graph attention mechanisms, such as dot product attention, calculate the weighted average of embedded code, and higher weights are assigned to the most relevant code. Information can be integrated for further processing by using the final memory state of the recursive unit or by applying a graph attention mechanism to the output vector set:

$$g_i = \sum_{j \in A(i)} a_{ij} e_j, \quad a_{ij} \geq 0 \quad for \quad j \in A(i) \tag{2}$$

In this work, recursive cells are realized by bidirectional gated recursive unit. The information related to the graph is embedded into the vectors by applying the exponential decay dot product to the graph weight matrix. In the equation above, g_i is the final representation of code c_i, $A(i)$ is the index of code c_i and its ancestors, e_j is the basic embedding of code c_j, and when calculating g_i, a_{ij} is the weight of concern for embedding e_j.

$$a_{ij} = \frac{exp(f(e_i, e_j))}{\sum_{k \in A(i)} exp(f(e_i, e_k))} \tag{3}$$

Algorithm 1. The GROM model

Randomly initialize diagnoses and procedures, medications and vital signs, and related time information embedding matrix DP, CP;
repeat
    for visit v_t in X **do**
        Calculate the knowledge graph embedded matrix G (see Section 2.2);
        Fusion state information, DP, CP and G;
        Make prediction yˆt using Softmax function;
    end for
    Calculate the prediction loss L;
    Update parameters according to the gradient of L;
until convergence

The $f(e_i, e_j)$ is a scalar value representing the basic embedding compatibility of e_i and e_k, and calculation formula of $f(e_i, e_j)$ is as follows:

$$f(e_i, e_j) = u_a^T tanh(W_a \begin{bmatrix} e_i \\ e_j \end{bmatrix} + b_a) \tag{4}$$

In the equation above, W_a is the weight matrix splicing e_i and e_j, b is the bias vector, and u_a is the weight vector generating scalar values. All the obtained g_i are connected to obtain the embedded representation of the required diagnostic code, and then the embedding matrix G is sent to the graph attention layer of the model for processing. To help with subsequent interpretation without changing network capacity, the vector of fixed size generated by the graph attention mechanism is reduced to a fraction of two scalar values (one related to diagnosis&procedure and the other related to medication&vital signs). Use a fully connected layer with linear activation functions.

3   Experiment

In this section, we performed several comparison experiments on the large public medical electronic medical records MIMIC-III data set[1] to evaluate the performance in ICU readmission prediction of the proposed GROM. This section includes three parts: Data Description, Experiments Setup and Results and Discuss.

3.1   Data Description

Data Set. The algorithm was evaluated on publicly available MIMIC-III data set (no ethical approval is required). In our experiment, the supervised learning task consist of predicting whether the patient will be readmitted to the ICU within 30 days from discharge for a given ICU stay. The final data set comprised of 45,298 ICU stays for 33,150 patients, labelled as either positive (N = 5,495) or

---
[1] https://mimic.physionet.org/.

negative (N = 39,803) depending on whether a patient did or did not experience readmission within 30 days from discharge. To develop and evaluate algorithms, patients based on patient identification were randomly subdivided into training and validation (90%) and test sets 10%.

Data Pre-processing. The data of a patient can be represented as a set of significant static variables and timestamped codes. In our research, static variables included the patient's gender, age, ethnicity, insurance type, marital status, the previous location of the patient prior to arriving at the hospital, and whether the patient was admitted for elective surgery. The importance of static data had a similar characteristic proportion in both positive and negative samples. Data types of timestamped codes included international classification of diseases and related health problems (ICD-9) diagnose and procedure codes, prescribed medications, and patient vital signs. Overall, the models were trained using 23 static variables, 992 unique ICD-9 diagnostic codes, 298 unique ICD-9 program codes, 586 unique medication therapy codes, and 32 codes related to vital signs. The record for each patient contained up to 552 ICD-9 diagnose and procedure codes, as well as 392 medications and vital signs codes related to the current ICU hospitalization.

3.2   Experiment Setup

Baseline Models. To verify the predictive performance of the proposed GROM, we compared it with the following four methods:

GROM. Dynamics in the time of embeddings were modelled using graph attention layer and neural ODEs, embeddings were passed to RNN layers, the final memory states were used for further processing.

ODE+RNN+Attention. Dynamic time in the patient embedding information was modelled using the neural ODE, the modeled information was passed through the RNN layer, the final memory state of the RNN was used for further processing.

ODE+RNN. Dynamics in the time of embeddings were modelled using neural ODEs, embeddings were passed to RNN the layers, the final memory states were used for further processing.

SVM. Support Vector machines.

RNN. The embedding information of patient was directly through the RNN layer, the final memory state was used for further processing.

Implementation. To compare several neural network architecture's classification accuracy in training, the maximum likelihood estimation of network parameters were obtained using log-loss cost function in the training data. The RNN and graph attention layer were embedded by dropout of 0.5, and the Adam optimizer with random gradient descent was used (batch size was 128 and the learning rate was 0.001) [7]. Considering the imbalance between classes, the proportionally increased misclassification overhead was allocated to fewer classes [16]. The training ended after 80 epochs because with the additional training of epochs (based on the average accuracy of the validation data), the over-fitting of the training data became apparent.

Ablation Study Design. In order to obtain the results of data ablation, the model deals with the detailed structure of different types of data. For dynamic data of diagnosis, prescription information sequence and event information sequence, ordinary differential equation can effectively improve the accuracy of the model. In addition, for the patient static information represented by the ICD-9 diagnostic code, the graph attention mechanism is used to reduce adjacent noise. To validate the results of data ablation, our experiment use static data, dynamic data, and graph attention information constructed using diagnostic code, which in turn contain sequences of diagnostic information and program code, as well as sequences of prescription information and event information.

3.3   Results and Discussions

Table 1. Summary statistics for the different algorithms used to predict readmission within 30 days of discharge from the intensive care unit.

	Average precision	AUROC	F1	Sensitivity	Specificity
GROM	0.375 [0.366,0.384]	0.786 [0.366,0.384]	0.422 [0.416,0.427]	0.74 [0.734,0.746]	0.707 [0.7,0.713]
ODE + RNN + Attention	0.314 [0.306,0.321]	0.739 [0.736,0.741]	0.376 [0.371,0.381]	0.685 [0.666,0.704]	0.697 [0.681,0.711]
ODE + RNN	0.331 [0.323,0.339]	0.739 [0.737,0.742]	0.372 [0.367,0.377]	0.672 [0.659,0.686]	0.697 [0.683,0.711]
RNN	0.196 [0.19,0.203]	0.602 [0.599,0.605]	0.251 [0.248,0.254]	0.582 [0.561,0.603]	0.582 [0.561,0.603]
SVM	0.265 [0.256,0.274]	0.655 [0.651,0.658]	0.303 [0.297,0.309]	0.565 [0.552,0.577]	0.679 [0.668,0.691]

Overall Performance. Table 1 reports the average accuracy, AUROC, F_1-SCORE, sensitivity and specificity of deep learning architectures and support vector machines. GROM obtained the highest average accuracy of 0.375, the highest average AUROC of 0.786 and the highest average F1 score of 0.422. In general, the prediction accuracy of neural network was significantly higher

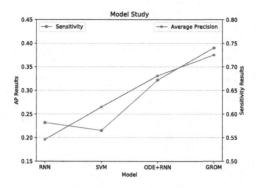

Fig. 3. We use SVM as a reference model to compare it with RNN, ODE+RNN and GROM, verifying that ODE module has processed dynamic data and graph attention mechanism reduces the RNN sensitivity of data noise.

than that of baseline models such as SVM. As shown in Fig. 3, it can be seen that the sensitivity of the RNN was higher than that of SVM, and the effect of its other indicators was significantly lower than that of SVM. This result showed that the sensitivity of RNN in missing detection result was better than that of SVM. However, fitting issues had more false positive examples, causing data noise interference to prediction and further resulting in that the highest average accuracy of RNN was significantly lower than that of SVM. And we could deal with dynamic data through the ODE module and utilize graph attention mechanism to reduce noise, obtaining a good prediction improving effect.

The results of the ODE&RNN and RNN showed that the deep learning model RNN performed better in processing sequential data, but it lacked the ability to process irregular interval information. It is seen that the combination of the ODE module and the RNN achieved higher precision than the RNN model alone. Particularly, we noted that the ODE module had a significant increase in the accuracy of readmission prediction, with an average accuracy increase of 13.5% and an accuracy increase of nearly 69%. This allows us to believe that the ODE module is suitable for processing dynamic data in the model, making full use of valuable information for patient readmission prediction. Therefore, it can be concluded that the introduction of ODE based on RNN can take advantage of the modeling capability of irregular interval to better play the role of sequential data processing.

Secondly, GROM was compared with the ODE&RNN, and we can see that GROM achieved better precision than ODE&RNN model. Particularly, we noted that the GROM had the highest accuracy in readmission prediction, which gave us confidence in using graph knowledge to understand patient relationships in the absence of sufficient data. In addition, it is clear that the graph attention mechanism provided valuable information with embedding of CCA information in the prediction of patient readmission. Specifically, GROM improved the prediction accuracy of readmission by 4.4%, indicating that the robust representation of the

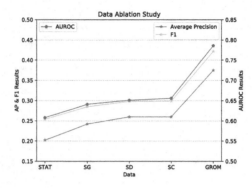

Fig. 4. We gradually add dynamic data and external prior information to static data to analyze the applicability of each part of the data in the model.

codes had learned significantly improved the prediction accuracy of readmission, and that the introduction of graphs contributed to data balance. It provided a more effective attention mechanism on existing information, and made better use of the value of information.

Finally, we compared GROM with ODE&RNN&Attention baseline model, the effect of adding an attention layer to the time series was poor, indicating that the use of knowledge graphs instead of the underlying attention mechanism was effective. The applicability of the time series attention structure in predicting reentry risk was poor, and the introduction of this layer in the model may lead to the performance decline of the model. The goal of this model was to extract knowledge from a given knowledge graph using attention mechanisms rather than adding attention mechanisms to past visits. Models with a graph attention layer (average precision range: 0.366–0.384) were slightly better than models based on a time attention layer (average precision range : 0.306–0.321). Instead of directly using the final memory state of RNN, a graph attention layer was applied to the output of RNN at each time step, increasing the association between records and improving prediction performance through data balance. This verifies the validity of the theory that the proposed graph attention mechanism can enhance the model prediction performance by enhancing the correlation between data.

Data Ablation Study. Figure 4 shows that based on static data, we used the attention layer building by the diagnostic codes associated by external CCS prior knowledge, with the prediction precision increased by 4%, and the usage of dynamic data set could effectively increase the precision by 5.8%. Moreover, combined with the static data and dynamic data, and introduced to an external priori knowledge, a complete GROM model could effectively enhance prediction precision, F1-score and AUROC, increasing the precision by about 86%, compared with a model merely using static data. Analysis of the experimental results showed static patient information alone was the worst predictive factor, because static information is only some of the static attributes of patients entering ICU and has a poor correlation with readmission. And patients' dynamic physiologic measurements had the greatest impact on the readmission prediction because these dynamic physiologic measurements are recorded in the patient's hospitalization, and changes in the patient's condition are closely related, which are valuable readmission prediction information. In addition, the patient's diagnostic information had a significant impact on the prediction task, as these diagnostic codes are given by the physician based on the patient's current condition and are highly relevant to the patient's readmission. Finally, the result shows that the introduction of external knowledge graph improved the prediction performance of the model, which makes us have reason to believe that external knowledge graph does contribute to the prediction of patient readmission.

Discussions. There are three major limitations in this study that could be addressed in future research. First, since all data in the MIMIC-III data set are shifted to protect patient confidentiality, it is not possible to ascertain which patients are admitted after 2001 and have at least 12 months of prior data, possibly leading to some incorrect values for the number of ICU admissions in the year preceding discharge. Second, information from clinical notes [8] is not included and the simplifying assumption is made that various diagnose and procedure-related codes are available immediately at the time of discharge. Third, the weak interpretability due to the continuous processing of patients' dynamic data by neural ODEs is difficult to analyze the influence of patient characteristics on the prediction effect.

4   Conclusion

In this paper, we proposed a based graph attention ordinary differential equation recurrent neural network (GROM) to predict readmission in ICU. The model framework was comprised of a recurrent neural network used to be the basic prediction model, adding neural ODE to process the irregular interval sequence information. Besides, our model also introduced a graph attention mechanism for using external knowledge to learn robust and reasonable representations of patient diagnostic codes to reduce noise interference between data. As demonstrated by experiment results, GROM produced better representations, which was validated by being used in a large open source MIMIC-III data set, effectively improving the prediction performance of readmission in ICU.

Acknowledgment. This work was supported in part by the Beijing Information Science and Technology University Research Level Improvement Project under grant no. 2020KYNH214, Qin Xin Talents Cultivation Program under grant no. QXTCPC202112, and Beijing Educational Science Planning Project of China under grant no. CHCA2020102.

References

1. Barbieri, S., Kemp, J., Perez-Concha, O., Kotwal, S., Jorm, L.: Benchmarking deep learning architectures for predicting readmission to the ICU and describing patients-at-risk. Sci. Rep. **10**(1), 1–10 (2020)
2. Chen, R., Rubanova, Y., Bettencourt, J., Duvenaud, D.: Neural ordinary differential equations (2018)
3. Choi, E., Bahadori, M.T., Song, L., Stewart, W.F., Sun, J.: GRAM: graph-based attention model for healthcare representation learning. In: the 23rd ACM SIGKDD International Conference (2016)
4. Dupont, E., Doucet, A., Teh, Y.W.: Augmented neural odes (2019)
5. Garland, A., Olafson, K., Ramsey, C.D., Yogendran, M., Fransoo, R.: Epidemiology of critically ill patients in intensive care units: a population-based observational study. Crit. Care (London, England) **17**(5), R212 (2013)
6. Johnson, A., et al.: MIMIC-III, a freely accessible critical care database. Sci. Data **3**, 1–9 (2016)
7. Kingma, D., Ba, J.: Adam: a method for stochastic optimization. Comput. Sci. (2014)
8. Liu, J., Zhang, Z., Razavian, N.: Deep ehr: chronic disease prediction using medical notes (2018)
9. Ma, F., You, Q., Xiao, H., Chitta, R., Jing, G.: Kame: knowledge-based attention model for diagnosis prediction in healthcare. In: the 27th ACM International Conference (2018)
10. Peng, X., Long, G., Pan, S., Jiang, J., Niu, Z.: Attentive dual embedding for understanding medical concepts in electronic health records. In: 2019 International Joint Conference on Neural Networks (IJCNN), pp. 1–8. IEEE (2019)
11. Peng, X., Long, G., Shen, T., Wang, S., Jiang, J.: Self-attention enhanced patient journey understanding in healthcare system. arXiv preprint arXiv:2006.10516 (2020)
12. Peng, X., Long, G., Shen, T., Wang, S., Jiang, J., Blumenstein, M.: Temporal self-attention network for medical concept embedding. In: 2019 IEEE International Conference on Data Mining (ICDM), pp. 498–507. IEEE (2019)
13. Rajkomar, A., et al.: Scalable and accurate deep learning for electronic health records. NPJ Digit. Med. **1**(1), 18 (2018)
14. Slee, V.N.: The international classification of diseases: ninth revision (ICD-9). Ann. Int. Med. **88**(3), 424–426 (1978)
15. Stearns, M.Q., Price, C., Spackman, K.A., Wang, A.Y.: Snomed clinical terms: overview of the development process and project status. In: Proceedings/AMIA ... Annual Symposium. AMIA Symposium, p. 662 (2001)
16. Weiss, G.M., Mccarthy, K., Zabar, B.: Cost-sensitive learning vs. sampling: which is best for handling unbalanced classes with unequal error costs? In: International Conference on Data Mining (2007)
17. Xiao, C., Edward, C., Sun, J.: Opportunities and challenges in developing deep learning models using electronic health records data: a systematic review. J. Am. Med. Inform. Assoc. **25**(10), 10 (2018)
18. Xue, Y., Klabjan, D., Luo, Y.: Predicting ICU readmission using grouped physiological and medication trends. Artif. Intell. Med. **95**(APR), 27–37 (2019)

Detecting SDCs in GPGPUs Through an Efficient Instruction Duplication Mechanism

Xiaohui Wei, Nan Jiang, Xiaonan Wang, and Hengshan Yue[(✉)]

College of Computer Science and Technology, Jilin University, Changchun, China
weixh@jlu.edu.cn, {nanjiang19,xnwang19,yuehs18}@mails.jlu.edu.cn

Abstract. As General-Purpose Graphics Processing Units (GPGPUs) are widely used in High-Performance Computing (HPC) applications, the vulnerability of GPGPUs to soft errors becomes a critical concern. In this paper, we propose an efficient instruction duplication mechanism that merely duplicates SDC vulnerable instructions for reliability overhead saving. We first observe that the SDC proneness of individual instruction is related to its instruction type, fault propagation, and whether it affects shared memory. Then, leveraging these observed factors, we utilize machine learning to intelligently identify all the SDC vulnerable instructions of GPU applications and efficiently protect them. Experimental results show that our method achieves a 90.45% SDC coverage only duplicating 37.8% of static instructions, which achieves a significant improvement in terms of performance and SDC detection capability compared to the state-of-the-art duplication technique in GPUs.

Keywords: GPGPUs · Silent Data Corruptions (SDCs) · Instruction duplication · Soft error · Machine learning · Parallel computing

1 Introduction

Graphics Processing Units (GPUs) are emerging as accelerators for High Performance Computing (HPC) applications because of their high concurrency and improved programmability [1]. With the development of the manufacturing process, the highly integrated GPU platform is more susceptible to the collision of high-energy particles, causing transient bit-flipping in logic units, also called soft errors. Unlike graphic applications that naturally exhibit error tolerance, General-Purpose GPUs (GPGPUs) have strict requirements on result correctness [2]. As a result, soft errors have gradually become the bottleneck of improving the reliability of GPGPUs. Soft errors may cause Silent Data Corruptions

This work is supported by the National Natural Science Foundation of China (NSFC) (Grants No. 61772228, No. U19A2061), National key research and development program of China under Grants No. 2017YFC1502306 and Interdisciplinary Research Funding Program for Doctoral Students of Jilin University under Grants No. 101832020DJX063, No. 101832020DJX007.

© Springer Nature Switzerland AG 2021
H. Qiu et al. (Eds.): KSEM 2021, LNAI 12817, pp. 571–584, 2021.
https://doi.org/10.1007/978-3-030-82153-1_47

(SDCs) in GPGPUs, which is the most critical error type as there is no indication that the program outputs are corrupted. Therefore, to ensure the reliability of GPGPU programs, in this work, we focus on proposing an efficient strategy to combat SDCs.

Exhaustive instruction duplication is an intuitive method to detect SDCs [3]. By copying the specified instruction segment and comparing the results, a programmer can detect SDCs. However, performing instruction duplication on GPUs is facing tough challenges. First, additional registers should be allocated to threads for duplication, which will significantly limit the concurrency of threads and thus increase the runtime of GPGPU applications. Beyond that, error verification and notification will increase the number of instructions, which will further incur the performance overhead of the program [4,5].

To address the above challenges, in this paper, we propose an efficient instruction duplication mechanism that merely duplicates SDC vulnerable instructions for reliability overhead saving. To this end, the first essential task is to build a model that can accurately pinpoint the SDC vulnerable instructions in the program. We propose some heuristic factors to profile individual instruction's SDC proneness. First, we observe that the instruction type reveals the SDC proneness of the instruction to some extent. Second, we find that some instructions can mask or aggravate the error during its propagation, thus decreasing the instruction's SDC proneness. Finally, we observe that instructions that access shared memory exhibit a high SDC proneness.

Based on these observations and the development of machine learning [6,7], we build a machine learning classifier to intelligently identify all the SDC vulnerable instructions in the program while introducing a low fault injection overhead. We extract the instruction type, fault propagation, and shared memory relevant features as the training set of the classifier. Based on our machine learning-based SDC vulnerable instructions identification model, we put forward an efficient instruction duplication mechanism that builds duplication paths for the selected SDC proneness instructions and inserts a verification instruction at the end of each path. Hence, while reducing the number of duplicated instructions, we also reduce the overhead of verification instructions.

In summary, our main contributions in this article are as follows:

- First, we observe that instruction type, fault propagation, and shared memory relevant features can help us figure out the SDC proneness of individual instructions.
- Based on our observations, we propose a machine learning-based SDC vulnerable instructions identification model.
- Lastly, we propose an efficient instruction duplication mechanism that merely duplicates SDC vulnerable instructions for reliability overhead saving.

2   Background

2.1   GPU Architecture and Programming Model

We describe the NVIDIA GPU in this section as our method is implemented on it. However, the method proposed in this article can be scaled to other GPU architectures.

Streaming Multiprocessors (SMs) are the basic units of NVIDIA GPU. The multiprocessor schedules and executes threads in groups called warps where threads execute in SIMT (single-instruction, multiple-threads) fashion. Resources such as shared memory and register file are provided to threads by an SM. The improved programmability of GPU allows users to write parallel programs. After profiling the parallel programs using a front-end compiler, we get the immediate code PTX (Parallel Thread Execution). PTX will continually be profiled into machine codes that run on the device. We perform our feature analysis and instruction duplication at PTX level in this article avoiding rescheduling instructions and register allocation [4].

2.2   Fault Model

Many architectural methods are used to improve the performance of cache, register files, and DRAM. For example, Qiu et al. proposed a novel pre-cache schema for high performance Android system in 2016 [8] and low-power low-latency data allocation approach for hybrid scratch-pad memory in 2014 [9]. In addition, architectural methods such as ECC are used to protect memory space from transient hardware faults [10]. In this work, we consider soft errors occurring in the functional units (i.e., the ALUs, SFUs, etc.) during the pipeline stage. We only focus on single-bit flip errors since they are the most common errors among all the error types [11]. Besides, the multi-bits flip errors have the similar behavior on programs with the single-bit flip errors [12,13]. As previous work [13] did, we assume that at most one transient fault occurs in each program execution.

We perform fault injection campaign to simulate the soft errors occurring during the program execution. According to the behavior of the corrupted program, we divide the outcomes of fault injections into three categories: (1) Masked, which means that there is no difference between the corrupted outcome and the correct output. (2) SDCs, which means that the program executes with no exception but the corrupted output deviates from the correct output. (3) DUEs, which means that system errors lead to obvious symptoms such as crashes or hangs of a program.

3   Key Observations

To design efficient instruction duplication technology, we merely protect the SDC vulnerable instructions selectively. However, to accurately obtain the SDC proneness of each instruction, a tremendous number of fault injections is required

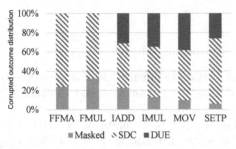

(a) Outcome of different instruction types.   (b) An example of loop control.

Fig. 1. The corrupted outcome distribution of different instruction types and an example of loop control in 2 mm benchmark.

[14], which can be highly time-consuming. In this section, we propose some heuristic observations from various perspectives that help us figure out the SDC proneness of individual instructions.

3.1   Observation on Instruction Type

In this section, we analyze the SDC proneness of different instruction types in GPGPUs. To this end, we inject errors into the destination register of each type of instruction to simulate soft errors occurring. Figure 1a shows the corrupted outcome distribution of different instruction types.

First, we observe FFMA (Floating-point Fused Multiply-Add) and FMUL (Floating-point MULtiply) exhibit high SDC proneness. As shown in Fig. 1a, the SDC rate of FFMA and FMUL reaches 76.1% and 67.7%, respectively. FFMA and FMUL are commonly used numerical calculation. Thus, when in errors, they only silently corrupt the program outcome. Second, Fig. 1a reveals that SETP (compare two numeric values and return a predicate value) also shows a high SDC proneness. The reason behind this is that SETP is usually used for branch controlling in the program. Since these branches originally exist in the program, an incorrect branch selection will lead the program to deviate from the fault-free execution trace, resulting in an erroneous result silently.

By comparison, IADD (Integer ADD) and IMUL (Integer MULtiply) have lower SDC rates while showing higher DUE rates. This is because IADD and IMUL are frequently used for address calculation. Soft errors in the address calculation instructions may lead the program to access the non-existent address and cause the application to crash. In addition, we find that MOV (set the value of register variable) also exhibits a low SDC proneness. This is because they are usually used for loop controlling in GPGPU programs. For example, Fig. 1b shows a code example from 2 mm benchmark. The main body of the loop is basic block 2 (BB2) and the loop control instructions are highlighted (*line 2, line 4*). MOV (*line 2*) is used for initial value assignment and IADD (*line 4*) summarizes loop variables. Hence, a bit-flip in MOV and IADD can change the loop times, which may incur excessive execution, manifesting as program hangs.

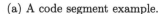

```
1   mad.lo.s32    %r3 , %r2 , 512 , %r1;

2   shl.b32       %r4 , %r3 , 8;

      ......

3   cvt.s64.s32   %rd1 , %r4;

4   add.s64       %rd3, %rd2, %rd1;

      ......

5   ld.global.f32 %f1, [%rd3+4];
```

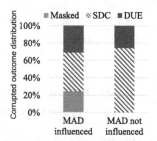

(a) A code segment example.   (b) Comparison of two instructions.

Fig. 2. (a) Shows a code segment in *bicg* which demonstrates how I_{mask} and I_{due} affect the fault propagation and (b) shows the corrupted outcome distribution of two types of MAD.

Observation-1: The type of instructions is effective in representing the SDC proneness of individual instructions.

3.2 Observation on Fault Propagation

Soft errors that occur in the target instruction will propagate to other instructions along the program dependency chain. In this section, we analyze the correlation between instruction's SDC proneness and fault propagation.

We extract dependency information of instruction I by building its static slice [15]. A slice of a specific instruction I is the set of instructions that I influenced. We call this instruction set the Instruction Dependency Set (IDS) of I. We observe there are two kinds of instructions in the IDS which can decrease the SDC proneness of the target instruction: 1) I_{mask}: Instructions that can inherently mask errors. 2) I_{due}: Instructions that are easy to trigger a crash when an error is propagated to it.

I_{mask} includes logical and shift operation instructions such as SHL (shift bits left, zero-fill on right), AND, OR, etc. and I_{due} mainly consists of address calculation instruction. As an example, Fig. 2a shows a code example from *bicg* benchmark to explain how these instructions influence the SDC proneness of the target instruction. We assume that a soft error occurring during the execution of instruction MAD (multiply two values and add a third value) (*line 1*), the error may propagate to other instructions (marked in blue in the figure). Because SHL in *line 2* shifts the content of *%r3* left for 8 bits, errors occurring in these shifted bits are masked. If the error is not masked, the error will propagate to address calculation instruction in *line 4*, which may result in an address out-of-bound (*line 5*). Figure 2b further compares the outcome distribution difference of influenced MAD (by I_{mask} and I_{due}) and not influenced MAD in *bicg*. We observe that about 25% error cases become Masked in the former, while the latter shows a zero rate of Masked. In addition, the DUE rate of MAD influenced is higher than the other instruction.

```
1   _shared_ float s1[size][size];

2   s1[ty][tx] = g1[index]

    ......

3   if():

4   {s1[ty][tx] = F(s1[S][tx] , s1[N][tx] ,
                    s1[ty][E] , s1[ty][W]);}
```

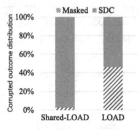

(a) An example using shared memory.   (b) Comparison of two instructions.

Fig. 3. (a) Shows a simplified example of using shared memory in `Hotspot` benchmark and (b) shows the SDC rate of share-LOAD and LOAD.

Observation-2: The existence of I_{mask} and I_{due} in the propagation chain will lower the SDC proneness of an instruction.

3.3   Observation on Shared Memory

GPGPU programs spawn thousands of parallel threads. To enable multiple threads to communicate, GPGPU equips a kind of on-chip memory of GPU, shared by all scalar processor cores (i.e., threads within a block). We find that shared memory-relevant instructions exhibit high SDC proneness since all threads in a block have the permission to write to the shared memory, which provides an extra chance for error propagation among threads.

For example, Fig. 3a shows a code segment of `hotspot`, which is a widely used tool for processor temperature estimation. Given the conductivity of heat, `hotspot` calculates the temperature of a spot based on its neighbor spots. As can be seen in Fig. 3a, shared array *s1* is initialized by global array *g1*. The value of $s1[ty][tx]$ (the temperature of the spot) is calculated by the nearest areas which are calculated by other threads (*line4*). Hence, errors occurring in shared memory will not only propagate within a thread but also among threads. We compare the SDC proneness of shared-LOAD (load data from shared memory) and LOAD (load data from thread private memory) in *hotspot*. As shown in Fig. 3b, shared-LOAD reaches an SDC proneness of over 95%, while the SDC rate of the LOAD is much lower (53.8%).

Observation-3: Shared memories allow errors to spread widely, which results in a high SDC proneness.

4   Implementation

In the previous chapter, we conduct a detailed analysis of the features that determine the SDC proneness of an instruction. In this chapter, we first leverage these features to intelligently pinpoint the SDC vulnerable instructions using machine learning. Then we propose a duplication strategy to efficiently duplicate all the SDC vulnerable instructions.

Table 1. Features collected for individual instruction.

	Type	Description		Type	Description
Instruction	INT	Instruction type	Propagation	INT	Number of instructions in the IDS
	BOOL	Is floating-point instruction		INT	Number of I_{mask} in the IDS
	BOOL	Is integer instruction		INT	Number of I_{due} in the IDS
	BOOL	Is value calculation instruction	Shared memory	BOOL	Is shared-load instruction
	BOOL	Is address instruction		BOOL	Is shared-store instruction
	BOOL	Is branch control instruction		INT	Number of shared-load in the IDS
	BOOL	Is loop control instruction		INT	Number of shared-store in the IDS

4.1 SDC Vulnerable Instruction Identification

Based on our observations, we consider features from the perspective of instruction type, error propagation, and shared-memory respectively as shown in Table 1. The first category includes the inherent properties of an instruction. The second category covers the propagation features. The last category includes features related to shared memory.

There are two types of machine learning models, classification and regression. Our problem is a classification problem because we make a judgement on the individual instruction whether it is an SDC vulnerable instruction or not. Fault Injection (FI) campaign are performed to provide a data set for the machine learning classifier. For individual instruction, we extract its feature vector composed of all the features shown in Table 1. Then we label the instruction as SDC vulnerable instruction (*Class 1*) or SDC non-vulnerable instruction (*Class 2*) according to the fault injection result. To efficiently pinpoint all the SDC vulnerable instructions in the program, we randomly inject faults into part of the instructions to train the classifier to classify new instructions.

4.2 Instruction Duplication

The basic idea of instruction duplication is to duplicate instructions and insert comparison and notification instructions at a certain place, often at the end of the basic block or before a store instruction. We decide where to apply duplication according to the machine learning results.

Our duplication method follows three steps. First, we refer to a basic block as the atomic unit to apply duplication. Second, we build at least one duplication path in a basic block. As shown in Fig. 4b, the selected instructions are not in the same slice, so we build two duplication paths to contain all the selected instructions due to their slices (e.g., instruction 2 and 3 are in the slice of instruction 1, so they are in a duplication path). A duplication path is defined as a sequence - $\{i_1, i_2, i_3,..., i_N\}$. The result of each instruction i_i is used by at least one subsequent instruction, except for i_N (the end of the path). Third, we perform duplication on each path as Fig. 4a demonstrates. We duplicate the operand register of each original instruction. At the end of each duplication path, there is a comparison instruction to verify whether an error has occurred. The results of the comparison instructions will accumulate to a signature register, which will

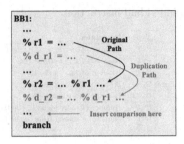
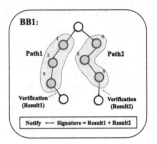

(a) A duplication path.   (b) Duplication paths in a basic block.

Fig. 4. Duplication methodology.

be used by a notification instruction at the end of the basic block as shown in Fig. 4b. Note that, for instructions that have no dependencies with other instructions, we also treat it as a path and add a comparison instruction right behind the duplicate instruction.

5   Experiment Methodology

5.1   Fault Injection

We choose 10 benchmarks from `Polybench` [16] and `Ronidia` [17] to evaluate our method. These benchmarks cover various domains such as linear algebra, data mining, deep learning, and physics simulation, and are widely used for previous GPGPU application resiliency and protection researches [4,18].

To accurately simulate soft errors in the execution units in GPGPUs, as previous works did [11,13], we inject single-bit flips into the destination register of a randomly selected instruction (one fault during one application runtime). We randomly perform 2500 fault injection trials for each benchmark to prepare the training set as prior work did [19]. Experimental results show that it is sufficient for to train the classifier.

5.2   Machine Learning

When choosing a machine learning model, we concern with the following two requirements. First, the model should manifest good adaptability on small-scale samples. The number of fault injection is limited because of the resource- and time-overhead. Second, an eligible classifier should not be sensitive to the data structure. Our problem space has a classification imbalance because SDC vulnerable instructions account for a small portion in some benchmarks. Considering the above challenges, we utilize Support Vector Machines (SVMs) to train the classifier because SVMs perform well in processing small-scale samples and imbalanced data in previous work [19].

Table 2. Prediction accuracy

Benchmark	2 mm	bicg	convolution	correlation	fdtd2d	gesummv	hotspot	syr2k	gaussian	mvt	AVG
Recall	92.86	92.71	92.57	94.44	96.30	92.31	93.75	94.12	95.13	97.62	94.18
Precision	93.57	91.67	97.61	95.24	96.47	95.36	97.73	94.52	95.26	91.67	94.93
F1-score	92.82	91.78	93.45	94.54	96.20	93.81	95.50	93.63	95.19	94.24	94.12

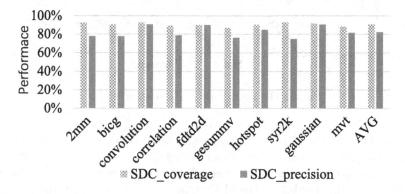

Fig. 5. The SDC_coverage and SDC_precision of our method.

6 Evaluation

In this section, we present the evaluation results for our method. We first evaluate the accuracy of the classifier. Then we evaluate the SDC detection capability and the duplication overhead of our method. Finally, we compare our method with the state-of-the-art duplication method on GPUs.

6.1 Prediction Accuracy

We use the metrics, *Recall, Precision,* and *F1-score* to quantify the performance of our classifier. *Recall* reveals the ratio of identified SDC vulnerable instructions to the ground truth. *Precision* defines the percentage of correct predictions in all predictions. *F1-score* is a harmonic average of *Precision* and *Recall* for the purpose of balancing *Recall* and *Precision*. Table 2 shows that we achieve good accuracy in predicting SDC vulnerable instructions with the *F1-score* of 94.12% on average.

6.2 SDC Detection Capability

In this section, we evaluate the SDC detection capability of our method from the aspect of the SDC coverage and SDC precision. SDC coverage reveals the ratio of SDC detected to the ground truth. Similar to the definition of *Precision* in Sect. 6.1, SDC precision is the ratio of SDC detected to all detected cases (including Masked, SDC, and DUE detected). We first focus on the SDC coverage of our method. As shown in Fig. 5, our method shows good performance

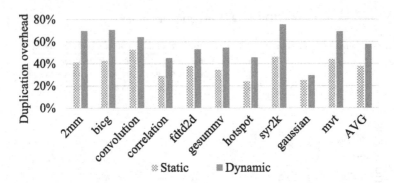

Fig. 6. The instruction duplication overhead.

on detecting SDCs on each benchmark and achieves an SDC coverage rate of 90.45% on average. However, we observe that there are remaining undetected SDCs. There are two main reasons behind this phenomenon. First, our classifier can not accurately predict all the SDC vulnerable instructions. Second, instructions with a low SDC proneness are unprotected by our method, but there is still a low probability for them to generate SDCs. In practice, the proportion of SDCs undetected by our method is partially acceptable in many circumstances because some scientific computations are resilient to inaccuracies during execution [11].

Except for SDC coverage, SDC precision is an important metric to evaluate the SDC detection capability of our method. In practice, a detected case means a warning notification to the system, and the system should take action to deal with it, such as checkpoint mechanism. Invalid warnings (Masked and DUE detected) will greatly increase the additional time and resource overhead of the system [4]. Excitingly, our method manifests a relatively high SDC precision of 82.2% on average. The high SDC coverage and SDC precision demonstrate that our method performs well in accurately detecting SDCs.

6.3   Instruction Duplication Overhead

We first measure the duplication rate of our method. As shown in Fig. 6, the range of duplicated static instructions varies from 24.3–52.8%, with an average coverage of 37.8%. We observe that *convolution* shows the highest duplication ratio of 52.8%. This is because there are many value calculation instructions in the program, and on the other hand, the program has a simple execution flow with no loops. Based on our observation, these two reasons lead to a high duplication ratio of *convolution*. On the contrary, *hotspot* shows the lowest duplication ratio of 24.3% which is attributed to 1) value calculation instructions account for a small proportion of total instructions, 2) complicated execution flow with multiple nested loops in the program, 3) many logical instructions in the program which can mask the error.

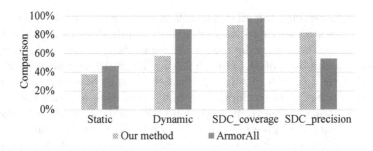

Fig. 7. A comparison of our method and ArmorAll.

Next, we evaluate the dynamic instruction overhead of our method. Figure 6 shows the increase in dynamic instructions to the baseline which do not perform any duplication. The increase of dynamic instructions includes the duplicated instruction, the verification, and notification instructions. On average, the increase of dynamic instructions attains 57.5%, 1.5x of the duplicated static instructions due to the additional verification and notification instructions.

6.4   Comparing with ArmorAll

We further compare our proposed method with ArmorAll [5], which selectively protects the address and values used by memory instructions. Figure 7 shows the comparison of instruction duplication overhead and SDC detection capability of our method and ArmorAll. The SDC coverage and SDC precision are normalized to the baseline that does not perform duplication the same as Sect. 6.2.

On average, our method shows lower SDC coverage than ArmorAll, however, we do a greater job in SDC precision. The increase of dynamic instructions achieves 85.5%, 1.85x of the duplicated static instructions in ArmorAll, which means our method is more efficient at transforming static duplicate rate into dynamic instruction overhead. Since in ArmorAll, there is an additional verification instruction that increases the overhead of dynamic instructions. As can be seen, our method shows fewer SDC coverage than ArmorAll, however, we do a greater job than ArmorAll in instruction overhead and SDC precision. The reason that ArmorAll has a lower SDC precision is that it overprotects the address-related instructions (always lead to DUEs). On considering instruction overhead and SDC detection capability, we achieve improvement to the state-of-the-art duplication technique in GPUs.

7   Related Work

With the requirement for performance of CPU applications [20] and cloud computing [21], data placement and duplication becomes a hot topic [22,23]. There are a couple of prior works that provide redundancy mechanisms to protect CPU applications [3,19,24]. SWIFT [3] proposed a compiler-based technique to detect faults leveraging the idled parallelism processors to deal with the redundancy overhead. Shoestring [24] proposed a compiler-based approach to selectively duplicate the error-vulnerable code segments that are easily to generate user-visible faults but not symptom behavior. IPAS [19] considered that only a subset of SDCs (i.e., SOCs) actually affect the output of applications and protection only needs to be performed on SOC-generating instructions. However, due to the complexity of error propagation within and among threads, the above mechanisms are not completely applicable for GPGPU applications.

A limited set of recent researches make effort on exploring duplication schemes on GPUs [4,5]. ArmorAll [5] proposed a selective, portable, and lightweight method to perform instruction duplication on GPUs. ArmorAll is composed of several compiler-based duplication schemes to intelligently select the eligible subset of instructions that needed protection. ArmorAll achieves an over 98% SDC detection rate on average. However, ArmorAll also detects over 90% Masked cases which is invalid detection and will greatly increase the additional overhead to the system in practice. SInRG [4] explored an efficient hardware-software combination methodology to perform instruction duplication on GPUs. Researchers extend the ISA to simplify the verification and notification process to reduce the additional instructions. Unlike our work, SInRG duplicates the same classes of instructions for each program but does not selectively duplicate the SDC vulnerable instruction which will cause unnecessary overhead.

8   Conclusion

In this paper, we proposed an efficient instruction duplication method that is able to protect GPU applications from SDCs in the output. The insight of our work is that we explored the inherent characteristics of instruction and the behavior of error propagation to profile the SDC proneness of individual instruction. Our method utilized machine learning to pinpoint all the SDC vulnerable instructions that we selected to protect. Our evaluations showed, our method can detect 90.45% SDCs by only duplicating 37.8% instructions on average.

References

1. Grauer-Gray, S., Killian, W., Searles, R., Cavazos, J.: Accelerating financial applications on the GPU. In: 6th Workshop on General Purpose Processor Using Graphics Processing Units, New York, NY, USA, pp. 127–136 (2013)
2. Gao, Y., Iqbal, S., Zhang, P., Qiu, M.: Performance and power analysis of high-density multi-GPGPU architectures: a preliminary case study. In: IEEE 17th International Conference on High Performance Computing and Communications (HPCC), pp. 29–35 (2015)
3. Reis, G.A., Chang, J., Vachharajani, N., Rangan, R., August, D.: Swift: software implemented fault tolerance. In: International Symposium on Code Generation and Optimization, pp. 243–254 (2005)

4. Mahmoud, A., Hari, S., Sullivan, M.B., Tsai, T., Keckler, S.W.: Optimizing software-directed instruction replication for GPU error detection. In: International Conference for High Performance Computing, Networking, Storage, and Analysis (2018)
5. Kalra, C., Previlon, F., Rubin, N., Kaeli, D.: ArmorAll: compiler-based resilience targeting GPU applications. ACM Trans. Archit. Code Optim. **17**(2), 1–24 (2020)
6. Gai, K., Qiu, M.: Optimal resource allocation using reinforcement learning for IoT content-centric services. Appl. Soft Comput. **70**, 12–21 (2018)
7. Gai, K., Qiu, M.: Reinforcement learning-based content-centric services in mobile sensing. IEEE Netw. **32**(4), 34–39 (2018)
8. Zhao, H., Chen, M., Qiu, M., Gai, K., Liu, M.: A novel pre-cache schema for high performance android system. Future Gener. Comput. Syst. **56**, 766–772 (2016)
9. Qiu, M., Chen, Z., Liu, M.: Low-power low-latency data allocation for hybrid scratch-pad memory. IEEE Embed. Syst. Lett. **6**(4), 69–72 (2014)
10. Wei, X., Yue, H., Tan, J.: LAD-ECC: energy-efficient ECC mechanism for GPGPUs register file. In: Design Automation Test in Europe Conference Exhibition (DATE), pp. 1127–1132 (2020)
11. Wei, X., Yue, H., Gao, S., Li, L., Zhang, R., Tan, J.: G-SEAP: analyzing and characterizing soft-error aware approximation in GPGPUs. Future Gener. Comput. Syst. **109**, 262–274 (2020)
12. Sangchoolie, B., Pattabiraman, K., Karlsson, J.: One bit is not enough: an empirical study of the impact of single and multiple bit-flip errors. In: 47th IEEE/IFIP International Conference on Dependable Systems and Networks (DSN), pp. 97–108 (2017)
13. Hari, S., Tsai, T., Stephenson, M., Keckler, S.W., Emer, J.: Sassifi: an architecture-level fault injection tool for GPU application resilience evaluation. In: IEEE International Symposium on Performance Analysis of Systems and Software (ISPASS), pp. 249–258 (2017)
14. Anwer, A., Li, G., Pattabiraman, K., Sullivan, M., Tsai, T., Hari, S.: GPU-trident: efficient modeling of error propagation in GPU programs. In: SC'20: International Conference for High Performance Computing, Networking, Storage and Analysis, pp. 1–15 (2020)
15. Weiser, M.: Program slicing. IEEE Trans. Softw. Eng. **SE–10**(4), 352–357 (1984)
16. Pouchet, L.N.: Polybench: the polyhedral benchmark suite (2012). http://www.cs.ucla.edu/pouchet/software/polybench
17. Che, S., et al.: Rodinia: a benchmark suite for heterogeneous computing. In: IEEE International Symposium on Workload Characterization (IISWC), pp. 44–54 (2009)
18. Kalra, C., Previlon, F., Li, X., Rubin, N., Kaeli, D.: PRISM: predicting resilience of GPU applications using statistical methods. In: International Conference for High Performance Computing, Networking, Storage, and Analysis (2018)
19. Laguna, I., Schulz, M., Richards, D.F., Calhoun, J., Olson, L.: IPAS: intelligent protection against silent output corruption in scientific applications. In: International Symposium on Code Generation and Optimization, NY, USA, New York, pp. 227–238 (2016)
20. Niu, J., Liu, C., Gao, Y., Qiu, M.: Energy efficient task assignment with guaranteed probability satisfying timing constraints for embedded systems. IEEE Trans. Parallel Distrib. Syst. **25**(8), 2043–2052 (2013)
21. Qiu, M., Ming, Z., Wang, J., Yang, L.T., Xiang, Y.: Enabling cloud computing in emergency management systems. IEEE Cloud Comput. **1**(4), 60–67 (2014)

22. Guo, Y., Zhuge, Q., Hu, J., Yi, J., Qiu, M., Sha, E.H.M.: Data placement and duplication for embedded multicore systems with scratch pad memory. IEEE Trans. Comput.-Aided Design Integr. Circuits **32**, 809–817 (2013)
23. Dai, W., Qiu, L., Wu, A., Qiu, M.: Cloud infrastructure resource allocation for big data applications. IEEE Trans. Big Data **4**(3), 313–324 (2016)
24. Feng, S., Gupta, S., Ansari, A., Mahlke, S.: Shoestring: probabilistic soft error reliability on the cheap. SIGARCH Comput. Archit. News **38**(1), 385–396 (2010)

GAN-Enabled Code Embedding for Reentrant Vulnerabilities Detection

Hui Zhao[1], Peng Su[1], Yihang Wei[2], Keke Gai[3(✉)] [iD], and Meikang Qiu[4]

[1] School of Software, Henan University, Kaifeng 475000, China
zhh@henu.edu.cn
[2] School of Computer Science and Technology, Beijing Insititute of Technology,
Beijing 100081, China
3120201079@bit.edu.cn
[3] School of Cyberspace Science and Technology, Beijing Insititute of Technology,
Beijing 100081, China
gaikeke@bit.edu.cn
[4] Texas A&M University–Commerce, Commerce, TX 75428, USA
qiumeikang@ieee.org

Abstract. As one of the key components of blockchain, smart contract is playing a vital role in achieving auto-functions; however, reentrant attacks are threatening the implementation of smart contracts, which limits the adoption of blockchain systems in various scenarios. To address this issue, we propose a reentrant vulnerability detection model based on word embedding, similarity detection, and Generative Adversarial Networks (GAN). Additionally, we provide a new approach for dynamically preventing reentrant attacks. We also implement experiments to evaluate our model and results show our scheme achieves 92% detecting accuracy for reentrant attack detection.

Keywords: Blockchain · Smart contract · Reentrant attack · Vulnerability detection · Generative adversarial networks

1 Introduction

With the development of big data and cloud computing, security and privacy become a critical issue in our daily life [5]. The competition between attackers and defenders is an ever-lasting process [15]. In recent years, blockchain has emerging as a hot topic in researches and applications. Blockchain technology has many applications in modern information technologies and computing environments [7]. This technology utilizes key characteristics such as decentralization, distribution, and tamper resistance to harness the power of distributed computational resources [6]. A smart contract is a predefined logic segment which automatically execute, control and document relevant events in blockchain. Key functions of smart contacts ensure that transactions are authenticated, disputes are resolved, and malicious activities are detected and reduced [10]. Although

© Springer Nature Switzerland AG 2021
H. Qiu et al. (Eds.): KSEM 2021, LNAI 12817, pp. 585–597, 2021.
https://doi.org/10.1007/978-3-030-82153-1_48

the applications of smart contracts are extensive, there is no unified standard for the sequence to invoke functions in blockchain systems. The lack of implementation standards in smart contracts is often exploited as a vulnerability to penetrate blockchain systems.

Reentrant attack is one of the most destructive attacks in blockchain systems caused by contract vulnerabilities [3]. A reentrant attack occurs when the attacker drains funds from the target by recursively calling the target's `withdraw()` function. When the contract fails to update its state, a victim's balance, prior to sending funds, the attacker can continuously call the withdraw function to drain the contract's funds. A famous real-world reentrant attack is "TheDAO" attack which caused a loss of 60 million US dollars [3,4].

There are some methods for vulnerability detection, but these methods have some limitations. First, these methods only focus on whether there are certain types of vulnerabilities in the contract. There are no other extensions. Rodler et al. [16] only aimed at dynamic detection of reentrant vulnerabilities. There is no more detailed function extension for the detected vulnerabilities, such as locating vulnerabilities and locating attackers. Second, these methods require specific defect patterns or specification rules defined by experts. Hence, it is not feasible to defend attack when a new type of vulnerability occurs [21]. Permenev et al. [13] formalized the contract by setting rules. This method only detected contracts that meet the specific rules. Qiu et al. proposed a dynamic scalable blockchain based communication architecture for IoT [14] and a secure digital evidence framework using blockchain [17]. These approaches are only used for specific areas.

To break these bottlenecks, we propose a model to detect reentrant vulnerabilities based on code embedding, space vector comparison and GAN. Through semantic analysis and code embedding technology. By using FastText [2] tool we get the vector representation of the contract sentence and detect contract vulnerabilities by similarity comparison. In addition, we classify the types of vulnerability statements and pinpoint the actual location. Through vector similarity comparison, we collect all the vulnerability statements in the smart contract library and use the data set to train the discriminator in GAN. The model we proposed solves the shortcomings of traditional manual data collection and manual annotation.

We briefly describe the main contributions made by this work in the following: (i) This paper proposes a model for learning the characteristics of smart contracts and detecting reentrant vulnerabilities. The type and location of vulnerability statements are detected by embedding word vectors and comparing space vectors, which enhances the expansibility of the model. (ii) We propose a scheme to prevent reentrant attacks. We conclude the characteristics of the smart contract when it is attacked and develop an anti-attack model. Using this model, reentrant attacks can be detected by checking the correctness of critical function (such as `transfer()` and `withdraw()`) invocation. (iii) We collect all the vulnerability statements in the smart contract library and construct a data set and use the data set to train the discriminator in GAN through code embedding and similarity detection technology. Experimental results show that our discriminator has better performance compared with others trained by existing models.

The remainder of this paper is organized in the following order. Section 2 describes the design of the proposed model and our design for detecting reentrant attacks. In Sect. 3, we describe our proposed algorithm named as LLT, which Locates the actual Location and Type of vulnerability statement. LLT is shown in Algorithm 1. We analyze the results of the experiment in Sect. 4 and conclude the paper in Sect. 5.

2   Proposed Model

2.1   Overview

Our proposed model is shown in Fig. 1. Figure 1(a) shows the step of collecting vulnerability statements and building discriminator. The system relies on code embedding and space vector comparison for vulnerability detection to verify whether there is a statement with reentrant vulnerability threat in the smart contract and check the type and location of the vulnerability statement. Then it collects all the detected vulnerability statements and uses the vulnerability statement set as the training set of the discriminator in GAN. Through semantic analysis, the vulnerability statement is transformed into word sequence. The system uses the FastText [2] tool to train it into word vector and get the statement vector matrix by summation. Through the results of similarity detection,

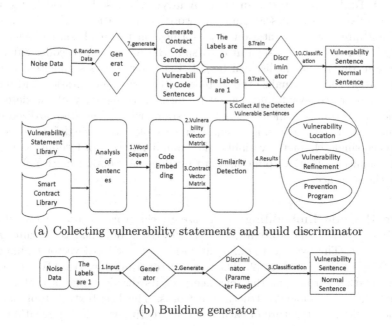

(a) Collecting vulnerability statements and build discriminator

(b) Building generator

Fig. 1. Proposed model

the system locates and classifies the vulnerabilities and gives the scheme to prevent the vulnerability. The system collects the detected vulnerability statements when detects the vulnerability of each smart contract. Then the system sets the label of each vulnerability statement to 1. After that, the collected set of vulnerability statements is input to the discriminator for training. In summary, this method solves the shortcomings of traditional manual data collection and manual marking.

Figure 1 (b) shows that the discriminator parameters are fixed, the system trains the generator with noise data. Under the constant confrontation between generator and discriminator, discriminator can well judge whether a sentence is a vulnerable sentence. We will explain the model design and the scheme of vulnerability prevention in the following.

2.2   Model Design

The design scheme of the model mainly consists of six phases. Text input and semantic analysis will be completed in phase I; phase II is responsible for code embedding; contract statement matrix and vulnerability statement matrix will be generated in phase III; phase IV is responsible for detailed detection; building of the discriminator will be completed in phase V; building of the generator will be completed in phase VI. The diagram of the model construction method is shown in Fig. 2. We will describe these phases respectively in the following.

Phase I Text Input and Semantic Analysis. Phase I is divided into three steps: regular expression segmentation, word segmentation and normalization. Regular expression segmentation is performed on the read source code, using the '\n' character as the separator to split the whole source code. After segmentation, the statement list can be got. Each sentence is segmented by using segmentation tool. Normalize the sentence after word segmentation and remove some semantic irrelevant information to ensure the accuracy of the detection. The normalization treatment refers to the standard [9]. The standardized information is as follows. For single character variables, the "single" word is used to replace single character variables. For numbers, the word "num" is used to replace numbers. Remove punctuation that does not contain much information about the sentence.

Phase II Code Embedding. In Phase II, the word vector is trained with FastText [2] tool. The statement vector matrix is obtained by summing the word vectors. The two most commonly used tools for word vector training are Word2Vec [12] and FastText [2]. The word vector trained by Word2Vec is helpful to predict the words near the sentence, but its disadvantage is that it can't capture the morphological structure of words. The FastText [2] tool captures the morphological structure of each word by treating it as an aggregation of its

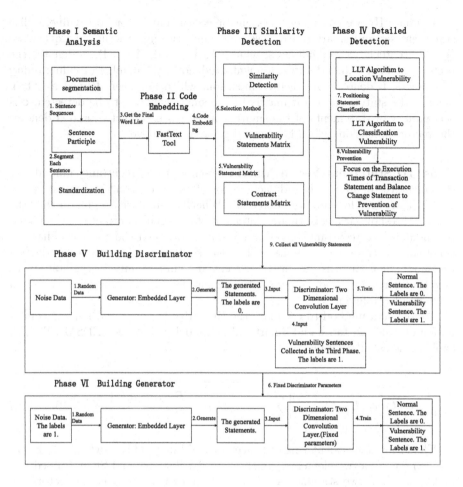

Fig. 2. The diagram of the model construction method.

children. The sub word can be regarded as the n-gram of the word, and the word vector trained by FastText [2] tool is actually the sum of all the n-gram vectors. The experimental results of literature [9] show that FastText [2] tool performs better than Word2Vec tool at the sentence level. Therefore, this paper uses FastText [2] tool for word vector training, and sets the vector dimension to 20, which is to ensure that the training speed is fast enough and reduce the occupation of memory space. The definition of sentence vector is as follows.

Definition 1. *Given a statement s, each word in the statement is w, the sentence vector of the statement is:*

$$S(vector) = \sum_{w \in s} w(vector). \tag{1}$$

In phase III, we construct a statement vector matrix for both vulnerability statement set and smart contract source code. Through the use of Eq. (1), we get two sentence vector matrices, which are **L** (**a b**), **T** (**c d**). **L** denotes the vector matrix of vulnerability statements, **a** denotes the number of vulnerability statements, **b** denotes the vector dimension, which has been defined as 20. **T** denotes the statement vector matrix of the smart contract to be detected, **c** is the number of statements of the smart contract to be detected, and **d** denotes the vector dimension, which has been defined as 20 above.

Phase III Statement Vector Matrix. Each vector of reentrant vulnerability statement vector matrix **L** and each vector of smart contract statement vector matrix **T** are used for similarity detection. When the similarity is greater than the defined threshold, it means that a statement of the smart contract to be detected is similar to the reentrant vulnerability statement, then the statement has the threat of reentrant vulnerability. When the similarity is less than the defined threshold, then there is no threat of reentrant vulnerability in the statement. Due to different methods of similarity calculation, the corresponding threshold value will be different.

We define a method to calculate the similarity in this work, namely combination of Euler Distance and SmartEmbed Model [8] method (EDSM). We will explain the calculation method.

$$distance(E1, E2) = \sqrt{\sum_{i=1}^{n}(e1_i - e2_i)^2} \times \frac{Euclidean(e1, e2)}{||e1|| + ||e2||} \times 10. \quad (2)$$

The formula for calculating distance of EDSM method is shown in (2). Equation (2) contains two elements, which are Euler distance and SmartEmbed formula [8]. Given two statements $E1$ and $E2$ and the corresponding vectors are $e1$ and $e2$. Euler distance makes the values of the corresponding positions of two vectors subtract and then square. SmartEmbed [8] is to find the euclidean value of two vectors first, and then get the sum of module length of two vectors and the $distance(E1, E2)$ is got by dividing the above two elements. Using this approach, the characteristics of the two elements can be got simultaneously.

$$Similarity(E1, E2) = 1 - distance(E1, E2). \quad (3)$$

Equation (3) is used to calculate the similarity according to the calculated vector distance using EDSM method.

Phase IV Detailed Detection. Phase IV is divided into three parts, namely location, vulnerability statement type classification and vulnerability prevention. We will describe our proposed Locating the actual Location of vulnerability statement and Type of vulnerability statement (LLT) algorithm in Sect. 3, which is shown in Algorithm 1.

We present a count-based reentrant vulnerability correction scheme for critical vulnerabilities. Developers can customize their own code according to the error correction scheme. The principle of count-based reentrant vulnerability correction scheme is to check whether the execution times of transaction statement and balance change statement are equal. When the transaction functions have been executed, the balance change function will be skipped and the transaction statement will be executed recursively where a reentrant attack occurs. As a result, the inconsistency of the execution times of the transaction statement and the balance change statement. When there is no reentrant attack, the execution times of transaction statement and balance change statement are consistent.

Phase V Building Discriminator. In this phase, we build a GAN. The generator is used to generate realistic sentences. The discriminator is used to judge whether a sentence is a vulnerability sentence. Through the confrontation between the two, the ability of discriminator is improved continuously. Referring to the literatures [19], we build an embedded layer as generator and two-dimensional convolution layer as discriminator [20]. We use 100×10 matrix as noise data. It means 100 sentences with 10 words in each sentence. For randomly generated noise sentences, when the number of words is more than 10, the redundant words are deleted. When the number of words is less than 10, 0 will be added by default. Through the generator, the noise data generates the sentences represented by vectors. The label of each sentence is 0. In the phase III, we collect all the vulnerable statements and convert them into vector form. We set the tag of all vulnerability statements to 1. The generated statements and vulnerability statements are used as input training discriminator.

Phase VI Building Generator. We build an embedded layer as a generator to generate realistic vulnerability statements. We use $100 * 10$ matrix as noise data. The matrix shows that there are 100 sentences with 10 words in each sentence. We set the label of each noise data to 1. Meanwhile, we set the parameters of the discriminator to be immutable. Then, we use noise data to train the generator.

Through vector similarity comparison, we can automatically collect vulnerability statements. Through the confrontation between generator and discriminator, the discriminator has strong discriminating ability.

3 Algorithm

In this section, we will describe our proposed Locating the actual Location of vulnerability statement and Type of vulnerability statement (LLT) algorithm, which is shown in Algorithm 1. This algorithm is used for detailed detection in phase IV in our model. In the third phase, we get the contract statement matrix. Each row of the matrix represents a statement of the contract. Therefore, the subscript of the matrix element can represent the actual line of the statement in the contract. According to the characteristics of vulnerability statements,

Algorithm 1. Locating the actual Location of vulnerability statement and Type of vulnerability statement algorithm (LLT)

Input: Reentrant vulnerability statement vector matrix: **L**; Smart contract statement vector matrix: **T**; Smart contract statement partition matrix: **S**; Vulnerability type characteristic matrix: **B**; Similarity comparison value: threshold
Output: A collection of vulnerable statement lines: Listline; A collection of vulnerability statement types: Listtype;

```
1:  function FIND(T,L,S,B,threshold)
2:      for t1, t2, ...in T do
3:          for l1, l2, ...in L do
4:              similar ← Similarity(t, l)
5:              if similar > threshold then
6:                  call Listline.add(t)
7:              end if
8:          end for
9:      end for
10:     Delete the duplicate number in Listline
11:     for a1, a2, ...in Listline do
12:         for s1, s2, ...in S[a] do
13:             if s in B[0] then
14:                 call Listtype.add("Serious threat")
15:                 return
16:             else if s in B[1] then
17:                 call Listtype.add("Mild threat")
18:                 return
19:             else
20:                 call Listtype.add("potential threat")
21:                 return
22:             end if
23:         end for
24:     end for
25:     return Listline, Listtype
26: end function
```

---

we divide vulnerability statements into severe vulnerability statements, mild vulnerability statements and potential vulnerability statements.

Complexity Analysis: Because each vulnerability statement has to calculate the similarity with all contract statements. The location of vulnerability statements is located by similarity results. Therefore, two loops are needed to represent the vulnerability statement matrix and the contract statement matrix respectively. Hence, the time complexity of the algorithm is $O(n^2)$.

Table 1. Experiment settings

Contract sources	70 Reentrant vulnerability smart contracts on *Etherscan* platform. Data collection method reference [1]
Divider	newline ('\n')
Word segmentation tool	Jieba
Training vector parameters	$n-gram = 3$ $minCount =1$ $wordNgrams = 1$ $lr = 0.05$ $dim = 20$ $loss =$ ns
Threshold	0.92

4 Experiment and the Results

4.1 Experiment Configuration

To evaluate the vulnerability detection ability of the model, we collected 70 solidity smart contracts on *Etherscan* platform. 20 smart contracts were taken out for observation. We extracted the statements related to the reentrant vulnerabilities. We extracted 32 statements and put in the vulnerability statement as TXT file. The remaining 50 smart contracts are used for attack detection.

We ran the evaluation in the following environment. Remix platform 0.7.5 with solidity compiler (v0.5.1) established a software configuration. The segmentation tool we used is stutter segmentation, which is developed in the Python. We also use Python (v3.7) to implement our model in the IDE of Pychar. The hardware platform was a Lenovo ideapad 300-15ISK notebook with Windows 10 operate system, a CPU with 2.3GHz, an i5 version Inter Core, and an 8GB of 2691MHz LPDDR3 memory.

The experiment settings are shown in Table 1. The contracts used in the experiment were collected from the *Etherscan* platform. In experiments, we used the detecting accuracy to evaluate the performance of our proposed methods, which is defined as: $Accuracy = \mathbf{c}/(\mathbf{c} + \mathbf{d}) \times 100\%$, where $\mathbf{c}$ is the number of vulnerability contracts are successfully detected, $\mathbf{d}$ is the number of vulnerability contracts are failed detected. The detecting accuracy is enough to evaluate the performance of the model since the statement will not be marked as a vulnerability statement when a normal statement is predicted as a vulnerability statement. This is because it does not meet the vulnerability statement characteristics and the wrong prediction will not affect our experiment.

In GAN, the discriminator constructs a Two-Dimensional Convolution layer (TDC). In order to measure the performance of the discriminator, we build One-Dimensional Convolution layer (ODC) and embedded layer (Embed) for comparison. In order to evaluate the performance of our proposed EDSM method, we compared the detecting accuracy of existing contract vulnerability detection methods with our method to evaluate the performance of our EDSM method. Selected existing methods included SmartEmbed [8] and Eth2Vec [1] detect vulnerabilities based on vector space. Oyente [11] and Securify [18] detect vulnerabilities based on symbolic execution. Mythril is a vulnerability security scanning tool.

4.2   Experiment Results

The experimental results are shown in Fig. 3. Figure 3(a) illustrated comparison between discriminators. The detecting accuracy of discriminator trained by our

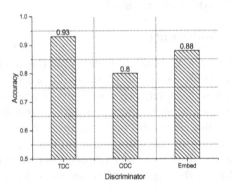

(a) Discriminator comparison

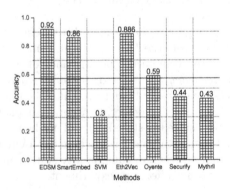

(b) Comparison of existing methods

Fig. 3. Experiment results of contract vulnerability detection using different methods.

model (TDC) reached 93% whereas detecting accuracy of discriminator ODC and Embed respectively reached 80% and 88%, which indicated that TDC has better performance compared with others trained by existing models.

Figure 3(b) depicted the result of the comparison with the other methods under the data set collected in this paper. The detecting accuracy of proposed EDSM method reached 92% detecting accuracy whereas the detection accuracy of the selected existing methods did not reach 90% in our experiment. The detection accuracy of SmartEmbed [8] method was the highest among the selected methods, reaching 88.2%. Most of selected existing methods had detection accuracy of around 40% to 50%. The results shown that the proposed method has high accuracy in detecting contract vulnerabilities and its performance is better than most existing methods.

We got a phenomenon that the attack detection model we proposed can effectively detect smart contracts with vulnerability. Hence, the proposed model had the ability to detect the whole function in the contract and return the result accurately. Additionally, the performance of our proposed methods was better than existing.

5   Conclusions

In this paper, we proposed a model to detect reentrant vulnerabilities based on code embedding and GAN. This model detected the vulnerability statements of smart contract using code embedding and space vector similarity comparison and classified the vulnerability statements. We also located the actual line of code for the vulnerable statement. In addition, we provided a method based on our proposed model to detect the vulnerability. We collected vulnerability statements detected by vector space comparison and used it as a data set to train the discriminator in GAN. This method effectively solved the shortcomings of traditional manual data collection and manual annotation. Experiments shown that the model and methods were feasible and effective for reentrant vulnerabilities attack detection. For future work, we will increase the number of types of vulnerabilities our model can detect and improve the detecting accuracy of our proposed model.

Acknowledgement. This work is partially supported by National Natural Science Foundation of China (Grant No. 61972034), Natural Science Foundation of Beijing Municipality (Grant No. 4202068), Natural Science Foundation of Shandong Province (Grant No. ZR2019ZD10, ZR2020ZD01).

References

1. Ashizawa, N., Yanai, N., Cruz, J., Okamura, S.: Eth2Vec: learning contract-wide code representations for vulnerability detection on ethereum smart contracts. In: the 3rd ACM International Symposium on Blockchain and Secure Critical Infrastructure, Hong Kong, China, pp. 47–59 (2021)

2. Bojanowski, P., Grave, E., Joulin, A., Mikolov, T.: Enriching word vectors with subword information. Trans. Assoc. Comput. Linguist. **5**, 135–146 (2017)

3. Dong, C., Li, Y., Tan, L.: A new approach to prevent reentrant attack in solidity smart contracts. In: Si, X., et al. (eds.) CBCC 2019. CCIS, vol. 1176, pp. 83–103. Springer, Singapore (2020). https://doi.org/10.1007/978-981-15-3278-8_6

4. Gai, K., Qiu, M., Zhao, H., Tao, L., Zong, Z.: Dynamic energy-aware cloudlet-based mobile cloud computing model for green computing. J. Netw. Comput. Appl. **59**, 46–54 (2016)

5. Gai, K., Wu, Y., Zhu, L., Qiu, M., Shen, M.: Privacy-preserving energy trading using consortium blockchain in smart grid. IEEE Trans. Ind. Inf. **15**(6), 3548–3558 (2019)

6. Gai, K., Wu, Y., Zhu, L., Zhang, Z., Qiu, M.: Differential privacy-based blockchain for industrial Internet-of-Things. IEEE Trans. Ind. Inf. **16**(6), 4156–4165 (2019)

7. Gai, K., Guo, J., Zhu, L., Yu, S.: Blockchain meets cloud computing: a survey. IEEE Commun. Surv. Tutor. **22**(3), 2009–2030 (2020)

8. Gao, Z., Jayasundara, V., Jiang, L., Xia, X., Lo, D., Grundy, J.: SmartEmbed: a tool for clone and bug detection in smart contracts through structural code embedding. In: IEEE International Conference on Software Maintenance and Evolution (ICSME) (2019)

9. Gao, Z., Jiang, L., Xia, X., Lo, D., Grundy, J.: Checking smart contracts with structural code embedding. IEEE Trans. Softw. Eng. **PP**(99), 1–1 (2020)

10. Griggs, K.N., Olya, O., Kohlios, C.P., Baccarini, A.N., Howson, E.A., Thaier, H.: Healthcare blockchain system using smart contracts for secure automated remote patient monitoring. J. Med. Syst. **42**(7), 130 (2018). https://doi.org/10.1007/s10916-018-0982-x

11. Luu, L., Chu, D., Olickel, H., Saxena, P., Hobor, A.: Making smart contracts smarter. IACR Cryptol. ePrint Arch. **2016**, 633 (2016)

12. Mikolov, T., Chen, K., Corrado, G., Dean, J.: Efficient estimation of word representations in vector space. Computer Science (2013)

13. Permenev, A., Dimitrov, D., Tsankov, P., Drachsler-Cohen, D., Vechev, M.: Verx: safety verification of smart contracts. In: IEEE Symposium on Security and Privacy (2020)

14. Qiu, H., Qiu, M., Memmi, G., Ming, Z., Liu, M.: A dynamic scalable blockchain based communication architecture for IoT. In: Qiu, M. (ed.) SmartBlock 2018. LNCS, vol. 11373, pp. 159–166. Springer, Cham (2018). https://doi.org/10.1007/978-3-030-05764-0_17

15. Qiu, H., et al.: All-or-nothing data protection for ubiquitous communication: challenges and perspectives. Inf. Sci. **502**, 434–445 (2019)

16. Rodler, M., Li, W., Karame, G., Davi, L.: Sereum: protecting existing smart contracts against re-entrancy attacks. arXiv preprint arXiv:1812.05934 (2018)

17. Tian, Z., Li, M., Qiu, M., Sun, Y., Su, S.: Block-DEF: A secure digital evidence framework using blockchain. Inf. Sci. **491**, 151–165 (2019)

18. Tsankov, P., Dan, A.M., Drachsler-Cohen, D., Gervais, A., Bünzli, F., Vechev, M.T.: Securify: practical security analysis of smart contracts. In: ACM SIGSAC Conference on Computer and Communications Security (CCS) 2018, Toronto, Canada, pp. 67–82 (2018)

19. Wang, K., Tao, J., Zhu, J., Ye, Z., Qiu, B., Xu, J.: Compressed sensing MRI reconstruction using generative adversarial network with enhanced antagonism. In: 12th International Conference on Intelligent Computation Technology and Automation, pp. 282–285 (2019)

20. Xin, R., Zhang, J., Shao, Y.: Complex network classification with convolutional neural network. Tsinghua Sci. Technol. **25**(4), 447–457 (2020)
21. Zhuang, Y., et al.: Smart contract vulnerability detection using graph neural network. In: IJCAI-PRICAI-20 (2020)

Attention Based Short-Term Metro Passenger Flow Prediction

Ang Gao[1], Linjiang Zheng[1][✉], Zixu Wang[2], Xuanxuan Luo[2], Congjun Xie[2], and Yuankai Luo[2]

[1] Chongqing University, Chongqing 400044, China
zlj_cqu@cqu.edu.cn
[2] Chongqing No. 8 Secondary School, Chongqing 400030, China

Abstract. Accurate short-term passenger flow prediction can help metro managers optimize train scheduling and formulate useful operation plan, so as to reduce metro transportation pressure and improve passenger comfort. However, existing research can't fully explore the dynamic spatial-temporal correlation of passenger flow in metro network, and don't fully consider the external characteristics such as weather and geographical, which affect the accuracy of metro passenger flow prediction. This paper proposes an attention based metro spatial-temporal convolution model (AMSTCN) for short-term passenger flow prediction. Firstly, aiming at the problem that the existing methods don't fully consider the dynamic correlation of passenger flow between stations, the model uses the spatial-temporal convolution block with attention mechanism to capture the spatiotemporal dynamic transferability of passenger flow between stations; Secondly, in view of the shortcomings of the existing graph convolutional network that does not fully consider the topology of the metro network, the adjacency matrix is constructed by using passenger flow transfer information; Finally, the model captures the characteristics of external factors through the external module, and the learning ability is enhanced. Experimental results show that not only the dynamic spatial-temporal dependence of metro network passenger flow is captured, but also the prediction accuracy is further improved after considering the external factors. The model is effective and stable in predict short-term and mid-term outbound passenger flow.

Keywords: Graph convolution network · Metro passenger flow prediction · Spatial-temporal

1 Introduction

With the expansion of cities and the increase of urban residents, cities are facing many problems such as traffic congestion and environmental pollution. Urban rail transit, with its low cost and energy consumption, high carrying capacity, comfort and convenience, plays an increasingly important role in passenger transport. However, the rapid increase in urban population and the increasingly severe congestion of urban ground transportation have caused rail transit to face greater transportation pressure.

© Springer Nature Switzerland AG 2021
H. Qiu et al. (Eds.): KSEM 2021, LNAI 12817, pp. 598–609, 2021.
https://doi.org/10.1007/978-3-030-82153-1_49

Timely and accurate passenger flow prediction of metro station can help managers optimize train scheduling and formulate useful operation plan, so as to reduce metro transportation pressure and improve passenger comfort. At the same time, it can also help the operation and management department to deal with possible emergencies in advance.

In the early days, researchers mainly used statistical methods to process and predict historical traffic data, such as ARIMA and its variants models [1]. Since most of the statistical methods are based on linear assumptions, and the changes in traffic data are non-linear in nature (mainly due to frequent traffic switching between free and congestion), the performance and application of the model are restricted. In order to deal with the nonlinear characteristics of traffic data effectively, various methods based on machine learning are proposed. Now, neural network prediction methods have been widely used in the field of traffic flow prediction due to their powerful fitting capabilities for complex functions [2–4].

However, the above models ignored the spatial correlation between roads. In actual traffic road scenes, the traffic flow at a certain road will be affected by near roads, and in the metro passenger flow prediction scenario, and passenger flow of a certain station will be affected by the upstream stations.

As deep learning has achieved a lot of results in different fields such as natural language processing, computer vision, and speech recognition, researchers apply it to capture the spatial correlation in traffic flow prediction. Some scholars [5, 6] use manual feature extract network to capture spatial correlation based on LSTM model. And some scholars [7] divided the city into grid, use CNN to capture the spatial correlation in the data. However, the above models ignore the traffic network topology or rely too much on the knowledge of the transportation domain. Recently, researchers have turned their attention to graph convolutional network (GCN) and proposed many GCN based models, such as STGCN [8], Conv-GCN [9], ASTGCN [10].

In general, the existing research ignore the spatial correlation and topological property of the entire metro network, and does not fully extract the characteristics of external factors.

The mainly contributions of this paper are as follows:

(1) We use the spatial-temporal convolution block with attention mechanism to capture the spatial-temporal dynamic transfer of passenger flow between stations.
(2) In view of the existing graph convolution network does not fully consider the topology of metro network, the adjacency matrix is constructed by using passenger flow transfer information.
(3) Our model fully considers the factors that can affect the passenger flow, mainly including weather, geographical factors, etc. and the learning ability is enhanced.

2 Method

2.1 Metro Passenger Flow Prediction

Given a graph-based metro network $G = (V, E, A)$, where V represents the set of stations, $V = \{v_1,..., v_n\}$, E represents the connection between stations, and A is adjacency matrix. Let $x_i^{c,t}$ denote the value of c attributes in the t-th period of station i, where c is the inbound passenger flow, outbound passenger flow, weather, POI, etc. $X_I^t = \{x_1^t, x_2^t, \ldots, x_{|I|}^t\}$ represents all the attribute values of all stations at time t, and $Y_I^t = \{y_1^t, y_2^t, \ldots, y_{|I|}^t\}$ represents the passenger flow of all stations at time t. The problem of metro short-term passenger flow prediction can be defined as finding a function f, which can obtain the predicted value of passenger flow for all stations I from $t + 1$ to $t + \Delta$ in the future to satisfy $(Y_I^{t+1}, Y_I^{t+2}, \ldots, Y_I^{t+\Delta}) = f(X_I^{t-P}, X_I^{t-p+1}, \ldots, X_I^t)$.

2.2 Model

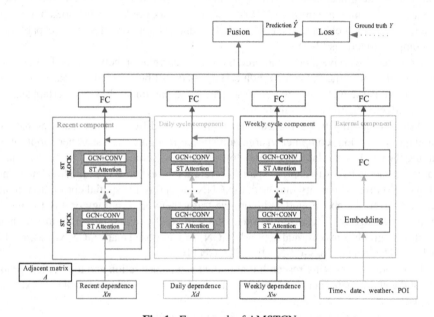

Fig. 1. Framework of AMSTCN

Figure 1 shows the architecture of the attention-based metro spatial-temporal convolutional network (AMSTCN) proposed in this paper, which is composed of four components: recent dependent module, daily cycle module, weekly cycle module and external module. The structure of the first three components is consistent. Each component is connected by multiple spatial-temporal blocks in the form of residuals, and each block is composed of spatial-temporal attention layer and spatial-temporal convolution layer. Then, a fully connected layer is used to make the output of each component have the same size and shape as the predicted target. At the same time, external data is also taken into account in the framework. The external module components extract external features of time, date, weather, and POI data through the embedding layer and the fully connected network. Finally the results of four components are fused using the fully connected layer to get predict value.

Spatial-Temporal Attention
The change of metro passenger flow is spatial-temporal dynamic. This paper uses spatial-temporal attention to capture the spatial-temporal dynamic correlation of passenger flow.

(1) Spatial attention

Define the query vector *Query*, $Query = x^T W_q$, and the key vector *Key*, $Key = x W_{k1} W_{k2}$, and the formula of spatial attention matrix s is as follows:

$$S = V_s \cdot \sigma((KeyQuery^T) + B_S) \tag{1}$$

Where $x \in R^{N \times C \times T}$ is the input, $W_{k1} \in R^{C \times T}, W_{k2} \in R^T, W_q \in R^C, V_s, B_S \in R^{N \times N}$ are the weight matrix that can be trained and learned, σ is the activation function, $S \in R^{N \times N}$ is the scoring matrix of the correlation between stations, $S_{i,j}$ represents the correlation score of station j to station i.

$$S'_{i,j} = \frac{\exp(S_{i,j})}{\sum_{j=1}^{N} \exp(S_{i,j})} \tag{2}$$

Then, the SoftMax function is used to normalize the spatial attention score matrix by column to ensure that the total attention weight of each node is 1. In the subsequent graph convolution, we use S' and adjacency matrix A to dynamically adjust the weight of impact between nodes.

(2) Temporal attention

Define the query vector *Query*, $Query = W_q x$, and the key vector *Key*, $Key = x^T W_{k1} W_{k2}$, and the formula of temporal attention matrix E is as follows:

$$E = V_e \cdot \sigma((Key^T Query) + B_e) \tag{3}$$

Where $x \in R^{N \times C \times T}$ is the input, $W_{k1} \in R^N, W_{k2} \in R^{C \times N}, W_q \in R^C, V_e, B_e \in R^{T \times T}$ are the weight matrix that can be trained and learned, σ is the activation function, $E \in R^{T \times T}$ is the scoring matrix of the correlation between time slices, $E_{i,j}$ represents the correlation score of time slice j to time slice i.

$$E'_{i,j} = \frac{\exp(E_{i,j})}{\sum_{j=1}^{N} \exp(E_{i,j})} \tag{4}$$

Multiply E' and input x to get $\hat{x} = xE'$, and dynamically adjust the input by merging related information.

Spatial-Temporal Convolution Block
The spatial-temporal convolution block includes two parts: the spatial-temporal attention layer and the spatial-temporal convolution layer. The attention layer applies attention to

the input so that the network automatically pays relatively more attention to valuable information. The convolution layer includes a graph convolution in the spatial dimension, which obtains spatial correlation from the neighborhood, and a convolution in the time dimension, using time correlation between adjacent time slices.

In this study, the metro network is a graph structure, and the characteristics of each node can be seen as a signal on the graph, so we use graph convolution based on the spectrogram theory to process the signal on each time slice. The spectral method transforms the graph into algebraic form to analyze the topological properties of the graph. In spectrogram analysis, the graph is represented by the Laplacian matrix L, $L = D - A$, where A is the adjacency matrix, I_N is a unit matrix, and D is the degree matrix. Perform eigen-decomposition on the Laplacian matrix $L = U\Lambda U^T$, where Λ is the diagonal matrix composed of eigenvalues, and U is the orthogonal matrix composed of eigenvectors. The eigenvector of the Laplacian matrix can be used as the basis of the Fourier transform, and the eigenvalue represents the frequency. Graph convolution is a kind of convolution operation, according to the convolution theorem, it can be implemented by using a linear operator diagonalize in the Fourier domain to replace the classic convolution operator. However, it is very costly to decompose the matrix in each forward propagation of neural network. Therefore, this paper uses Chebyshev polynomials to approximate the convolution kernel [11].

$$g\theta * Gx = g\theta(L)x = \sum_{k=0}^{K-1} \beta k T k(\tilde{L})x \tag{5}$$

Where β_k is the polynomial coefficient vector, $\tilde{L} = \frac{2}{\lambda_{max}}L - I_N$ is the rescaled diagonal matrix of eigenvalues, λ_{max} is the maximum eigenvalue of L, $T_k(\cdot)$ is the k-order Chebyshev polynomial.

In order to dynamically adjust the connection between nodes, Hadamard operation is performed on each term of Chebyshev polynomial and spatial attention matrix S', and then the above definition is extended to the multi-channel graph signal with temporal attention $\hat{x} \in R^{N \times C \times T}$.

$$g\theta * G\hat{x} = g\theta(L)x = \sum_{k=0}^{K-1} \beta k (Tk(\tilde{L}) \odot S')\hat{x} \tag{6}$$

At this point, the graph convolution has captured the dynamic spatial correlation between stations, and further performs standard convolution operations in the time dimension to update the node's signal by merging information at adjacent time slices. The spatial-temporal convolution formula of the r-th layer of a certain component is:

$$\hat{x}^{(r)} = ReLU(\Phi * (ReLU(g\theta * G\,\hat{x}^{(r-1)}))) \tag{7}$$

Where * represents the convolution operation, Φ is the parameter of the temporal-dimension convolution kernel, and the activation function is ReLU.

Adjacent Matrix Construction Based on the Metro Transfer Passenger Flow

Adjacency matrix A represents the connection status between stations, if station i has a connection with station j, $A_{i,j}$ is 1, otherwise it is 0. Different from the traffic flow propagation mode of the road network, the passenger flow propagation of metro network is less related to the real metro network. In rail transportation, passengers will not affect the passenger flow of the passing rail station before they departure. Therefore, the distance between stations with obvious upstream and downstream relationship may be very close or far.

Figure 2 is the construction schematic diagram of a metro adjacency matrix. (a) shows the transfer of passenger flow between stations within a certain time slice. The darker the arrow color, the larger the proportion of transferred passenger amount to the target station outbound passenger amount. When the passenger flow of station a suddenly increases at a certain moment, then the outbound passenger flow of station f will increase in adjacent time slice, and the adjacency matrix $A_{a,f}$ related to station a is 1. Although there is also a transfer of passenger flow from stations c to d, the proportion of passenger flow transfer is very small, so there is no connection between stations c and d.

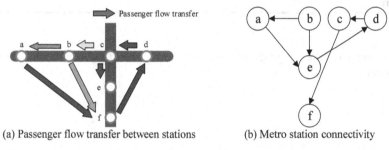

(a) Passenger flow transfer between stations   (b) Metro station connectivity

Fig. 2. Construction of adjacency matrix

Due to the different characteristics of the metro network and the road network, we adopt the adjacency matrix construction method based on the station passenger flow transfer matrix. The adjacenct matrix calculation algorithm pseudo code is as follows (Table 1):

External Feature Extraction Considering Geographic Factors

In spatial feature extraction, it does not consider that other stations may have similar passenger flow at the same time, that is, they have similar passenger flow changes due to the similar factors of geographical environment. As shown in Fig. 3, (a) is the operation diagram of metro, in which Shapingba, Guanyinqiao, Lianghekou and xiaoshizi have similar geographical environment. (b) is the change of four stations inbound passenger flow and shows that the change trend of passenger flow has obvious similarity. Therefore,

Table 1. Algorithm of adjacency matrix construction

Input: Smart card record $R = \{R_1, R_2,..., R_n\}$, station set $stopList = \{S_1, S_2,..., S_n\}$
Output: Adjacent matrix A

Steps:
Initialize adjacent matrix A, frequency threshold λ, station connection Dic;
while *beginDay <endDay* **do:**
  for each a $\in$ *stopList* **do:**
    Initialize the connection set T_a, sum=0;
    calculate all the records that the outbound station is a, and group statistics according to
        the inbound station number to get Dic_a;
    Sort Dic_a in descending order of frequency;
    for each item $\in Dic_a$ **do:**
      if $sum \leq \lambda$ **then:**
        put the station ID of item into set T_a;
      end if
    $Dic[a] = Dic[a] \cup T_a$
  end for
end while
for each a $\in Dic.keys()$ **do:**
  for each b $\in Dic[a]$ **do:**
    $A_{a,b}=1$
END

---

it is necessary to take the geographical environment around the station into account in the model.

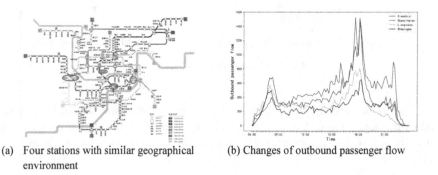

(a) Four stations with similar geographical   (b) Changes of outbound passenger flow
    environment

Fig. 3. Influence of geographical factors on station passenger flow

As one of the basic data of urban spatial analysis, POI (Point of Interest) directly and effectively reflects the agglomeration of various urban elements, so we use POI distribution around metro station as its spatial geographical factor. We used Baidu map API to obtain POI data of main city area, which covers 13 major categories, specific 24 sub-categories. In this paper, we reclassify 24 categories into 7 categories according to the "Urban Land Classification and Planning and Construction Land Standards". The results are shown in Table 2.

Table 2. POI data types of Chongqing urban area

Land use type	Sub-categories	Amount	Proportion (%)
Entertainment	Food, shopping, sports, leisure and entertainment	83037	62.44
Traffic	Entrances and exits, traffic facilities, roads	4283	3.22
Business	Finance, company, office building, media	36603	27.52
Public Service	Government, medical services, car services	87939	8.6
Residence	Residential area, dormitory, hotel	8057	6.06
Education	Education and training organizations	570	0.43
Tour	tourist attraction	250	0.18

3 Experiments and Results

3.1 Experiments Set

This paper uses the Chongqing metro smart card data set to verify the accuracy of AMSTCN. The data set includes 141 stations, and the time span is 214 days from June 1, 2018 to December 31, 2018. In this paper, we select 10 min as time slice for passenger flow statistics, considering that the departure time interval of some stations in Chongqing is more than 5 min, if we choose a smaller time interval of 5 min, the traffic of these stations may be very small (even zero) in a short time interval, which is very difficult for the training of the prediction model, and will cause the accuracy of the prediction results to decline significantly.

The input of the recent dependent component is X_n, $X_n = \{X^{t-j}, X^{t-j+1}, \ldots, X^t\} \in R^{N \times C \times j}$, j is the length of the selected historical period. The input of the daily cycle dependent component is X_d, $X_d = \{X^{t-d*q+1}, \ldots, X^{t-d*q+T_p}, X^{t-(d-1)*q+1}, \ldots, X^{t-(d-1)*q+T_p}, X^{t-q+1}, \ldots, X^{t-q+T_p}\} \in R^{N \times C \times (d*T_p)}$, where T_p is the length of the time slice that needs to be predicted, q is the number of time slices in a day, and d is the historical data spanning the same period of d days. The input of the weekly cycle dependent component is X_w, $X_w = \{X^{t-w*m+1}, \ldots, X^{t-w*m+T_p}, X^{t-(w-1)*m+1}, \ldots, X^{t-(w-1)*m+T_p}, X^{t-m+1}, \ldots, X^{t-m+T_p}\} \in R^{N \times C \times (w*T_p)}$, where T_p is the length of the time period that needs to be predicted, m is the number of time slices in one week, and w is the data of the same time slice of history w weeks.

Based on experience, the related parameters j, d, and w selected in this paper are 18, 3, and 2, respectively. In this paper, the data set is standardized to eliminate the large data gap that leads to abnormal model training. We divide the 214-day data set into training set, validation set and test set according to the ratio of 6:2:2.

In this paper, after using the Chebyshev polynomial to replace the convolution kernel, the value of K needs to be set. K is the receptive field of the convolution kernel. For the metro stations, the outbound flow of each station is only affected by the upstream station. Considering that some passengers may make outbound transfers, we set convolution kernel receptive field K to 2. The size of the temporal convolution layer convolution kernel is set to 5, and all the graph convolution layers in the model use 64 convolution kernels. The number of spatial-temporal convolution blocks is set to 2. In the training process, the Adam optimizer is used to optimize the model parameters, the learning rate is 0.001, and the loss function uses MAE.

We choose three time series prediction methods: ARIMA, LSTM, GRU, and two spatial-temporal prediction models: STGCN, ASTGCN as the baseline model, and compare them with AMSTCN.

3.2 Results

(1) Performance comparison

Compare our model with the five baseline models, the experiment results are shown in Table 3. It can be seen from the table that the prediction model proposed in this paper is significantly better than the comparison model for the prediction results at different time steps.

Table 3. Prediction performance of different algorithms for outbound passenger flow

Model	10 min			30 min			60 min		
	MAE	RMSE	MAPE	MAE	RMSE	MAPE	MAE	RMSE	MAPE
ARIMA	58.63	80.56	86.96	74.85	128.36	97.56	88.41	141.30	110.54
LSTM	19.03	42.49	57.26	21.23	47.44	63.41	25.52	57.87	78.19
GRU	18.45	39.88	53.33	20.68	43.17	57.99	25.18	55.96	74.53
STGCN	14.42	28.41	42.19	15.98	31.08	44.45	17.55	33.83	45.59
ASTGCN	12.98	26.16	37.59	13.88	28.51	38.74	15.03	29.77	40.47
AMSTCN	11.77	23.71	34.56	11.87	24.10	34.84	12.12	24.88	35.85

First of all, it can be seen from the table that the overall prediction effect of the model without considering the spatial characteristics is biased. The ARIMA model has poor performance in fitting volatile data, and its accuracy is very low even if the differential smoothing process is performed. The prediction results of LSTM and GRU that can capture the long-term and short-term time of metro passenger flow are similar, and the RMSE and MAPE of the prediction in next 10 min are 42.49, 57.26% and 39.88, 53.33%, respectively. Taking spatial correlation between stations into consideration has greatly improved the model, three evaluation indexes of STGCN reached 12.98, 26.16, and 37.59%. ASTGCN captures the dynamic spatiotemporal characteristics by using the attention based spatial-temporal block, and the model prediction accuracy is further improved. When predicting the outbound passenger flow in next 10 min, MAE, RMSE, and MAPE were reduced to 12.98, 26.16, and 37.59, respectively. The AMSTCN model proposed in this paper, taking into account the dynamic spatial-temporal characteristics of metro passenger flow and the influence of external factors, the predicted MAE, RMSE, and MAPE for 10 min are reduced to 11.77, 23.71, and 34.56%. In order to visually display the accuracy of each prediction model, this paper visualizes the prediction results of three time steps, and the results are shown in Fig. 4.

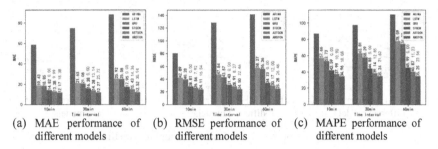

(a) MAE performance of different models

(b) RMSE performance of different models

(c) MAPE performance of different models

Fig. 4. Performance comparison of different models

Figure 4 shows the performance improvement of ASTGCN and AMSTCN based on the prediction accuracy of the STGCN model. It can be seen from the figure that ASTGCN is significantly improved, three evaluation indexes decrease about 10% in next 10 min prediction. With the increase of prediction time interval, the accuracy of ASTGCN is increased more, MAE, RMSE and MAPE are decreased about 13%, 10% and 12% in next 30 min and 60 min prediction. On the basis of attention mechanism, considering the characteristics of subway passenger flow and external factors, the prediction accuracy is further improved. MAE has been improved by 18.38%, 25.72% and 30.94% in three time slices, and RMSE has been improved by 16.54%, 22.46% and 26.46%, and MAPE has been improved by 18.08%, 21.62% and 23.56%. With the increase of time interval, the performance of the model is improved more and more, which shows that the external factors and the unique characteristics of metro passenger flow have a greater impact on the passenger flow prediction. Full consideration of these two factors can improve the accuracy of model.

Figure 5 shows the performance of different algorithms in short-term and medium-term prediction. On the whole, with the increase of time interval, the difficulty of prediction increases, and the prediction accuracy of each model shows a downward trend. It can be seen from the figure that the LSTM and GRU models, which can only capture temporal correlation, perform well in predicting short-term passenger flow. While the predict time interval increases, the prediction performance drops sharply. For the model that can capture the spatial correlation, the performance is stable and just declines slightly with the increase of the prediction time interval, indicating that the spatial transfer of metro passenger flow has a great impact on the overall prediction effect over time. Compared with STGCN, which does not consider the dynamic spatial-temporal correlation between stations, the prediction accuracy of ASTGCN's multi-component attention model is higher, which indicates that the transfer of passenger flow between stations will change dynamically with time. Compared with ASTGCN which uses spatial direct connection as the connection between stations, AMSTCN constructs the adjacency matrix by considering the passenger flow transfer relationship between stations. At the same time, the accuracy of the model is further improved by adding external factors.

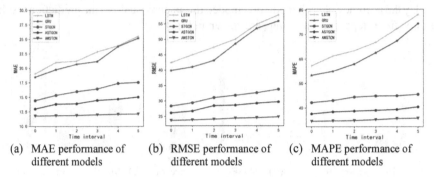

(a) MAE performance of   (b) RMSE performance of   (c) MAPE performance of
     different models   different models   different models

Fig. 5. Line chart of model performance changing with time interval

(2) Spatial-temporal attention visualization

In order to observe the role of attention mechanism in our model, we select all the stations in three different time slices to observe. Figure 6 shows the thermal diagram of spatial-temporal attention matrix in three time slices, in which line i represents the impact of other stations on station i, and the deeper the color represents the greater the impact degree. It can be seen from the figure that for each station, the spatial and temporal impact of other stations on the station is different. At the same time, we can notice that the grid thermal value near the diagonal from the upper left corner to the lower right corner is higher, but there are many grids with high thermal value far away from the diagonal, which indicates that the influence degree and distance between stations have certain relationship, but the distance is not the decisive factor. It can be proved that the adjacency matrix construction method based on passenger flow transfer proposed in this paper can more effectively extract the dynamic spatiotemporal correlation between stations.

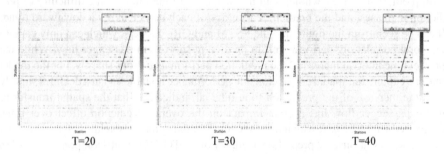

T=20   T=30   T=40

Fig. 6. Spatiotemporal attention matrix of different time slices

4 Conclusion

In this paper, we proposed an attention-based metro spatial-temporal convolution network, called AMSTCN, for metro passenger flow prediction. By using attention based spatial-temporal convolution block, the model can capture the dynamic spatial-temporal characteristics in passenger flow. By constructing adjacency matrix based on passenger flow transfer, the model fully extracts the topology information of subway network. The learning ability of model is further enhanced with the help of fully extracting external factors characteristics. Experimental results show that the model has a good and stable effect in short and medium term passenger flow forecast.

The model eliminated in this paper can be further improved and optimized from the following points: (1) emergency events in or around metro stations can be considered and input into model; (2) the spatial-temporal correlation between stations is approximate correlation. By considering average travel time information between stations can solve this problem and reduce the model parameters and training time.

References

1. Voort, M.D., Dougherty, M., Watson, S.: Combining Kohonen maps with arima time series models to forecast traffic flow. Transp. Res. C: Emerg. Technol. **4**(5), 307–318 (1996)
2. Vlahogianni, E.I., Karlaftis, M.G., Golias, J.C.: Optimized and meta-optimized neural networks for short-term traffic flow prediction: a genetic approach. Transp. Res. C: Emerg. Technol. **13**(3), 211–234 (2005)
3. Wei, Y., Chen, M.-C.: Forecasting the short-term metro passenger flow with empirical mode decomposition and neural networks. Transp. Res. C: Emerg. Technol. **21**(1), 148–162 (2012)
4. Li, H., Wang, Y., Xu, X., Qin, L., Zhang, H.: Short-term passenger flow prediction under passenger flow control using a dynamic radial basis function network. Appl. Soft Comput. **83**, 105620 (2019)
5. Liu, Y., Liu, Z., Jia, R.: DeepPF: a deep learning based architecture for metro passenger flow prediction. Transp. Res. C: Emerg. Technol. **101**, 18–34 (2019)
6. Zhang, H., He, J., Bao, J., Hong, Q., Shi, X.: A hybrid spatiotemporal deep learning model for short-term metro passenger flow prediction. J. Adv. Transp. **2020**, 4656435 (2020)
7. Zhang, J., Zheng, Y., Qi, D., Li, R., Yi, X., Li, T.: Predicting citywide crowd flows using deep spatio-temporal residual networks. Artif. Intell. **259**, 147–166 (2018)
8. Yu, B., Yin, H., Zhu, Z.: Spatio-temporal graph convolutional networks: a deep learning framework for traffic forecasting. In: Proceedings of the 27th International Joint Conference on Artificial Intelligence (IJCAI-18), pp. 3428–3434. Morgan Kaufmann (2018)
9. Zhang, J., Chen, F., Guo, Y., Li, X.: Multi-graph convolutional network for short-term passenger flow forecasting in urban rail transit. IET Intell. Transp. Syst. **14**(10), 1210–1217 (2020)
10. Guo, S., Lin, Y., Feng, N., Song, C., Wan, H.: Attention based spatial-temporal graph convolutional networks for traffic flow forecasting. In: Proceedings of 33rd AAAI Conference on Artificial Intelligence, pp. 922–929. AAAI (2019)
11. Simonovsky, M., Komodakis, N.: Dynamic edge-conditioned filters in convolutional neural networks on graphs. In: Proceedings of 30th IEEE Conference on Computer Vision and Pattern Recognition, pp. 29–38. IEEE (2017)

Thematic Analysis of Twitter as a Platform for Knowledge Management

Saleha Noor[1] (ID), Yi Guo[1,2,3](✉) (ID), Syed Hamad Hassan Shah[4] (ID),
and Habiba Halepoto[5] (ID)

[1] School of Information Science and Engineering, East China University of Science and
Technology, Shanghai 200237, People's Republic of China
guoyi@ecust.edu.cn
[2] Business Intelligence and Visualization Research Center, National Engineering Laboratory for
Big Data Distribution and Exchange Technologies,
Shanghai 200436, People's Republic of China
[3] Shanghai Engineering Research Center of Big Data & Internet
Audience, Shanghai 200072, People's Republic of China
[4] Glorious Sun School of Business and Management, Donghua University, Shanghai, China
[5] College of Information Science and Technology, Donghua University, Shanghai, China

Abstract. The purpose of this study is to conduct a thematic analysis of Twitter-related publications in knowledge management (KM) discipline and explore different research themes of KM Twitter-related publications. These publications were retrieved from Web of Science (WoS) during time span of 2009–2020 and thematic analysis was conducted through VOSviewer. Different methodologies were used according to the nature of bibliometric analysis and explained in each section. Three themes were emerged from these publications indicating Twitter users' explicit contribution in KM through big data and text mining, knowledge sharing through communities' collaboration and KM through machine learning. This is the first bibliometric study to explore overall contribution of Twitter-related publications in KM field at a glance.

Keywords: Twitter · VOSviewer · Thematic Analysis · knowledge management

1 Introduction

Twitter is challenging new source of information for data mining techniques and it has become "what's-happening-right-now" tool that enables interested parties to follow individual users' thoughts and commentary on real-time events. This knowledge discovery in Twitter has been focused by different researchers in different domains. Due to this, the number of twitter publications is dramatically increasing on average rate of 6.57 publications per day (2017) and has cross the limit of 15000 in Web of Science (WoS) in less than a decade 2009–2018. Noor et al. [1] explored major research themes and hotspots of Twitter-related publications through bibliometric analysis, such as sentiment analysis as knowledge sharing, political findings as knowledge seeking,

© Springer Nature Switzerland AG 2021
H. Qiu et al. (Eds.): KSEM 2021, LNAI 12817, pp. 610–618, 2021.
https://doi.org/10.1007/978-3-030-82153-1_50

health care awareness as both knowledge seeking and sharing and twitter role in crisis and emergency risk communication as knowledge collaboration and these findings were consistent with prior bibliometric study [2]. These previous studies established significant role of Twitter with KM therefore it became essential to explore specific research themes of Twitter-related publications in KM field. Therefore, we conducted thematic analysis of 216 Twitter-related publications which have substantial link with KM to find out explicit KM twitter research themes in this study.

Despite of this, there are two motivations to conduct this bibliometric study. First, we found only two bibliometric studies exploring overall research dynamics and thematic analysis of Twitter-related publications. First, Fausto and Aventurier [2] conducted a bibliometric analysis of 2,338 Twitter related publications to explore yearly growth output, most influential authors, institutions and countries who published about Twitter in time span of 2006–14. Moreover, they also explored "Hot topics" and their evolution in literature about Twitter related publications. Moreover, Kapoor et al. [3] conducted a bibliometric study of 12000 Social Media (SM) publications between 1997–2017 using VOSviewer. They found seven major themes through author co-citation analysis and five themes through text Analysis. This study also indicated that almost all publications related to knowledge sharing during natural disasters and critical events focus only on Twitter data [3, p. 24,10]. This sparked our interest to determine the sole contribution of Twitter-related publications in KM research academia to explore its significant and vital role in different sectors of life.

Second, previous studies also conducted a bibliometric analysis of specific research areas under the umbrella of SM especially Twitter. For example, bibliometric of event detection [4], SM trends in psychology [5] and the role of Twitter in health promotion [6]. Despite these bibliometric analyses, prominent studies also found significant embeddedness of SM (Twitter) in KM system; e.g., Ford and Mason [7] determined perceived tensions to KM through Twitter at an individual level, group level and organizational level [7]. Nisar et al. [8] found that virtual community and groups' discussion (Knowledge sharing) positively affects organizational performance through embedded SM. Scuotto et al. [9] found a significant role of Twitter networks through mass collaborative KM in small and medium-sized enterprises productivity [9]. Sigala and Chalkiti [10] determined employee creativity by adopting KM approach through SM [10]. The above studies clearly express the implementation of SM especially Twitter to leverage and improve KM initiatives and processes. But there is scarcest study to provide a complete and comprehensive overview of KM through Twitter-related publications. To fulfill this gap, we investigated mapping analysis of KM publications under Twitter platform to find out significant emerging themes in these publications (see methodology section).

2 Thematic Mapping Overview

Thematic mapping investigations have been used frequently to explore evolution, growth and prominence of many research fields in the research academia through bibliometric analysis [6, 11–13]. Pritchard [14] defined bibliometric analysis as a way of applying mathematics and statistics to the media of written communication in order to understand the nature and course of development of a discipline [14]. The traditional bibliometric methods usually focus on the citation and content analysis, whereas the emerging bibliometric network analysis often analyzes the relationships among keywords, countries, research institutes, and authors [15].

VOSviewer has been extensively used to conduct bibliometric mapping analyses as compared with other bibliometric software tools in different research areas, e.g., social media in KM [16], Twitter [1] and prosumption [11]. Actually, VOS analysis represents enormous information in one single graphical plot which is based on the visualization of similarities-VOS technique. Thus, the map built by the text-mining is comprised of related terms and hence make one cluster or theme. Consequently, researchers may get themes or clusters of countries, institutions, and keywords used in title and abstract of published papers through citations links, bibliographic coupling links and co-occurrence analysis. These themes represent the closeness of specific keywords, authors, journals, organizations or countries with one color which indicate their relatedness in specific research streams and thus help researchers to explore various dimensions of an underlying research discipline [17].

3   Data and Method

The methodology and structure of this are mainly inspired by the methodologies used by two recent bibliometric studies; value co-creation Shah et al. [12] and Noor et al. [16]. This methodology has also been applied by diverse disciplines such as social media in KM [16], prosumption [18] and Twitter [1].

To identify and retrieve relevant articles for inclusion, we employed a screening routine in Web of Science (WoS) as employed extensively in prior studies such as Shah et al. [12] and Noor et al. [6]. WoS database allowed us to identify the best optimal research publications as it is a top-quality database comprising top journals of basic Science, social science, arts and humanities disciplines. It contains more than 22,000 journals, 50 million publications data in 70 languages and 151 research categories. Therefore, this study is focused on the WoS database despite other research engines, such as Google Scholar, SCOPUS or Scientific Electronic Library Online (SciELO).

In order to quantitatively analyze the Twitter research related to KM, first of all, we selected WoS core collection database and inserted keyword "Twitter" in the "topic" section and, second, we mentioned the time period between 2009 and 2020 in WoS. Consequently, 19107 of Twitter research papers were retrieved. After that, we sorted these 19107 Twitter-related publications data with respect to "knowledge management" and consequently got only 216 publications data. Then we extracted these 216 publications data in text document file containing valuable information about each publication such as subject category, journal name, publication type, country, organization and keywords. This study enabled us to answer following research question that what are the emerging themes and Twitter hotspots in 216 Twitter-related publications in KM field?

4   Results and Discussion

4.1   Co-occurrence of Keywords in Twitter and KM Publications

The main objective of this paper to conduct the thematic analysis of Twitter-related publications related to KM through the co-occurrence of keywords founded in the titles, keywords and abstracts of the 216 retrieved publications. We conducted cartography analysis to determine significant research areas where these KM Twitter-related publications played an important role and how they can be grouped together in a systematic way. We chose the type of analysis as "co-occurrence" and unit of analysis as "All keywords" in VOSviewer. Furthermore, we chose 3 minimum numbers of occurrences of a keyword as threshold level. The keyword network visualization map was constructed based on the co-occurrence frequencies of top 25 keywords out of total 533 retrieved keywords as shown in Fig. 1. Three prominent themes have been emerged in this cartography analysis (see Fig. 1 and Table 1).

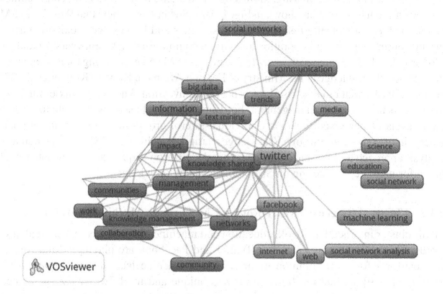

Fig. 1. Most occurred keywords in Twitter and KM research.

4.1.1 Cluster 1 (Blue): Twitter Role in KM Through Big Data and Text Mining

In this cluster social networks, big data, information, trends and text mining were prominent keywords as shown in Fig. 1. This cluster let us know that virtual communities through social networks not only use Twitter as knowledge-seeking platform but also generate a lot of information in the form of user-generated content to capture, integrate and convey cultural knowledge [19]. Consequently, researchers access this big data for knowledge seeking, knowledge acquisition and knowledge disseminating through data mining. Zhao et al. [20] used big data for knowledge extraction from Twitter's data to illustrate the multi-dimensional relations (social networking) among users. Wang et al. [21] used Twitter as knowledge acquisition platform as a rich source for gleaning people's emotions, which is necessary for deeper understanding of people's behaviors and actions. Okazaki *et al.* [22] proposed a data mining approach on Twitter to explore customer engagement and electronic word-of-mouth (knowledge dissemination). Prior studies also used Twitter as platform to predict current and future trends and risk in financial business market. Huang *et al.* [23] also used Twitter as prediction tool for boosting financial trends. Aghababaei and Makrehchi [24] predicted crime trends in Chicago through Twitter sequential data mining. Lagos-ortiz [25] proposed a system (knowledge seeking) for trends detection on Twitter, to have knowledge about people's opinions and moods to enhance real-time decision making.

4.1.2   Cluster 2 (Red): Twitter Role in KM Through Collaboration and Knowledge Sharing

In this cluster knowledge sharing, knowledge management, networks and communities were prominent keywords as shown in Fig. 1. This cluster let us knew that Web 2.0 in SM landscape has dramatically reshaped digital societies and knowledge-seeking behavior through online network collaboration and virtual communities in recent years. Chaudhry [26] revealed that knowledge workers frequently use SM and networking tools to enhance their personal knowledge at the Ministry of Foreign Affairs in Kuwait. Kreiner et al. [27] analyzed Twitter data to discussed retrospective conversion (knowledge dissemination) of human-safety in crisis management. Ford and Mason [7] used Twitter data to resolve three levels of perceived tensions (individual-micro, group-meso and organizational-macro) in organizations through Knowledge sharing. Panahi et al. [28] used the thematic analysis approach to share and create tacit knowledge through qualitative study and found that information encountering on SM facilitates tacit knowledge.

4.1.3   Cluster 3 (Green): Twitter Role in KM Through Machine Learning

In this cluster internet, Facebook, education and machine learning were prominent keywords. This cluster let us knew that Twitter and Facebook are playing a vital role as KM platform for users' opinion mining through machine learning techniques. Abu-Salih et al. [29] applied machine learning technique and used Twitter user-generated contents to propose a framework for business-related applications to examine the voice of customer/market and recommendation systems. Wang [30] used a machine learning approach to detect the spammer in Twitter platform. Porshnev et al. [31] applied machine learning technique to discuss possibility to improve accuracy of stock market indicators predictions by using data about psychological states of Twitter users. As SM building has been constructed on two main pillars; Facebook and Twitter, therefore, we found significant contribution of Facebook data and Twitter data related to KM in this cluster. Twitter platform is also being used in education field for KM. Kassens-Noor [32] explored Twitter platform as an active, informal and outside-of-class learning tool for KM in higher education. Similarly, Menkhoff *et al.*, [33] examined Twitter an effective tool for collaborative knowledge creation by engaging students in group discussion and generate their own learning context.

Table 1. Themes in KM Twitter-related publications

Cluster name	Theme	Sub-theme	Examples from prior studies
1-Blue Cluster	Twitter role in KM through big data and text mining	Social networking through big data, customer feedback and electronic word-of-mouth, future trends in different business market segments, event detection, predict crime trends	Zhao et al. [20], Okazaki *et al.* [22], Huang *et al.* [23], Aghababaei and Makrehchi [24], Lagos-ortiz [25]
2-Red Cluster	Twitter role in KM through collaboration and knowledge sharing	Twitter in Personal KM Support, Communication in crisis KM, Twitter role in tacit knowledge	Chaudhry [26], Kreiner et al. [27], Ford and Mason [7]
3-Green Cluster	Twitter role in KM through machine learning	Twitter role in customer/market recommendation systems, detection of spammer in Twitter, Twitter inaccuracy of stock market predictions	Abu-Salih et al. [29], Wang [30], Porshnev et al. [31], Menkhoff et al., [33]

5   Conclusion

This article not only provided us an overall contribution of the KM Twitter research dynamics in academia but also examined the thematic analysis of Twitter-related publications with KM at a glance. The results indicated that Twitter research related to KM has been flourished gradually over the last decade but still in an early stage. Thematic analysis revealed that Twitter is no longer just a platform for socialization, but is being acknowledged as source of user-generated data to have a collective opinion (sentiment analysis) for knowledge sharing. Furthermore, KM Twitter-related publications revealed that Twitter is disseminating knowledge through big data text mining and machine learning.

5.1   Implications for Academia and Society

According to the KM literature of Twitter, this bibliometric study provides significant contributions of most productive journals, categories, countries, organizations and keywords evolution of underlying themes at a glance. These 216 Twitter studies of KM revealed that Twitter has been used as a practical tool to gather new ideas and public opinion through knowledge sharing and collaborative KM. Some implications for society are as follows: first, business community may use twitter as KM platform to glean customers' emotions to predict different trends in business market to enhance real-time decision making. Second, this study also provides implication for crisis control agencies to use twitter as knowledge disseminating platform in crisis and emergency to fan out information in digital communities through online collaboration. Furthermore, educationists can use twitter as a learning tool in education by engaging students in group discussions happening on twitter digital communities to share collaborative knowledge.

5.2   Limitations and Future Directions

Despite the significant contribution of this study in KM Twitter research, it has some limitations. First, as mentioned at the beginning of this study, this analysis is based on publication data provided by WoS, considered as most authenticated source of data but still we could not claim data is free of errors but accurate enough to support this bibliometric study. Moreover, publications data extracted from WoS through "topic" research query string may not provide 100% accurate results but again this methodology is sound enough to conduct bibliometric analysis. Furthermore, bibliometric analysis suggested in this paper can be expanded to databases other than SCI/SSCI index and other time periods. Second, this study did not conduct most influential authors in KM Twitter research domain, so future studies are needed to explore this domain. Third, this is the first bibliometric analysis, where citation links; bibliographic coupling and co-authorships links have been explicitly used to explore underlying significance of countries and institutions in KM Twitter research. Other researchers may use these bibliometric indicators in different research fields to explore underlying research areas. However, this study provides enormous information on Twitter research at a glance and its explicit role in KM, which open new avenues for other researchers to conduct Twitter research under different disciplines.

Funding.   This research is financially supported by The National Key Research and Development Program of China (grant number 2018YFC0807105), National Natural Science Foundation of China (grant number 61462073) and Science and Technology Committee of Shanghai Municipality (STCSM) (under grant numbers 17DZ1101003, 18511106602 and 18DZ2252300).

Conflict of Interest.   The authors declare no conflict of interest.

References

1. Noor, S., Guo, Y., Shah, S.H.H., Nawaz, M.S., Butt, A.S.: Research synthesis and thematic analysis of twitter through bibliometric analysis. Int. J. Semant. Web Inform. Syst. (2019, forthcoming)
2. Fausto, S., Aventurier, P.: Scientific literature on Twitter as a subject research: findings based on bibliometric analysi. Handb. Twitter Res. 2015 (2016). https://doi.org/10.5281/zenodo.44882
3. Kapoor, K.K., Tamilmani, K., Rana, N.P., Patil, P., Dwivedi, Y.K., Nerur, S.: Advances in social media research: past, present and future. Inform. Syst. Front. **20**(3), 531–558 (2017). https://doi.org/10.1007/s10796-017-9810-y
4. Chen, X., Wang, S., Tang, Y., Hao, T.: A bibliometric analysis of event detection in social media. Online Inf. Rev. **43**(1), 29–52 (2019). https://doi.org/10.1108/OIR-03-2018-0068

5. Zyoud, S.H., Sweileh, W.M., Awang, R., Al-Jabi, S.W.: Global trends in research related to social media in psychology: mapping and bibliometric analysis. Int. J. Ment. Health Syst. **12**(1), 4 (2018). https://doi.org/10.1186/s13033-018-0182-6

6. Noor, S., Guo, Y., Shah, S., Halepoto, H.: Bibliometric Analysis of Twitter Knowledge Management Publications Related to Health Promotion. In: Li, G., Shen, H.T., Yuan, Y., Wang, X., Liu, H., Zhao, X. (eds.) KSEM 2020. LNCS (LNAI), vol. 12274, pp. 341–354. Springer, Cham (2020). https://doi.org/10.1007/978-3-030-55130-8_30

7. Ford, D.P., Mason, R.M.: A multilevel perspective of tensions between knowledge management and social media. J. Organ. Comput. Electron. Commer. **23**(1–2), 7–33 (2013). https://doi.org/10.1080/10919392.2013.748604

8. Nisar, T.M., Prabhakar, G., Strakova, L.: Social media information benefits, knowledge management and smart organizations. J. Bus. Res. **94**, 264–272 (2019). https://doi.org/10.1016/j.jbusres.2018.05.005

9. Scuotto, V., Del Giudice, M., Omeihe, K.: SMEs and mass collaborative knowledge management: toward understanding the role of social media networks. Inform. Syst. Manag. **34**(3), 280–290 (2017). https://doi.org/10.1080/10580530.2017.1330006

10. Sigala, M., Chalkiti, K.: Knowledge management, social media and employee creativity. Int. J. Hosp. Manag. **45**, 44–58 (2015). https://doi.org/10.1016/j.ijhm.2014.11.003

11. Shah, S.H.H., Lei, S., Ali, M., Doronin, D., Hussain, S.T.: Prosumption: bibliometric analysis using HistCite and VOSviewer. Kybernetes **49**(3), 1–24 (2019). https://doi.org/10.1108/K-12-2018-0696

12. Shah, S.H.H., Noor, S., Ahmad, A.B., Butt, A.S., Lei, S.: Retrospective view and thematic analysis of value co-creation through bibliometric analysis. Total Qual. Manag. Bus. Excell., 1–25 (2021). https://doi.org/10.1080/14783363.2021.1890017

13. Noor, S., Guo, Y., Shah, S., Philippe Fournier-Viger, M., Nawaz, S.: Analysis of public reactions to the novel coronavirus (COVID-19) outbreak on Twitter. Kybernetes **50**(5), 1633–1653 (2020). https://doi.org/10.1108/K-05-2020-0258

14. Pritchard, A.: Statistical bibliography or bibliometrics? J. Doc. **25**(4), 348–349 (1969)

15. Van Eck, N.J., Waltman, L.: Appropriate similarity measures for author co-citation analysis. J. Am. Assoc. Inform. Sci. Technol. **59**(10), 1653–1661 (2008). https://doi.org/10.1002/asi.20872

16. Noor, S., Guo, Y., Shah, S., Saqib Nawaz, M., Butt, A.: Bibliometric analysis of social media as a platform for knowledge management. Int. J. Knowl. Manag. **16**(3), 33–51 (2020). https://doi.org/10.4018/IJKM.2020070103

17. Decker, R., Lenz, H.-J. (eds.): Advances in Data Analysis. SCDAKO, Springer, Heidelberg (2007). https://doi.org/10.1007/978-3-540-70981-7

18. Shah, S.H.H., Lei, S., Noor, S., Anjum, A.: Research synthesis and new directions of prosumption: a bibliometric analysis. Int. J. Inform. Manag. Sci. **31**(1), 79–98 (2020). https://doi.org/10.6186/IJIMS.20200331(1).0005

19. Nicolas-Rocca, T., Parrish, J.: Capturing and conveying chamorro cultural knowledge using social media. Int. J. Knowl. Manag. **9**(3), 1–18 (2013). https://doi.org/10.4018/ijkm.2013070101

20. Zhao, Y.W., van den Heuvel, W.-J., Ye, X.: Exploring Big Data in Small Forms: A Multilayered Knowledge Extraction of Social Networks (2013)

21. Wang, W., Chen, L., Thirunarayan, K., Sheth, A.P.: Harnessing Twitter 'big data' for automatic emotion identification. In: Proceedings – 2012 ASE/IEEE International Conference on Privacy, Security, Risk and Trust and 2012 ASE/IEEE International Conference on Social Computing, SocialCom/PASSAT 2012, pp. 587–592 (2012). https://doi.org/10.1109/SocialCom-PASSAT.2012.119

22. Okazaki, S., Díaz-Martín, A.M., Rozano, M., Menéndez-Benito, H.D.: Using twitter to engage with customers: a data mining approach. Internet Res. **25**(3), 416–434 (2015). https://doi.org/10.1108/IntR-11-2013-0249

23. Huang, Y., Zhou, S., Huang, K., Guan, J.: Boosting Financial Trend Prediction with Twitter Mood Based on Selective Hidden Markov Models. In: Renz, M., Shahabi, C., Zhou, X., Cheema, M.A. (eds.) DASFAA 2015. LNCS, vol. 9050, pp. 435–451. Springer, Cham (2015). https://doi.org/10.1007/978-3-319-18123-3_26

24. Aghababaei, S., Makrehchi, M.: Mining Twitter data for crime trend prediction. Intell. Data Anal. **22**(1), 117–141 (2018). https://doi.org/10.3233/IDA-163183

25. Valencia-García, R., Lagos-Ortiz, K., Alcaraz-Mármol, G., del Cioppo, J., Vera-Lucio, N. (eds.): CITI 2016. CCIS, vol. 658. Springer, Cham (2016). https://doi.org/10.1007/978-3-319-48024-4

26. Chaudhry, A.S.: Use of Social Media and Networks to Support Personal Knowledge Management: A Study of PKM Practices of Government Officers in Kuwait, pp. 136–139 (2013)

27. Kreiner, K., Immonen, A., Suominen, H.: Crisis Management Knowledge from Social Media, pp. 105–108 (2013). https://doi.org/10.1145/2537734.2537740

28. Panahi, S., Watson, J., Partridge, H.: Information encountering on social media and tacit knowledge sharing. J. Inform. Sci. **42**(4), 539–550 (2016). https://doi.org/10.1177/0165551515598883

29. Abu-Salih, B., Wongthongtham, P., Kit, C.: Twitter mining for ontology-based domain discovery incorporating machine learning. J. Knowl. Manag. **22**(5), 949–981 (2018). https://doi.org/10.1108/JKM-11-2016-0489

30. Wang, A.H.: Detecting Spam Bots in Online Social Networking Sites: A Machine Learning Approach. In: Foresti, S., Jajodia, S. (eds.) DBSec 2010. LNCS, vol. 6166, pp. 335–342. Springer, Heidelberg (2010). https://doi.org/10.1007/978-3-642-13739-6_25

31. Porshnev, A., Redkin, I., Shevchenko, A.: Machine learning in prediction of stock market indicators based on historical data and data from twitter sentiment analysis. In: Proceedings - IEEE 13th International Conference on Data Mining Workshops, ICDMW 2013 pp. 440–444 (2013). https://doi.org/10.1109/ICDMW.2013.111

32. Kassens-Noor, E.: Twitter as a teaching practice to enhance active and informal learning in higher education: The case of sustainable tweets. Act. Learn. High. Educ. **13**(1), 9–12 (2012). https://doi.org/10.1177/1469787411429190

33. Menkhoff, T., Chay, Y., Bengtsson, M., Jason Woodard, C., Gan, B.: Incorporating microblogging ("tweeting") in higher education: lessons learnt in a knowledge management course. Comput. Human Behav. **51**, 1295–1302 (2015). https://doi.org/10.1016/j.chb.2014.11.063

Cross-Chain-Based Decentralized Identity for Mortgage Loans

Tianxiu Xie[1], Yue Zhang[1], Keke Gai[2(✉)] (iD), and Lei Xu[2]

[1] School of Computer Science and Technology, Beijing Institute of Technology,
Beijing 100081, China
`2017141461102@stu.scu.edu.cn`, `3220201017@bit.edu.cn`
[2] School of Cyberspace Science and Technology, Beijing Institute of Technology,
Beijing 100081, China
{`gaikeke,6120180029`}`@bit.edu.cn`

Abstract. *Decentralized Identity* (DID) has been deemed an ideal mechanism for identity sharing and authentication, which allows users to process control over identity information. However, the centralized storage of DID hinders further expansion due to security issues. Combining the existing blockchain technology with the DID theory has a great development prospect in terms of privacy protection and security enhancement. In order to address the identity authentication issue of collateral in financial loans, this paper proposes the *Cross-chain Channel-based DID* (C3-DID) model, which realizes the distributed storage of DID and allows relay-based cross-chain data exchange. We deploy the loan process and the identity verification process on consortium blockchains, separately. In addition, a permission chain channel, called peer-to-peer *Matching Channel* (MC), is established to accomplish cross-chain data exchange. Our security analysis indicates that the proposed model can resist multiple threats.

Keywords: Decentralized identity · Blockchain · Cross-chain · Financial mortgage loan

1 Introduction

The scale of global *Identity and Access Management* (IAM) market has continued to expand in recent years [16]. However, there are a series of issues with centralized IAM system. Identity issuance and authentication are determined by the centralized organization, which leads to the risk of privacy leakage [22]. In addition, independent management of each organization makes it difficult to share identity information on different platforms [3,14]. *Decentralized Identity* (DID) advocates that digital identities are owned and controlled by users, who can optionally share digital identities to protect privacy. According to the definition given by the document of the World Wide Web Consortium (W3C) [12], the DID was a new type of identifier with the natures of global uniqueness, high

© Springer Nature Switzerland AG 2021
H. Qiu et al. (Eds.): KSEM 2021, LNAI 12817, pp. 619–633, 2021.
https://doi.org/10.1007/978-3-030-82153-1_51

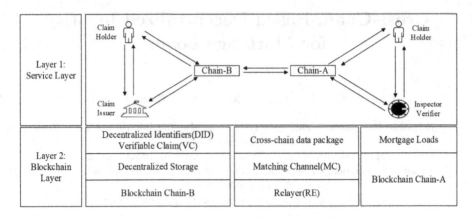

Fig. 1. The high level architecture of Cross-chain Channel-based DID .

availability, resolvability, and encryption verifiability [5,6,15]. The DID mechanism provides a novel alternative for the mortgage identity authentication in financial mortgage load. The application of blockchain in IAM, especially in the direction of DID, has received extensive attentions. Due to decentralized and tamper-resistant characteristics of blockchain, the storage security issue of DID can be solved [6].

Many companies have been trying to explore the practical application of DID in different fields. For example, *Identity Overlay Network* (ION) was a Microsoft's DID project [18], which adopted W3C DID standard.Similarly, Baidu introduced the Identity Hub technology in its own DID research project Grem to solve the authentication and authorization issues of different platforms for digital identity [11,21]. M. Qiu et al. proposed a secure digital evidence framework using blockchain [19] and a dynamic scalable framework [17]. Besides, the digital identity management network Sovrin [20] developed the DID programmes on Hyperledger instead of on Ethereum [25].

Motivated by the privacy protection of digital identity, our investigation finds that the critical challenge of DID is the security threat posed by centralized storage. DID is originally designed to break the monopoly of digital identities by centralized institutions. However, due to the complexity of distributed storage [4,8,10,23], DID generally adopts centralized storage (e.g., cloud storage) in practical deployments. Thus, service providers still control the identity information of users, resulting in DID cannot effectively exert advantages. The blockchain-based DID solution solves the problem of storage security. However, the scalability of the blockchain limits the development of DID in the financial field [9,24]. Besides, various financial institutions construct and utilize their blockchain systems. Valuable data are difficult to exchange and share between different chains, resulting in information isolation. In other words, the identity data of collateral are difficult to share on several blockchains constructed by different institutions, which hinders the development of DID verification in financial mortgage loans [7].

In order to address above issues of DID in financial mortgage loans [13], this paper proposes a *Cross-chain Channel-based DID* (C3-DID) model to ensure the secure storage and exchange of the collateral DID. The C3-DID separates the financial mortgage loan process and the collateral identity authentication process on two consortium blockchains. Data packages are exchanged between two chains through *Relayers* (RE). In the field of cross-chain research, the BTC relay [2] realized one-way cross-chain connection from Bitcoin to Ethereum based on the relayer scheme. The proposed model is composed of three parts, including two consortium blockchain systems and the intermediate RE. Figure 1 shows the high level architecture of C3-DID. Chain-A is designed to calculate and store the loan business information between users and banks. Chain-B is responsible for calculating the data of the collateral identity authentication business between users and trusted third parties. Chain-B is also used to store the collateral DID and related *Verifiable Claim* (VC). In addition, RE connects the two consortium chains Chain-A and Chain-B by establishing a peer-to-peer *Matching Channel* (MC). Each data exchange requires a lock-up period to ensure that the DID and VC stored by Chain-B can be successfully transmitted to Chain-A. The data packages (including DID and VC) can prove the integrity and validity of the collateral identity.

Main contributions and innovations of this paper are twofold:

1. Different from other centralized storage solutions, the proposed C3-DID adopts blockchain to store DID and VC data. C3-DID eliminates the control of digital identity by centralized institutions. Besides, users can selectively share identity information, which protects the privacy of identity-sensitive data.
2. Two consortium blockchains are used in C3-DID to separate the collateral identity authentication business and the mortgage loan business. Importantly, the C3-DID realizes the mutual trust connection between the two consortium blockchains through anchored RE. At the same time, the cross-chain data exchange is realized by MC between peer nodes on different chains.

The remainder of this paper is organized by the follows. Main concepts and proposed model statements are given in Sect. 2. Next, in Sect. 3, we give detailed descriptions about our DID generation algorithm and data transfer algorithm. Finally, security analysis of the proposed system and conclusions are given in Sect. 4 and Sect. 5, respectively.

2   Proposed Method

2.1   Definitions

In this section, we explained related definitions in C3-DID.

Verifiable Claim (VC). After the verifiable claim initiator verifies that the user's specific characteristics (such as gender, age, etc.) are correct, it initiates a VC

Table 1. Risks and potential attack vectors

Role	Threat			
	DLP	AT	IR	DOS
CH	–	Y	–	Y
IV	–	–	Y	Y
MCNode(MCN)	Y	–	–	Y
CH + MCN	–	–	–	Y
IV + MCN	Y	–	Y	Y

of the user's identity. Any trusted party (verifier) that needs to verify the user will receive the VC and verify its authenticity.

Claim Issuer (CI). An entity that owns user data and can release VCs, such as the governments, universities and other institutions or organizations. In this paper, it refers to a trusted third party.

Claim Holder (CH). An entity that requests, receives and holds VC from CI, then show VC to IV. The released VCs are stored in the Chain-B for convenient reuse in the future.

Inspector Verifier (IV). An entity that accepts and verifies VCs, then it can provide a certain type of service to CH. In this paper refers to the bank.

Relayers (RE). RE is the hub of the entire model. All consortium chains must be anchored by RE to connect with other chains. RE contains some nodes from Chain-A and Chain-B. The node cluster on the RE will participate in the matching of nodes between multiple chains and the creation of MC.

peer-to-peer Matching Channel (MC). RE can authorize the creation of a peer-to-peer matching channel among nodes for cross-chain data exchange through smart contracts. MC provides a dedicated communication channel among nodes on multiple chains. We suppose all nodes on MC are trusted.

Lock-up period (Tlock). The lock-up period is the data freeze period on Chain-A. The lock time is the duration of time that data is frozen on Chain-B before being transmitted to Chain-A. During the lock-up period, nodes in RE will verify the transaction from Chain-B to Chain-A. We define the lock period in Eq. (1), where *Plock* is the multi-parameter set by the user, and *Tblock* is the average block generation time.

$$Tlock = Plock \times Tblock. \tag{1}$$

2.2 Threat Model

Table 1 summarizes the risks and potential attack vectors. Since CI is a trusted third party in this system, we assume that CI will not commit fraud.

Notes. DLP means "Data Leakage during Program execution", which may occur during the execution of the data packet exchange smart contract on Chain-A, Chain-B or MC. AT means "Authority Transfer", which means that the ownership of the smart contract has been transferred. IR means "Information Reselling", that is the original information of CH is resold or forwarded to an unauthorized third-party. "Y" means *yes*.

DelegateCall Vulnerabilities. During the execution of the smart contract, the attacker uses the CALL and DELEGATE CALL functions to call other contracts to leak relevant sensitive data. Since nodes in the channel MC are randomly selected, there may be malicious MC nodes leaking DID and VC information through this vulnerability during the data package transmission (DLP). At the same time, when the execution of the smart contract is over, the dishonest IV may forward the packet information to an unauthorized third party after receiving it (IR). In the same way, the IV can collude with the MCN node to achieve the purpose of leaking or forwarding data, so it is a risk of DLP and IR.

Change of Contract Ownership. In some versions of smart contracts, the contract name and the constructor function name are required to be strictly consistent. When names are different, the constructor function can be called by other contracts. CH applies for the collateral DID on Chain-B. The attacker (maybe other dishonest CH) may use this method to attack the OWMER function and obtain the ownership of the current smart contract of CH, that is, the ownership of the DID can be transferred. CH has a risk of AT.

DOS Attack. The attacker can repeatedly call the contract or frequently initiate a lock-up period to exhaust the network communication resources in the system. All roles in C3-DID may launch DOS attacks.

The Threat of Multiple Mortgages. After a DID and VC have participated in the mortgage loan, the malicious node still uses the DID to apply for loans from other IVs before the VC expires and is revoked by CI. At the same time, the malicious node does not update the VC data on Chain-B, so what IV gets is VC data that has not been updated before. The attacker uses this method to obtain funds through multiple mortgages.

2.3   Model Design

This paper proposes C3-DID that provides a solution for realizing the exchange of information between multiple blockchains. The C3-DID not only record the cross-chain data without tampering, but also realize the cross-chain data exchange. Figure 2 illustrates the architecture of C3-DID, which contains four key components.

In our double-chain storage identity authentication system, Chain-A is used for mortage loan transactions. Chain-B is used for collateral identity authentication and store DID or VC at the same time. Both Chain-A and Chain-B are consortium chains developed by Tendermint and adopt Tendermint's consensus algorithm. Tendermint was a consensus algorithm commonly used in cross-chain

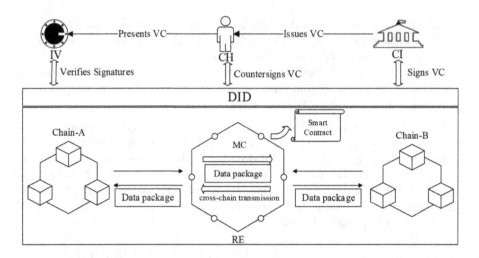

Fig. 2. The architecture of Cross-chain Channel-based DID.

based on relayers [1]. It had improved on the basis of PBFT, combined with POS consensus. The two chains A and B need to register with each other before performing the cross-chain data transmission. During the registration process, the two chains A and B will send their respective genesis block and ChainID using to represent different chains to each other. Since the genesis block contains the Validator information, the A and B chains will have the Validator information of the other chain and the block header information after registration.

Only stakeholders (i.e., CHs and CVs) can access the VC data on Chain-B. The two-way anchoring of Chain-A and Chain-B is realized by the mapping nodes. The anchor master nodes on the consortium chain accepted by the RE will form a mapping node in the RE, that is, the anchor master node *master-a* on the Chain-A will create its own mapping node *master-a'* in the RE. Similarly, the mapping node of *master-b* on the Chain-B is *master-b'*. The mapping nodes synchronize the information of original chain including chain ID, node ID, number of nodes and other blockchain data. The user accounts transmit data through the RE and MCs. The essence of the MC is a private permitted blockchain with a small number of random nodes. Each time the information of data package exchanged across the chain through the channel is recorded on the chain. After a node joins the same channel, it can share or manage all cross-chain data recorded in the channel. Every data transmission and exchange requires a lock-up period with the intention to ensure the successful transmission of data package in the MC.

This model can minimize the security risk on Chain-A. Loan transactions and identity data storage are carried out separately which can both simplify the storage, sharing or verification of personal data and eliminate redundant identity authority procedures. C3-DID proactively cater to supervision while reduce costs. Figure 3 shows main phases of C3-DID.

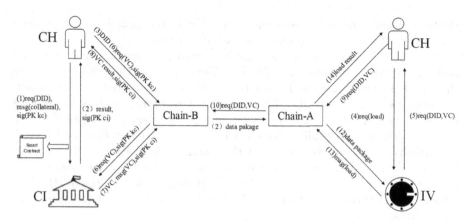

Fig. 3. The basic workflow of Cross-chain Channel-based DID .

Phase I: System Initialization. First, the system should be initialized. Individual users register through the third-party platform. After registration, both Chain-A and Chain-B will generate user accounts in the system and obtain the corresponding addresses. At the same time, a key pair is randomly generated. The chain-A key pair is (PK_{km}, SK_{km}) and the corresponding Chain-B key pair is (PK_{kc}, SK_{kc}). Next, the system will storage the smart contracts through submitting the transaction. Then the system will activate the mining process, and we can obtain the contract address after activating the mining process and successfully writing it into the block.

Phase II: Collateral Identity Authentication Process. Steps (1), (2), and (3) are the procedures for the CH to apply for the DID of the collateral by using the smart contract. Step (1). CH initiates a request for collateral DID to CI through a smart contract on Chain-B. The content of the smart contract includes objective data required for the application of the collateral and the related supporting documents msg (collateral). And CH uses the public key PK_{kc} to sign the contract. Step (2). CI verifies the data msg (collateral) in the smart contract, then responds to the request and returns the DID result of the application. Definitely, the contract also should have the signature of CI. When the respond consequence is passed, the DID application of CH is successful and the system allows CH collateral to be registered and used. Then these certification documents will get a capture method similar to the QR code and are stored in the CI local database for convenient reuse. Otherwise, the DID request fails and CH need to apply again. Step (3). When the application in step (2) is successful, the DID of the collateral will be generated based on the smart contract address produced in this application through the encryption algorithm (Algorithm 1) and will store in the DID document on Chain-B. We should pay attention that DID is not generated by CI and passed from CI to CH.

Phase III: Mortgage Loan Application Process. Steps (4)–(14) are the entire process of mortgage loan application, of which steps (6), (7), and (8) are the verification statement generation process (detailed explanation in 3.4.4), and steps (9)–(11) are the data cross-chain exchange process.

Step (4). CH applies for a mortgage loan from IV through a smart contract and signs it with the public key PK km. The content of the contract includes the required loan application information. Step (5). After receiving the request, IV sends the collateral verification request to CH. Step (6)–(8) is the process of CH applying for VC to CI after receiving request from IV. In step (9)–(11), when the VC is successfully released, CI initiates a request through Chain-A to Chain-B to display the VC and DID. Then Chain-B successfully responds it and transmits data package across the chain through MC. In steps (12)–(14), IV receives data package of VC and DID then verifies it. Finally, the loan information is transmitted to Chain-A after IV signs it, then CH receives the loan results.

Phase IV: VC Service Process. Steps (6)–(8) explain how the VC is generated. In step (6), CH first initiates a certificate request on Chain-B and then CI responds to it and processes it. Step (7). CI accepts the claim content from CH after it verifies that specific characteristics of the CH (such as gender, age, etc.) are correct according to the signature. Then CI produces VC and signs it, and stores the VC and claim content msg (VC) in Chain-B in order to transmit it to Chain-A next. Finally, in step (8), Chain-B issues VC to CH.

In order to prevent various hidden dangers that may exist in the VC service process, CI has the right to revoke the VC issued by itself. The following is the revocation process of VC. CI first checks the revocation status of the selected VC on Chain-B. If the VC has not been revoked, it initiates a smart contract to revoke it. The revocation result is stored as a block on Chain-B, and the same result will be broadcast to the CH node that owns the VC. The content of the contract needs to include the revocation method, CH address, and the VC address that need to be revoked. In order to prevent the threat of multiple mortgages, when the VC is issued by CI and stored on Chain-B for a specific period *effective time*, CH can revoke the expired VC.

Phase V: Cross-chain Data Exchange Process. Steps (9)–(11) are the cross-chain data exchange process. After Chain-B receives the request from Chain-A for VC and DID, it will transmission the data packet including cross-chain data, timestamp, VC and DID data and node signatures to Chain-A. The transmission method is building MC through RE.

MC is a channel created through smart contracts authorized by RE nodes. It is a private permitted chain containing a small number of random trusted nodes which are from Chain-A and Chain-B in RE. It is assumed that all random nodes are trusted nodes. Each block on the chain records the data information that is exchanged each time through the channel. These data information are jointly recorded and maintained by the nodes that join the channel and the two parties are allowed to participate in the chain. Each time the data information is regarded as it is a bookkeeping in the channel ledger system, and the data information is recorded in the form of blocks and stamped with a timestamp. Therefore, each data information is securely encrypted and stored in strict order.

Each block is connected in a strict timestamp sequence to form a general ledger or blockchain. When a node queries cross-chain historical data information, it can find the block corresponding to the timestamp node to read.

The MC contains multiple groups of nodes belonging to different chains. Nodes on different chains are added to the channel by executing the channel script file.

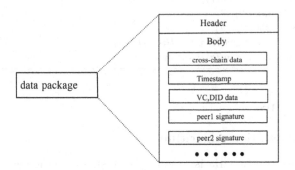

Fig. 4. The basic structure of data package.

Figure 4 shows the basic structure of data package. The data package submission process from Chain-B to Chain-A is as follows. First, in step (10), Chain-B receives a data request from Chain-A. If the required data has been recorded in the block through the consensus by Chain-B ,it will respond correctly. In addition, the data package is verified with the local ledger by 51% of the trusted nodes randomly selected by Chain-B in the MC and signed with the node's public key, and then the data exchange is initiated.

Second, the RE will enter a lock-up period after the data exchange is initiated. During the lock-up period, the node master-b will packet the cross-chain data and broadcast it in the MC to the nodes from Chain-A in the RE for verification. The nodes on Chain-A verify the node signatures in the data package. When the verification is passed, it will be fed back to the node master-a on Chain-A.

Then the information which consists of cross-chain data, node list, node signature and so on will be packaged into blocks linked to the blockchain in MC by master-a, and then master-a broadcast to all nodes in the MC for recording. Finally, in Chain-A, 51% of trusted nodes on Chain-A that join MC broadcast cross-chain data blocks to other nodes on Chain-A, and other nodes verify them on the broadcast area according to the Chain-B nodes signature. When the verification is valid, the data package is recorded locally and displayed to the IV. The system unlock at the same time. The cross-chain data exchange from Chain-B to Chain-A is completed through MC, and the authenticity of the data information is guaranteed.

When the data sending node is the same as the last node that sent the lock request, the time between two requests need to reach the freeze time.

Algorithm 1. DID Generation Algorithm

Require: User Address $uaddr$, User Public Key $PKkc$, CI Public Key $PKci$
Ensure: DID
  1: $scid \leftarrow \text{``} did:\text{''};$
  2: $mid \leftarrow \text{``} mor:\text{''};$
  3: $pHash = SHA256(PKkc)$
  4: $hash1 = SHA256(uaddr)$
  5: $hash2 = ripemd160(hash1)$
  6: $aBit = base58(hash2)$
  7: $cHash = SHA256(PKci)$
  8: $ms - id = Constructor(pHash, aBit, cHash);$
  9: $DID \leftarrow$ Connect $scid, mid, msid$ in order

---

3 Algorithms

3.1 DID Generation Algorithm

W3C stipulates that a DID is a simple text string consisting of three parts: 1) the did URI scheme identifier, 2) the identifier for the DID method, and 3) the DID method-specific identifier. We assume the first two parts $scid$ and mid are "did:" and "mor:" respectively. The text string $msid$ in the third part is composed of three key values, including $pHash$, $aBit$ and $cHash$. The $pHash$ means the SHA256 hash value of the user's public key PK kc.The $aBit$ means the value generated by the contract address $conaddr$ after hash, ripemd160 and base58 encryption and the $cHash$ means the CI public key SHA256 hash value of PK_{ci}. The DID generation algorithm is shown in Algorithm 1.

The input of the algorithm is Contrast Address $conaddr$, User Public Key (PK_{kc}) and CI Public Key (PK_{ci}). $conaddr$ means the smart contract address of the user to apply for DID. PK_{kc} means the public key on the user's chain-B chain, and PK_{ci} means the public key of CI. The output is the collateral DID, which is used when the user submit a collateral registration request to the bank.

Algorithm 1 encodes the public key into a byte array, and then converts the byte array into a hexadecimal string. It performs a SHA-256 hash operation on the string to obtain the hash value of the public key, that is, the value of the $pHash$ in the DID. Get the $cHash$ of the CI public key in the same way. In addition, the smart contract address may generate $aBit$ through a double hash encryption process similar to Bitcion. The $pHash$, the $aBit$ and the $cHash$ form the DID method-specific identifier. Finally, the existing fields are stored in the DID data, $scid$, mid and $msid$ included.

The analysis of time complexity of the DID Generation Algorithm is given below. First, the scales of $conaddr$, PK_{kc} and PK_{ci} are fixed. The length of $conaddr$ is 20 bytes, and the length of PK_{kc} and PK_{ci} are both 64 bytes. For any input smart contract address, user public key and CI public key, a certain number of encryption algorithms and a string concatenation operation are required to generate $msid$. In addition, $scid$ and mid only need to perform a certain assignment operation, and finally the generation of DID requires a string

---

Algorithm 2. Channel Lock-up Algorithm

Require: Sending Node Address *snaddr*, current lock node address *clnaddr*, last lock
    node address *llnaddr*, freeze time *ftime*, lock start time *lstime*

Ensure: Current lock node address *clnaddr*, last lock node address *llnaddr*, lock start
    time *lstime*.

 1: **if** *clnaddr*! = *address*(0) **then**
 2:    the channel cannot be locked;
 3: **end if**
 4: **if** (*lstime* + *ftime* >= *now*) and (*llnaddr* == *snaddr*) **then**
 5:    the channel cannot be locked;
 6: **end if**
 7: the Channel Lock-up request succeeded;
 8: current lock node address *clnaddr* ← *snaddr*;
 9: lock start time *lstime* ← *now*;

---

connection. Thus each process of the DID Generation Algorithm is completed in a constant time, so the time complexity is $O(1)$.

3.2 Channel Lock-Up Algorithm

In Algorithm 2, the sending node can lock the channel. This algorithm is implemented on the RE in chain-A, and the purpose is to provide locking services to achieve global consensus. The lock-up algorithm is activated during the interaction between the external node and the MC node.

The algorithm first checks the address of the current lock node. If the channel has been locked by a node, the channel lock-up request from other nodes may fail. Next, if the data sending node is the same as the last node which sent the channel lock-up request, the algorithm will check whether the time between the two requests meets the freeze time (*ftime*) requirement. A lock-up request transaction that meets all the above requirements is a valid lock-up request. Therefore, the contract records the current lock node address of the new lock channel and the new lock start time.

The length of the node address *snaddr*, *clnaddr*, and *llnaddr* is fixed at 20 bytes, and the values of *ftime* and *lstime* are also fixed. Only one operation is required in the two IF structures in the Channel Lock-up Algorithm. Therefore, each process in the Channel Lock-up Algorithm is finished in a constant time, and the time complexity of the algorithm is $O(1)$.

4 Security Analysis

In this section, we combine the security analysis with Table 1 in Sect. 2.3.

DelegateCall Vulnerabilities. A dishonest IV node can write a malicious smart contract to steal or forward the DID and VC data package. The malicious contract may call other smart contracts by executing CALL and DELEGATE CALL functions, thereby leaking data package information or forwarding received data package to unauthorized third parties. In order to solve this problem, we have made restrictions to on Chain-B and prohibit the ability of smart contracts to make calls or delegate calls. Since we assumed that MCN selected the trusted nodes in Chain-A and Chain-B during the modelling process, MCN may not have a risk of DLP and may not collude with dishonest IV.

In addition, DID and VC have strong confidentiality. The DID stored in the data package is the encrypted text string, and the text string itself does not have any meaning. The public key information of the user and CI is encrypted by the hash algorithm, so that the DID cannot reflect any private information. As for VC, we can adopt a zero-knowledge proof method to prove the integrity and validity of the collateral with as little and rough information as possible. Even if the data package is leaked, the attacker cannot obtain useful sensitive data.

Change of Contract Ownership. Dishonest CH has AI risk. Malicious CH nodes can change the ownership of the contract by attacking the hidden loopholes in the Chain-B contract code, in order to invade the DID of other CHs. One example is that in previous versions of smart contracts, the contract name is strictly the same as the constructor function name. If they are different, the constructor function can be called by other contracts. If the permission contract is named Owner and the constructor function is named owner(), the attacker can write other malicious contracts to call this function owner(), and then it can change the ownership of the contract.

In order to solve this problem, our smart contract adopts the version after 0.4.2. At the same time, the C3-DID application contract for DID strictly controls the variables and representations that characterize permissions, that is, these sensitive variables should also be controlled by function modifiers to ensure a closed loop of permissions.

DOS Attack. On the one hand, an attacker who can play any role in the system may call contracts repeatedly by applying for DID with the intention to consume network communication resources in Chain-B. The attacker can continuously broadcast his need through smart contracts and do not perform any subsequent operations. On the other hand, attackers on Chain-A can lock the system by sending a lock-up request, but they will not unlock it. It may result in the system being unable to meet the lock requests of other nodes.

In order to prevent the DOS attack, a token system can be introduced. The smart contract in the Chain-B will charge certain tokens as an additional broadcast fee. When a node in Chain-A initiates a smart contract and requests to lock the channel, the node must pay some tokens as a collateral. The tokens will be consumed when the node ether starts the smart contract but unintentionally completes subsequent operations or locks the channel but do not want to unlocks it. In this way, the attacker will be punished. The introduction of the token system is a further research direction.

The Threat of Multiple Mortgages. The malicious node encapsulates the unupdated data of DID and VC on Chain-B into data package and transmits it to Chain-A and then displays the data package to different IVs. Its purpose is to use the same collateral for multiple mortgages and fraudulent funds.

To avoid the risk of multiple mortgages, C3-DID sets up three verification processes. The first is the verification of VC data on Chain-B. When the storage time of a VC on Chain-B exceeds the *effective time*, CI will revoke it after checking the status of the VC to the VC from being stored on Chain-B for too long. Then, the RE verifies the validity of the VC. The MC in the RE records each exchanged data package on the local blockchain. When Chain-A requests the DID and VC data package from Chain-B, the MC node will first check whether there is a data package record related to the DID on the RE blockchain. If so, it proves that DID has participated in other mortgage loans, and a new VC is needed to prove the validity of collateral. Finally, the VC contains the declared expiration time, so when the data package is displayed to the IV, the IV will verify whether the VC has expired through the expiration time data of the VC. C3-DID guarantees the validity of the transmitted VC through three verification processes, avoiding the occurrence of multiple mortgages as much as possible.

5 Conclusions

In this paper, we deployed the loan process and the identity verification process on consortium blockchains separately and implemented mortgage loans on the blockchain. A novel method of using the C3-DID and RE was proposed to ensure the secure distributed storage of mortgage DID authentication, and the method of lock-up period was proposed to ensure the cross-chain exchange of data package. The analysis showed that the C3-DID can effectively resist multiple mortgages and some other threats, so that C3-DID had good security performance.

Acknowledgements. This work is partially supported by National Natural Science Foundation of China (Grant No.s 61871037, 61972034), Natural Science Foundation of Shandong Province (Grant No.s ZR2019ZD10, ZR2020ZD01), Natural Science Foundation of Beijing Municipality (Grant No. 4202068), Ministry of Education - China Mobile Research Fund Project (Grant No. MCM20180401).

References

1. Assiri, B., Khan, W.Z.: Enhanced and lock-free tendermint blockchain protocol. In: 2019 IEEE International Conference on Smart Internet of Things (SmartIoT), Tianjin, China, pp. 220–226 (2019)
2. Chow, J.: Btc relay. btc-relay (2016)
3. Dai, W., Qiu, M., Qiu, L., Chen, L., Wu, A.: Who moved my data? Privacy protection in smartphones. IEEE Commun. Mag. **55**(1), 20–25 (2017)
4. Gai, K., Guo, J., Zhu, L., Yu, S.: Blockchain meets cloud computing: a survey. IEEE Commun. Surv. Tutor. **22**(3), 2009–2030 (2020)

5. Gai, K., Wu, Y., Zhu, L., Qiu, M., Shen, M.: Privacy-preserving energy trading using consortium blockchain in smart grid. IEEE Trans. Ind. Inf. **15**(6), 3548–3558 (2019)
6. Gai, K., Wu, Y., Zhu, L., Zhang, Z., Qiu, M.: Differential privacy-based blockchain for industrial internet-of-things. IEEE Trans. Ind. Inf. **16**(6), 4156–4165 (2019)
7. Gai, K., Qiu, M., Sun, X., Zhao, H.: Security and privacy issues: a survey on FinTech. In: SmartCom, pp. 236–247 (2016)
8. Gao, F., Zhu, L., Gai, K., Zhang, C., Liu, S.: Achieving a covert channel over an open blockchain network. IEEE Network **34**(2), 6–13 (2020)
9. Gervais, A., Karame, G.O., Wüst, K., Glykantzis, V., Ritzdorf, H., Capkun, S.: On the security and performance of proof of work blockchains. In: Proceedings of the 2016 ACM SIGSAC Conference on Computer and Communications Security, Vienna, Austria, pp. 3–16 (2016)
10. Guo, J., Gai, K., Zhu, L., Zhang, Z.: An approach of secure two-way-pegged multi-sidechain. In: Wen, S., Zomaya, A., Yang, L.T. (eds.) ICA3PP 2019. LNCS, vol. 11945, pp. 551–564. Springer, Cham (2020). https://doi.org/10.1007/978-3-030-38961-1_47
11. Hughes, A., Sporny, M., Reed, D.: A primer for decentralized identifiers-an introduction to self-administered identifiers for curious people. (w3c credentials community group) (2019)
12. Laborde, R., et al.: A user-centric identity management framework based on the W3C verifiable credentials and the FIDO universal authentication framework. In: IEEE 17th Annual Consumer Communications & Networking Conference (CCNC), Las Vegas, USA, pp. 1–8 (2020)
13. Qiu, M., Cao, D., Su, H., Gai, K.: Data transfer minimization for financial derivative pricing using monte Carlo simulation with GPU in 5G. IEEE Int. J. Commun. Syst. **29**(16), 2364–2374 (2016)
14. Qiu, M., Gai, K., Xiong, Z.: Privacy-preserving wireless communications using bipartite matching in social big data. FGCS J. **87**, 772–781 (2018)
15. Reed, D., et al.: Decentralized identifiers (DIDs) v1. 0. Draft Community Group Report (2020)
16. Schrimpf, A., Drechsler, A., Dagianis, K.: Assessing identity and access management process maturity: first insights from the German financial sector. Inf. Syst. Manag. **38**(2), 94–115 (2021)
17. Shao, Z., et al.: Real-time dynamic voltage loop scheduling for multi-core embedded systems. IEEE Trans. Circuits Syst. II **54**(5), 445–449 (2007)
18. Simons, A.: Toward scalable decentralized identifier systems. Microsoft Tech Community (2019). https://techcommunity.microsoft.com/t5/Azure-Active-Directory-Identity/Toward-scalable-decentralized-identifiersystems/ba-p/560168
19. Tian, Z., Li, M., Qiu, M., Sun, Y., Su, S.: Block-DEF: a secure digital evidence framework using blockchain. Inf. Sci. **491**, 151–165 (2019)
20. Windley, P., Reed, D.: Sovrin: a protocol and token for self-sovereign identity and decentralized trust. Whitepaper, The Sovrin Foundation, USA (2018)
21. Yoon, C., Hwang, J., Cho, M., Lee, B.G.: Study on did application methods for blockchain-based traffic forensic data. Appl. Sci. **11**(3), 1268 (2021)
22. Zhang, Y., Gai, K., Qiu, M., Ding, K.: Understanding privacy-preserving techniques in digital cryptocurrencies. In: Qiu, M. (ed.) ICA3PP 2020. LNCS, vol. 12454, pp. 3–18. Springer, Cham (2020). https://doi.org/10.1007/978-3-030-60248-2_1
23. Zhu, L., Wu, Y., Gai, K., Choo, K.: Controllable and trustworthy blockchain-based cloud data management. Future Gener. Comput. Syst. **91**, 527–535 (2019)

24. Zhu, X., Badr, Y.: A survey on blockchain-based identity management systems for the internet of things. In: IEEE iThings/GreenCom/CPSCom/SmartData, Halifax,Canada, pp. 1568–1573 (2018)
25. Zyskind, G., Nathan, O., Pentland, A.: Decentralizing privacy: using blockchain to protect personal data. In: IEEE Symposium on Security and Privacy Workshops (SPW), San Jose, USA, pp. 180–184 (2015)

Blockchain-Based Privacy-Preserving Medical Data Sharing Scheme Using Federated Learning

Huiru Zhang[1], Guangshun Li[1], Yue Zhang[2], Keke Gai[3(✉)] [iD], and Meikang Qiu[4]

[1] College of Computer Science, Qufu Normal University, Rizhao 276800, China
guangshunli@qfnu.edu.cn
[2] School of Computer Science and Technology, Beijing Institute of Technology,
Beijing 100081, China
3220201017@bit.edu.cn
[3] School of Cyberspace Science and Technology, Beijing Institute of Technology,
Beijing 100081, China
gaikeke@bit.edu.cn
[4] Texas A&M University-Commerce, Commerce, TX 75428, USA
qiumeikang@ieee.org

Abstract. With the booming development of big data technology and health care applications, data in the medical field is characterized by explosive growth, and medical data is valuable, which is the privacy data of patients. However, the characteristics and storage environment of medical big data have brought great challenges to the realization of privacy protection of medical data. In order to ensure the protection of data privacy when sharing medical data, we propose a medical data privacy protection framework based on blockchain (MPBC). In this framework, we protect privacy by adding differential privacy noise into federated learning. In addition, the growing volume of medical data could make blockchain storage problematic. Therefore, a storage mode is proposed to reduce the storage burden of blockchain. The raw data are stored locally and only the hash value calculated by IPFS are stored in blockchain. To enhance the performance, a mechanism is used to validate transactions and aggregate the model. Security analysis shows that our method is a safe and effective way to implement medical data.

Keywords: Blockchain · Medical data · Privacy protection · Federated learning

1 Introduction

With the rapid development of *the Internet of Things* (IoT), cloud computing, machine learning [5,6], and other technologies, the era of big data has arrived [2]. Smart devices and digital medical instruments are rapidly popularized, and a large number of personal health data are continuously generated [33]. These

© Springer Nature Switzerland AG 2021
H. Qiu et al. (Eds.): KSEM 2021, LNAI 12817, pp. 634–646, 2021.
https://doi.org/10.1007/978-3-030-82153-1_52

personal data contain valuable information and are related to patients privacy [7,9]. In the process of data collection, storage, sharing and analysis, privacy information might be leaked [3]. Moreover, in addition to possessing 4V (Volume, Velocity, Variety and Value) characteristics of big data [2,17], medical big data is also incomplete and highly sensitive. Medical big data is directly related to human life and health when compared with other fields, so that it is necessary to have stricter requirements on safety [1,8]. Therefore, it is of great practical significance to explore medical data privacy protection strategies in the big data environment [12,21].

Due to network security isolation and industry privacy, data barriers exist between different industries and departments, leading to the formation of isolated islands of data, which cannot be shared safely [22]. Moreover, the performance of machine learning model based on independent data training of each department cannot reach the goal of global optimization. In order to solve this issue, Google proposed Federated Learning (FL) technology [32]. FL uses distributed machine learning and deep learning technologies to build a public virtual model on the basis of data within the domain. During the entire process of training and interaction, the data of each party is always kept in the local area. Instead of exchanging and merging raw data, only gradient updates are exchanged [14,34].

One of the most obvious advantages of FL is to build federated models without sharing raw data. However, there are also some security challenges.

- In the training process, the updated information of the model is constantly reported to the third party or the central server. The third party can continuously collect the data of all participants in different rounds and has the opportunity to analyze and derive the original information, which is prone to be a single-point failure.
- Although the gradient is transmitted in the training process rather than the original information, there is still a risk of exposing sensitive information, and there is still a chance to deduce user data from the update of gradient and model parameters.

In order to overcome theses challenges, a decentralized FL systems agency should be established. Blockchain technology enables the system to store learning models and updates them without a central server [15]. Security multi-party computation can also be used to achieve the aggregation of gradient updates, so that the security of the system is improved. In view of the information leakage risk that may be brought by gradient update in the latter challenge we propose above, differential privacy, encryption protection and other technical means can be added to protect sensitive information.

The contributions of our proposed method are threshold.

- This paper proposes a blockchain-based healthcare data privacy protection framework (MPBC), which uses federated learning technology to co-model the data without leaving the local area.
- To avoid a potential single-point failure on the central server, we use blockchain to store and share global models instead of aggregators in federated learning. The differential privacy noise is added in the local model

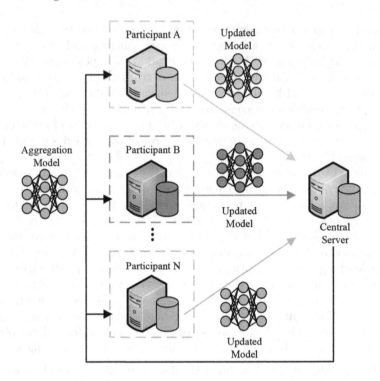

Fig. 1. Traditional federated learning system model.

training process to prevent the attacker from inferring the user's sensitive information by using the learned model.
- In order to reduce the storage pressure on the blockchain, the trained local model is uploaded to the Interplanetary File System (IPFS). Besides, hashes are calculated and uploaded to the blockchain as transactions, and the global model is aggregated and stored in the blockchain after verification by committees.

The remainder of this paper is organized as follows. In Sect. 2, we briefly review some background concepts and work related to this article. Section 3 illustrates our proposed model. Section 4 introduces the algorithm of adding differential privacy noise in federated learning. In Sect. 5, our method is experimented and analyzed. Finally, we conclude the paper in Sect. 6.

2   Background and Related Work

2.1   Federated Learning

FL aims to establish a federated learning model based on distributed data sets. An example of a traditional FL system is shown in Fig. 1. The central server can send the initial model to each participant, who will train the model with their own data set, and send the model weight update to the central server. The central server aggregates the model updates received from the participants and sends the aggregated model updates back to the participants. This process will be repeated until the model converges, the maximum number of iterations is reached, or the maximum training time is reached.

FL is used to build machine learning models with the following characteristics [30]:

1. Each participant has a large amount of training data for training the model.
2. During FL model training, data does not leave the local area.
3. It is necessary to ensure that no party can infer the original data of any other party.
4. The machine learning model obtained by the centralized training of all the training data sets should be able to fully approximate the ideal model.

In this architecture, the raw data of the participants never leaves itself. This method not only protects the privacy and data security of users, but also reduces the communication overhead caused by sending original data. In order to ensure data privacy and network security, Safa Otoum et al. [20] introduced a solution that integrates federated learning and blockchain and proposed a framework to decentralize mutual machine learning models on interrupt devices, effectively improving throughput and reducing latency. Lu et al. [18] proposed a federated learning framework for blockchain authorization, which enhanced security and privacy by integrating blockchain into a federated learning scheme to maintain trained parameters. Qu et al. [23] proposed a new blockchain-supported federated learning scheme that combines blockchain with federated learning to achieve decentralized privacy protection and prevent a single point of failure in fog computing scenarios.

2.2   Differential Privacy (DP)

The central idea of differential privacy is to confuse individual information when an adversary tries to query it from a database, making it impossible for an adversary to discern an individual-level sensitivity from the query results. ε-Differential privacy is defined as follows [30]:

Definition 1 (ε-Differential Privacy). For two datasets D and D' (adjacent datasets) where only one record is different, a randomization mechanism M can provide ε-differential privacy, and for all datasets $S \subset Range(\mathrm{M})$ that have:

$$Pr[\mathrm{M}(D) \in S] \leq Pr[\mathrm{M}(D') \in S] \times e^{\varepsilon}. \tag{1}$$

Pr represents the probability of the set composed of all possible outputs of the mechanism M, and ε represents the privacy budget. The smaller ε is, the higher the privacy protection density; The larger ε is, the higher the data availability is but the lower the retention density is.

There are two main ways to achieve differential privacy by adding noise to the data [31]. Another is to increase the noise according to the sensitivity of the function, that is the Laplace mechanism; One is to select the noise according to the exponential distribution of discrete values, that is the exponential mechanism.In the model [10], Laplace mechanism is used to add noise to the energy cost concentration, and differential privacy technology is implemented in the blockchain system to prevent the information on the block from being attacked based on data mining. In addition, Yin et al. [31] proposed a location privacy protection method satisfying the differential privacy constraint, which used Laplace operator to add noise to the access frequency of selected data to protect the location data privacy.

Generally, the overall research of blockchain technology is still in hot spot. How to directly or indirectly use differential privacy technology to protect the privacy information of blockchain will become the next research focus. Wan et al. proposed the blockchain-based solution designed for enhancing security and privacy in smart factory [27]. And Liu et al. also discussed the privacy in blockchain-enabled data collection and sharing for IIoT with the help of reinforcement learning [16].

2.3 Blockchain-Based IPFS

In a blockchain system, all nodes are equally involved in data recording, which is open and transparent to all nodes. It is easier to trace than traditional storage systems and can avoid the possibility of a single point of failure caused by a single node being controlled or bribed. In addition, because there are enough nodes, in theory, unless all the nodes are destroyed, the data records will not be lost, thus ensuring the security of the data [25, 26].

IPFS has following advantages [29]:

1. Content addressable: Content is hashed to make it easier to find and trace.
2. No duplicate content: the hash value in the system is unique, and the same content will produce the same hash value, so it will be judged as duplicate and deleted in time.
3. Content cannot be tampered with: the content of the system needs to pass the hash verification, if the content is tampered with, the hash value will naturally change.

IPFS technology uses hashing encryption to generate immutable permanent IPFS addresses for massive data and then stores the address information on the blockchain. This is equivalent to simplifying the original data into IPFS addresses and then uploading them to the chain, so as to realize off-chain storage without sacrificing decentralization and security. This method provides a feasible solution to the impossible triangle problem in the blockchain (that is, the blockchain cannot achieve scalability, decentralization and security at the same time).

Combining the characteristics of blockchain and IPFS, [19] complements IPFS with blockchain technology, providing a clear path to use blockchain as a service to track all activities related to a given file, thus improving the reliability of the data. Chen et al. [4] proposed an improved P2P file system based on IPFS and blockchain, which effectively improved the reliability and availability of data. Gaganjeet et al. [24] proposed a mechanism that allows hospitals and patients around the world to connect with each other using a licensed blockchain to store records using IPFS, ensuring that records are not deformed, which can effectively address the privacy and security issues existing in the current electronic health record (EHR) system.In order to solve the privacy threat brought by the use of a centralized storage model to store sensitive information, Randhir Kumar et al. [11] suggested using IPFS and blockchain technology to store medical data in a distributed off-chain. While protecting patient privacy, healthcare providers can easily access medical data, achieving consistency, integrity, and availability.In order to improve the scalability of the blockchain, Mathis Steichen et al. [25] proposed a modified version of IPFS, which uses the Ethereum smart contract to provide access-controlled file sharing, which can store and share large files more effectively.

3   Proposed Model

3.1   Design Goals

Privacy: We are focused on using a federated learning collaboration model to store healthcare data locally. Each participant controls its own data throughout the training and interaction and the data remains local. Since the data itself does not move, the privacy of medical data can be better ensured. At the same time, differential privacy noise is added in the local training to prevent the gradient information from leaking and achieve the purpose of privacy protection.

Traceability: Effectively aggregate the value of medical data obtained from various institutions through federal learning, and promote the further development of medicine. Institutional vandalism is inevitable throughout the learning process. IPFS uses hashes to identify people, and blockchain has traceability, so when a system is compromised, it can be traced to the person who broke it.

Extensibility: In order to ensure that the blockchain is open, transparent and non-tamperable, any node must be given equal rights and obligations. The performance of the system is limited by a single node, so scalability and throughput become a bottleneck. However, the idea of IPFS is consistent with the idea of blockchain, whether it is decentralized structure or information encryption technology. Therefore, we use the approach of IPFS + blockchain, which not only retains the advantages of decentralization and security of blockchain, but also solves the scalability problem that has been plagued for a long time.

3.2   Model Design

This section discusses the workflow of the proposed method, as shown in Fig. 2.

1. **Distribute model**: FL requires a central server to aggregate the local models, and a failure of this central server directly and seriously affects the training

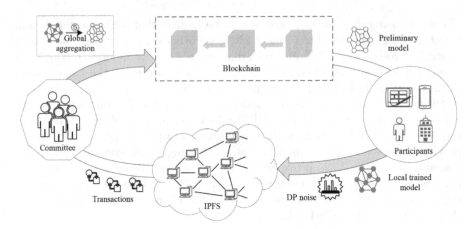

Fig. 2. Overview of our MPBC.

of the global model. Blockchain provides a trusted mechanism for various participants in federated learning. This paper uses blockchain to store an initial model with randomly selected parameters and each participant can send a request to obtain the model.

2. **Local training**: With the advent of big data, healthcare data are constantly being generated. Mobile devices, wearable devices and medical institutions used by users all have a large amount of medical and health data, which contains rich value. Each participant obtains the latest available model from the blockchain, uses the local data for training, and updates the local model.

3. **Add noise**: DP is a strict and provable privacy protection method. For a large scale of medical data, if the sensitivity of the query function can be controlled in a low range, a small amount of noise can be added to achieve the purpose of privacy protection. The noise calibrated by sensitivity s is added to the trained local model, and the Laplace mechanism is applied to the local data model m' to achieve differential privacy.

$$m' = m_i + Laplace(s/\varepsilon), \tag{2}$$

where s is the value of sensitivity, as shown in Eq. (3)

$$s = \max_{D,D'} \| M(D) - M(D') \|. \tag{3}$$

Then, the model m' with added noise is uploaded to IPFS. IPFS calculates the model parameters, calculates the hash and sends it to the blockchain as a transaction.

4. **Varify transaction**: Transactions are validated before they are added to the blockchain, so we set up a committee of several honest nodes that are responsible for validating transactions and block generation. After verification by the committee, only eligible transactions can be packaged onto the blockchain.

5. **Global Aggregation**: As a classic federated learning algorithm, federated average algorithm is widely used [13]. After the committee verifies and passes the transaction, the federated average algorithm is used to aggregate average the model. When the model parameters converge, model training can be completely stopped and the obtained global model can be uploaded to the blockchain and stored.

Table 1. List of Symbols

Symbols	Meaning
w_0	The nitial model parameters
C_t	A set of randomly selected participants
t	Training round
K	The number of participants
ρ	The percentage of users calculated in each round
k	The kth participant
$\bar{w}_t$	The latest model parameters
P_k	An index set of data points at uer k
n_k	The base of P_k
n	The number of training data
$w_{1,1}^{(k)}$	The latest model parameters obtained from the server
I	The number of iterations
D_k	A data set owned by the kth participant
M	The batch
b	The batch number
B	The number of batches
η	The learning rate
$g_k^{(b)}$	The batch gradient
S	The privacy sensitivity of DP
ε	The privacy budget of DP
$w_{t+1}^{(k)*}$	The latest model parameters added to DP

4   Algorithm

Table 1 presents the list of symbols used in this paper.

Based on federated average algorithm, this paper applies blockchain technology and combines this algorithm with differential privacy. Here, we assume that there are K participants (also known as data owners or clients) in a federated learning system, each with its own fixed set of local data. Algorithm 1 gives the details of the secure federated learning algorithm.

In Algorithm 1, the users use the mini-batch SGD (B batches) algorithm locally. For a typical implementation of distributed gradient descent with a fixed learning rate η, when updating global model parameters in round t, the kth participant will calculate the average gradient of the local data at the current model parameters, aggregate these gradients and use the updated information of the model parameters according to the following formula:

$$w_{t+1} \leftarrow w_t - \eta \sum_{k=1}^{K} \frac{n_k}{n} g_k. \tag{4}$$

The blockchain nodes can then send the updated model parameters w_{t+1} to each participant. Alternatively, the average gradient $\bar{g}_t = \sum_{k=1}^{K} \frac{n_k}{n} g_k$ can be sent to each participant and participants will calculate the updated model parameters according to Eq. (4). Each participant performs gradient descent locally on existing model parameters $\bar{w}_t$ using local data according to Eq. (5) and adds Laplace noise to locally updated model parameters $w_{t+1}^{(k)}$ through Eq. (6). Then, the weighted average calculation of the model results is carried out according to Eq. (7) and the aggregated model parameters $\bar{w}_{t+1}$ are sent to IPFS.

$$\forall k, w_{t+1}^k \leftarrow \bar{w}_t - \eta g_k, \tag{5}$$

$$w_{t+1}^{(k)*} = w_{t+1}^{(k)} + Laplace(0, S^2/\varepsilon), \tag{6}$$

$$\bar{w}_{t+1} \leftarrow \sum_{k=1}^{K} \frac{n_k}{n} w_{t+1}^{(k)*}. \tag{7}$$

5   Experiment and the Results

In order to verify the effectiveness of the design method in this paper, we used MNIST data set mentioned in literature [28] and set the number of participating nodes as 10. The MNIST dataset has a total of 70,000 images, of which 60,000 are used for training the neural network and 10,000 are used for testing. Each image is a hand-written digital picture of 0 9 with 28×28 pixels. This dataset is widely used in machine learning and deep learning to test the effectiveness of algorithms.

We compared our performance with federated learning training and training with individual nodes, as shown in Fig. 3. The experimental results showed that the federated learning method can effectively help the participants to obtain the model with higher accuracy. The improvement degree of model accuracy was also increasing with the continuous training. In addition, we combined federated learning with blockchain, based on the decentralized nature of blockchain, so there was no single point of failure. In the process of training, even if some nodes no longer participate in training, the remaining other nodes can continue

Algorithm 1. Secure FederatedAveraging Algorithm

Blockchain Node:
    initialize w_0, broadcast the w_0 to all participants
    for round t=1,2,...do
        $C_t = \max(K\rho, 1)$
        for each participant $k \in C_t$ do in parallel
            $w_{t+1}^{(k)^*} \leftarrow$ParticipantUpdate$(k, \bar{w}_t)$
        end for
        $\bar{w}_{t+1} \leftarrow \sum_{k=1}^{K} \frac{n_k}{n} w_{t+1}^{(k)^*}$
    endfor
ParticipantUpdate$(k, \bar{w}_t)$:
    $w_{1,1}^{(k)} = \bar{w}_t$
    for local iteration i from 1 to I do
        batches←(Randomly divide the data set D_k into the size of batch M)
        $w_{1,i}^{(k)} = w_{B,i-1}^{(k)}$ //Get local model parameters from the last iteration
        for b from 1 to $B = \frac{n_k}{M}$ do
            Calculate $g_k^{(b)}$
            $w_{b+1,i}^{(k)} \leftarrow w_{b,i}^{(k)} - \eta g_k^{(b)}$
        end for
    end for
    $w_{t+1}^{(k)} = w_{B,I}^{(k)}$
    $w_{t+1}^{(k)^*} = w_{t+1}^{(k)} + Laplace(0, S^2/\varepsilon)$

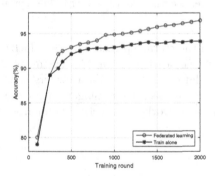

Fig. 3. Model accuracy when samples are sufficient.

to train and get good training results, as shown in Fig. 4. Figure 5 showed the effect of adding differential privacy to federated learning.

The experiment showed that we use federated learning instead of ordinary machine learning training model and the data remained local, which not only protected the privacy of user data, but also made the model sample more sufficient. Replacing a centralized server in federated learning with a blockchain removed the centralized trust to prevent a single point of failure. Differential privacy allowed gradient updates to be better protected from opponents inferring the original information. The addition of IPFS improved the scalability of

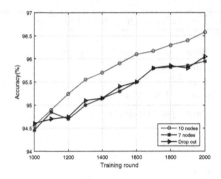

Fig. 4. Model accuracy when a part of nodes drop out.

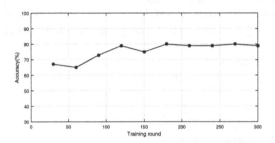

Fig. 5. Model accuracy compared with differential privacy.

the system and relieved the storage pressure on the blockchain. Only the hashes calculated by IPFS were uploaded to the blockchain, while the real data were stored locally by each data owner. The data owners can control the authority of their data and realize the security management of the data. Therefore, the implementation of our framework can effectively enhance the privacy protection capability.

6   Conclusions

In this paper, we design a blockchain-based healthcare data privacy protection framework. It decentralizes the system and avoids the risks of a centralized server. We built the framework using several advanced technologies, including blockchain, federated learning, and IPFS. In order to further protect data privacy from disclosure, we add differential privacy noise to better protect data privacy. Finally, the commission will verify records before they are uploaded to the blockchain, thereby preventing malicious users.

Acknowledgements. The authors would like to thank all anonymous reviewers for their valuable comments and suggestions to improve this paper. This work is partially supported by National Natural Science Foundation of China (Grant No. s 61972034, 61832012, 61771289), Natural Science Foundation of Shandong Province

(Grant No. ZR2019ZD10), Natural Science Foundation of Beijing Municipality (Grant No. 4202068), Ministry of Education - China Mobile Research Fund Project (Grant No. MCM20180401).

References

1. Aguiar, E.J.D., Faiçal, B.S., Krishnamachari, B., Ueyama, J.: A survey of blockchain-based strategies for healthcare. ACM Comput. Surv. **53**(2), 1–27 (2020)
2. Chen, M., Zhang, Y., Qiu, M., Guizani, N., Hao, Y.: SPHA: smart personal health advisor based on deep analytics. IEEE Commun. Mag. **56**(3), 164–169 (2018)
3. Chen, M., Qian, Y., Chen, J., Hwang, K., Mao, S., Hu, L.: Privacy protection and intrusion avoidance for cloudlet-based medical data sharing. IEEE Trans. Cloud Comput. **8**(4), 1274–1283 (2020)
4. Chen, Y., Li, H., Li, K., Zhang, J.: An improved P2P file system scheme based on IPFS and blockchain. In: Nie, J., et al. (eds.) 2017 IEEE International Conference on Big Data, BigData 2017, Boston, MA, USA, 11–14 December 2017, pp. 2652–2657. IEEE Computer Society (2017)
5. Gai, K., Qiu, M.: Optimal resource allocation using reinforcement learning for IoT content-centric services. Appl. Soft Comput. **70**, 12–21 (2018)
6. Gai, K., Qiu, M.: Reinforcement learning-based content-centric services in mobile sensing. IEEE Network **32**(4), 34–39 (2018)
7. Gai, K., Wu, Y., Zhu, L., Qiu, M., Shen, M.: Privacy-preserving energy trading using consortium blockchain in smart grid. IEEE Trans. Ind. Inf. **15**(6), 3548–3558 (2019)
8. Gai, K., Wu, Y., Zhu, L., Xu, L., Zhang, Y.: Permissioned blockchain and edge computing empowered privacy-preserving smart grid networks. IEEE Internet Things J. **6**(5), 7992–8004 (2019)
9. Gai, K., Zhu, L., Qiu, M., Xu, K., Choo, K.: Multi-access filtering for privacy-preserving fog computing. IEEE Trans. Cloud Comput. **PP**(99), 1 (2019)
10. Gai, K., Wu, Y., Zhu, L., Zhang, Z., Qiu, M.: Differential privacy-based blockchain for industrial internet-of-things. IEEE Trans. Ind. Inform. **16**(6), 4156–4165 (2020)
11. Kumar, R., Marchang, N., Tripathi, R.: Distributed off-chain storage of patient diagnostic reports in healthcare system using IPFS and blockchain. In: 2020 International Conference on COMmunication Systems & NETworkS, COMSNETS 2020, Bengaluru, India, 7–11 January 2020, pp. 1–5. IEEE (2020)
12. Li, Y., Gai, K., Qiu, L., Qiu, M., Zhao, H.: Intelligent cryptography approach for secure distributed big data storage in cloud computing. Inf. Sci. **387**, 103–115 (2017)
13. Li, Y., Zhou, Y., Jolfaei, A., Yu, D., Zheng, X.: Privacy-preserving federated learning framework based on chained secure multi-party computing. IEEE Internet Things J. **PP**(99), 1–1 (2020)
14. Lia, D., Togan, M.: Privacy-preserving machine learning using federated learning and secure aggregation. In: 2020 12th International Conference on Electronics, Computers and Artificial Intelligence (ECAI) (2020)
15. Lim, W.Y.B., et al.: Federated learning in mobile edge networks: a comprehensive survey. IEEE Commun. Surv. Tutor. **22**(3), 2031–2063 (2020)
16. Liu, C.H., Lin, Q., Wen, S.: Blockchain-enabled data collection and sharing for industrial IoT with deep reinforcement learning. IEEE Trans. Ind. Inform. **15**(6), 3516–3526 (2019)

17. Lu, R., Jin, X., Zhang, S., Qiu, M., Wu, X.: A study on big knowledge and its engineering issues. IEEE Trans. Knowl. Data Eng. **31**(9), 1630–1644 (2018)
18. Lu, Y., Huang, X., Zhang, K., Maharjan, S., Zhang, Y.: Blockchain and federated learning for 5g beyond. IEEE Network **35**(1), 219–225 (2021)
19. Nyaletey, E., Parizi, R.M., Zhang, Q., Choo, K.R.: BlockIPFS - blockchain-enabled interplanetary file system for forensic and trusted data traceability. In: IEEE International Conference on Blockchain, Blockchain 2019, Atlanta, GA, USA, 14–17 July 2019, pp. 18–25. IEEE (2019)
20. Otoum, S., Ridhawi, I.A., Mouftah, H.T.: Blockchain-supported federated learning for trustworthy vehicular networks. In: IEEE GLOBECOM 2020-2020 IEEE Global Communications Conference, Taiwan, pp. 1–6 (2020)
21. Qiu, H., Qiu, M., Lu, Z.: Selective encryption on ECG data in body sensor network based on supervised machine learning. Inf. Fus. **55**, 59–67 (2020)
22. Qiu, H., Qiu, M., Liu, M., Memmi, G.: Secure health data sharing for medical cyber-physical systems for the healthcare 4.0. IEEE J. Biomed. Health Inform. **24**(9), 2499–2505 (2020)
23. Qu, Y., et al.: Decentralized privacy using blockchain-enabled federated learning in fog computing. IEEE Internet Things J. **7**(6), 5171–5183 (2020)
24. Reen, G., Mohandas, M., Venkatesan, S.: Decentralized patient centric e-health record management system using blockchain and IPFS. CoRR abs/2009.14285 (2020)
25. Steichen, M., Pontiveros, B., Norvill, R., Shbair, W., State, R.: Blockchain-based, decentralized access control for IPFS. In: The 2018 IEEE International Conference on Blockchain (Blockchain-2018) (2018)
26. Tian, Z., Li, M., Qiu, M., Sun, Y., Su, S.: Block-DEF: a secure digital evidence framework using blockchain. Inf. Sci. **491**, 151–165 (2019)
27. Wan, J., Li, J., Imran, M., Li, D.: A blockchain-based solution for enhancing security and privacy in smart factory. IEEE Trans. Ind. Inform. **15**(6), 3652–3660 (2019)
28. Wu, X., Wang, Z., Zhao, J., Zhang, Y., Wu, Y.: FedBC: blockchain-based decentralized federated learning. In: 2020 IEEE International Conference on Artificial Intelligence and Computer Applications (ICAICA) (2020)
29. Xu, J., et al.: Healthchain: a blockchain-based privacy preserving scheme for large-scale health data. IEEE Internet Things J. **6**(5), 8770–8781 (2019)
30. Yang, Q., Liu, Y., Cheng, Y., Kang, Y., Chen, T., Yu, H.: Federated Learning. Synthesis Lectures on Artificial Intelligence and Machine Learning, Morgan & Claypool Publishers, Williston (2019)
31. Yin, C., Xi, J., Sun, R., Wang, J.: Location privacy protection based on differential privacy strategy for big data in industrial internet of things. IEEE Trans. Ind. Inform. **14**(8), 3628–3636 (2018)
32. Zhan, Y., Li, P., Qu, Z., Zeng, D., Guo, S.: A learning-based incentive mechanism for federated learning. IEEE Internet Things J. **7**(7), 6360–6368 (2020)
33. Zhang, J., Liang, X., Zhang, Z., He, S., Shi, Z.: Re-DPoctor: real-time health data releasing with w-day differential privacy. In: IEEE GLOBECOM 2017-2017 IEEE Global Communications Conference, Singapore (2017)
34. Zhang, Y., Gai, K., Qiu, M., Ding, K.: Understanding privacy-preserving techniques in digital cryptocurrencies. In: Qiu, M. (ed.) ICA3PP 2020. LNCS, vol. 12454, pp. 3–18. Springer, Cham (2020). https://doi.org/10.1007/978-3-030-60248-2_1

An Edge Trajectory Protection Approach Using Blockchain

Meiquan Wang[1], Guangshun Li[1], Yue Zhang[2], Keke Gai[3(✉)] ⓘ,
and Meikang Qiu[4]

[1] College of Computer Science, Qufu Normal University, Rizhao 276800, China
guangshunli@qfnu.edu.cn
[2] School of Computer Science and Technology, Beijing Institute of Technology,
Beijing 100081, China
3220201017@bit.edu.cn
[3] School of Cyberspace Science and Technology, Beijing Institute of Technology,
Beijing 100081, China
gaikeke@bit.edu.cn
[4] Texas A&M University–Commerce, Commerce, TX 75428, USA
qiumeikang@ieee.org

Abstract. With the popularity of edge-based trajectory applications, application providers have accumulated a large amount of user trajectory data. However, direct use of trajectory data containing rich privacy information has the risk of leaking user privacy. In this paper, we propose an edge trajectory protection approach using the technique of blockchain. This protection mechanism not only takes account of users information protection and identity authentication in block generation, but considers the screening mechanism to ensure the integrity of most authorized nodes. We propose trajectory entropy suppression method that combines it with a cost function evaluation sequence and achieve collaboration between regions by deploying smart contracts. Our experimental results demonstrate the efficiency and effectiveness of our proposed model.

Keywords: Blockchain · Edge trajectory · Anonymity · Location privacy

1 Introduction

Edge devices have the advantage of making computing more flexible and controllable, so it has become a widely used technology in many enterprises. These edge devices can exchange information with each other, but most trading platforms are centralized and their data processing [2] and scheduling control relies on trusted third-party. There are some challenges, such as single-point attacks and data leakage [3,6,17].

Blockchain has characteristics of tamper-resistance, traceability and decentralization. It is one of the most promising techniques for building a safe and

ⓒ Springer Nature Switzerland AG 2021
H. Qiu et al. (Eds.): KSEM 2021, LNAI 12817, pp. 647–658, 2021.
https://doi.org/10.1007/978-3-030-82153-1_53

trusted trading platform. As a matter of fact, many recent studies have explored the integration of blockchain and edge trajectory, but there are few practical on-ground solutions. In this paper, we intend to combine edge trajectory with blockchain to establish a secure trajectory information data protection mechanism to solve the problem of edge trajectory protection in data sharing. In order to achieve the proposed goal, there is a main issue that have to be taken into account.

In the existing trajectory protection schemes, the influence of group feature extraction on clustering is not well considered and the problem of designing a cooperation mechanism among anonymous regions is ignored.

To solve the above problem, we have carried out researches on the high-confidence block generation, reliable blockchain construction and edge trajectory security of blockchain system. We extract regional features, cluster them into position sequences, design an encryption algorithms, formulate screening rules for authorized nodes, construct trajectory entropy suppression evaluation cost functions and deploy smart contracts to achieve the efficiency, reliability and scalability of the blockchain system.

The main contribution of our work is threefold.

1. We extract the sensitive properties of the data and make improvements to enhance the confidence of fine-grained sensitive property blocks.
2. We develop a screening mechanism for authorized nodes, ensure the security of the key. Using neural network training data set to obtain a block recognition model and build a safe and efficient editable blockchain.
3. We study the relationship between security control mechanism and users location and design smart contract rules to solve the problem of edge trajectory protection in data sharing.

We organize the remainder of this paper in the following order. Section 2 provides a brief review of related work about blockchain and edge trajectory. System designs and main algorithms are shown in Sects. 3 and 4, respectively. Section 5 displays partial experiment results as well as main findings. Finally, Section 6 draws a conclusion of our work.

2   Related Work

In the process of block generation, using idle edge computing resources can effectively improve the efficiency of blockchain implementation [19]. Based on blockchain data tokens and energy tokens, Liu et al. [13] designed an electric vehicle cloud security model that integrates edge computing and blockchain. Gai et al. [8,9] proposed an edge Internet model based on blockchain and an edge blockchain model. These models fully combine the advantages of the two and optimize the block generation process.

For data-driven applications [14], encrypted data is regarded as a secure storage state and processing sensitive data in the encrypted domain can effectively prevent privacy leakage [7]. Li et al. [12] proposed a symmetric homomorphic encryption scheme. However, the algorithm is highly complex and it is difficult to effectively resist changeable attacks or thefts. Ding et al. [5] proposed a privacy protection data processing system based on homomorphic re-encryption, which can support seven basic operations based on ciphertext. Kuang et al. [11] proposed a fully homomorphic encryption hybrid operation based on tensor. The model uses the tensor law to perform mixed arithmetic operations within the real number range.

The construction of early blockchains mainly relied on traditional hash functional linking and traditional hash functions, which were so unitary that historical data could not be edited once confirmed. The emergence of editable blockchain [4] has opened up a new world for the development of blockchain.

At present, the interaction mechanism between nodes of editable blockchains needs to be further improved. Xu et al. [20] proposed a blockchain-based authentication management scheme to achieve user authentication and session key negotiation. Qiu et al. [16] proposed a dynamic scalable blockchain based communication architecture for IoT.

Ma et al. [15] proposed a budget allocation method based on regional privacy weights, which improves the privacy of real-time trajectory data. Wu et al. [18] proposed a location privacy protection system. The location privacy model is established to improve service efficiency. An et al. [1] designed a decentralized privacy protection model based on blockchain double verification and consensus to protect user identity privacy. Keshk et al. [10] proposed a privacy protection framework reduce the probability of data being attacked.

3   Proposed Model

3.1   Design Goals

In this paper, the design goals are distributed as follows.

First, high-confidence block generation. In response to the threat of privacy leakage to users, the user's sensitive information is divided, while taking into account the accuracy of property extraction and the efficiency of legal supervision.

Second, safe and efficient construction of editable blockchain. Aiming at the efficiency and security of blockchain construction, we adopt a reasonable screening mechanism of authorized nodes to improve the security of blockchain construction, which not only guarantees the high integrity of authorized nodes, but maintains the randomness of node selection.

Third, edge trajectory protection with trajectory entropy suppression. In response to the privacy leakage of edge trajectories in data sharing, according to the trajectory privacy and data access frequency, the trajectory entropy suppression evaluation cost function is designed to achieve the balance between the user's privacy protection cost and the benefit.

3.2   Threat Model

The threats to trajectory privacy information are multifaceted. According to the knowledge of the attacker, it is mainly divided into the following categories.

Trajectory Detection. Based on the precise location of the user at a certain moment, this type of threat further attempts to analyze the trajectory characteristics of the location data. When the attacker obtains enough positions, even if the specified privacy can be guaranteed with each position refresh, the trajectory characteristics can still be recognized from continuous observations.

Anit-anonymization Attack. Attackers are usually required to have a large amount of location data, which mainly threatens location privacy when location big data is released, but it can pose a certain threat to location privacy in the mobile Internet scenario.

Continuous Query Attack. The continuous query attack is in the K-anonymity method. When a mobile user continuously sends a request to the server, the attacker connects multiple anonymous boxes constructed by the anonymizer to form the approximate shape of the mobile user's trajectory, thereby inferring private information.

3.3   Model Design

First, verify the user's identity and extract its fine-grained sensitive properties. Use double encryption technology for encryption processing. Use improved Merkle tree to generate high-confidence blocks. Second, optimize the chameleon hash function, design a block recognition model and build a secure and efficient editable blockchain. Finally, the group features are extracted to generate anonymous regions and the location information is clustered into trajectory entropy sequences to obscure the user's real information and protect the edge privacy trajectory.

High-Confidence Block Generation. First, fine-grained sensitive properties extraction. The data has n properties, forming a set $X = \{x_1, x_2, ..., x_n\}$. Assuming that the user's expected value of protection for the sensitive property i is p_i, then the expected value set of all property protect is $P = \{p_1, p_2, ...p_n\}$. The entropy of each property is

$$E_i = -\ln(n)^{-1}\sum_{i-1}^{n} p_i \ln p_i. \tag{1}$$

The weight of each property is

$$W_i = \frac{1 - E_i}{n - \sum E_i}(i = 1, 2, ..., n). \tag{2}$$

Second, design an integer polynomial ring and construct a double encryption algorithm. $F_p[x]$ is a set of integer polynomials, $f(x)$ is an integer polynomial and $f(x) \in F_p(x)$, design a double encryption algorithm based on $f(x)$.

One time encryption: Key generation: Choose random integers $a_i, r_i \in Z(Z$ is a set of integers). The public keys $pk = <b_0, b_1, ..., b_n>$ and b_i satisfy $b_i = a_i f_i(x) + r_i$, where $i = 1, 2, ..., n$ and b_0 are the largest elements in the public key pk.

Re-encryption: Key generation: Take the prime number $p, k \in Z$ arbitrarily and define $x_p = \lceil \frac{2^k}{p} - \frac{1}{2} \rceil$ and $u_i \in (0, 2^k)$ satisfies

$$\sum_{i \in S}^{n} u_i = x_p \bmod 2^k. \tag{3}$$

Let $v_i = \frac{u_i}{2^k}$, get the new public key $pk' = < pk, v_1, v_2, ..., v_n >$.

Encryption: Input ciphertext c_i and new public key pk', output new cipher-text $z = < z_1, z_2, ..., z_m >$, where $z = [c_i \cdot v_i] \bmod 2$.

Third, build a Merkle tree to generate blocks. The greater the weight $W_i (i = 1, 2, ..., n)$ of the fine-grained sensitive property, the higher the sensi-tivity. Sum the weights of all sensitive properties in the data D_i to obtain the sensitivity S_i of the data. The m data $D_i (i = 1, 2, ..., m)$ is hashed $hash(D_i)$ and stored in m leaf nodes. Then select the two most sensitive leaf nodes and perform hash operation to generate intermediate nodes. The hash operation is $hash(hash(D_i) + hash(D_j))$. Repeat the process until the intermediate node is merged with the least sensitive leaf node to generate the root node and finally the Merkle tree is obtained. As shown in Fig. 1, the more sensitive the data is hashed, the more security it is.

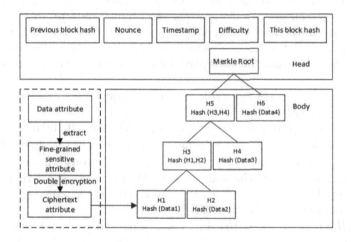

Fig. 1. High-confidence block construction process.

Blockchain Construction. First, authorized node screening mechanism. S is the set of all nodes and S_i represents the set of nodes whose credibility is in the top $\frac{1}{3}$. The authorized node consists of two parts, A and B. A and B satisfy:

$$\begin{cases} A \subset S_1. \\ B \subset (S - A). \\ A \bigcap B = \emptyset. \end{cases} \tag{4}$$

Assuming that the ratios of the number of nodes in A and B to the total number of authorized nodes are a and b respectively, then

$$\begin{cases} a = \dfrac{|A|}{|A| + |B|} \times 100\%. \\ b = \dfrac{|B|}{|A| + |B|} \times 100\%. \end{cases} \tag{5}$$

where $|A|, |B|$ respectively represent the number of nodes in the set A and B. a and b satisfy:

$$\begin{cases} a + b = 1. \\ a > 3b. \end{cases} \tag{6}$$

It can be seen that the authorized nodes with high integrity account for the vast majority ($> \frac{4}{3}$). A and B are respectively composed of authorized nodes randomly selected from the set S_1 and $(S - A)$. Since authorized nodes are randomly selected from the set that meets the conditions each time, targeted attacks from malicious nodes can be effectively avoided.

Second, construction method of Loop-sequence Chameleon Hash (LCH) based on ring sequence calculation. For the original data m and any random number r, the authorized node performs a ring sequence calculation to obtain the key and calculates the new random number r' to make the hash value of the original data m and the encrypted data m' equal. The design process is as follows:

$LCH.Setup(\lambda) \to (Par_{LCH})$: Input safety parameter λ and output system parameter Par_{LCH}.

$LCH.KeyGen(Par_{LCH}) \to ((c_1 \cdot \ldots \cdot c_k), hk)$: After inputting Par_{LCH}, k authorized nodes perform ring sequence calculation: The ith member chooses a $Z_q^* \xrightarrow{R} c_i$ as the trapdoor key. Set $t_i = c_i$, pass t_i to the $(i+1)th$ member, calculate $t_{i+1} = t_i \cdot c_{i+1}$ to the next member. After k rounds of the ring sequence, output the public key $hk = g^{(c_1 \Delta_2 \ldots \Delta_k)}$ and the private key $(c_1 \Delta_2 \ldots \Delta_k)$, where g is the generator of the cyclic group.

$LCH.Hash(hk, m, r) \to (h)$: Input safety parameter λ and output system parameter Par_{LCH}.

$LCH.Forge((c_1 \cdot \ldots \cdot c_k), (m, h, r), m') \to (r')$: Input private key $(c_1 \cdot \ldots \cdot c_k)$, tuple (m, h, r) and encrypted data m'. Output a new random number r' such that

$$LCH.Hash(hk, m, r) = LCH.Hash(hk, m', r'). \tag{7}$$

Third, block verification algorithm based on neural network. Each block contains identity information $R_i = \{ID_i, H_i\}$, where ID_i is the identification number of the block and H_i is the reliability index metric extracted from the block and cannot be copied. When a block in the blockchain needs to be modified, the identity information $R_i = \{ID_i, H_i\}$ of the known legal block i and the identity information $R_i = \{ID_i, H_i\}$ of the unknown block j are extracted. Compare whether the ID of block i and block j are the same. If $ID_i \neq ID_j$, block j is not a cloned block; otherwise, combine the reliability metrics of known legal blocks and cloned blocks to form a data set

$$S = \{(x_1, y_1)(x_2, y_2)...(x_n, y_n)\}. \tag{8}$$

The neural network is used to train the data set and generate a model satisfying the recognition rate. If the output of the neural network model is $r = 1$, then the unknown block j is a legal block; otherwise, block j is an illegal block. Replace the original damaged block with a legal block to ensure the integrity of the blockchain. The block recognition construction process is shown in Fig. 2.

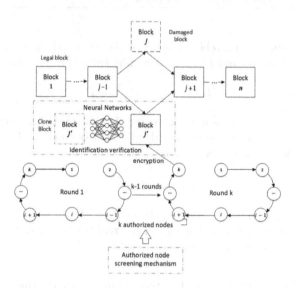

Fig. 2. Block recognition construction process.

Design of Edge Trajectory Protection Based on Smart Contract. First, extract group features and generate anonymous regions. Define the location of the user at time t as loc_t, calculate the trajectory change

$$L = \sum_{t=1}^{n} |loc_t - loc_{t-1}|. \tag{9}$$

Equation 9 is based on the time dimension information, cluster the calculation results and extract its dynamic feature λ_c. Let $S = \frac{1}{\lambda_c} L$ form the spatial sequence $< S_1, S_2, ..., S_n >$. According to the spatial sequence, the location is divided to form anonymous area, which can confuse the real data of users, avoid the leakage of the user's real location and protect edge privacy information.

Second, design of trajectory entropy suppression method. The probability of user trajectory T_i is

$$P_i = \sum_{i}^{n} e_i f_i. \tag{10}$$

Algorithm 1. Spurious Trajectory Generation

Input: Area $n \times n$ grids, real trajectory $U\{X_0, X_1, X_2, ..., X_m\}$, maximum moving speed v_{max}, service request time point Δt;
Output: k trajectories forming an anonymous set;
1: Divide $n \times n$ grids;
2: Use X_i and $d = v_{max} \times \Delta t$ to generate a spurious position;
3: **repeat**
4: $X_0, X1, X_2, ..., X_m$;
5: $X_i, X_{i+1} \rightarrow Pi, X_{is}$;
6: Generate spurious trajectory;
7: return k trajectories forming an anonymous set;

where e_i represents the correlation between the area and the user, f_i represents the frequency of access and $i = 1, 2, ..., n$. The trajectory entropy of user k is

$$H_k = -\sum_{i=1}^n P_i^{-1} \log P_i. \tag{11}$$

The trajectory entropy measures the degree of chaos of the trajectory. The lower the trajectory entropy is, the more orderly the trajectory is. The cost function of malicious node attack trajectory is

$$S(i, \omega) = 2\omega e_i^{\frac{i}{\omega}} \omega. \tag{12}$$

where ω is the cost parameter. When the entropy of all trajectories is similar, it is difficult for the attacker to distinguish the real trajectory of the user, so as to achieve the purpose of protection.

Set Smart Contract Rules. For the original data m, the sender uses the encryption function $En[sk, m]$ to obtain the encrypted data m'(where sk represents the key) and stores it on the blockchain. User u sends demand information according to the sharing protocol and broadcasts the demand to the node network. The smart contract updates the feedback information after the transaction and matches. The amount of information obtained is

$$I_u = \sum_{m=1}^M exp\{-\frac{e^{\frac{MR}{m}-1}}{S}\}. \tag{13}$$

where R represents the sending frequency, S represents the matching degree of user information and M represents the total amount of data required by the receiver. After receiving the information, the receiver uses $De[m']$ to decrypt it. Smart contract management nodes are used to protect the processing results through trusted nodes to ensure that each record can be traced. If the user violates the sharing agreement, the user is restricted from obtaining the remaining information.

Algorithm 2. *FormCloakArea*

Input: Unique cell identifier for each cell cid,$cloaked_set$, k users satisfying anonymity concentration;
  Output: Anonymous area $outrect$;
1: **for** $i = 0$ to $k - 1$ **do**
2:    $S\_uid \leftarrow cloaked\_set[i]$;
3:    $S\_cid \leftarrow$ the cell where S_uid is located;
4:    $rect[i] \leftarrow$ the coordinates of the cell $S\_cid\{lx_i, ly_i, rx_i, ry_i\}$;
5:    $outrect \leftarrow$ the smallest area covered by all elements in the array $rect[i]$;
6: **end for**
7: return $outrect$;

4 Algorithms

This section introduces spurious trajectories generation and the sub-function *FormCloakArea*() in the anonymous algorithm in the edge trajectory protection.

Spurious Trajectory Generation Algorithm. In the description of the spurious trajectory algorithm, assuming that the user moves in $n \times n$ grids, the user determines the real movement trajectory according to the known background information, current location and destination and the user's maximum moving speed is defined as v_{max}. According to the user's real trajectory, it is divided into several time points and it is determined that the user sends a service request every time at Δt. The setting of Δt can be determined by setting the time interval of the system. The pseudo codes are given in Algorithm 1.

According to the divided $n \times n$ grids, we obtain the historical sending probability. Find the grids that are close to the historical transmission probability of the true location point in the circular area and generate a spurious location in these grids. Calculate the position transition probability between two real positions, select the trajectory segment closest to the position transition probability and connect them to form a spurious trajectory.

Anonymous Area Generation Algorithm. Calculate the anonymous area based on the given anonymity set. The anonymous area should be the smallest area that includes all users. The location of each user can be represented by the corresponding area. Therefore, the algorithm first obtains the area corresponding to the user. The areas corresponding to each user in the anonymity set is merged one by one to form the final anonymous area. The pseudo codes are listed in Algorithm 2.

5 Experiment and the Results

In order to verify the effectiveness and efficiency of the solution in this paper, the experimental details are as follows. The experimental environment is Lenovo T430, the CPU is Intel Core i5, 8 GB memory and the operating system is Windows 10 64 bit.

We use the sensors and video cameras in the multi-functional light pole to collect the location and other trajectory information of the mobile user, collecting it every 5 s. The main event location is Rizhao's 50 users' movement trajectory for a week as historical location information. A total of 672 pieces of data are stored in a computer-simulated big data platform.

We use the sensors and video cameras in the multi-functional light pole to collect the location and other track information of the mobile user, collecting it every 5 s. The main event location is Rizhao's 50 users' movement trajectory for a week as historical location information, a total of 672 pieces of data, stored in a computer-simulated big data platform. The parameters involved in the experiment include: anonymity level k, usually set to 0–30. The number of time points on the track $m = 15$. Δt means that the GPS system sends a request every 2 s and obtains the service information of the query request. The longitude of the regional grid is 1000×1000 and each grid represents 10 m. The diameter of the circular area is $d = 20$ m.

In order to verify the performance of the mechanism proposed in this paper, the data selected in the experiment is obtained by taking a real user trajectory from big data. According to factors such as access frequency, we use trajectory entropy to suppress the cost function to train the neural network model according to factors such as access frequency. As shown in Fig. 3, the solid line represents the solution in this paper and the dotted line represents the solution in [15]. Compared with the traditional k-anonymity and trajectory frequency, our scheme considers the study of regional collaboration information sharing in complex user trajectory changes. With the increase of user access frequency, the higher the trajectory entropy value of the anonymous set generated according to the cost function is, the lower the probability of the user's real location being broken, which has a good effect on the privacy protection of the user's location trajectory. We evaluated the real data set used in the experiment and increased the anonymous level k from 5 to 25. According to the algorithm design, the time

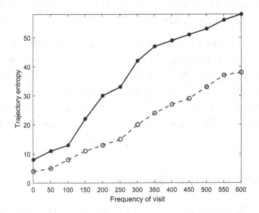

Fig. 3. The influence of the frequency of visits on the entropy of the trajectory.

cost is mainly derived from the content in the cache. As the number of users increases, there are more contents in the cache and more possibilities need to be traversed when selecting a location. The time complexity is $O(n)$, where n represents the representation of the anonymous level in the algorithm. As shown in Fig. 4, with the increase of anonymity level, the running time of the two algorithms increases linearly, which is consistent with the analysis results. We can further improve the results by swaping space for time and increasing time complexity by expanding memory and improving CPU performance.

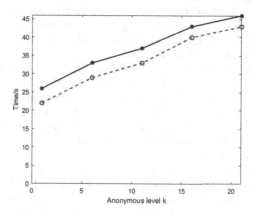

Fig. 4. The impact of anonymity level k on execution time.

6 Conclusions

This paper proposed a mechanism of trajectory protection based on blockchain to solve the privacy problem of user edge trajectory. We considered the problem that fine-grained sensitive properties of users were vulnerable to attack, starting from the key issues such as sensitive property selection and key generation of mobile edge device information. By studying the generation method of high-confidence blocks and the secure construction and verification recognition of trusted blockchain. Smart contracts were deployed based on the selected appropriate plan to achieve inter-regional collaboration. Through experiments, the security of the user's trajectory privacy information was effectively improved and the purpose of protecting the edge trajectory was achieved.

Acknowledgement. This work is partially supported by National Natural Science Foundation of China (Grant Nos. 61972034, 61832012, 61771289), Natural Science Foundation of Shandong Province (Grant No. ZR2019ZD10), Natural Science Foundation of Beijing Municipality (Grant No. 4202068), Ministry of Education - China Mobile Research Fund Project (Grant No. MCM20180401).

References

1. An, J., Yang, H., Gui, X., Zhang, W., Gui, R., Kang, J.: TCNS: node selection with privacy protection in crowdsensing based on twice consensuses of blockchain. IEEE Trans. Netw. Serv. Manag. **16**(3), 1255–1267 (2019)

2. Dai, W., Qiu, L., Wu, A., Qiu, M.: Cloud infrastructure resource allocation for big data applications. IEEE Trans. Big Data **4**(3), 313–324 (2016)

3. Dai, W., Qiu, M., Qiu, L., Chen, L., Wu, A.: Who moved my data? privacy protection in smartphones. IEEE Commun. Mag. **55**(1), 20–25 (2017)

4. Deuber, D., Magri, B., Thyagarajan, S.A.K.: Redactable blockchain in the permissionless setting. In: 2019 IEEE Symposium on Security and Privacy, SP 2019, San Francisco, CA, USA, 19–23 May 2019, pp. 124–138. IEEE (2019)

5. Ding, W., Yan, Z., Deng, R.H.: Encrypted data processing with homomorphic re-encryption. Inf. Sci. **409**, 35–55 (2017)

6. Gai, K., Guo, J., Zhu, L., Yu, S.: Blockchain meets cloud computing: a survey. IEEE Commun. Surv. Tutor. **22**(3), 2009–2030 (2020)

7. Gai, K., Qiu, M.: Blend arithmetic operations on tensor-based fully homomorphic encryption over real numbers. IEEE Trans. Ind. Info. **14**(8), 3590–3598 (2018)

8. Gai, K., Wu, Y., Zhu, L., Xu, L., Zhang, Y.: Permissioned blockchain and edge computing empowered privacy-preserving smart grid networks. IEEE Internet Things J. **6**(5), 7992–8004 (2019)

9. Gai, K., Wu, Y., Zhu, L., Zhang, Z., Qiu, M.: Differential privacy-based blockchain for industrial internet-of-things. IEEE Trans. Ind. Info. **16**(6), 4156–4165 (2020)

10. Keshk, M., Turnbull, B., Moustafa, N., Vatsalan, D., Choo, K.R.: A privacy-preserving-framework-based blockchain and deep learning for protecting smart power networks. IEEE Trans. Ind. Inform. **16**(8), 5110–5118 (2020)

11. Kuang, L., Yang, L.T., Feng, J., Dong, M.: Secure tensor decomposition using fully homomorphic encryption scheme. IEEE Trans. Cloud Com. **6**(3), 868–878 (2018)

12. Li, L., Lu, R., Choo, K.R., Datta, A., Shao, J.: Privacy-preserving-outsourced association rule mining on vertically partitioned databases. IEEE Trans. Inf. Forensics Secur. **11**(8), 1847–1861 (2016)

13. Liu, H., Zhang, Y., Yang, T.: Blockchain-enabled security in electric vehicles cloud and edge computing. IEEE Netw. **32**(3), 78–83 (2018)

14. Lu, R., Jin, X., Zhang, S., Qiu, M., Wu, X.: A study on big knowledge and its engineering issues. IEEE Trans. on Know. and Data Eng. **31**(9), 1630–1644 (2018)

15. Ma, Z., Zhang, T., Liu, X., Li, X., Ren, K.: Real-time privacy-preserving data release over vehicle trajectory. IEEE Trans. Veh. Technol. **68**(8), 8091–8102 (2019)

16. Qiu, H., Qiu, M., Memmi, G., Ming, Z., Liu, M.: A dynamic scalable blockchain based communication architecture for IoT. In: SmartBlock, pp. 159–166 (2018)

17. Sharma, V., You, I., Palmieri, F., Jayakody, D.N.K., Li, J.: Secure and energy-efficient handover in fog networks using blockchain-based DMM. IEEE Commun. Mag. **56**(5), 22–31 (2018)

18. Wu, Z., et al.: A location privacy-preserving system based on query range cover-up or location-based services. IEEE Trans. Veh. Technol. **69**(5), 5244–5254 (2020)

19. Xie, J., et al.: A survey of blockchain technology applied to smart cities: research issues and challenges. IEEE Commun. Surv. Tutor. **21**(3), 2794–2830 (2019)

20. Xu, J., et al.: An identity management and authentication scheme based on redactable blockchain for mobile networks. IEEE Trans. Veh. Technol. **69**(6), 6688–6698 (2020)

Approach Based on Ontology and Machine Learning for Identifying Causes Affecting Personality Disorder Disease on Twitter

Mourad Ellouze[(✉)], Seifeddine Mechti, and Lamia Hadrich Belguith

ANLP Group MIRACL Laboratory, FSEGS, University of Sfax, Sfax, Tunisia

Abstract. This paper presents an approach for the detection of the reason that causes a personality disorder (PD) among Twitter users. A reason is the subject of a tweet that is recorded with an inappropriate mood by an individual having already a PD. For this reason, we will focus on our work on the identification of the tweet's topic and the mood of the tweet's writer. Our approach includes a step to cluster topics based on an unsupervised recursive learning method. Besides, a step for elaborating for each leaf obtained from the previous step an ontology which will be used later for decision making by querying it using the different rules obtained automatically. Our proposed method benefits from both natural language processing (NLP) techniques and artificial intelligence (AI) algorithms. These techniques gave us the opportunity to obtain an explanatory result in the form of a hierarchical tree destined for an open lexicon. As an evaluation result, we got an F-score equals to 73% for the evaluation of topic identification and 92% for mood detection.

Keywords: Personality disorder reasons · Mood identification · Machine learning · Natural language processing · Ontology · Twitter

1 Introduction

In our days there is an impressive evolution of people having personality disorders in the world [6]. The negative impact of this disease on humanity and countries [1, 13] pushes the world organizations to invest and put a lot of resources to ensure the surveillance. Furthermore, to decrease the number of infected people in order to fight against the negative effects, including violence and suicide [5]. In this context, Canada announced in 2020 an investment of $100 million to improve the provision of psychosocial and mental health care and services for the people of Quebec[1]. This is justified by the fact that in 2041, the total number of Canadians with mental illness will reach 8.9 million, which will generate additional costs

---

[1] https://www.quebec.ca/nouvelles/actualites/details/sante-mentale-le-ministre-car mant-annonce-un-investissement-majeur-de-100-m.

© Springer Nature Switzerland AG 2021
H. Qiu et al. (Eds.): KSEM 2021, LNAI 12817, pp. 659–669, 2021.
https://doi.org/10.1007/978-3-030-82153-1_54

that exceed \$306 billion in this period[2]. This encourages researchers to work more on the sciences related to the study of personality and especially psychological problems. In this context, [17] proposes an i-RISE system for anxiety disorders furthermore, [8] proposes a polymer sensor embedded for long-term monitoring of sleep disordered breathing. Among the obstacles found in dealing with this type of problem are physical means that require significant financial resources to analyze a limited number of people. Despite the existence of persons with personality disorders as a result of a common cause (unemployment, poverty, etc.). In this context, 20% of people around the world have been psychologically infected during the outbreak of the Covid-19 pandemic[3]. Thus, the supervision of people with PD is sensitive since we can't predict their behavior towards a specific situation. Generally, the best way to behave with a person having a PD is when he feels free and not in a situation of control or attack [7]. One of the favorable environments that allows people to express themselves freely about any situation is social networks. Although the data of social networks are very large, varied and not structured, their processing is becoming more and more feasible with the advancement of new technologies such as Big Data, AI, NLP, etc. In this context, we propose an approach that takes advantage of these technologies to analyze in real time the variety of the enormous volume of textual production of Internet users. Besides, to understand the reasons that make people in a trouble situation. This will ensure the surveillance of several persons at the same time. To achieve our objectives, we have followed these steps:

1. Categorize the tweets extracted from Twitter by a hierarchical clustering technique using recursive unsupervised learning (UL) methods.
2. Model the lexicon linked to a specific topic extracted from the previous step by an ontology constructed automatically.
3. Build rules automatically in order to query the ontology for decision making (detection the topic and the mood expressed in the tweet).

This approach provides as a result a hierarchical representation that shows the topic of a tweet with the mood of the user when he is entering it. The organization of this manuscript is carried out as follows: the next section is devoted to the presentation of related works. In Sect. 3, we describe our proposed methodology in more detail for the detection of PD causes from Twitter. Sect. 4 presents the details of the data, the results of our experiments with the evaluation part. Finally, we close our work with a conclusion and some perspectives in Sect. 5.

2   Related Work

In recent years, several research works are being done on the study of personality given their interest in humanity and the whole world. This makes it until to

---

[2] https://www.mentalhealthcommission.ca/sites/default/files/Investing_in_Mental_He alth_FINAL_FRE_0.pdf.

[3] https://www.leaders.com.tn/article/31396-les-troubles-psychologiques-en-periode-de-covid-19-facteurs-de-risques-effets-et-comment-s-en-premunir.

today a very evolutionary axis of research. However, there are several problems related to this area as the variety of criteria that can influence the personality, such as the family situation. This variety makes psychiatrists in a critical situation that requires an interaction with each patient differently and giving for each patient a personalized treatment. Several studies have focused on detecting of PD by applying different machine learning (ML) methods such as [15,16]. These works have used the classical ML algorithms (SVM, random forest) to detect depressed and antisocial people on social media. Other researchers [9,10] have used neural approaches to detect the degree of stress among social networks users by combining a convolutional neural network model (CNN) with the neural network model (DNN). Besides, [2] has benefited of a neural approach that combines a multi-layer perception model (MLP) and an LSTM model to detect the deception in people on social media. Despite the importance of these works, they remain limited because saying that a person is sick without giving an explanatory reason makes the results unreliable. For that, several researchers have focused on finding the factors that may cause the disease in order to give a deep diagnosis. In this context, [3] seeks to detect factors that may affect behavior disorders over time. This is done by getting advantage of a graphical pattern of behavior (sbGraph) which is composed by nodes indicating keywords such as interest, work, etc. These nodes are linked by semantic arcs that are extracted from existing resources such as Wikidata. Finally, this graphic model is enriched with linguistic information in the form of keywords that can affect the personality at the affective and cognitive level. In the same context, [14] took advantage of association rule mining (ARM) techniques to find the dependency links between borderline diseases and psychological problems. This analysis is done on data composed of 1460 patients obtained from the Taiwan National Health Insurance Research Database. The Expert System can be a solution that shows links between the different elements since it is based on cause and effect rules. In this context [11] has proposed rules composed of symptoms, type of the disease and the treatment to be followed for the diagnosis of bipolar individuals. Besides, [18] worked on the detection of psychological diseases using rules in the form of links between symptoms and diagnosis that are obtained automatically by applying the Rosetta system tool on AFIMH[4] data. After the literature study, we note that most of the research works are done on the detection of the disease rather than looking for the reason of their decision [2,15,16]. Even researchers who have worked on the relations symptoms, diagnose they have chosen to work on medical data that are structured as data from medical reports [11,18]. We note also an excessive use of ML algorithms [2,9,10,15,16] which makes the results very abstracts, lack of explanation, difficult to interpret since the ignorance of the semantic aspect.

---

[4] Francophone Association for Human-Machine Interaction.

3 Proposed Approach

As mentioned above, we offer an approach comprising three main parts to detect the reasons that cause PD for people on Twitter as is shown in the Fig. 1.

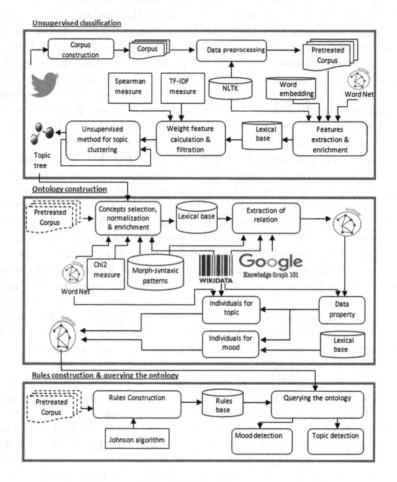

Fig. 1. Work process.

3.1 Unsupervised Classification

Data Preprocessing and Features Processing (extraction, Enrichment, Filtering and Weight Calculation). In this step, we have applied the different classical techniques of text cleaning, which involves the elimination of symbols and empty words, the normalization of the text by transforming words into lemmas using NLTK library. Next, we proceeded to segment the document into a set of fragments, which represents in our case a set of tweets, with invariant lengths. This is done by applying a hybrid technique that combines both: (1) a lexico-semantic technique that consists of: (i) first detecting simple and compound words (1,2,3 Gram) that are repeated more than once in the text and that are not prepositions, (ii) enriching in a second time this lexicon by getting advantage of the resources available on Word embedding and WordNet. This enrichment is to associate for each word that appears in the lexicon a set of context words using the existing relations such as synonyms, hypernyms, synsets. (2) Next, we took advantage of the static TF-IDF measurement to calculate the meaning of each word in the corpus. Finally, we proceeded to eliminate the attributes (lexicon) that don't make the distinction between classes since there are words that are appearing in the corpus independently of the class. This step was done by applying the Spearman measure.

Clustering. This step consists of combining tweets with the same or similar topics (having a similar or close lexicon). Among the specificities of our corpus is the variety of subjects (not related to a specific domain) which makes it impossible to predict neither the subjects nor the number of subjects. For this reason, we have hierarchically categorized these subjects by applying recursively UL algorithms such as K-means. We repeated the clustering phase (categorization of tweets by topic) several times. This technique helps to get as a result a hierarchical categorization in the form of a tree that illustrates in detail the sub-categorization of tweets' subjects. While setting from the start the number of classes at each hierarchical level (required by some algorithms such as k for k-means) and the depth level (stop condition for the recursive loop). After an empirical study, we set the value of K to 2 and the stop condition, according to the score result between the set of the most frequent words calculated by Google Knowledge (in any case this number does not exceed 5).

3.2 Ontology Construction

After the recursive topic clustering step, we assume at this level that each node in our arborescent (output of the previous step) represents a topic. For that, we will move on to associate for each topic, a list of words that are related to this field. This is done by elaborating for each subject a domain ontology that contains the lexicon used which is linked by semantic relations.

Concepts Selection, Normalization and Enrichment. Our concept selection technique is based on a hybrid method that combines both statistical and linguistic techniques. The linguistic method relies on the creation of morphosyntaxic patterns to detect simple and compound words. The statistical method consists of detecting the sequences of words that frequently appear together using the Chi2 measure. After extracting the concepts found in the corpus, we move on to group these concepts according to a class example (Paris, Marseille by city) using the hypernym relation existing in WordNet (WOLF [12] for the

French language). Then by making the enrichment of our lexical base (concepts) by words of contexts using the Wikidata[5] resource.

Extraction of Relations. In this step, we will be interested in extracting the relations between concepts. To do that, we have used the 3 different methods bellow:

1. Resources that contain standard semantic relations related to a domain such as Wikidata.
2. Our corpus by defining a set of morpho-syntaxic patterns such as *Noun(Concept1) Verb(Relation) Noun(Concept2)*.
3. Google Knowledge Graph[6] to treat exceptional cases in our corpus such as a segment that contains more than two concepts.

For inheritance relations, we first used existing subclass relations in Wikidata and in a second time we defined rules. For example, if the word "x" appears in the list of 1-Gram and 2-Gram or 3-Gram we consider it as a compound word. If the word "x" appears differently in the list of 2-Gram or 3-Gram (in the form of "y" and "z"). We will consider that the words "y" and "z" are subclass of the word "x". (economic crisis, health crisis are two sub-classes of the crisis class.)

Data Property. In this step, we will define for each concept a set of explanatory properties. In fact, we will assign for each concept the list of attributes existing in the Wikidata resource (including label, description,...) to ensure the explanatory specificity concepts of our ontology. For example, the class COVID-19 description: respiratory syndrome and infectious disease in humans, caused by SARS coronavirus 2, label: COVID-19.

Individuals. We have divided the step of filling the ontology into two sub-parts:

A. Topic The individuals of topics is done using: (1) the Wikidata resource that already contains the list of names of each concept, e.g. the list of symptoms of Covid-19 disease are cough, fever, respiratory failure, headache, etc. ,(2) the Word-Net resource using hyperonymy and synonymy resources to feed each concept in our ontology.

B. Mood After an empirical study, we have noticed that adjectives are the best way to describe the mood of the person. For this reason, we have given automatically for each concept two lists: one that contains adjectives which show the bad mood and the others indicate positive and neutral adjectives using the annotation of mood made it by our expert, while dealing with the problem of negation.

---

[5] https://www.wikidata.org/.

[6] Is a knowledge base used by Google and its services to enhance its search engine's results with information gathered from a variety of sources.

3.3 Rules Construction & Querying Our Ontology

The detection of the subject and the mood of the person is done using the rules of reasoning (SWRL), the explicit way to obtain these rules is done based on the following process: For the first classification, we have transformed each tweet into a vector that it's represented as a binary numerical sequence indicating whether the concept exists in the tweets. After that, we move on to extract rules automatically by taking benefit of the Johnson algorithm existing in the Rosetta system which takes as input the list of vectors with their labels and it provides as an output a list of rules. Similarly, for detecting the mood of people, just at the level of the transformation of the textual data into vectors: If the concept appears with an adjective that appears in the list of inappropriate mood this concept will take the negative value. If the concept appears with a positive adjective we will grant the positive value and if the concept does not appear in the tweet we will assign the neutral value.

4 Experimental Results

4.1 Corpus

We have applied our method on data composed of 6180 tweets (last 20 tweets of 309 users) that are obtained from Twitter in real time by using the Spark Streaming tool in a non-successive way to have more variety. These tweets are written in the French language and contain keywords manually defined which may indicate that this person has a PD. Then, we kept only the 20 tweets of people with PD according to the judgment of our expert. These tweets talk about different topics sports, politics, Covid-19, etc. Our expert has affected the annotation step (4 times) one before the execution of our approach to select the profile of person with PD according to their last 20 tweets. For the others, he did it after the recursive unsupervised classification step in order to: First, evaluate the UL part. Second, detect tweets that talk about Covid-19 since we chose to focus on this topic and at the third time to detect the mood of people. We chose to do the annotation step each time with a binary classification to decrease the variation and the degree of the overlap, e.g. Is the tweet talking about the Covid-19 topic (Yes or No). The following table described in more details the distribution of our corpus in each step (Table 1).

4.2 Results

We developed our approach using Python programming language. The Fig. 2 shows an extract from the result of the unsupervised classification step. The following Fig. 3 shows the results of the automatic ontology construction step for the topic "Covid-19".

Table 1. The distribution of our corpus by step.

Description	Corpus size per tweet
Size for the 1st clustering	6180 tweets (309 users)
Size for the 2nd clustering	3160 tweets
Size for the 3rd clustering	1300 tweets
Size for ontology construction	700 tweets talking about Covid-19
COVID-19 Topic Corpus Size	700 tweets
Corpus size for mood classification	700 tweets

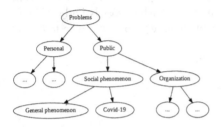

Fig. 2. Extract of our result of the unsupervised ML.

Fig. 3. Our Covid-19 ontology obtained.

4.3 Evaluation

Operational Evaluation. The performance of our system is measured using the 3 metric classic evaluations as the following: recall, precision and f-measure. We present in the Table 2 the different values obtained from each step in our work process.

Table 2. The evaluation of our approach.

	Unsupervised recursive learning								
	1st clustering			2st clustering			3st clustering		
	Recall	Preci.	F-sco.	Recall	Preci.	F-sco.	Recall	Preci.	F-sco.
K-means	71	72	**71**	58	63	60	75	86	**80**
Agglomotive Clustering	69	71	70	66	66	**66**	74	86	80
Spectral Clustering	57	56	56	48	46	47	52	81	66

Topic and mood identification			
	Recall	Precision	F-score
Topic Covid-19 detection	81	65	**73**
People mood towards Covid-19 detection	97	88	**92**

Human Expert Evaluation. After the construction of our ontology, we asked our expert to evaluate it according to the Gruber criteria. Our expert stated that our ontology is clear since it's represented by terms coming from the study field. Thus, our ontology is extensible by the fact that is ready for any type of modification. Moreover, the minimum ontology commitment is ensured by the presence of most of the terms covering the field studied, besides the coherence and the encoding minimum deformation of our ontology are also insured. All these criteria will guarantee the sharing of knowledge related to this field.

4.4 Discussion

In this work, we proposed a hybrid approach that allows us to detect the cause (reason) that pushed the patient to have a PD. We have responded to the extracted limits at the level that in our work: (i) we are looking for the causes of PD in order to understand with more details the person's situation, which will facilitate the follow-up afterwards, (ii) we tried to solve the problems related to ML techniques such as (a) the neglect of the semantic part by the use of an ontology, (b) their results are not explanatory by a representation of the results in the form of a tree. This evaluation is still to be discussed since we have made the evaluation according to the interpretation of our expert about the meaning of the clusters. For the rules obtained, we obtained the best results with the mood since the lexicons used to express mood is less overlap. On the other hand, in the detection of the topic Covid-19, some terms appear in more than one cluster such as the term *economic crisis*. According to our expert our results are acceptable. This acceptation due to the fact that the mood is the trigger to ensure the monitoring of a patient. So, if our system is non-robust it may abandon a sick case or launch an unnecessary treatment for a normal person. In our future work, we plan to apply the neural networks model RWNN [4] to improve the relationship between the different elements.

5   Conclusion

In this paper, we have proposed a hybrid approach that permits us to identify reasons affecting PD disease for users of Twitter. This work takes advantage of the different techniques of NLP (lexical, ontology), AI (ML, rules) and statistics. This leads our approach to benefit of the mentioned techniques in terms of preserving both semantic and mathematical aspects. In addition, this makes our results more interpretable and detailed. The results obtained will push us to apply our approach on other fields with other languages and other challenges. In our future work, we aim to integrate an analytical module to provide Twitter the ability to create dashboards that show the most anxious topics in the world and to identify the geographical areas with more infected people by PD.

References

1. Al-Atwi, A.A., Cai, Y., Amankwah-Amoah, J.: Workplace ostracism, paranoid employees, and service performance: a multilevel investigation. J. Manag. Psychol. (2020)
2. An, G., Levitan, S.I., Hirschberg, J., Levitan, R.: Deep personality recognition for deception detection. In: INTERSPEECH, pp. 421–425 (2018)
3. Beheshti, A., Moraveji-Hashemi, V., Yakhchi, S., Motahari-Nezhad, H.R., Ghafari, S.M., Yang, J.: Personality2vec: enabling the analysis of behavioral disorders in social networks. In: Proceedings of the 13th International Conference on Web Search and Data Mining, pp. 825–828 (2020)
4. Cao, W., Hu, L., Gao, J., Wang, X., Ming, Z.: A study on the relationship between the rank of input data and the performance of random weight neural network. Neural Comput. Appl. 32(16), 12685–12696 (2020). https://doi.org/10.1007/s00521-020-04719-8
5. Chanen, A.M., Nicol, K., Betts, J.K., Bond, G.R., Mihalopoulos, C., Jackson, H.J., Thompson, K.N., Jovev, M., Yuen, H.P., Chinnery, G., et al.: Individual vocational and educational support trial (invest) for young people with borderline personality disorder: study protocol for a randomised controlled trial. Trials 21(1), 1–12 (2020)
6. Botella, V.G., García-Palacios, A., Miñana, S.B., Baños, R., Botella, C., Marco, J.H: Exploring the effectiveness of dialectical behavior therapy versus systems training for emotional predictability and problem solving in a sample of patients with borderline personality disorder. J. Pers. Disord. 35(Supplement A), 21–38 (2021)
7. Henry, J., Collins, E., Griffin, A., Zimbron, J.: Treatment of severe emotionally unstable personality disorder with comorbid ehlers-danlos syndrome and functional neurological disorder in an inpatient setting: a case for specialist units without restrictive interventions. Case Rep. Psychiatry, 2021 (2021)
8. Jayarathna, T., Gargiulo, G.D., Breen, P.P.: Polymer sensor embedded, iot enabled t-shirt for long-term monitoring of sleep disordered breathing. In: 2019 IEEE 5th World Forum on Internet of Things (WF-IoT), pp. 139–143. IEEE (2019)
9. Lin, H., et al.: User-level psychological stress detection from social media using deep neural network. In: Proceedings of the 22nd ACM International Conference on Multimedia, pp. 507–516 (2014)
10. Lin, H., et al.: Detecting stress based on social interactions in social networks. IEEE Trans. Knowl. Data Eng. 29(9), 1820–1833 (2017)
11. Muhammad, A., Hendrik, B., Iswara, R.: Expert system application for diagnosing of bipolar disorder with certainty factor method based on web and android. J. Phys. Conf. Ser. 1339, 012020 IOP Publishing (2019)
12. Sagot, B., Fišer, D.: Building a free French wordnet from multilingual resources. In OntoLex (2008)
13. Scocco, P., Preti, A., Totaro, S., Corrigan, P., Castriotta, C., Team, S., et al.: Stigma, grief and depressive symptoms in help-seeking people bereaved through suicide. J. Affect. disord. 244, 223–230 (2019)
14. Shen, C.-C., Hu, L.-Y., Hu, Y.-H.: Comorbidity study of borderline personality disorder: applying association rule mining to the taiwan national health insurance research database. BMC Med. Inform. Decis. Mak. 17(1), 1–10 (2017)
15. Singh, R., et al.: A framework for early detection of antisocial behavior on twitter using natural language processing. In: Barolli, L., Hussain, F.K., Ikeda, M. (eds.) CISIS 2019. AISC, vol. 993, pp. 484–495. Springer, Cham (2020). https://doi.org/10.1007/978-3-030-22354-0_43

16. Stankevich, M., Latyshev, A., Kuminskaya, E., Smirnov, I., Grigoriev, O.: Depression detection from social media texts. In: Elizarov, A., Novikov, B., Stupnikov., S (eds.) Data Analytics and Management in Data Intensive Domains: XXI International Conference DAMDID/RCDL, pp. 352 (2019)
17. Sundaravadivel, P., Goyal, V., Tamil, L.: I-rise: an iot-based semi-immersive affective monitoring framework for anxiety disorders. In: 2020 IEEE International Conference on Consumer Electronics (ICCE), pp. 1–5. IEEE (2020)
18. Umar, A., Qamar, U.: Detection and diagnosis of psychological disorders through decision rule set formation. In: 2019 IEEE 17th International Conference on Software Engineering Research, Management and Applications (SERA), pp. 33–37. IEEE (2019)

QBT: Efficient and Flexible Resource Allocation Method for Data Center of State Grid Scenario

Zhengdong Ren[1], Jun Wang[1], Guangxian Lyu[2], Peng Liu[2], Wang Zhou[3(✉)], and Yu Huang[3]

[1] State Grid Corporation of China, Beijing, China
{zhengdong-ren,junwang}@sgcc.com.cn
[2] State Grid Shanghai Energy Interconnection Research Institute, Beijing, China
{lvgx,liupeng1}@epri.sgcc.com.cn
[3] Peking University, Beijing, China
{1801210925,hy}@pku.edu.cn

Abstract. With the rapid development of computer technology, service platforms have increasingly become the industry's first choice for building service center. In order to use resources more efficiently, flexible resource allocation is a very important part of the service platform construction. In the service of State Grid, the issue of flexible resource allocation is super important. However, the business of the State Grid is very complicated, and the service will include the invocation of various business logics, and resource allocation cannot be simply carried out. In order to solve this problem, this paper designs an efficient and flexible resource allocation scheme-QBT (quota boosting task) based on this project. QBT has designed three functional modules: log collection, log analysis, and flexible resource allocation. Log collection and log analysis will restore the real request path and construct it as a DAG. The system will count the QPS of each DAG, and calculate the load corresponding to the service on the DAG. Based on this information, the elastic resource allocation will perform elastic resource allocation in the two situations when the remaining resources are sufficient and insufficient. The experimental results show that the QBT design scheme can successfully solve the resource scheduling problem of the National Grid Service Platform.

Keywords: Service center · Flexible resource allocation · Log collection · Log analysis · DAG

1 Introduction

Both the Internet industry and the traditional power industry have the problem of resource waste, and related industries are also affected, such as transportation [1], medical [2, 3], banking [4, 5], communications [6–8] And computing systems [9, 10]. Services have peak and low peak periods, and the duration of the low peak period [11] is much longer than the peak period, which causes a huge waste of resources. If elastic resource allocation [12–18] is made to services, the service center platform will support more service.

© Springer Nature Switzerland AG 2021
H. Qiu et al. (Eds.): KSEM 2021, LNAI 12817, pp. 670–683, 2021.
https://doi.org/10.1007/978-3-030-82153-1_55

The business scenario of the power grid is very complex, each service is not independent, and each service is interdependent. In addition, the response of flexible resource allocation should be fast. If the elastic resource allocation is too slow during the service peak period, in extreme cases, it will cause the service to collapse and have a serious impact. Therefore, big data processing [19–21] and artificial intelligence [22, 23] have great potential in power grid resource allocation.

There are two main types of flexible resource allocation, namely feedback triggering and forward forecasting. Feedback triggers are passive, and forward predictions are active. The research on feedback trigger mode mainly concerns system performance detection, real-time resource monitoring [24, 25], real-time log analysis [26–28] and so on. System performance testing [29] is to ensure the healthy operation of services. When the system load is high, the system needs to expand the service capacity. Monitoring technology is the basis of feedback triggering, and most researches have made improvements from the aspects of monitoring granularity [30–32] and self-sensing technology [33–36]. The elastic services of Amazon EC2, Alibaba Cloud EC, Baidu Cloud EC and Meituan are all designed based on feedback triggers. Forward forecasting is to analyze the operating status of the service, predict the usage of resources in the future, and allocate resources in advance to reduce latency. At present, forward-looking forecasting mainly adopts the transformation of resource forecasting problems into forecasting models, the use of AR and MA forecasting models [37–39], or the transformation into deep learning for forecasting.

2 QBT Service

2.1 QBT Overall Design Scheme

Flexible resource allocation is a core part of the service center [40–42]. Flexible resource allocation can save a lot of resources for the service center, and reduce the cost of enterprises [43–45]. The services of the power grid are very complex, and there are mutual calls between services. From the perspective of power grid business, this article designs QBT services. QBT contains three modules, namely log collection module, log analysis module and elastic resource allocation module. The overall design of QBT is shown in Fig. 1.

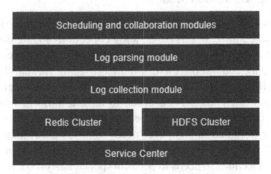

Fig. 1. QBT overall architecture diagram

As shown in the figure above, QBT mainly contains three modules, which are log collection module, log parsing module, elastic resource allocation module and so on. A brief overview of the three modules is given below.

2.1.1 Log Collection Module

The log collection module is the basis of QBT elastic resource allocation, and all subsequent resource allocation strategies are based on the log collection. The lower the delay of elastic resource allocation, the better the performance of QBT. Therefore, the log collection module needs to have timeliness. The log collection is divided into two parts, the aging log and the normal log. The aging logs are stored in a REIDS cluster. The Redis cluster stores the log information for a certain period of time, and the logs will be deleted when they are expired. Normal logs are stored in the form of common log files, which are stored on an hourly basis and are periodically stored in the HDFS cluster.

2.1.2 Log Parsing Module

Log parsing module needs to rely on the log acquisition module, these two parts constitute the collection and analysis of the log, for the elastic resource allocation module is very important. In the service center, the service is divided into three types, which are independent external service, basic service and dependent external service. For dependent external services, the service dependency invokes the underlying service. Thus, the path of the entire request forms a Directed Acyclic Graph (DAG). Log parsing needs to figure out how many request paths are included in the request and which request path each request belongs to. In addition, log parsing also needs to parse out information such as how many times each service was accessed over a period of time.

2.1.3 Elastic Resource Allocation Module

Elastic resource allocation module is the soul of QBT. This module mainly allocates elastic resources according to the data parsed by the log parsing module. The main work of the elastic resource allocation module is to allocate system resources for the peak service and recover the redundant system resources for the low peak service.

2.2 Design of Log Acquisition Module

Log collection module is the basis of the whole service, which is very important for flexible resource scheduling. In this paper, a log collection module is designed to solve the problem of log collection among various services. The log collection module needs to meet the following conditions. First, a unified logging format. The service center packages many different types of services. In order to process logging efficiently, the logging specification for each service needs to have a uniform format. Second, the lower the service delay of elastic resource scheduling, the better. Therefore, the log acquisition module designed in this paper needs to have high response, low delay and other characteristics. Third, log maintenance. The system needs to maintain the log of the service in case a technician needs to perform special analysis or troubleshoot the log for problems.

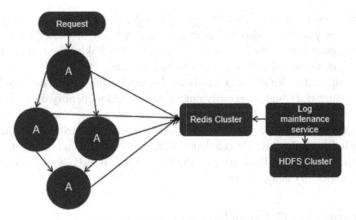

Fig. 2. QBT log collection module

After the above analysis, this paper designs the log collection module as shown in Fig. 2 below. In order to achieve low delay of log collection, the log is stored in the Redis cluster, and the Redis cluster only stores log information within a certain period. When the logs in Redis expire, the system stores the expired log information in the HDFS cluster. To solve the problem of logging unification, this article encapsulates the logging to the Redis cluster into an API that each service calls when it needs to log. This design is relatively simple, and the developer involved only needs to add a single line of code. Figure 2 mainly introduces the processing logic of log collection, and the following article will introduce the detailed design of each sub-function.

2.2.1 Log Specification Design

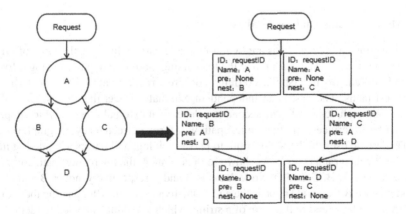

Fig. 3. Request path to log conversion

The specification of the log is particularly important for log collection. Log collection needs to reflect the request path. For a standalone external service, the request path is simpler and the log contains only itself. For a dependent external service, its request path includes not only itself but also the underlying service being invoked. In order to unify the logging specification, the logs need to reflect the full link of the request as well as information about the individual services being accessed.

In this paper, the idea of multi-tree is used to design the service log. Each request contains a requestId, which is globally unique and is used to identify different requests. This is followed by Name, Pre, and Next. Name represents the Name of the node, Pre represents the level above the request, and Next represents the next node in the request. As shown in Fig. 3, the left side is a demo of the request path, and the right side is the format of the request log. Each node on the request path inserts the log into the Redis, marked by a globally unique requestId.

2.2.2 Design of Log Collection Interface

A service center contains many types of services. For logging, the service must be logging in the same way. This article encapsulates the logging function as a software package, and each service invokes the relevant interface to do the logging.

2.2.3 Log Maintenance Design

Redis logs only for a period of time, and expired logs will be stored in the HDFS cluster. In order to maintain these logs, this paper designs a log maintenance module. What is kept in Redis is the full link log of a request. The log module stores these logs separately for different external services. The log file will then contain two types of logs, one for independent external services and one for dependent external services. A separate external service log that contains only the service's own log conditions. The dependent external service log contains the logs of the service itself, as well as the logs associated with its calls to other underlying services.

2.3 Design of Log Analysis Module

Log collection and log analysis are two inseparable parts, which are the basis of QBT's distribution strategy. The main job of the log parsing module is to parse the log information in Redis and distinguish it according to different request paths. There are two types of request paths. The first is an independent external service, the request path of the service only includes itself. The second is a dependent external service, which depends on other basic services, and the request path will form a directed acyclic graph (DAG).

This article uses the BFS algorithm to parse each log, and parses a single log into a directed acyclic graph (DAG). As shown in Figs. 3 and4, the log request path contains 4 nodes, namely A, B, C, and D. Node A visits B and C respectively, nodes B and C visit D node respectively, and D node is the end of the request path. After parsing the request, the DAG will be stored in the form of a string, which is unique and used to identify the request path. As shown in the right part of the figure below, the parentheses are the list of child nodes, sorted in alphabetical order, and the node nodes are separated by ";".

The log analysis module refers to each request path as a request strategy. The service will count the number of occurrences of the request policy in a period of time. The

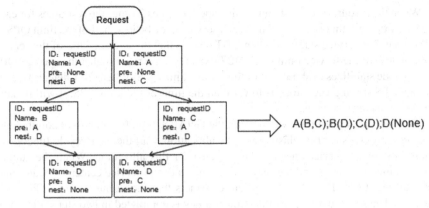

Fig. 4. The request path is converted to a unique identifier

elastic resource allocation module allocates and reclaims resources according to the request strategy and the QPS information of the service.

2.4 Design of Elastic Resource Allocation Module

Flexible resource allocation is the core module of QBT. It is stated in advance that when the service is in its peak period, its excess resources cannot be recycled and allocated to other services. Because this will only increase the entropy of the entire system, making the system more unstable. In the service center, each service has peak and low peak periods. During low peak periods, services require fewer resources. During the peak period, the service requires more resources, even 5–10 times the resources during the low peak period. In order to make the service run normally most of the time, the traditional way is to allocate sufficient resources for the service (satisfying the load during high staging). This method caused a lot of waste of resources. Therefore, for service centers, flexible resource allocation is essential.

The following is to design the elastic resource allocation module from two aspects, namely, the elastic resource allocation with sufficient resources and the elastic resource allocation with insufficient resources.

2.4.1 Flexible Resource Allocation with Sufficient Resources

The flexible resource allocation strategy when the remaining resources of the service center are sufficient is relatively simple, that is, sufficient server resources are allocated for each service. However, there is a problem with allocation. How does the system determine that a certain service needs to be expanded? Here is an introduction process. Before the service goes online, the tester will test the QPS of a single node service with acceptable delay, and then calculate how many nodes are needed based on the total amount of QPS requested. This QPS is very important in the flexible resource allocation service. This article refers to this QPS as the limit QPS. When the average QPS of a service is greater than the QPS, QBT will allocate server resources for the service.

When the resources are sufficient, this paper allocates 2 times the resources for each service by default, that is, the QPS that each service node bears is half of the limit QPS of the service. For service stability, when QBT detects that the average QPS of the service is about 80% of the service limit QPS, QBT expands the service so that the average QPS of each node stabilizes to about half of the service limit QPS. When QBT detects that the average QPS serving each node is lower than the limit of the limit QPS, it will reclaim the excess server resources.

As shown in Algorithm I, we first call the GetAllocation function to obtain the total allocated resources for this elastic resource allocation. Call the GetRecycle function to obtain how many services need to be recycled for this allocation. When the sum of the remaining resources and the recycled resources of the service center is greater than the resources to be allocated, the system considers that the resources are sufficient at this time. The flexible resource allocation strategy is completed in two steps. First, first recover the excess resources of the service during the low peak period. Second, allocate server resources for each request strategy and related services along the request path. First, create a new allocation task for each request strategy, then add the allocation task to the large allocation queue, and finally perform resource allocation (Fig. 5).

Algorithm 1 Flexible resource allocation with sufficient resources

1: allocation = GetAllocation()

2: recycle = GetRecycle()

3: amount = GetAmount()

4: **if** $recycle + amount > allocation$ **then**

5:    RecoveryResource(StrategyConfigList)

6:    **for** $StrategyeConfig\ from\ StrategyConfigList$ **do**

7:        task = DistributeTask(StrategyeConfig)

8:        append task to the Distribution of the queue

9:    **end for**

10: **end if**

Fig. 5. Flexible resource allocation strategy with sufficient resources

2.4.2 Flexible Resource Allocation With Insufficient Resources

The flexible resource allocation in the case of insufficient resources is meaningless in a sense. At this time, the most reasonable operation should be to expand the entire service center. There are two types of insufficient service resources. In the first type, some services in the system are in high staging period and a small part of services are in low peak period. At this time, the service center has no remaining server resources. If the system is to perform flexible resource allocation, it can only recycle the excess resources of the service in the low peak period and allocate it to the service in the high installment period. At this time, the resource recovery for the service in the low peak period is slightly different from the recovery when the resource is sufficient. During the low peak period, the system guarantees that the average QPS of the service is half of the limit QPS. For recycling when resources are insufficient, the system will limit the average QPS of the service to approximately 80% of the limit QPS, and the remaining server resources will be recycled for allocation to peak services. In the second type, most of the services in the service center are in peak periods. At this time, flexible resource allocation is meaningless. Therefore, this situation is not considered.

The elastic resource allocation module divides all services into two types: peak period and low peak period. Services during peak periods require the system to allocate resources. Service surplus resources during low peak periods will be recycled by QBT. The service classification when resources are insufficient is slightly different from the classification when resources are sufficient. When resources are insufficient, this article defines the service with a QPS of approximately the limit QPS as a peak period service, and the service with a QPS less than 80% of the limit QPS as a low peak period service.

The classification of services when resources are insufficient is shown in the figure below (Fig. 6).

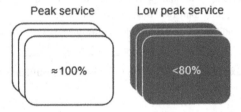

Fig. 6. Service classification when resources are insufficient

The following is mainly about two aspects. First, how to recycle resources. Second, how to allocate the recovered resources.

(1) **Resource Recovery**

In the case of insufficient resources, QBT defines services whose QPS is lower than 80% of the limit QPS as low-peak services. QBT will maintain the average QPS of the service during the low peak period at about 80% of the limit QPS, and the remaining server resources will be recycled. The resource recovery strategy is shown in the figure below (Fig. 7).

Algorithm 2 Resource recycle

1: **for** *RecycledService from RecycledServiceList* **do**

2:    task = RecycleTask(RecycledService)

3:    append task to the Perform of the queue

4: **end for**

Fig. 7. The resource recovery of QBT

(2) **Resource Allocation**

See Fig. 8.

Algorithm 3 Flexible resource allocation with insufficient resources
---
1: Count = 0

2: RatioMap = Map()

3: **for** *BusyService from BusyServiceList* **do**

4:      cou = CalReq(BusyService)

5:      RatioMap[BusyService.Name] = cou

6:      Count += cou

7: **end for**

8: **for** *BusyService from BusyServiceList* **do**

9:      ratioTemp = RatioMap[BusyService.Name]/Count

10:      task = DistributeTask(BusyService, ratioTemp)

11:      append task to the Distribution of the queue

12: **end for**

Fig. 8. Flexible resource allocation strategy with insufficient resources

The elastic resource allocation strategy in this article is relatively simple when resources are insufficient. QBT will allocate the recovered server resources to peak service in proportion. First, QBT will calculate the number of system resources required for each peak period service of the service center. Different from sufficient resources, QBT calculates the server resources required for each peak period service based on the resources required to maintain its QPS at about 80% of the limit QPS. Then, QBT will allocate the remaining server resources according to the proportion of service demand resources in each peak period to the total demand resources. The flexible resource allocation strategy when resources are insufficient is shown in Algorithm 3.

3 Testing and Verification

The following two experiments are mainly used to verify the effect of QBT. Experiment 1: Flexible resource allocation in the case of sufficient resources. Experiment two, flexible resource allocation in the case of insufficient resources.

The services in the experiment are built using Django. Each service only contains requests and forwarding, with a calculation module in between. The calculation amount of the calculation module of each service is different, so that different services can be simulated. The experimental environment is a 16G, 8-core, 100G storage server. Deploy Kubernetes with version number 1.15 and Docker with version number 1.7 on the server. A total of 10 services were deployed in the experiment, and each service was deployed using Service and Deployment in Kubernetes. The dependencies of the 10 services are shown in Fig. 9.

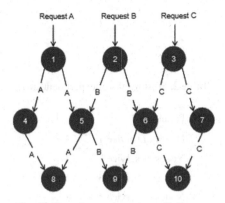

Fig. 9. Experimental service call diagram

As can be seen from the above figure, services 1, 2, and 3 are external services, and the remaining services are basic services. Services 1, 4, 5, and 8 form a request path. Services 2, 5, 6, and 9 form a request path. Services 3, 6, 7, and 10 form a request path. To facilitate testing, this article sets the default QPS of services 1–10 to 50.

3.1 Experiment I

In order to simulate real service scenarios, this article gives basic traffic with a QPS of 50 to services 1, 2, and 3 respectively. In the case of sufficient system resources, services 1, 2, 3, 4, and 7 all include two working nodes in the cluster, and services 5, 6, 8, 9, and 10 all include 4 nodes. The experiment uses different QPS to perform stress testing on the request path of service 1, and the experiment records the number of nodes on the request path when the service is stable and the time it takes to restore the service smoothly. Pressure measurement is carried out on the basic flow (Table 1).

Table 1. Test results of experiment one.

QPS	Nodes of service 1	Nodes of service 4	Nodes of service 5	Nodes of service 8	Stable service time (S)
100	6	6	10	10	2.16
150	8	8	12	12	2.22
200	10	10	14	14	2.50

It can be seen from the above table that the pressure test on the request path of service 1 shows that the service only takes about 2.5S to reach a stable state. The number of nodes when services 1, 4, 5, and 8 return to normal state is in line with expectations. Therefore, the scheduling of QBT with sufficient resources is in line with expectations.

3.2 Experiment II

See Table 2.

Table 2. Test results of experiment two.

Parameter	Value
Nodes of service 1	3
Nodes of service 2	3
Nodes of service 3	3
Nodes of service 4	3
Nodes of service 5	6
Nodes of service 6	6
Nodes of service 7	3
Nodes of service 8	6
Nodes of service 9	6
Nodes of service 10	6
Stable service time (S)	4.3

In order to simulate the elastic resource allocation in the case of real resource shortages, the experiment puts an upper limit on the amount of resources of the entire service, and a maximum of 45 containers can be built in the cluster. As in the previous experiment, the experiment gave a basic traffic with a QPS of 50 for the request paths corresponding to services 1, 2, and 3. Then, services 1, 2, 3, 4, and 7 all include two working nodes in the cluster, and services 5, 6, 8, 9, and 10 all include 4 nodes. The experiment performed stress testing on the request paths corresponding to services 1, 2, and 3 to ensure that the QPS on each request path was about 200. At this time, the resources of the system cannot satisfy all services. The experiment records the number of nodes finally allocated for each service and the time it takes for the service to recover and stabilize.

In the case of insufficient resources in the cluster, resource allocation is based on the proportion of the number of machines required for each service to the total number of machines required to allocate the remaining number of machines. It can be seen from the test results in the above table that the node allocation for each service is correct, and it only takes about 4.3S to restore the stability of the service. Therefore, the elastic resource allocation when resources are insufficient is also in line with expectations.

4   Conclusion

In order to solve the problem of flexible resource allocation of the State Grid Service Platform, this paper proposes a service that can efficiently perform flexible resource allocation-QBT. QBT proposes a way to automatically analyze the request path, analyze the load of the service in the request path, and efficiently allocate elastic resources. All in all, QBT not only solves the problem of flexible resource allocation of the State Grid Service Platform, but also provides an effective solution to this type of problem.

Acknowledgment. This work financially supported by Science and Technology Program of State Grid Corporation of China under Grant No.: 5700-202055183A-0-0-00, which named Research on Technology of Big Data Monitoring Analysis in Power Grid by Coordination of Data Middle platform & Edge Calculation. Without their help, it would be much harder to finish the program and this paper.

References

1. Zhu, M., et al.: Public vehicles for future urban transportation. IEEE Trans. Intell. Transp. Syst. **17**(12), 3344–3353 (2016)
2. Zhang, Q., Huang, T., Zhu, Y., Qiu, M.: A case study of sensor data collection and analysis in smart city: provenance in smart food supply chain. Int. J. Distribut. Sensor Netw. **9**(11), 382132 (2013)
3. Qiu, M., et al.: RNA nanotechnology for computer design and in vivo computation. Philos. Trans. R. Soc. A: Math. Phys. Eng. Sci. **371**(2000), 20120310 (2013)
4. Tao, L., Golikov, S., Gai, K., Qiu, M.: A reusable software component for integrated syntax and semantic validation for services computing. In: IEEE Symposium on Service-Oriented System Engineering (SOSE), pp. 127–132 (2015)
5. Gai, K., Qiu, M., Sun, X., Zhao, H.: Security and privacy issues: a survey on FinTech. In: International Conference on Smart Computing and Communication, pp. 236–247 (2016)
6. Qiu, M., Zhang, K., Huang, M.: An empirical study of web interface design on small display devices. In: IEEE/WIC/ACM International Conference on Web Intelligence (WI 2004), pp. 29–35 (2004)
7. Dai, W., Qiu, M., Qiu, L., Chen, L., Wu, A.: Who moved my data? Privacy protection in smartphones. IEEE Commun. Mag. **55**(1), 20–25 (2017)
8. Zhao, H., Chen, M., Qiu, M., Gai, K., Liu, M.: A novel pre-cache schema for high performance Android system. Futur. Gener. Comput. Syst. **56**, 766–772 (2016)
9. Shao, Z., et al.: Real-time dynamic voltage loop scheduling for multi-core embedded systems. IEEE Trans. Circuits Syst. II **54**(5), 445–449 (2007)
10. Qiu, H., Qiu, M., Memmi, G., Ming, Z., Liu, M.: A Dynamic Scalable Blockchain Based Communication Architecture for IoT. In: Qiu, M. (ed.) SmartBlock 2018. LNCS, vol. 11373, pp. 159–166. Springer, Cham (2018). https://doi.org/10.1007/978-3-030-05764-0_17
11. Gao, Y., Iqbal, S., Zhang, P., Qiu, M.: Performance and power analysis of high-density multi-GPGPU architectures: a preliminary case study. In: IEEE 17th International Conference on High Performance Computing (HPCC) (2015)
12. Schultz, J.C., Appel, H.M., Ferrieri, A.P., Arnold, T.M.: Flexible resource allocation during plant defense responses. Front. Plant Sci. **4**, 324 (2013)
13. Yaghubi-Namaad, M., Rahbar, A.G., Alizadeh, B.: Adaptive modulation and flexible resource allocation in space-division- multiplexed elastic optical networks. J. Opt. Commun. Netw. **10**(3), 240–251 (2018)
14. Katz, D., Schieber, B., Shachnai, H.: Flexible resource allocation to interval jobs. Algorithmica **81**(8), 3217–3244 (2019)
15. Sawyer, N., Smith, D.B.: Flexible resource allocation in device-to-device communications using Stackelberg game theory. IEEE Trans. Commun. **67**(1), 653–667 (2019)

16. Angalakudati, M., et al.: Business analytics for flexible resource allocation under random emergencies. Manage. Sci. **60**(6), 1552–1573 (2014)
17. Tang, X., Li, K., Qiu, M., Sha, E.H.-M.: A hierarchical reliability-driven scheduling algorithm in grid systems. J. Parallel Distribut. Comput. **72**(4), 525–535 (2012)
18. Dai, W., Qiu, L., Wu, A., Qiu, M.: Cloud infrastructure resource allocation for big data applications. IEEE Trans. Big Data **4**(3), 313–324 (2016)
19. Guo, Y., Zhuge, Q., Hu, J., Yi, J., Qiu, M., Sha, E.H.: Data placement and duplication for embedded multicore systems with scratch pad memory. IEEE Trans. Comput. Aided Des. Integr. Circuits Syst. **32**(6), 809–817 (2013)
20. Qiu, M., Ming, Z., Wang, J., Yang, L.T., Xiang, Y.: Enabling cloud computing in emergency management systems. IEEE Cloud Comput. **1**(4), 60–67 (2014)
21. Niu, J., Liu, C., Gao, Y., Qiu, M.: Energy efficient task assignment with guaranteed probability satisfying timing constraints for embedded systems. IEEE Trans. Parallel Distrib. Syst. **25**(8), 2043–2052 (2013)
22. Gai, K., Qiu, M.: Optimal resource allocation using reinforcement learning for IoT content-centric services. Appl. Soft Comput. **70**, 12–21 (2018)
23. Gai, K., Qiu, M.: Reinforcement learning-based content-centric services in mobile sensing. IEEE Netw. **32**(4), 34–39 (2018)
24. Kalliski, M., Engell, S.: Real-time resource efficiency indicators for monitoring and optimization of batch-processing plants. Can. J. Chem. Eng. **95**(2), 265–280 (2017)
25. Yadav, Y., Rama Krishna, C.: Real-time resource monitoring approach for detection of hotspot for virtual machine migration. Int. J. Inf. Technol. **11**(4), 639–646 (2018)
26. Vega, C., Roquero, P., Leira, R., Gonzalez, I., Aracil, J.: Loginson: a transform and load system for very large-scale log analysis in large IT infrastructures. J. Supercomput. **73**(9), 3879–3900 (2017)
27. Huang, M., Dong, H., Wang, C.: Web link and transaction log analyses of digital archive websites. Tʻu shu kuan hsüeh yü tzǔ hsün kʻo hsüeh **39**(2), 65–82 (2013)
28. DiCostanzo, D., Ayan, A., Woollard, J., Gupta, N.: SU-F-R-12: prediction of truebeam hardware issues using trajectory log analysis. Med. Phys. (Lancaster) **43**(6), 3375 (2016)
29. Brebner, P.C.: Is your cloud elastic enough performance modeling the elasticity of infrastructure as a service (IaaS) cloud applications. In: ICPE 2012 Proceedings of the 3rd ACM/SPEC International Conference on Performance Engineering, pp.263–266. New York, USA (2012)
30. Shen, Z., Subbiah, S., Gu, X.: CloudScale: elastic resource scaling for multi tenant cloud systems. In: Proceedings of the 2nd ACM Symposium on Cloud Computing, pp. 1–14. New York, USA (Oct. 2011)
31. Hadji, M., Zeghlache, D.: Minimum cost maximum flow algorithm for dynamic resource allocation in clouds. In: IEEE 5th International Conference on Cloud Computing (CLOUD), pp.876–882. Honolulu (2012)
32. Duong, T.N.B., Li, X., Goh, R.S.M.: A framework for dynamic resource provisioning and adaptation in IaaS clouds. In: IEEE Third International Conference on Cloud Computing Technology and Science (CloudCom), pp. 312–319. Athens (2011)
33. Rao, J., Bu, X., Wang, K.: Self-adaptive provisioning of virtualized resources in cloud computing. ACM SIGMETRICS Perform. Eval. Rev. **39**(1), 321–322 (2011)
34. Buyya, R., Garg, S.K., Calheiros, R.N.: SLA-oriented resource provisioning for cloud computing challenges, architecture, and solutions. In: International Conference on Cloud and Service Computing (CSC), pp. 1–10. Hong Kong, China (2011)
35. Kranas, P.: ElaaS: an innovative Elasticity as a Service framewor-k for dynamic management across the cloud stack layers. In: Proceedings of Complex, Intelligent and Software Intensive Systems (CISIS), pp. 1042–1049. Palermo, Italy, 4–6 July (2012)

36. He, S., Guo, L., Guo, Y., Wu, C., Ghanem, M., Han, R.: Elastic application container: a lightweight approach for cloud resource provisioning. In: 2012 IEEE 26th International Conference on Advanced Information Networking and Applications (AINA), pp. 15–22. Fukuoka (2012)

37. Gong, Z., Gu, X., Wilkes, J.: PRESS: predictive elastic resource scaling for cloud systems. In: Proceedings of Network and Service Management, pp. 9–16. Niagara Falls, USA, 25–29 Oct. (2010)

38. Jie, Y., Qiu, J., Li, Y.: A profile-based approach to just-in-time scalability for cloud applications. In: IEEE International Conference on Cloud Computing, pp.9–16. Bangalore (2009)

39. Xu, W., et al.: Predictive control for dynamic resource allocation in enterprise data centers. In: 10th IEEE/IFIP Date of Conference, pp.115–126. Vancouver, Canada, 3–7 April (2006)

40. Gai, K., Qiu, M., Zhao, H., Liu, M.: Energy-aware optimal task assignment for mobile heterogeneous embedded systems in cloud computing. In: IEEE 3rd International Conference on Cyber Security and Cloud Computing (CSCloud) (2016)

41. Chen, L., Duan, Y., Qiu, M., Xiong, J., Gai, K.: Adaptive resource allocation optimization in heterogeneous mobile cloud systems. In: IEEE 2nd International Conference on Cyber Security and Cloud Computing (CSCloud) (2015)

42. Xu, Y., Li, K., Khac, T.T., Qiu, M.: A multiple priority queueing genetic algorithm for task scheduling on heterogeneous computing systems. In: IEEE 14th International Conference on High Performance Computing (HPCC) (2012)

43. Thakur, K., Qiu, M., Gai, K., Ali, M.L.: An investigation on cyber security threats and security models. In: IEEE 2nd International Conference on Cyber Security and Cloud Computing (CSCloud) (2015)

44. Gai, K., Qiu, M., Elnagdy, S.A.: A novel secure big data cyber incident analytics framework for cloud-based cybersecurity insurance. In: IEEE 2nd International Conference on Big Data Security on Cloud (CSCloud) (2016)

45. Zhang, Z., Wu, J., Deng, J., Qiu, M.: Jamming ACK attack to wireless networks and a mitigation approach. In: IEEE GLOBECOM, pp. 1–5 (2008)

Author Index

Printed in the United States
by Baker & Taylor Publisher Services

Printed in the United States
by Baker & Taylor Publisher Services